DANICA NOVG

the
UNDErTAKING
OF LILY CHEN

:01

First Second
NEW YORK

Many thanks to my excellent readers Edith Freni, Quince Mountain, Blair Braverman, Jonathan Farmer, Casey Siemaszko, Matthew Stadelmann, Laurence Klavan, Jordan Mechner, Dawn Landes, and Chad Simpson. Thank you Mark, Calista, Colleen, Gina, and everyone at First Second. Thanks also to VCCA, and to the MacDowell Colony, where I started and finished this book.

~ D.N.

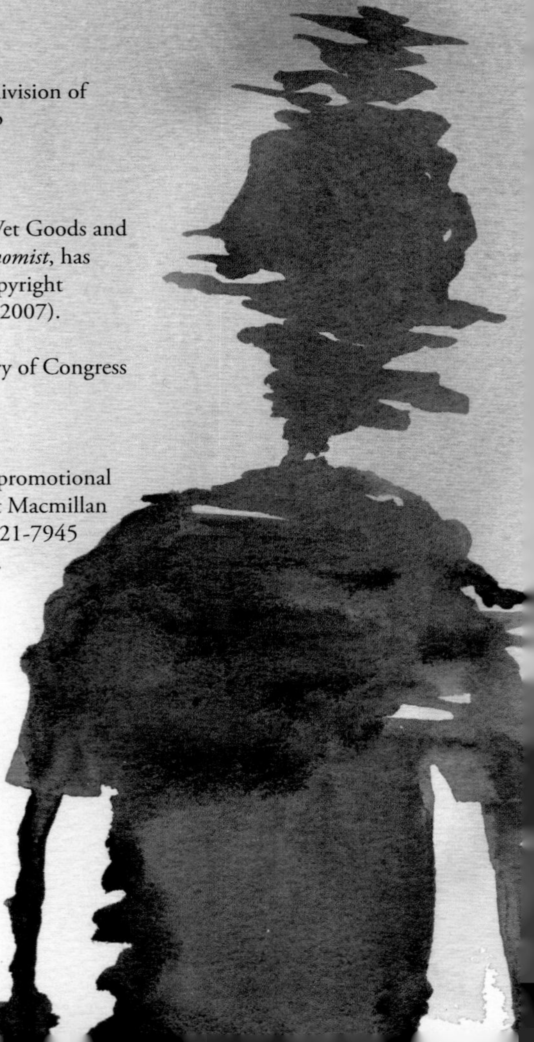

First Second

An excerpt from the article "China's Corpse Brides: Wet Goods and Dry Goods," from the July 26, 2007 issue of *The Economist*, has been used by permission of that publication and is copyright © The Economist Newspaper Limited, London (July 2007).

Cataloging-in-Publication Data is on file at the Library of Congress

ISBN: 978-1-59643-586-5

First Second books may be purchased for business or promotional use. For information on bulk purchases please contact Macmillan Corporate and Premium Sales Department at (800) 221-7945 x5442 or by email at specialmarkets@macmillan.com.

FIRST
EDITION

First edition 2014
Book design by Danica Novgorodoff
with Colleen AF Venable
Printed in China

10 9 8 7 6 5 4 3 2

BY ART
WE LIVE

To my grandparents,
Eugene and Ellen Chen Novgorodoff

Parts of rural China are seeing a burgeoning market for female corpses, the result of the reappearance of a strange custom called "ghost marriages." Chinese tradition demands that husbands and wives always share a grave. Sometimes, when a man died unmarried, his parents would procure the body of a woman, hold a "wedding," and bury the couple together . . . A black market has sprung up to supply corpse brides. Marriage brokers—usually respectable folk who find brides for village men—account for most of the middlemen. At the bottom of the supply chain come hospital mortuaries, funeral parlors, body snatchers—and now murderers.

—*The Economist*, July 26, 2007

Prologue

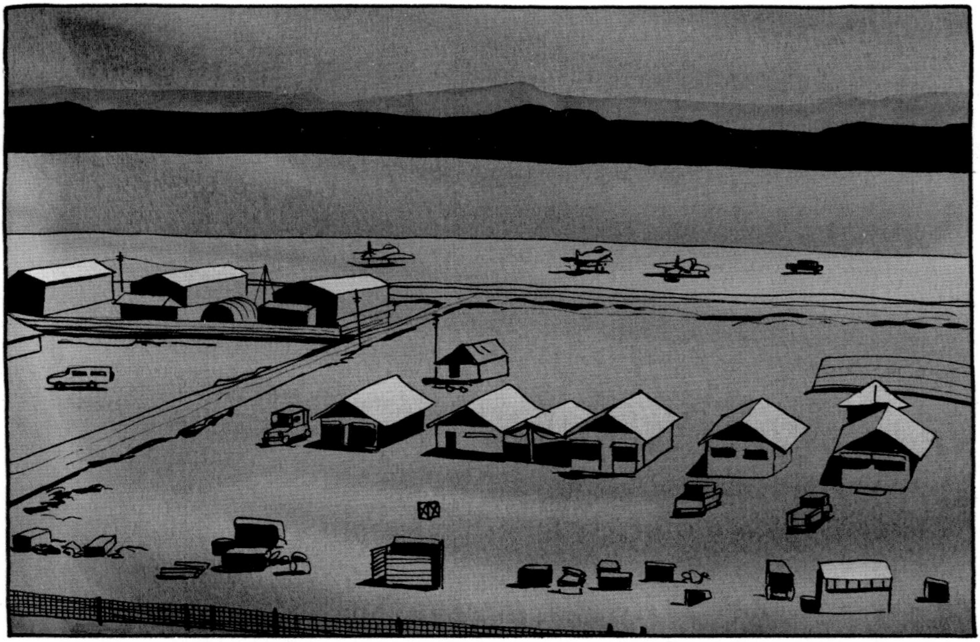

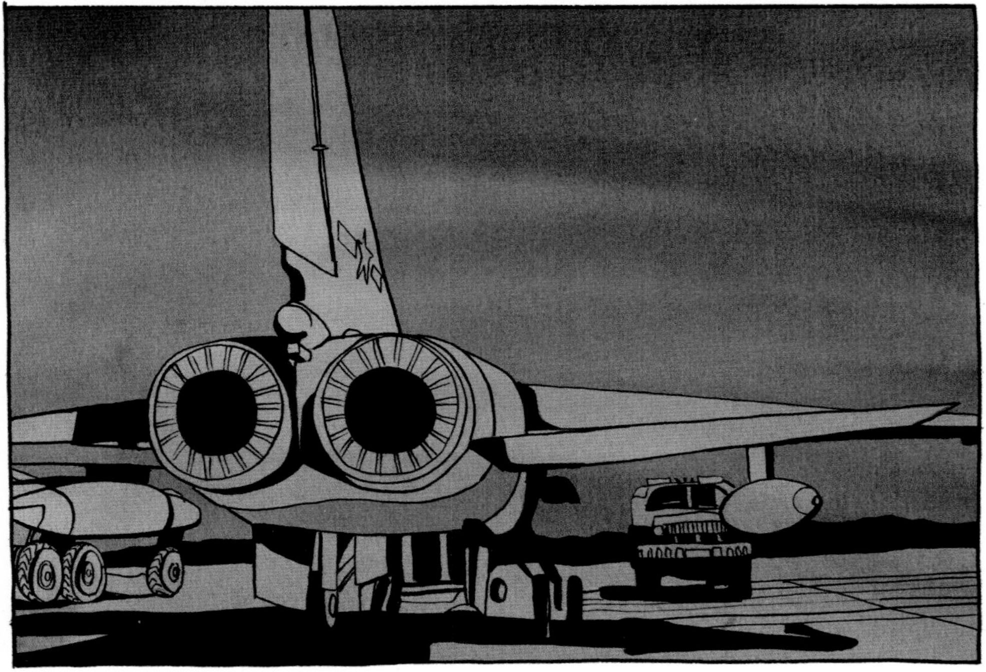

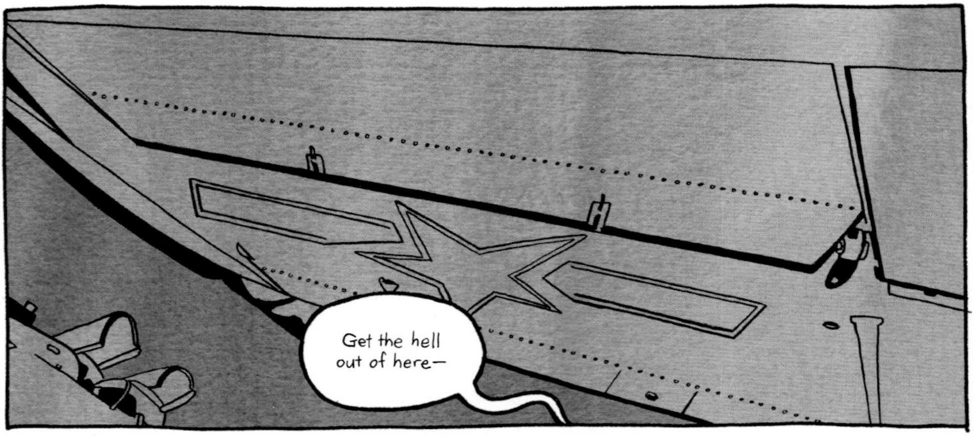
Get the hell out of here—

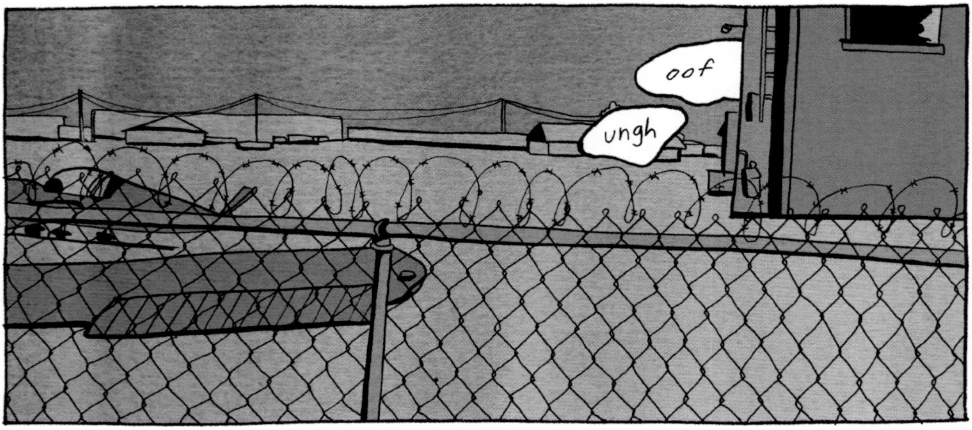
oof
ungh

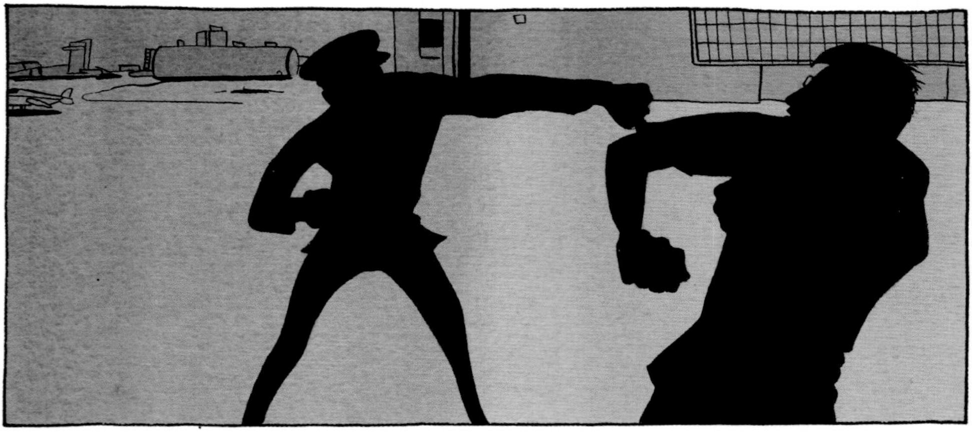

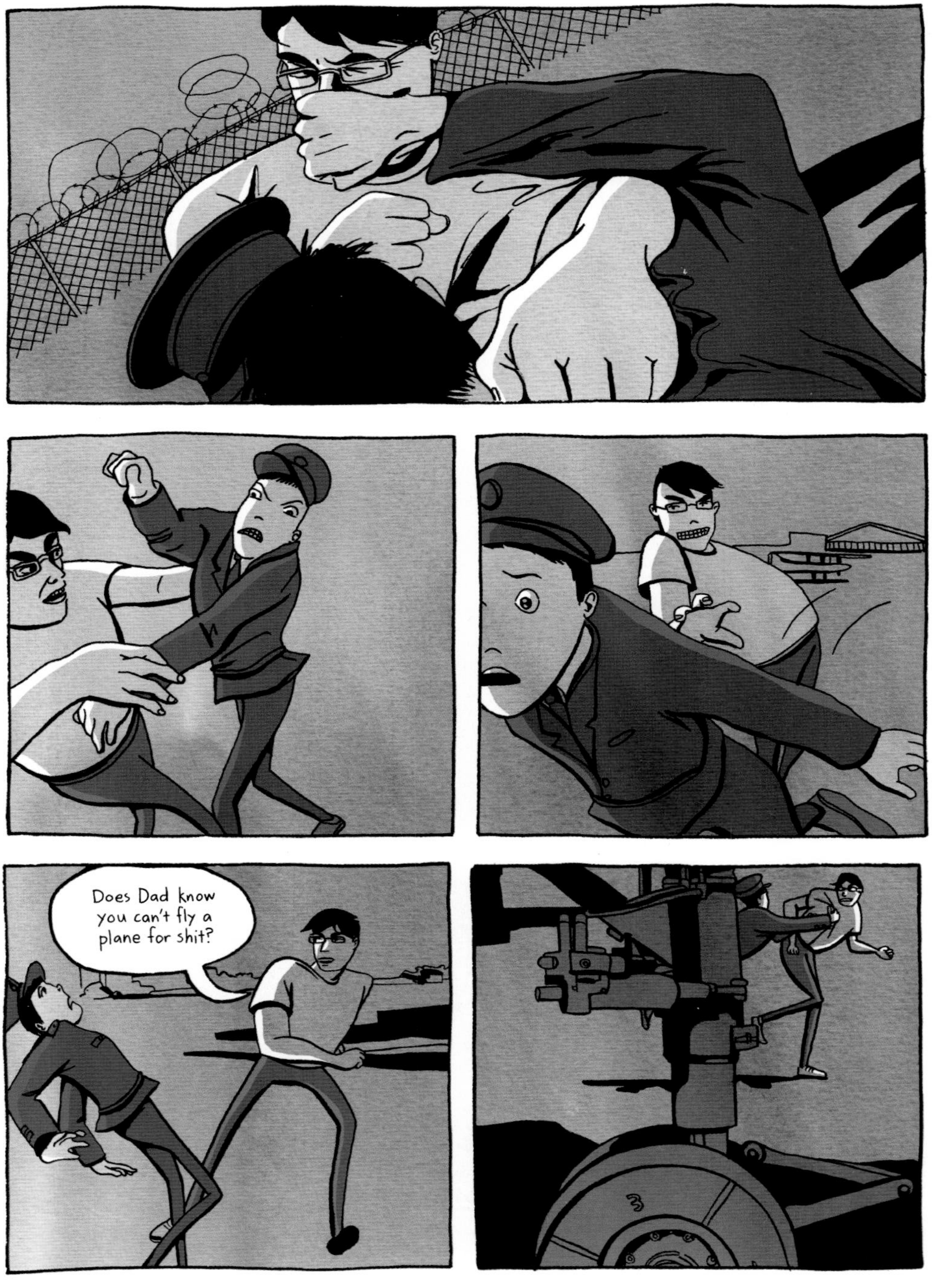
Does Dad know you can't fly a plane for shit?

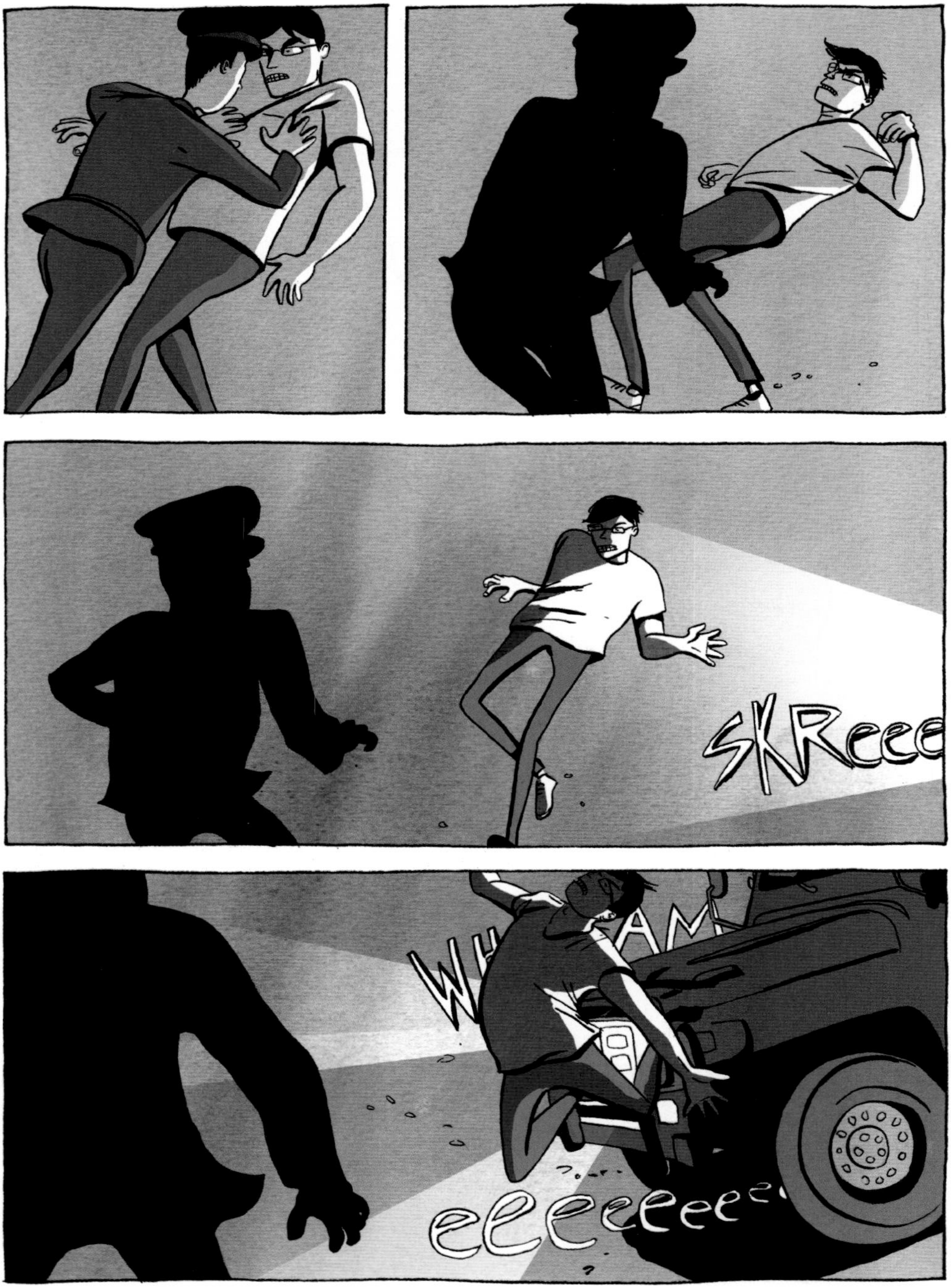
SKReee
WH
AM
eeeeeeee

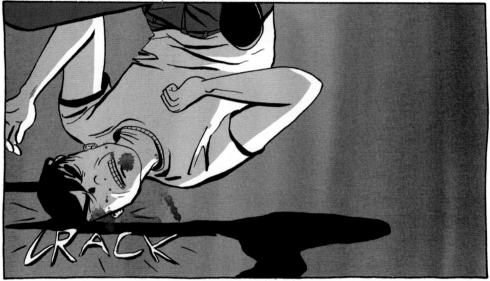

CRACK

Wei

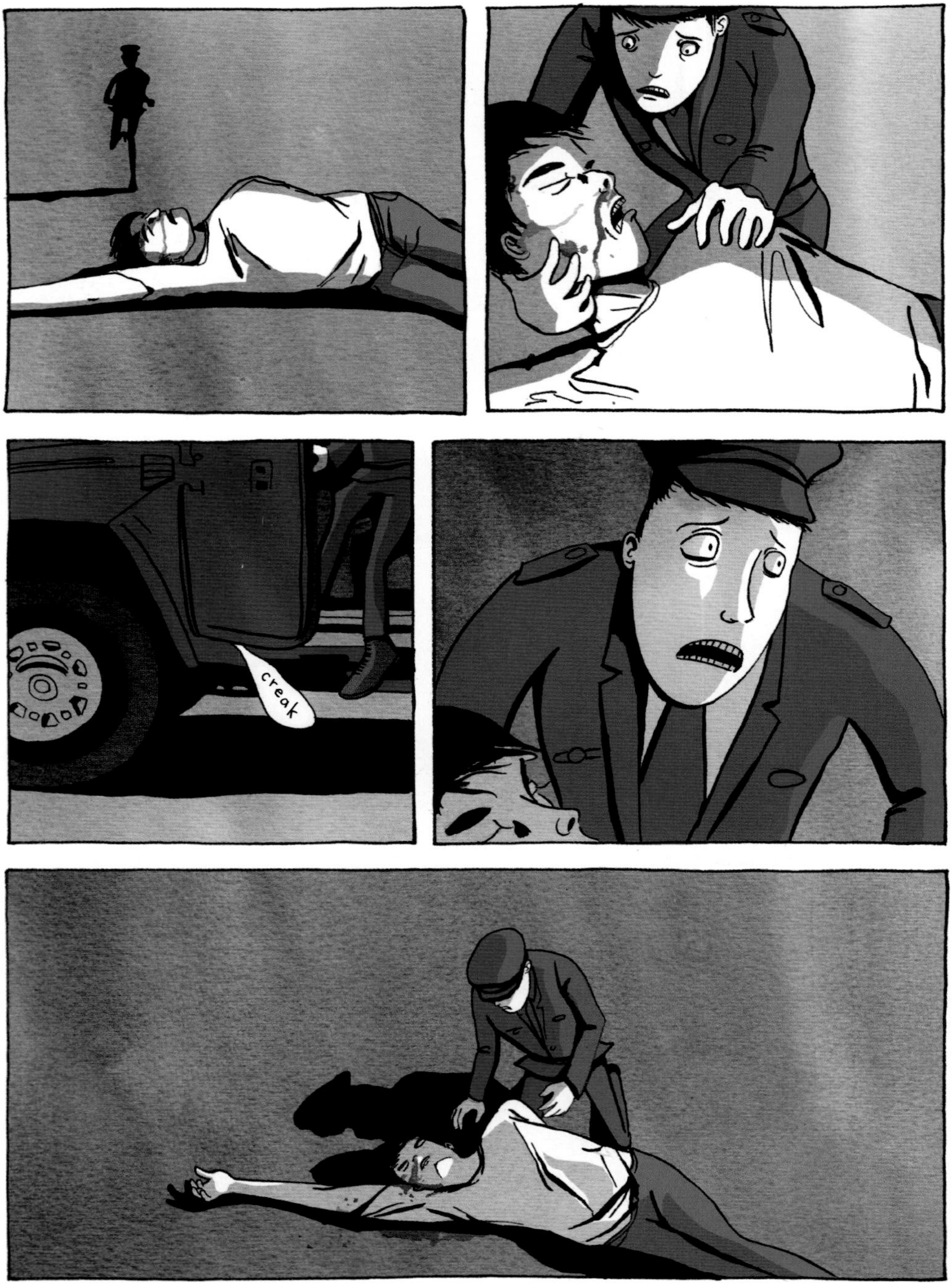
creak

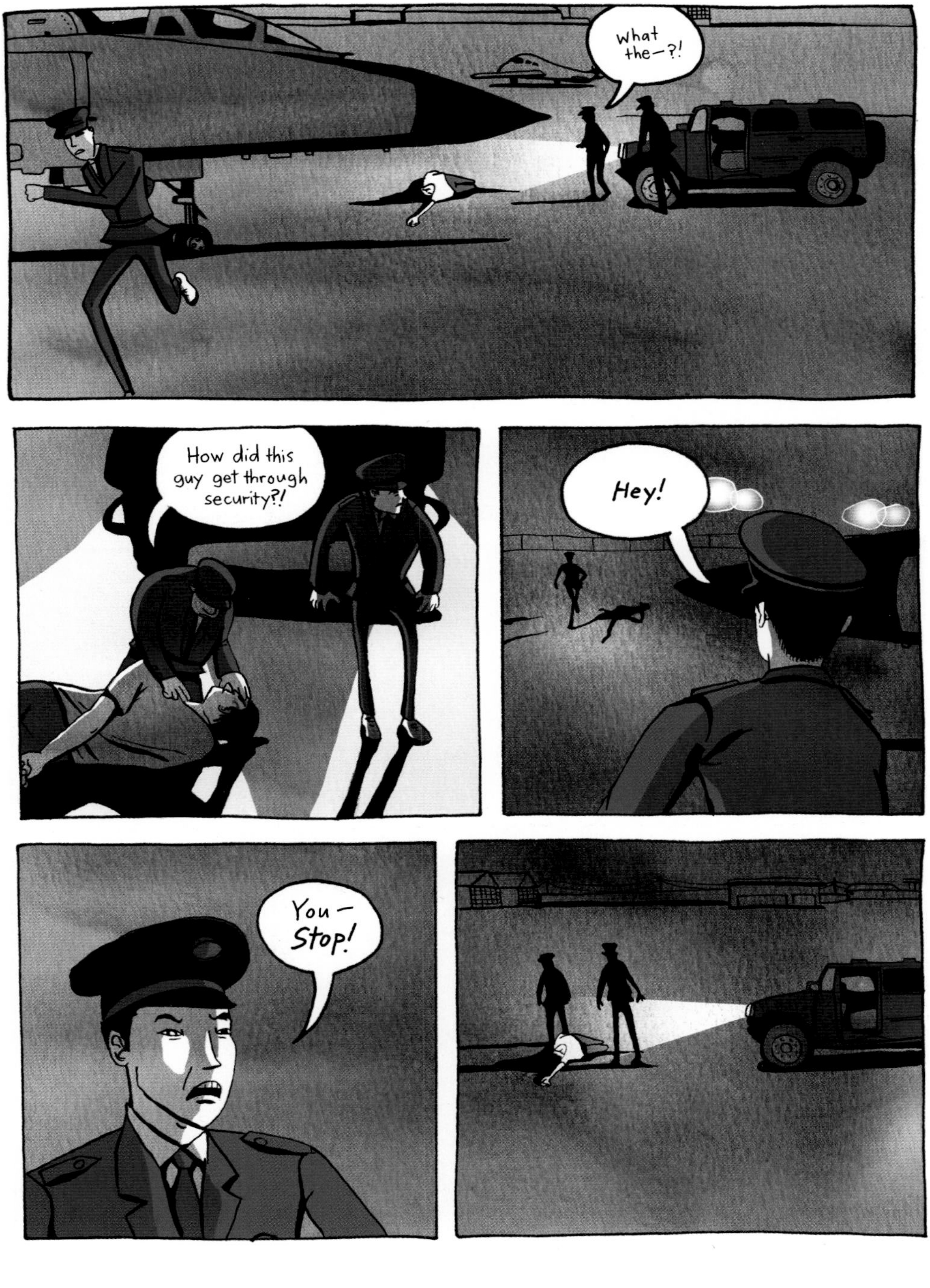
What the—?!
How did this guy get through security?!
Hey!
You— Stop!

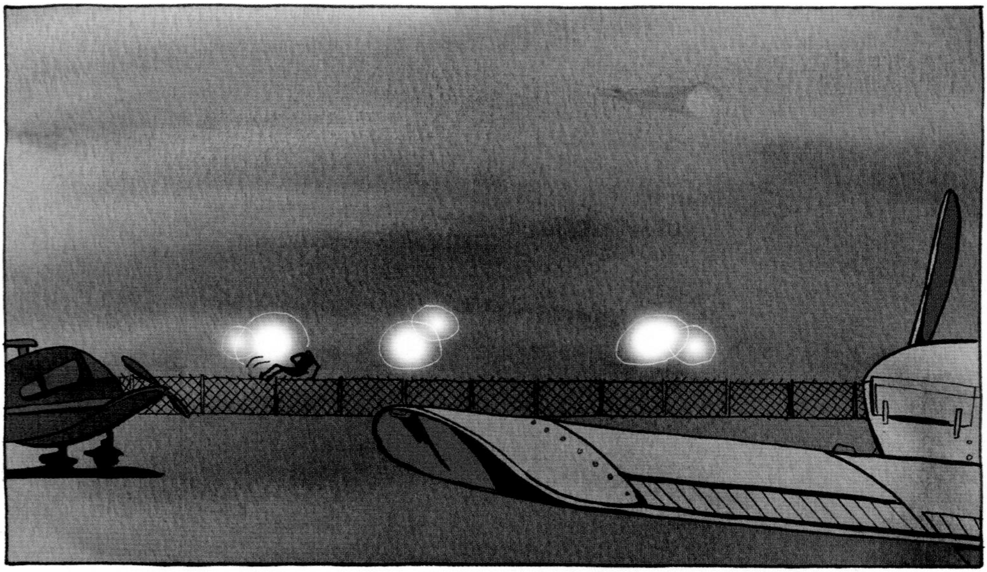

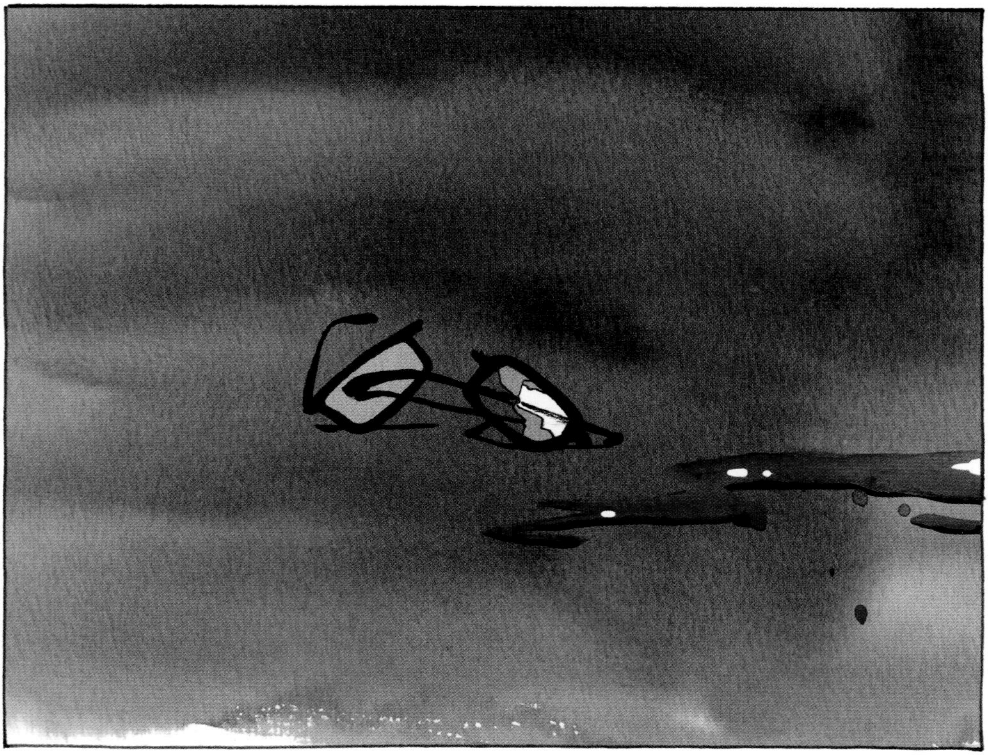

THIS STORY BEGINS WHERE
A YOUNG LIFE ENDS...

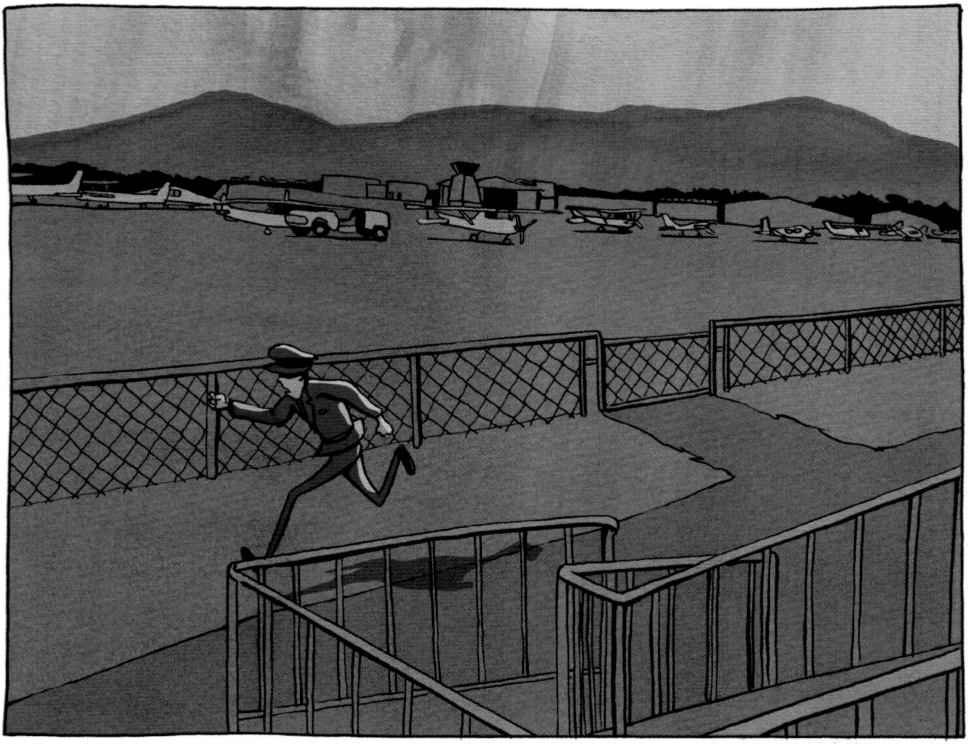

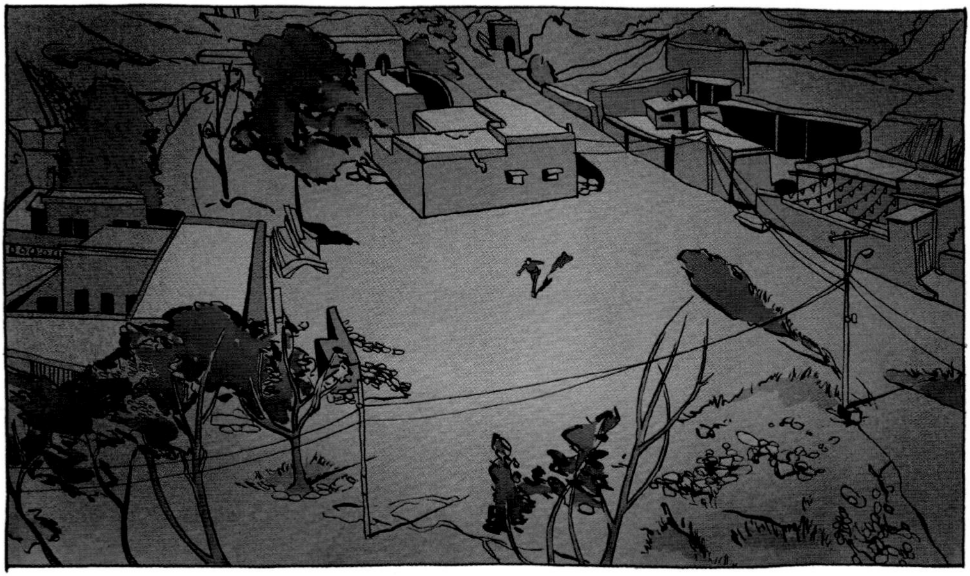

BUT THE JOURNEY BEGAN WITH OUR ANCESTORS MANY CENTURIES AGO.

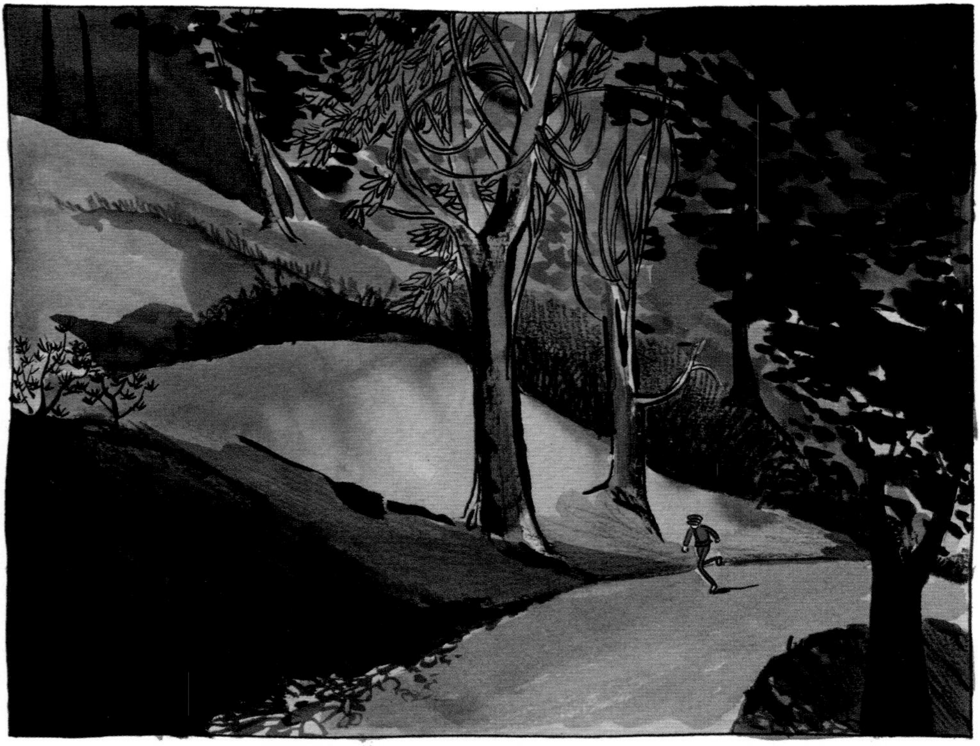

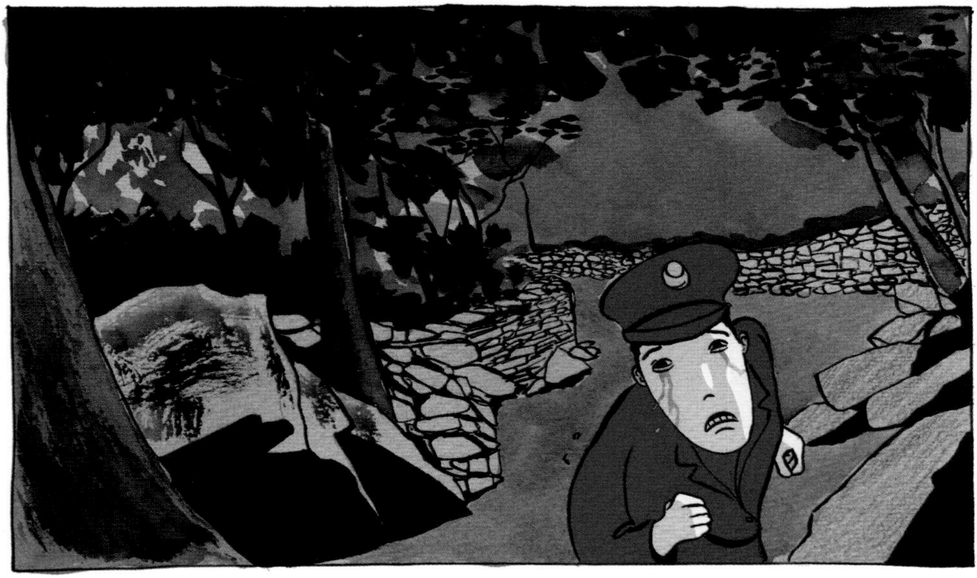

IN THE YEAR 208 AD, THE SON OF THE WARLORD CAO CAO BECAME GRAVELY ILL. CAO CAO SPARED NO EXPENSE OR EFFORT TO SAVE CAO CHONG, A CHILD PRODIGY AND HIS FAVORITE OF TWENTY-FIVE SONS;

NONETHELESS THE BOY DIED AT THE AGE OF THIRTEEN.

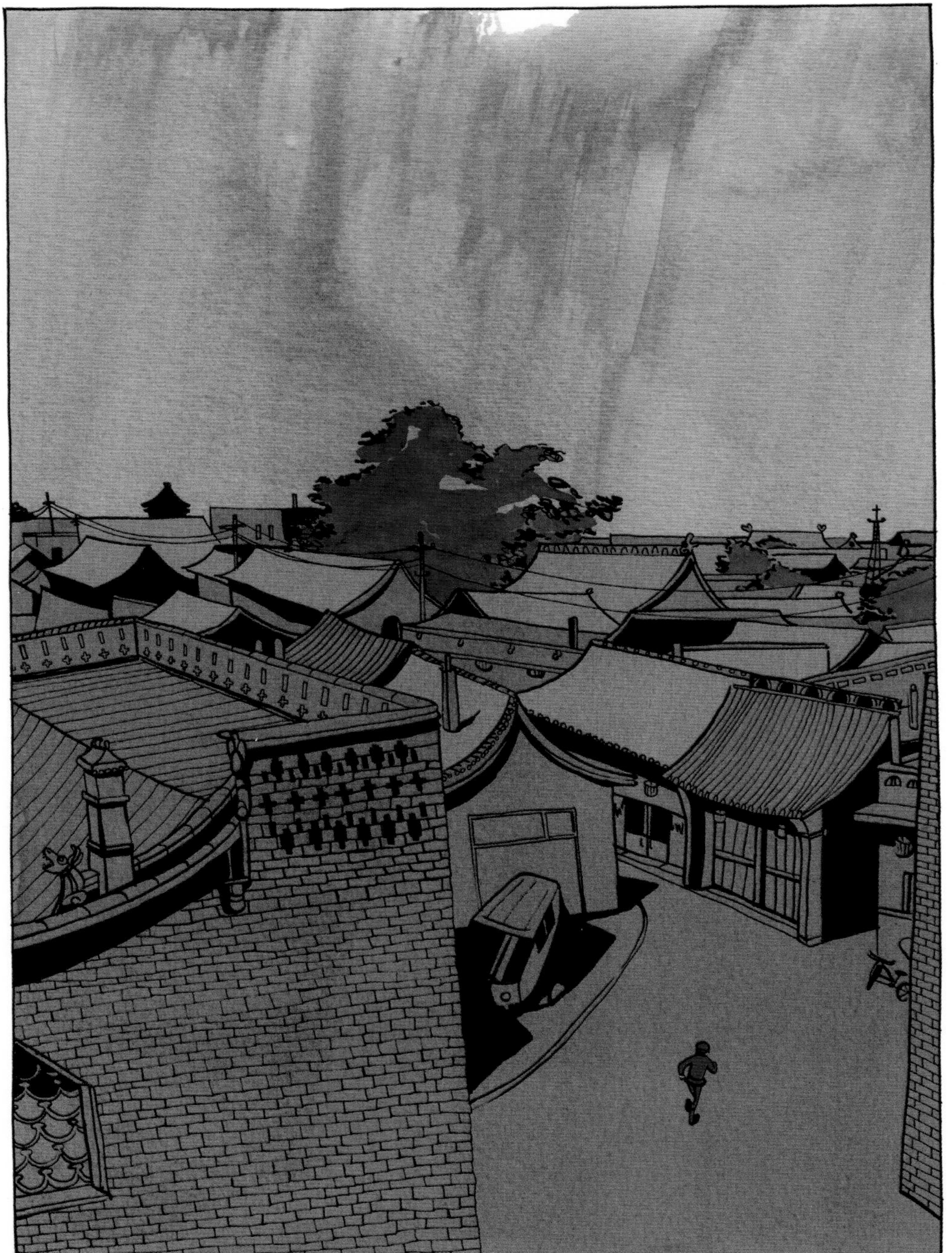

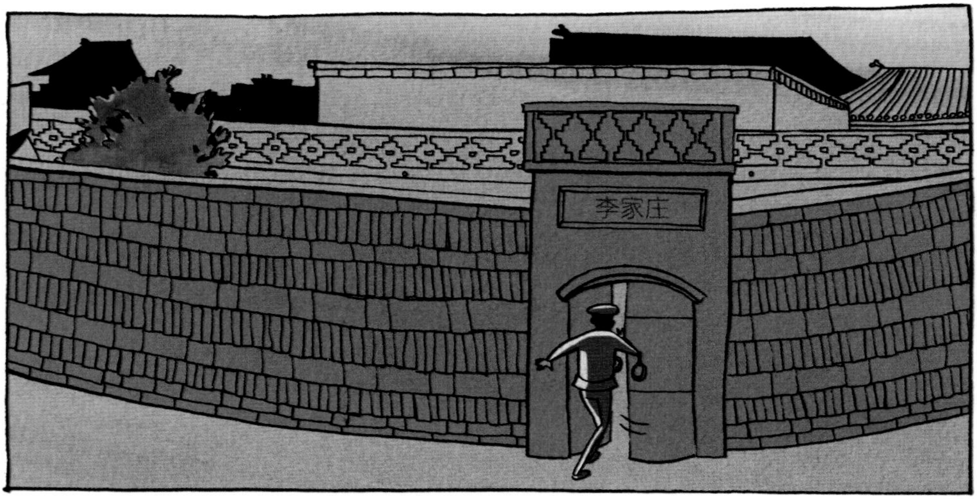
李家庄

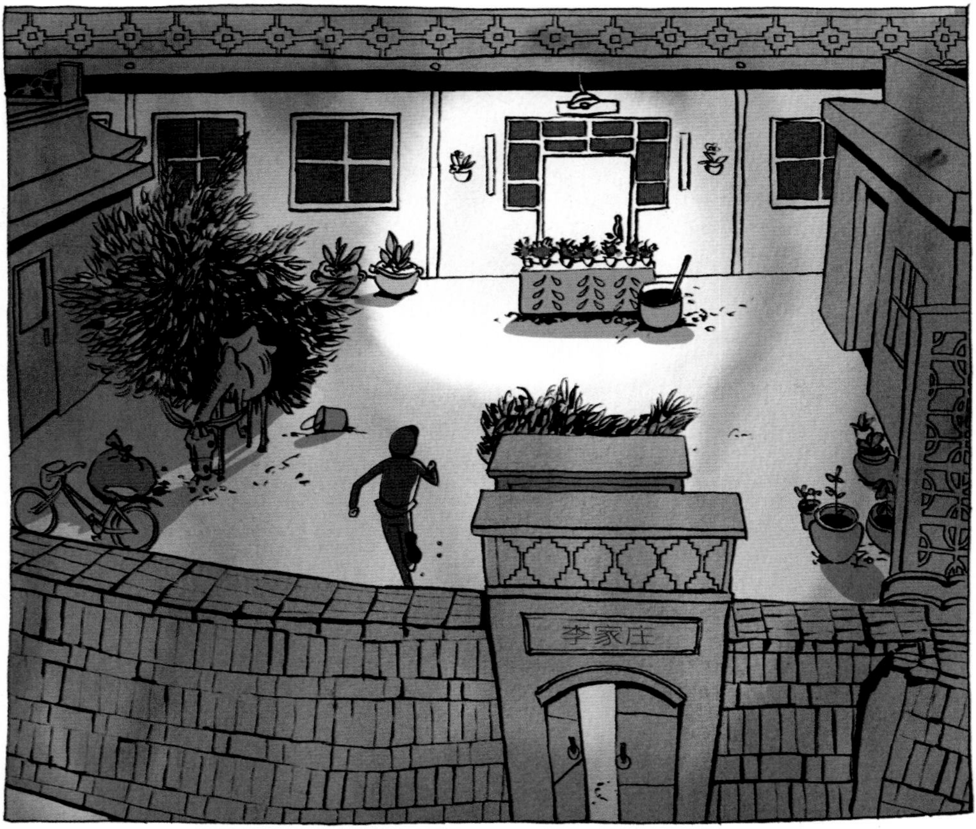
李家庄

Dear son, child not yet a man, who will hold your hand as you approach the gates of heaven?

Who will lie with you in the dark eternal bedroom?

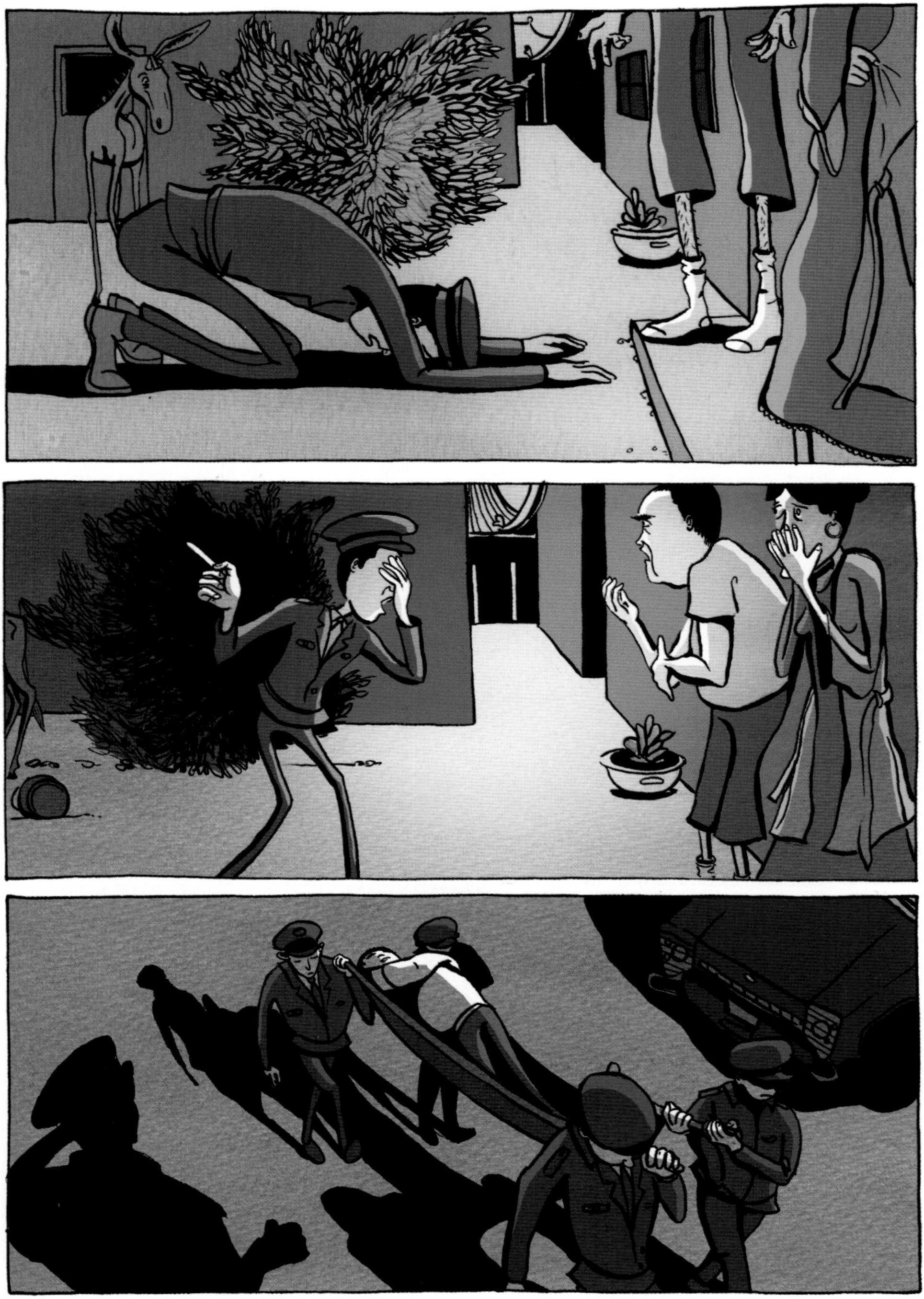

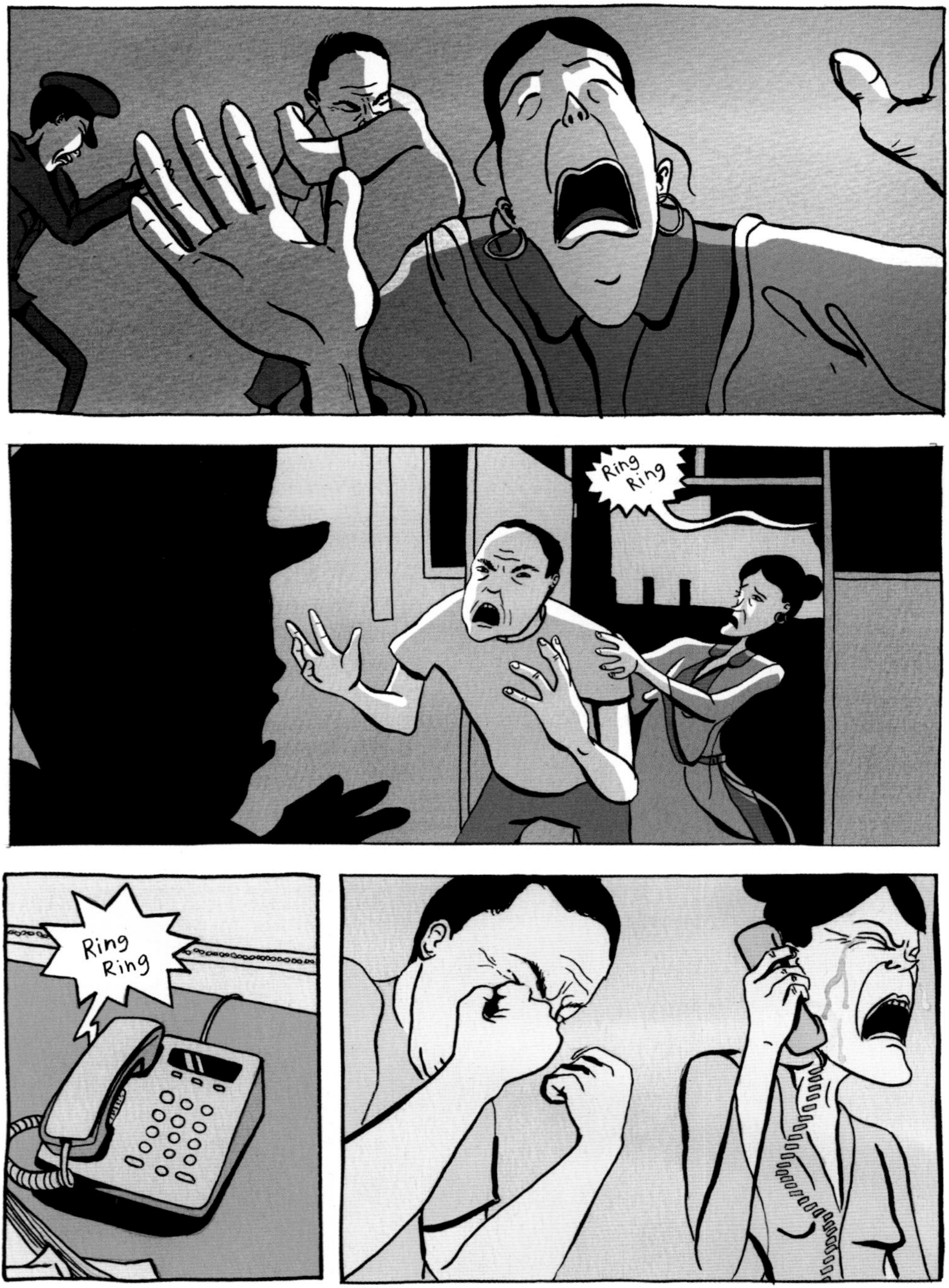
Ring Ring
Ring Ring

CAO CAO, THE BEREAVED, CALLED BEFORE HIM THE
MARRIAGE BROKERS, THE DOCTORS, THE UNDERTAKERS,
AND THE GRAVEDIGGERS OF HIS DOMINION.

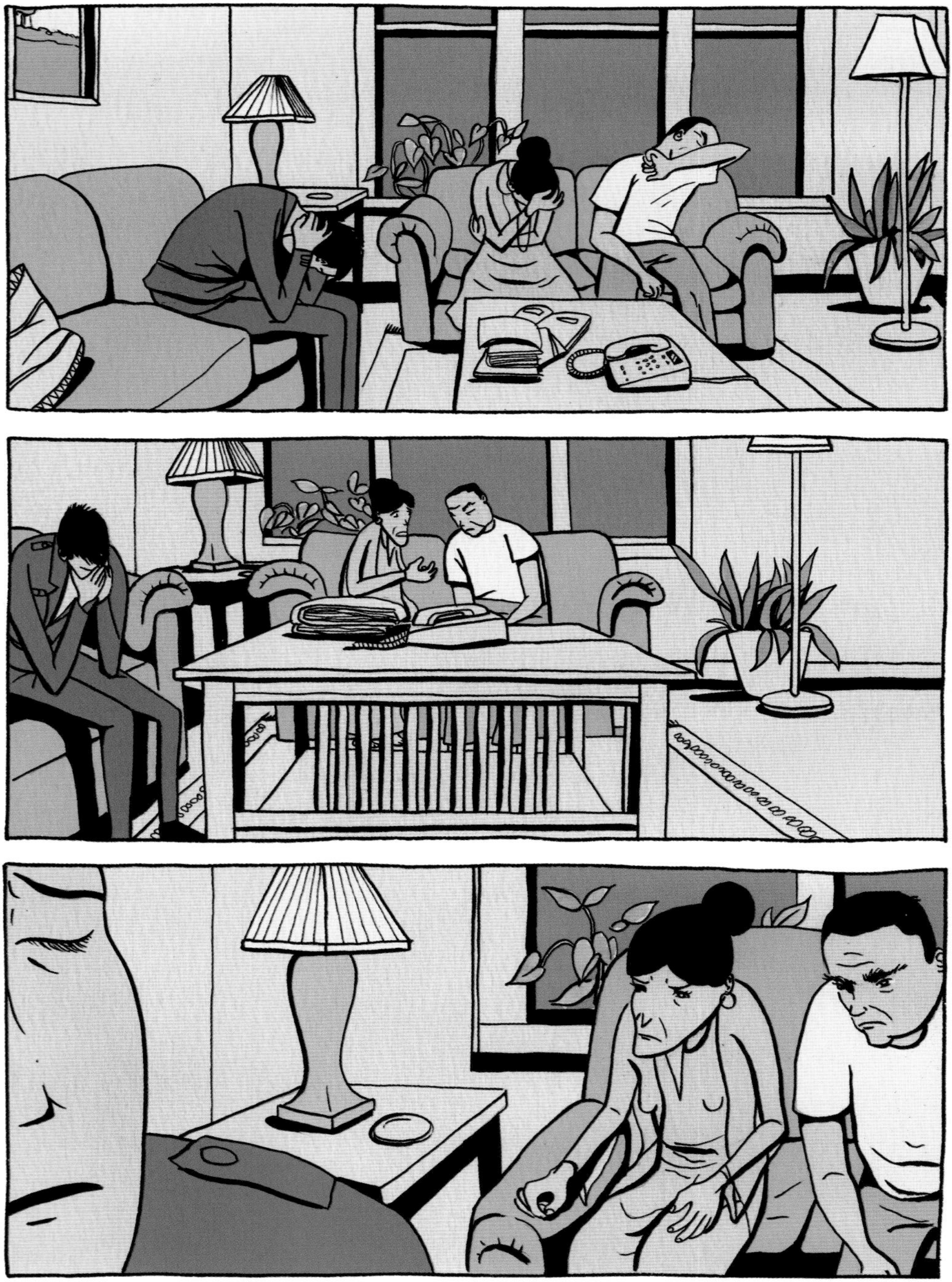

AND HE SAID TO THEM,

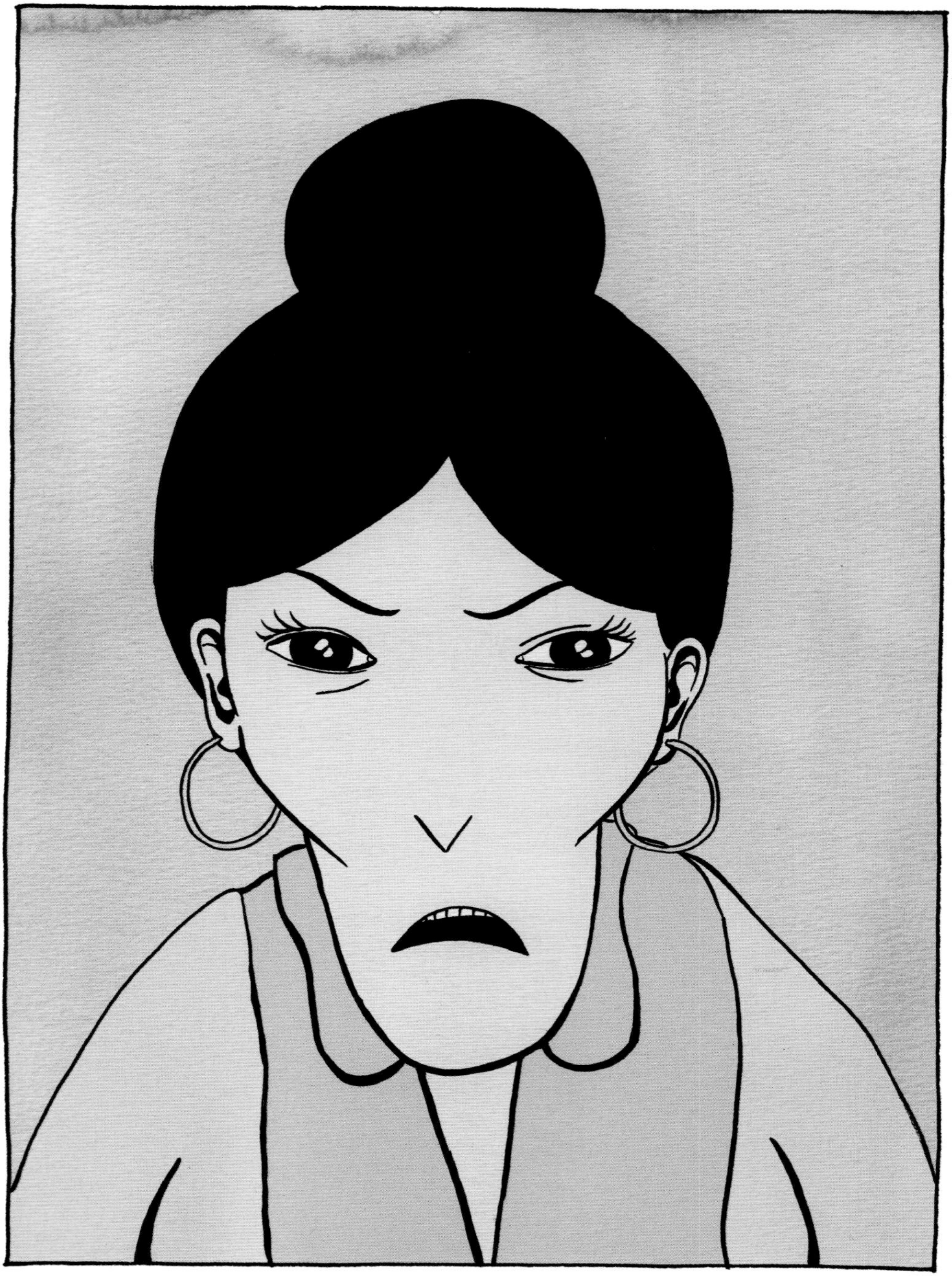

Find me the body of a woman.

AND THEY FOUND HIM THE BODY OF A WOMAN, A DECEASED DAUGHTER FROM THE ESTEEMED CLAN OF ZHEN. THE CORPSE BRIDE WAS PREPARED, AND THE GRIEVING FATHER PRESIDED OVER HIS SON'S GHOST MARRIAGE.

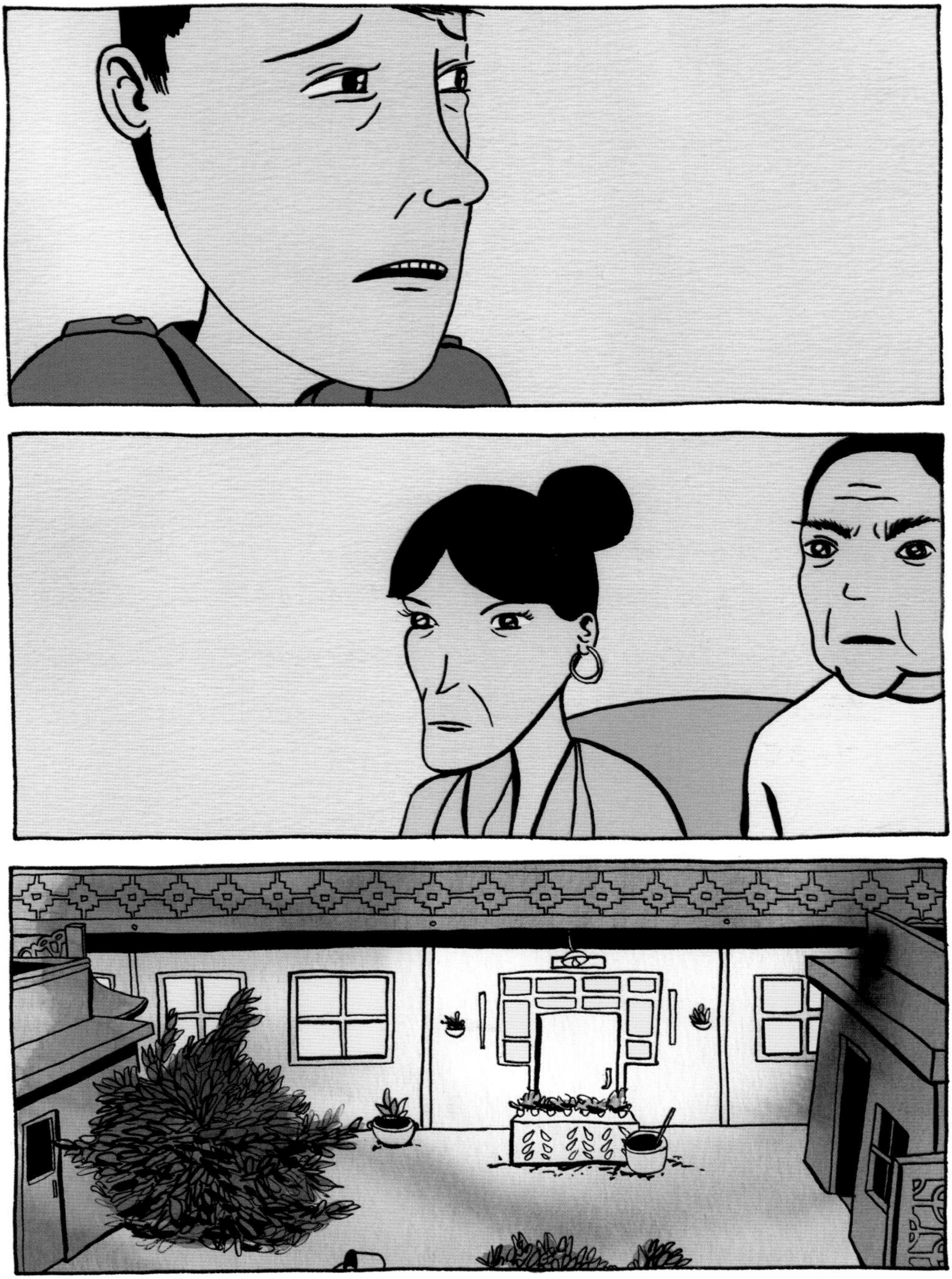

Sweet boy, you who have known so little of life, be brave, for you are not alone. Sleep long in the arms of your lover.

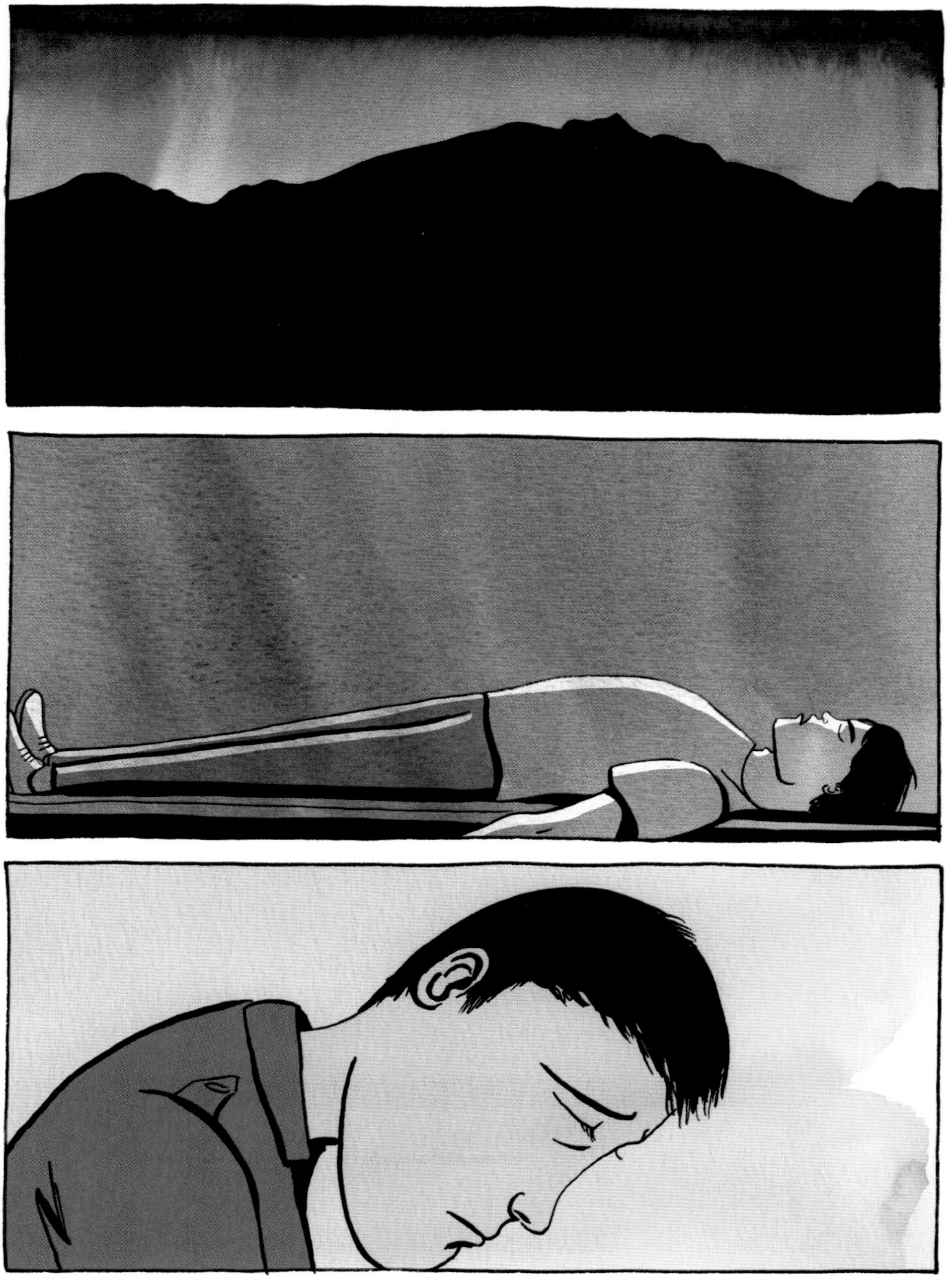

1. House of Li

SUNDAY

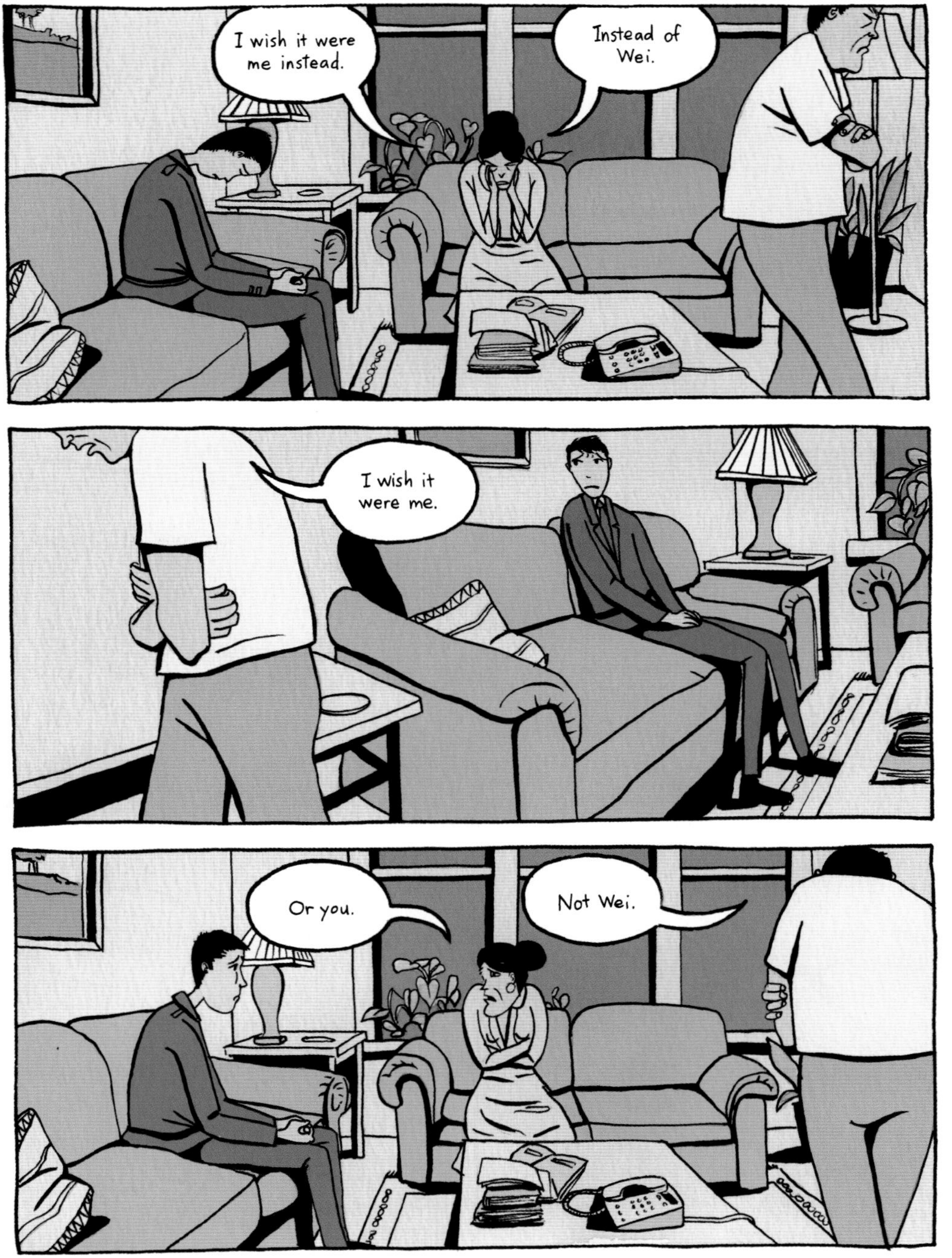
I wish it were me instead.
Instead of Wei.
I wish it were me.
Or you.
Not Wei.

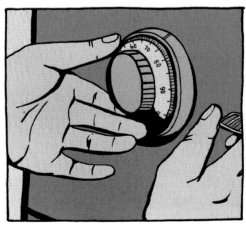

It's terrible, **terrible.**

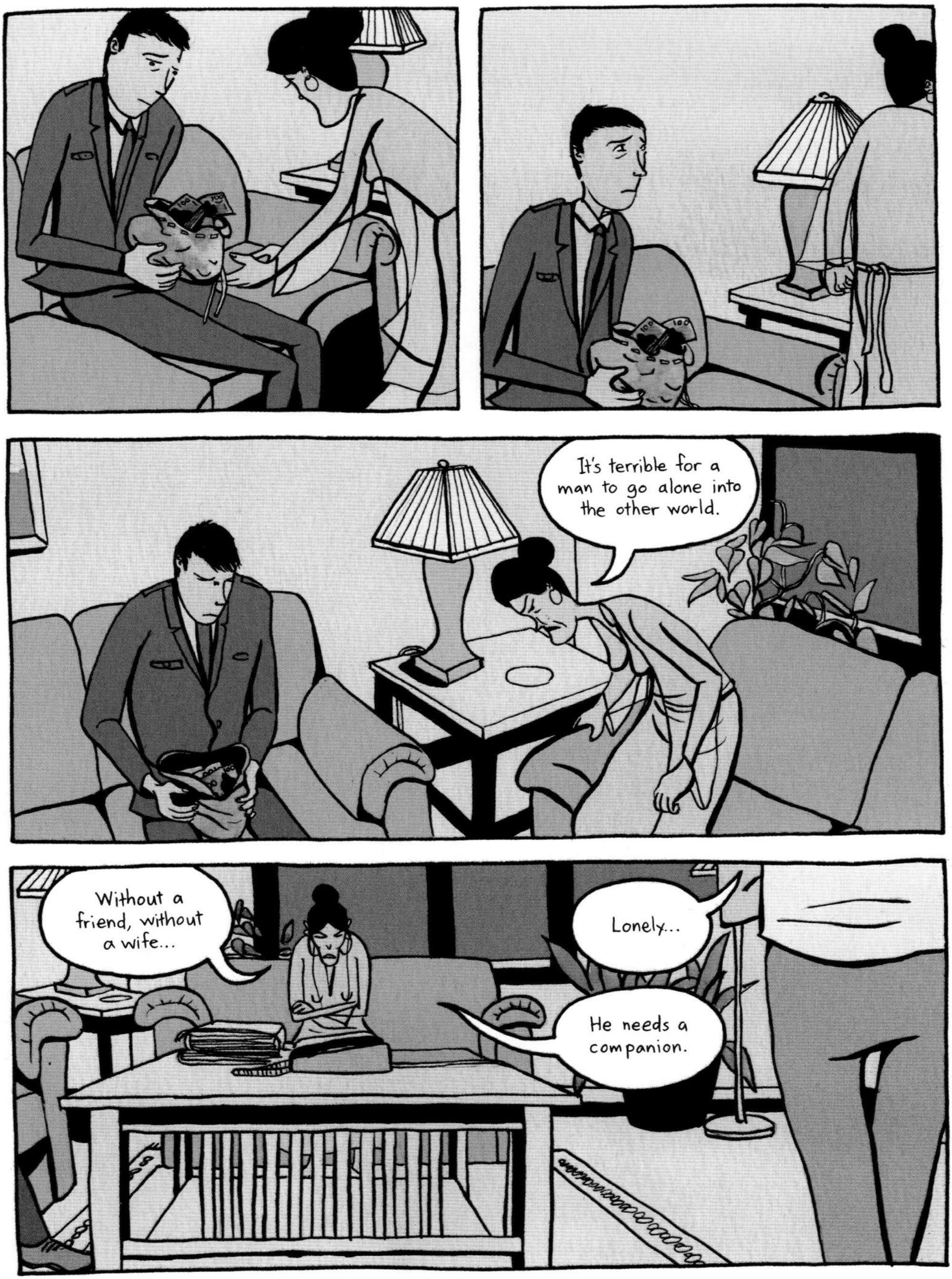
It's terrible for a man to go alone into the other world.
Without a friend, without a wife...
Lonely...
He needs a companion.

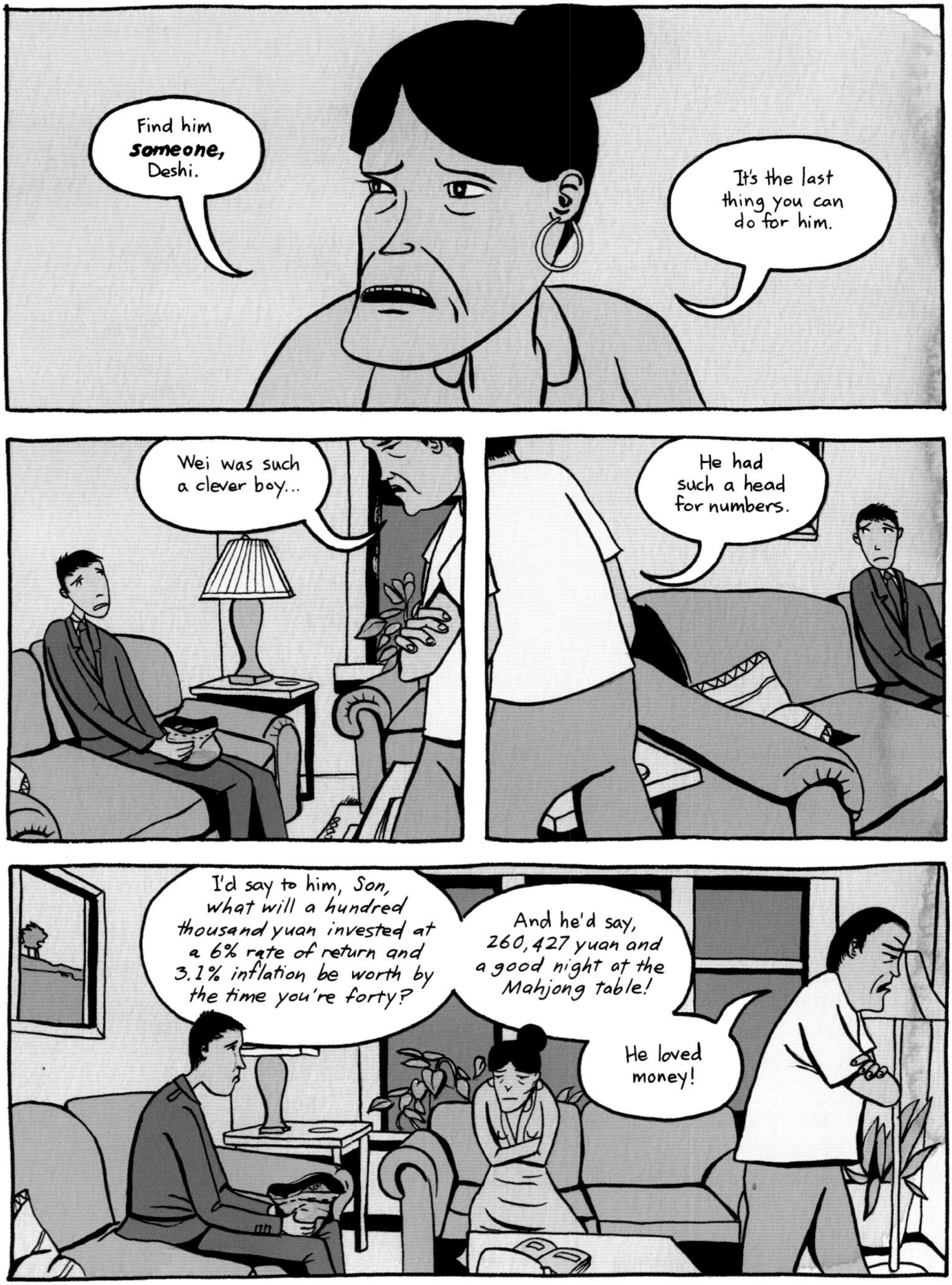
Find him **someone,** Deshi.
It's the last thing you can do for him.
Wei was such a clever boy...
He had such a head for numbers.
I'd say to him, Son, what will a hundred thousand yuan invested at a 6% rate of return and 3.1% inflation be worth by the time you're forty?
And he'd say, 260,427 yuan and a good night at the Mahjong table!
He loved money!

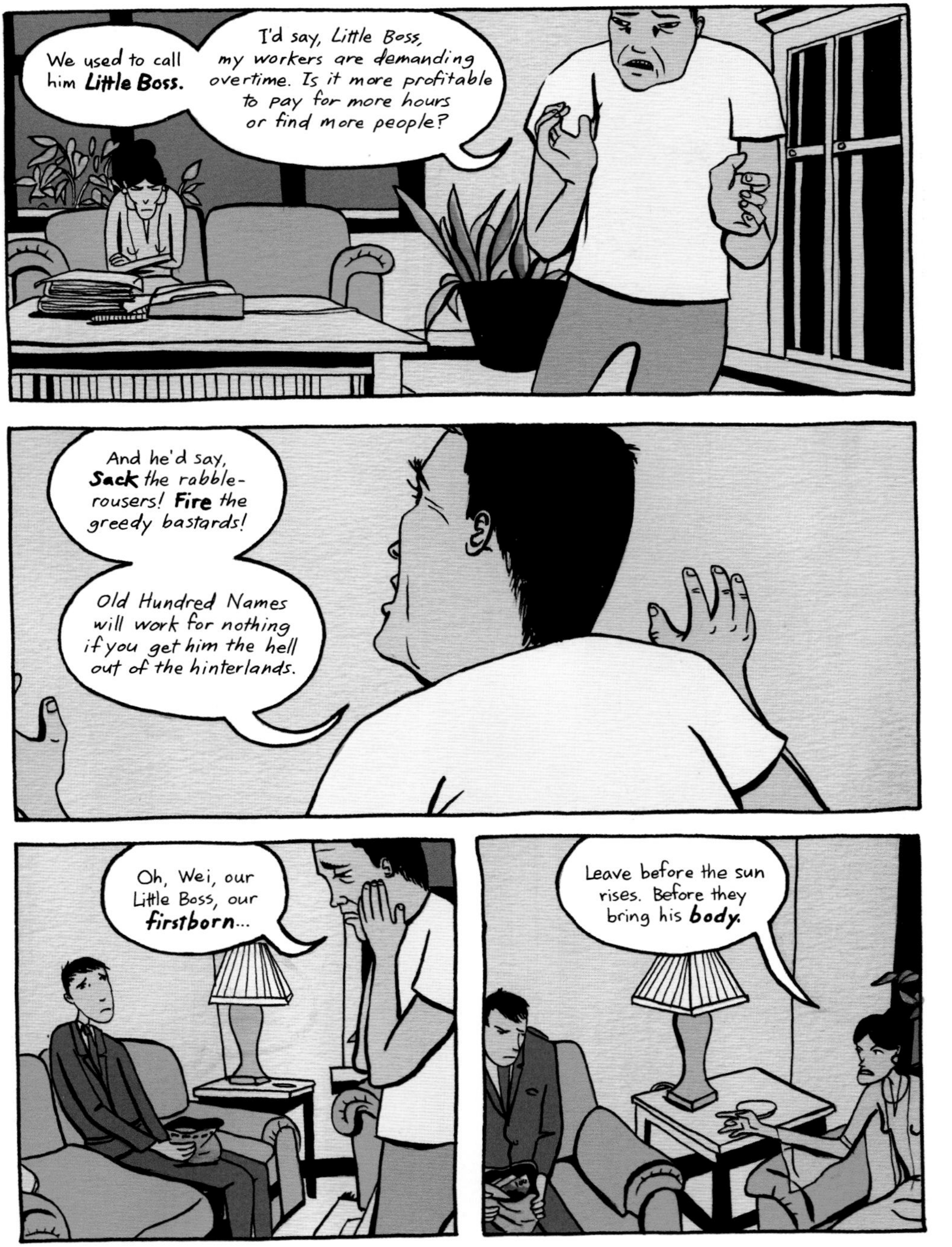
We used to call him **Little Boss.**
I'd say, *Little Boss, my workers are demanding overtime. Is it more profitable to pay for more hours or find more people?*
And he'd say, ***Sack** the rabble-rousers! **Fire** the greedy bastards!*
Old Hundred Names will work for nothing if you get him the hell out of the hinterlands.
Oh, Wei, our Little Boss, our **firstborn**...
Leave before the sun rises. Before they bring his **body.**

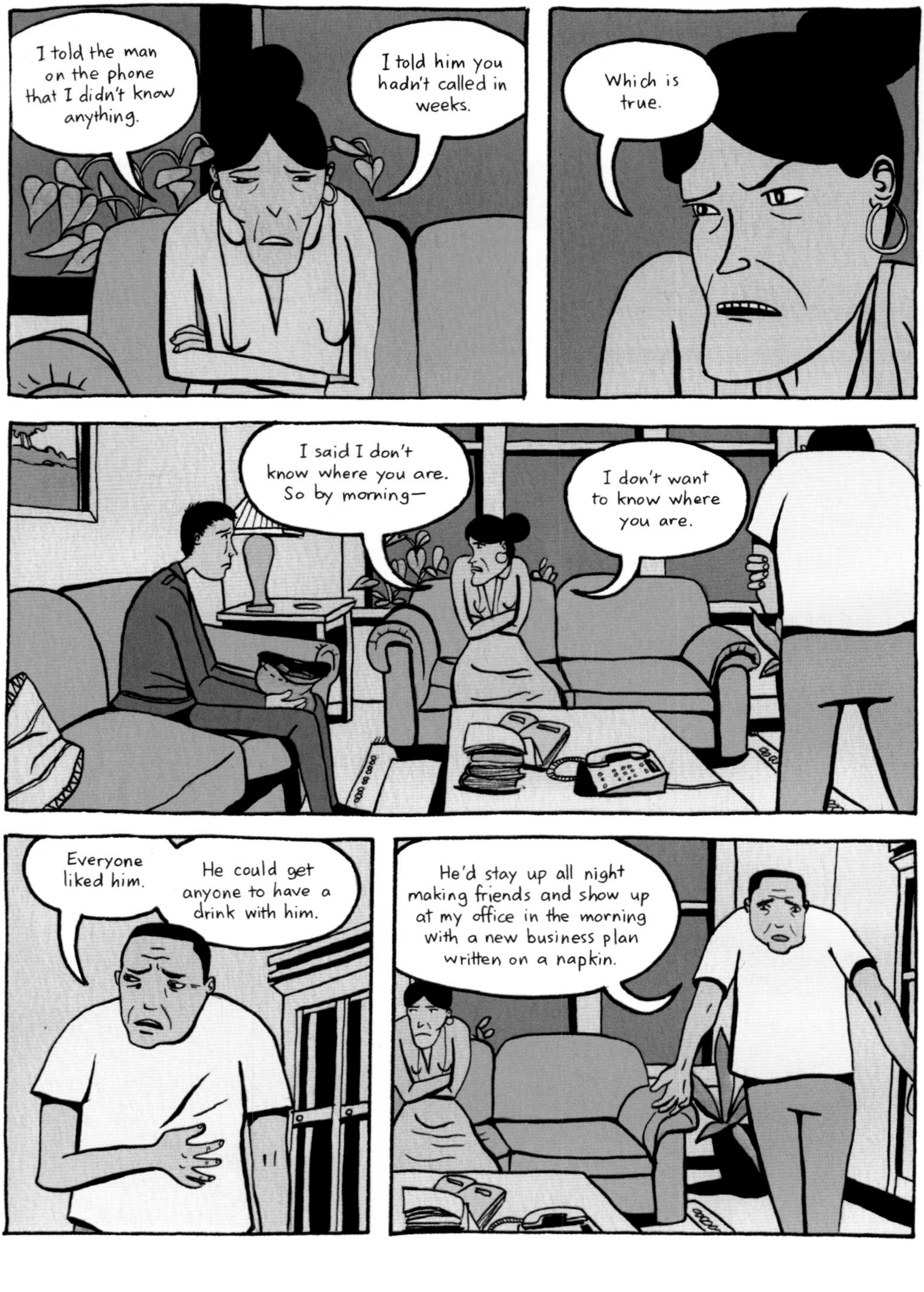
I told the man on the phone that I didn't know anything.
I told him you hadn't called in weeks.
Which is true.
I said I don't know where you are. So by morning—
I don't want to know where you are.
Everyone liked him.
He could get anyone to have a drink with him.
He'd stay up all night making friends and show up at my office in the morning with a new business plan written on a napkin.

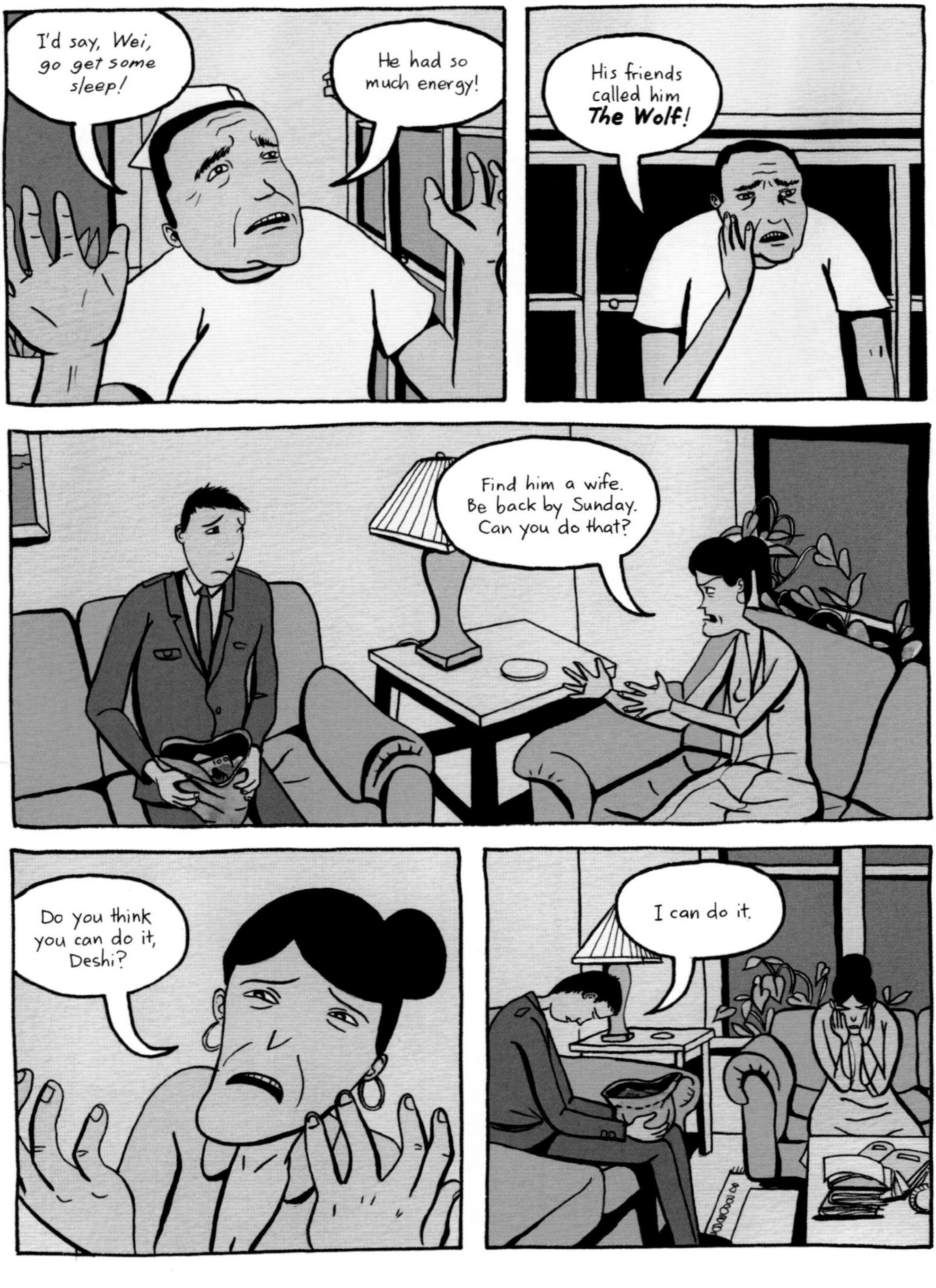
I'd say, Wei, go get some sleep!
He had so much energy!
His friends called him **The Wolf**!
Find him a wife. Be back by Sunday. Can you do that?
Do you think you can do it, Deshi?
I can do it.

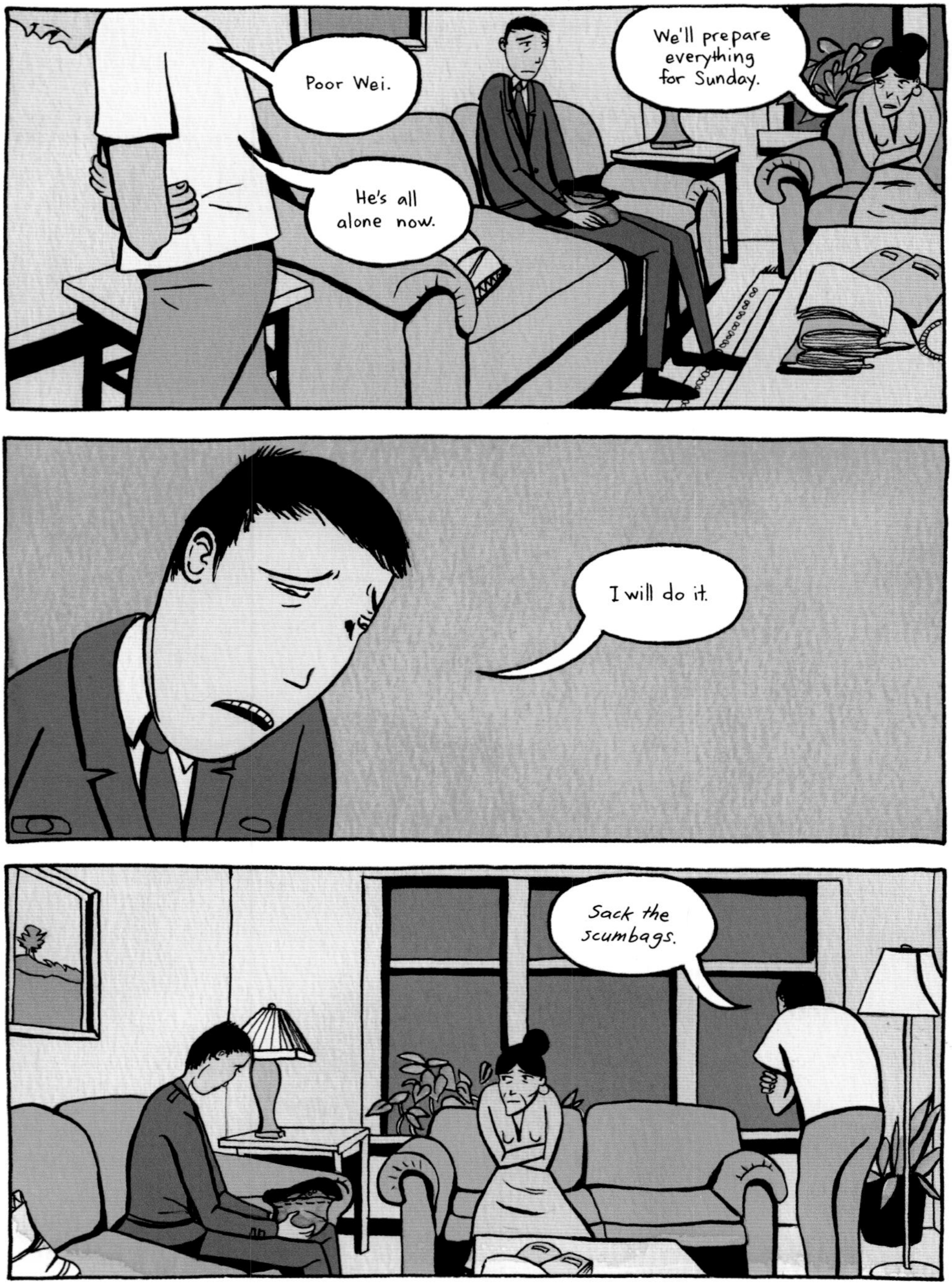
Poor Wei.
He's all alone now.
We'll prepare everything for Sunday.
I will do it.
Sack the scumbags.

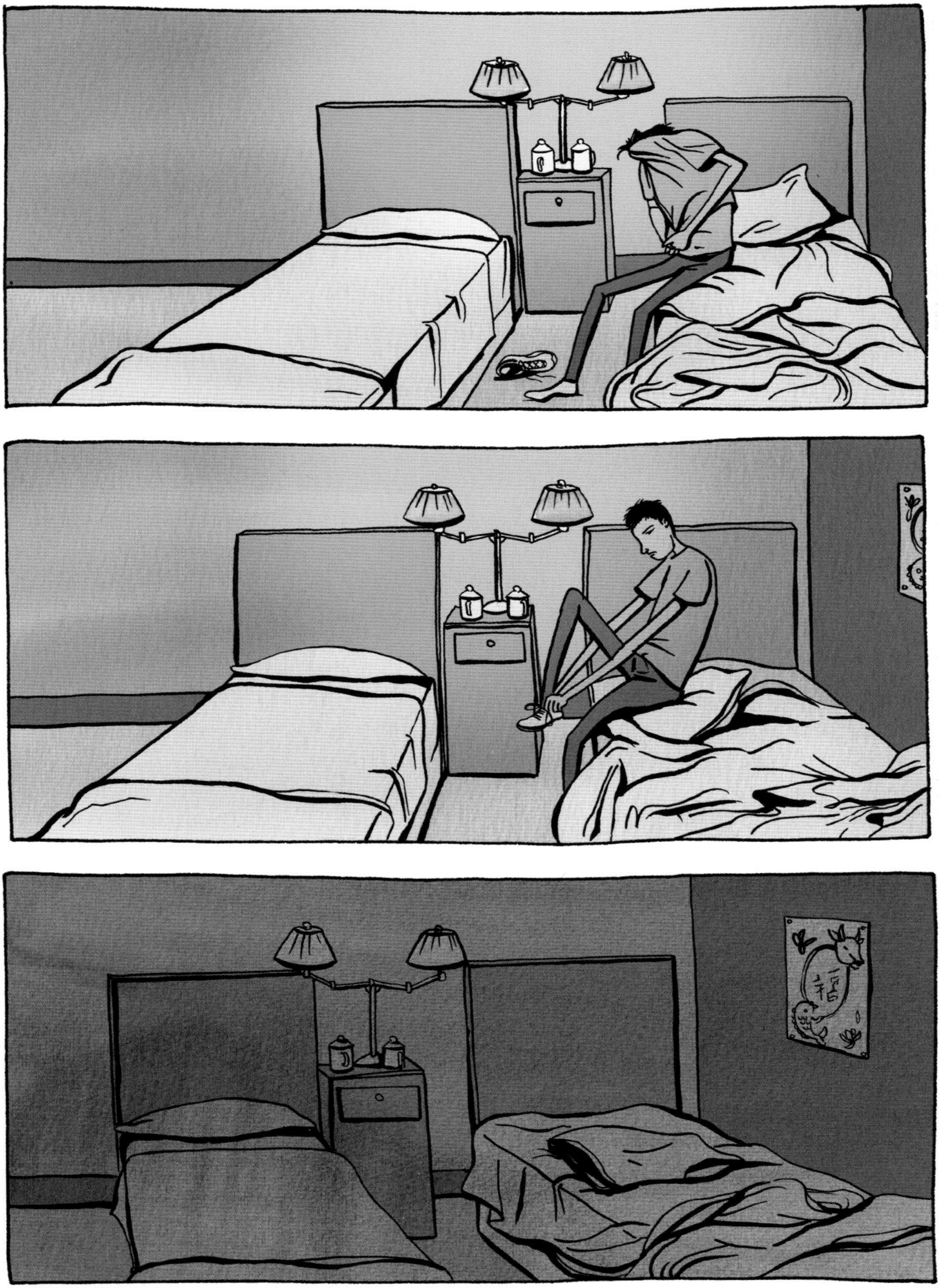

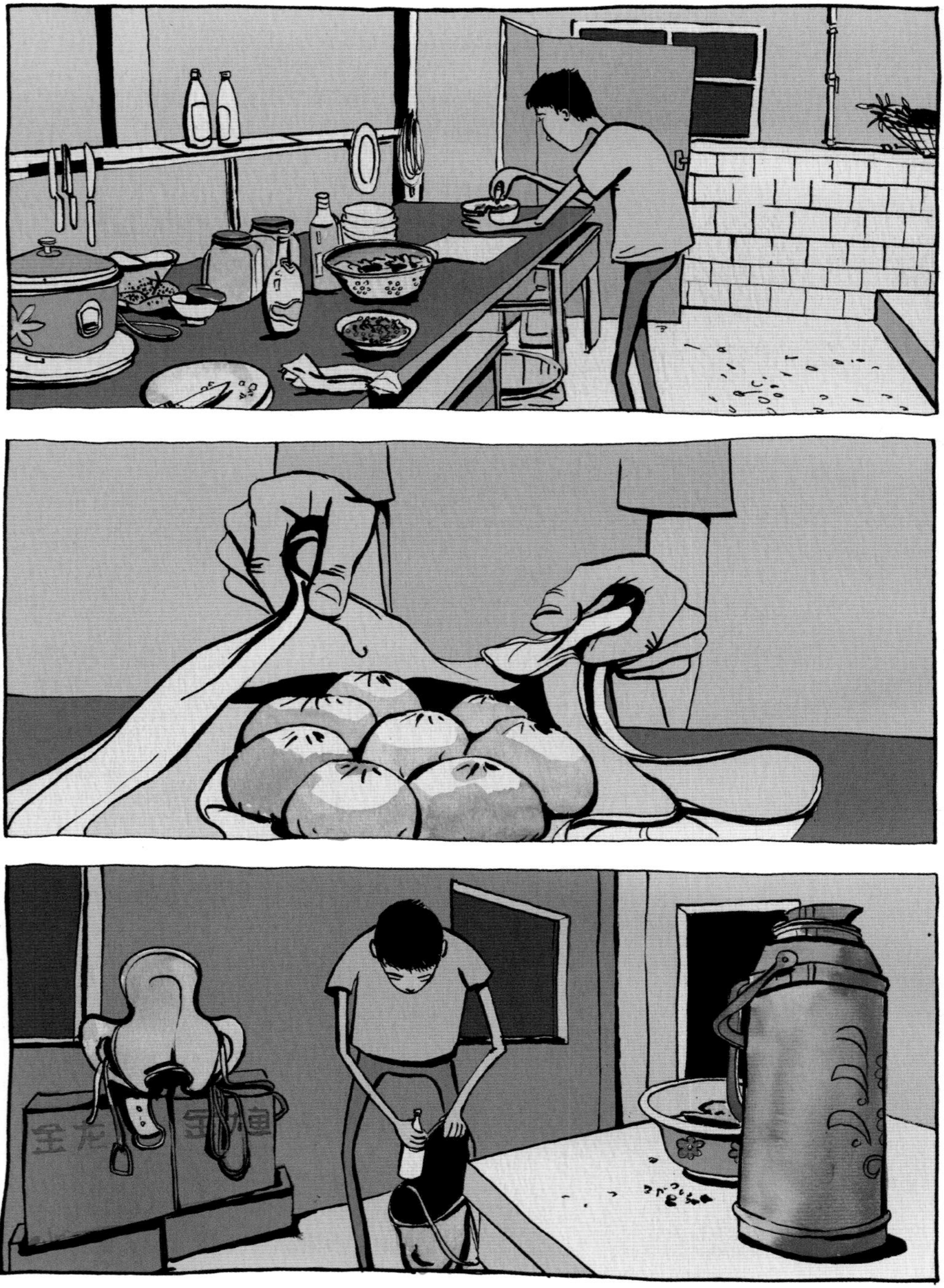

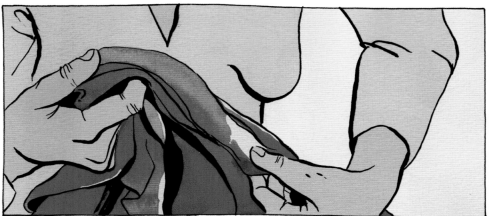

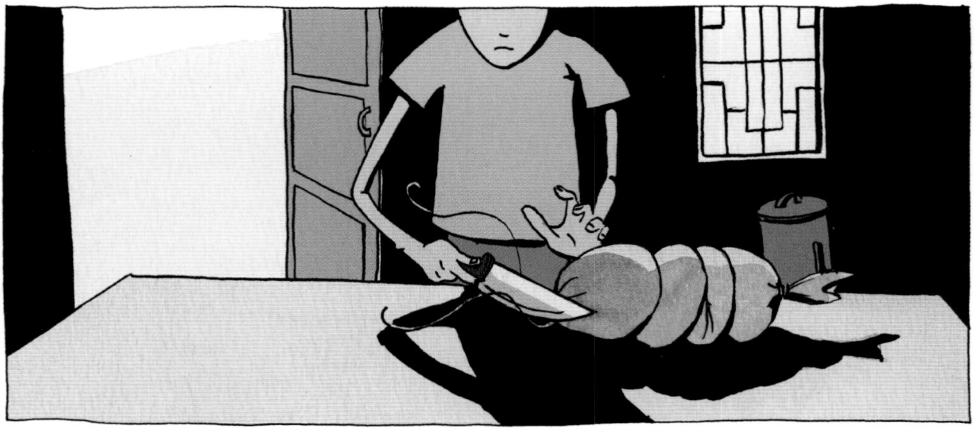
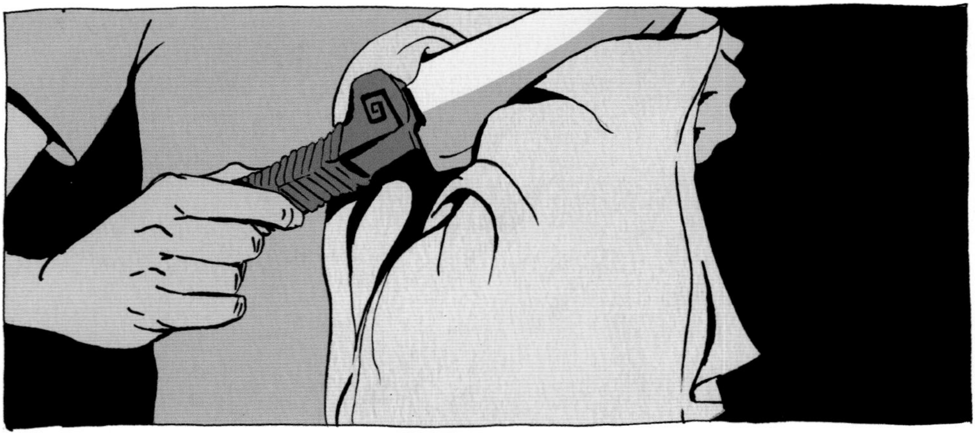
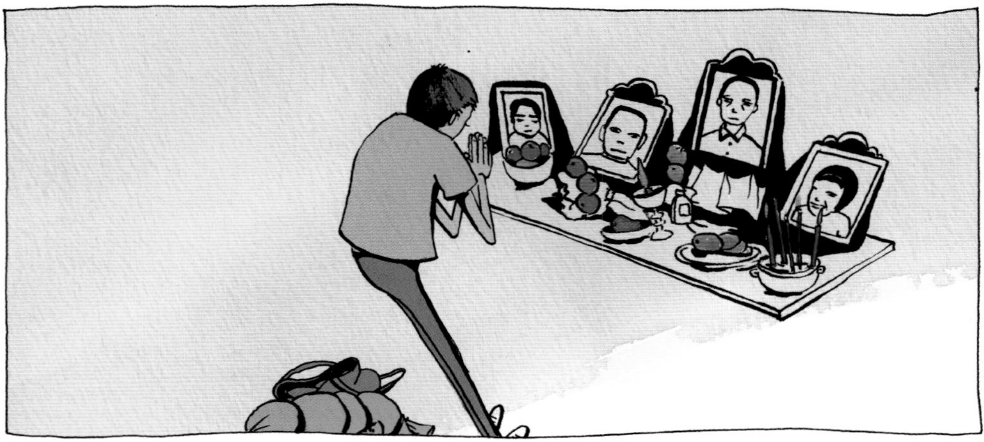

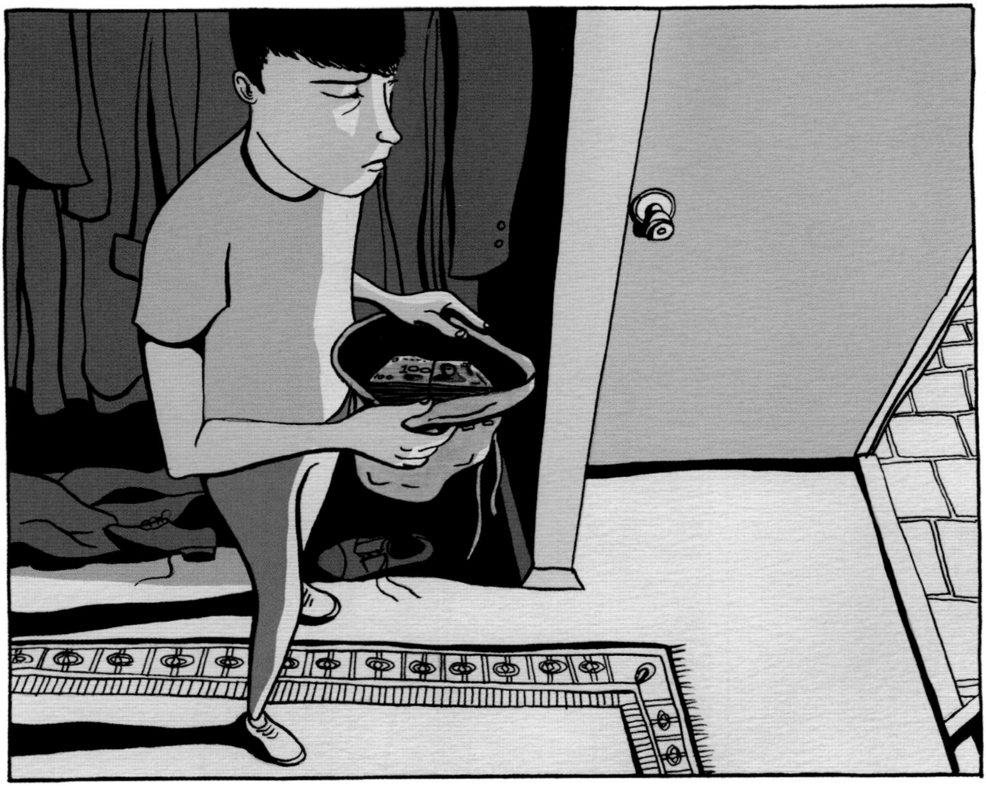

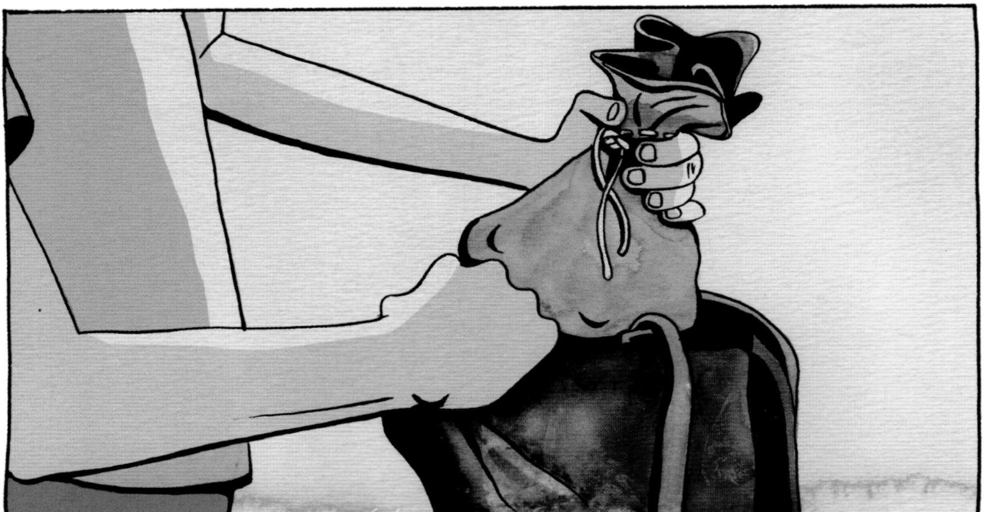

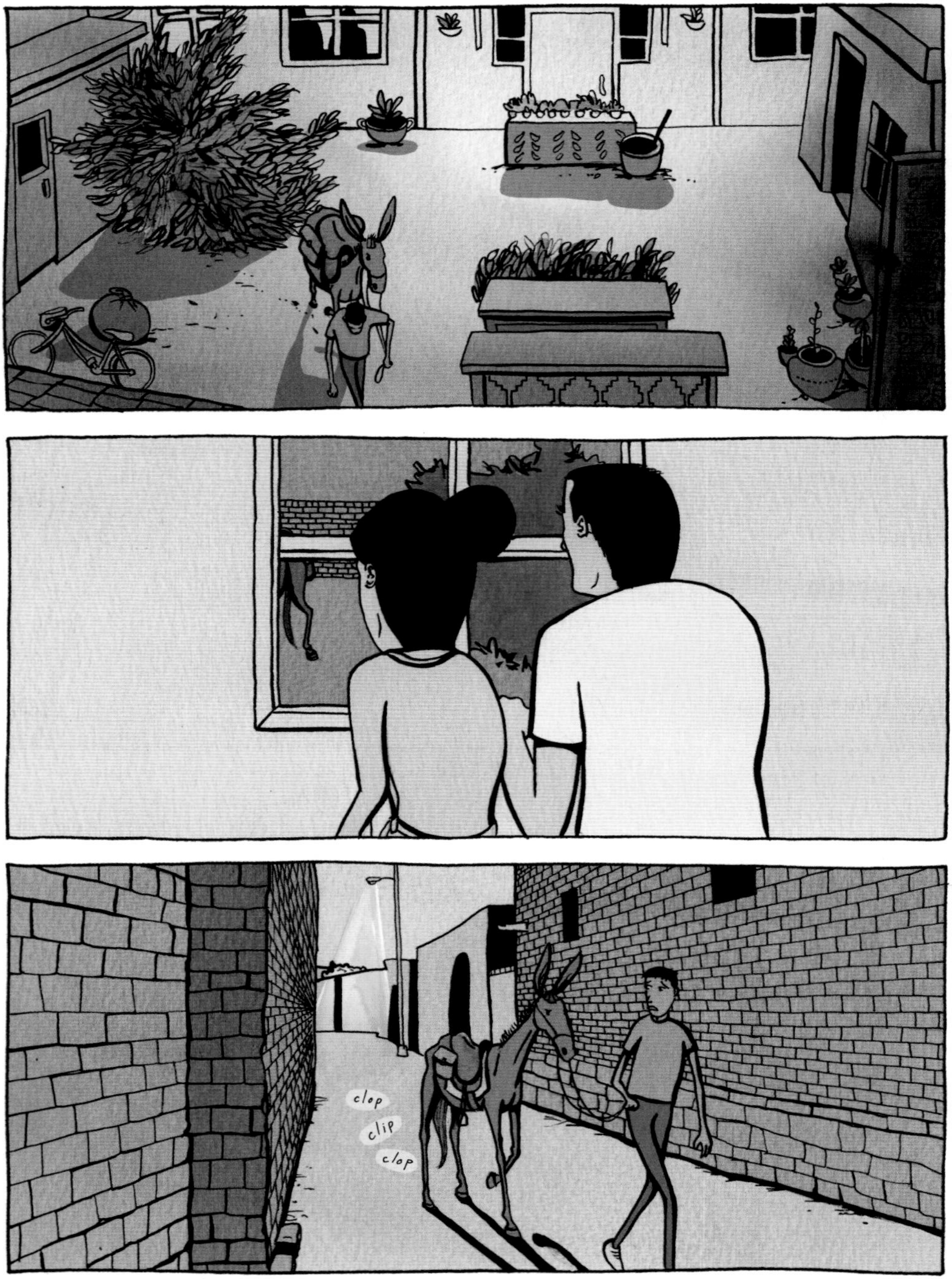
clop
clip
clop

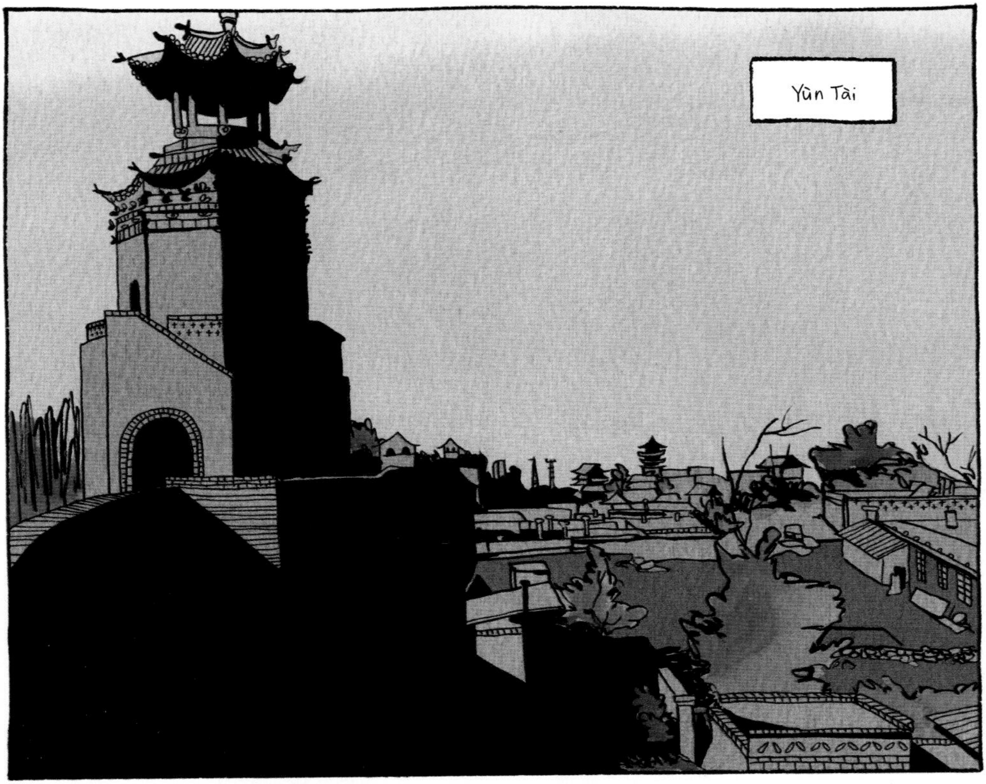
Yùn Tài

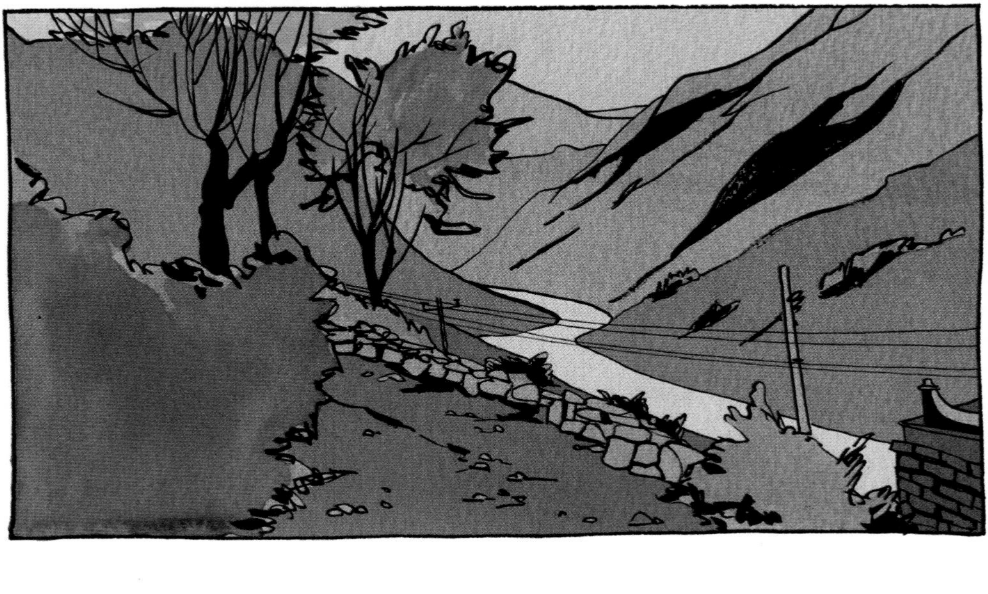

2. Matchmaker

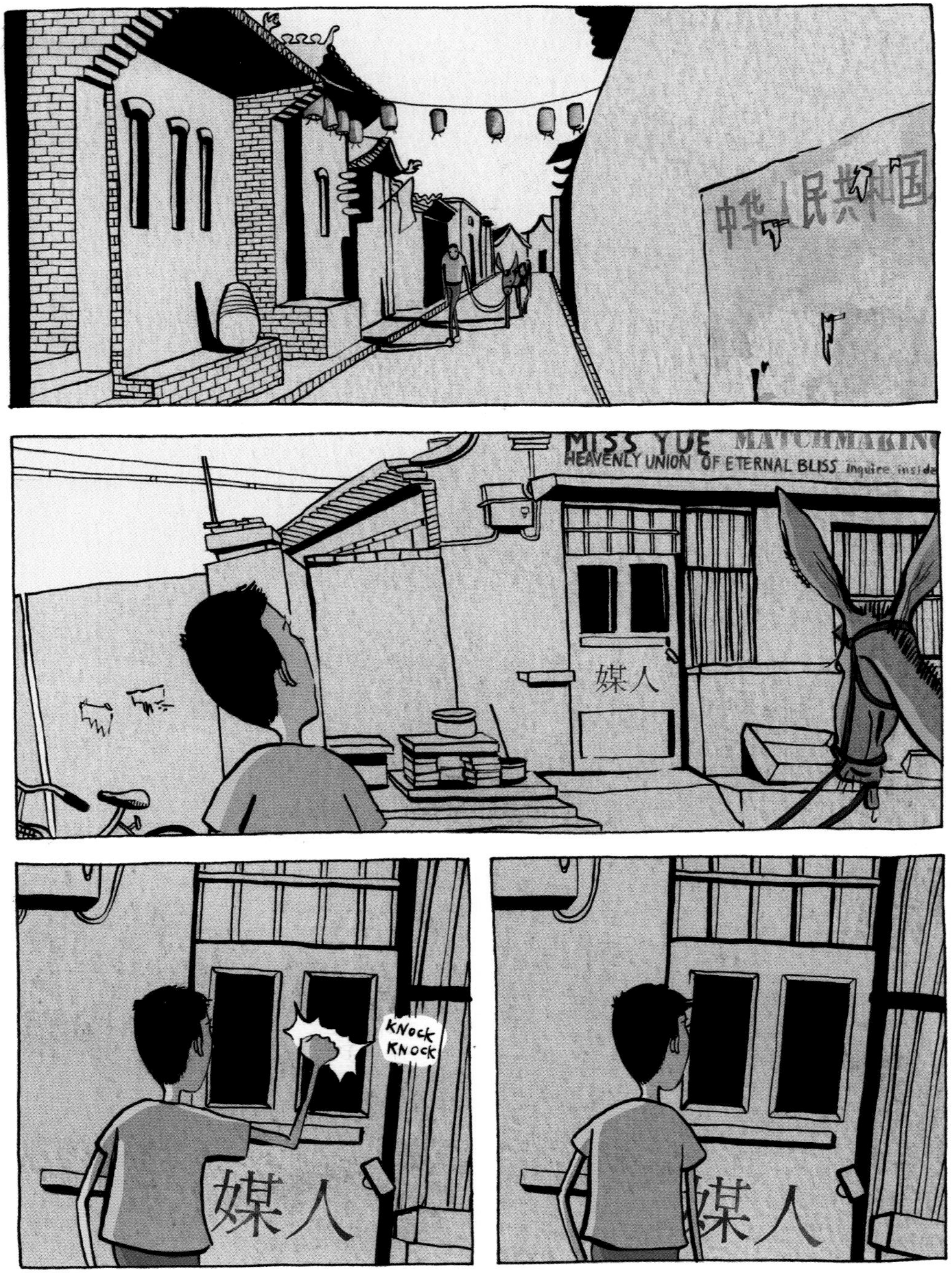
MISS YUE MATCHMAKIN
HEAVENLY UNION OF ETERNAL BLISS inquire insid
媒人
KNOCK KNOCK
媒人
媒人

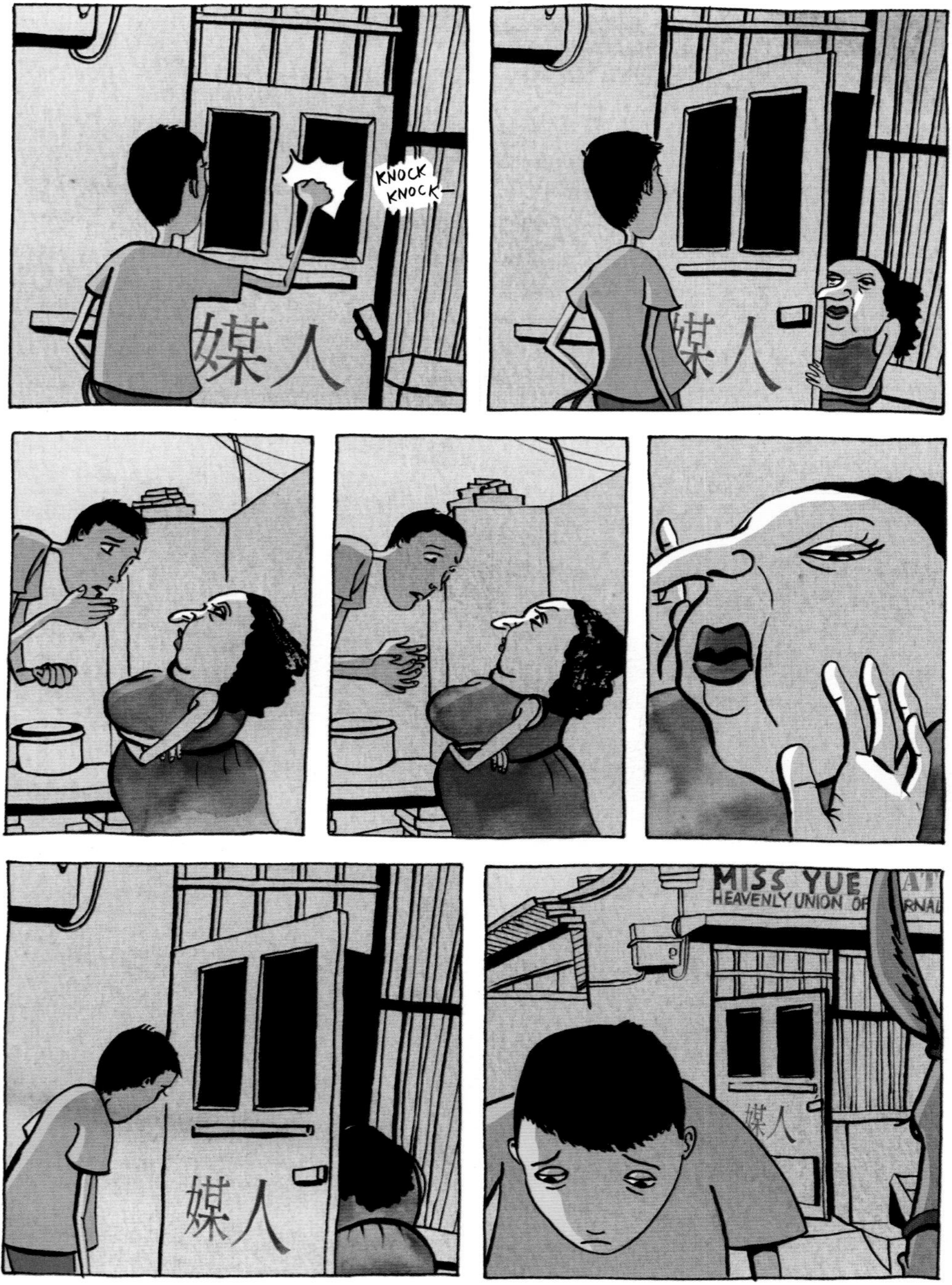
KNOCK KNOCK—
媒人
媒人
媒人
MISS YUE
HEAVENLY UNION
媒人

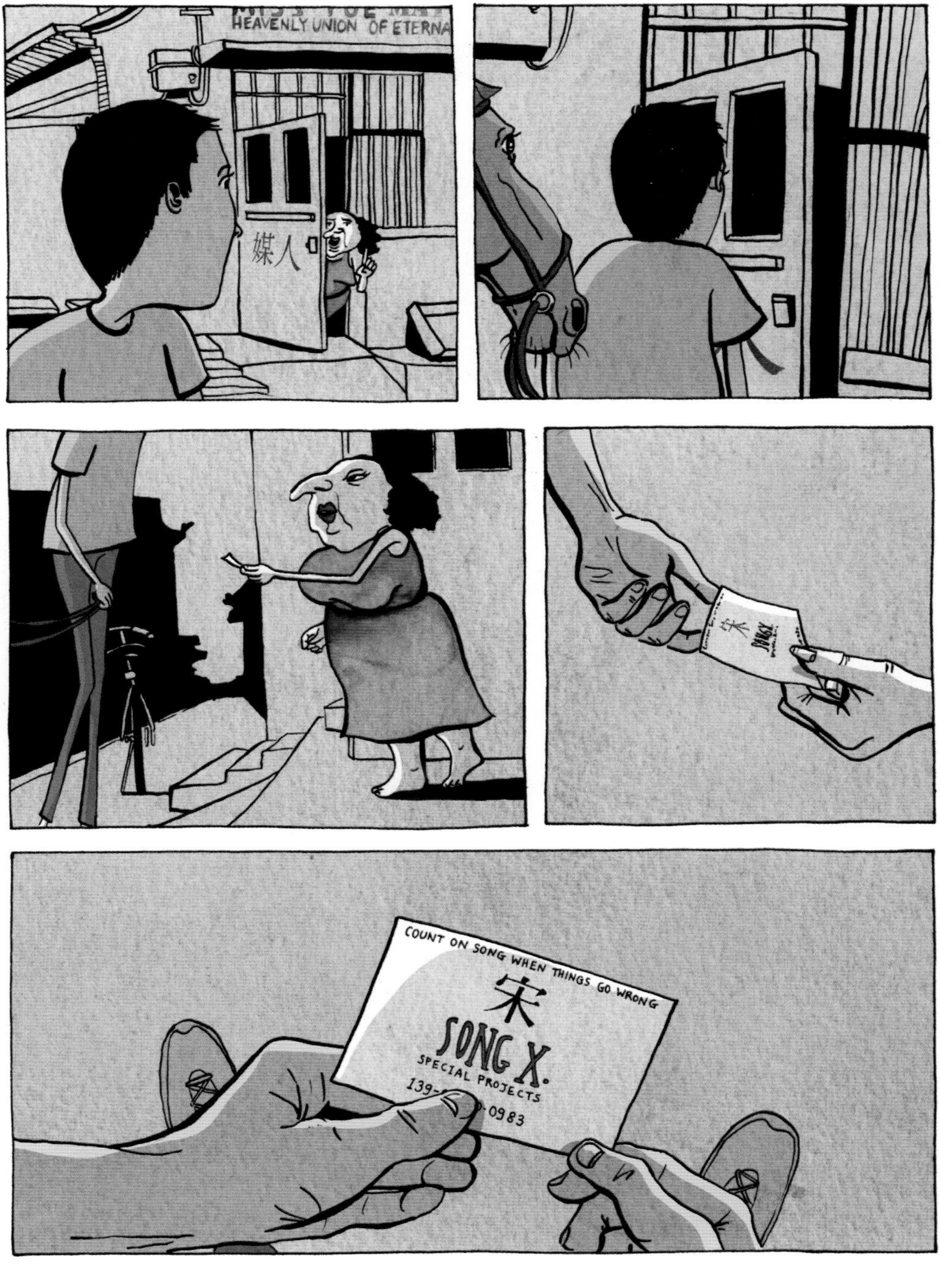
HEAVENLY UNION OF ETERNA
媒人
COUNT ON SONG WHEN THINGS GO WRONG
宋
SONG X.
SPECIAL PROJECTS

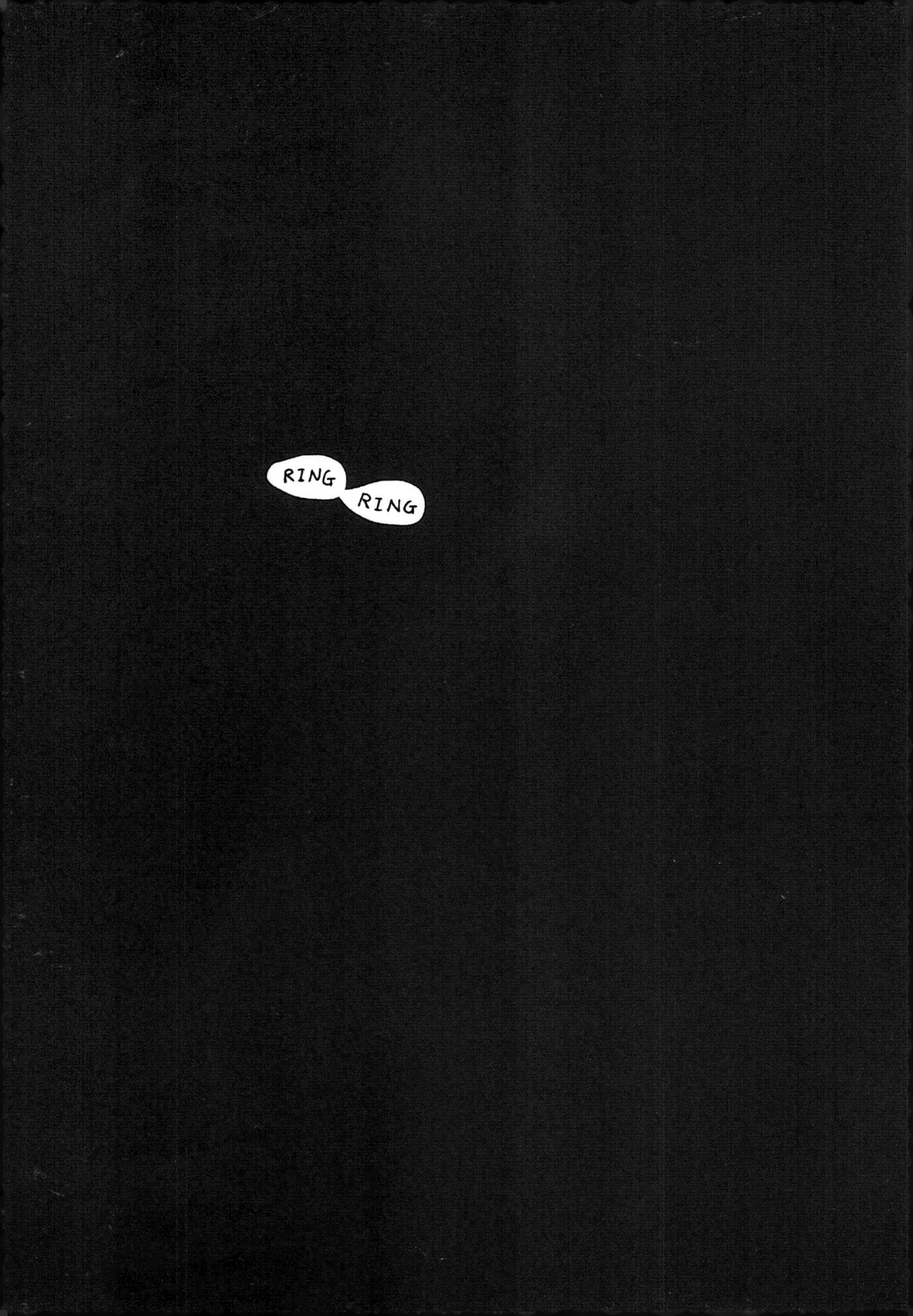
RING
RING

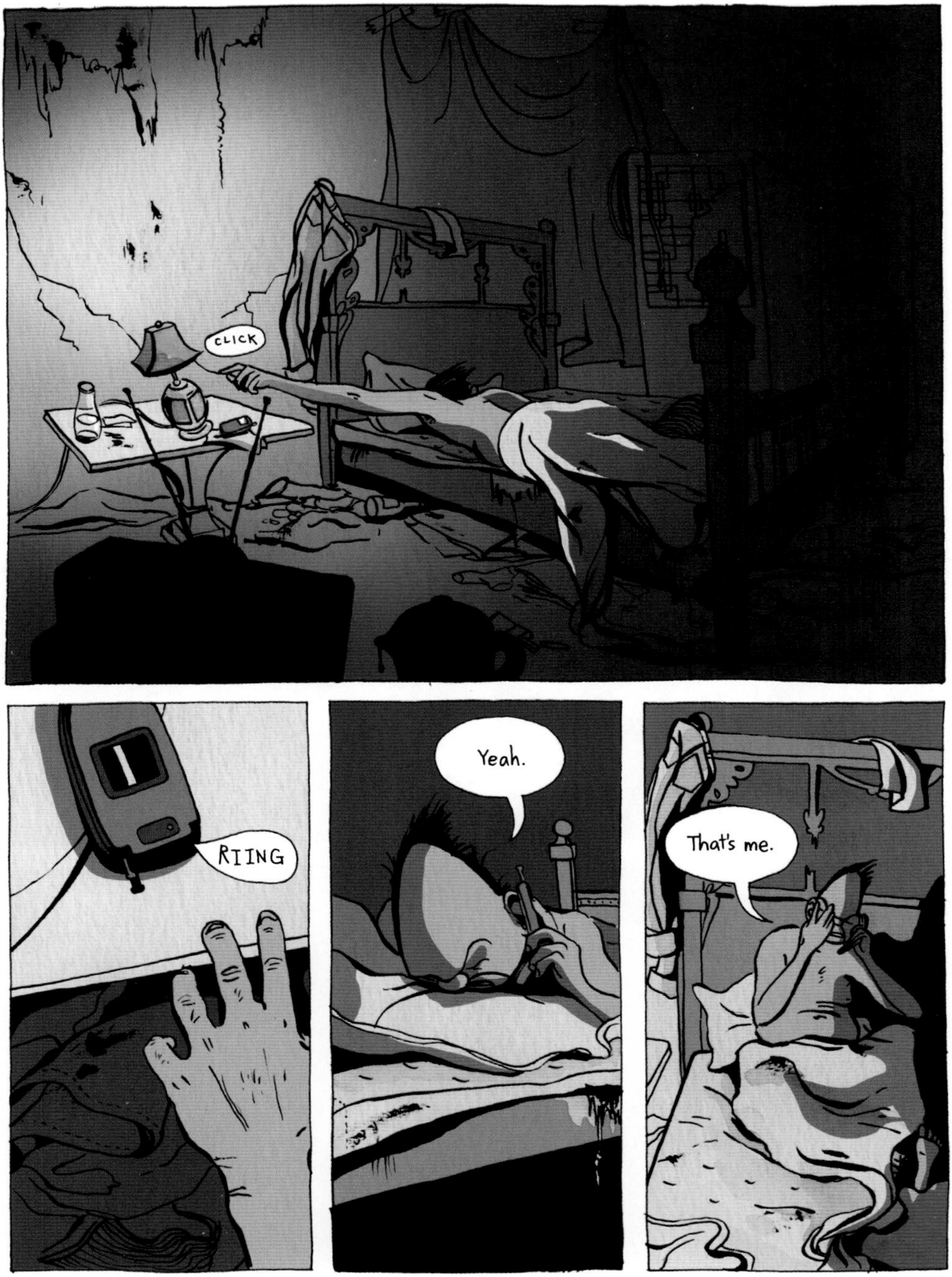
CLICK
RIING
Yeah.
That's me.

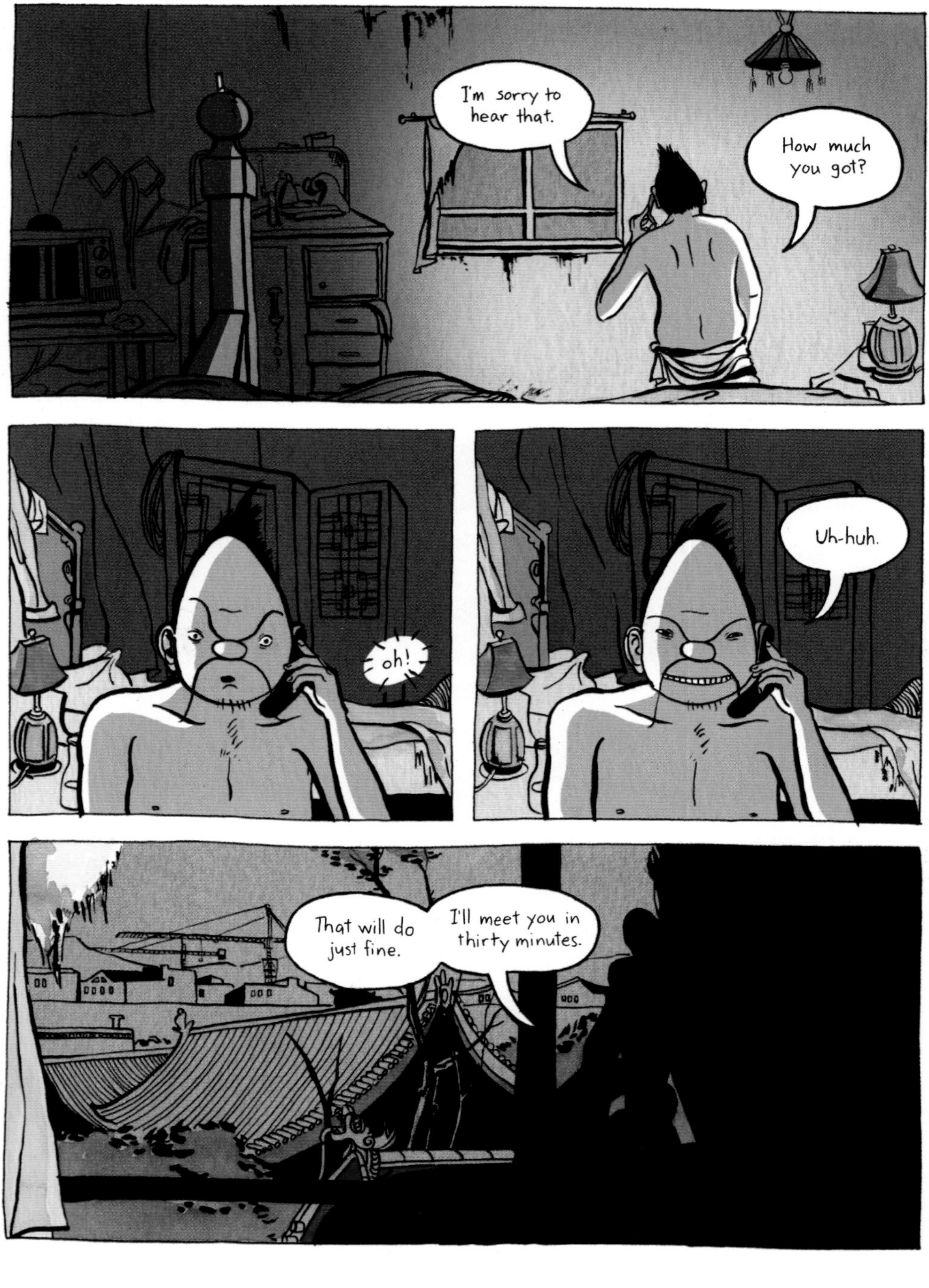
I'm sorry to hear that.
How much you got?
oh!
Uh-huh.
That will do just fine.
I'll meet you in thirty minutes.

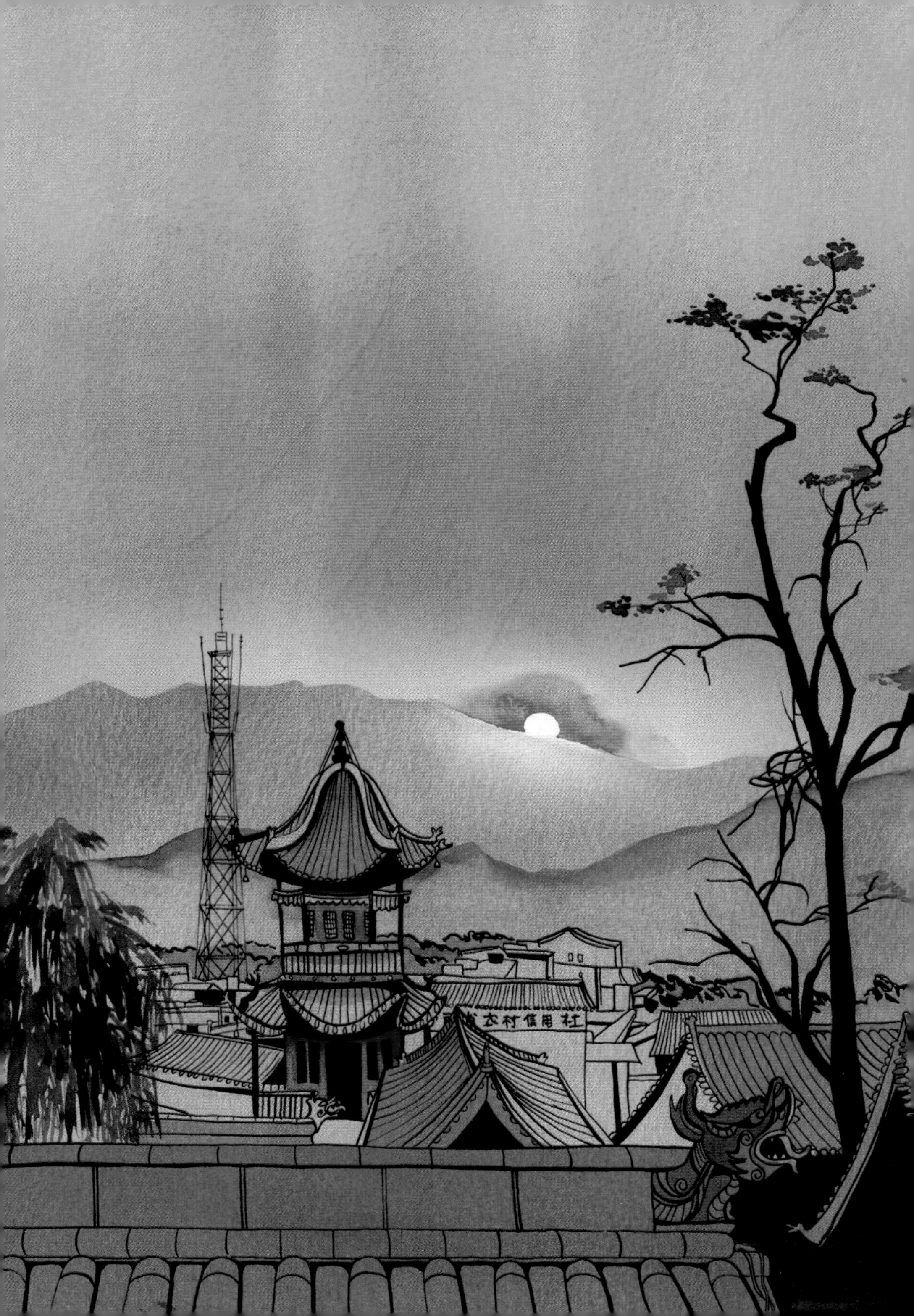
农村信用社

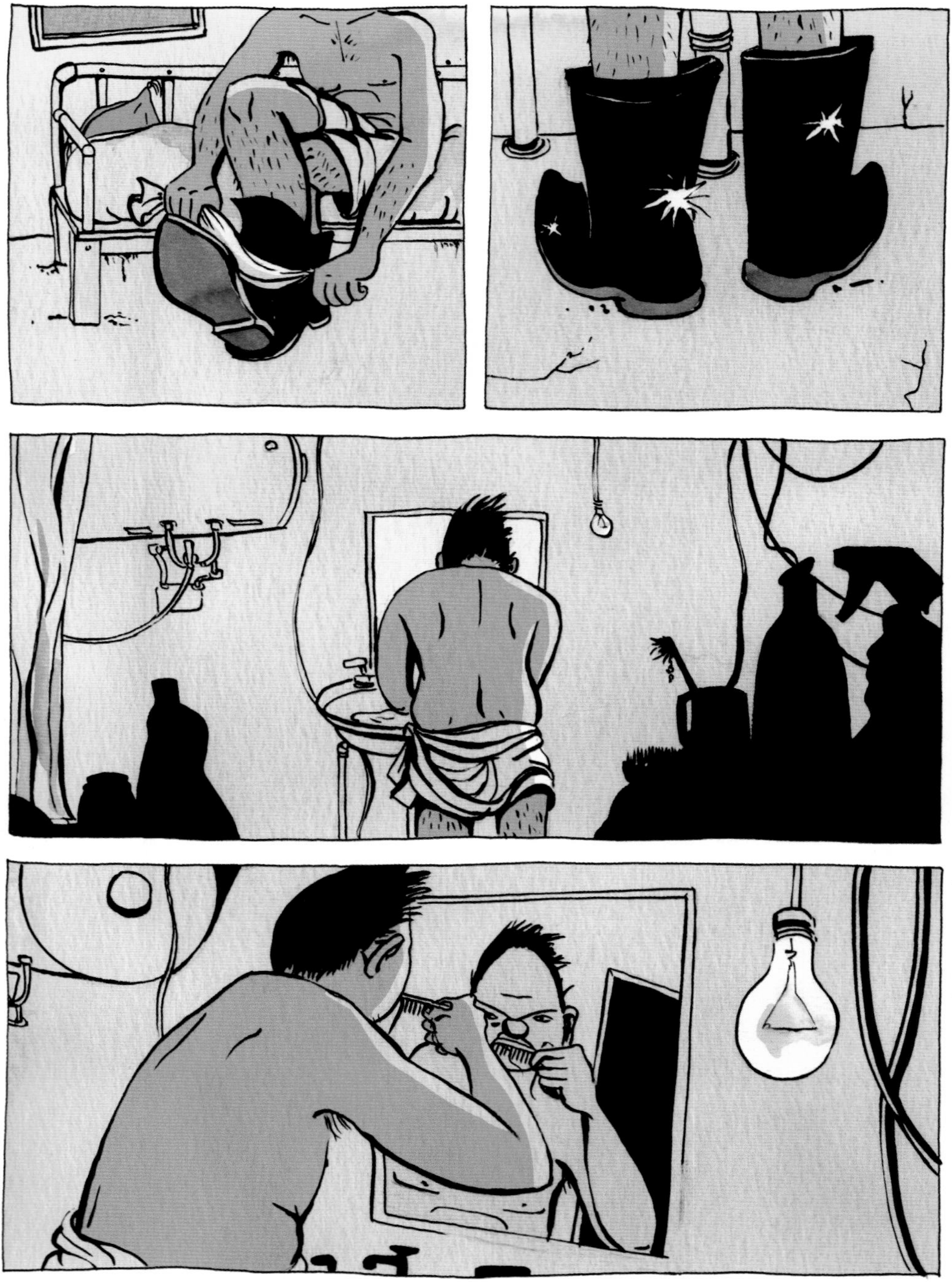

CLICK
6:17am

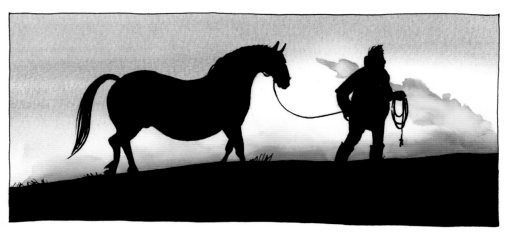

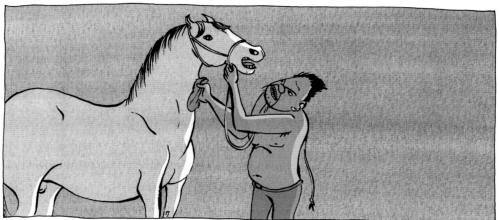

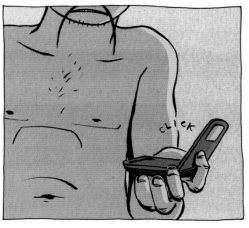

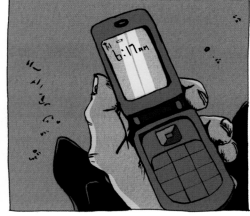

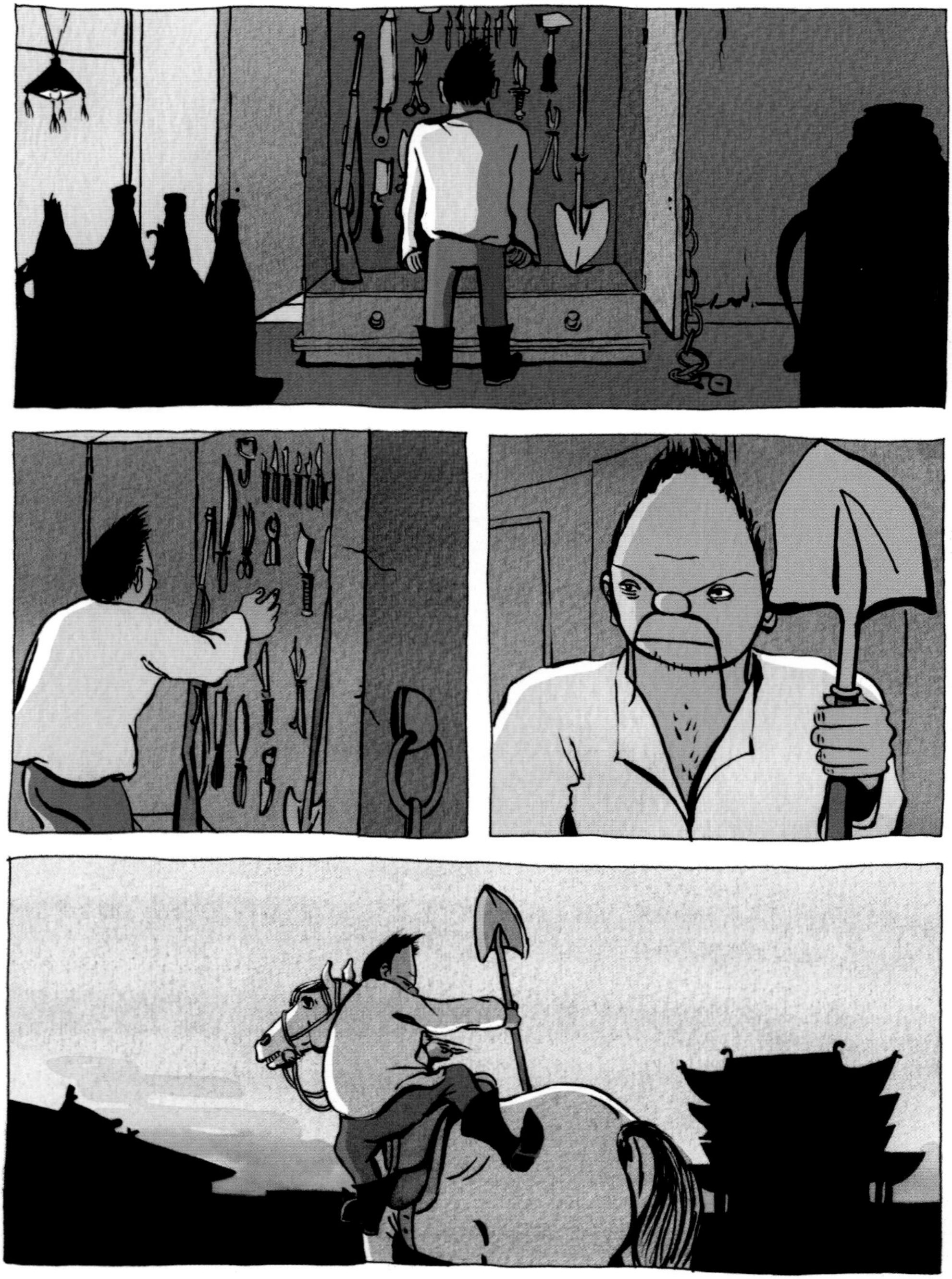

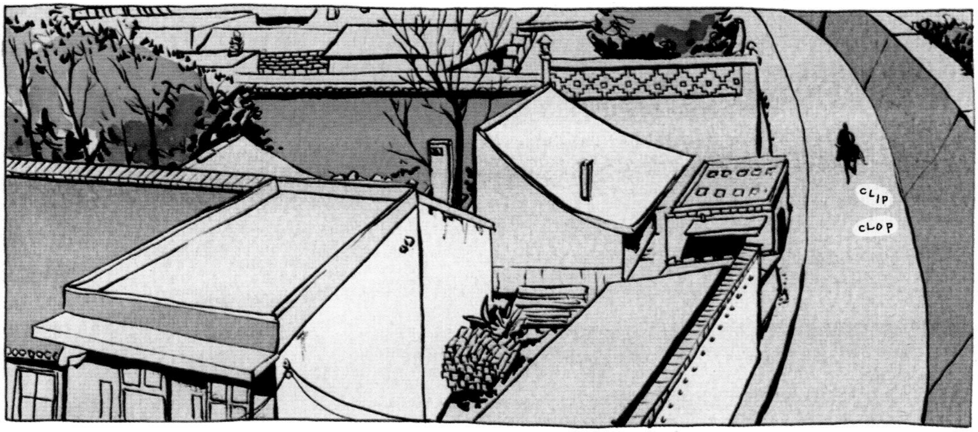
CLIP
CLOP

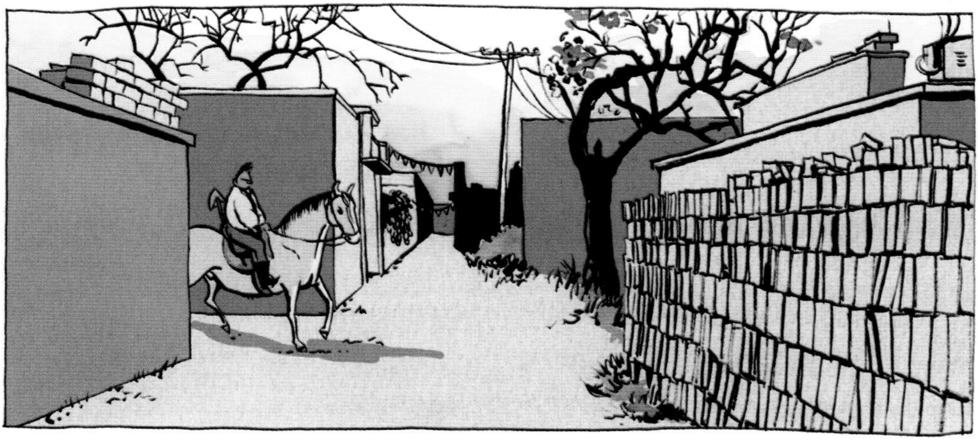

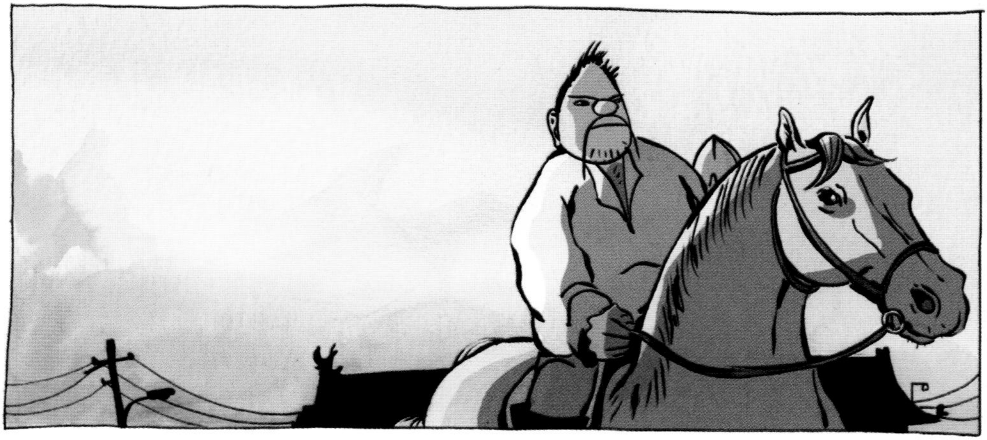

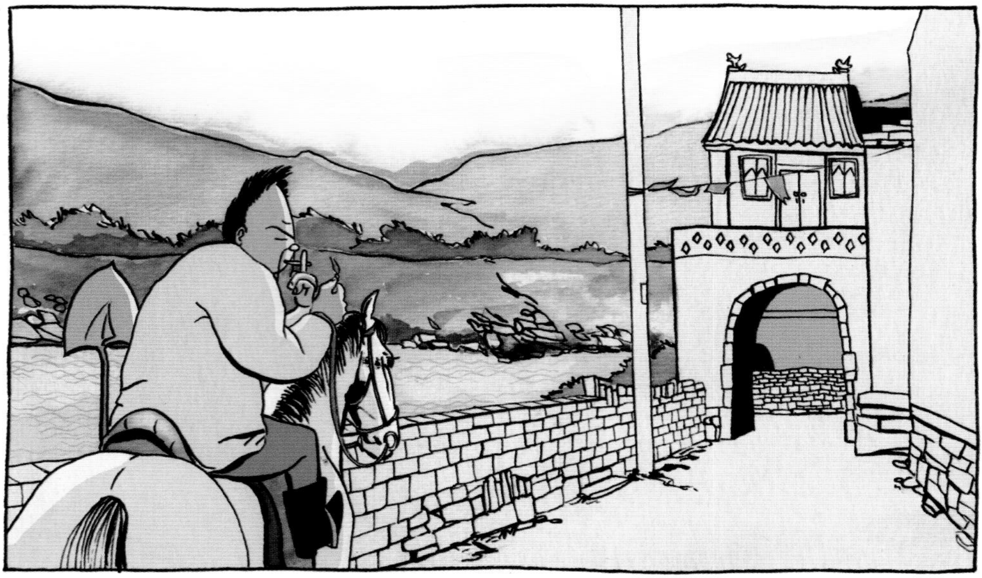

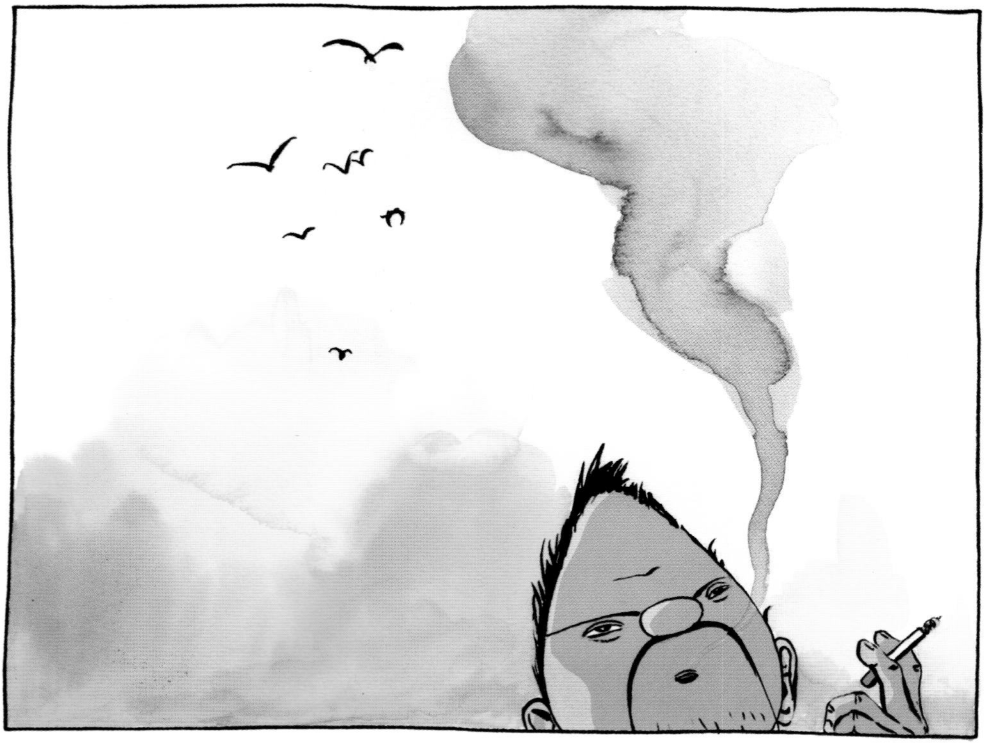

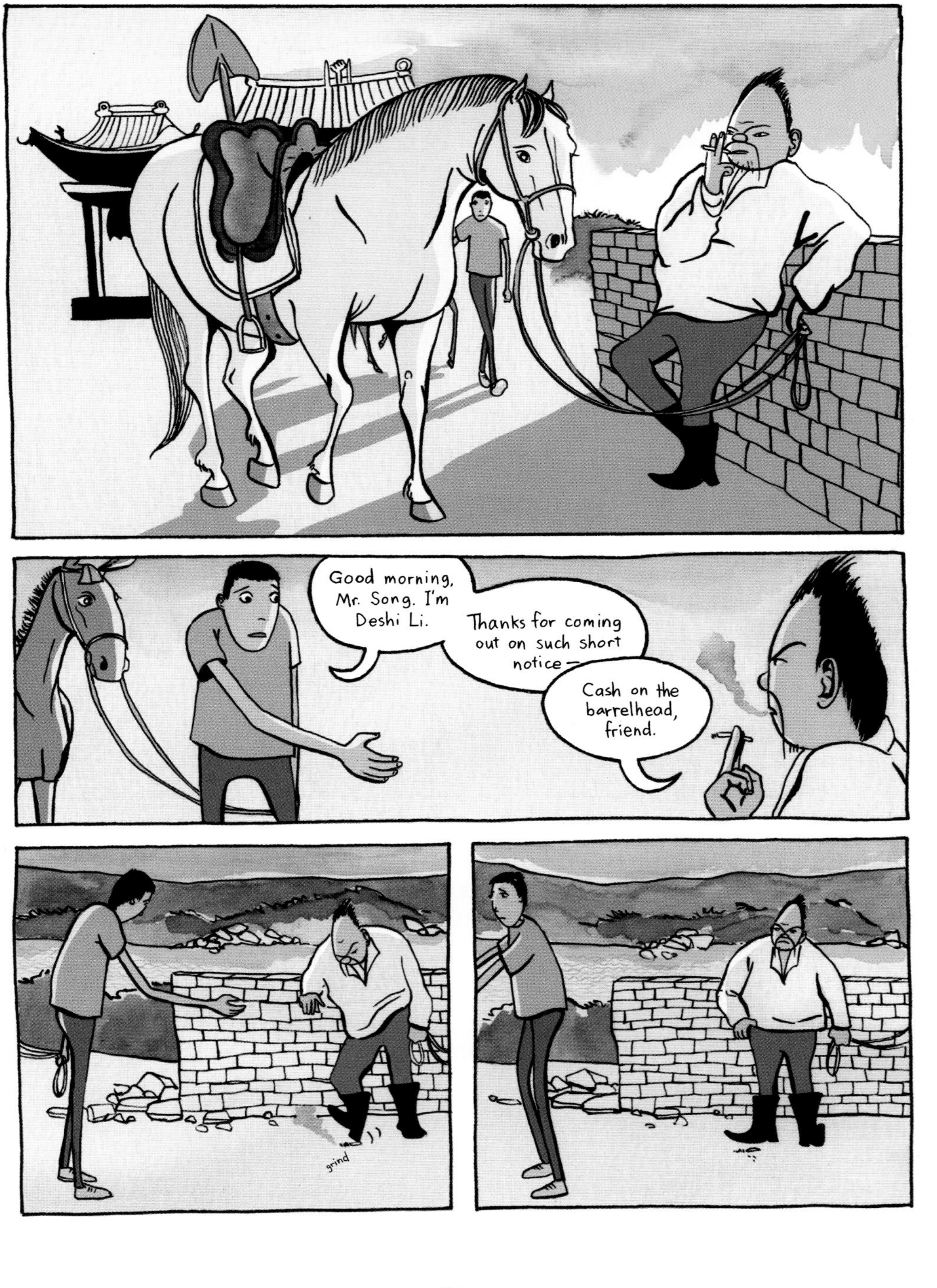
Good morning, Mr. Song. I'm Deshi Li.
Thanks for coming out on such short notice—
Cash on the barrelhead, friend.
grind

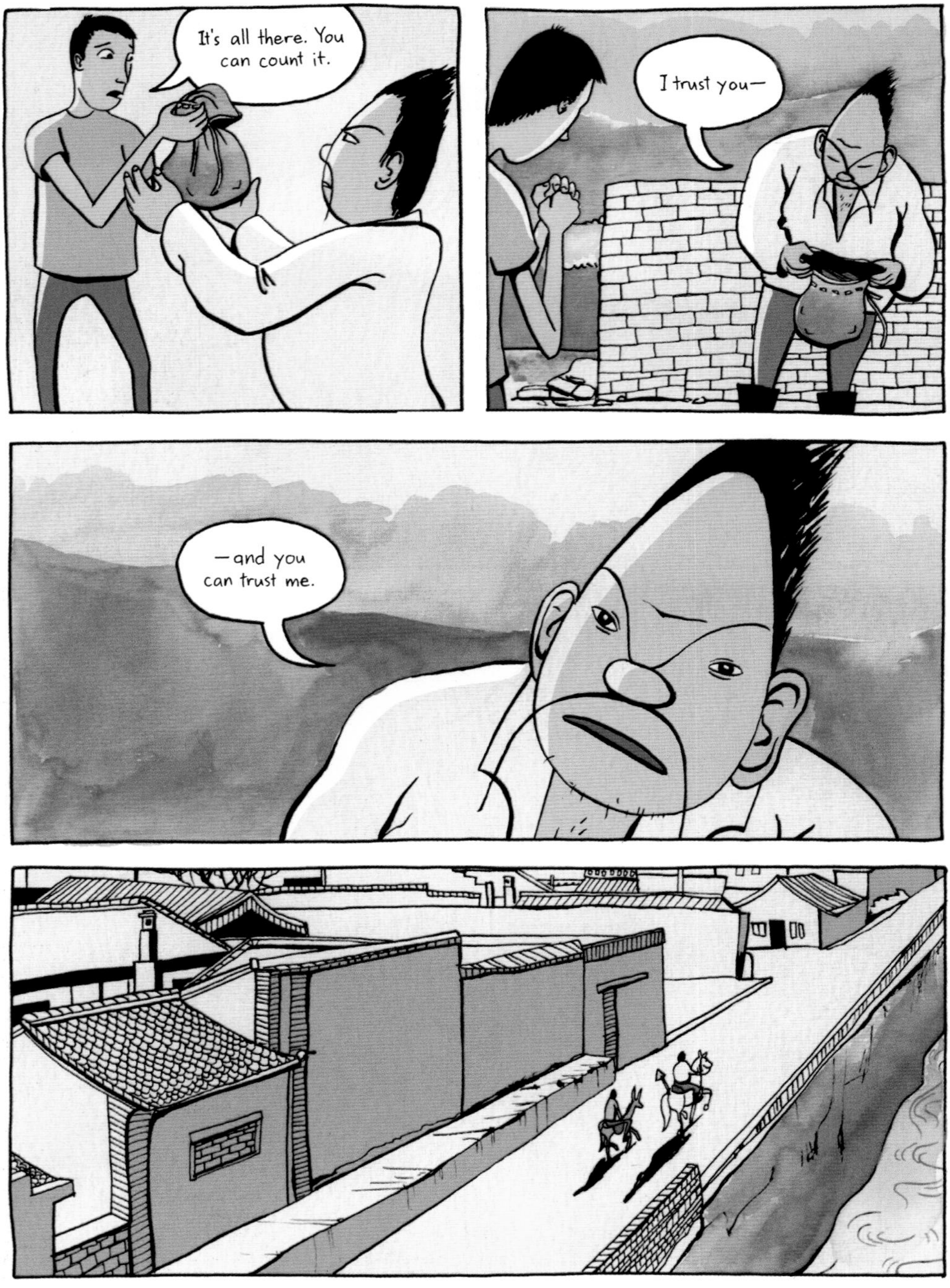
It's all there. You can count it.
I trust you—
—and you can trust me.

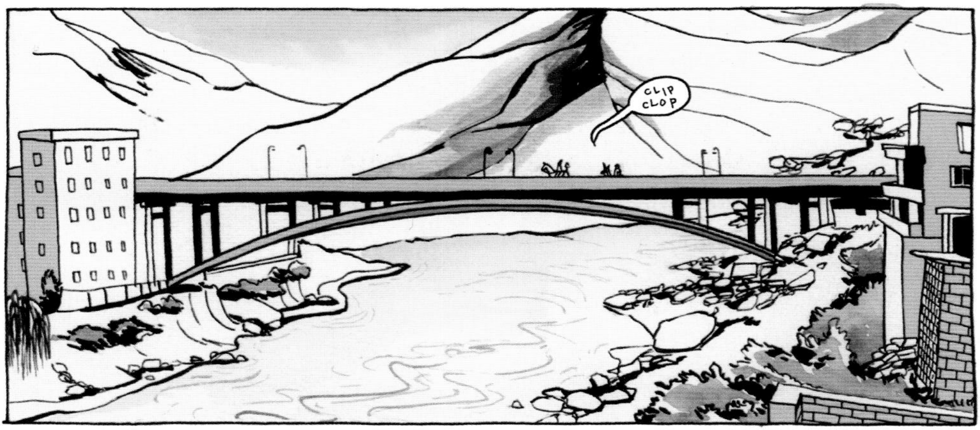
CLIP CLOP

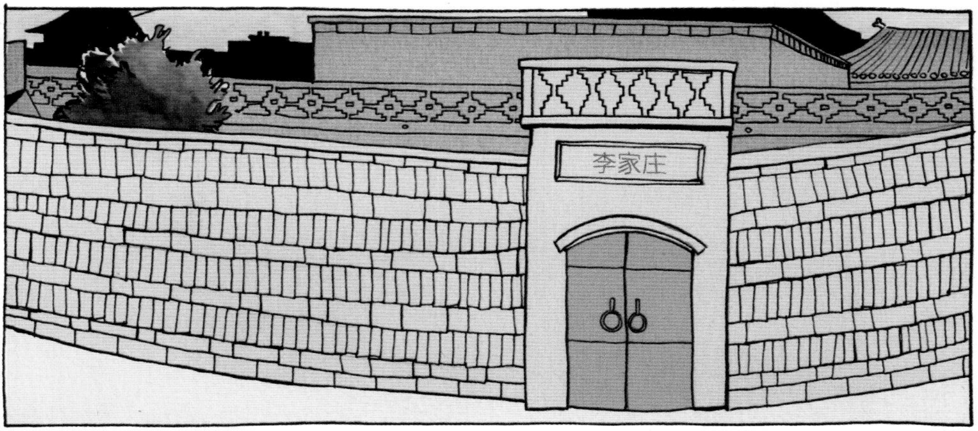
李家庄

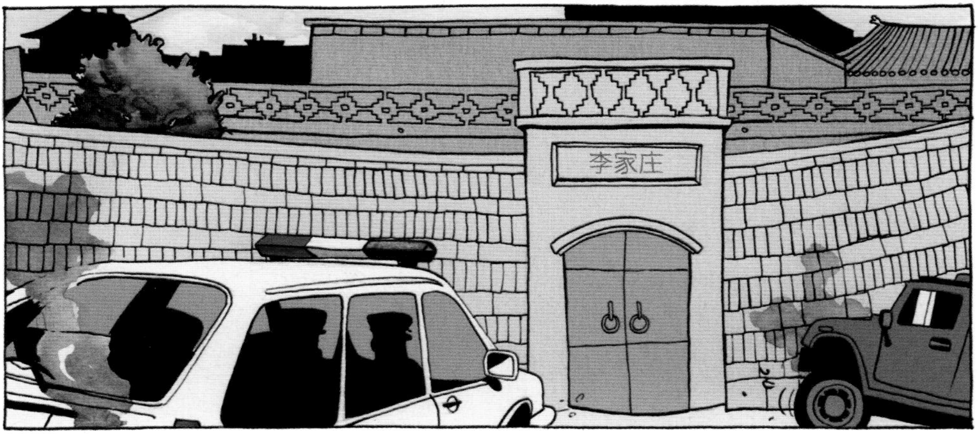
李家庄

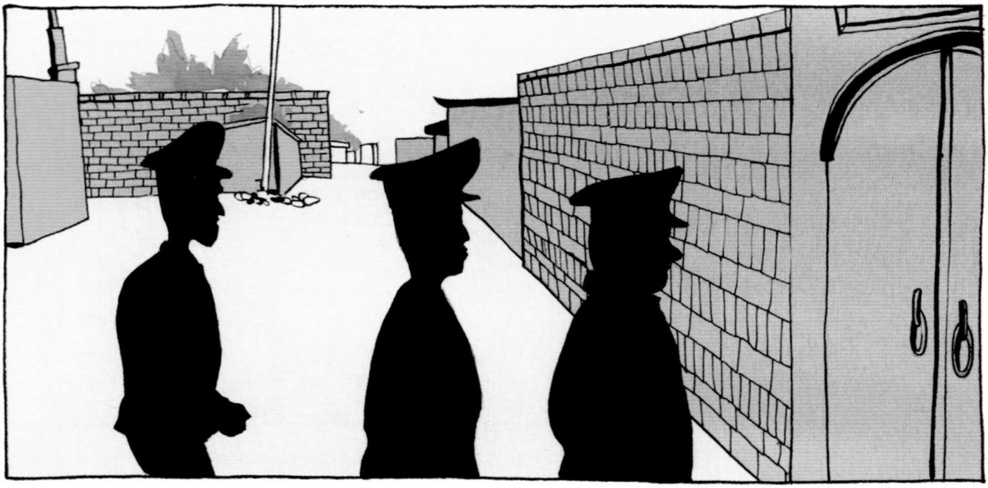

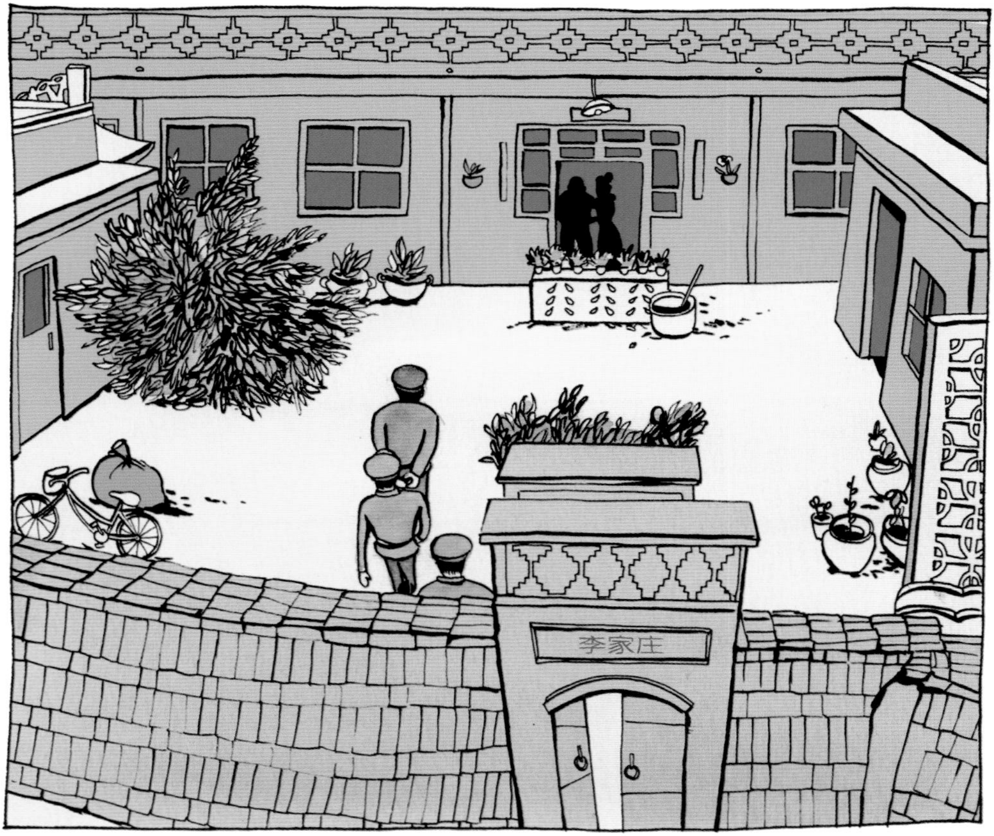
李家庄

3. Days of our Lives

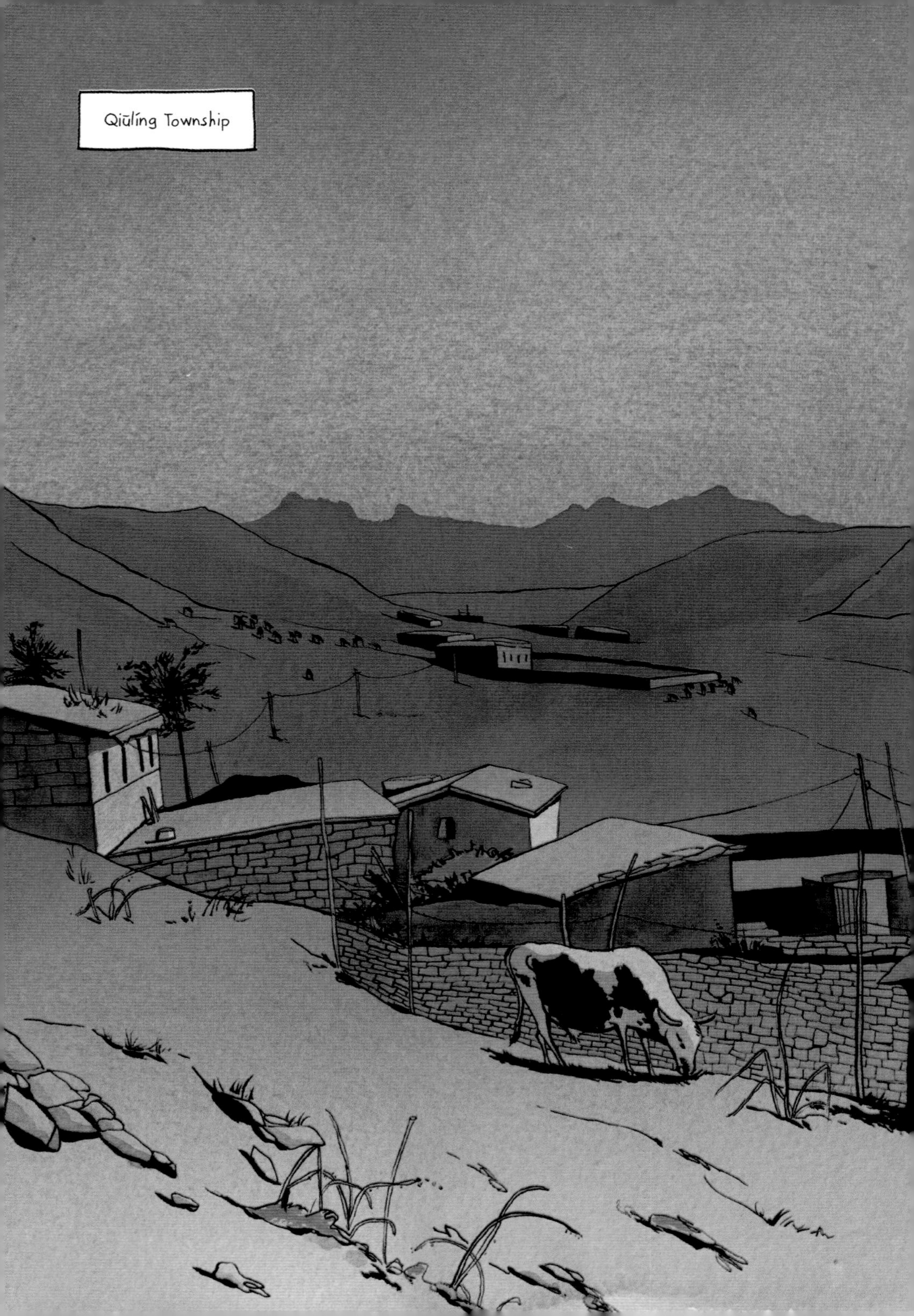
Qiūlíng Township

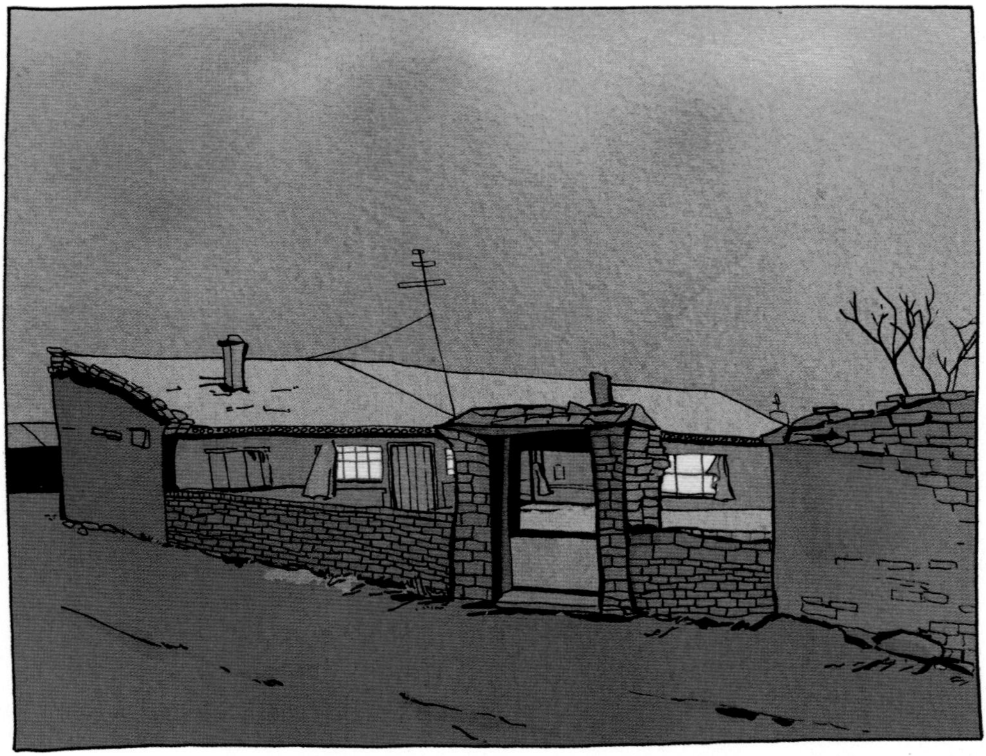

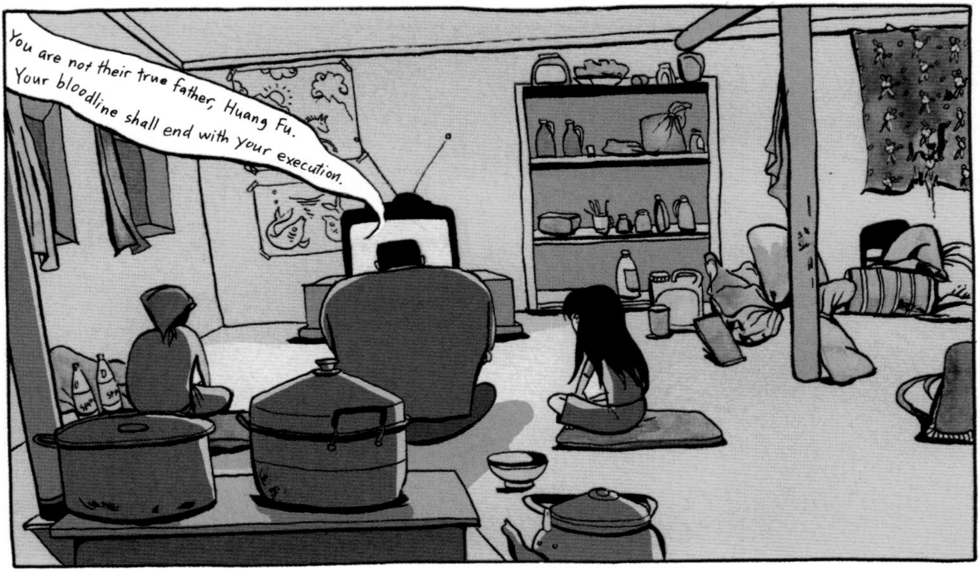
You are not their true father, Huang Fu. Your bloodline shall end with your execution.

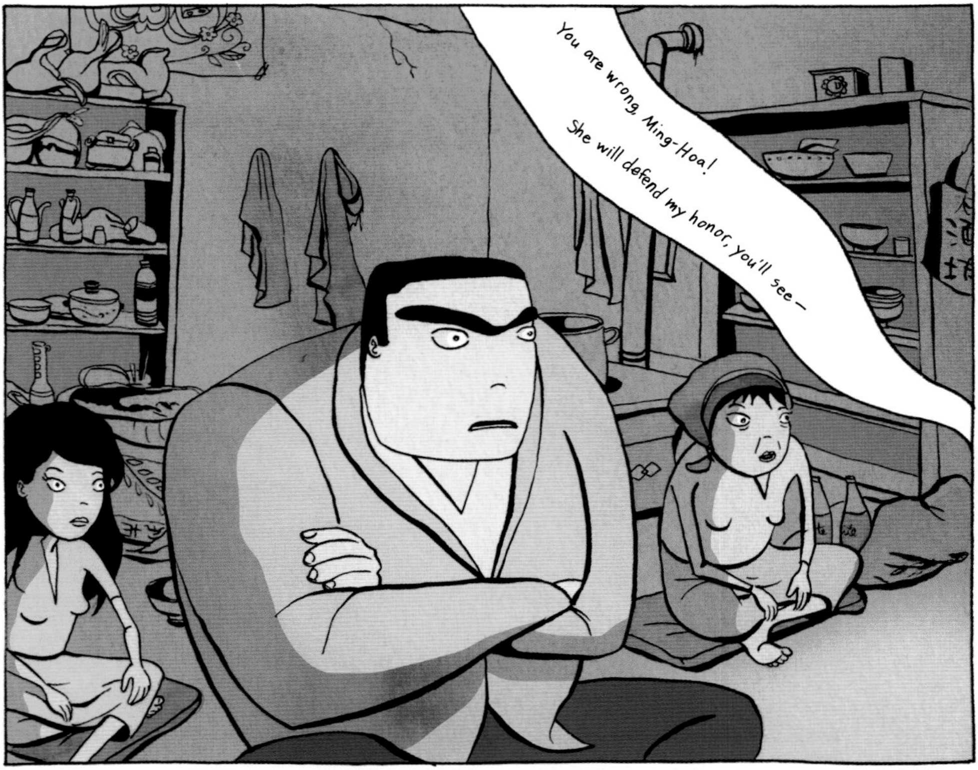
You are wrong, Ming-Hoa!
She will defend my honor, you'll see—

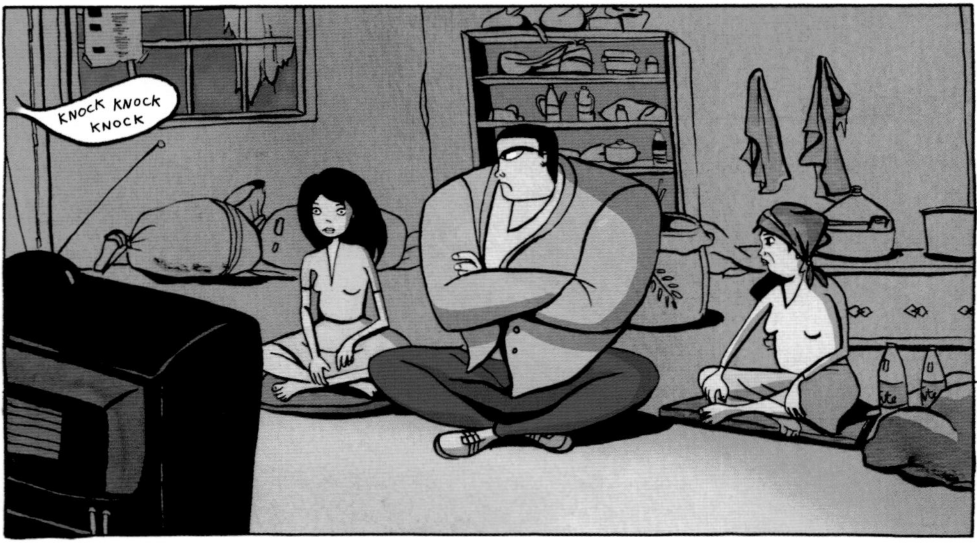
KNOCK KNOCK KNOCK

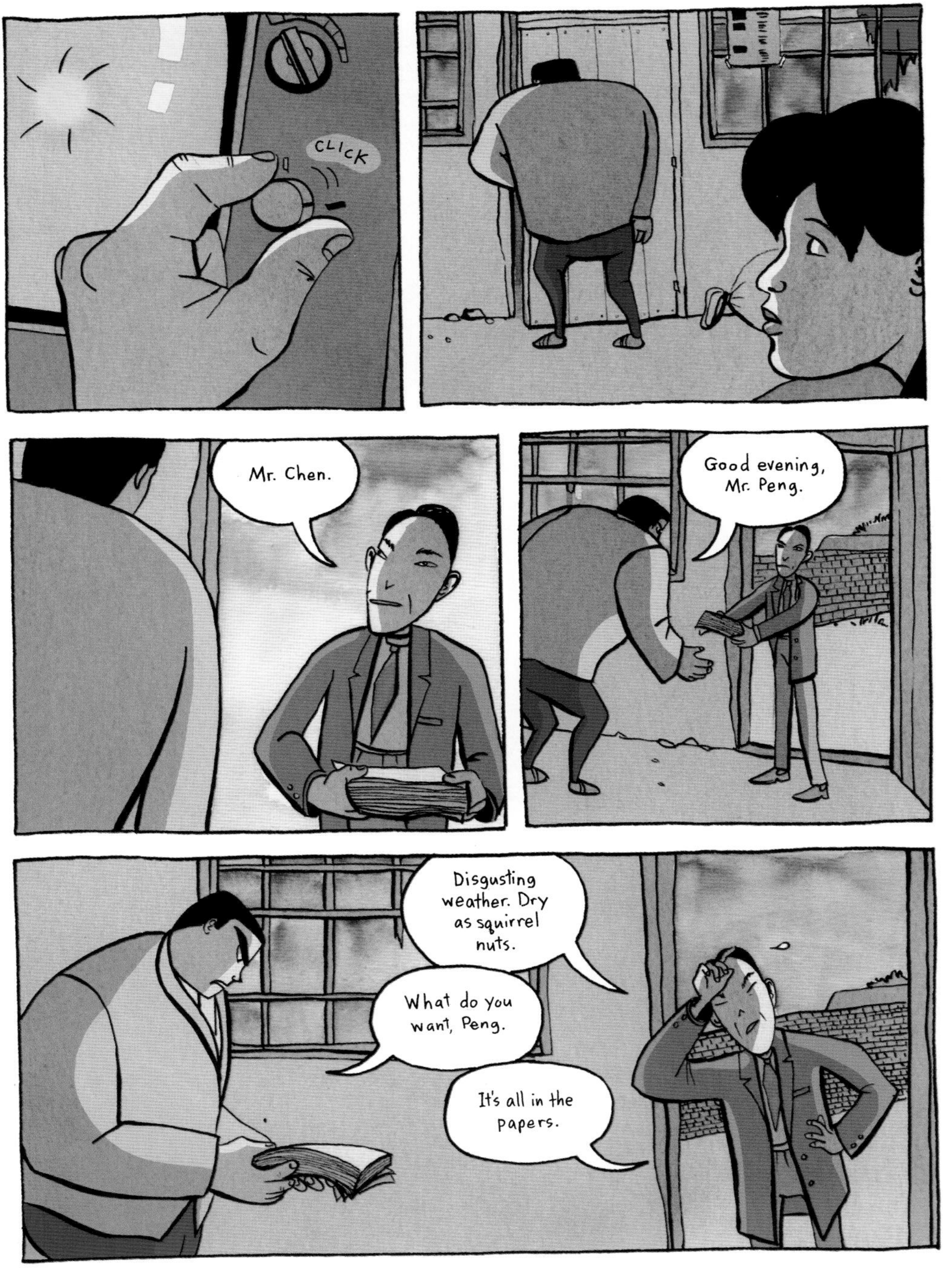
CLICK
Mr. Chen.
Good evening, Mr. Peng.
Disgusting weather. Dry as squirrel nuts.
What do you want, Peng.
It's all in the papers.

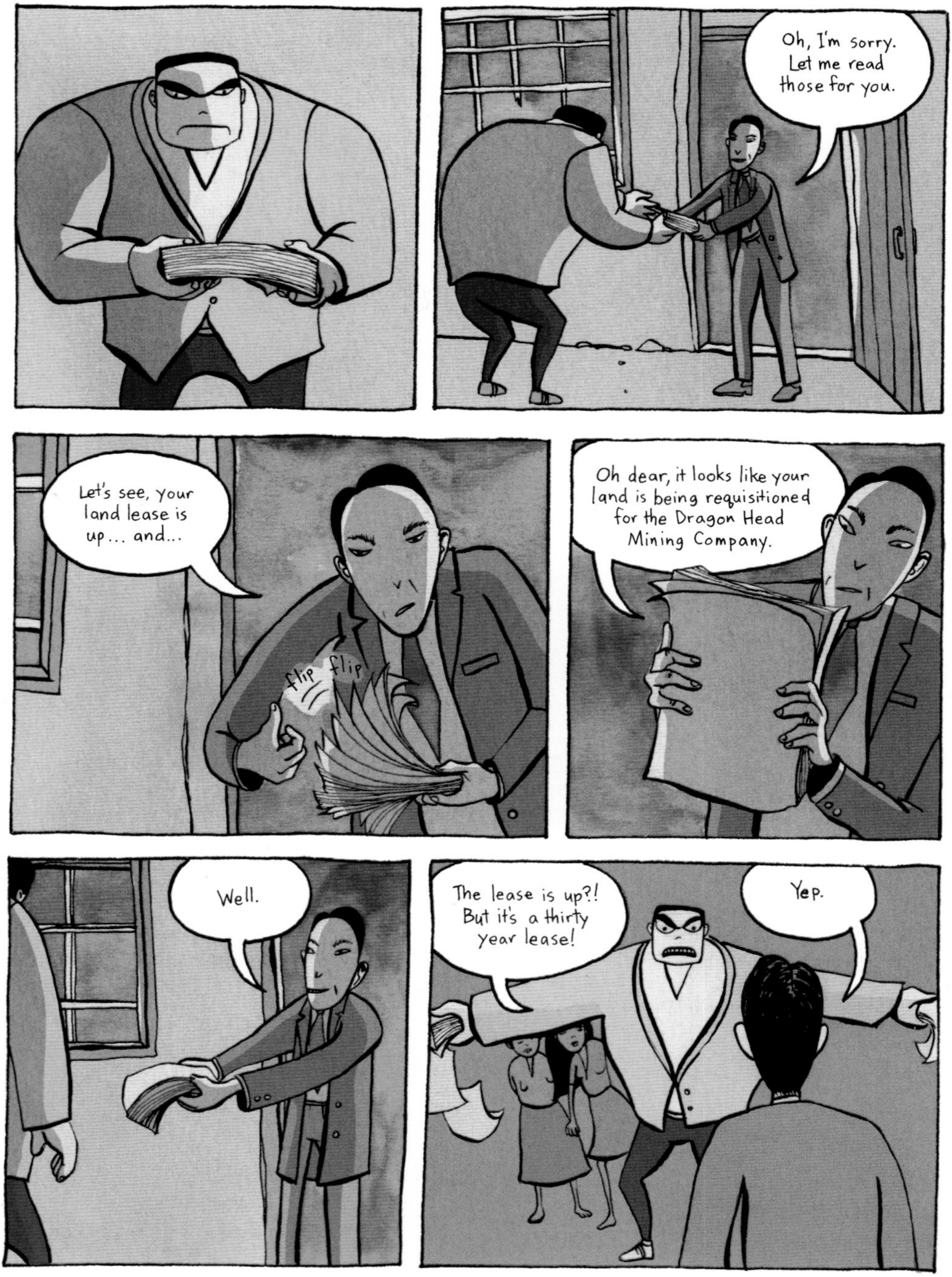
Oh, I'm sorry. Let me read those for you.
Let's see, your land lease is up... and...
flip flip
Oh dear, it looks like your land is being requisitioned for the Dragon Head Mining Company.
Well.
The lease is up?! But it's a thirty year lease!
Yep.

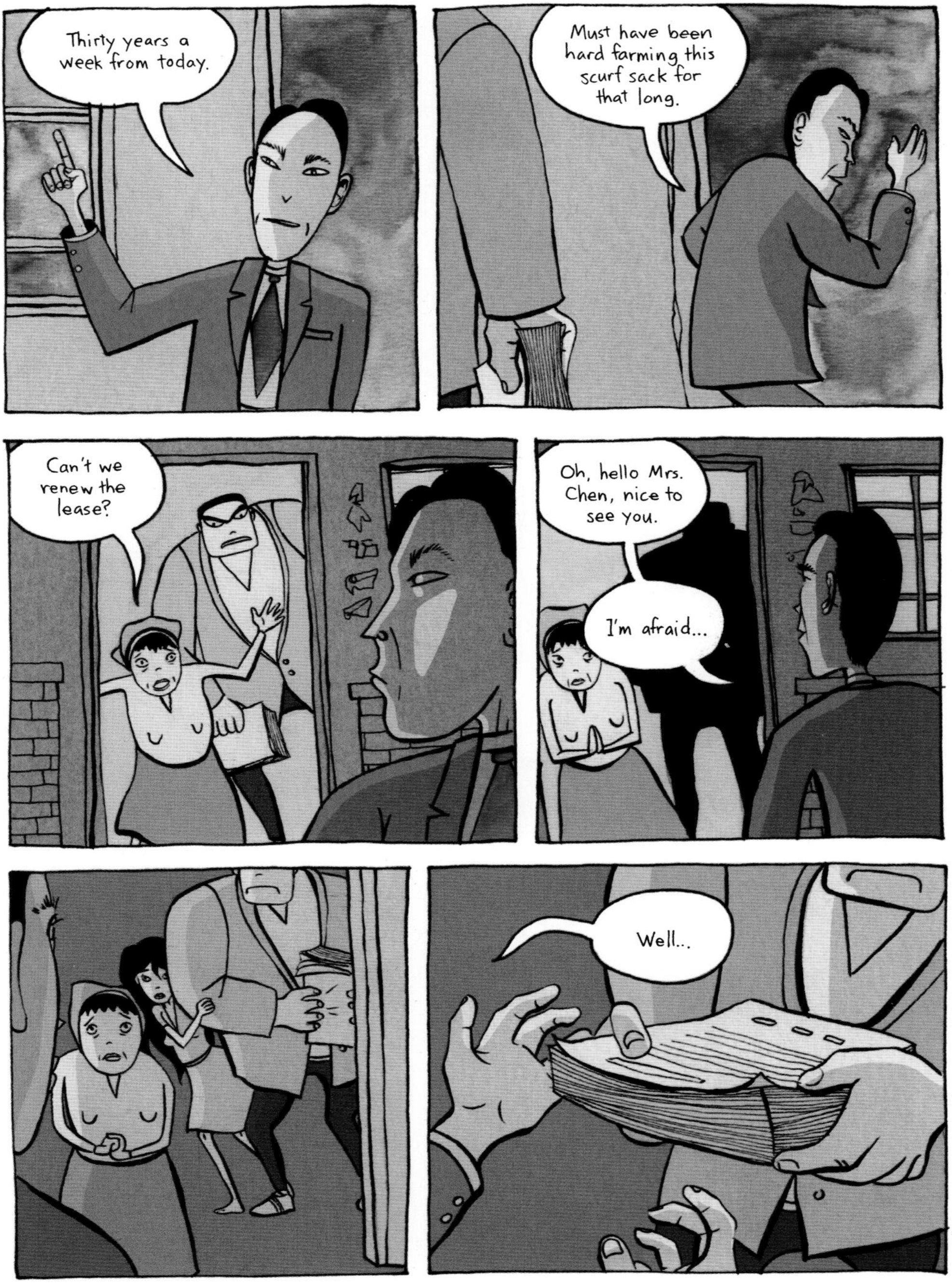
Thirty years a week from today.
Must have been hard farming this scurf sack for that long.
Can't we renew the lease?
Oh, hello Mrs. Chen, nice to see you.
I'm afraid...
Well...

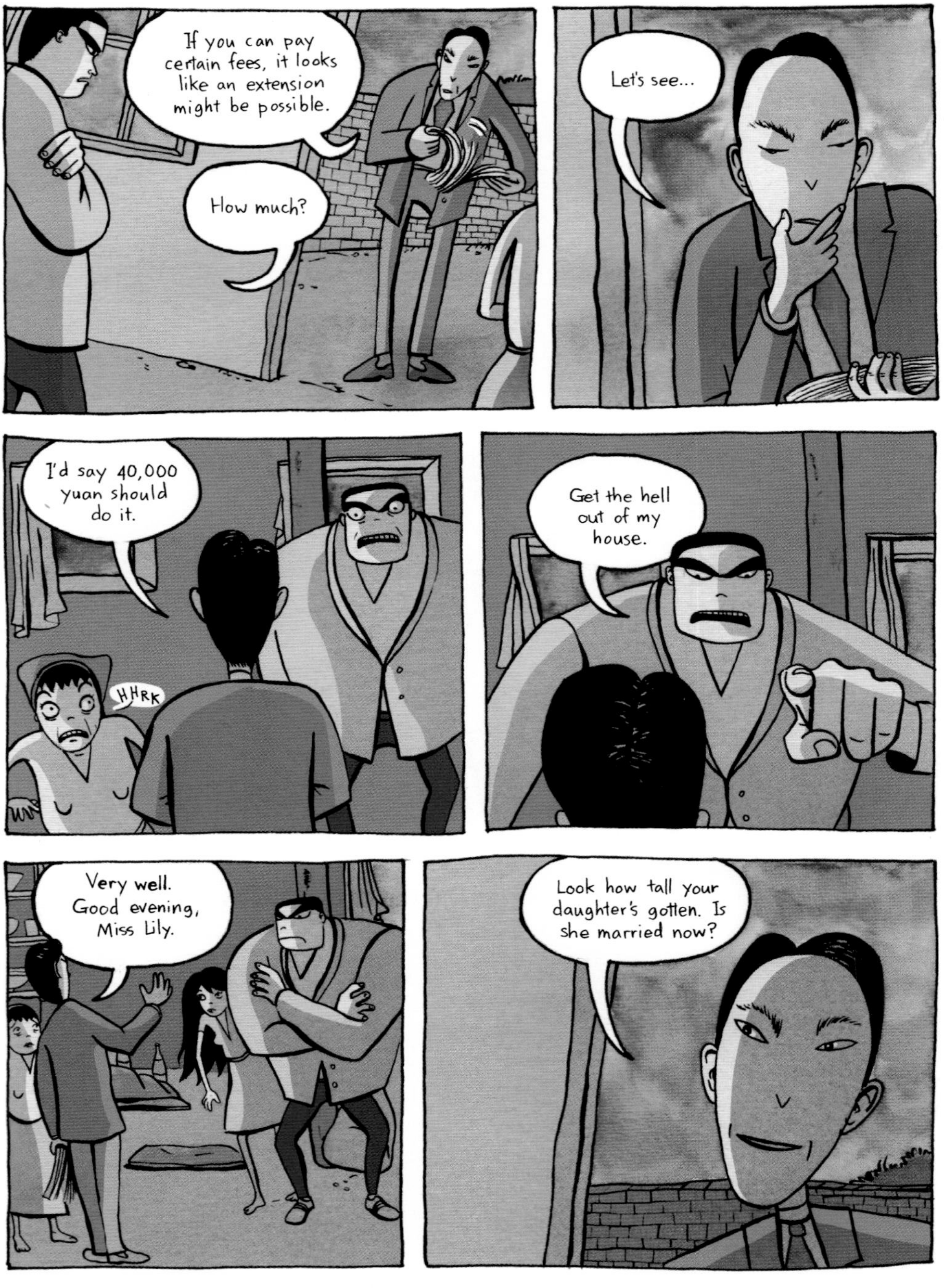
If you can pay certain fees, it looks like an extension might be possible.
How much?
Let's see...
I'd say 40,000 yuan should do it.
HHRK
Get the hell out of my house.
Very well. Good evening, Miss Lily.
Look how tall your daughter's gotten. Is she married now?

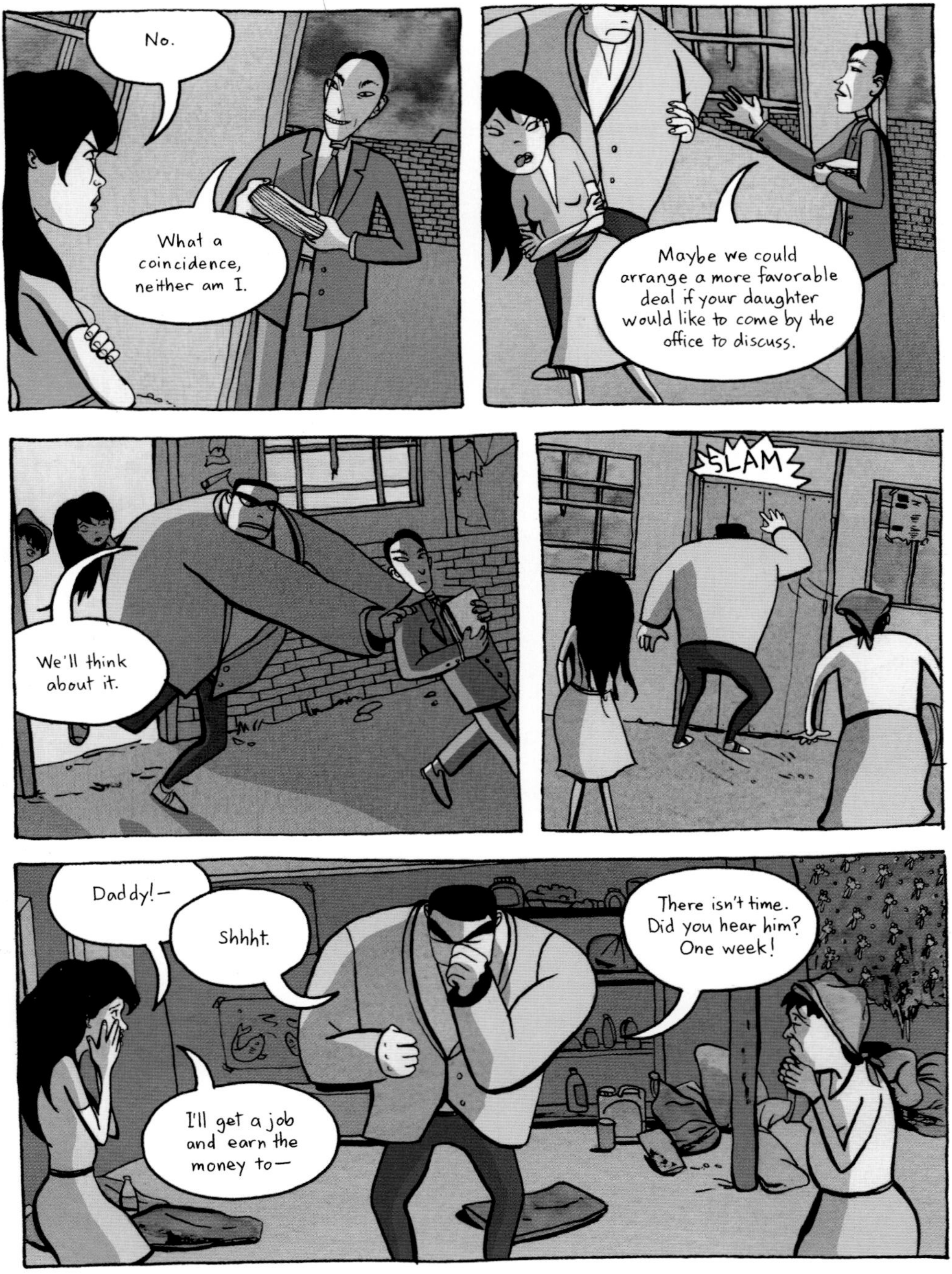
No.
What a coincidence, neither am I.
Maybe we could arrange a more favorable deal if your daughter would like to come by the office to discuss.
We'll think about it.
SLAM
Daddy!—
Shhht.
I'll get a job and earn the money to—
There isn't time. Did you hear him? One week!

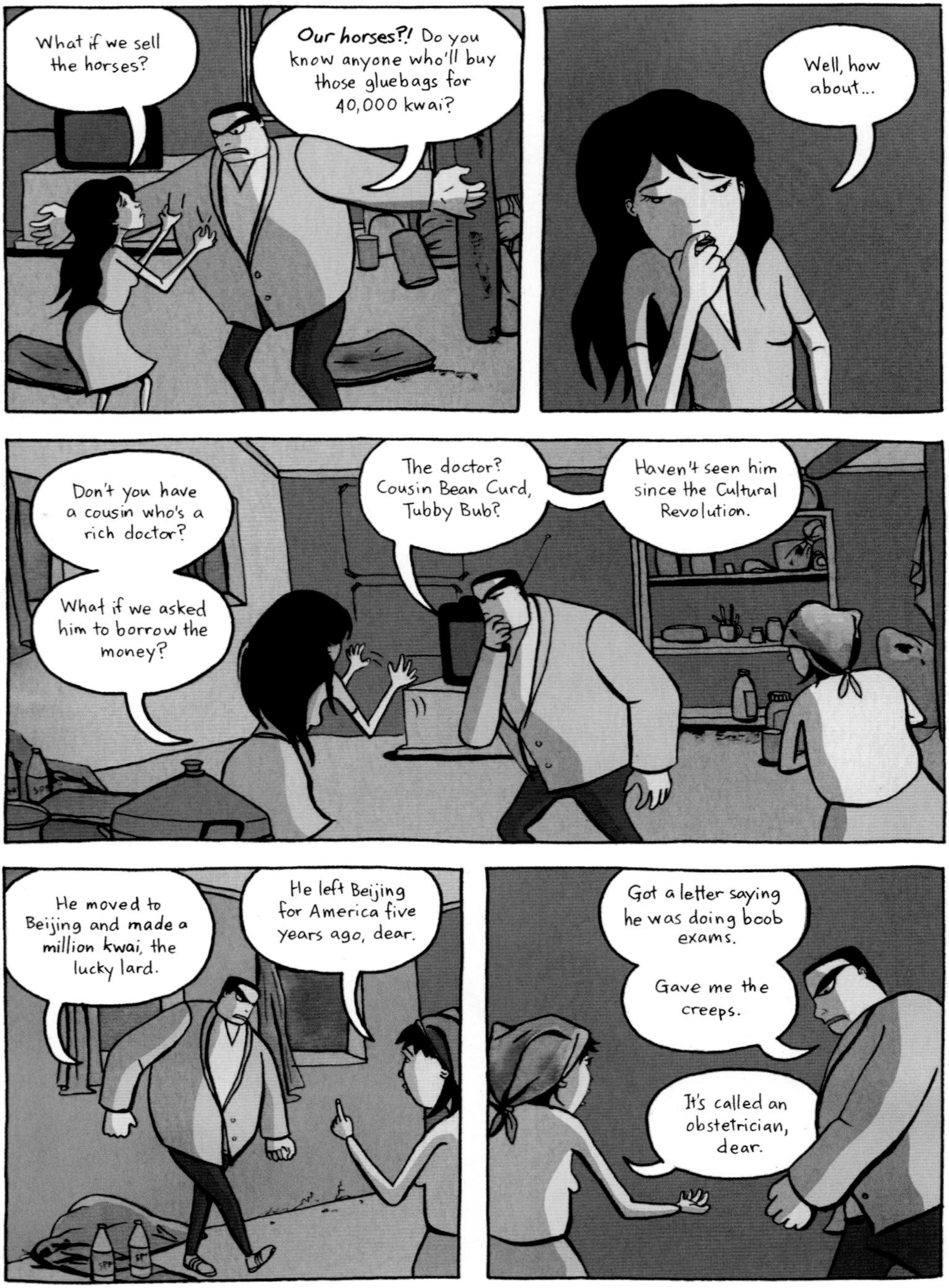
What if we sell the horses?
Our horses?! Do you know anyone who'll buy those gluebags for 40,000 kwai?
Well, how about...
Don't you have a cousin who's a rich doctor?
What if we asked him to borrow the money?
The doctor? Cousin Bean Curd, Tubby Bub?
Haven't seen him since the Cultural Revolution.
He moved to Beijing and made a million kwai, the lucky lard.
He left Beijing for America five years ago, dear.
Got a letter saying he was doing boob exams.
Gave me the creeps.
It's called an obstetrician, dear.

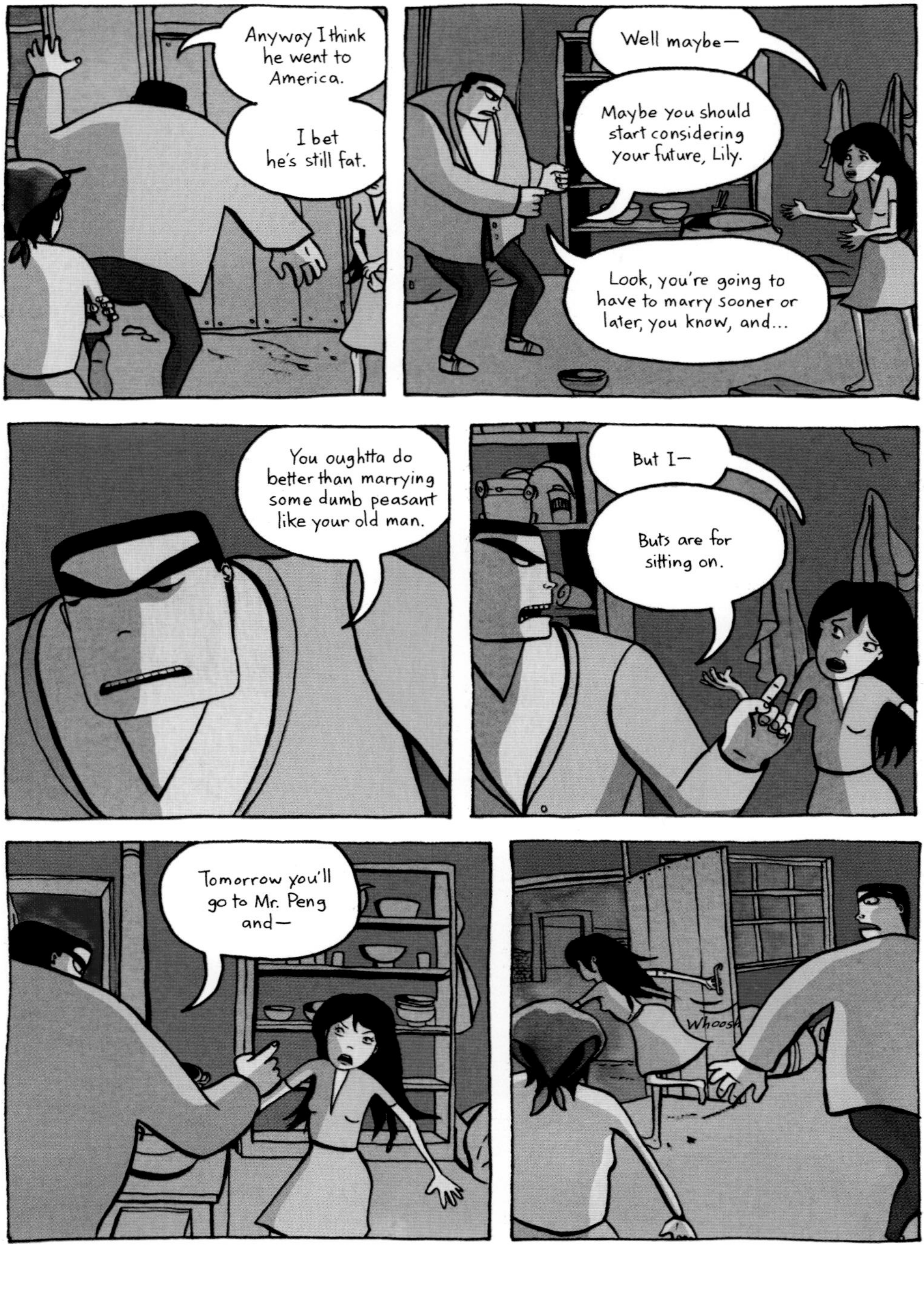
Anyway I think he went to America.
I bet he's still fat.
Well maybe—
Maybe you should start considering your future, Lily.
Look, you're going to have to marry sooner or later, you know, and...
You oughtta do better than marrying some dumb peasant like your old man.
But I—
Buts are for sitting on.
Tomorrow you'll go to Mr. Peng and—
Whoosh

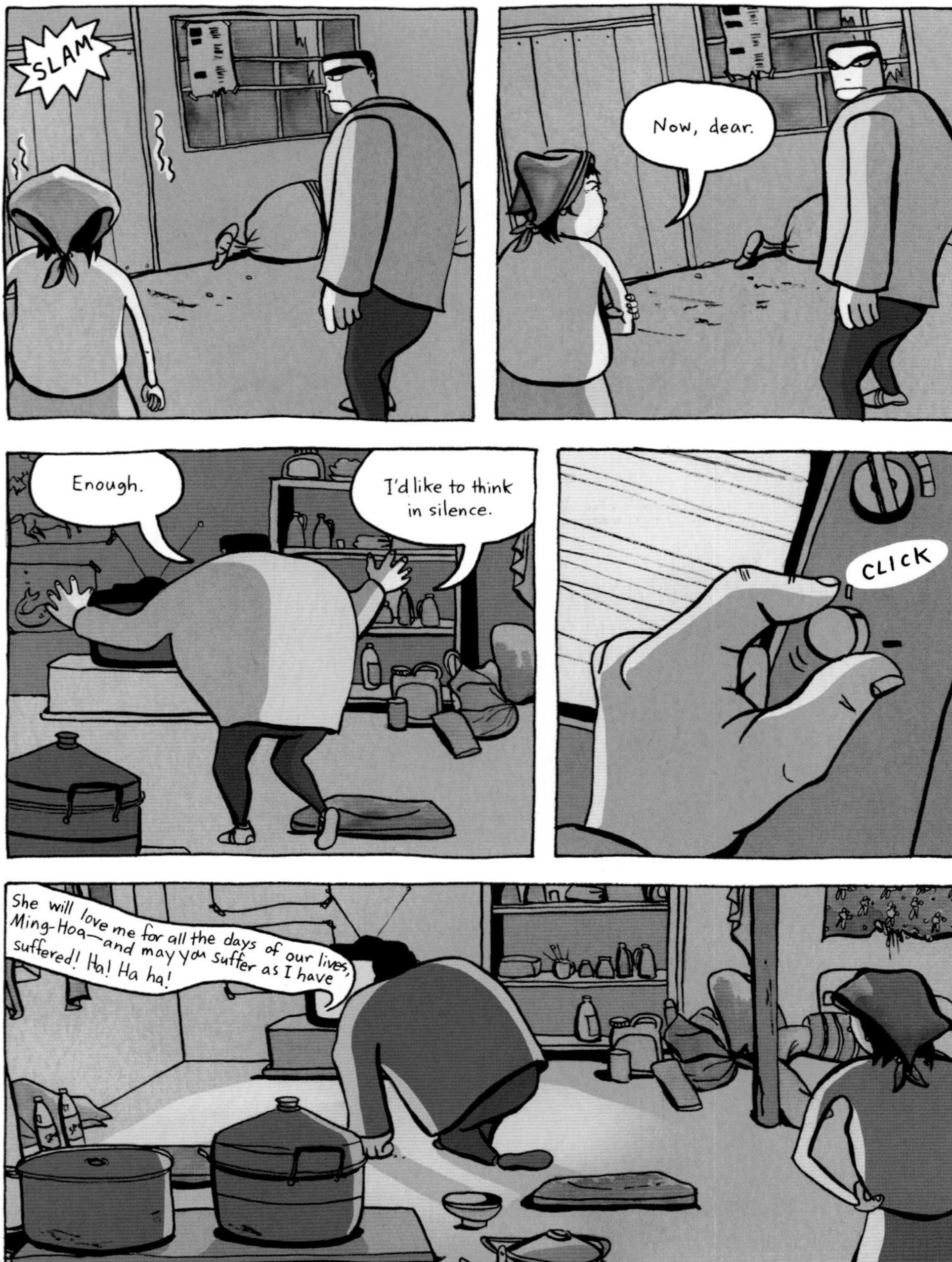
SLAM
Now, dear.
Enough.
I'd like to think in silence.
CLICK
She will love me for all the days of our lives, Ming-Hoa—and may you suffer as I have suffered! Ha! Ha ha!

4. Miles

MONDAY

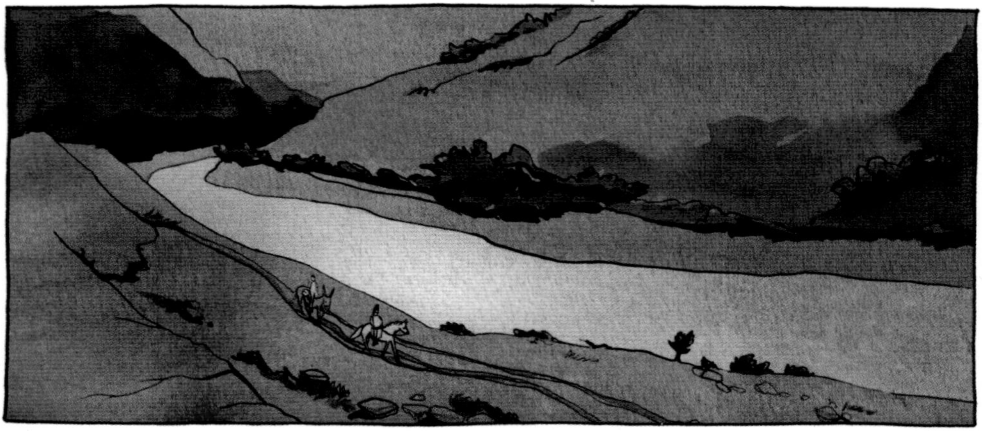

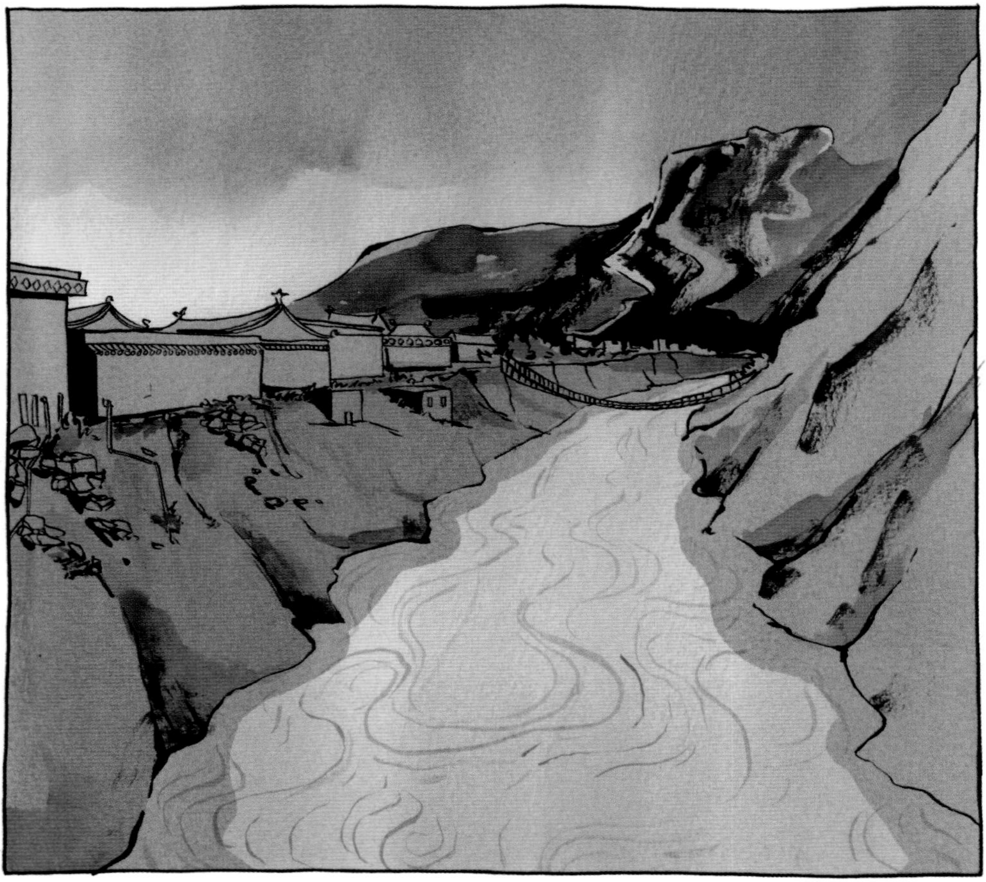

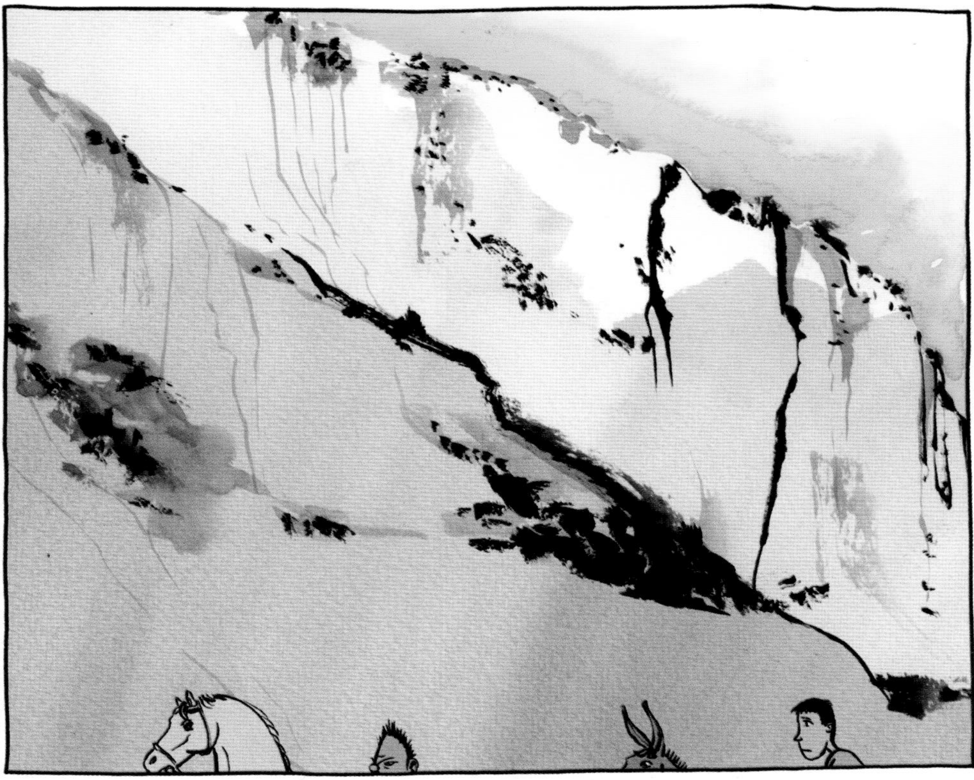

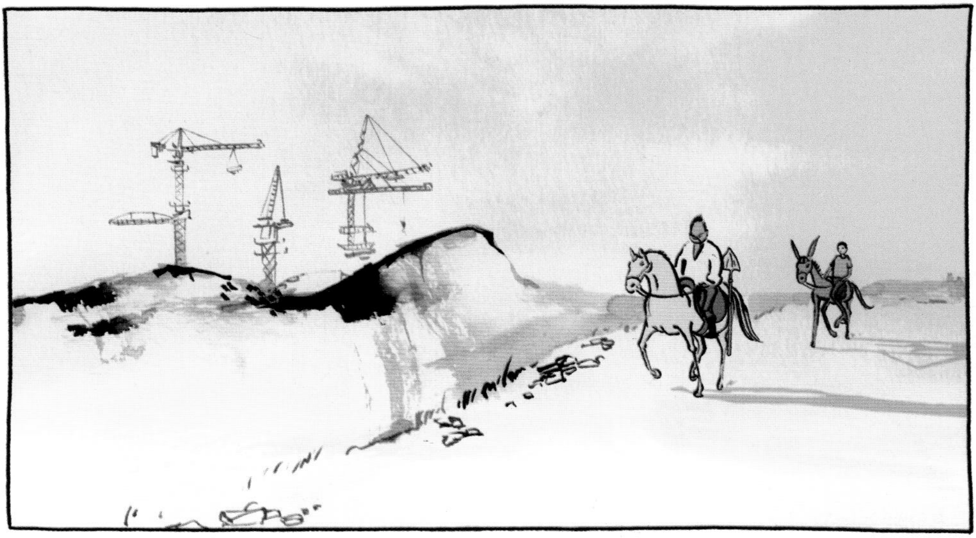

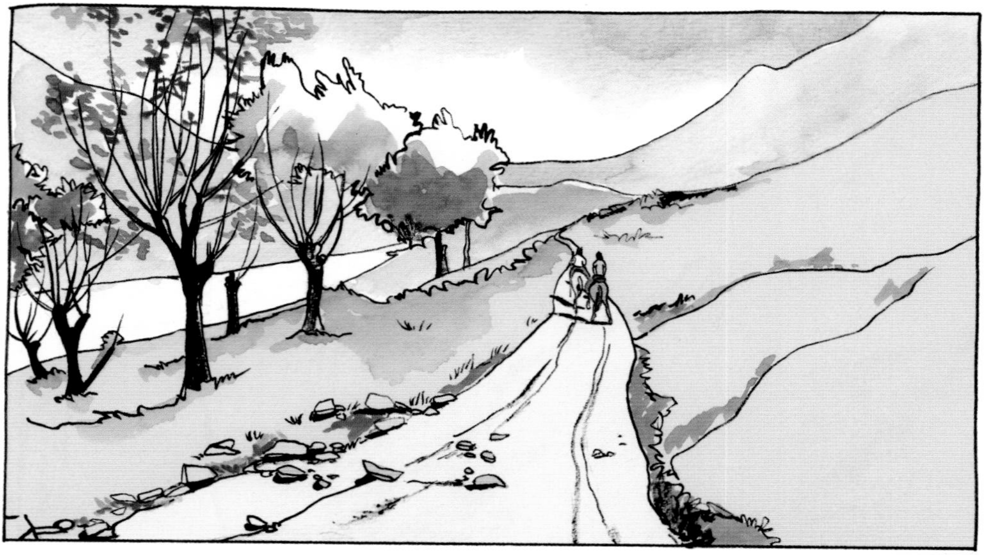

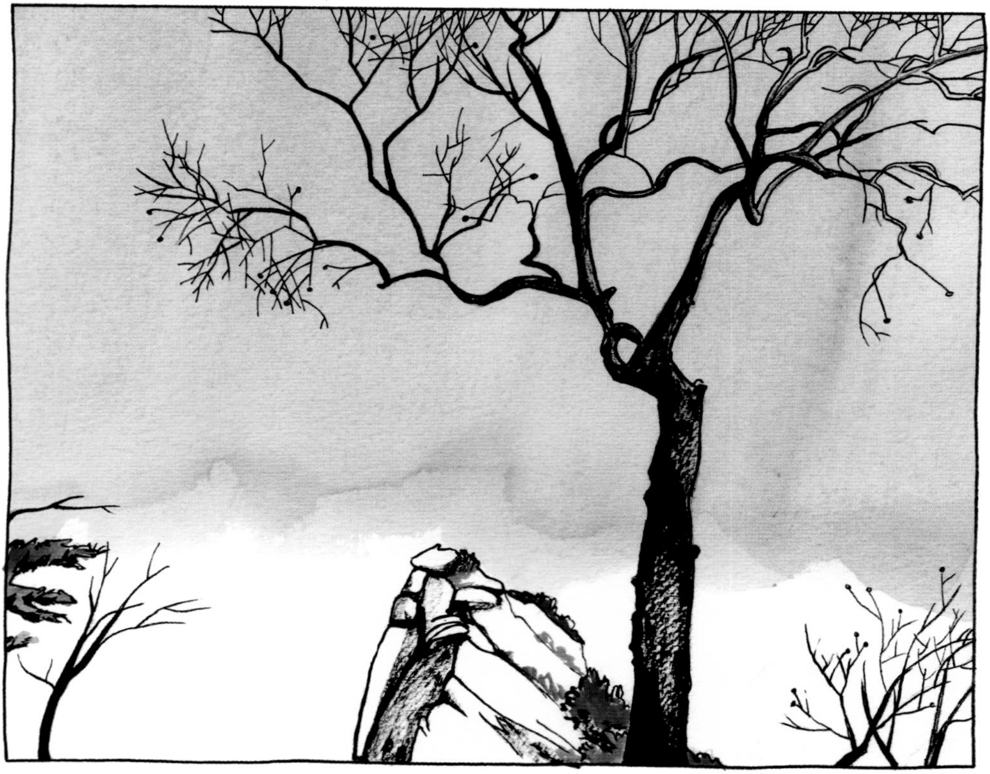

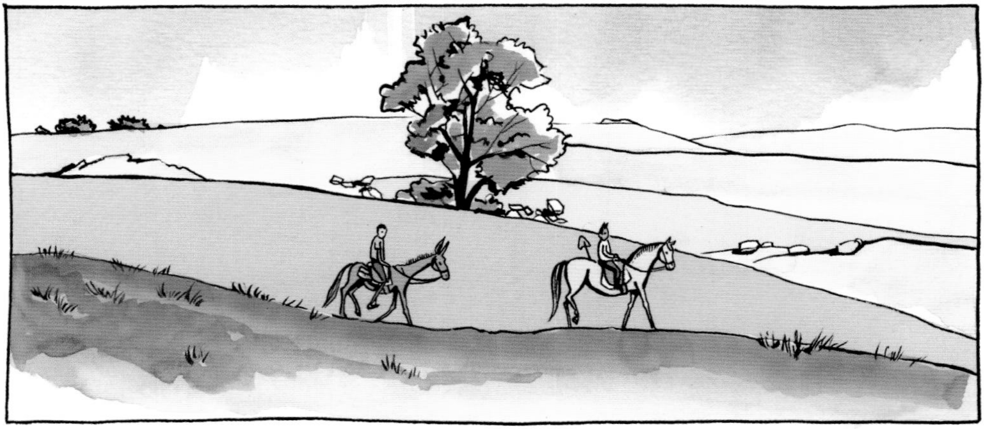
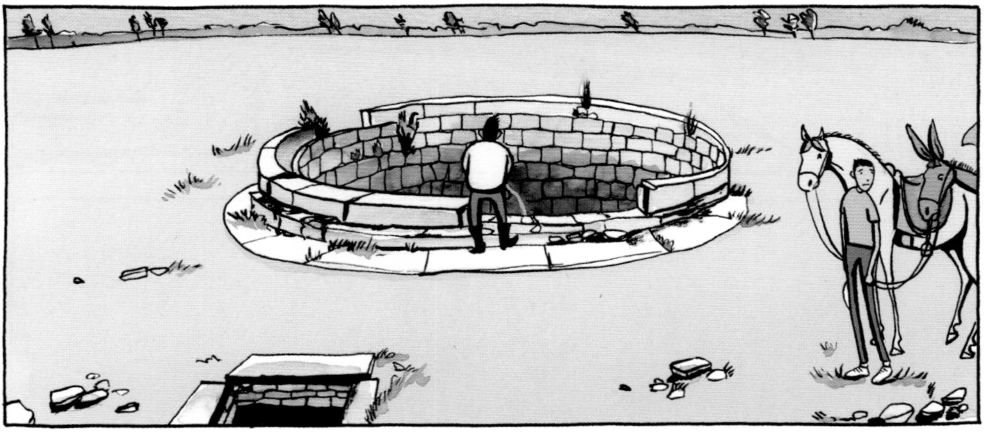
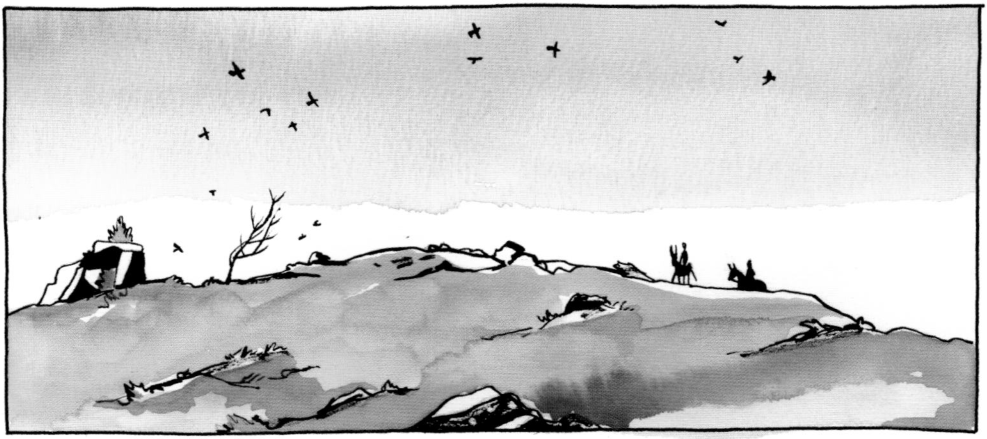

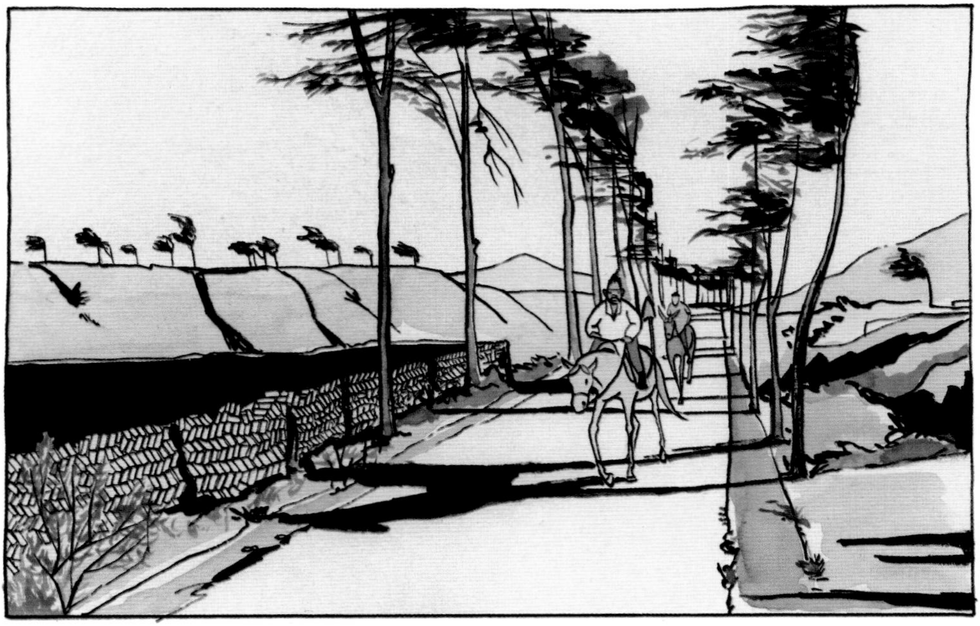

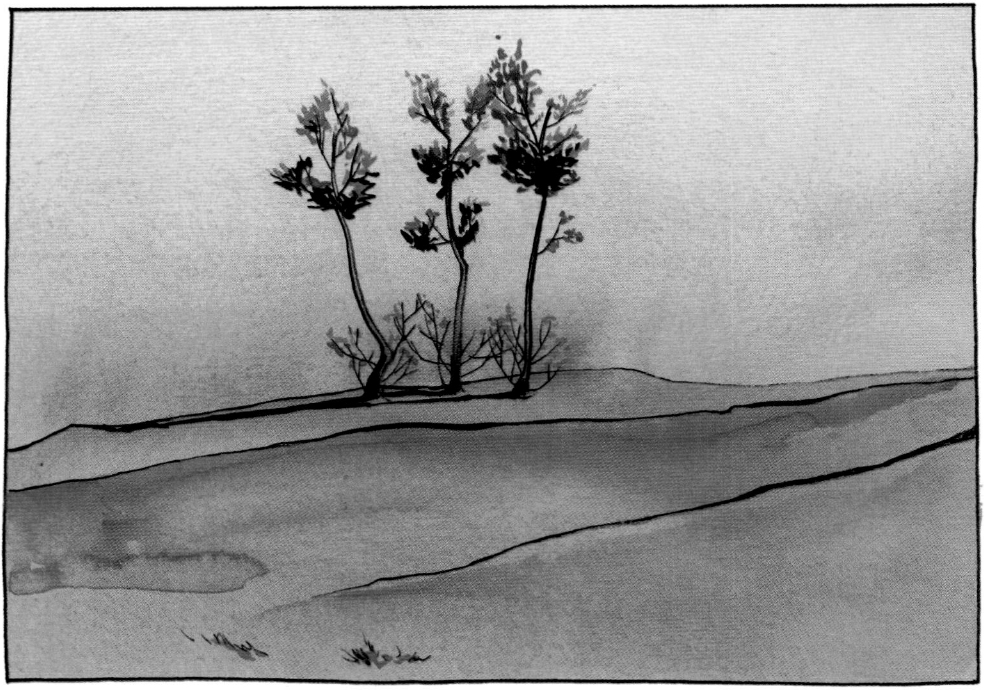

5. The Land

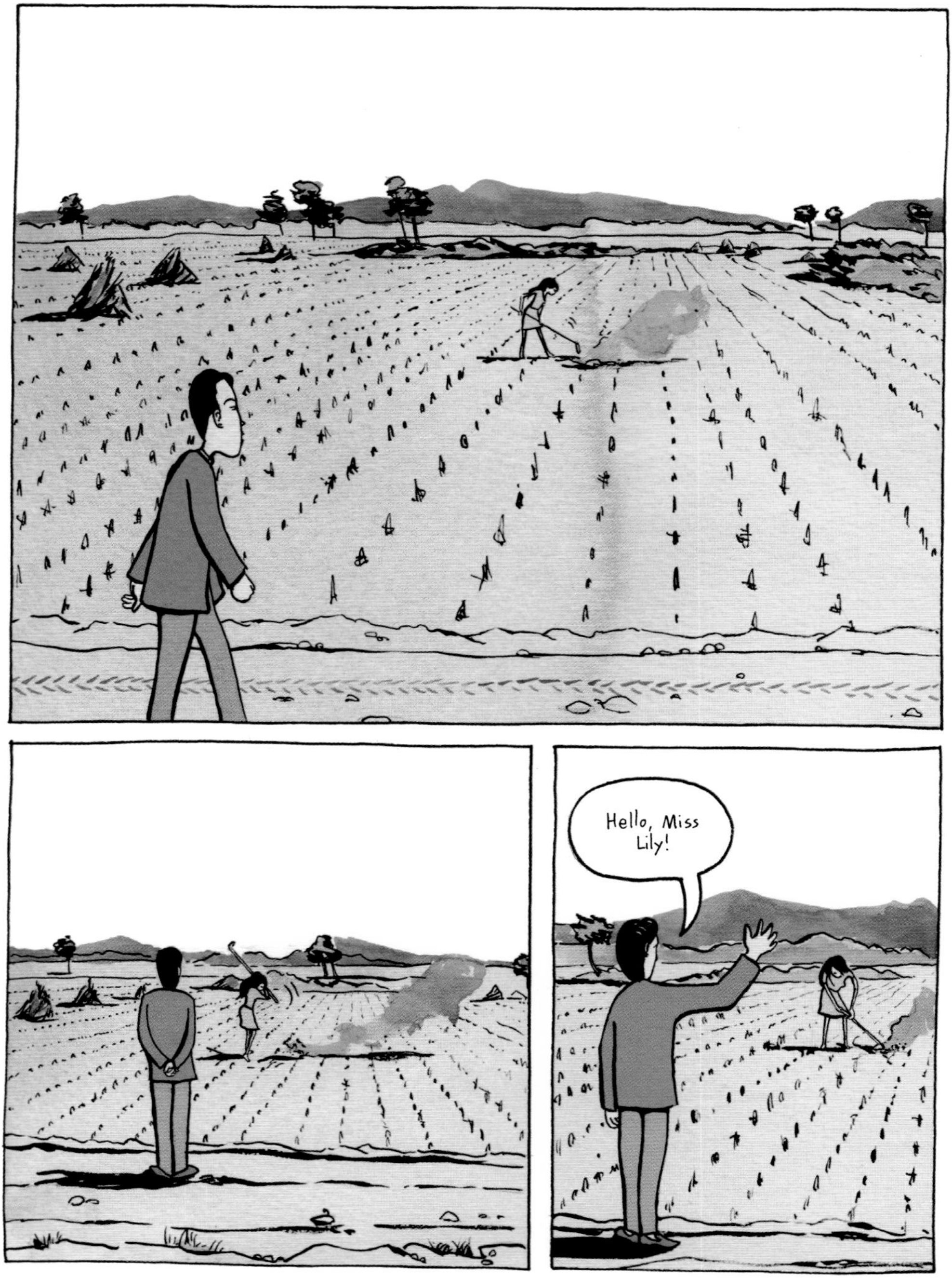
Hello, Miss Lily!

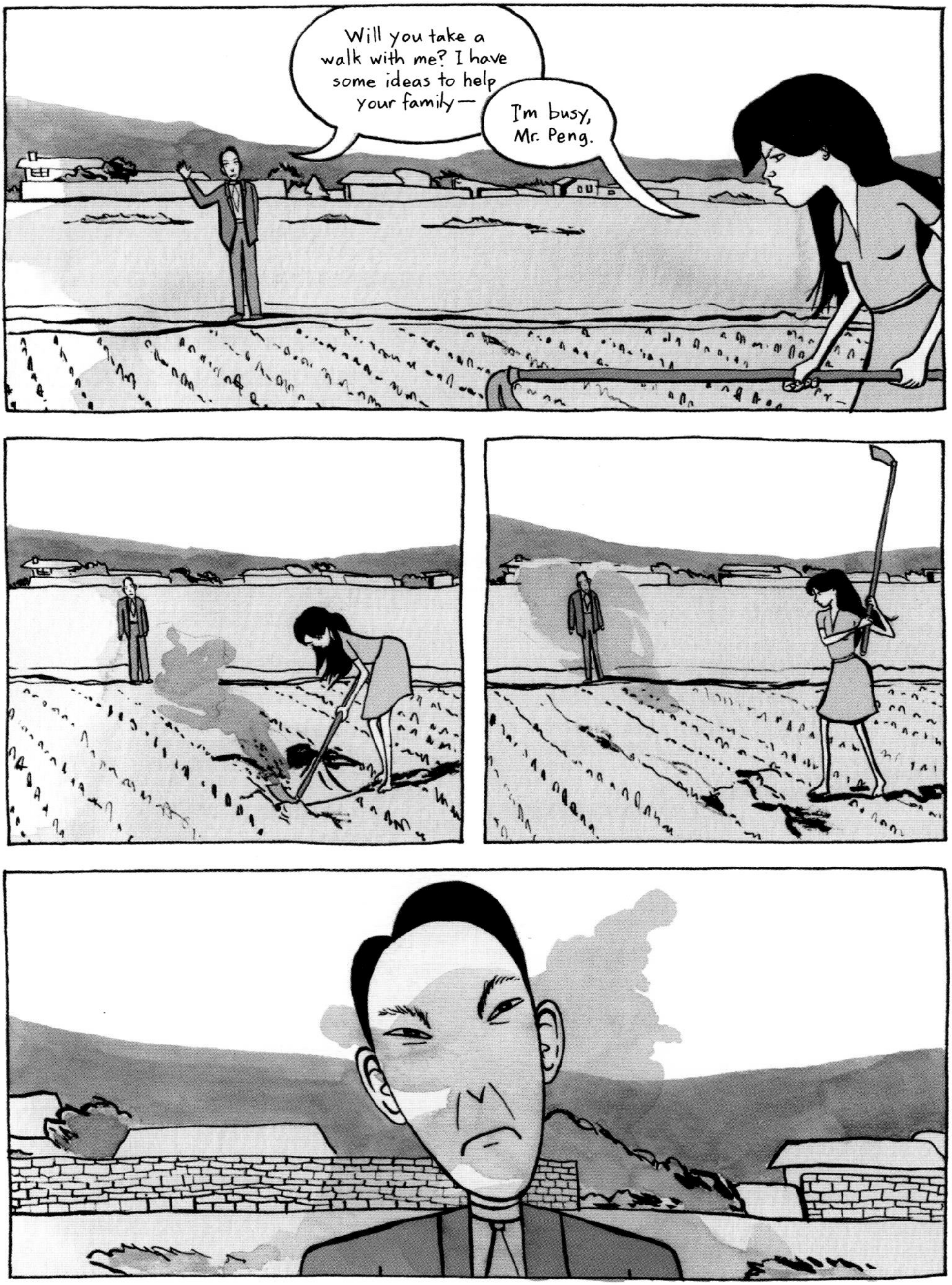
Will you take a walk with me? I have some ideas to help your family—
I'm busy, Mr. Peng.

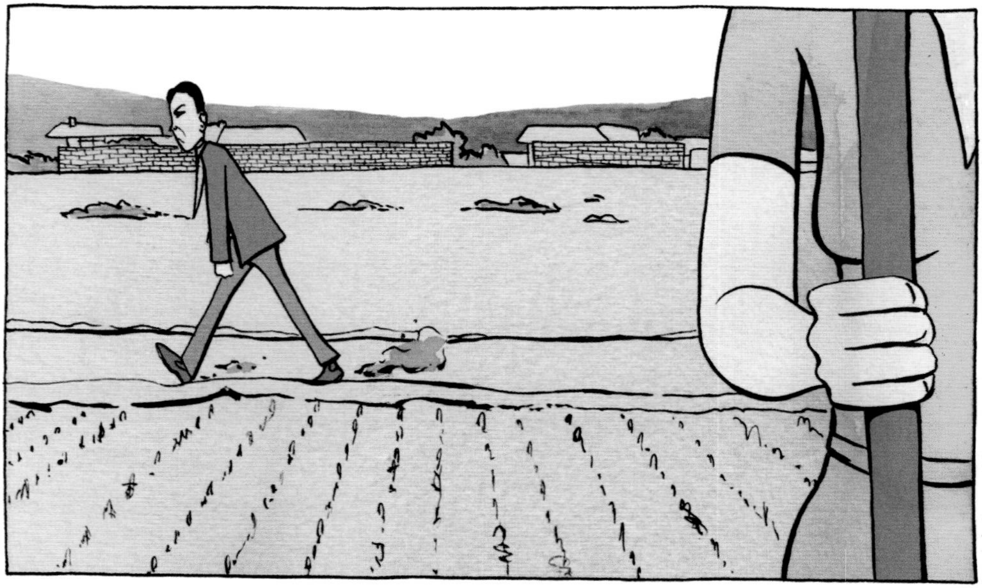

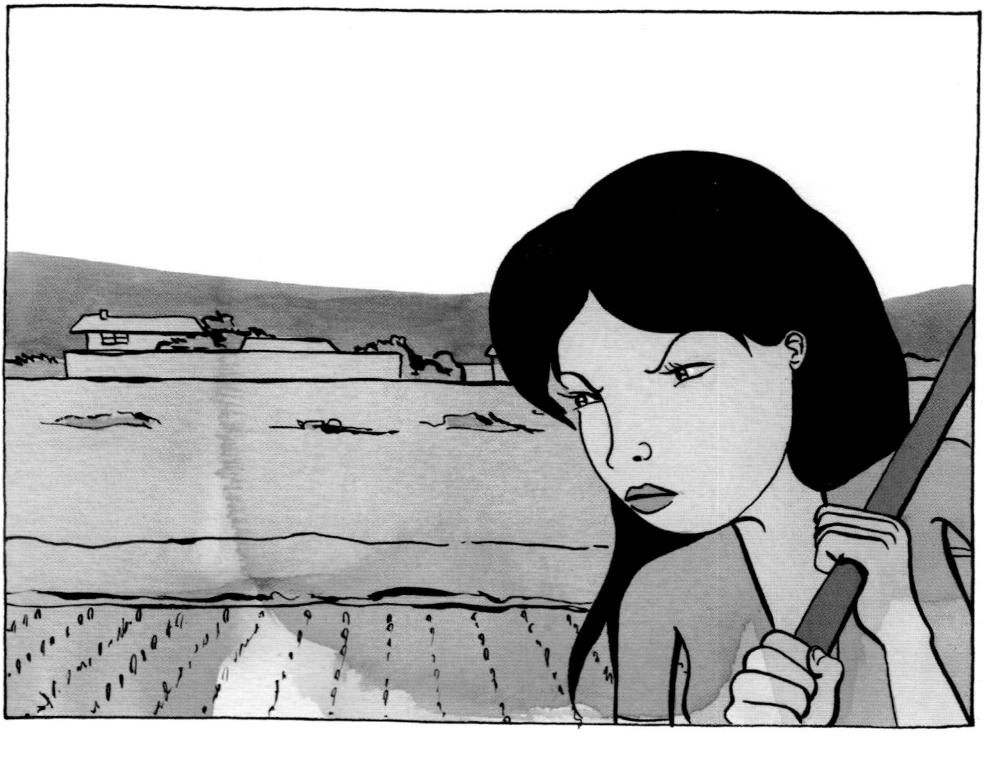

6. The Sleepers

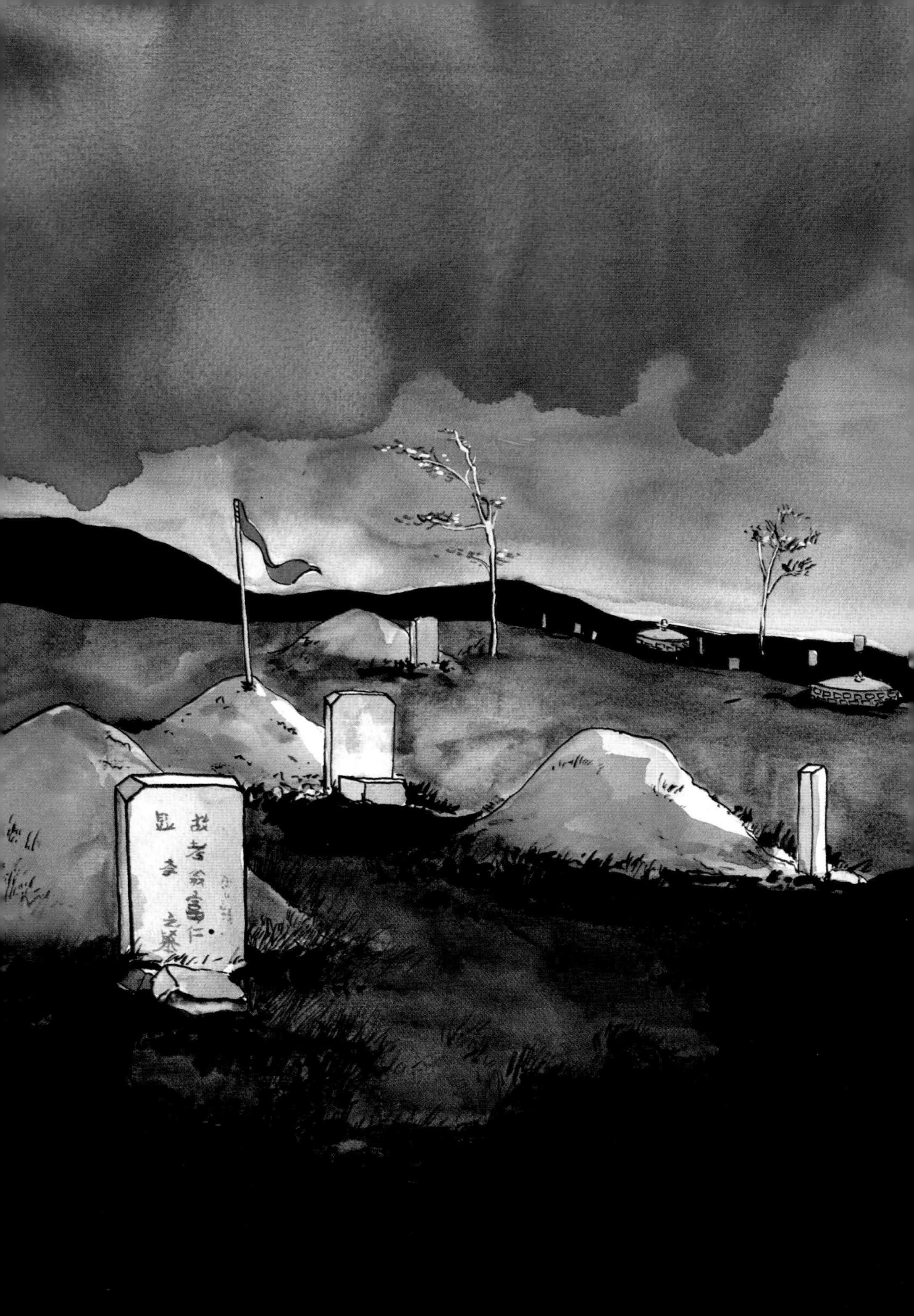
故老翁高仁

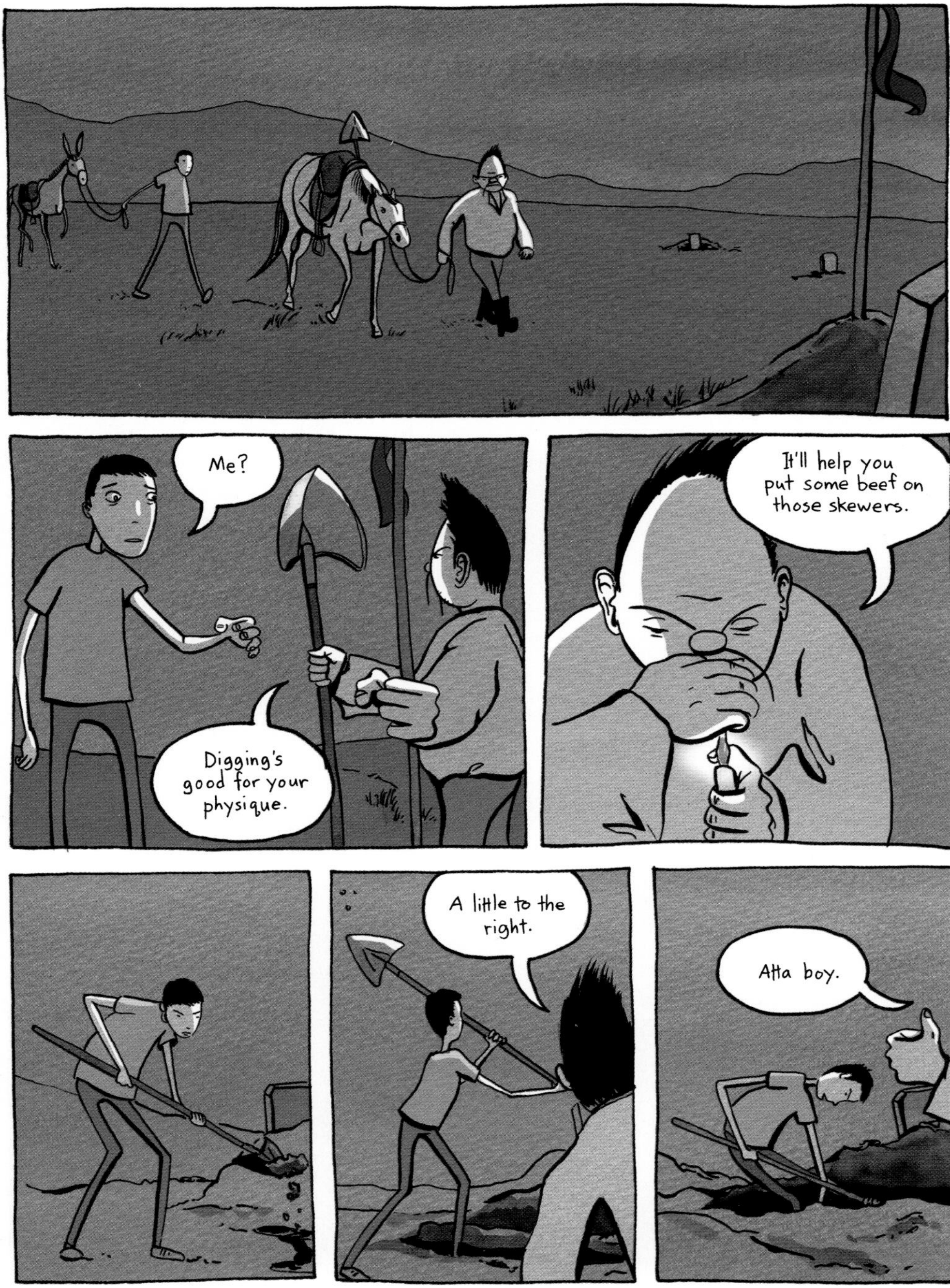

Me?
Digging's good for your physique.
It'll help you put some beef on those skewers.
A little to the right.
Atta boy.

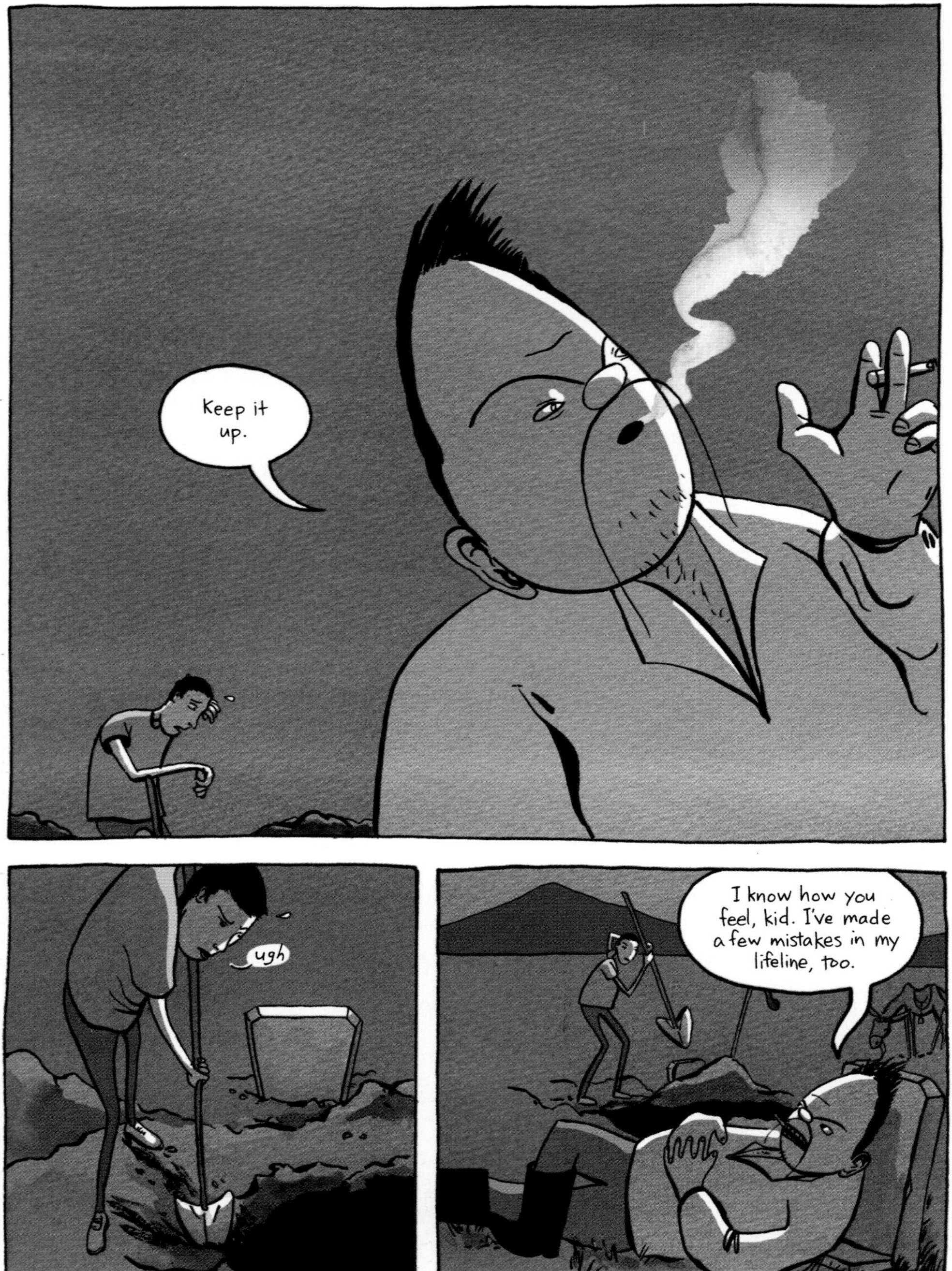
Keep it up.
ugh
I know how you feel, kid. I've made a few mistakes in my lifeline, too.

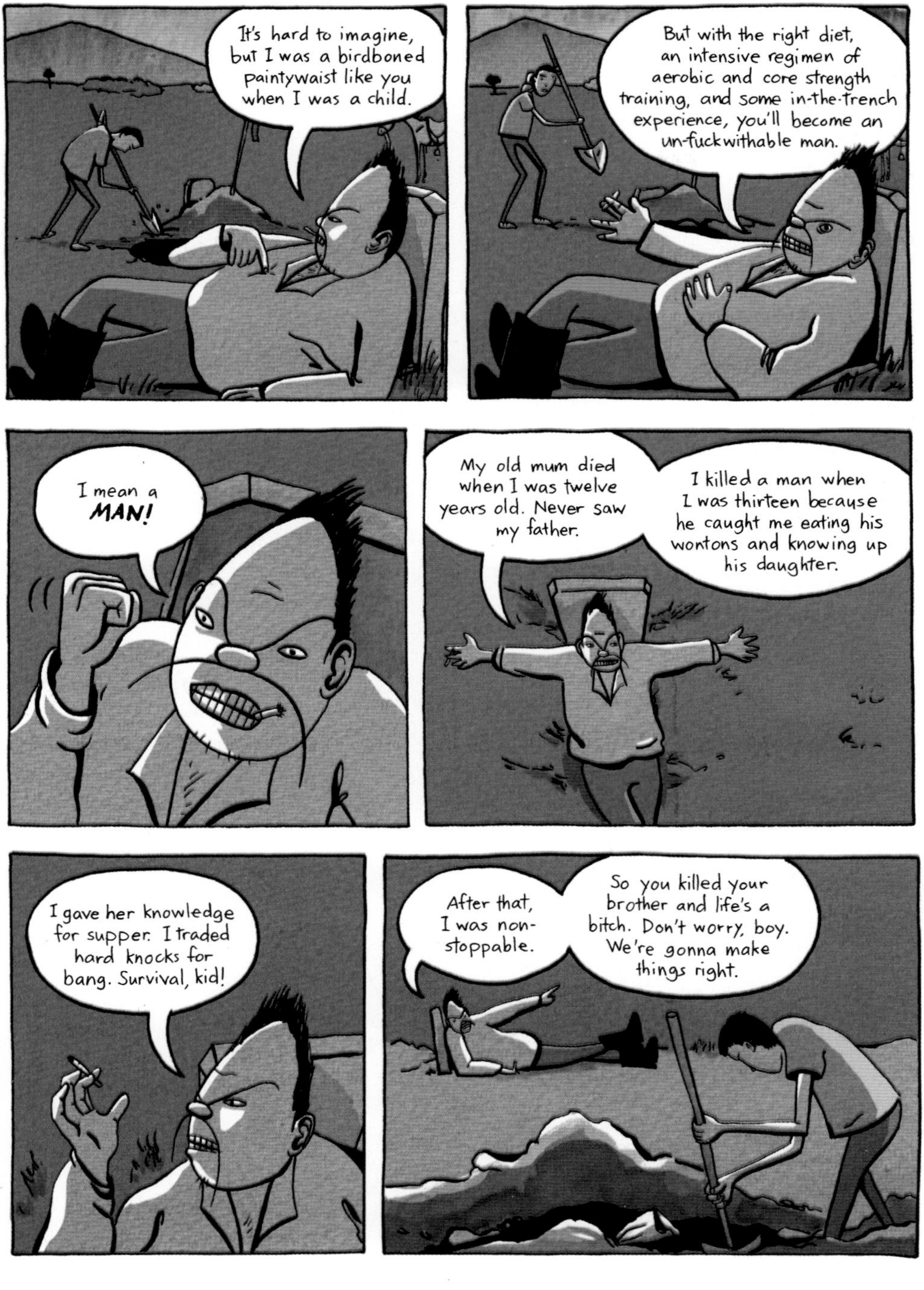
It's hard to imagine, but I was a birdboned paintywaist like you when I was a child.
But with the right diet, an intensive regimen of aerobic and core strength training, and some in-the-trench experience, you'll become an un-fuckwithable man.
I mean a **MAN!**
My old mum died when I was twelve years old. Never saw my father.
I killed a man when I was thirteen because he caught me eating his wontons and knowing up his daughter.
I gave her knowledge for supper. I traded hard knocks for bang. Survival, kid!
After that, I was non-stoppable.
So you killed your brother and life's a bitch. Don't worry, boy. We're gonna make things right.

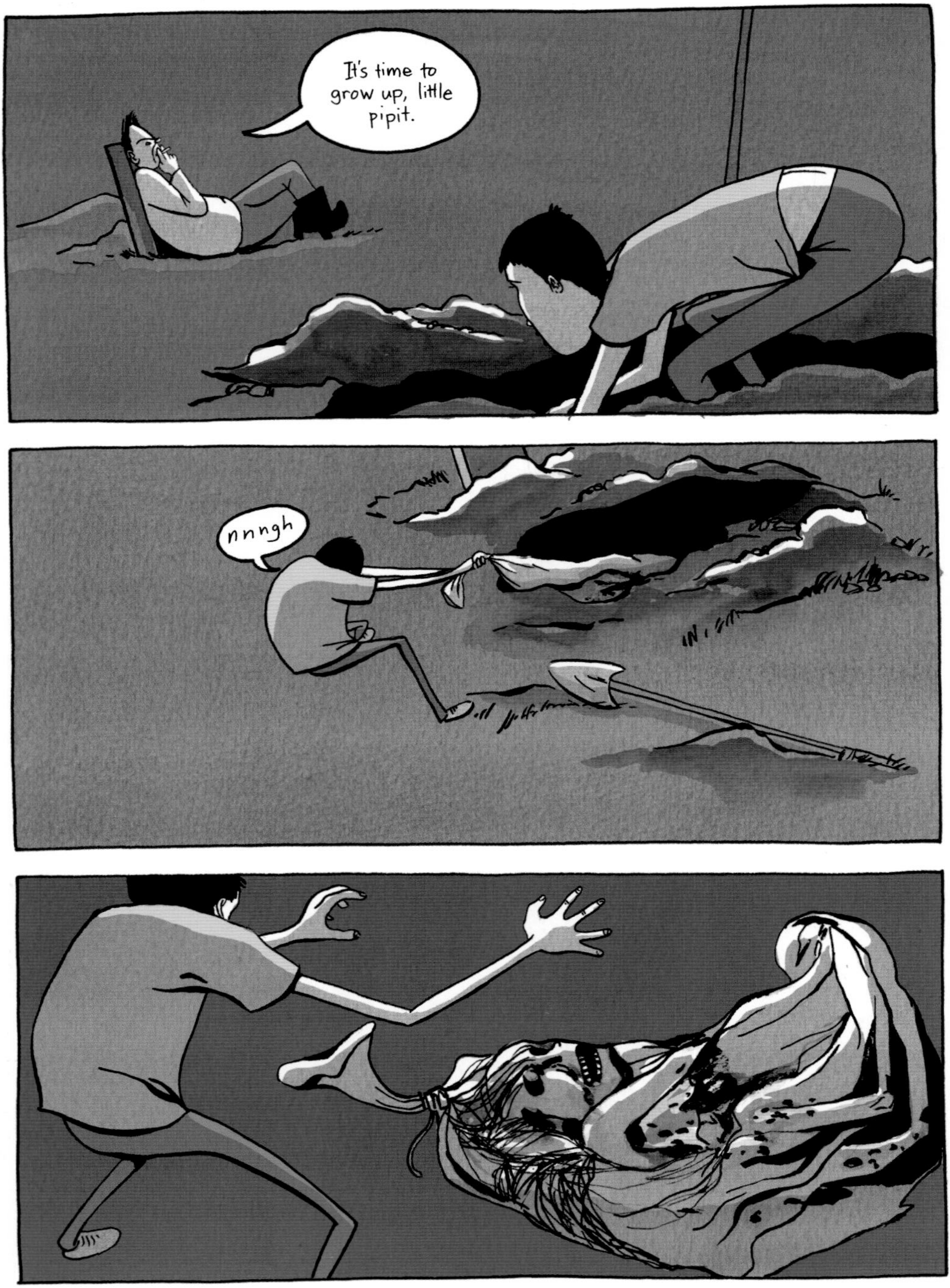
It's time to grow up, little pipit.
nnngh

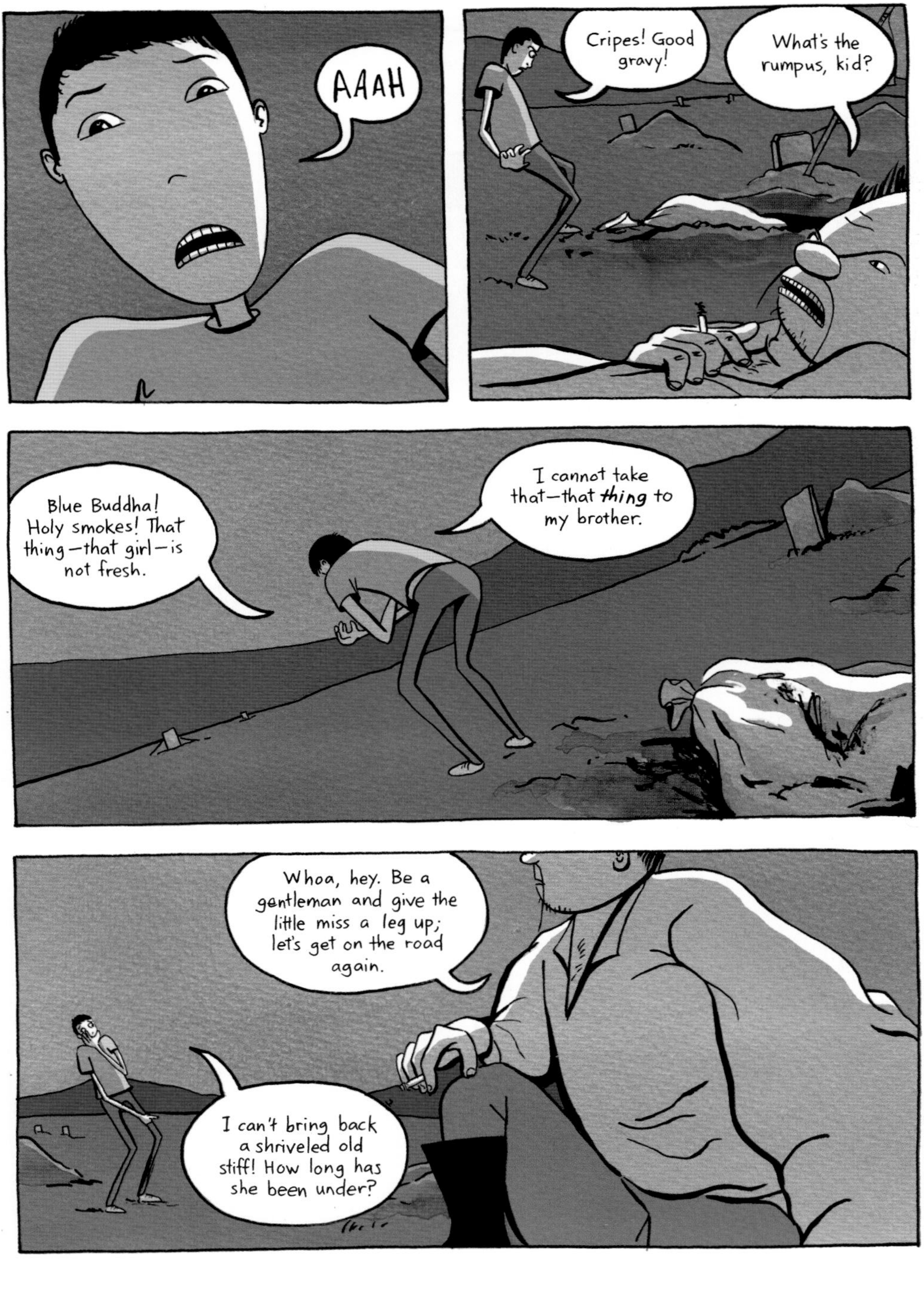
AAAH
Cripes! Good gravy!
What's the rumpus, kid?
Blue Buddha! Holy smokes! That thing—that girl—is not fresh.
I cannot take that—that *thing* to my brother.
Whoa, hey. Be a gentleman and give the little miss a leg up; let's get on the road again.
I can't bring back a shriveled old stiff! How long has she been under?

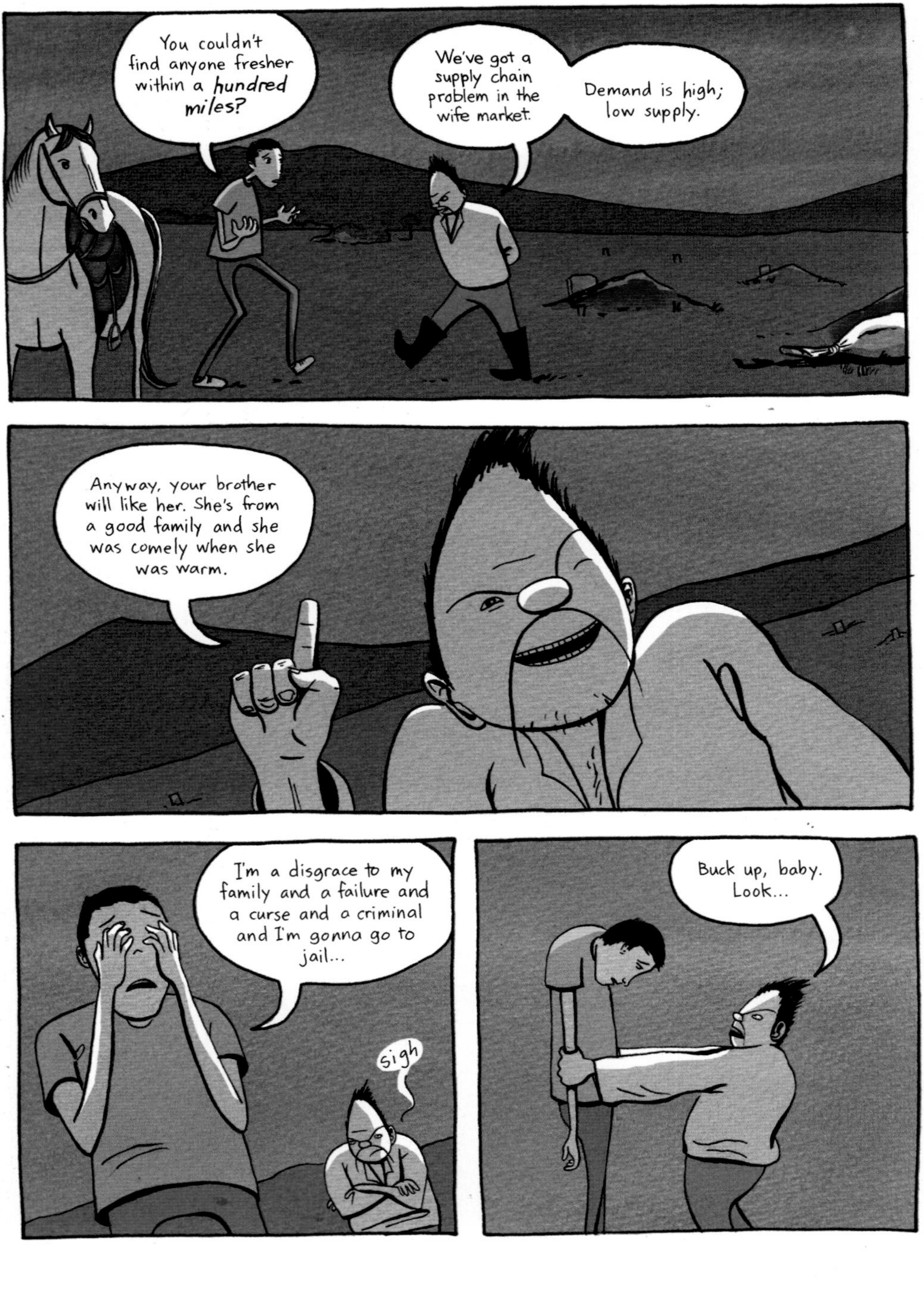
You couldn't find anyone fresher within a hundred miles?
We've got a supply chain problem in the wife market.
Demand is high; low supply.
Anyway, your brother will like her. She's from a good family and she was comely when she was warm.
I'm a disgrace to my family and a failure and a curse and a criminal and I'm gonna go to jail...
Sigh
Buck up, baby. Look...

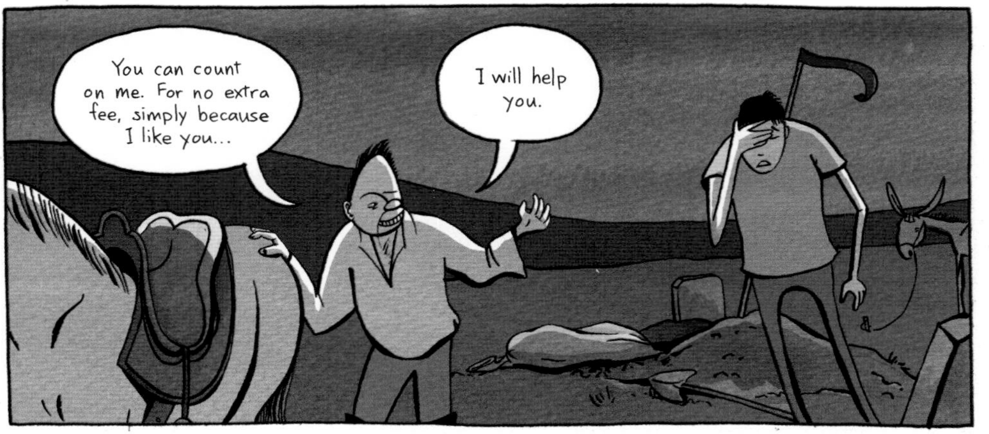
You can count on me. For no extra fee, simply because I like you...
I will help you.

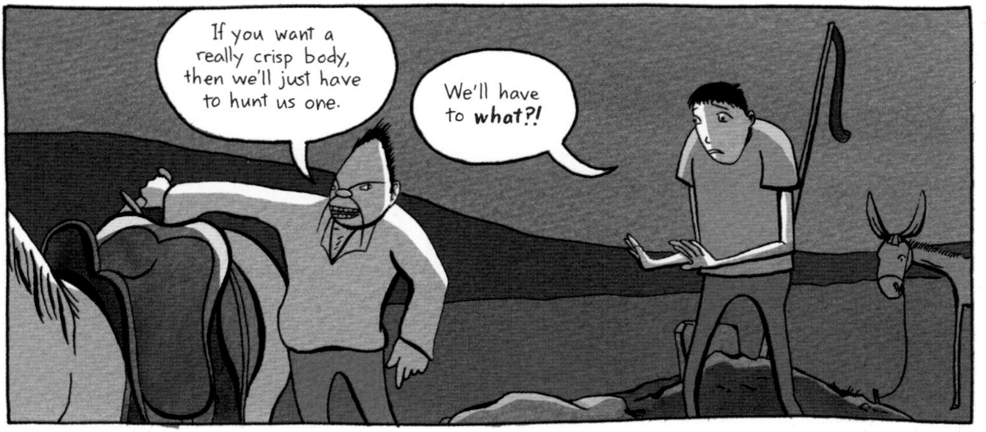
If you want a really crisp body, then we'll just have to hunt us one.
We'll have to **what?!**

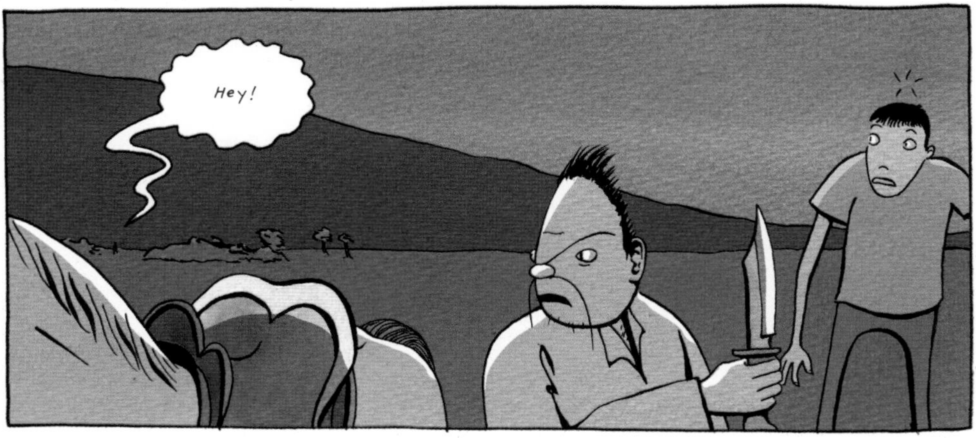
Hey!

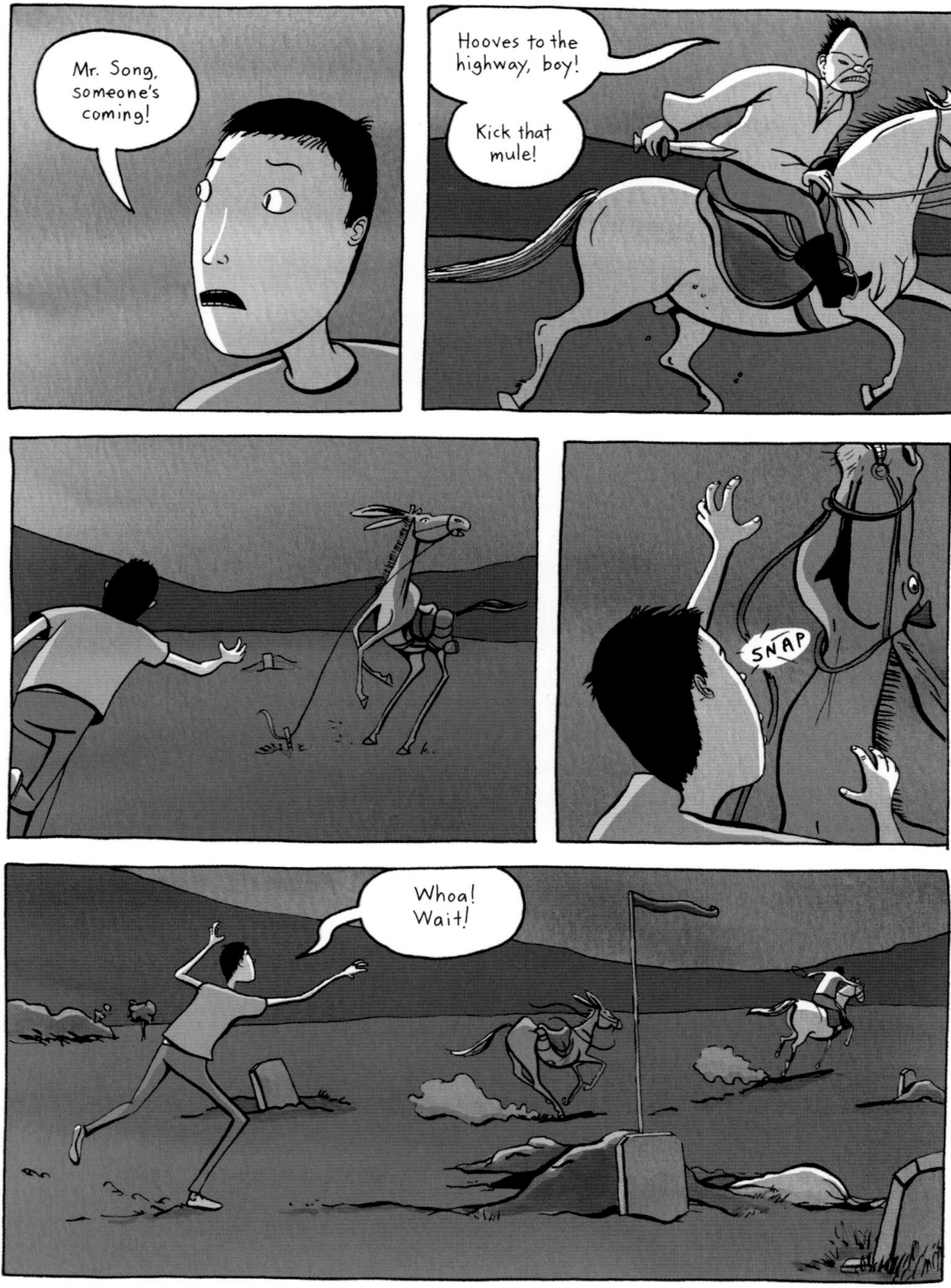
Mr. Song, someone's coming!
Hooves to the highway, boy!
Kick that mule!
SNAP
Whoa! Wait!

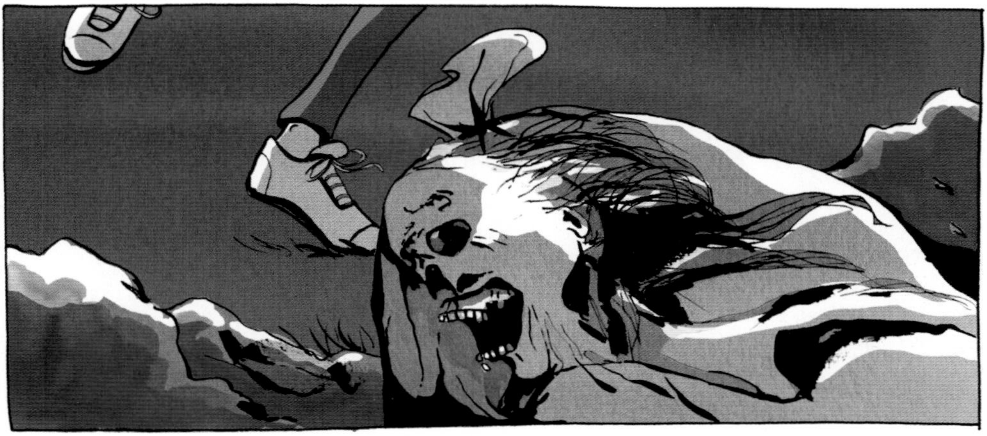

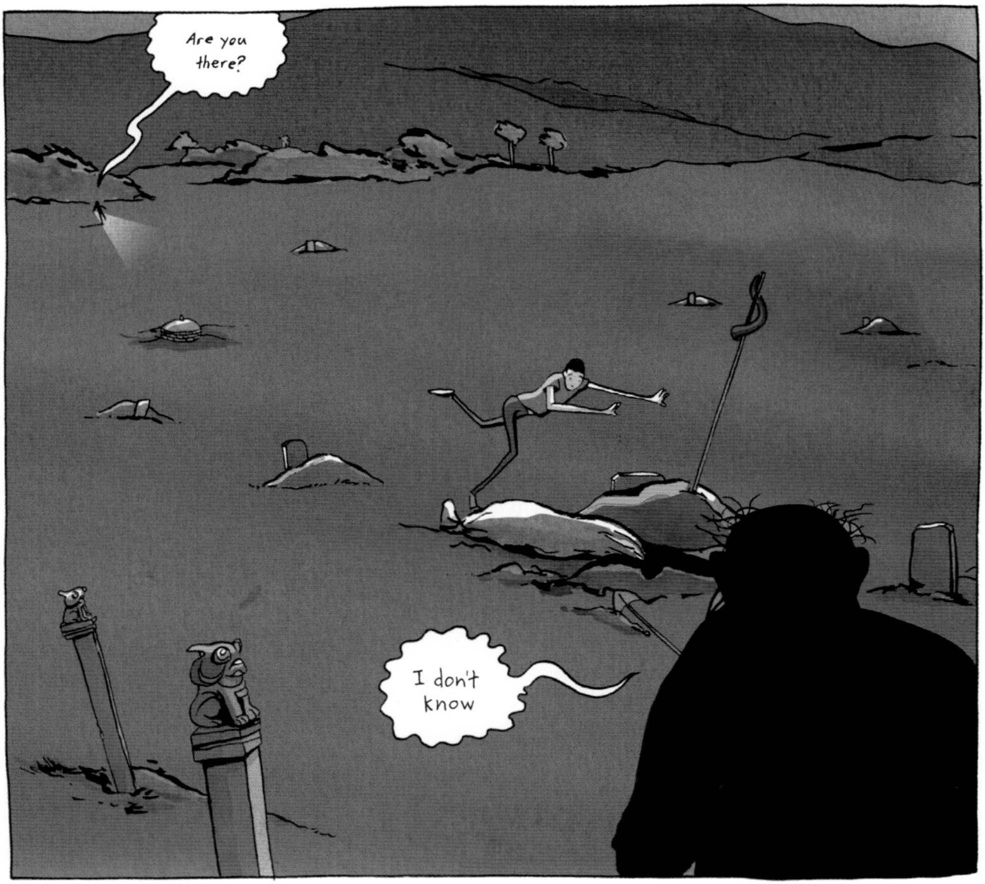
Are you there?
I don't know

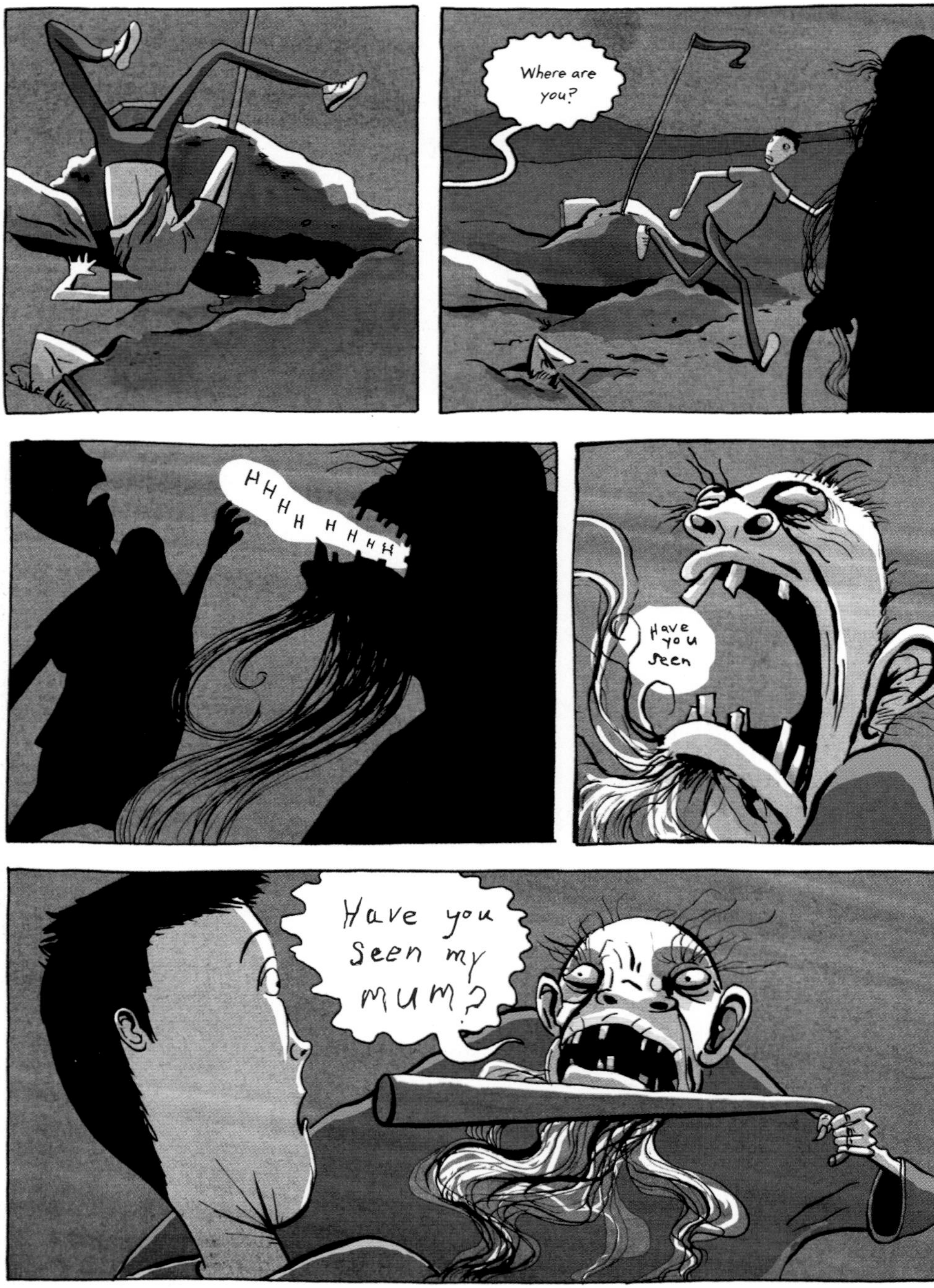
Where are you?
HHHH HHHHHHH
Have you seen
Have you seen my mum?

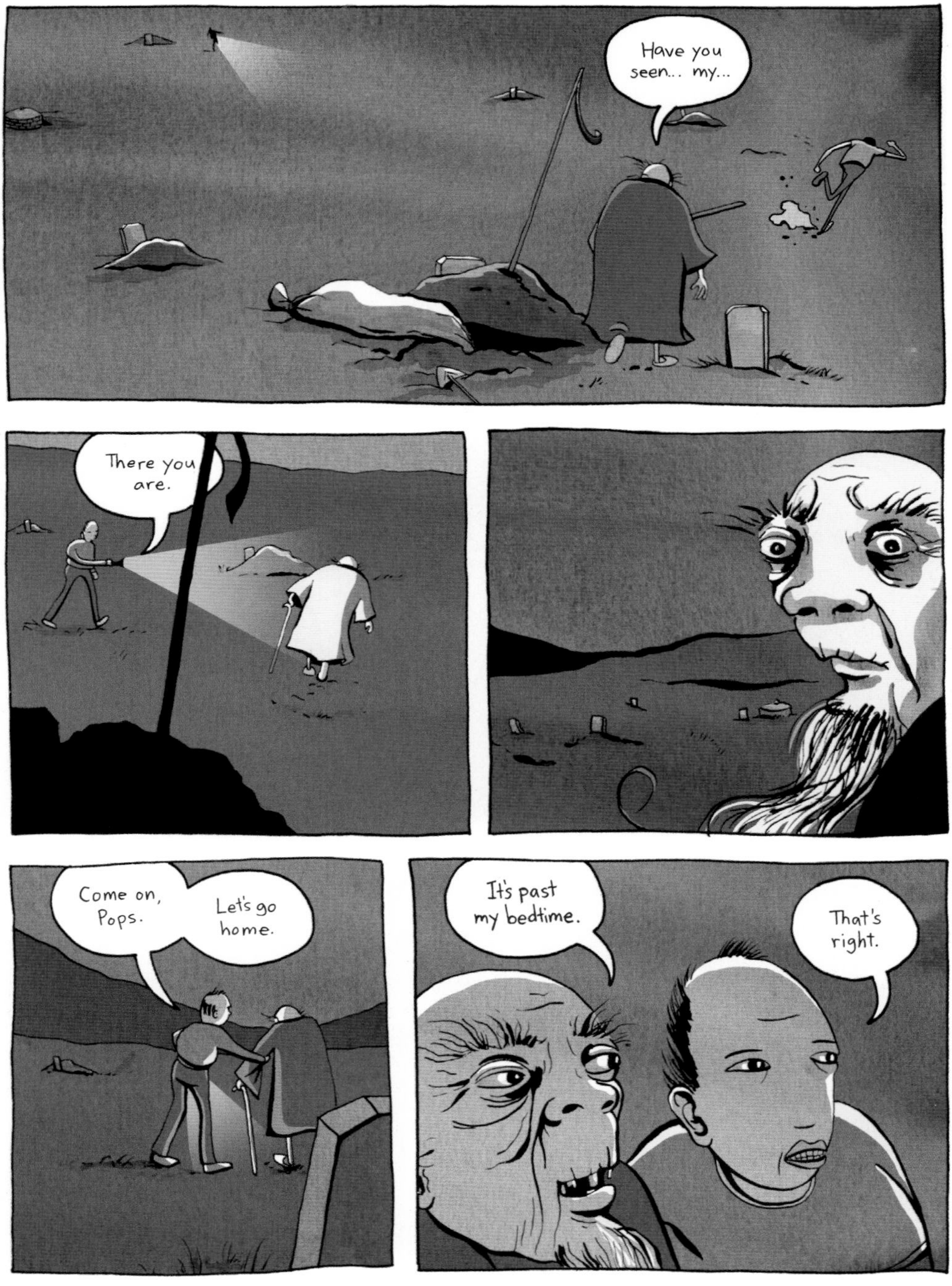
Have you seen... my...
There you are.
Come on, Pops.
Let's go home.
It's past my bedtime.
That's right.

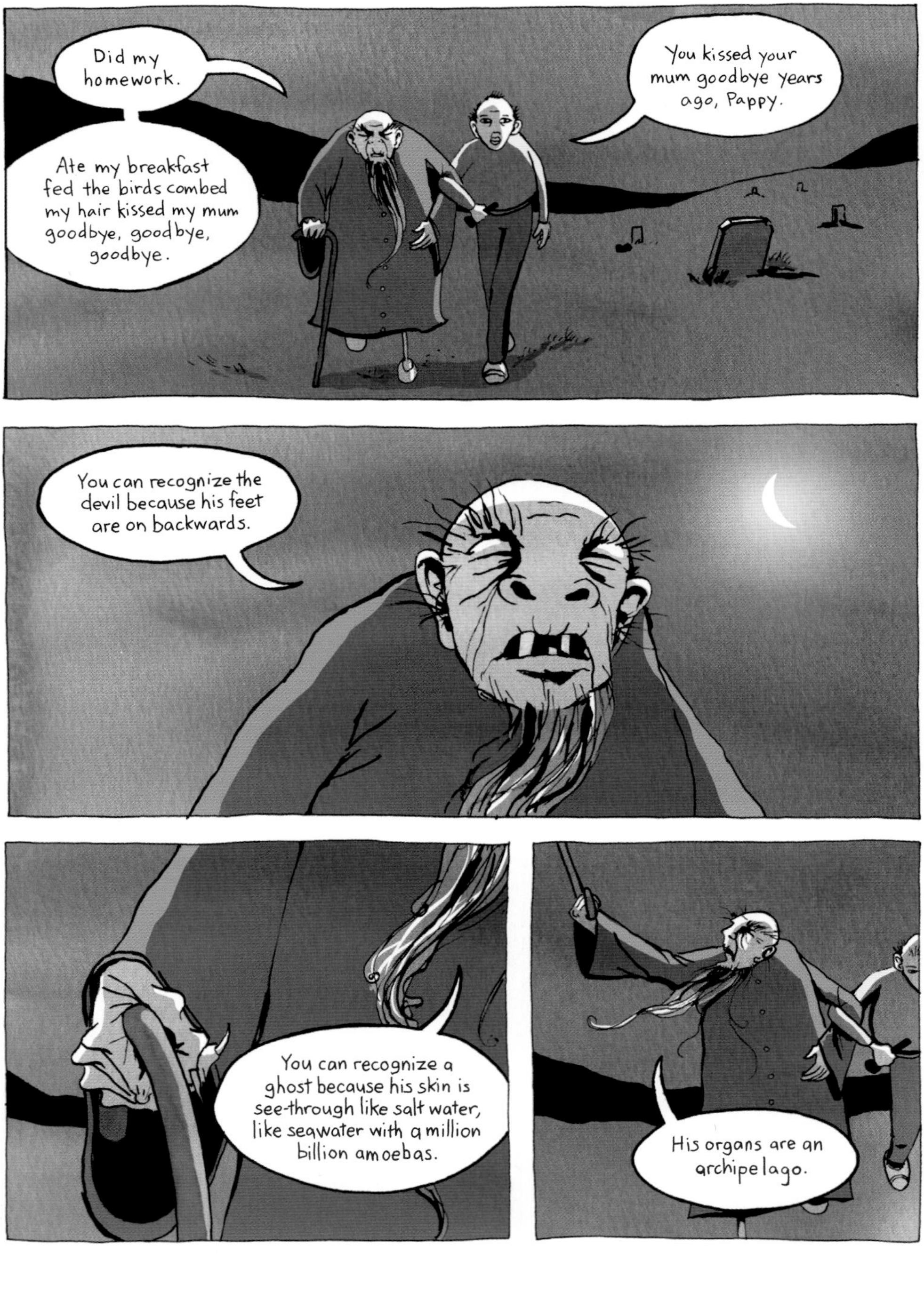
Did my homework.
Ate my breakfast fed the birds combed my hair kissed my mum goodbye, goodbye, goodbye.
You kissed your mum goodbye years ago, Pappy.
You can recognize the devil because his feet are on backwards.
You can recognize a ghost because his skin is see-through like salt water, like seawater with a million billion amoebas.
His organs are an archipelago.

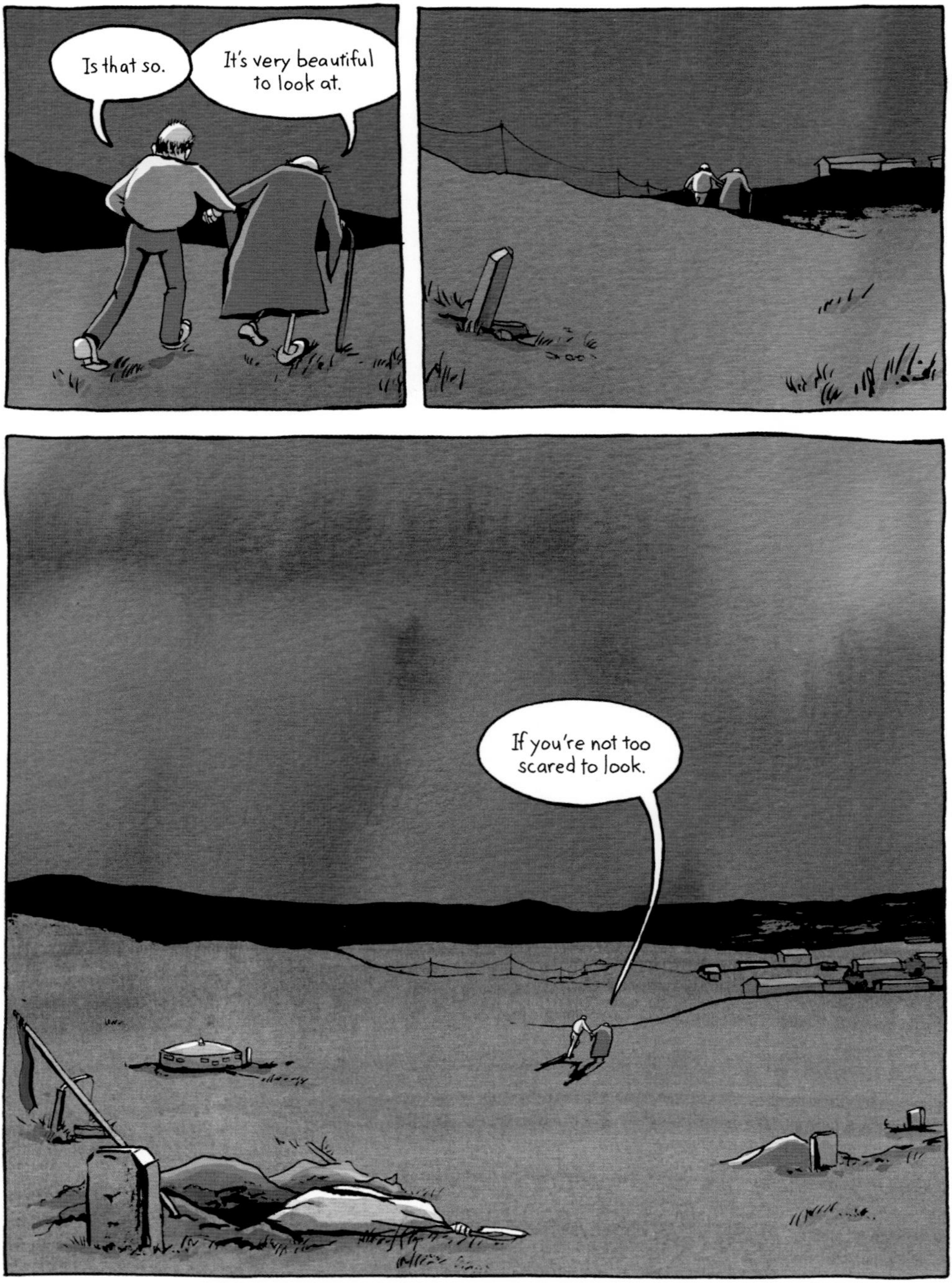
Is that so.
It's very beautiful to look at.
If you're not too scared to look.

7. All the King's Horses

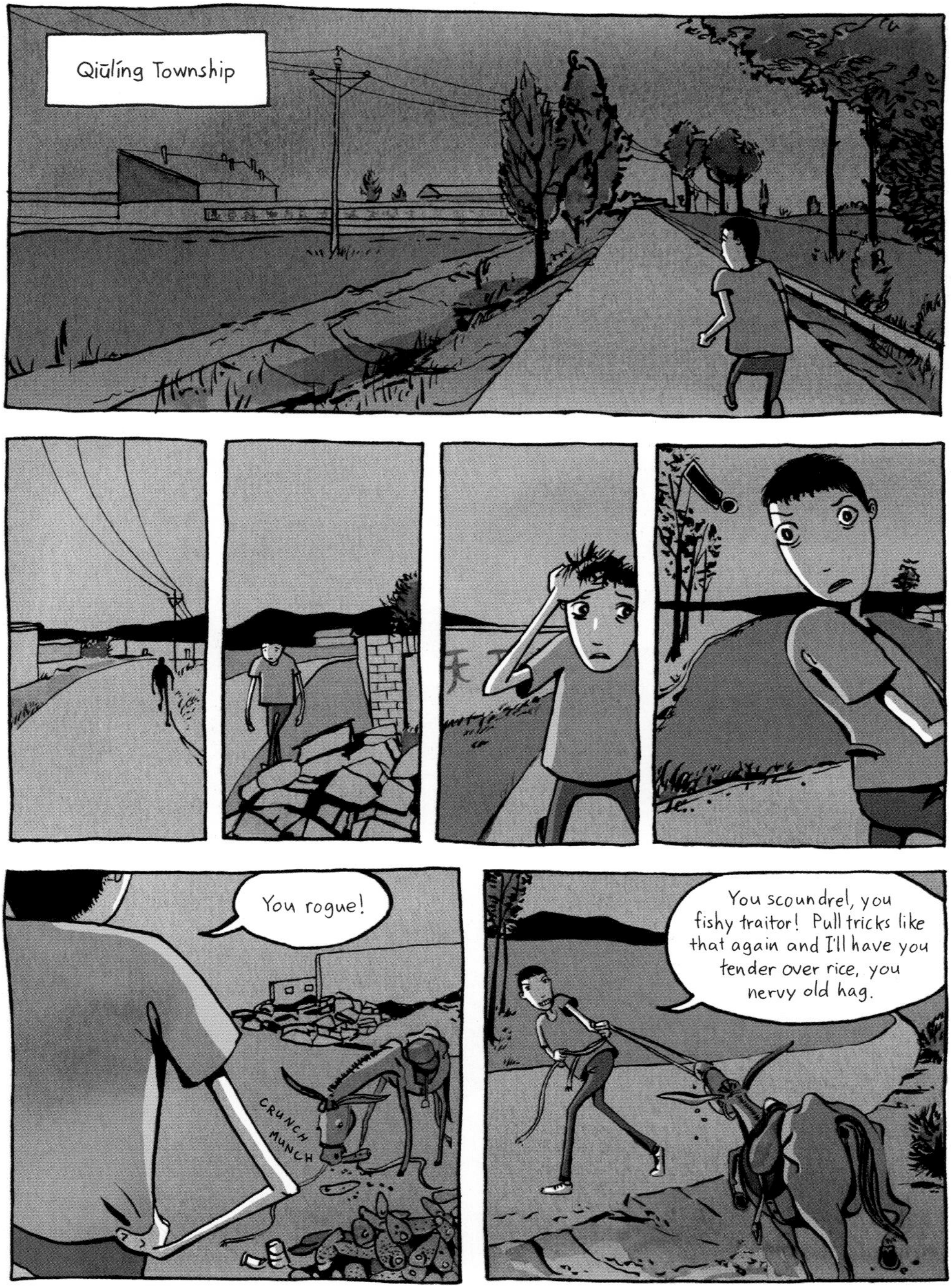
Qiūlíng Township
You rogue!
CRUNCH
MUNCH
You scoundrel, you fishy traitor! Pull tricks like that again and I'll have you tender over rice, you nervy old hag.

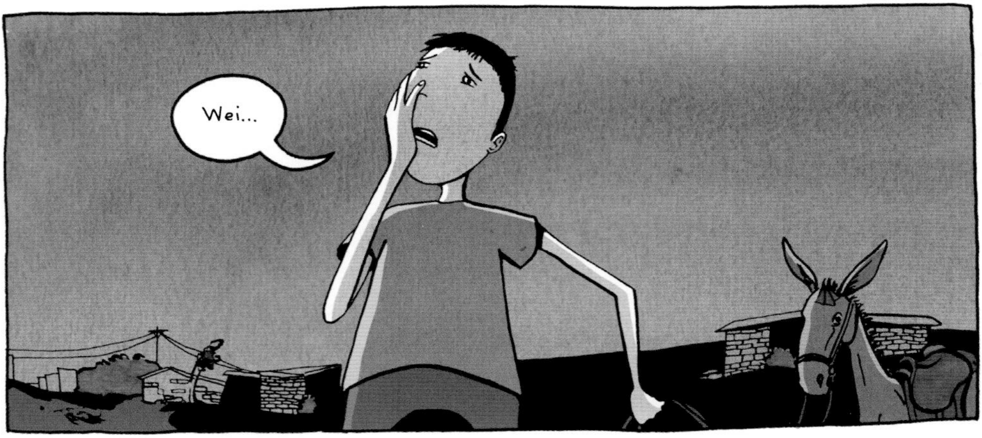
Wei...

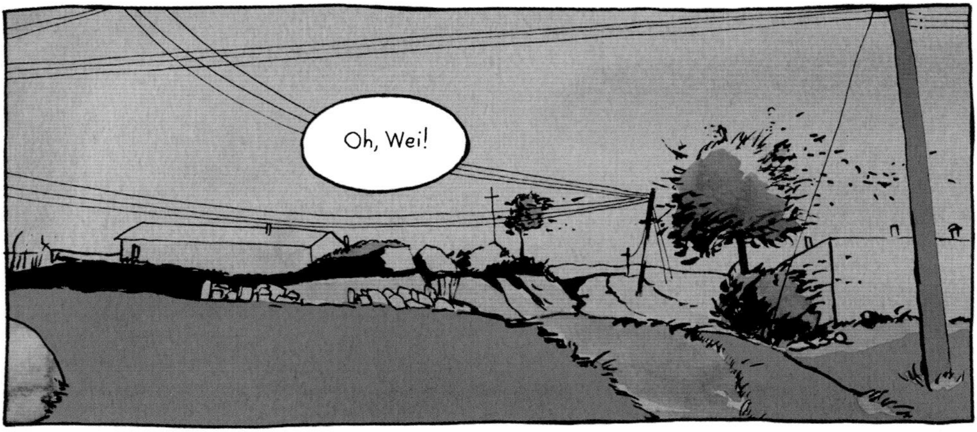
Oh, Wei!

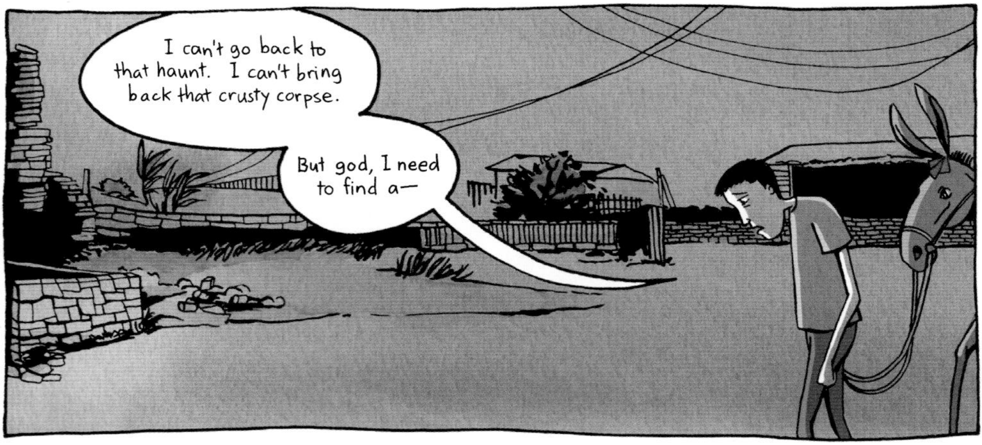
I can't go back to that haunt. I can't bring back that crusty corpse.
But god, I need to find a—

—body.

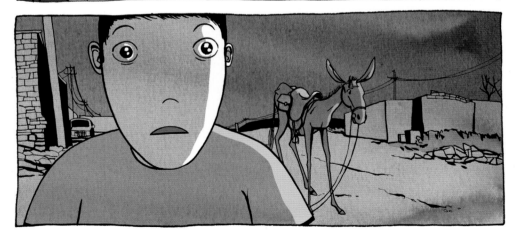

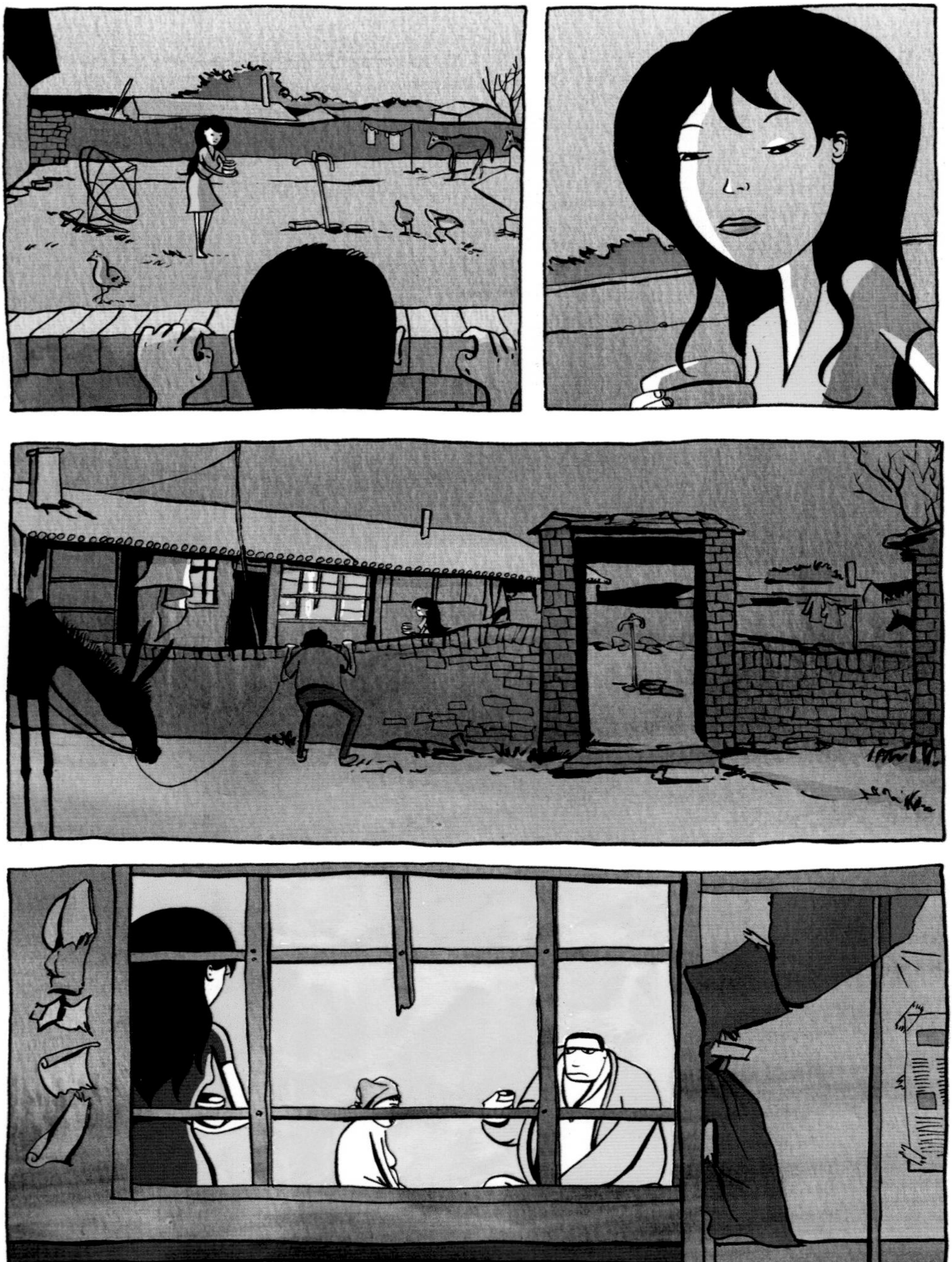

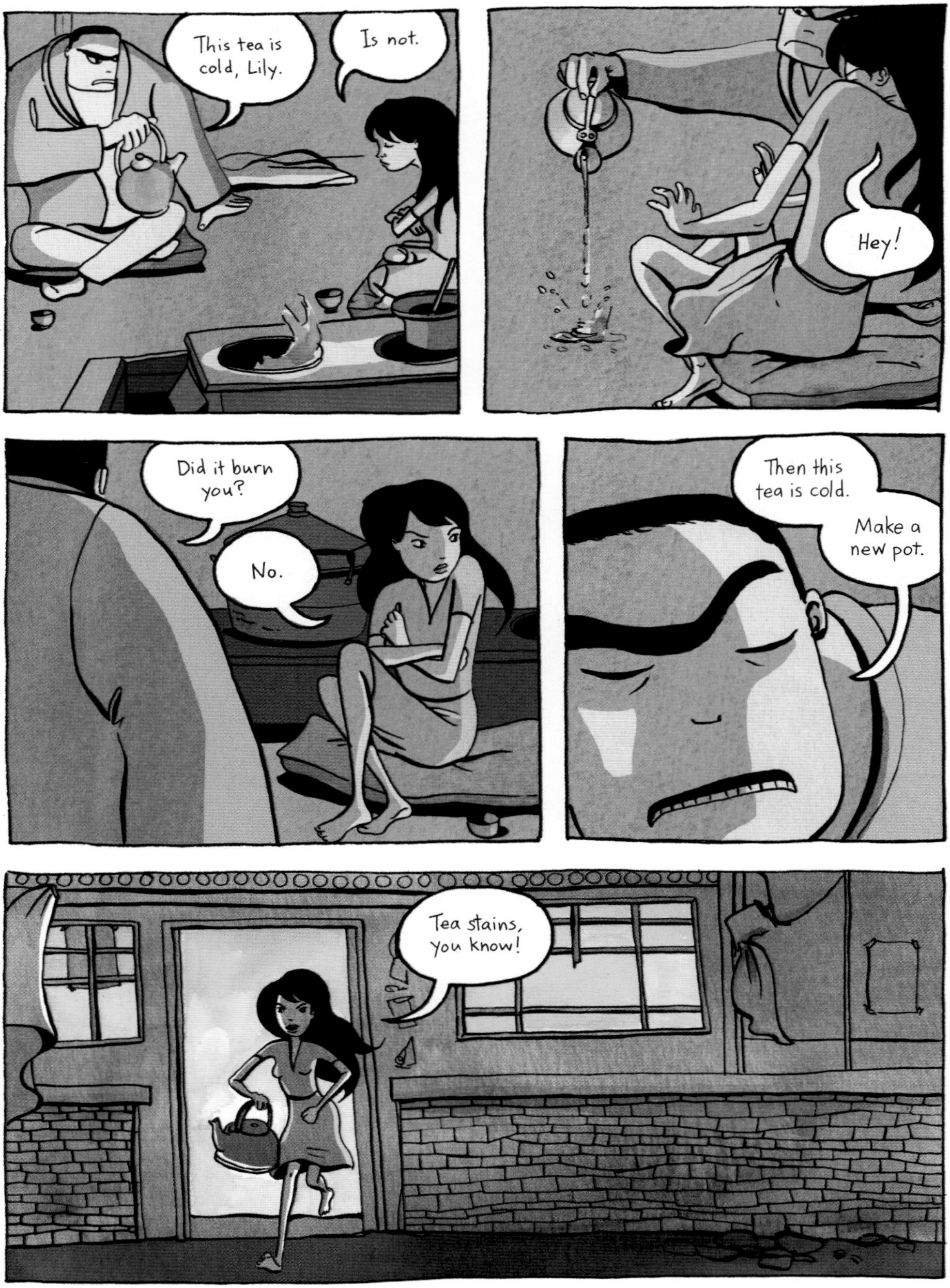
This tea is cold, Lily.
Is not.
Hey!
Did it burn you?
No.
Then this tea is cold.
Make a new pot.
Tea stains, you know!

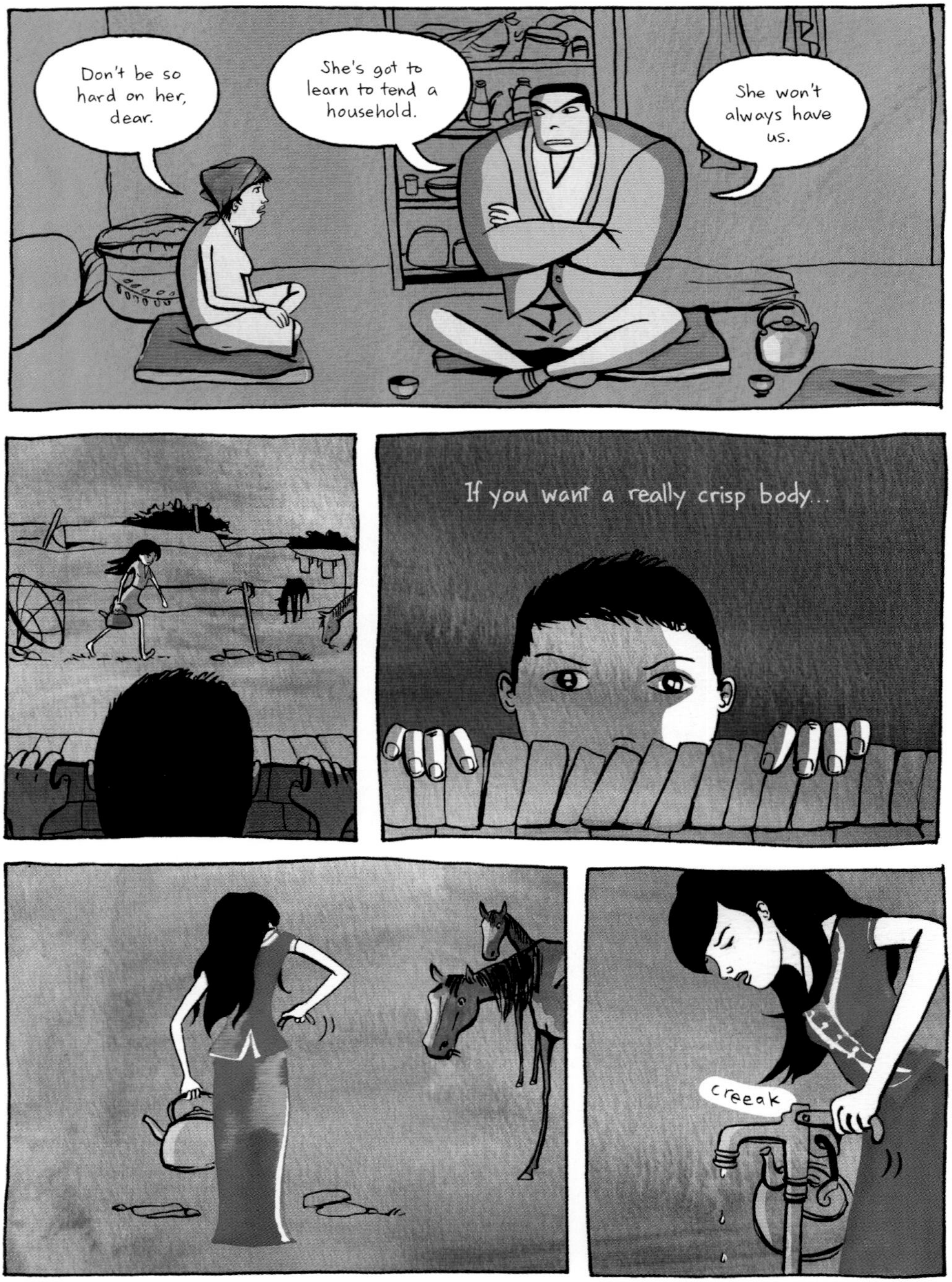
Don't be so hard on her, dear.
She's got to learn to tend a household.
She won't always have us.
If you want a really crisp body...
creeak

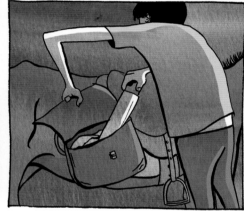

sigh

plink
plink

I'm going to the river!

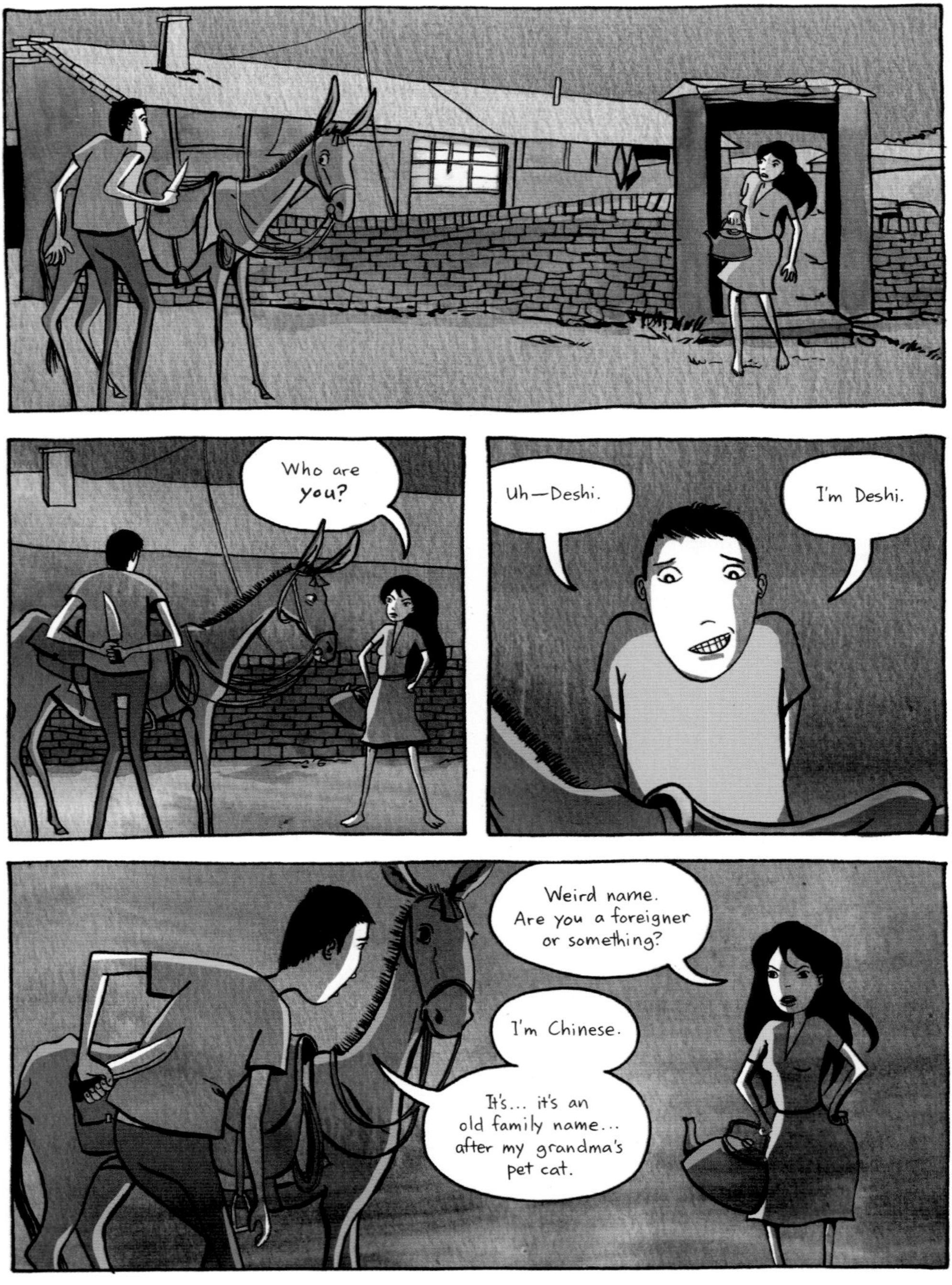
Who are you?
Uh—Deshi.
I'm Deshi.
Weird name. Are you a foreigner or something?
I'm Chinese.
It's... it's an old family name... after my grandma's pet cat.

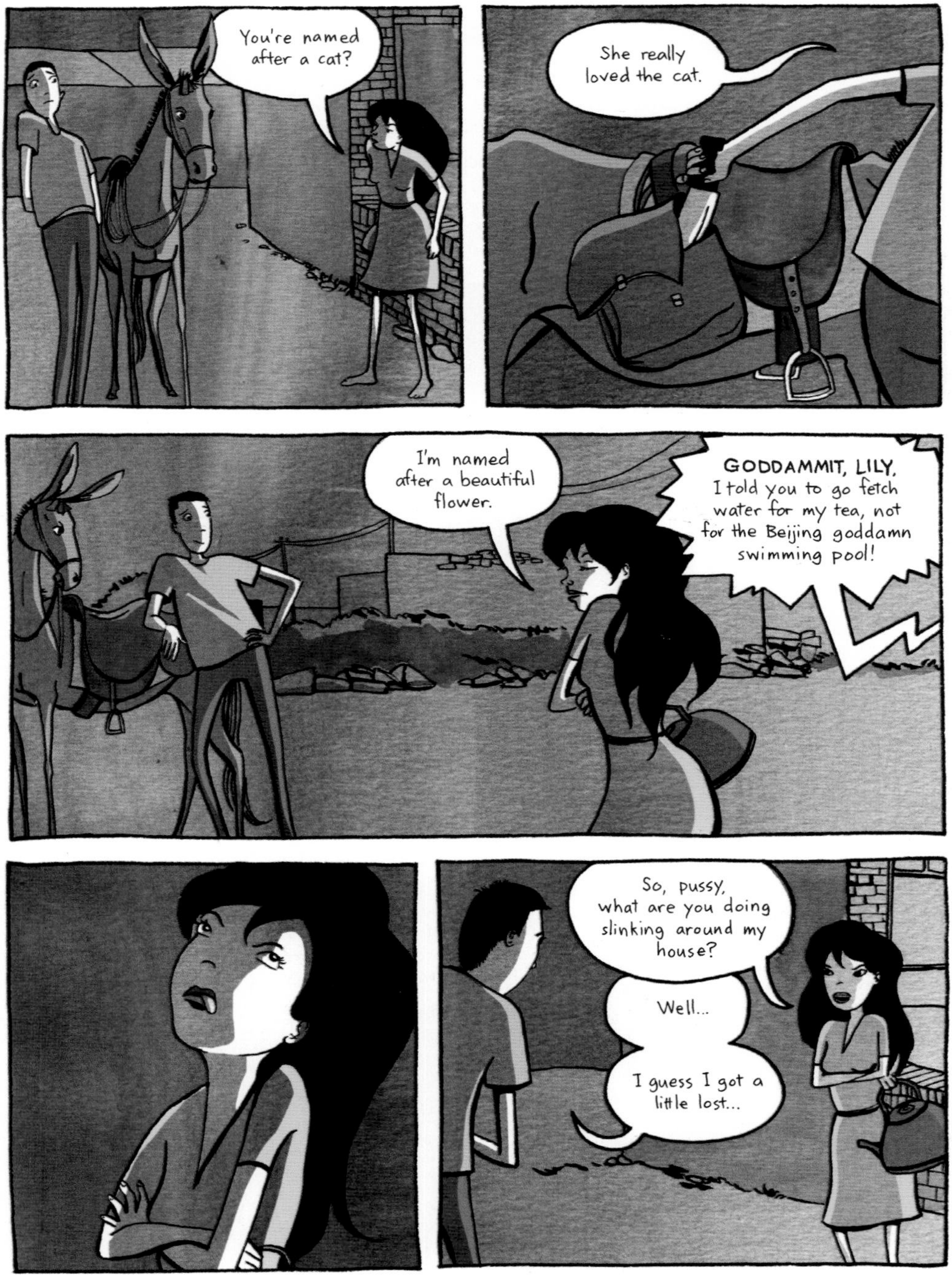
You're named after a cat?
She really loved the cat.
I'm named after a beautiful flower.
GODDAMMIT, LILY, I told you to go fetch water for my tea, not for the Beijing goddamn swimming pool!
So, pussy, what are you doing slinking around my house?
Well...
I guess I got a little lost...

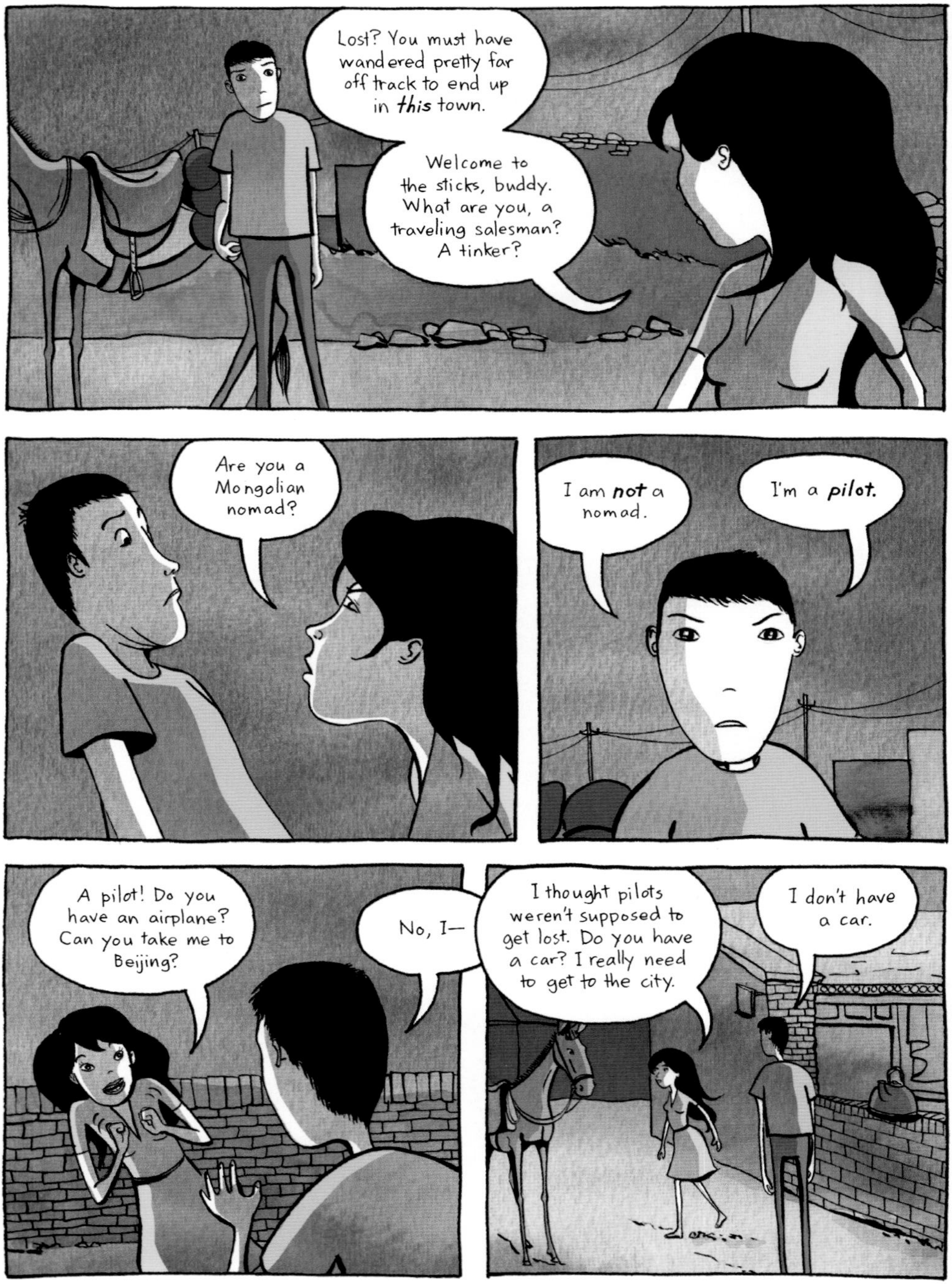
Lost? You must have wandered pretty far off track to end up in *this* town.
Welcome to the sticks, buddy. What are you, a traveling salesman? A tinker?
Are you a Mongolian nomad?
I am **not** a nomad.
I'm a ***pilot.***
A pilot! Do you have an airplane? Can you take me to Beijing?
No, I—
I thought pilots weren't supposed to get lost. Do you have a car? I really need to get to the city.
I don't have a car.

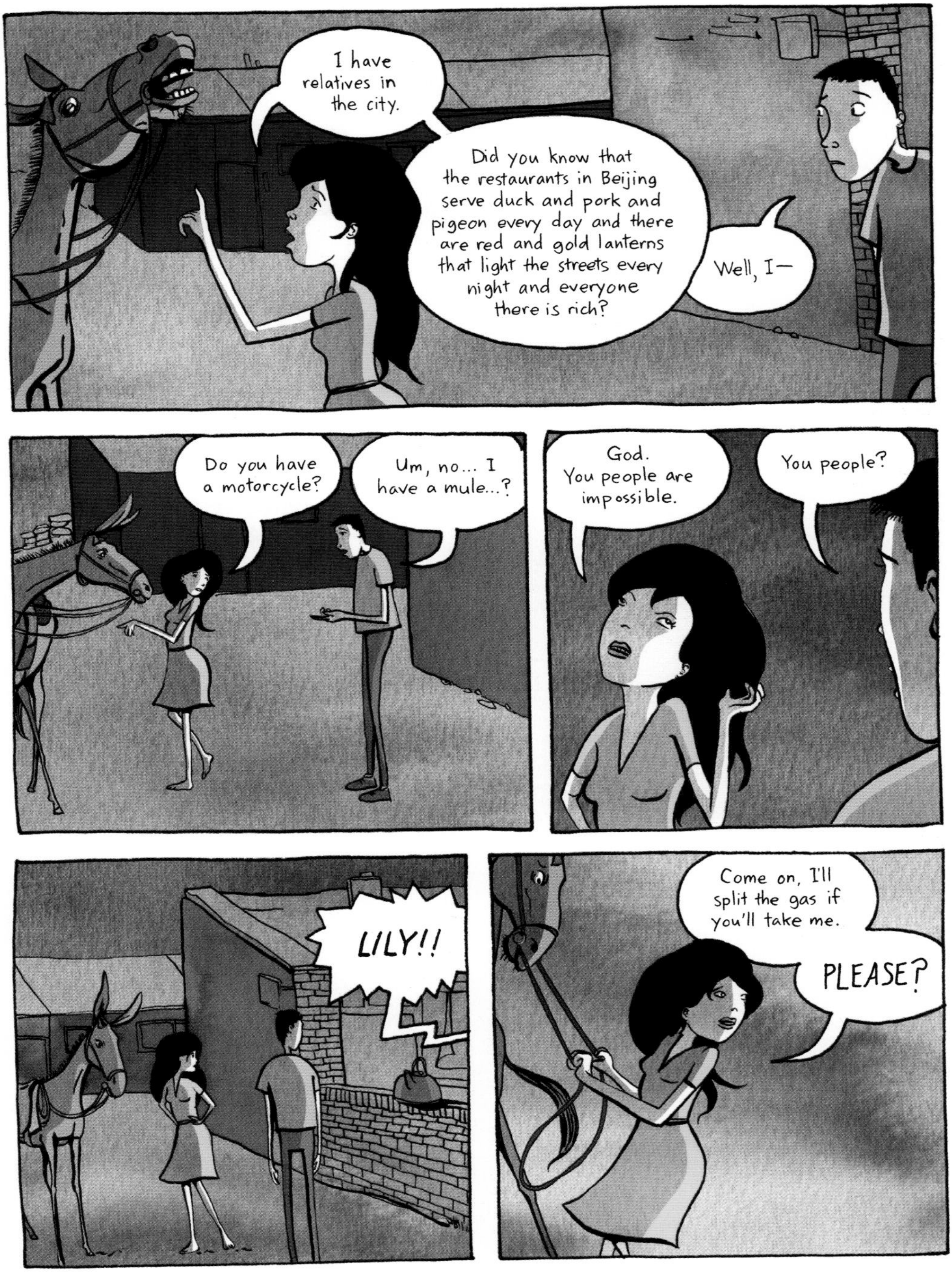

I have relatives in the city.
Did you know that the restaurants in Beijing serve duck and pork and pigeon every day and there are red and gold lanterns that light the streets every night and everyone there is rich?
Well, I—
Do you have a motorcycle?
Um, no... I have a mule...?
God. You people are impossible.
You people?
LILY!!
Come on, I'll split the gas if you'll take me.
PLEASE?

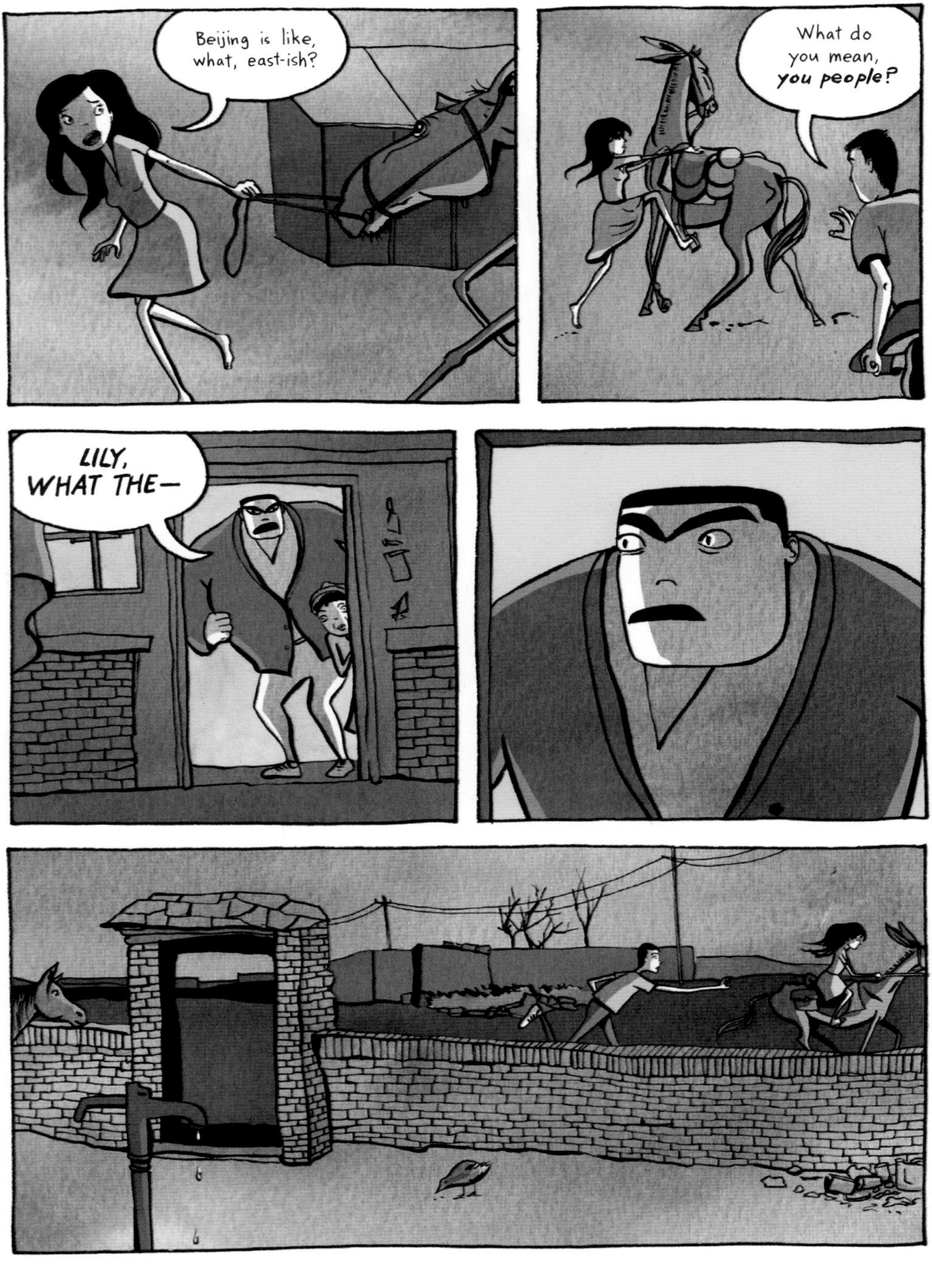
Beijing is like, what, east-ish?
What do you mean, **you people**?
LILY, WHAT THE—

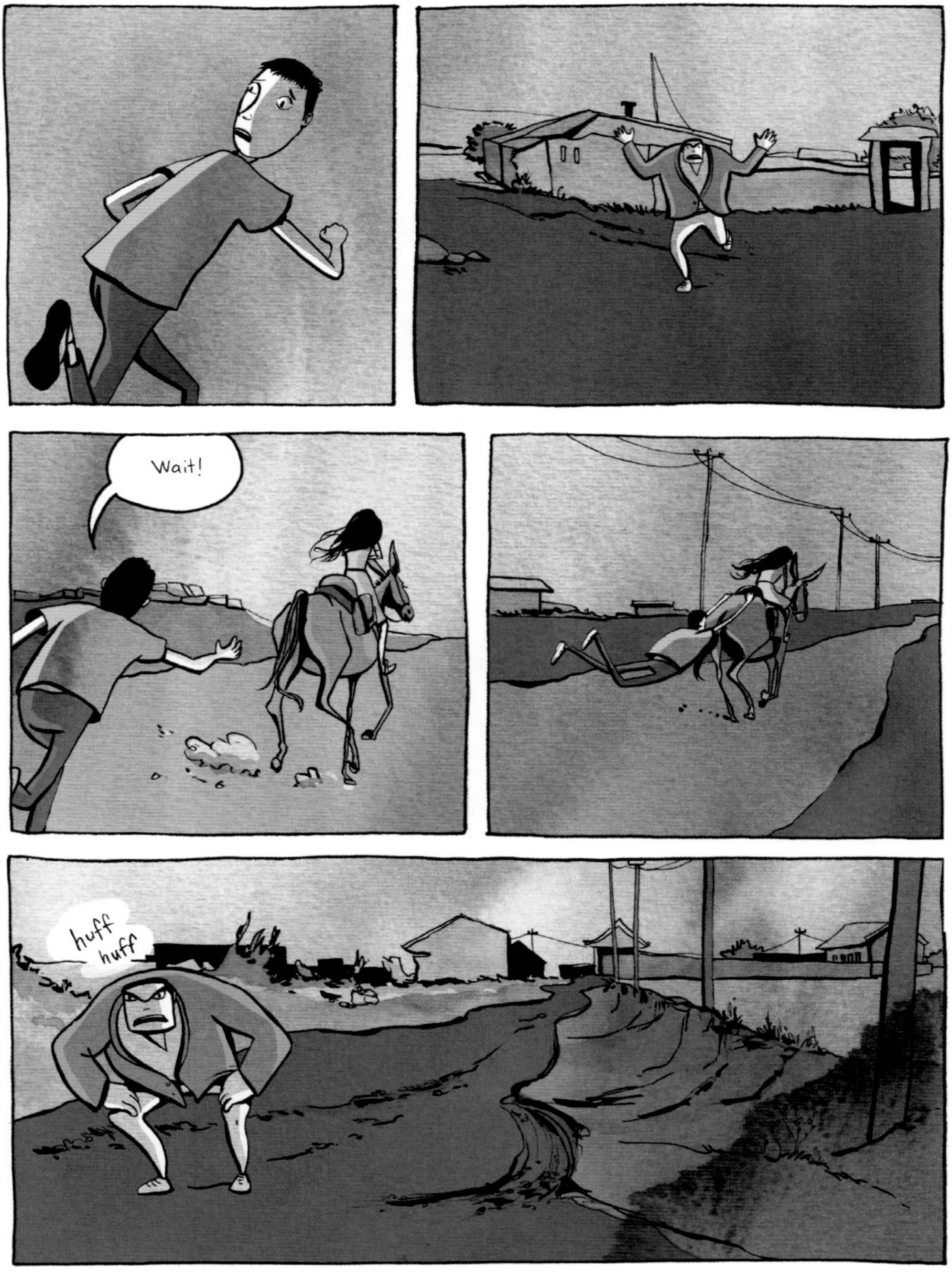
Wait!
huff
huff

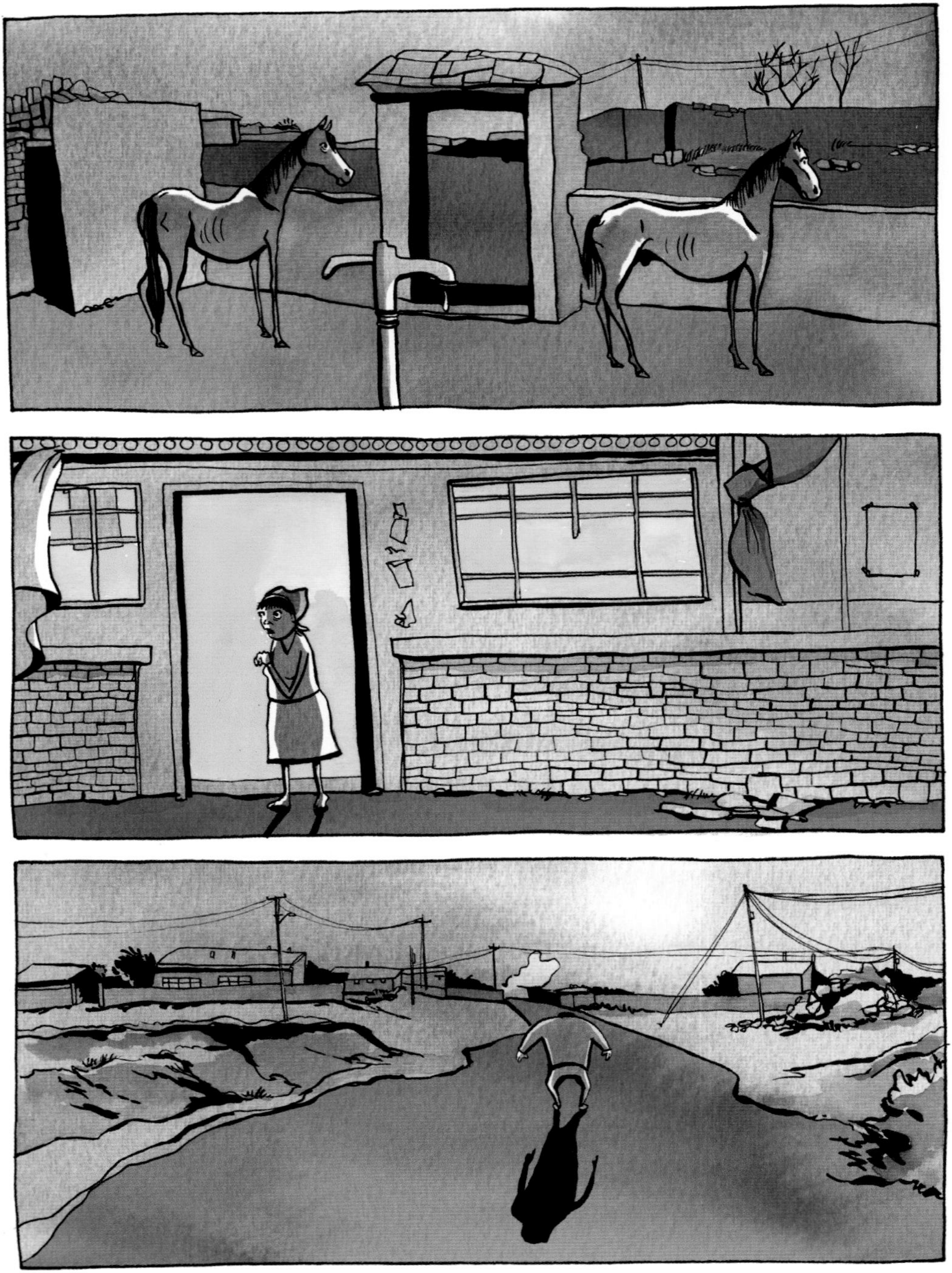

8. Booty Call

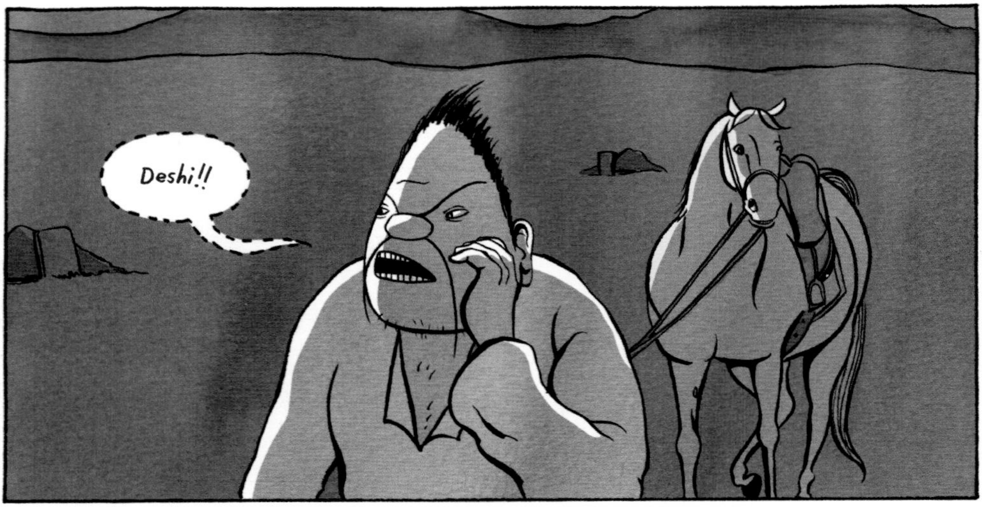
Deshi!!

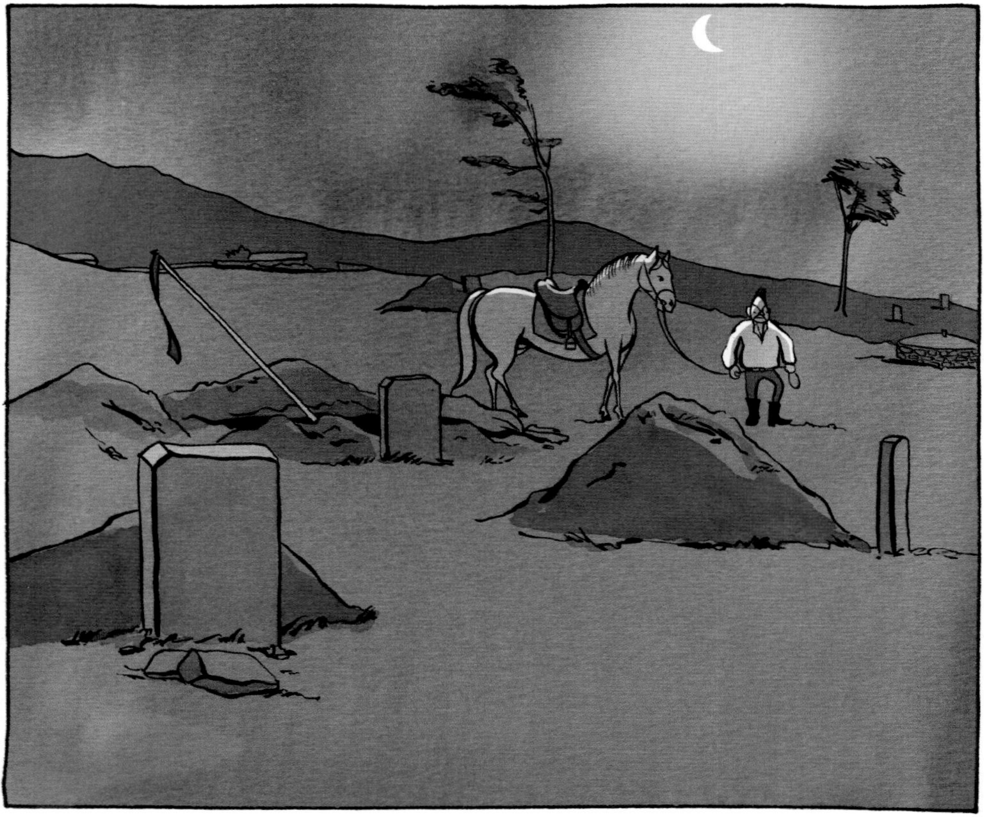

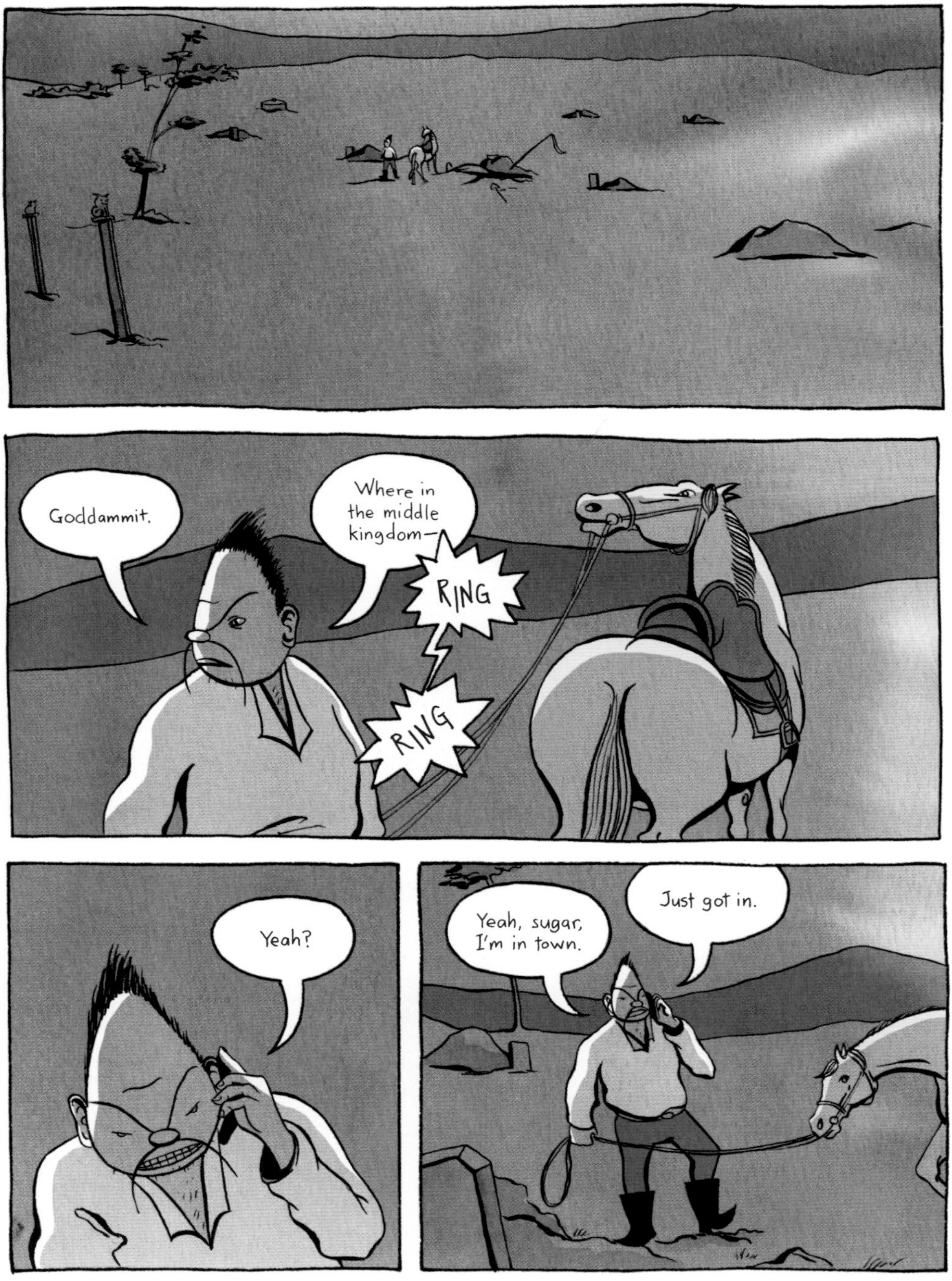
Goddammit.
Where in the middle kingdom—
RING
RING
Yeah?
Yeah, sugar, I'm in town.
Just got in.

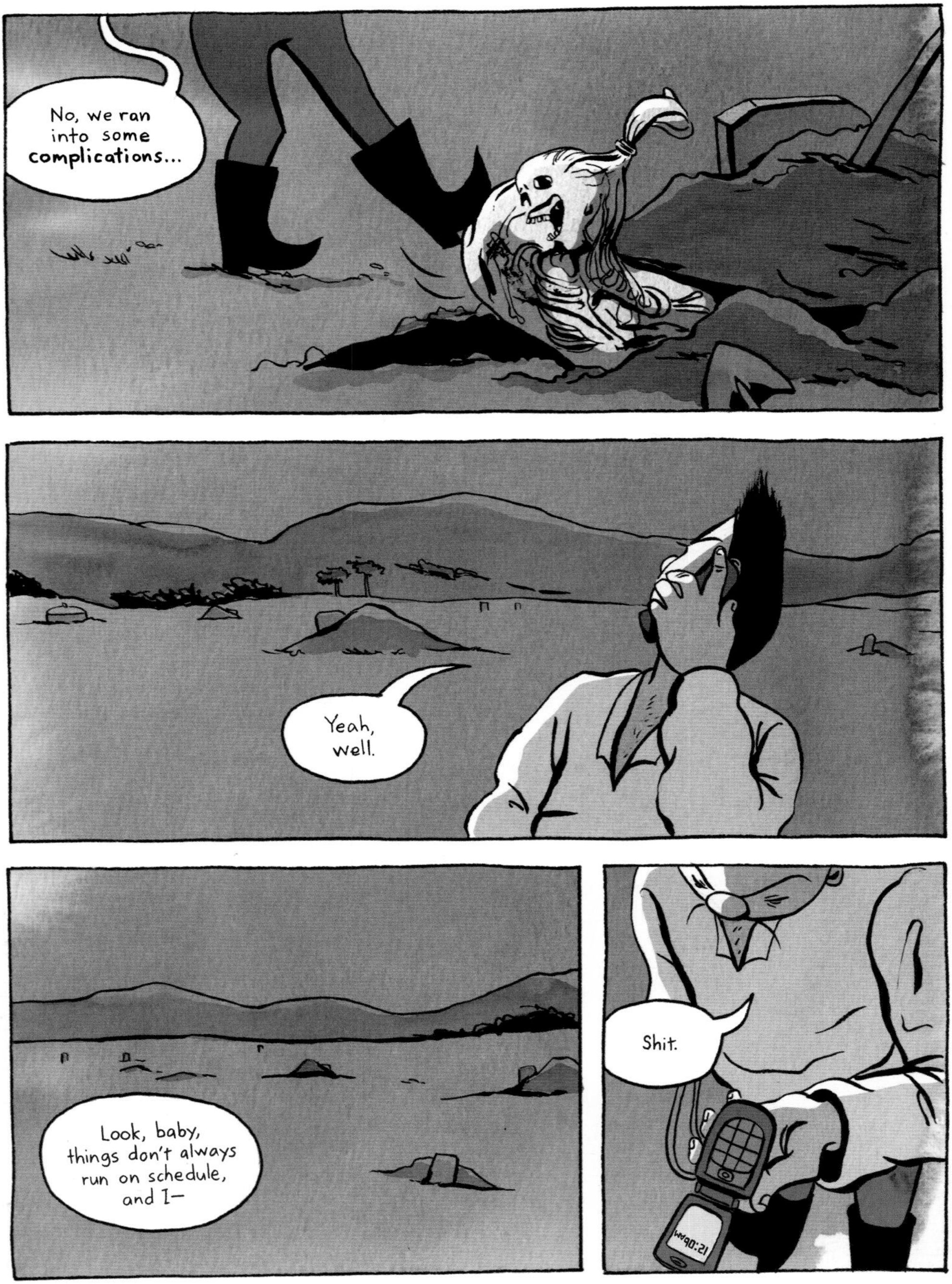
No, we ran into some **complications...**
Yeah, well.
Look, baby, things don't always run on schedule, and I–
Shit.
12:08am

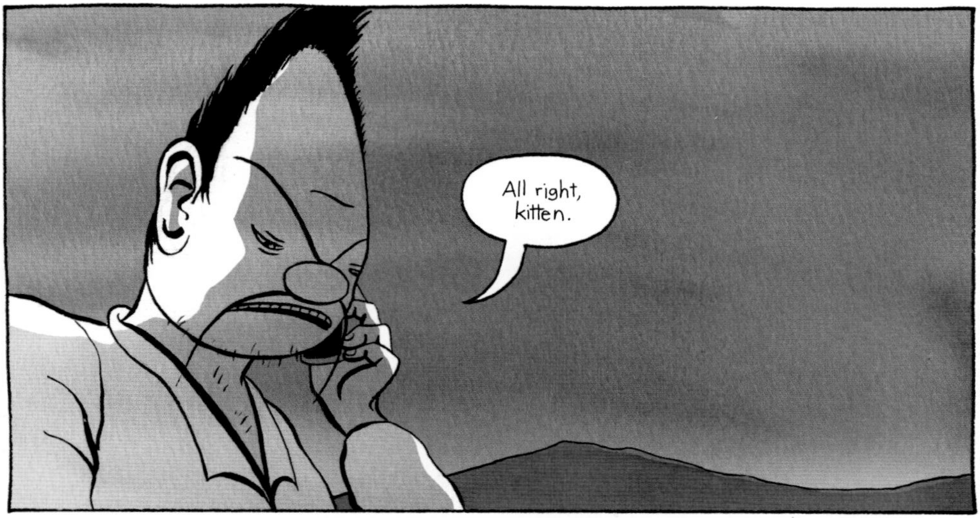
All right, kitten.

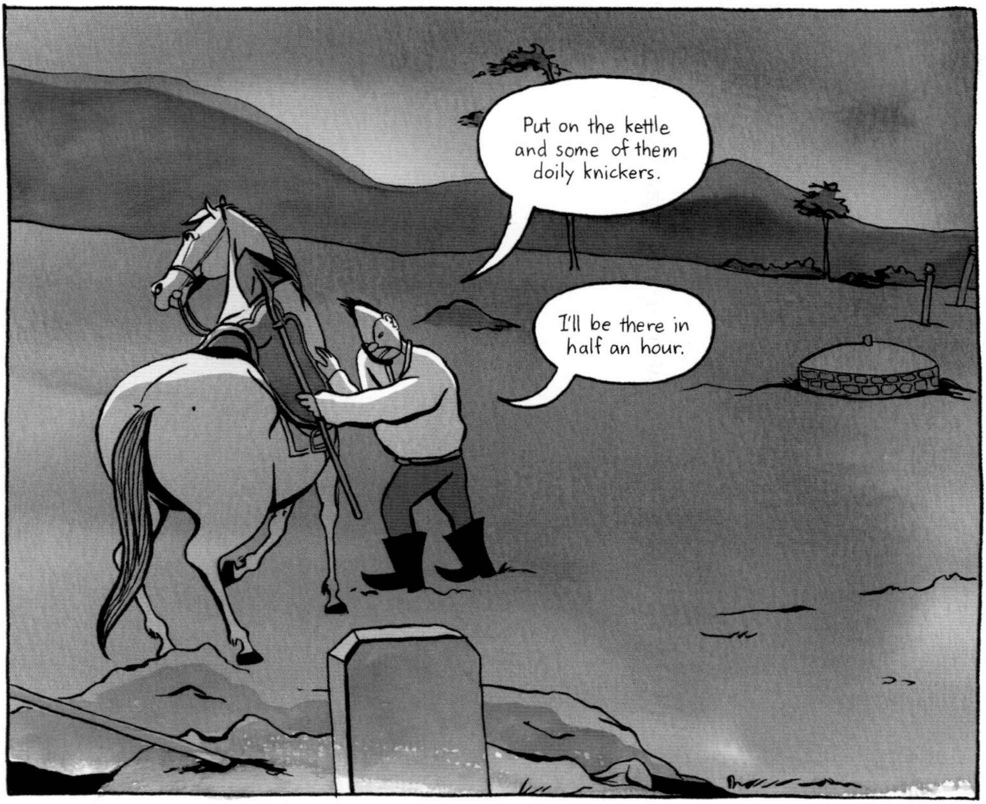
Put on the kettle and some of them doily knickers.
I'll be there in half an hour.

9. Fresh Goods

TUESDAY

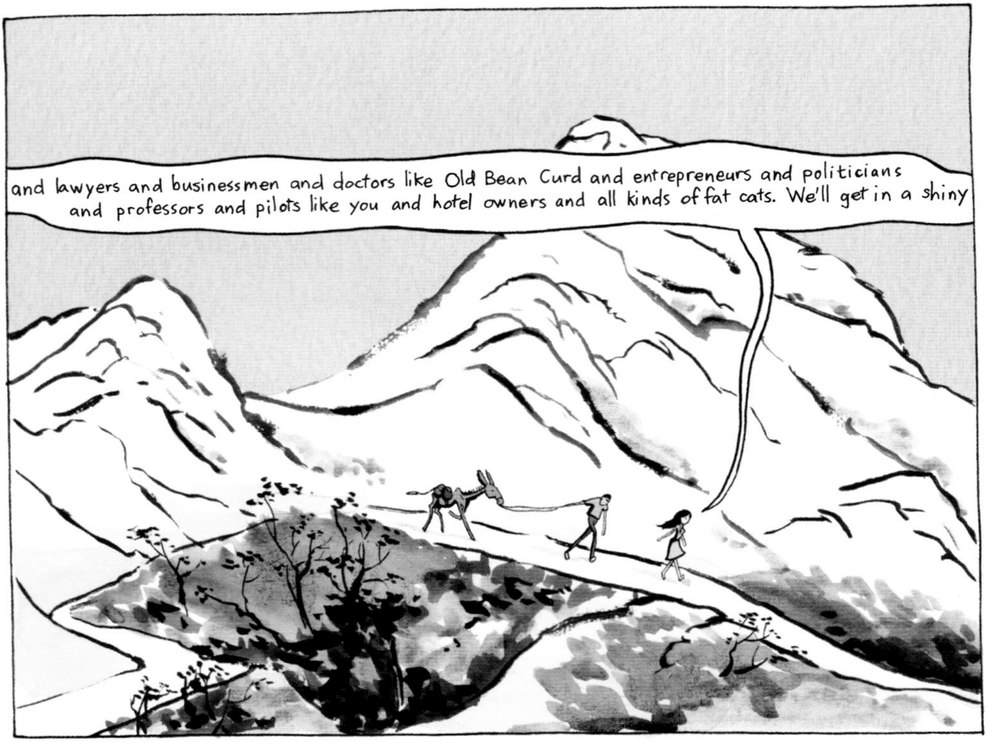
and lawyers and businessmen and doctors like Old Bean Curd and entrepreneurs and politicians and professors and pilots like you and hotel owners and all kinds of fat cats. We'll get in a shiny

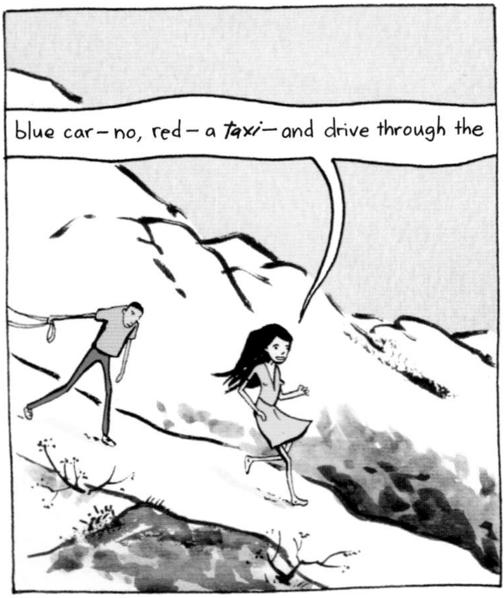
blue car—no, red—a *taxi*—and drive through the

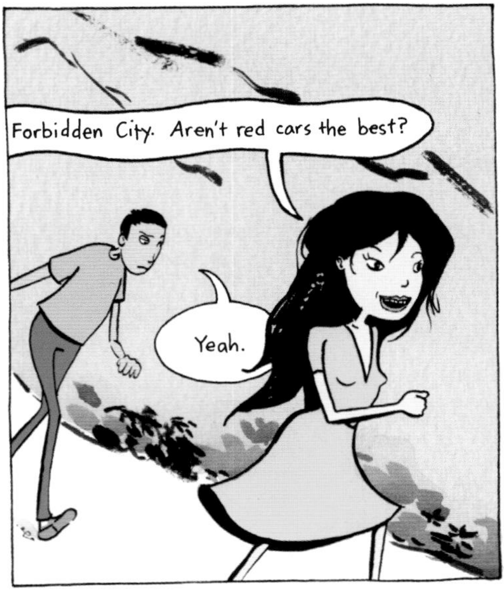
Forbidden City. Aren't red cars the best?
Yeah.

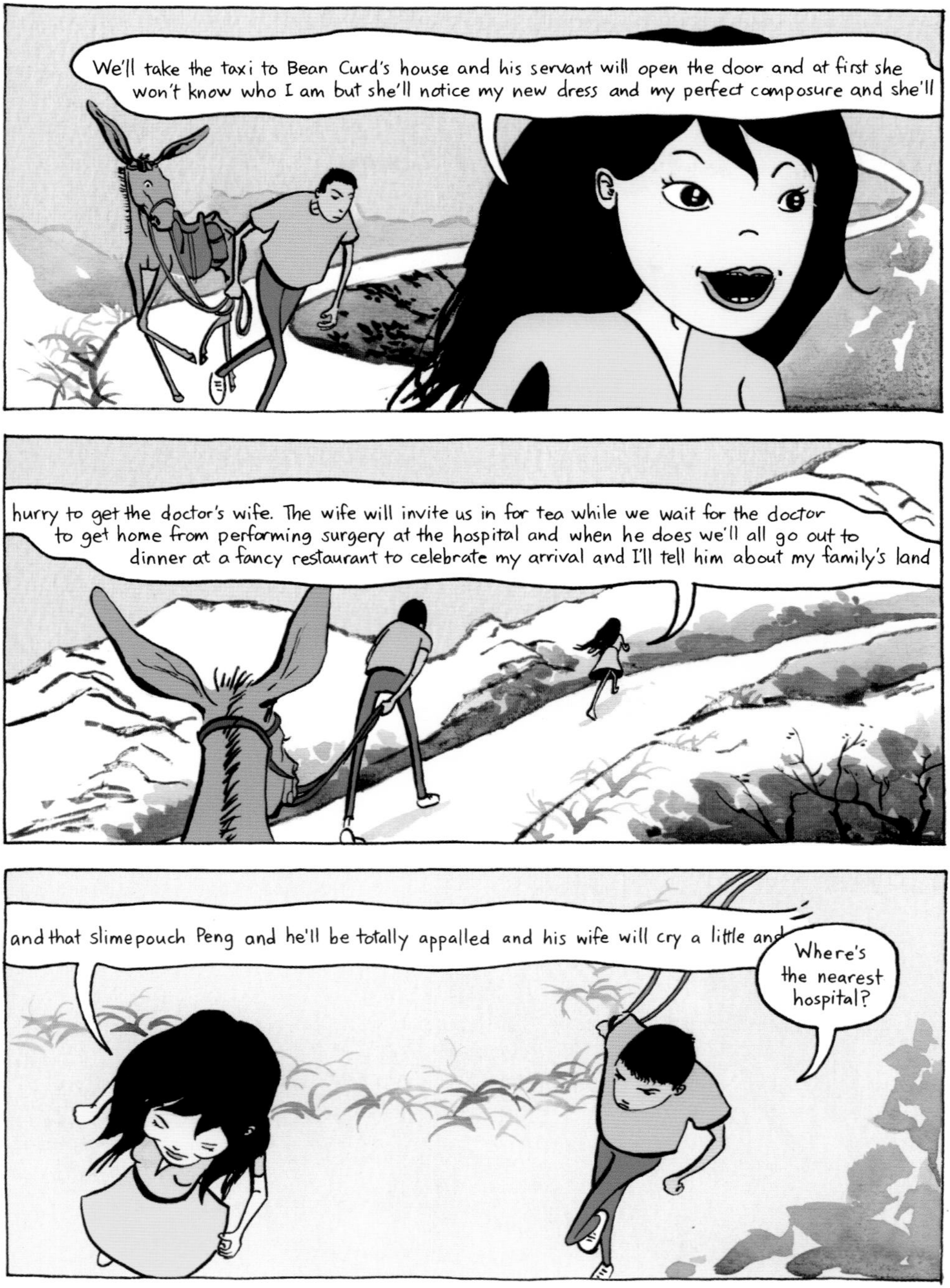
We'll take the taxi to Bean Curd's house and his servant will open the door and at first she won't know who I am but she'll notice my new dress and my perfect composure and she'll
hurry to get the doctor's wife. The wife will invite us in for tea while we wait for the doctor to get home from performing surgery at the hospital and when he does we'll all go out to dinner at a fancy restaurant to celebrate my arrival and I'll tell him about my family's land
and that slimepouch Peng and he'll be totally appalled and his wife will cry a little and
Where's the nearest hospital?

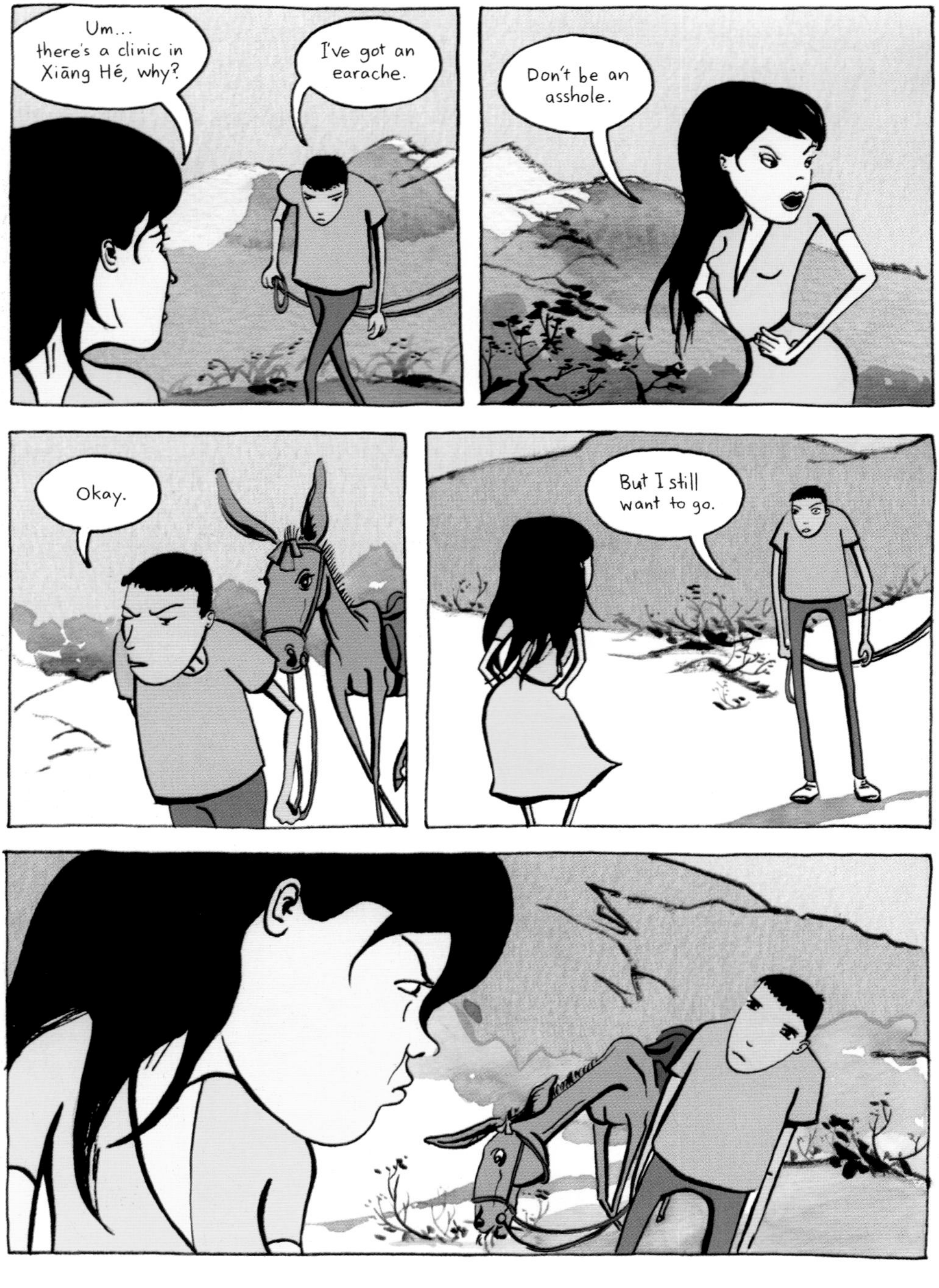
Um... there's a clinic in Xiāng Hé, why?
I've got an earache.
Don't be an asshole.
Okay.
But I still want to go.

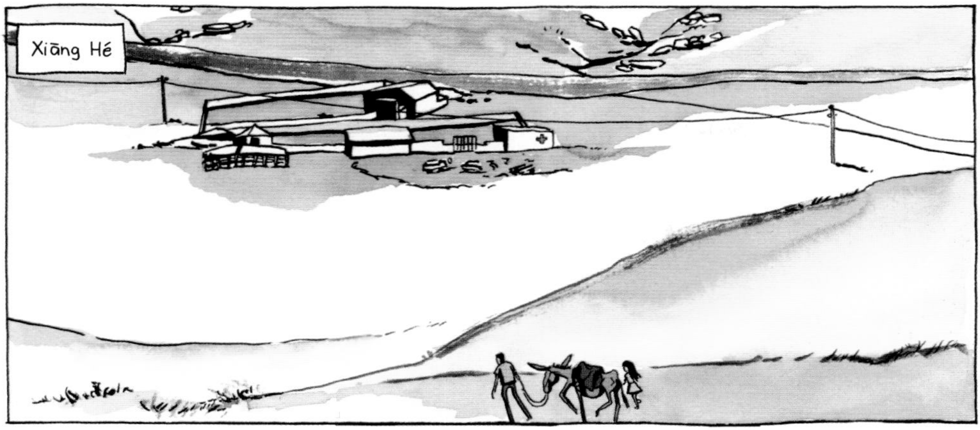
Xiāng Hé

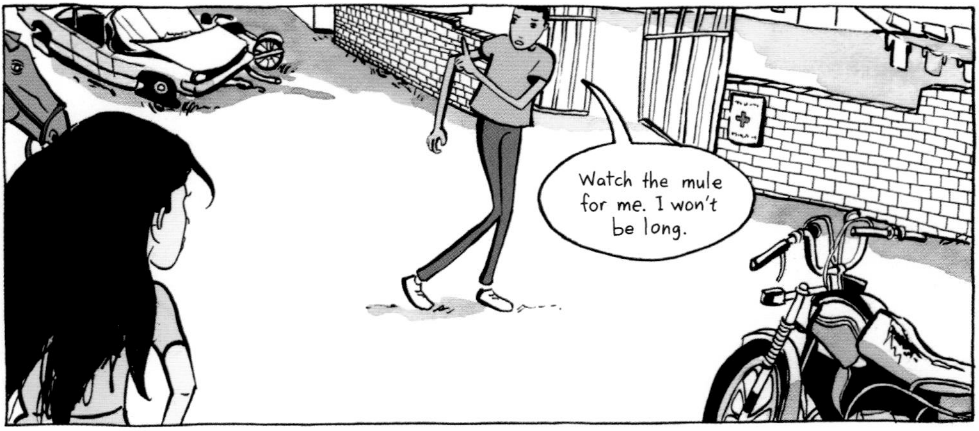
Watch the mule for me. I won't be long.

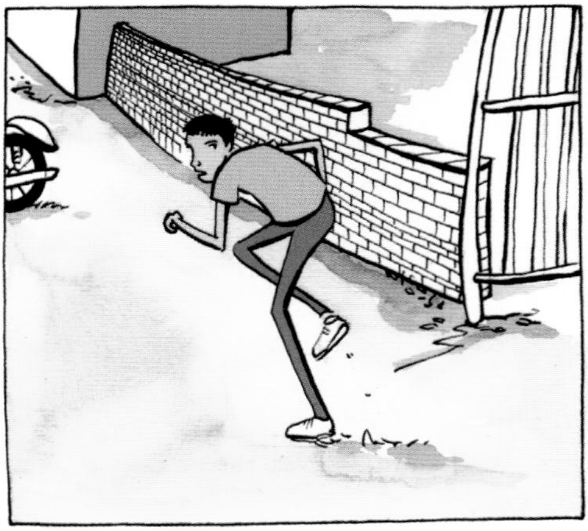

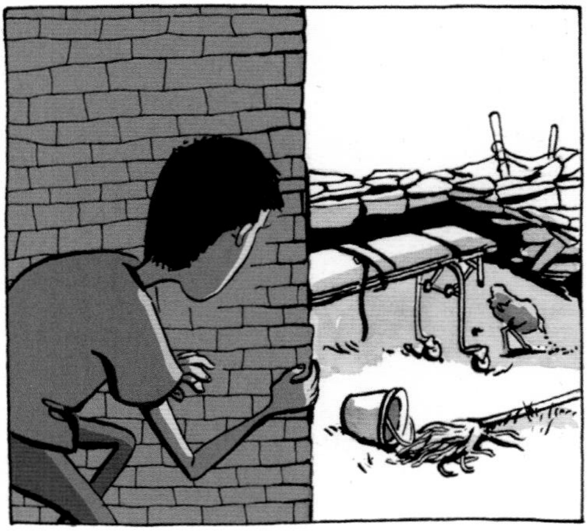

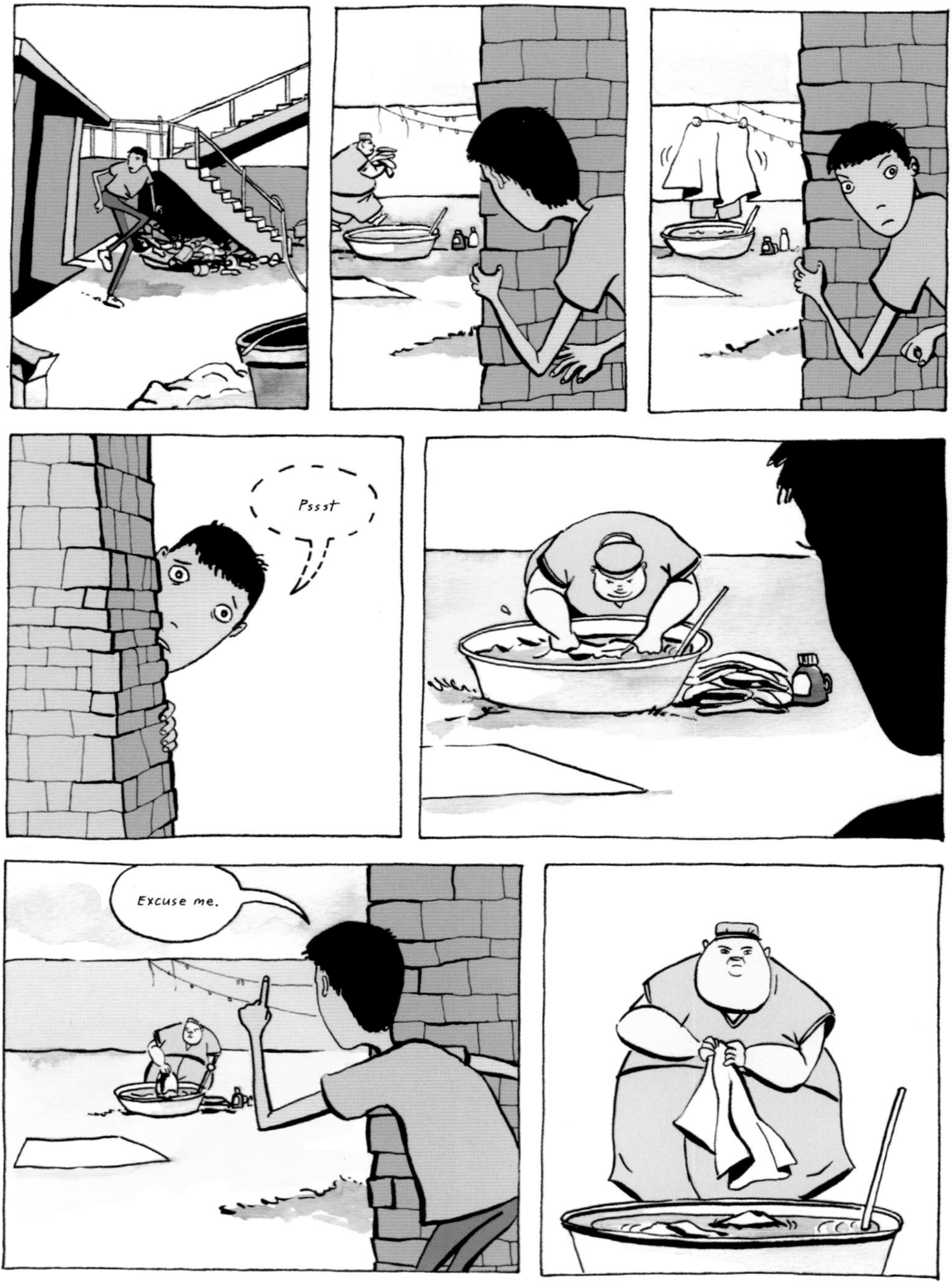
Pssst
Excuse me.

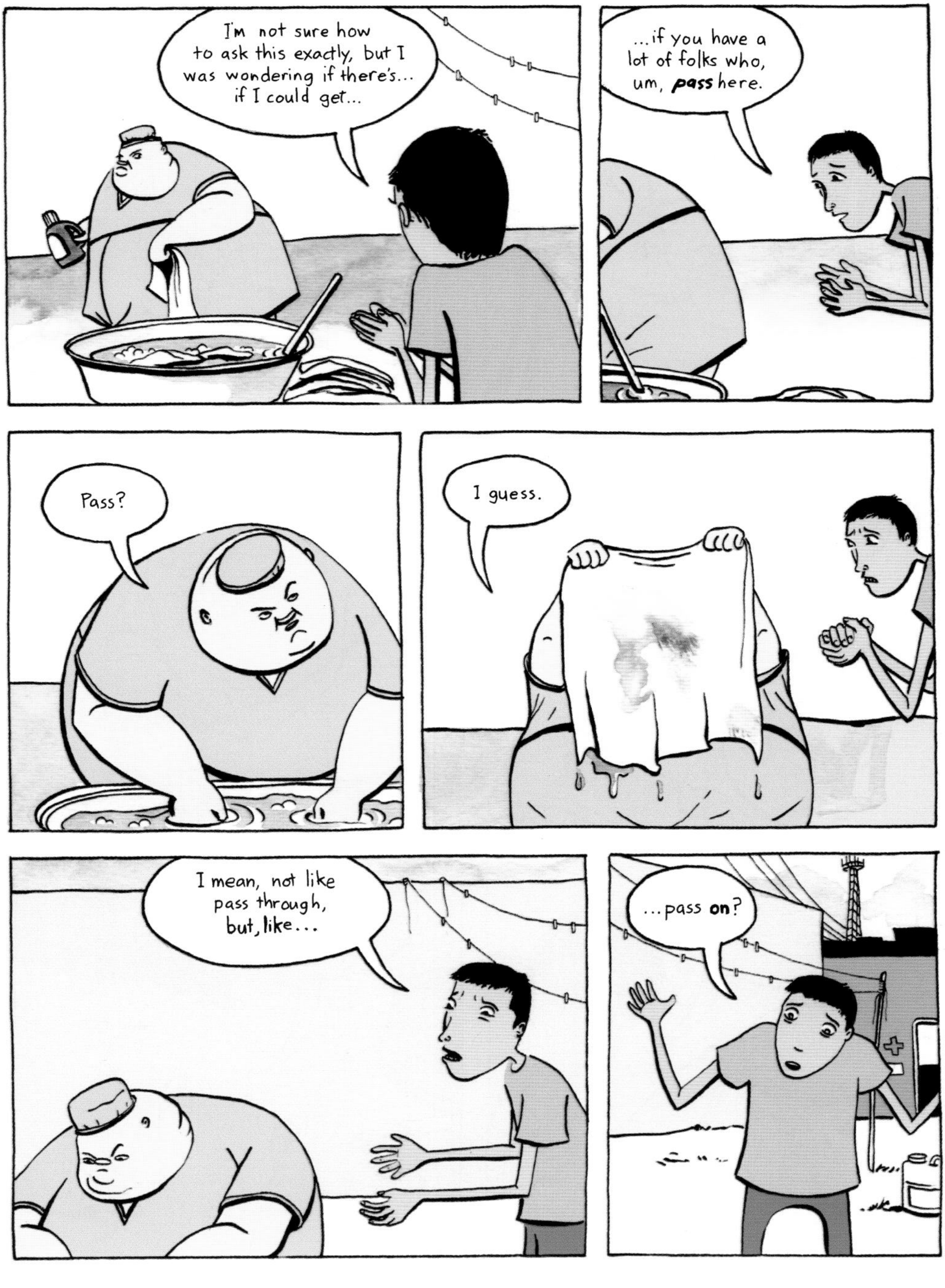
I'm not sure how to ask this exactly, but I was wondering if there's... if I could get...
...if you have a lot of folks who, um, **pass** here.
Pass?
I guess.
I mean, not like pass through, but, like...
...pass **on**?

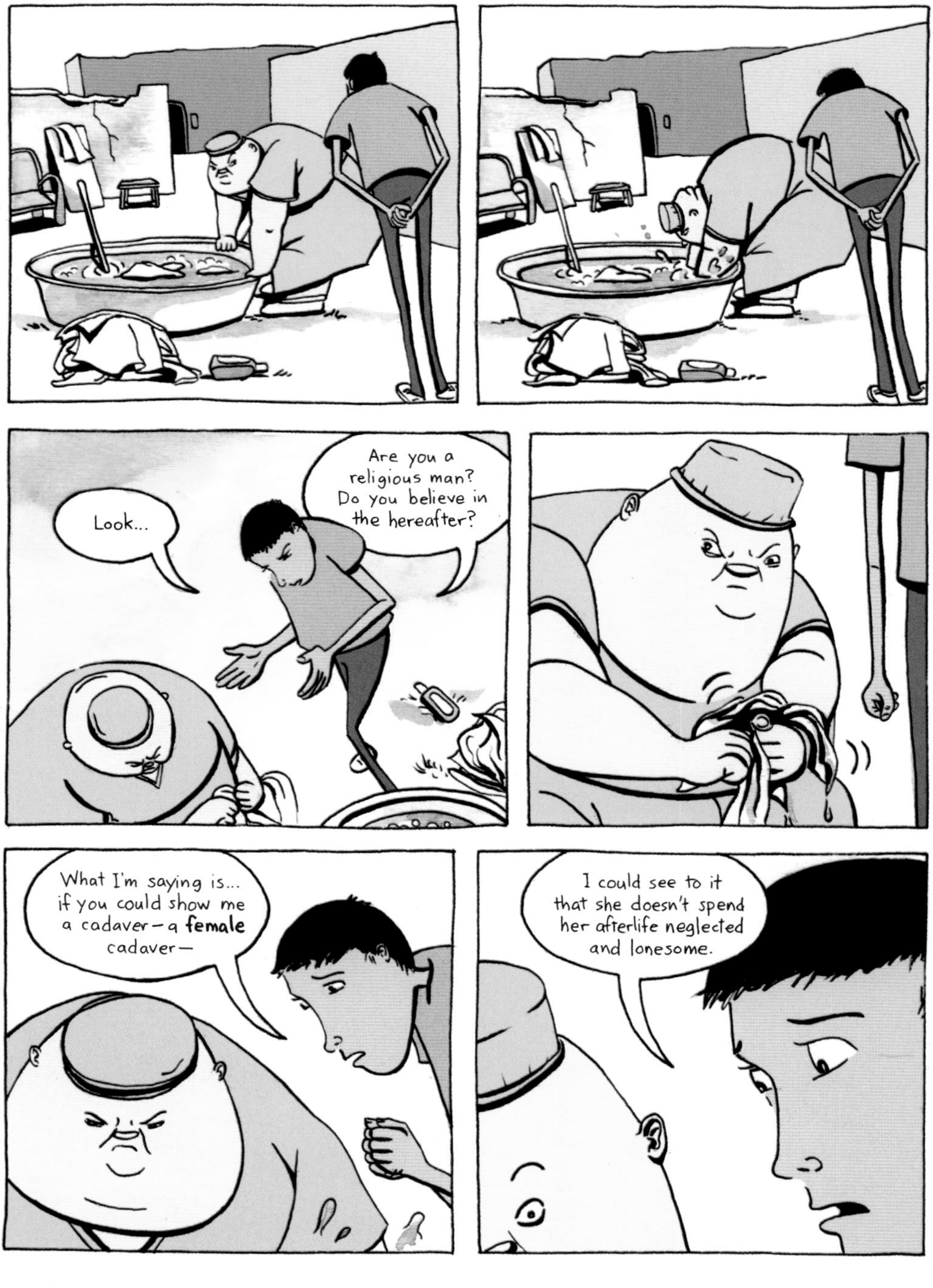
Look...
Are you a religious man? Do you believe in the hereafter?
What I'm saying is... if you could show me a cadaver—a **female** cadaver—
I could see to it that she doesn't spend her afterlife neglected and lonesome.

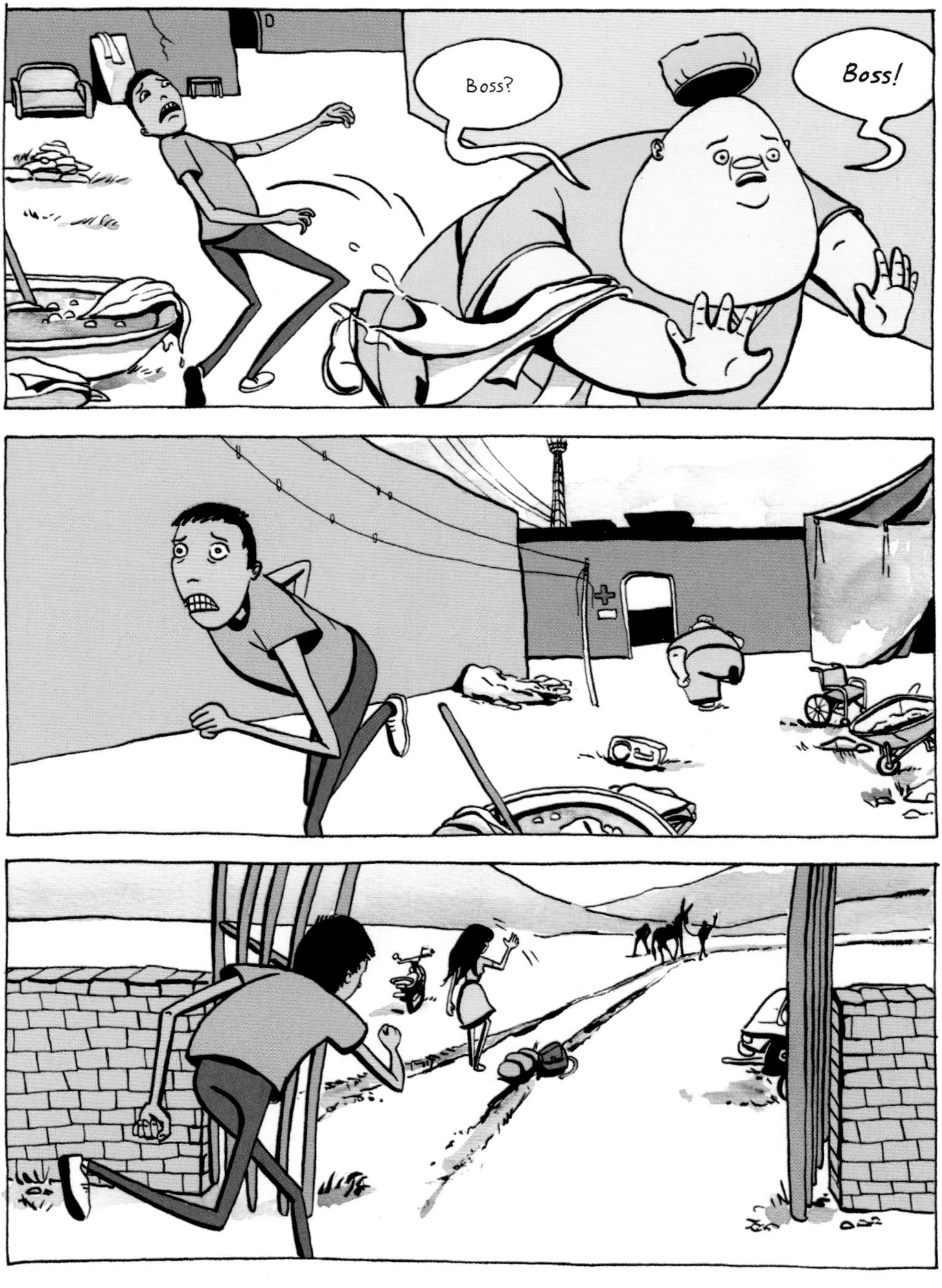
Boss?
Boss!

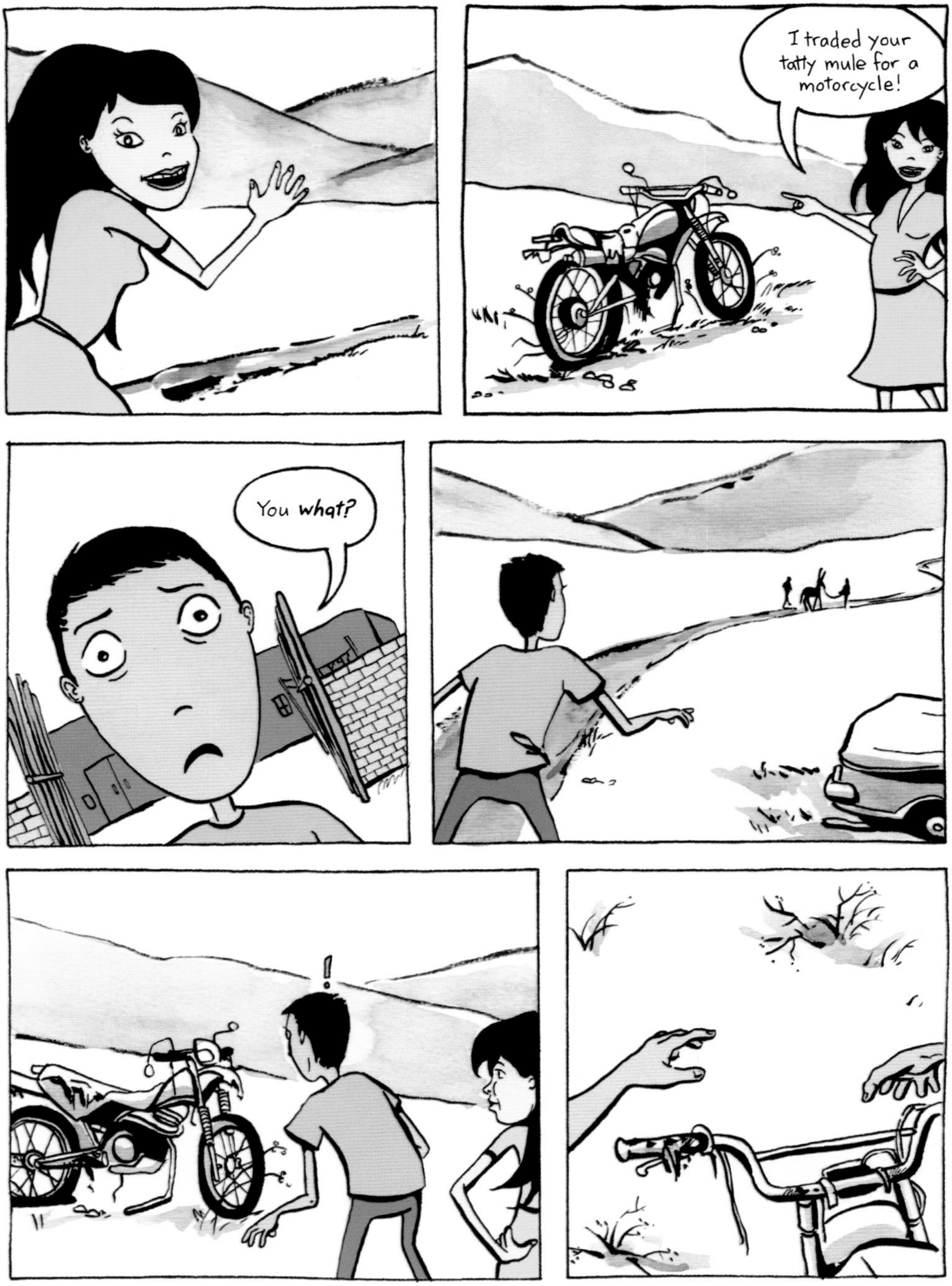
I traded your tatty mule for a motorcycle!
You what?
!

KA-CLUNK

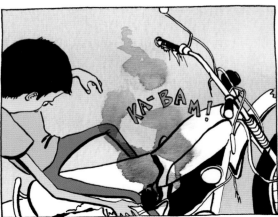

KA-BAM!

WHOOSH

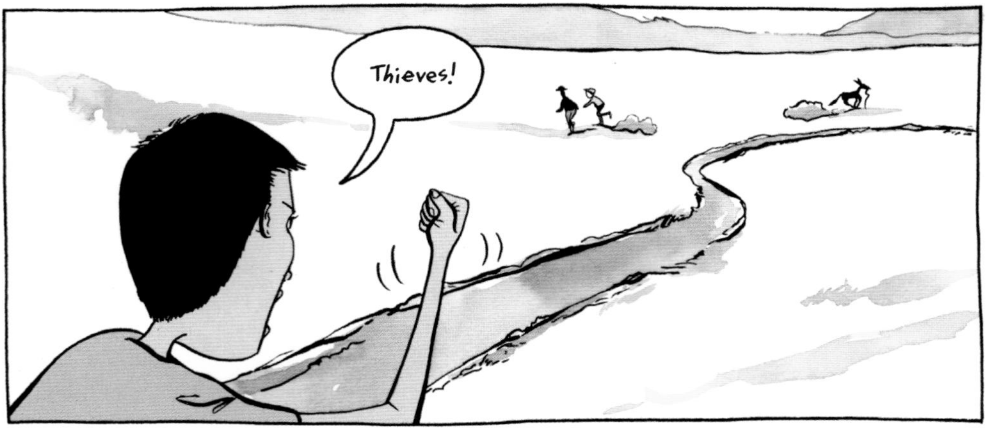
Thieves!

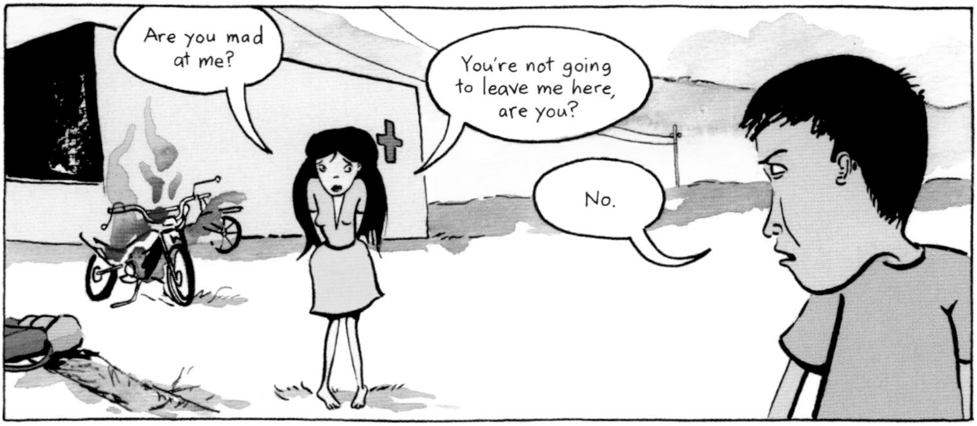
Are you mad at me?
You're not going to leave me here, are you?
No.

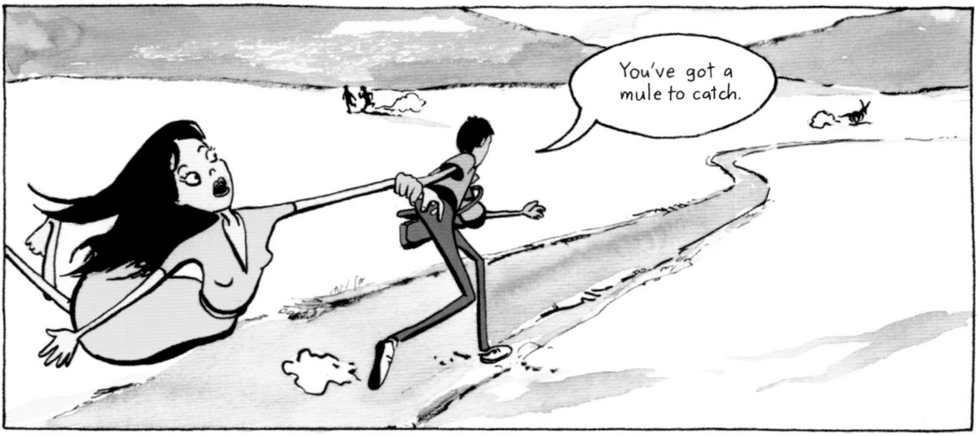
You've got a mule to catch.

10. All the King's Men

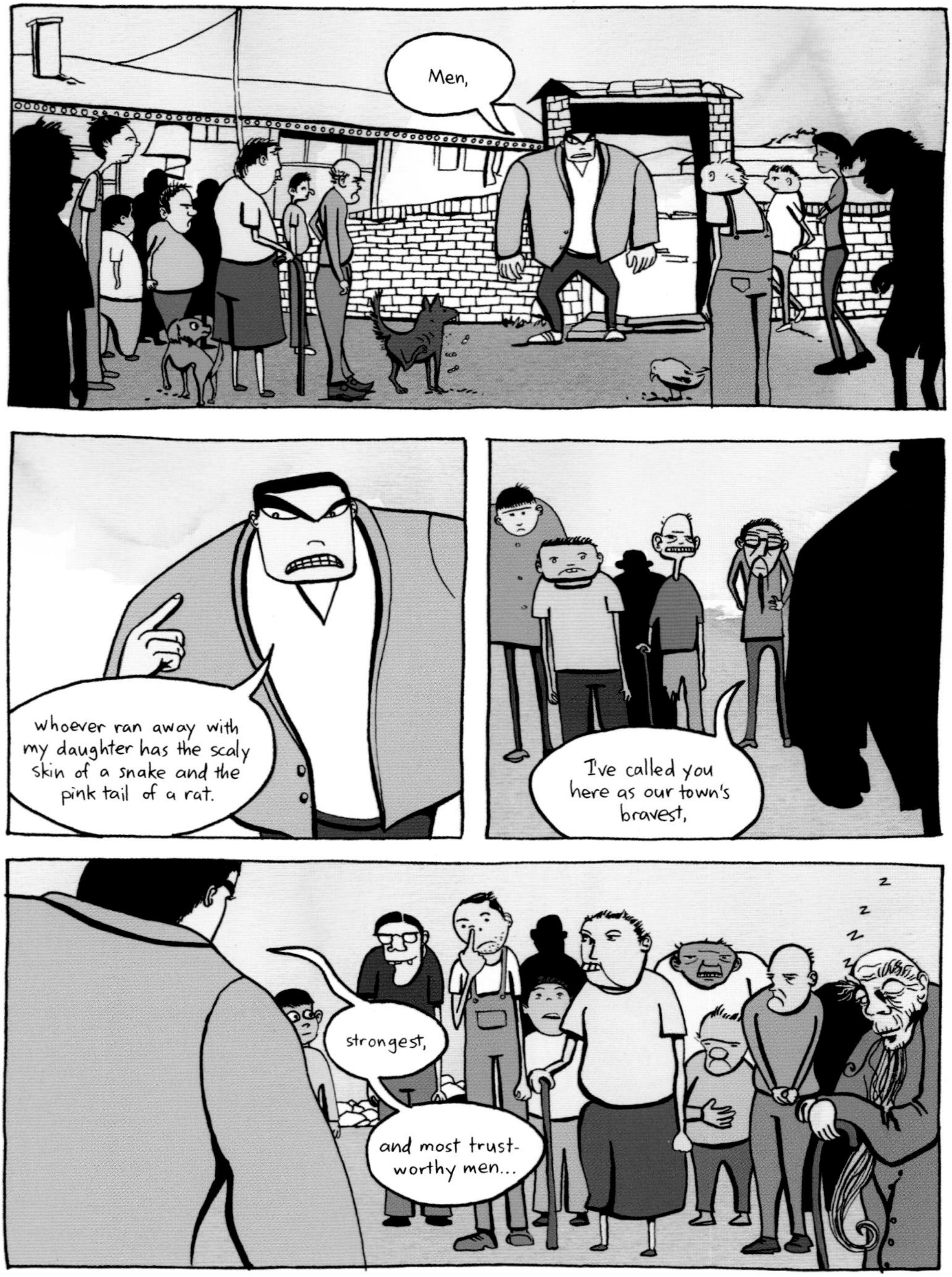

Men,
whoever ran away with my daughter has the scaly skin of a snake and the pink tail of a rat.
I've called you here as our town's bravest,
strongest,
and most trust-worthy men...

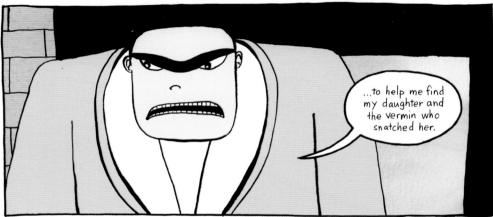

...to help me find my daughter and the vermin who snatched her.

I WANT REVENGE!!

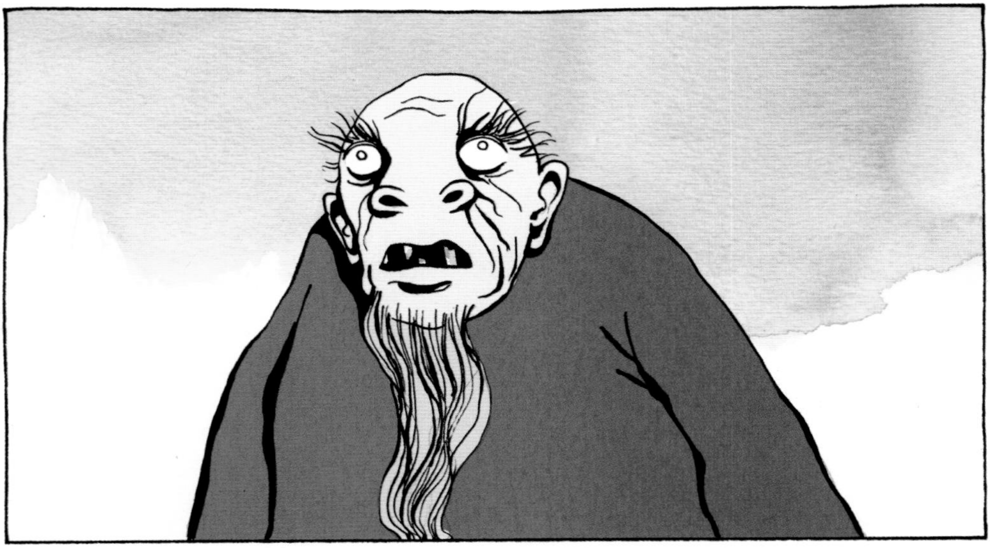

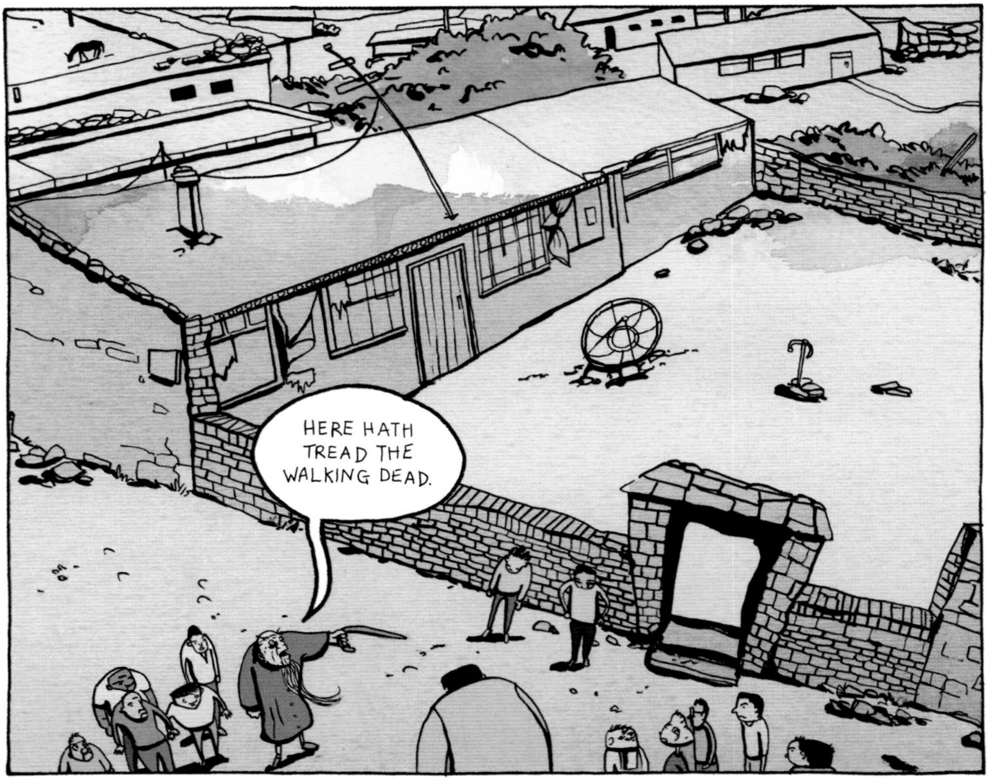
HERE HATH TREAD THE WALKING DEAD.

11. Dry Goods

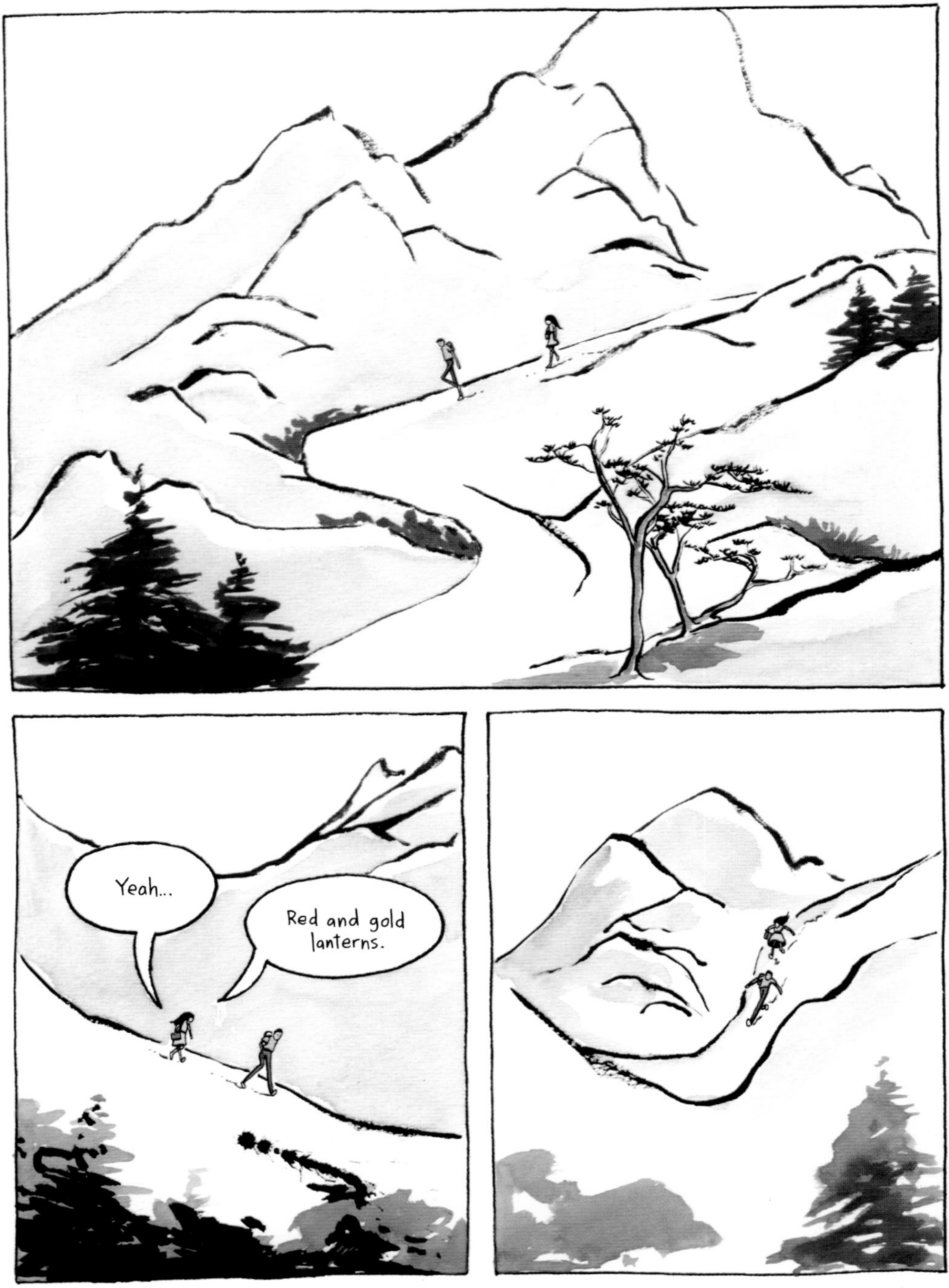
Yeah...
Red and gold lanterns.

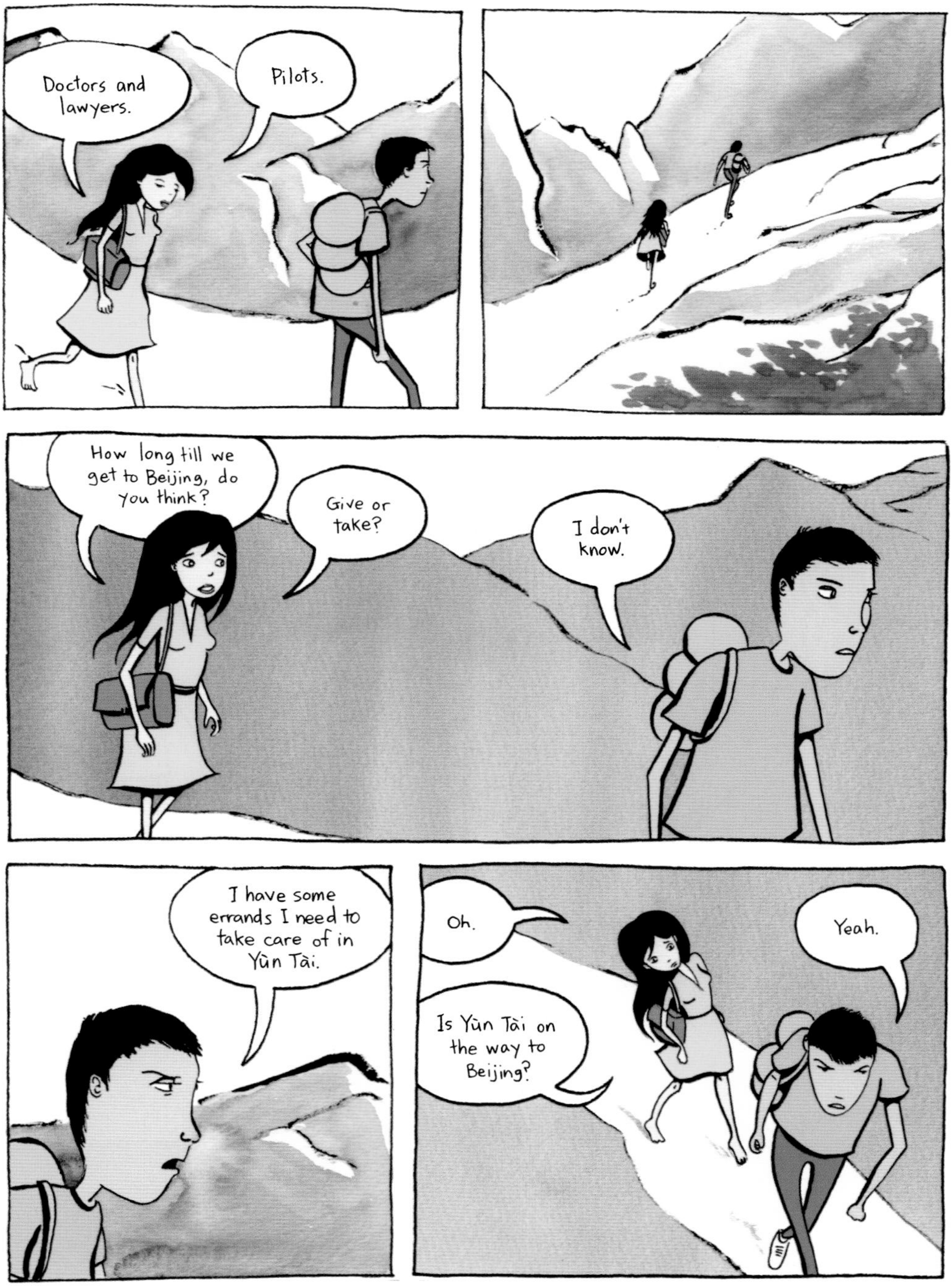
Doctors and lawyers.
Pilots.
How long till we get to Beijing, do you think?
Give or take?
I don't know.
I have some errands I need to take care of in Yùn Tài.
Oh.
Is Yùn Tài on the way to Beijing?
Yeah.

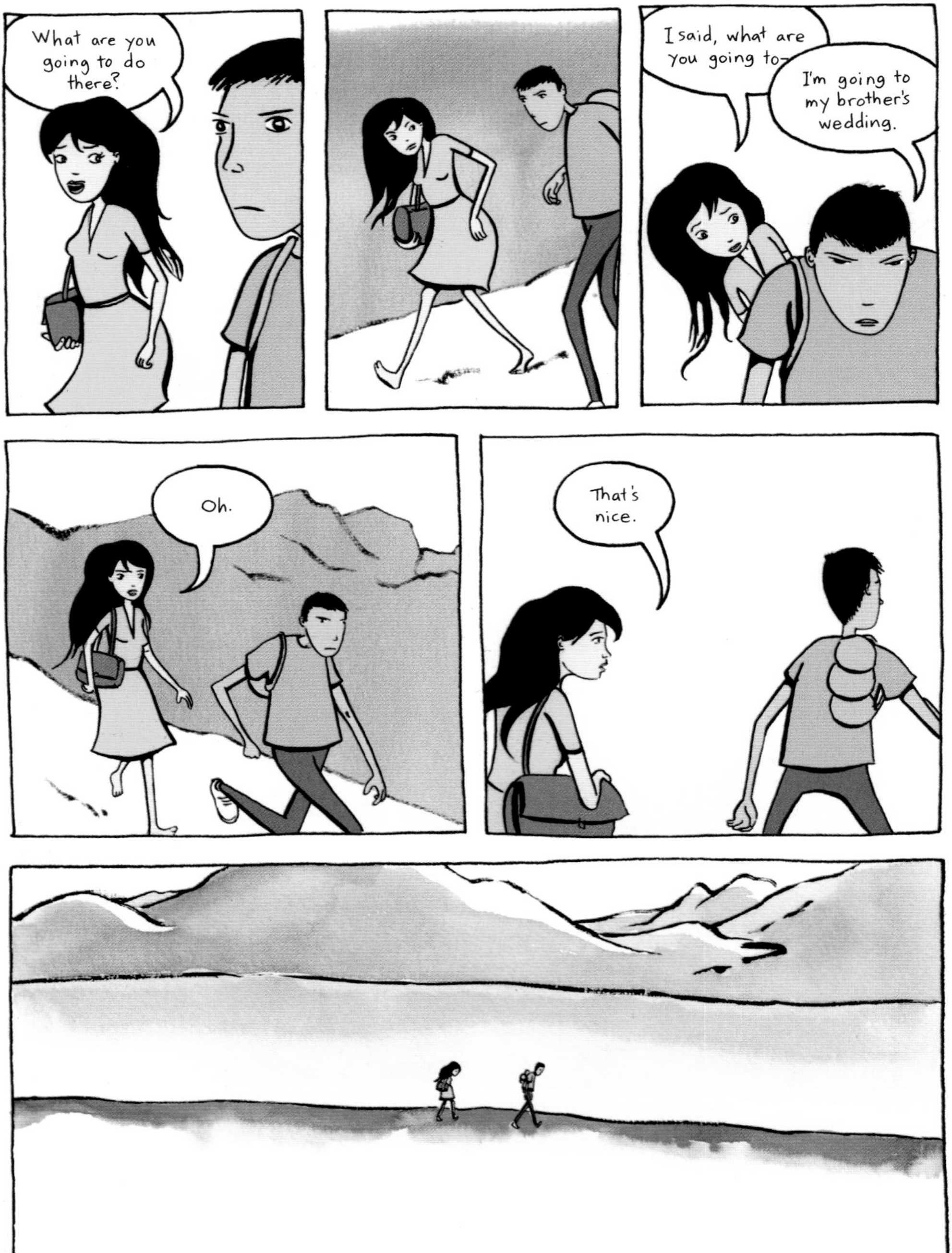

What are you going to do there?
I said, what are you going to—
I'm going to my brother's wedding.
Oh.
That's nice.

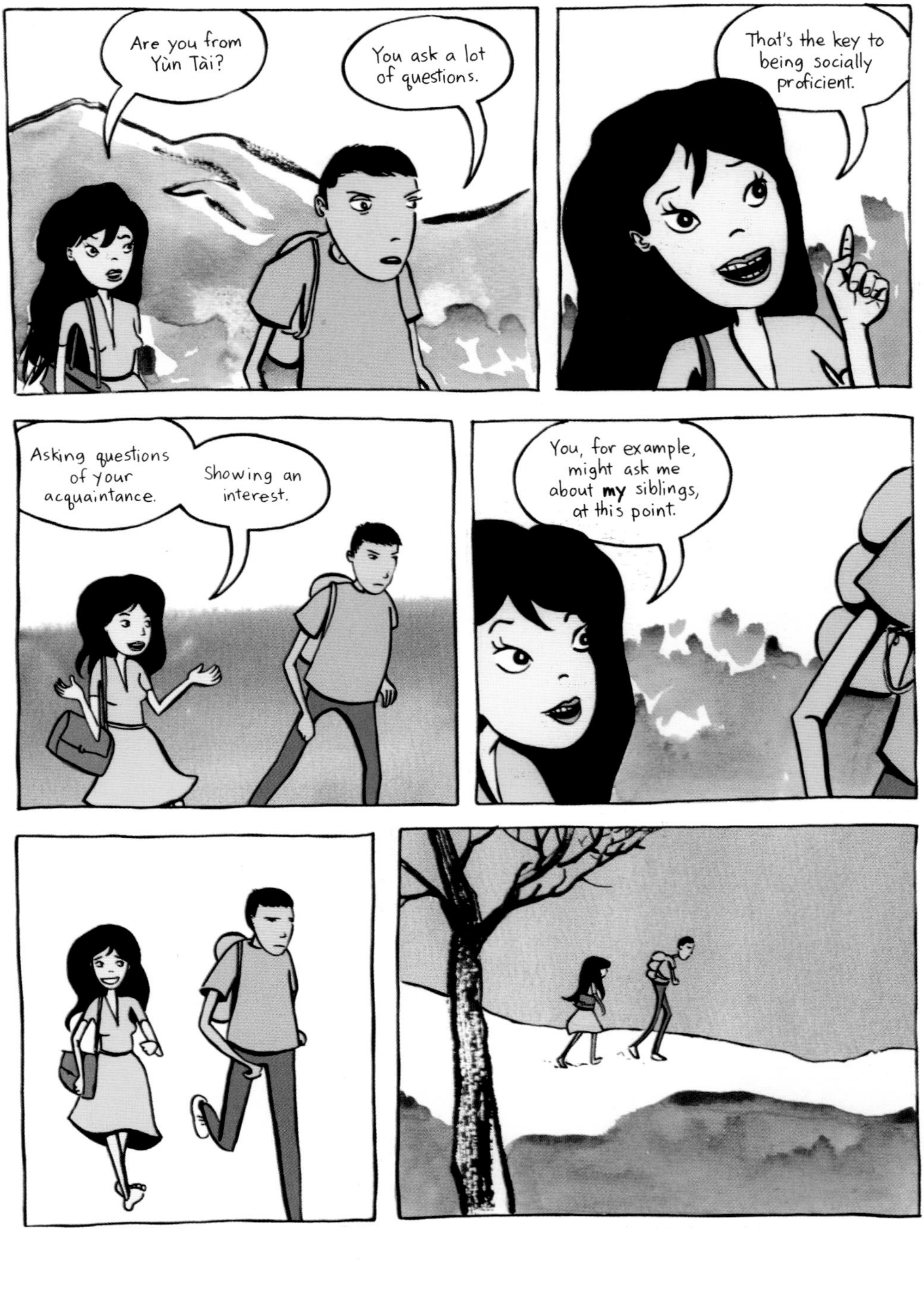
Are you from Yùn Tài?
You ask a lot of questions.
That's the key to being socially proficient.
Asking questions of your acquaintance.
Showing an interest.
You, for example, might ask me about **my** siblings, at this point.

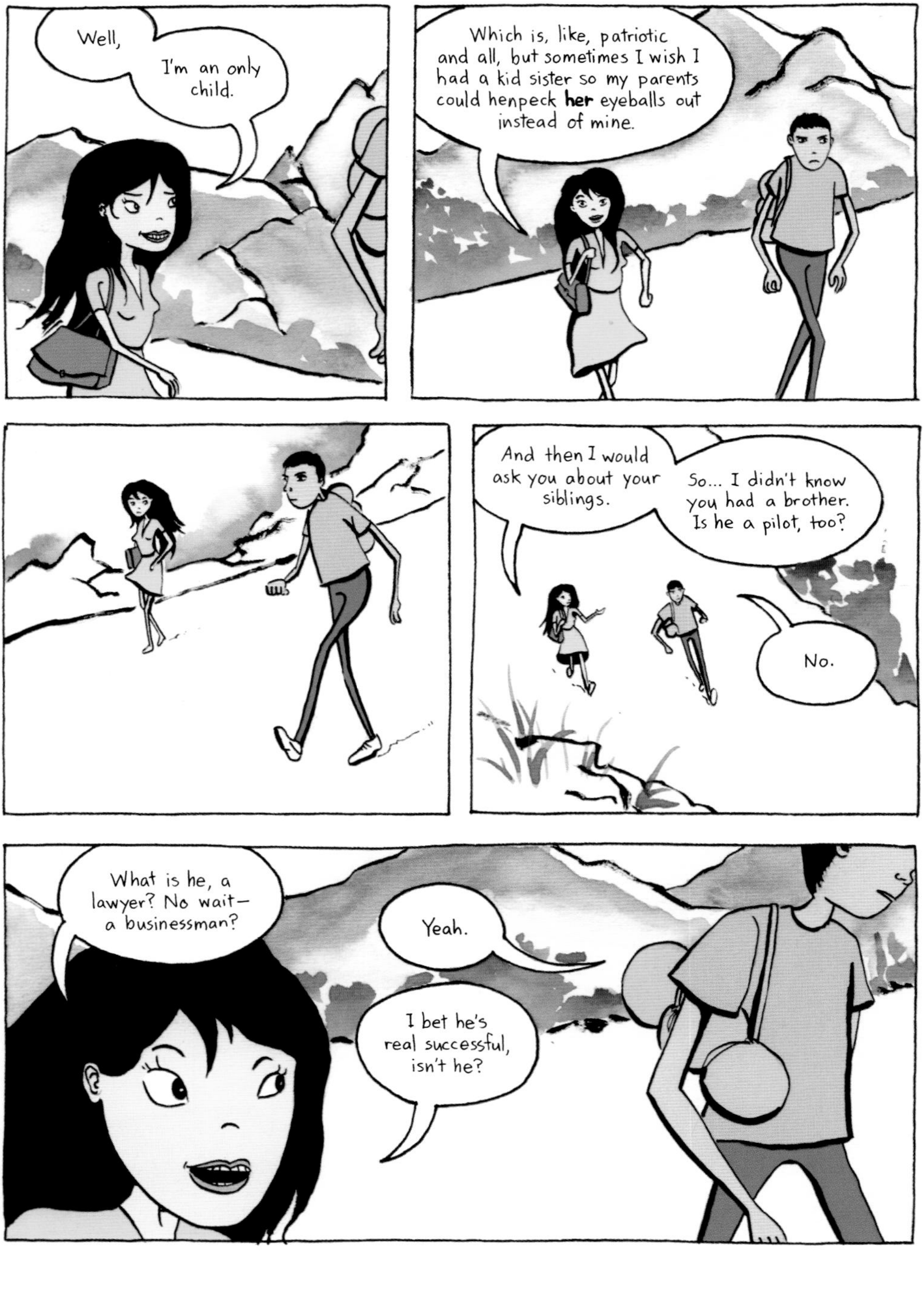
Well,
I'm an only child.
Which is, like, patriotic and all, but sometimes I wish I had a kid sister so my parents could henpeck **her** eyeballs out instead of mine.
And then I would ask you about your siblings.
So... I didn't know you had a brother. Is he a pilot, too?
No.
What is he, a lawyer? No wait— a businessman?
Yeah.
I bet he's real successful, isn't he?

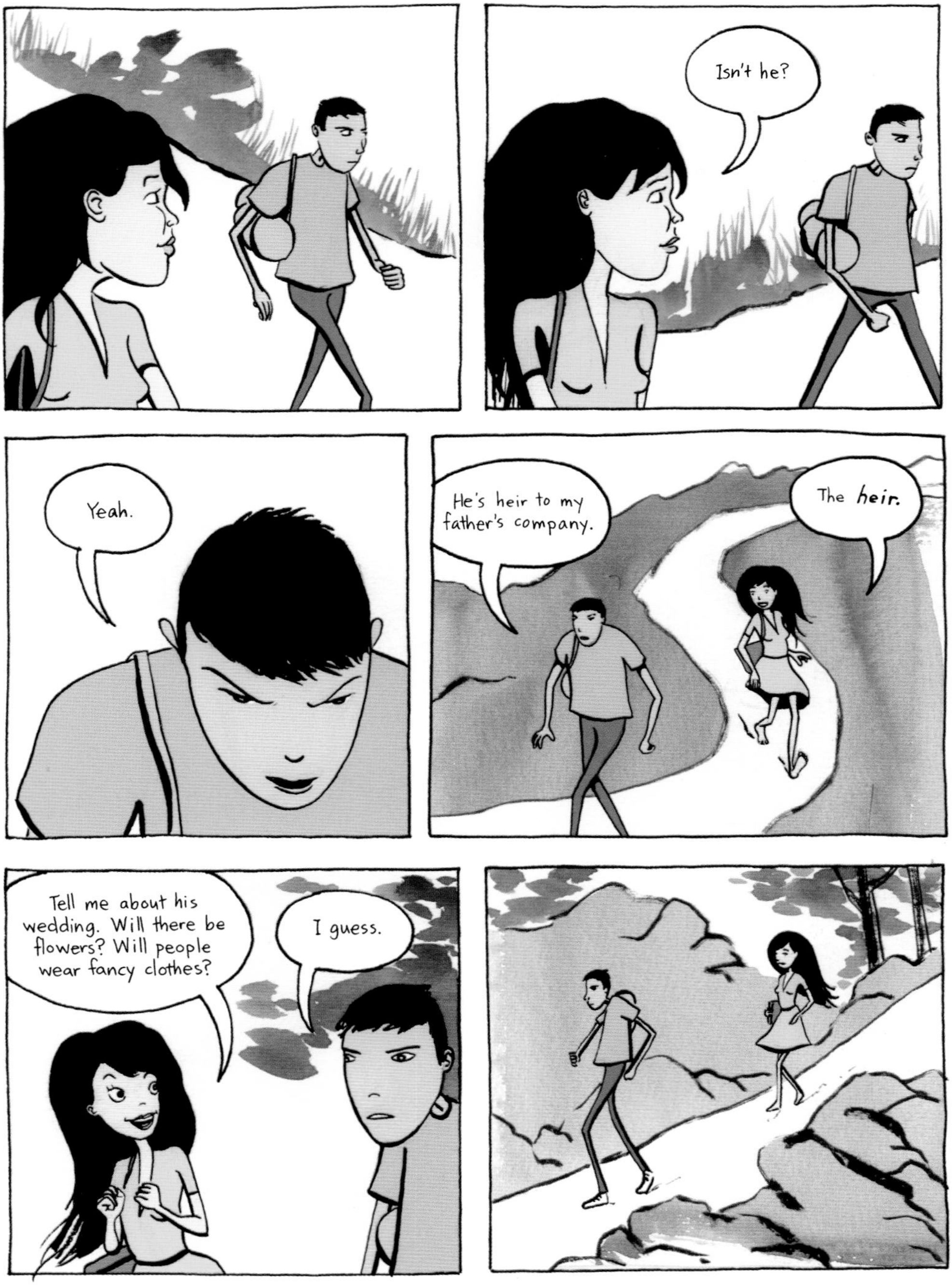

Isn't he?
Yeah.
He's heir to my father's company.
The heir.
Tell me about his wedding. Will there be flowers? Will people wear fancy clothes?
I guess.

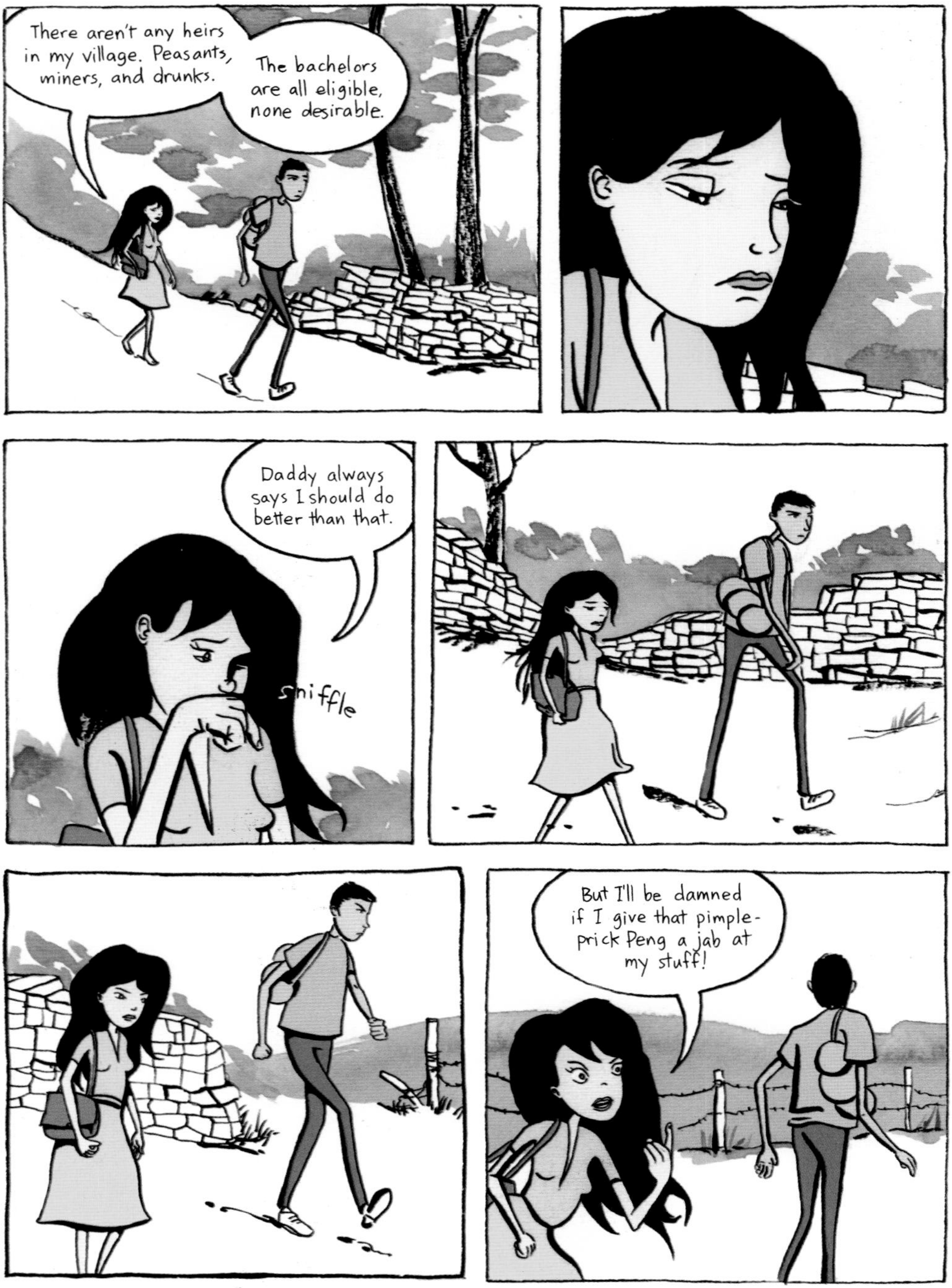
There aren't any heirs in my village. Peasants, miners, and drunks.
The bachelors are all eligible, none desirable.
Daddy always says I should do better than that.
sniffle
But I'll be damned if I give that pimple-prick Peng a jab at my stuff!

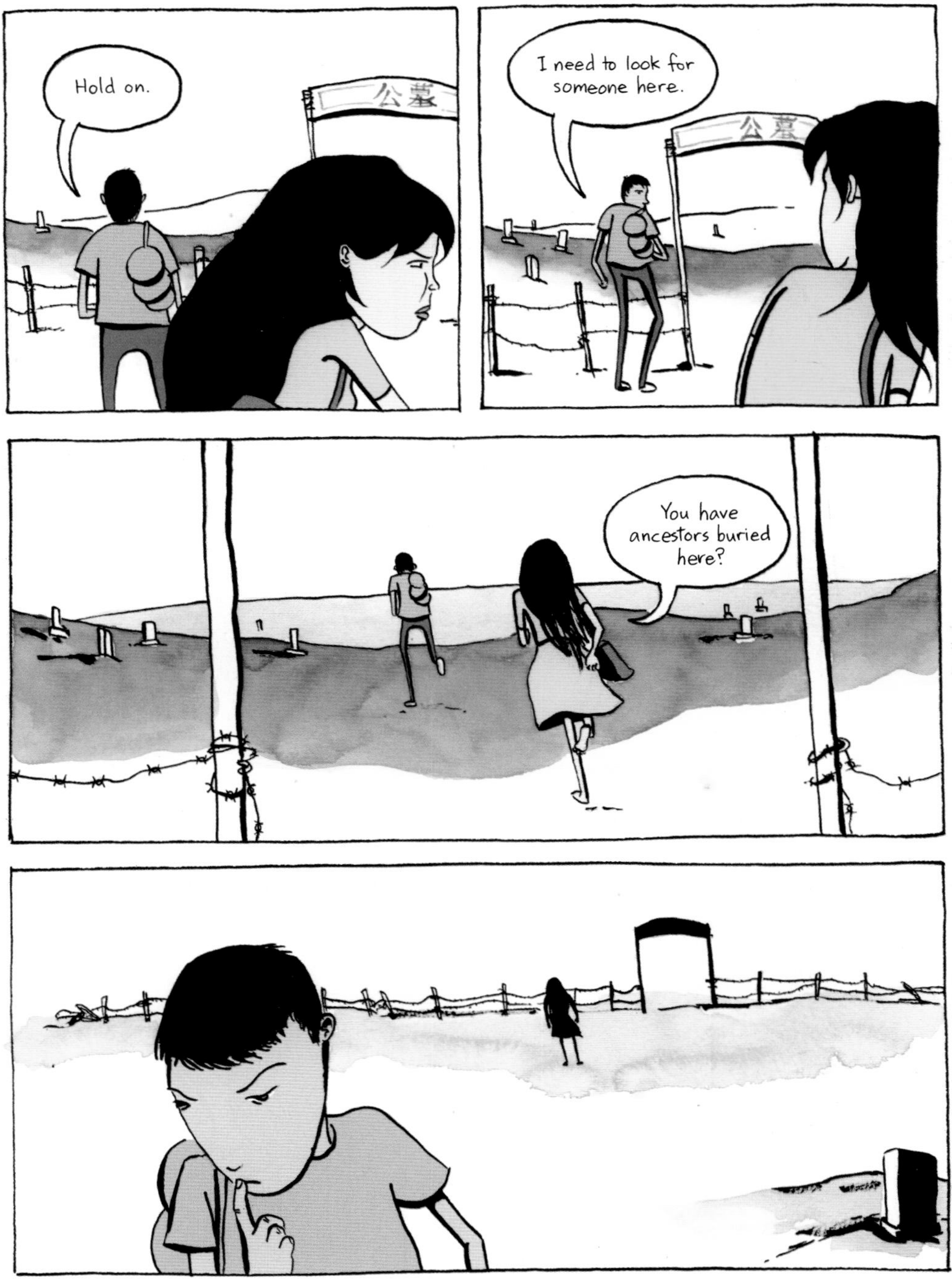
Hold on.
公墓
I need to look for someone here.
公墓
You have ancestors buried here?

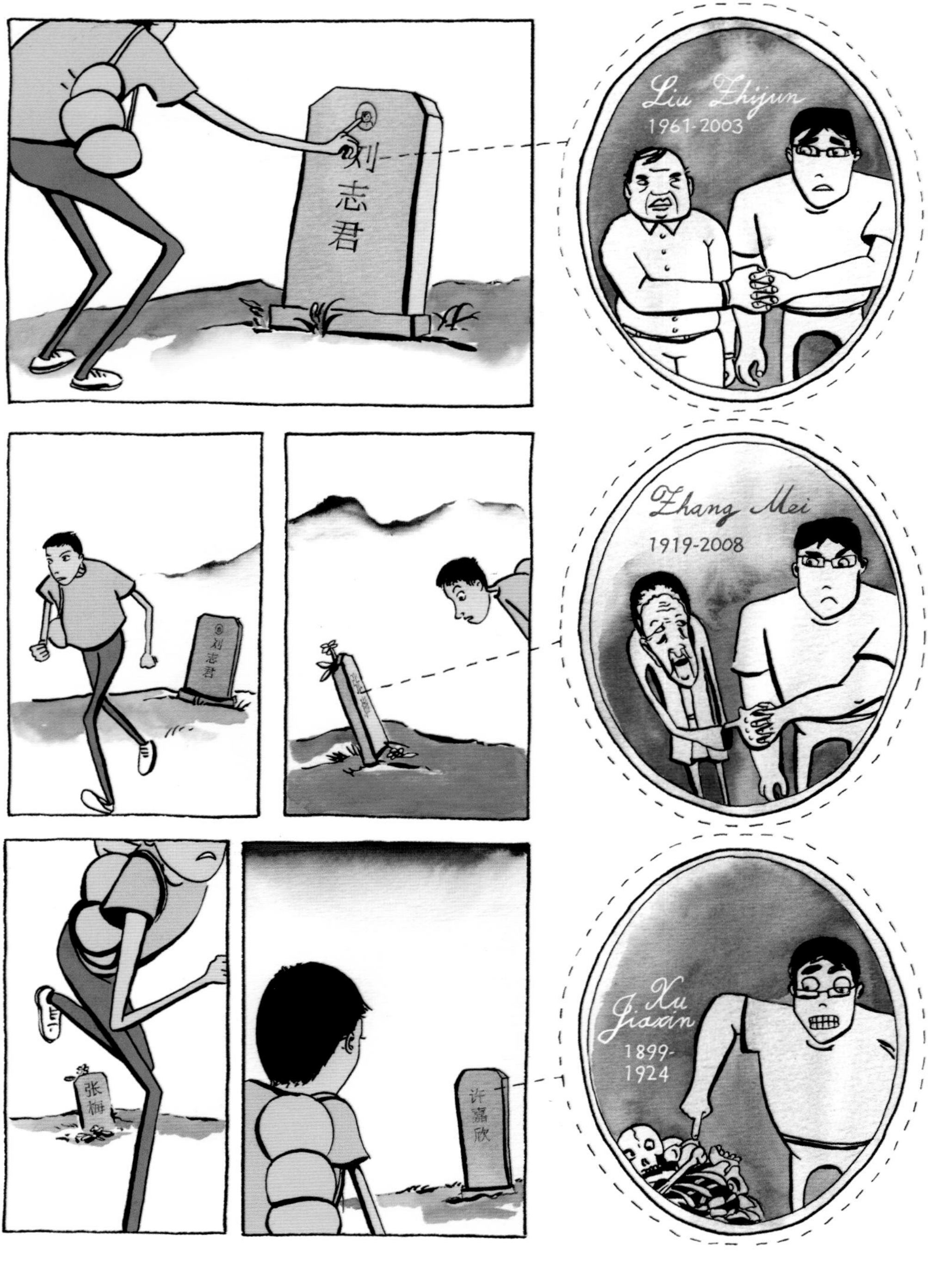

刘
志
君
Liu Zhijun
1961-2003
刘
志
君
Zhang Mei
1919-2008
张
梅
许
嘉
欣
Xu
Jiaxin
1899-
1924

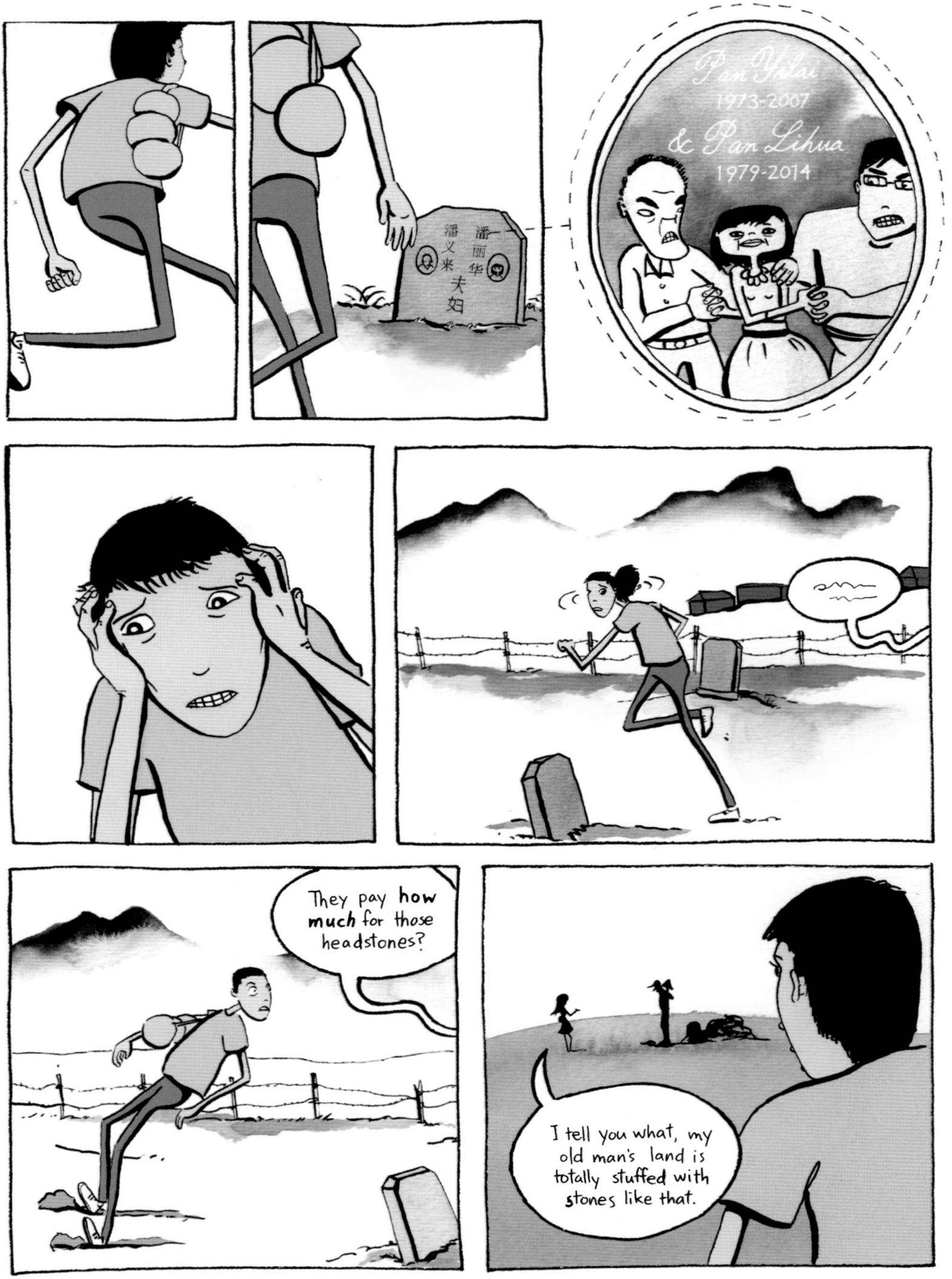
潘丽华
潘义来
夫妇
Pan Yilai
1973-2007
& Pan Lihua
1979-2014
They pay **how much** for those headstones?
I tell you what, my old man's land is totally stuffed with stones like that.

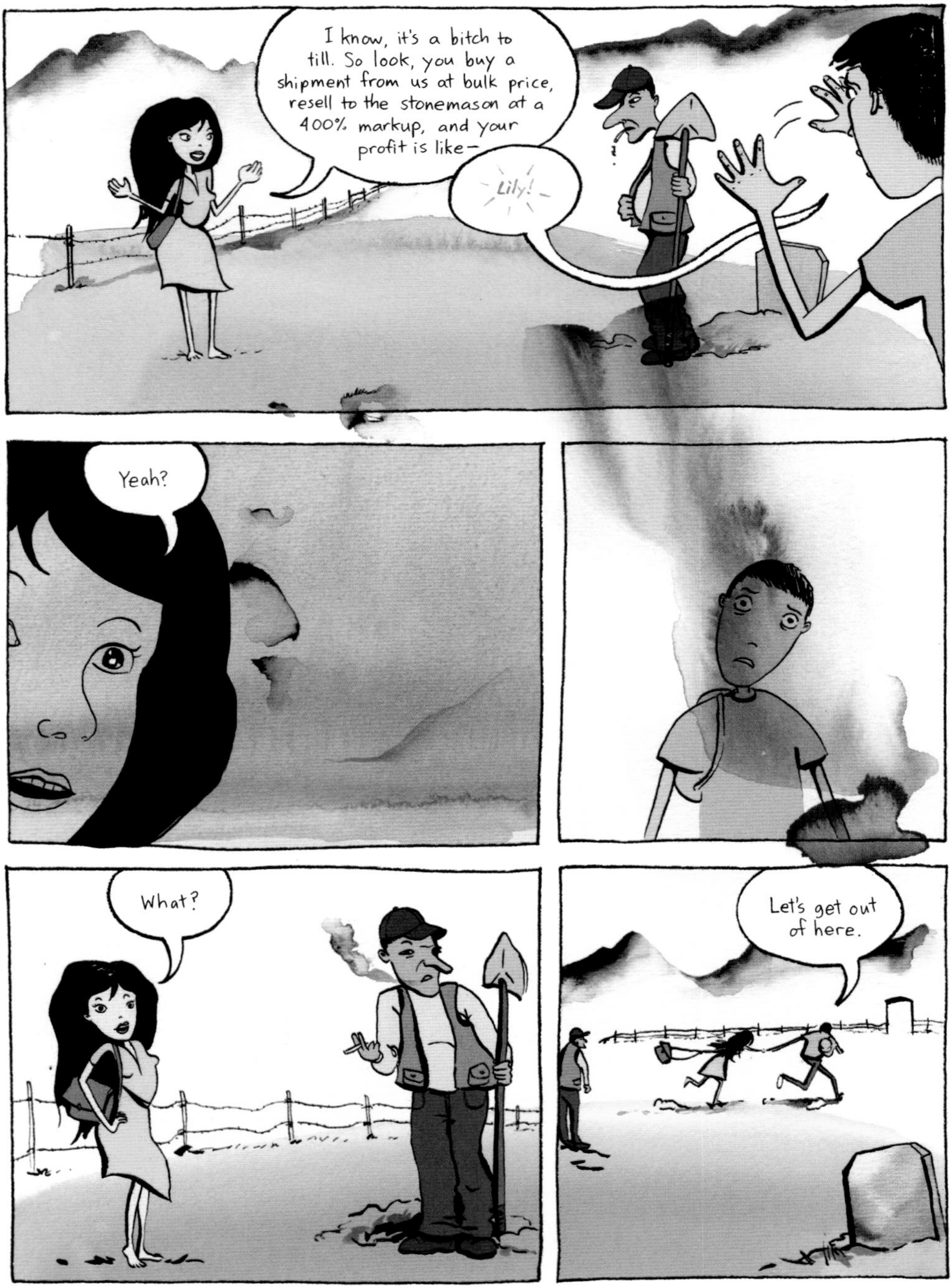
I know, it's a bitch to till. So look, you buy a shipment from us at bulk price, resell to the stonemason at a 400% markup, and your profit is like—
Lily!
Yeah?
What?
Let's get out of here.

12. The Avengers
WEDNESDAY

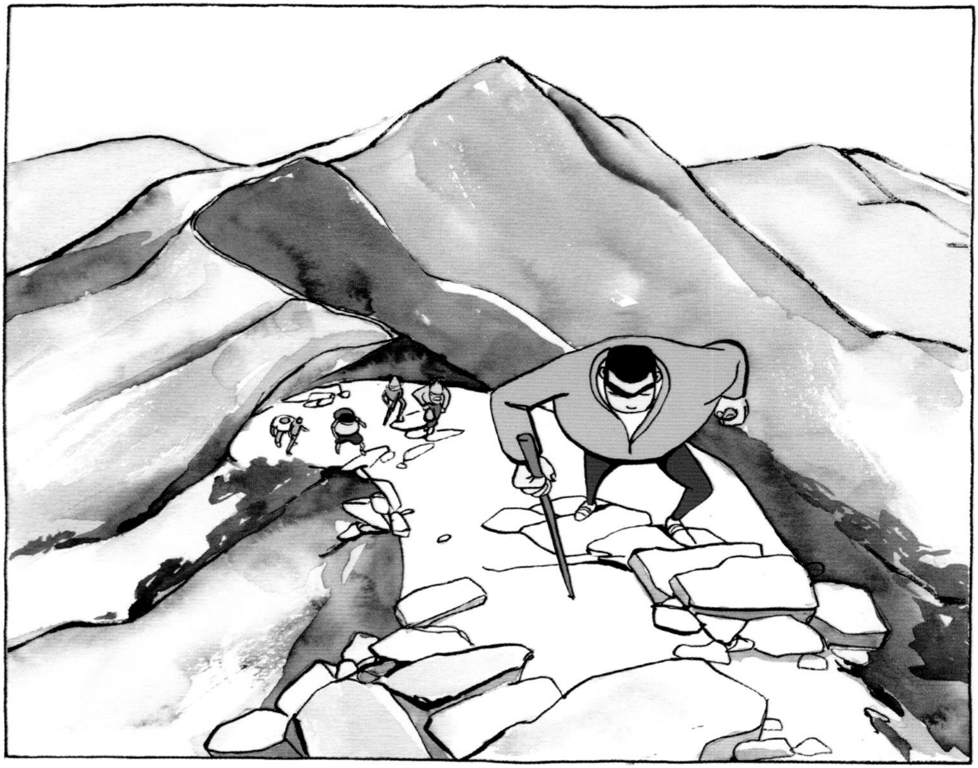

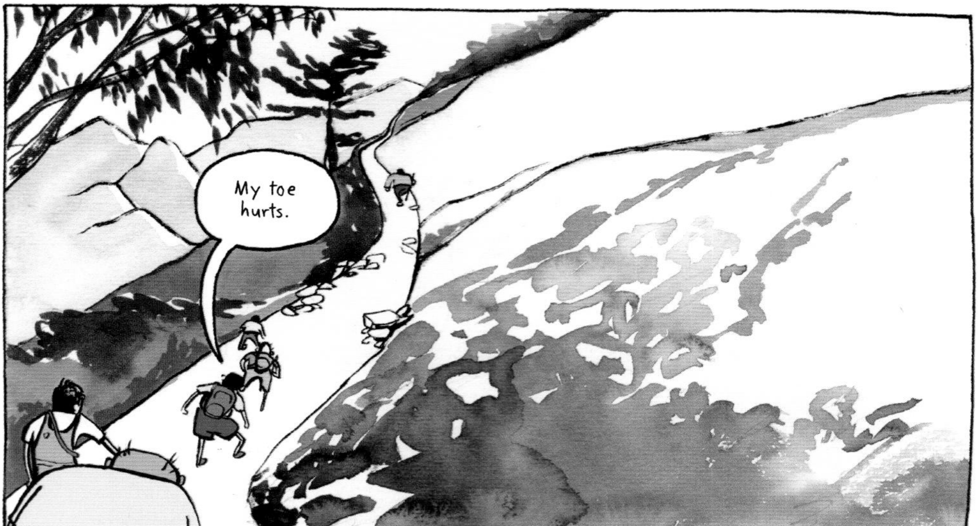
My toe hurts.

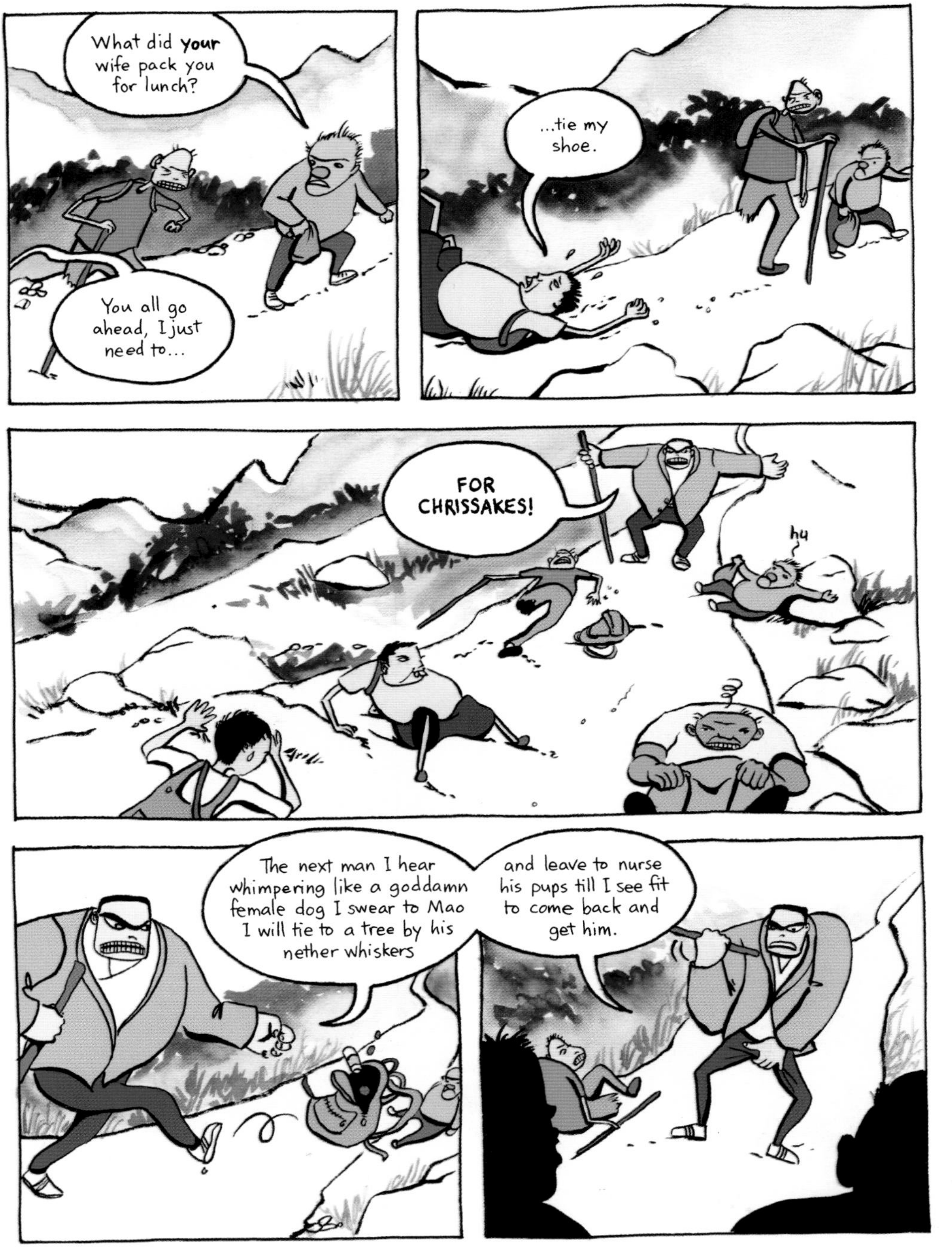

What did your wife pack you for lunch?
You all go ahead, I just need to...
...tie my shoe.
FOR CHRISSAKES!
hu
The next man I hear whimpering like a goddamn female dog I swear to Mao I will tie to a tree by his nether whiskers
and leave to nurse his pups till I see fit to come back and get him.

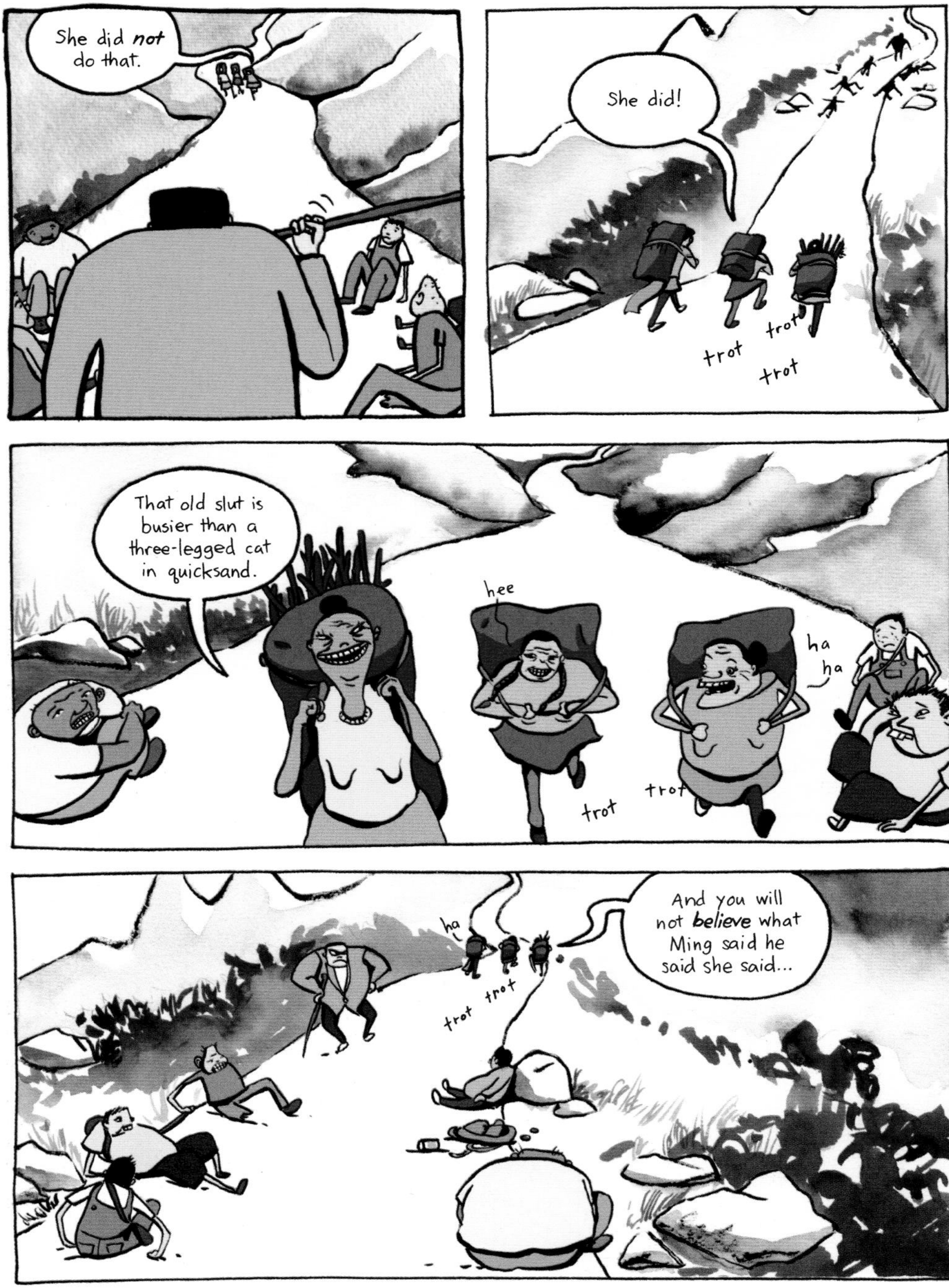
She did **not** do that.
She did!
trot
trot
trot
That old slut is busier than a three-legged cat in quicksand.
hee
ha
ha
trot
trot
ha
trot
trot
And you will not **believe** what Ming said he said she said...

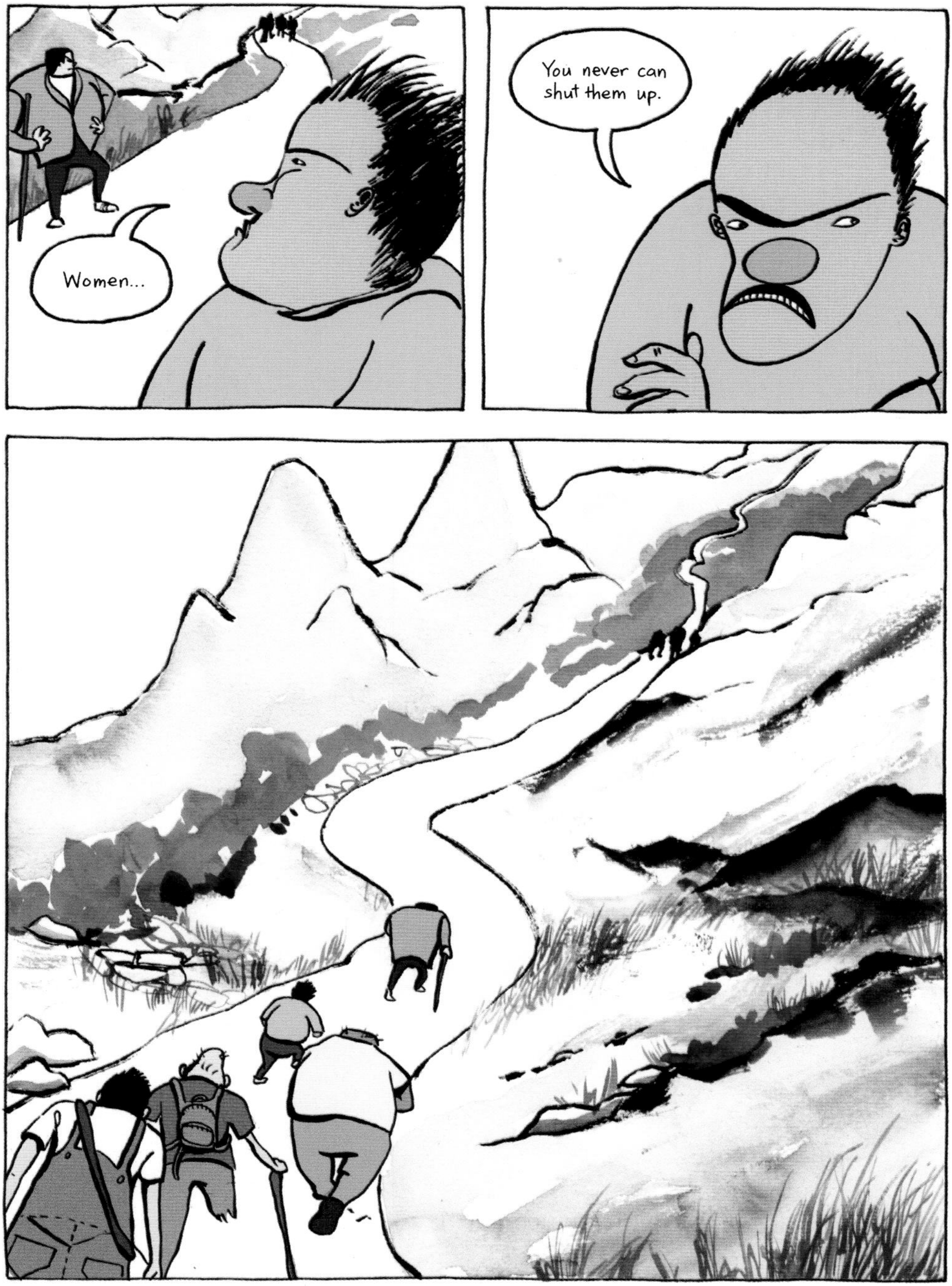

Women...
You never can shut them up.

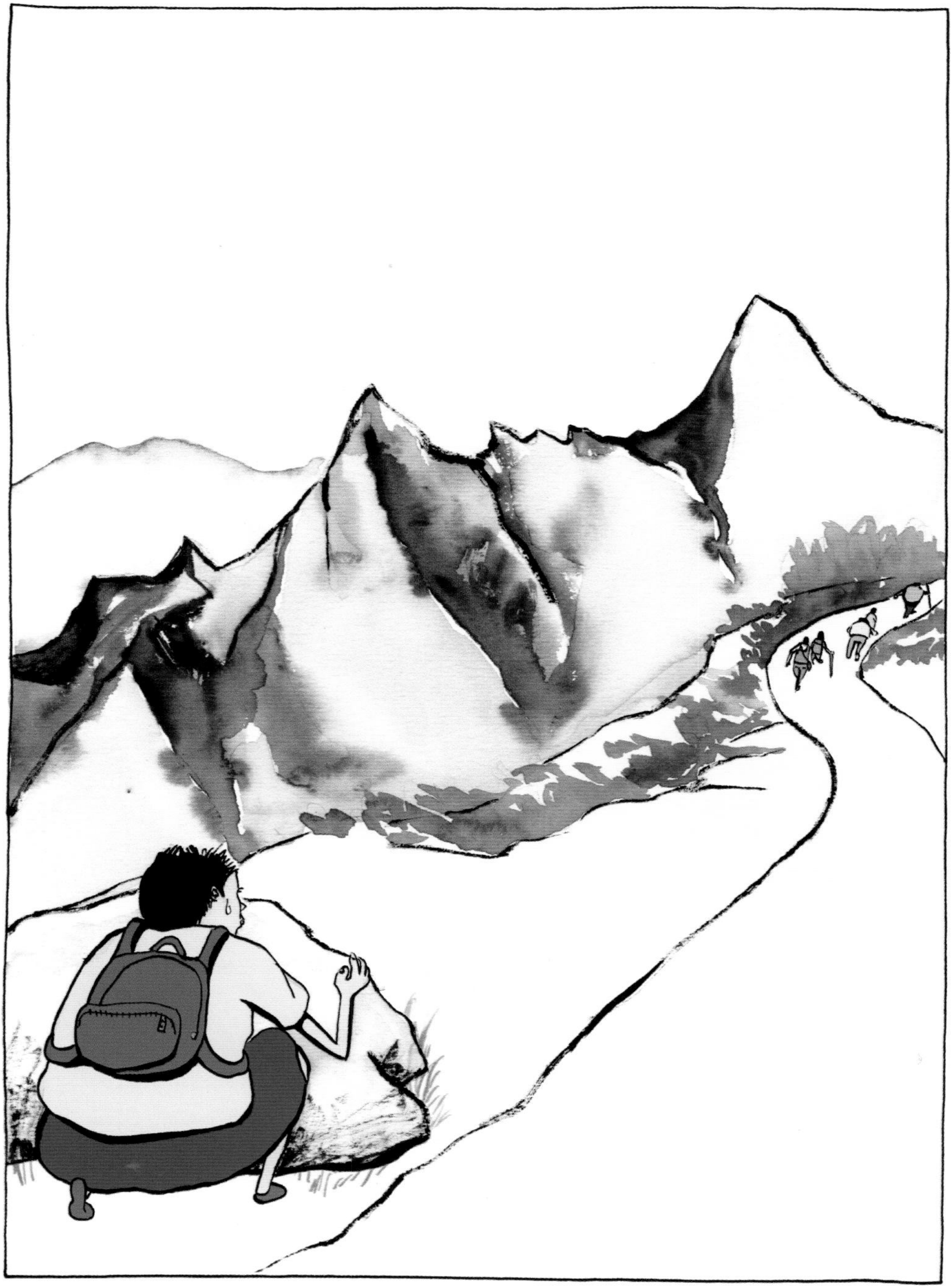

13. Layover

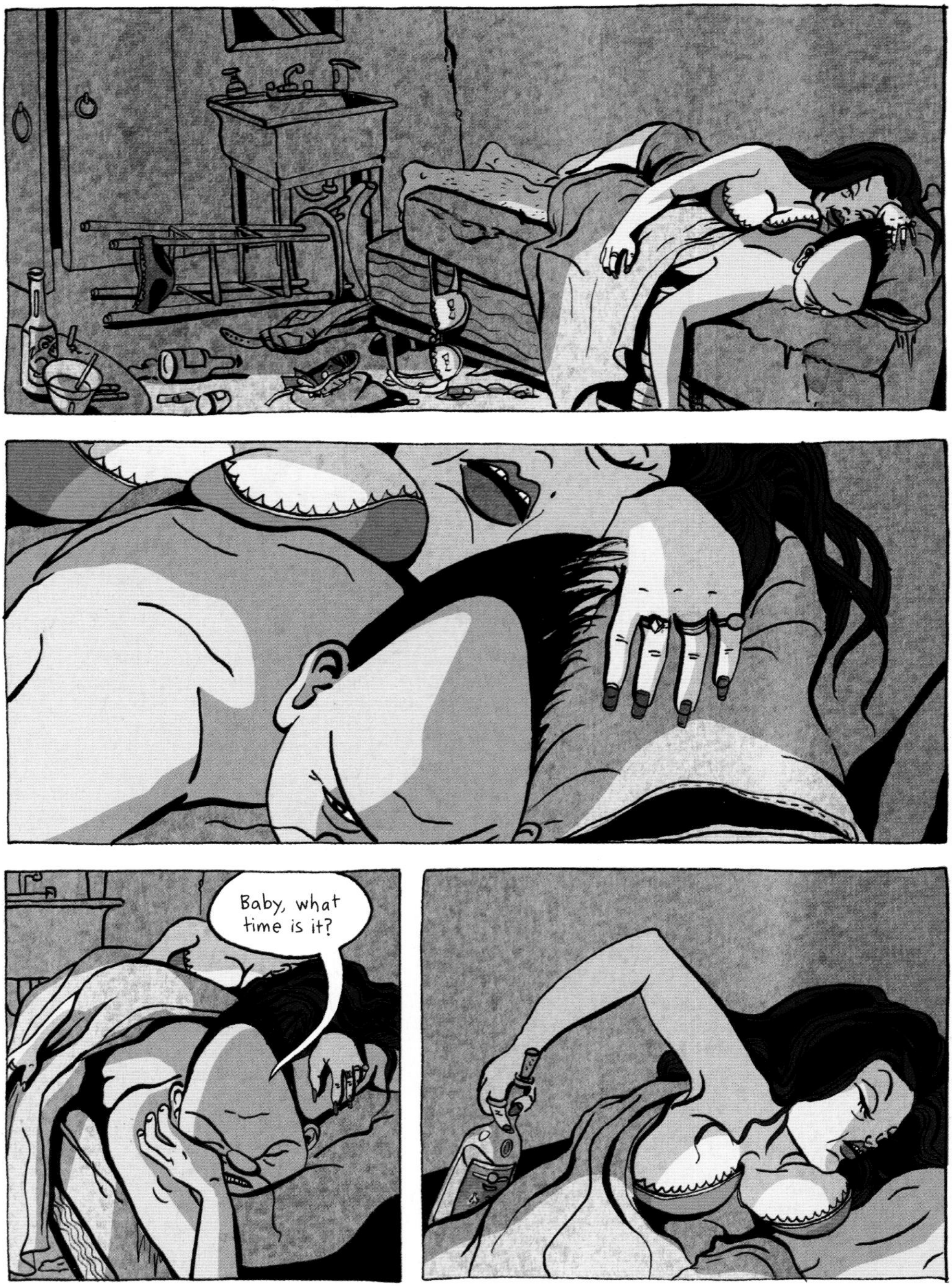
Baby, what time is it?

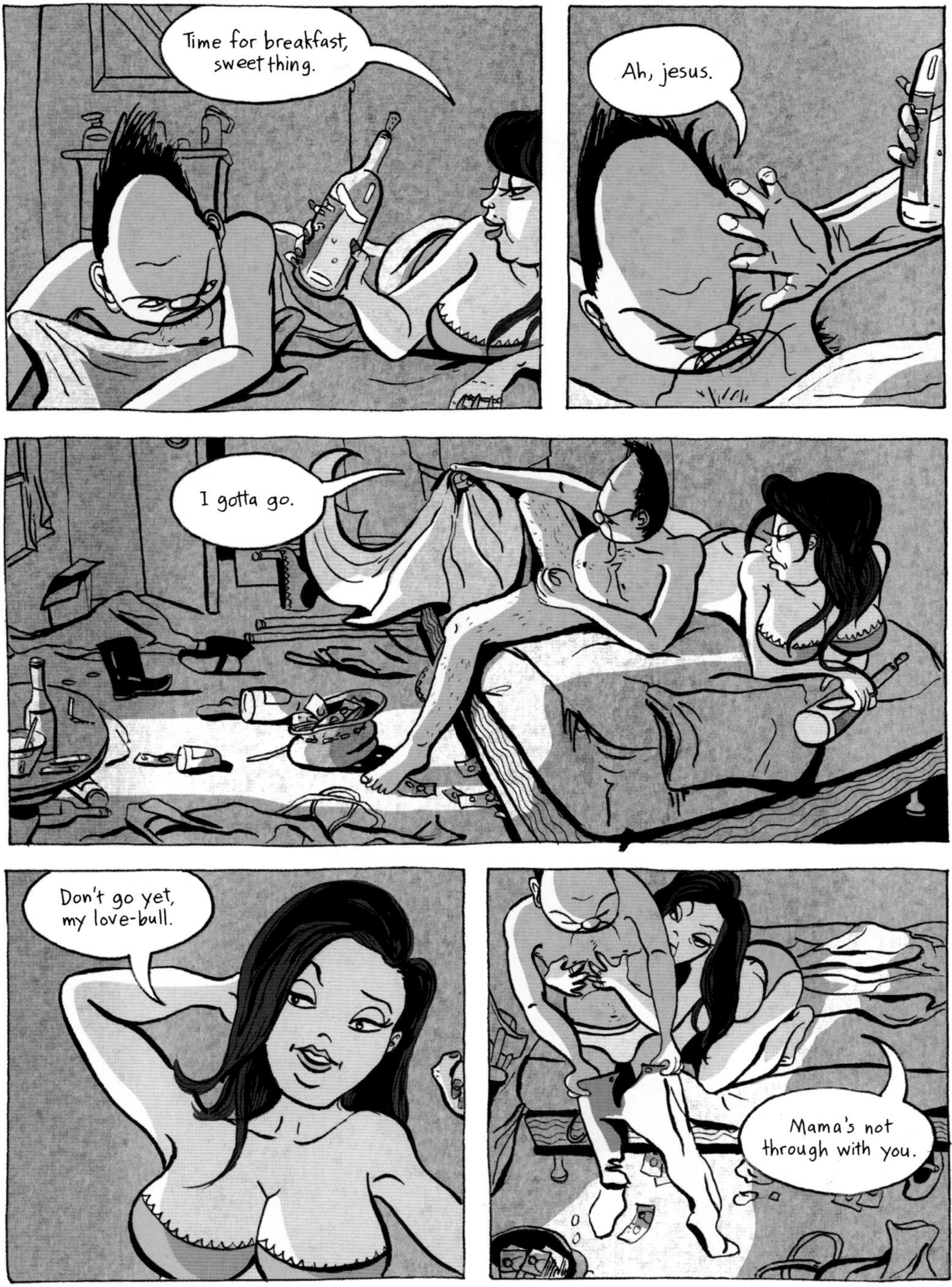
Time for breakfast, sweet thing.
Ah, jesus.
I gotta go.
Don't go yet, my love-bull.
Mama's not through with you.

I gotta find a guy, finish a deal.

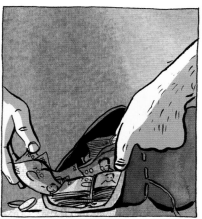

When I'm paid, I always see the job through.

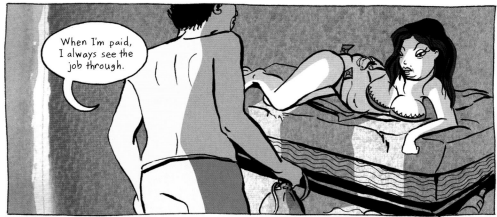

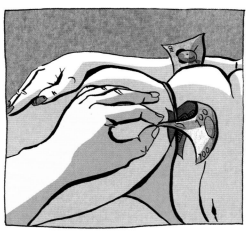

14. Fishing

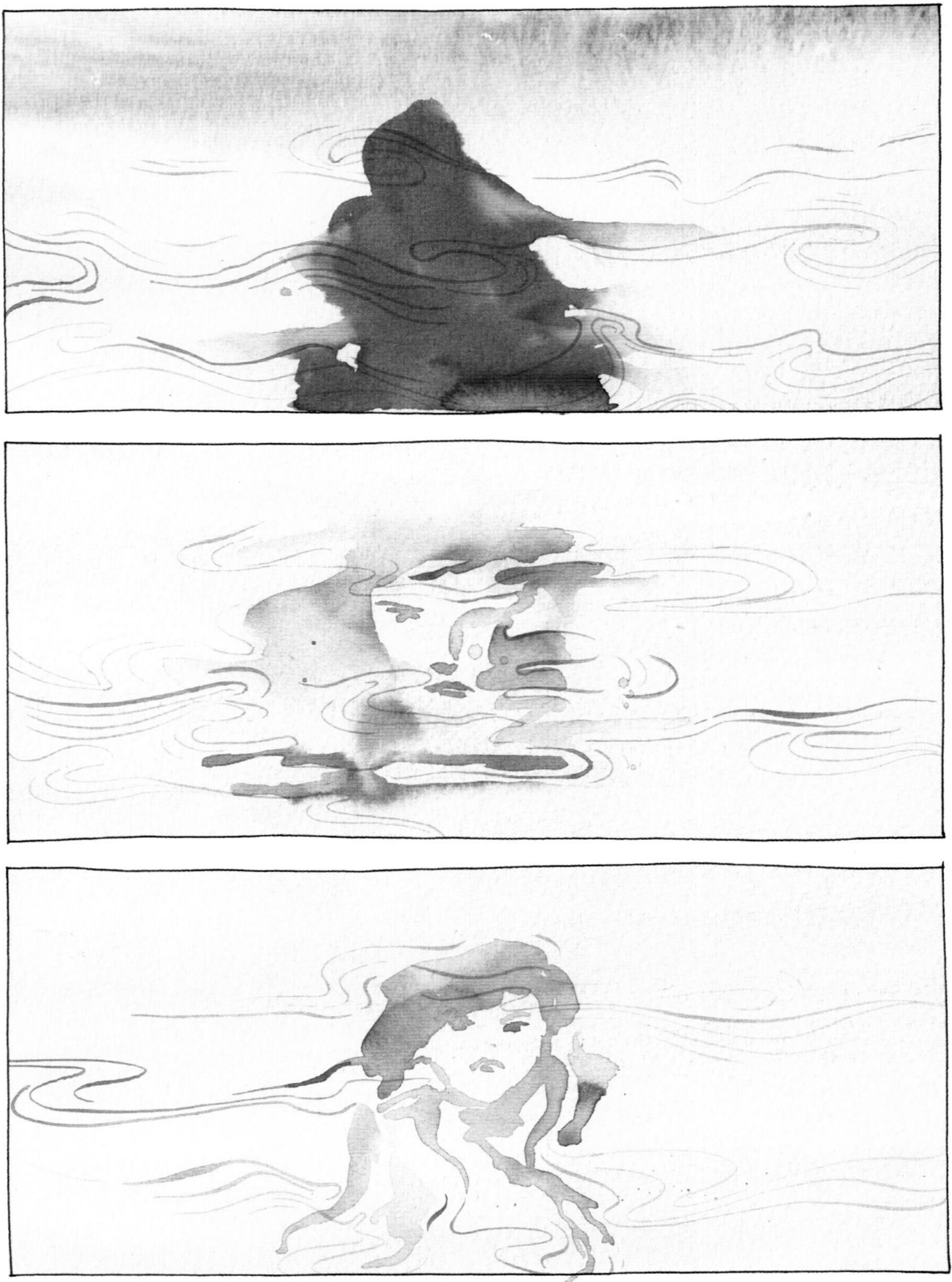

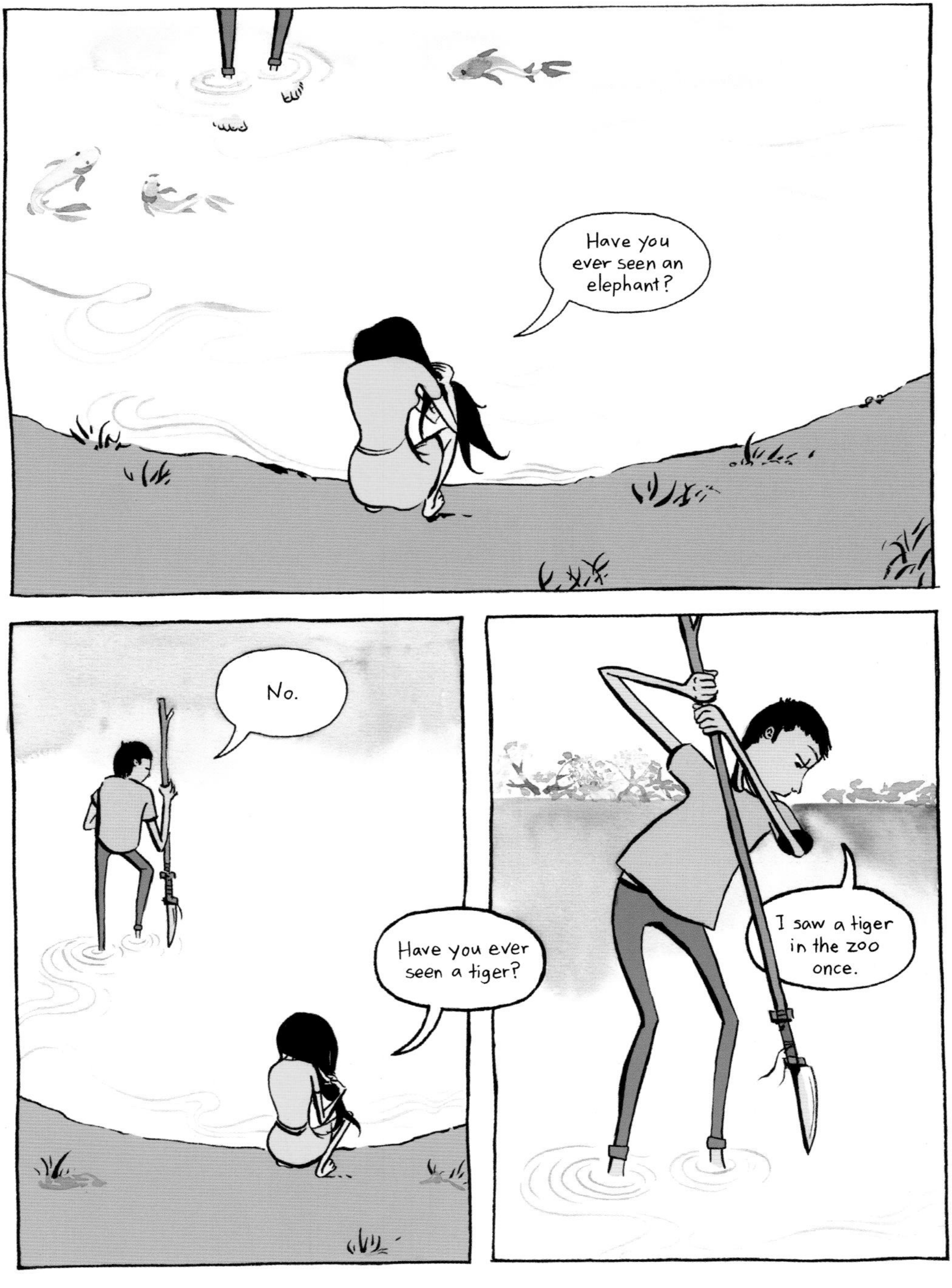
Have you ever seen an elephant?
No.
Have you ever seen a tiger?
I saw a tiger in the zoo once.

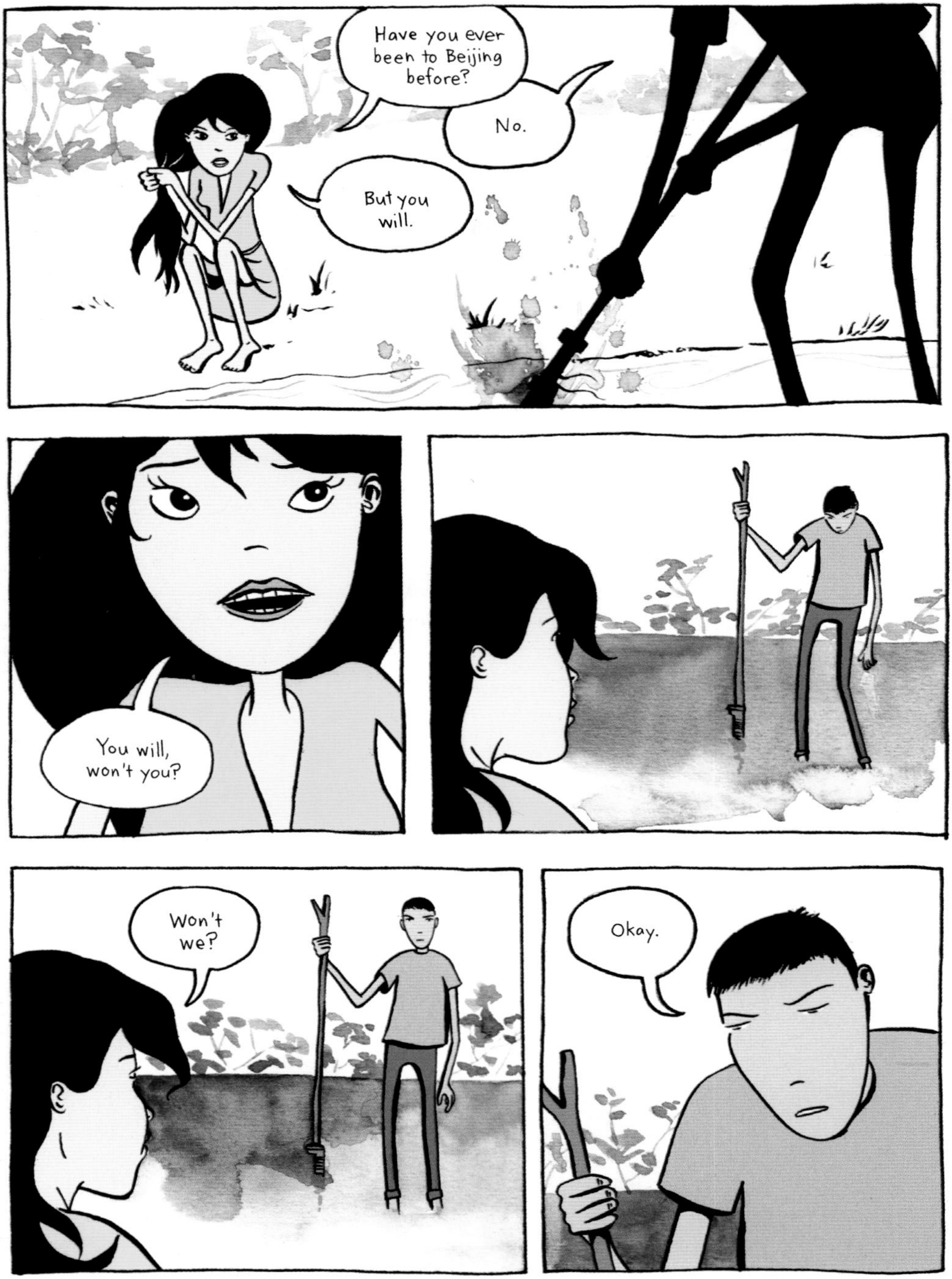
Have you ever been to Beijing before?
No.
But you will.
You will, won't you?
Won't we?
Okay.

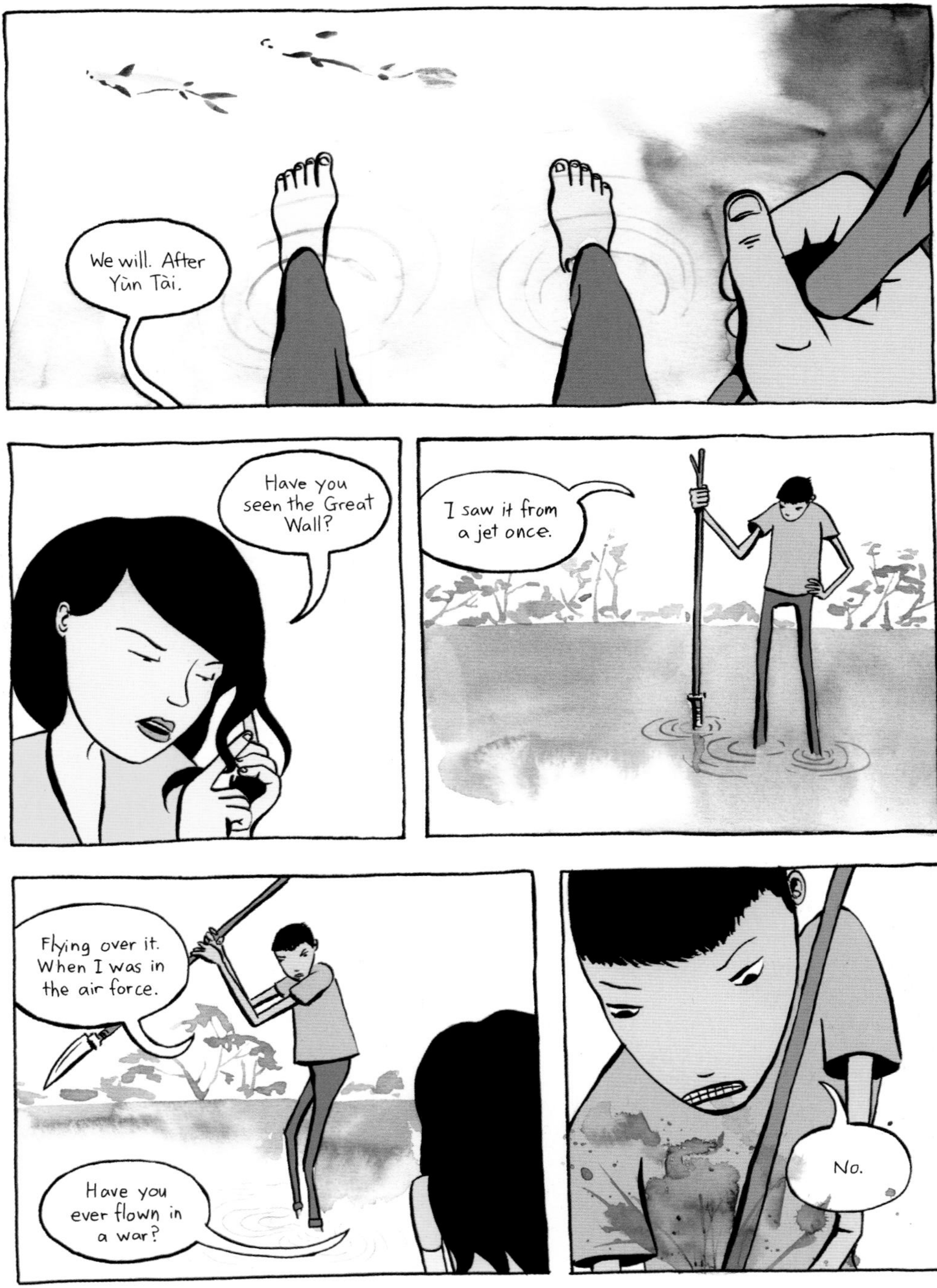

We will. After Yùn Tài.
Have you seen the Great Wall?
I saw it from a jet once.
Flying over it. When I was in the air force.
Have you ever flown in a war?
No.

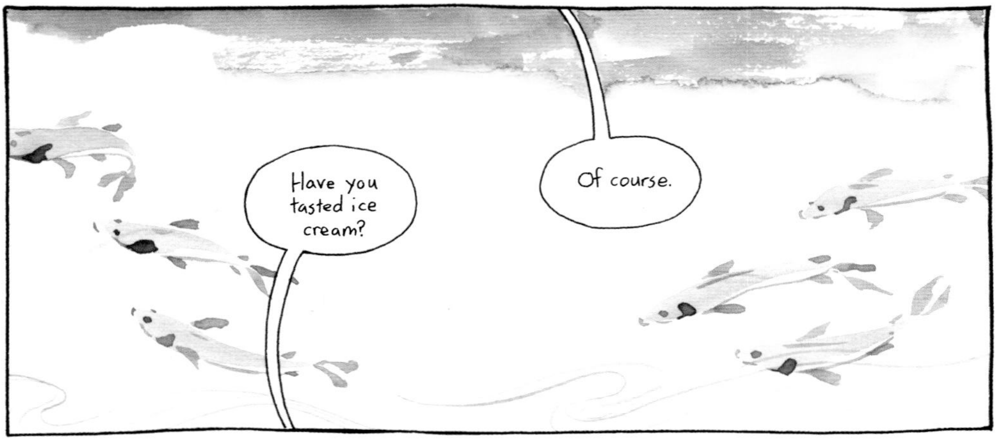
Have you tasted ice cream?
Of course.

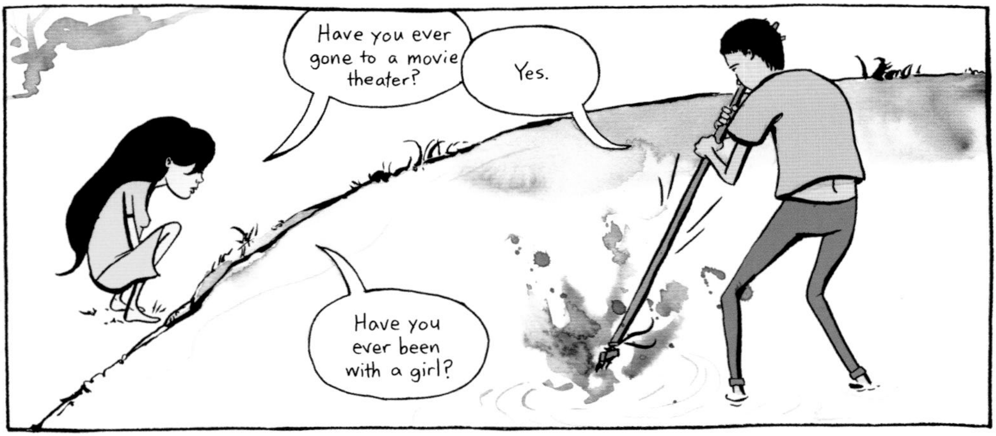
Have you ever gone to a movie theater?
Yes.
Have you ever been with a girl?

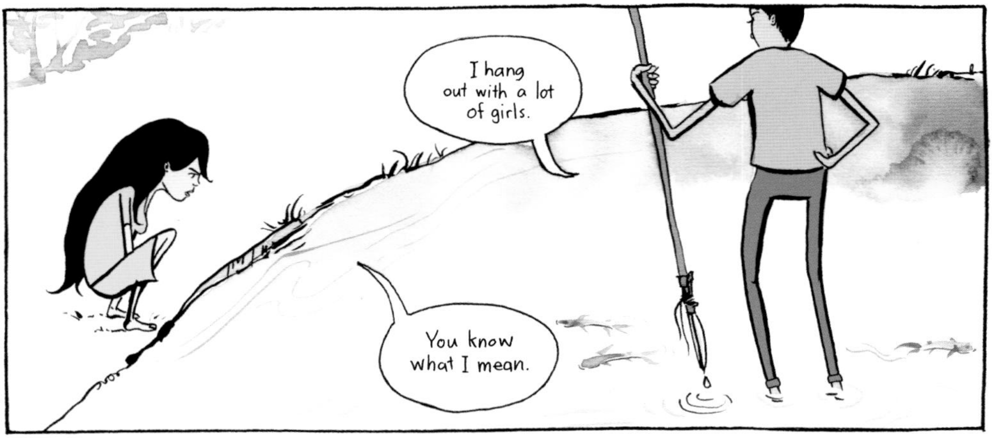
I hang out with a lot of girls.
You know what I mean.

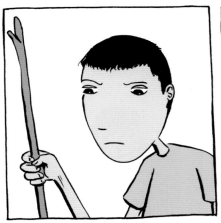

No.
I haven't.

Have you
ever been
hungry?

Sure.

I mean really,
really hungry.

No.

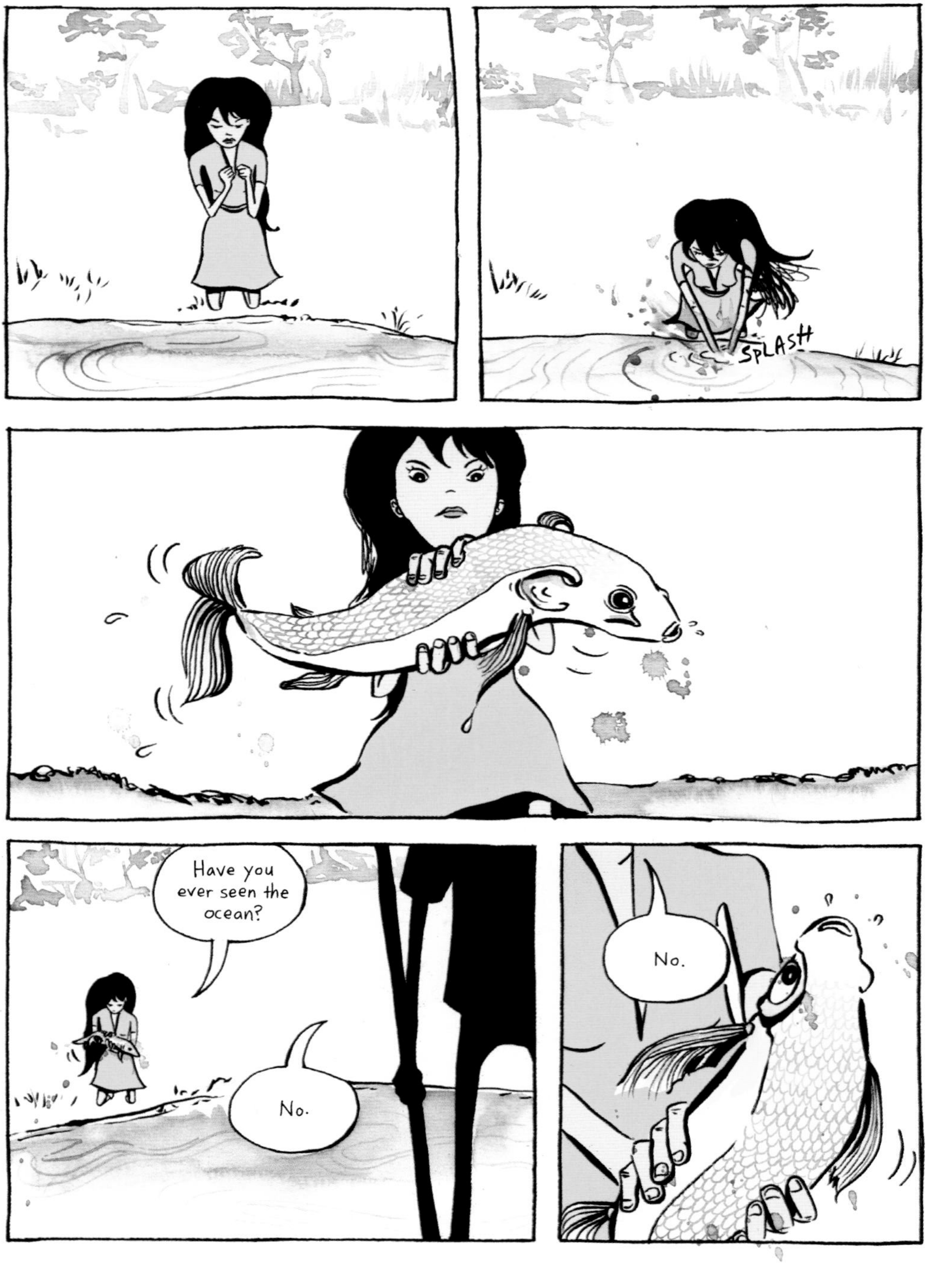
SPLASH
Have you ever seen the ocean?
No.
No.

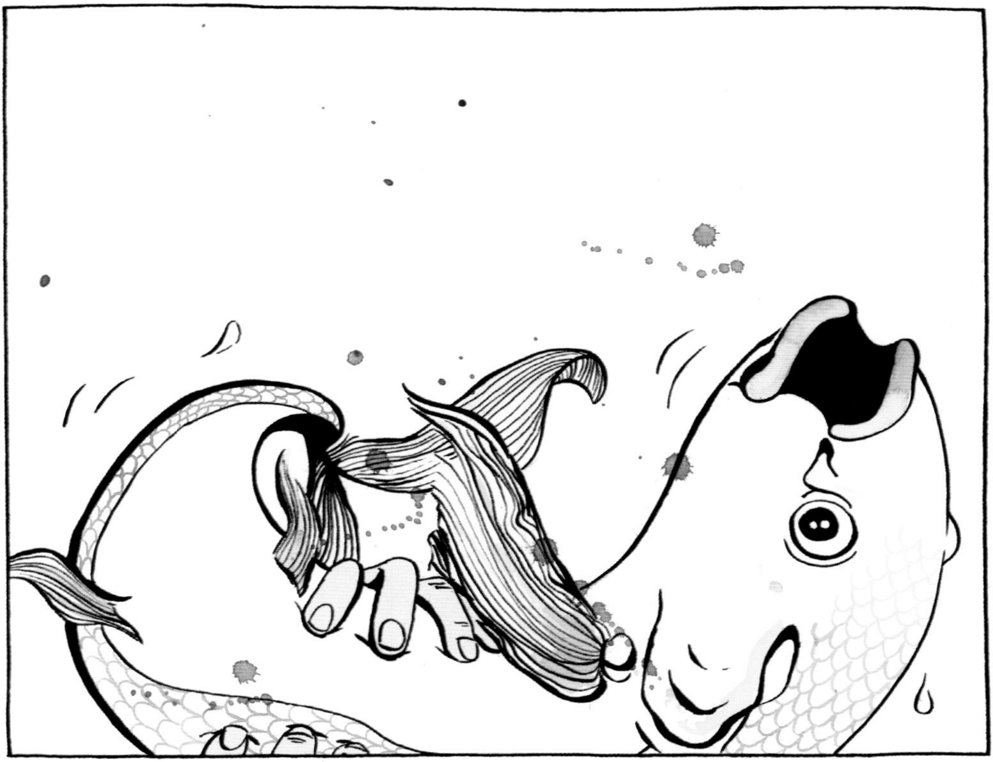

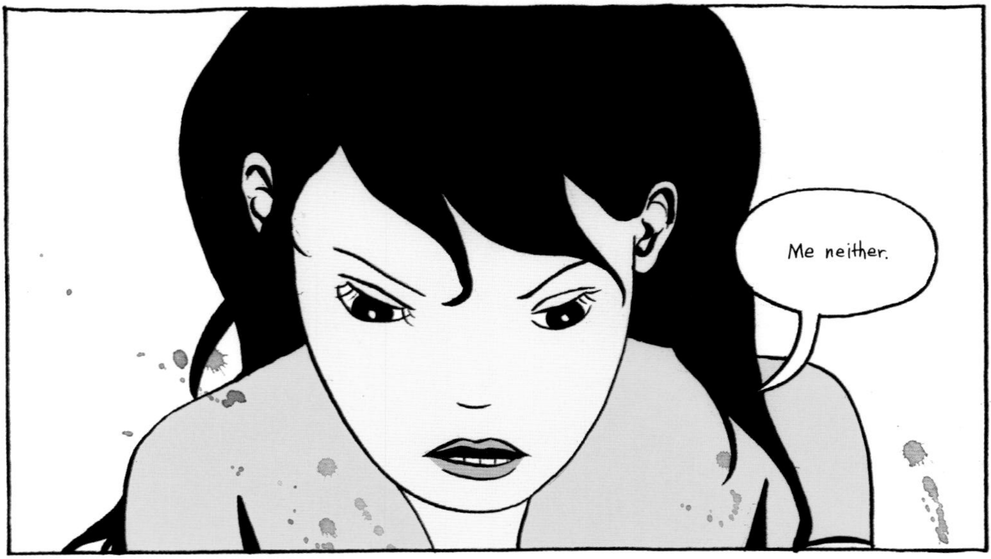
Me neither.

15. Luck

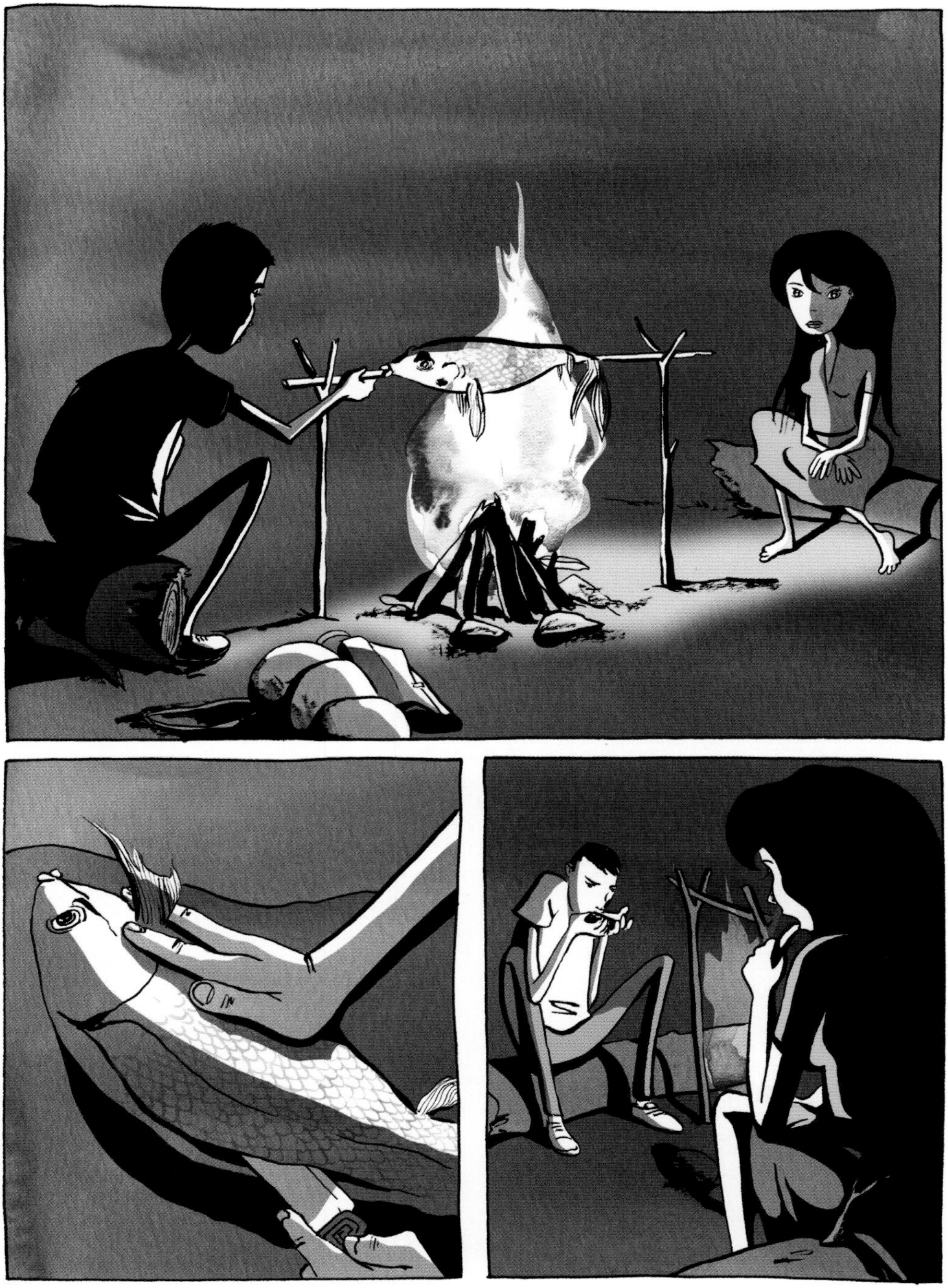

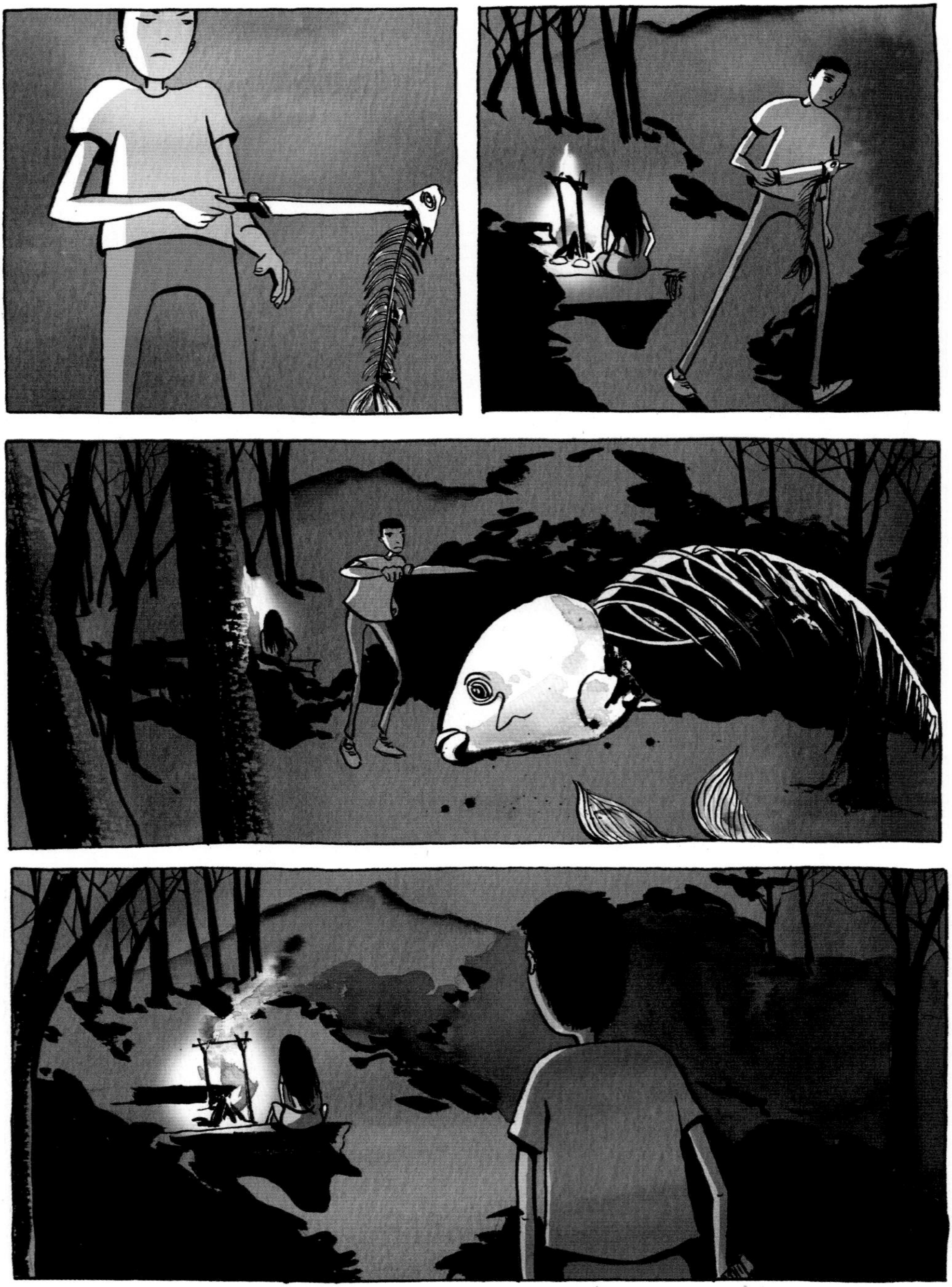

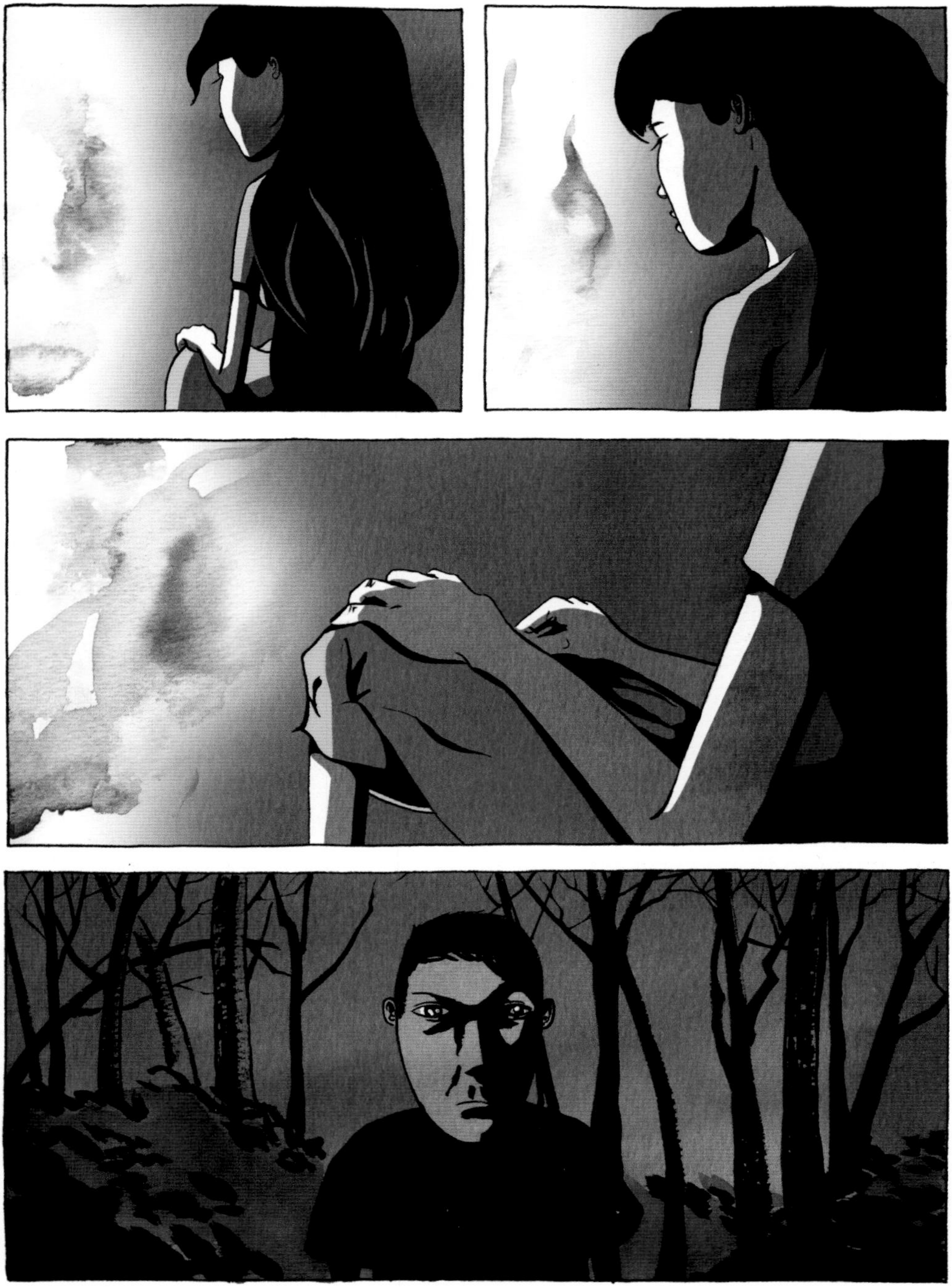

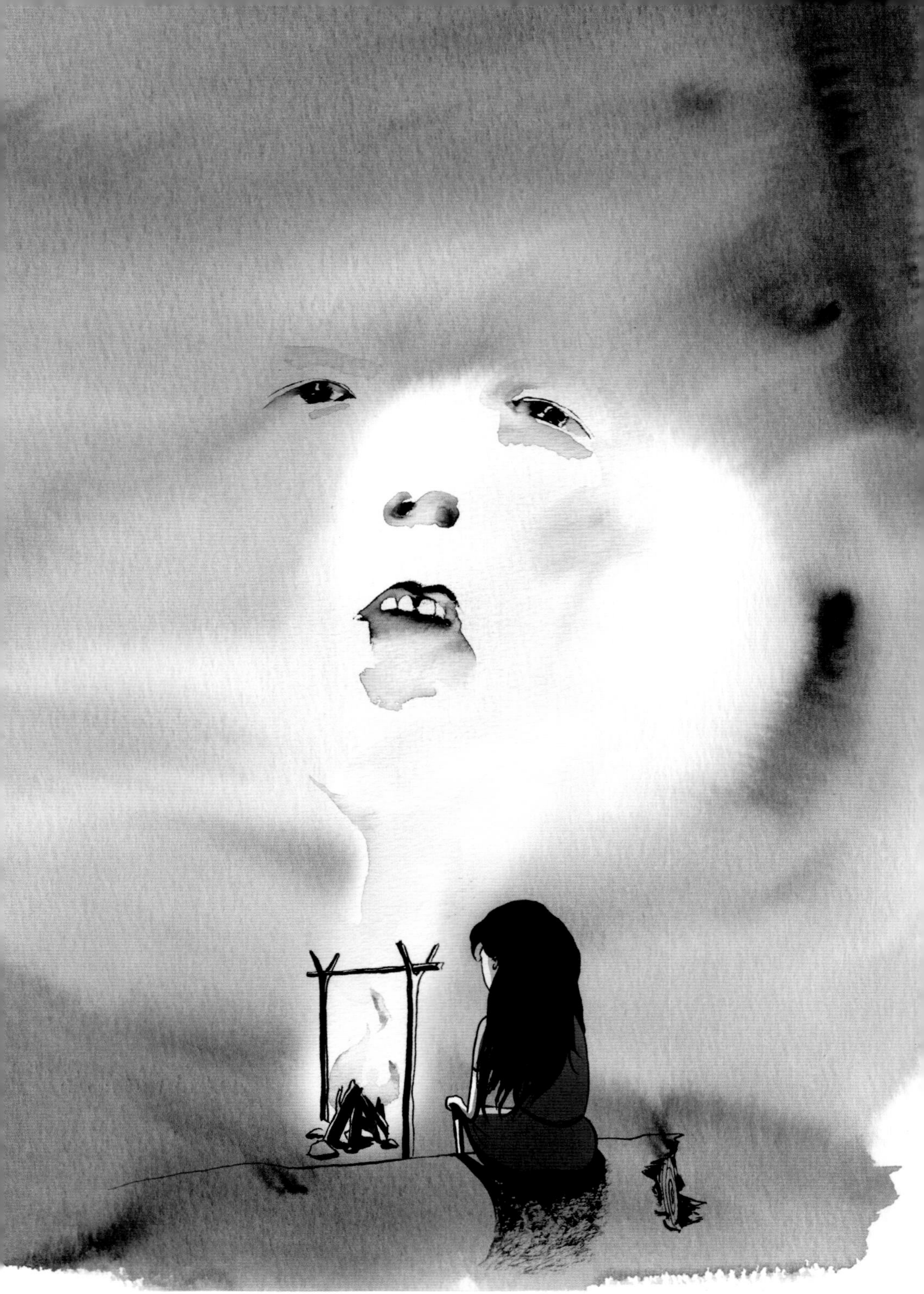

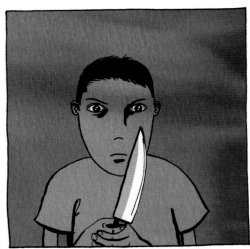

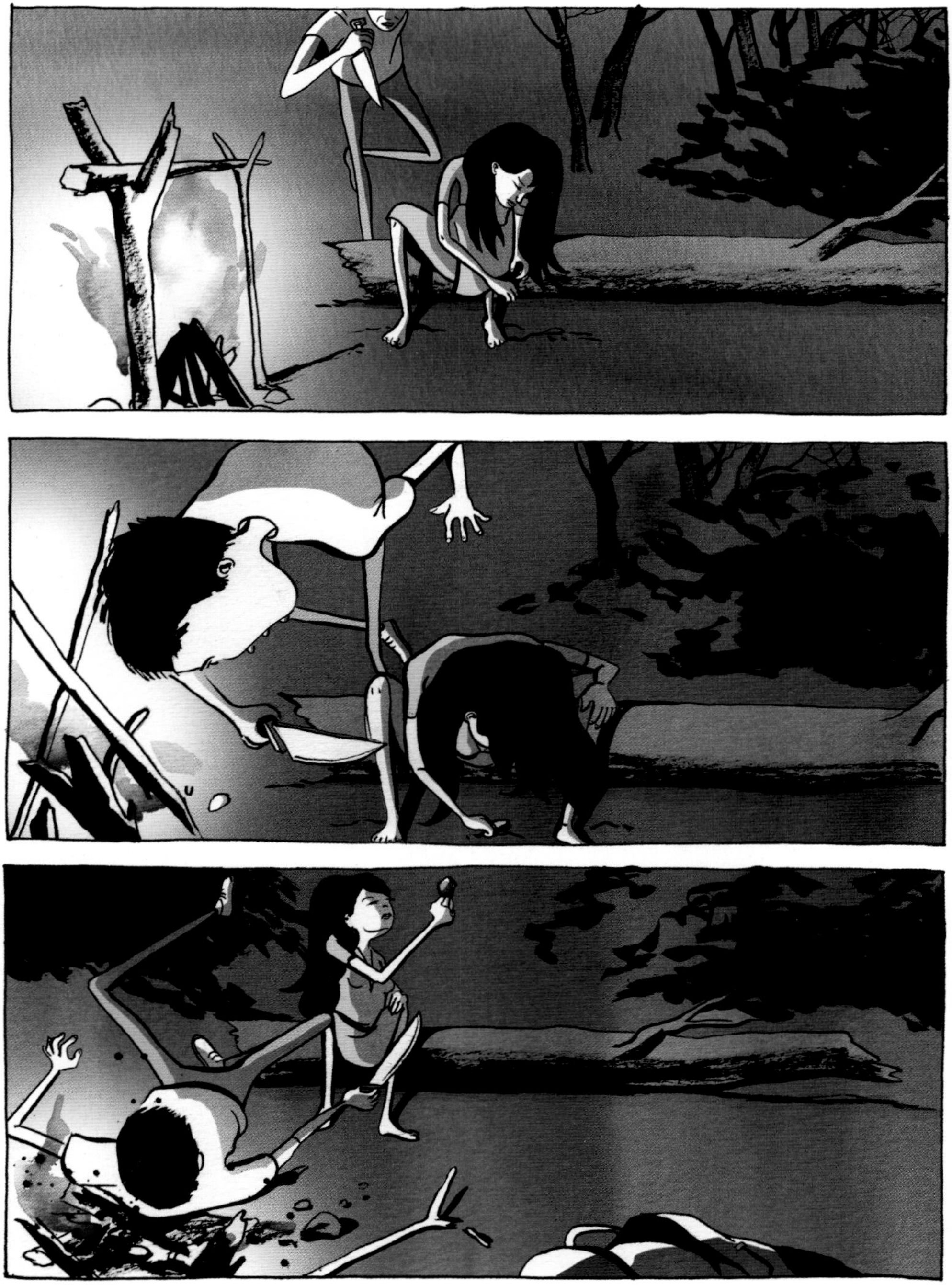

Would you look at that.

Here.

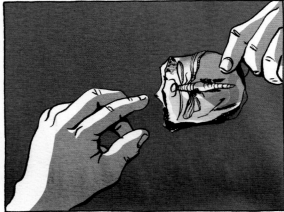

It's good luck.

I think you'll need it.

16. The Fortune House

THURSDAY

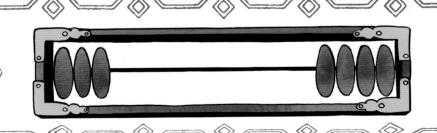

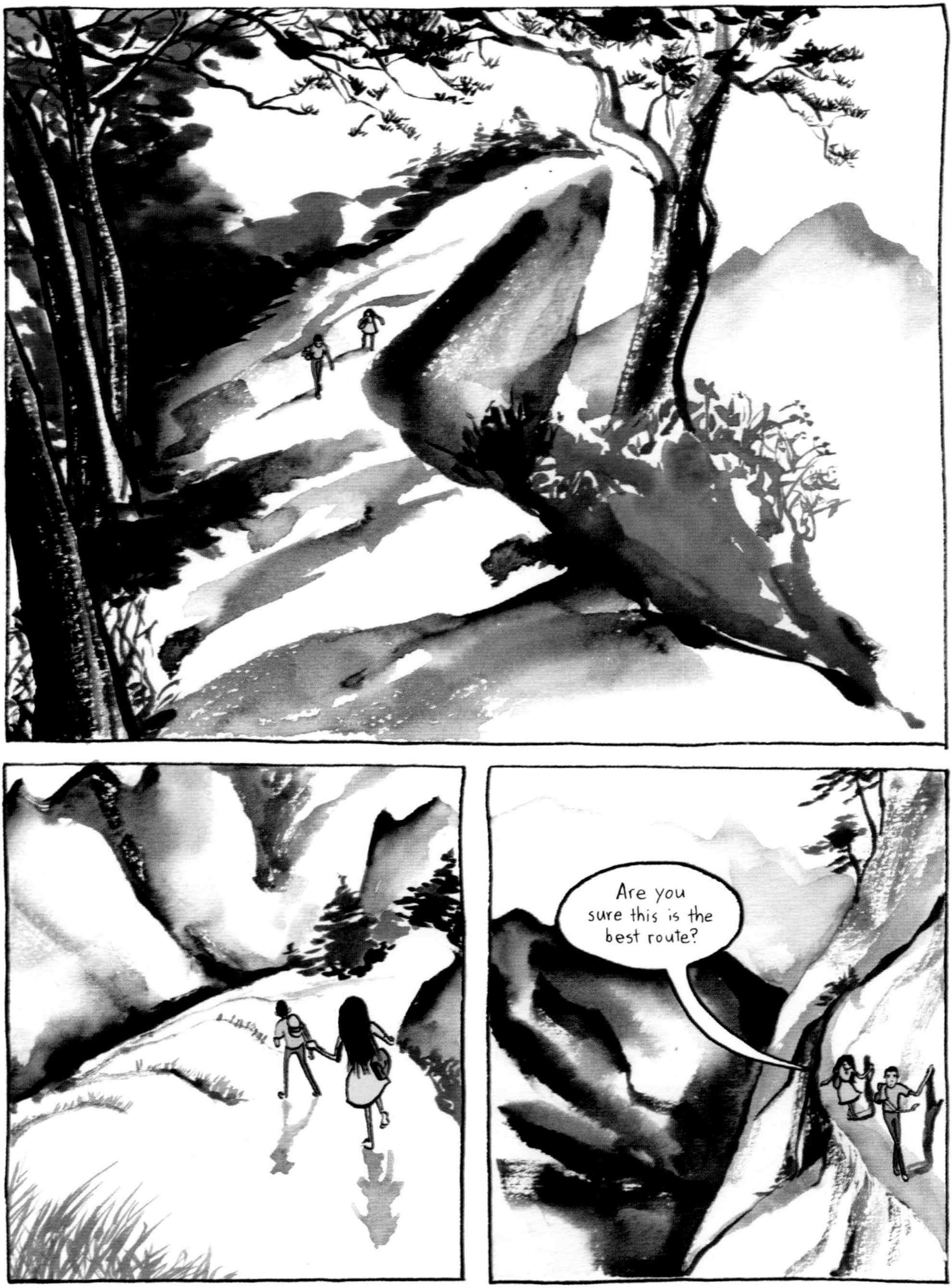
Are you sure this is the best route?

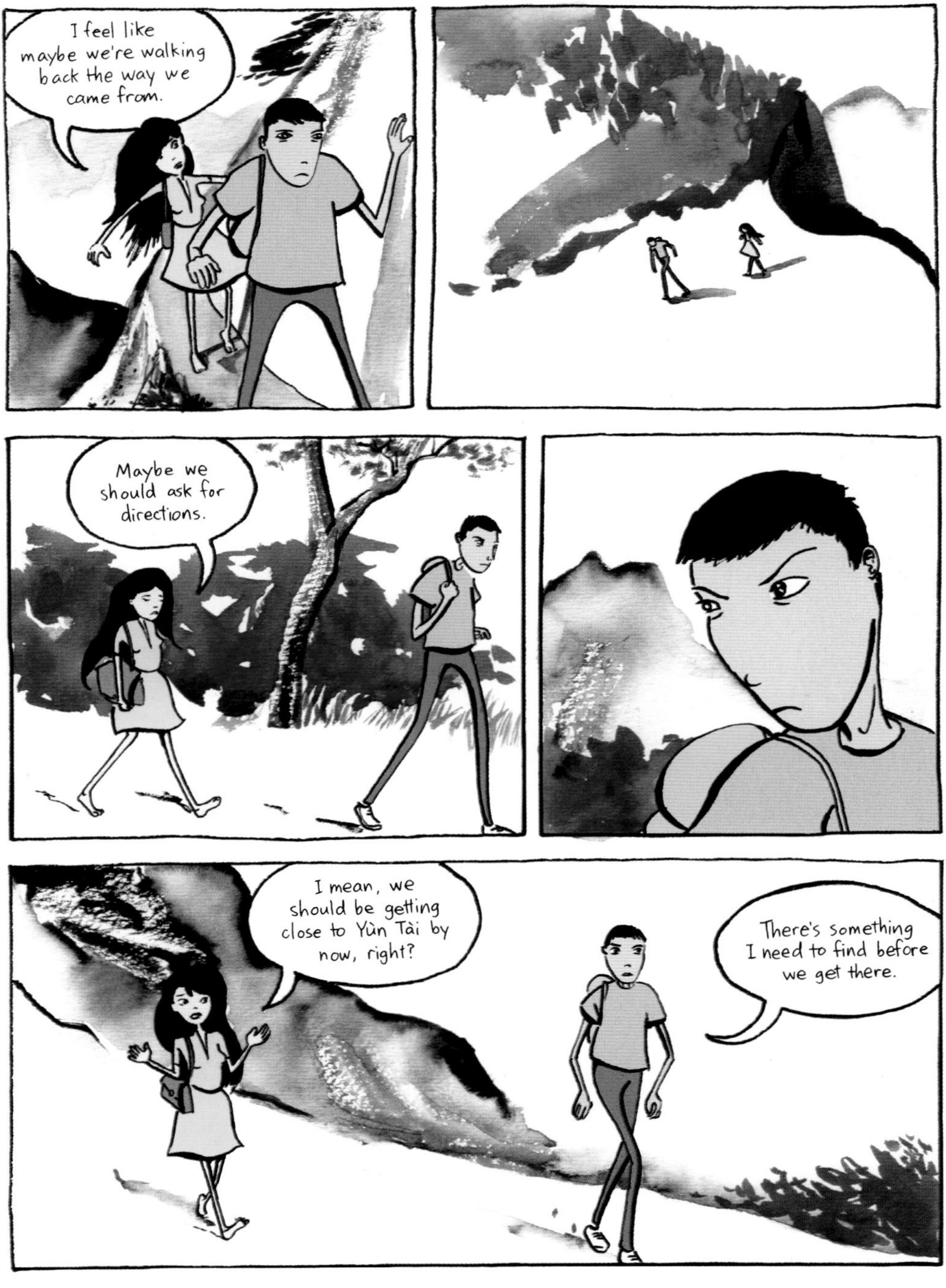
I feel like maybe we're walking back the way we came from.
Maybe we should ask for directions.
I mean, we should be getting close to Yùn Tài by now, right?
There's something I need to find before we get there.

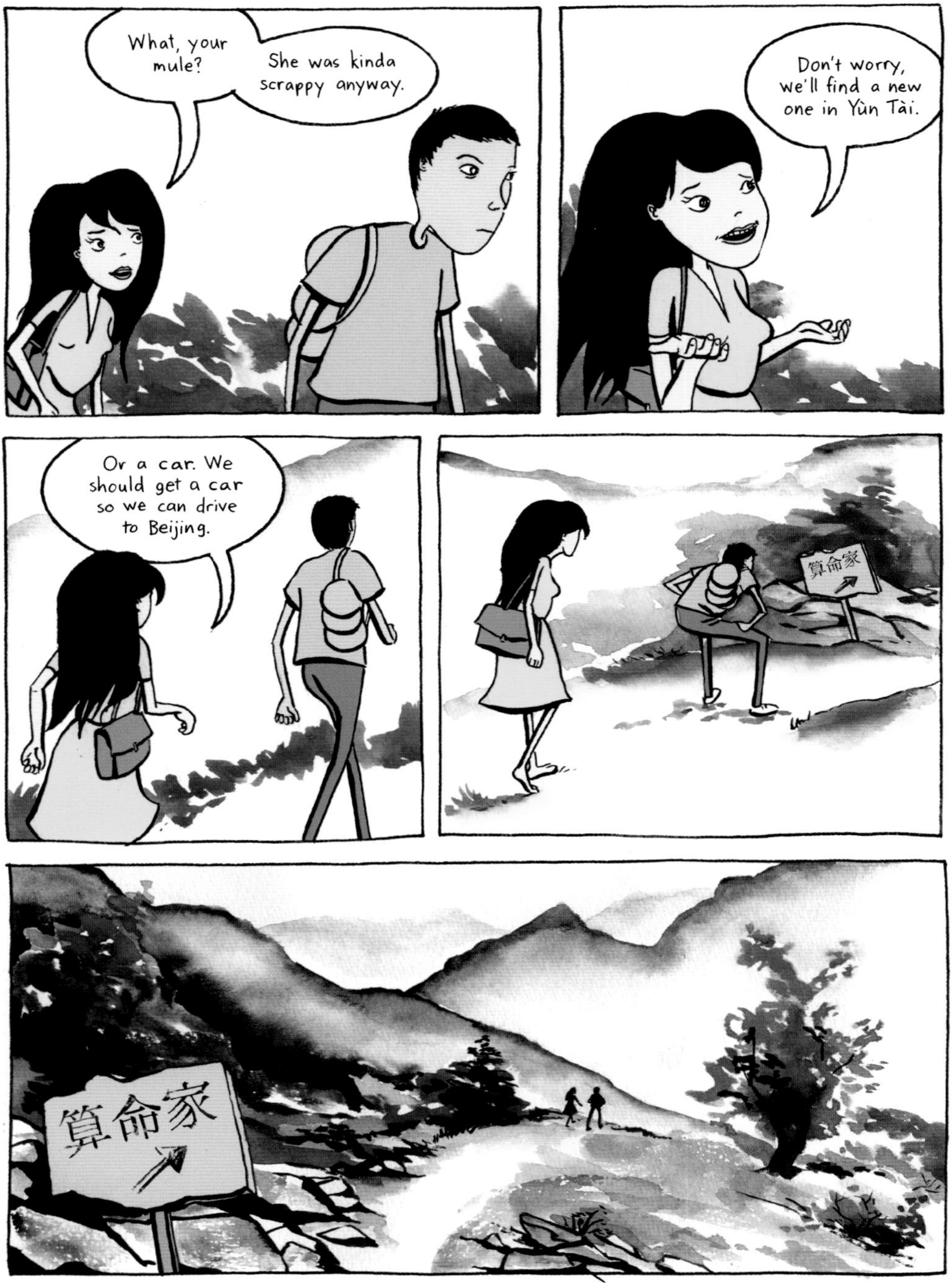
What, your mule?
She was kinda scrappy anyway.
Don't worry, we'll find a new one in Yùn Tài.
Or a car. We should get a car so we can drive to Beijing.
算命家
算命家

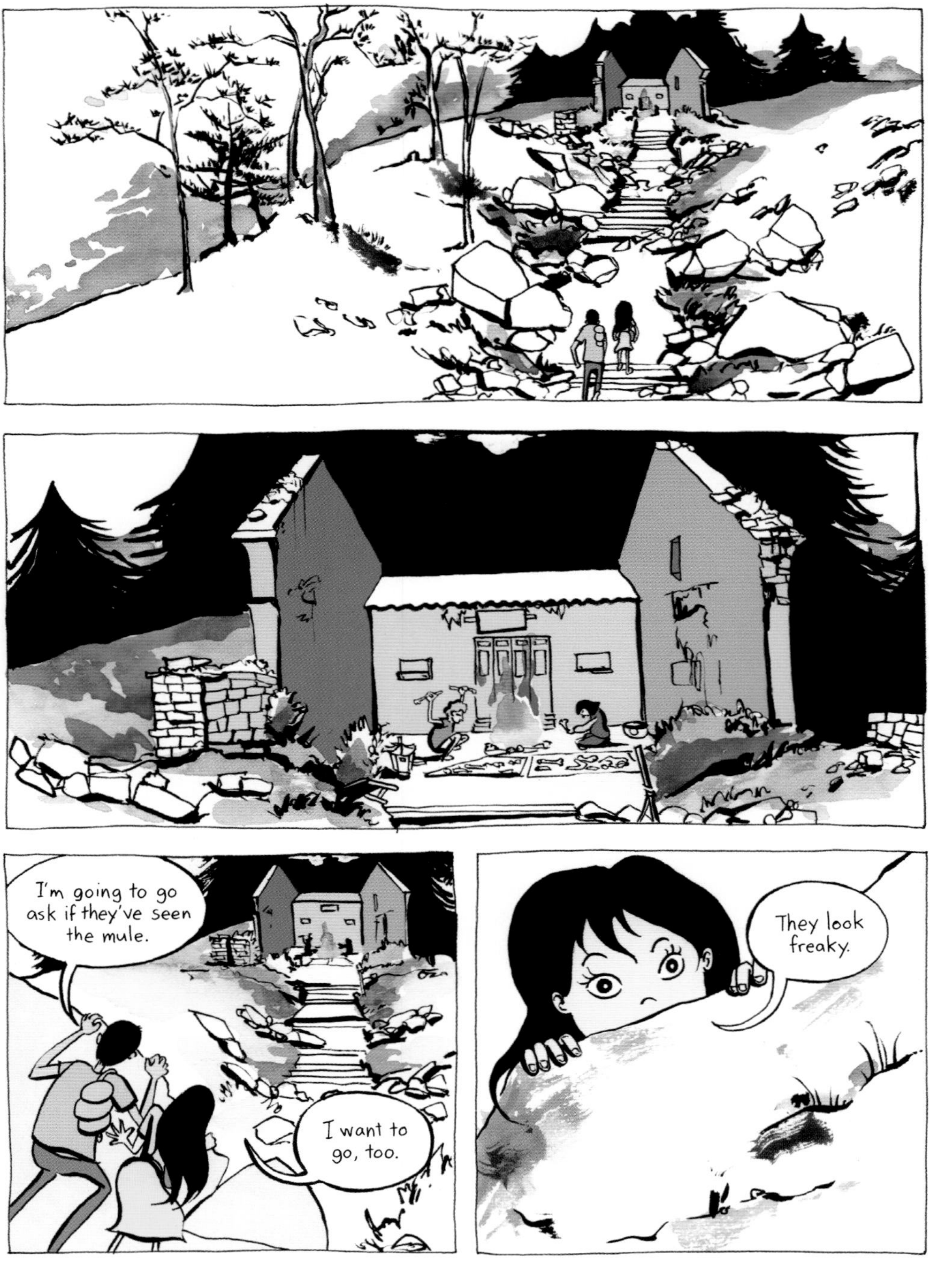
I'm going to go ask if they've seen the mule.
I want to go, too.
They look freaky.

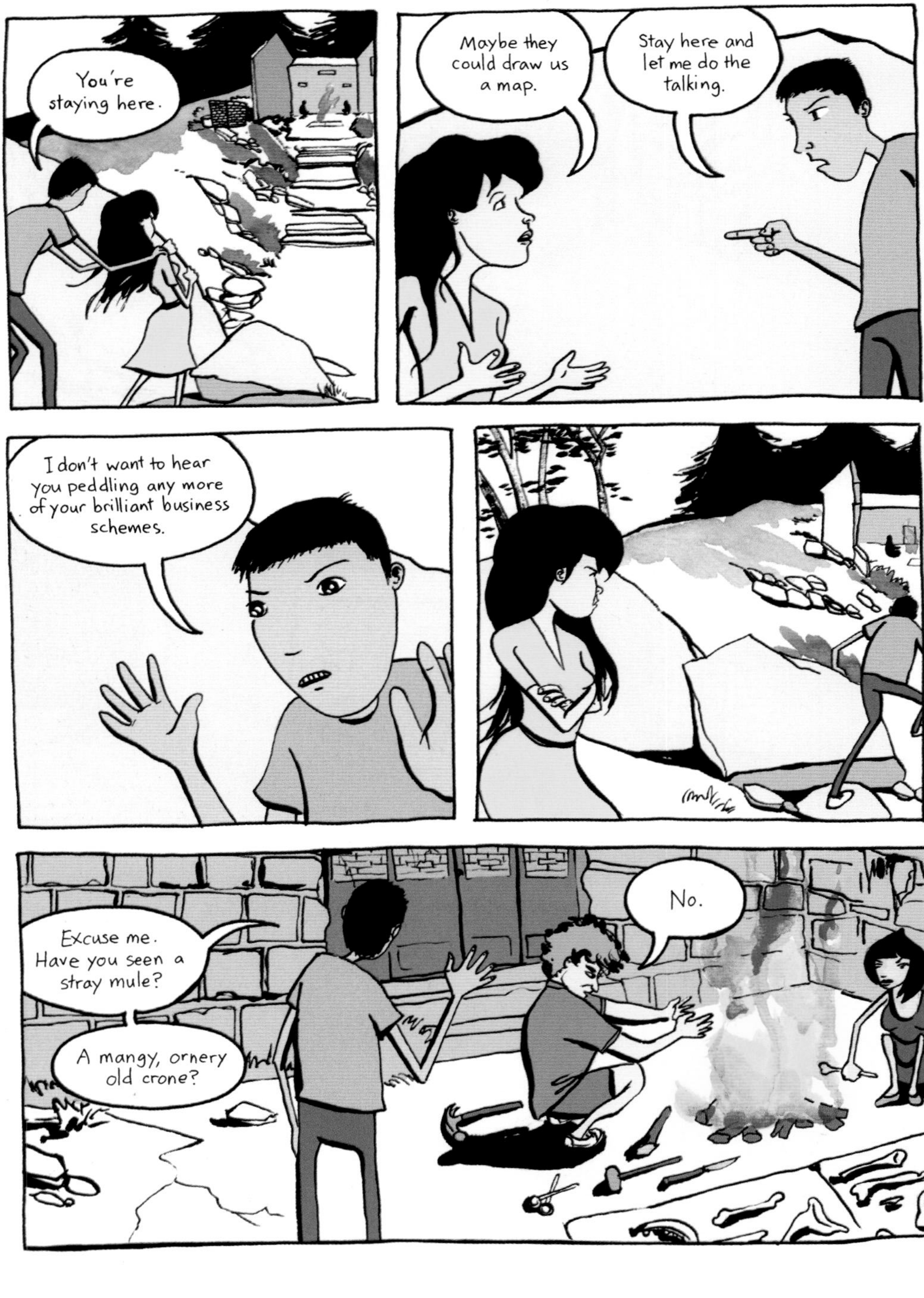
You're staying here.
Maybe they could draw us a map.
Stay here and let me do the talking.
I don't want to hear you peddling any more of your brilliant business schemes.
Excuse me. Have you seen a stray mule?
A mangy, ornery old crone?
No.

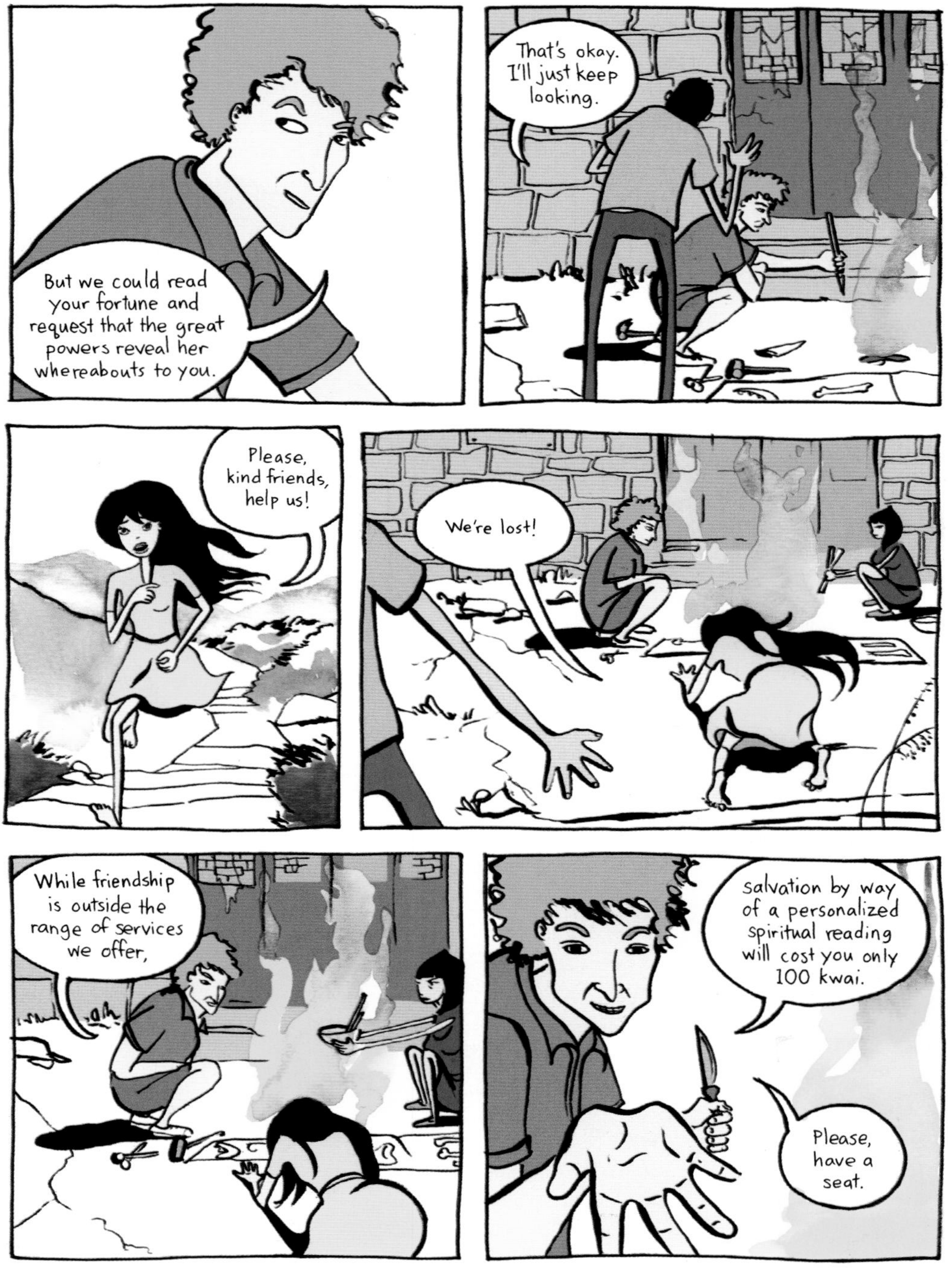
But we could read your fortune and request that the great powers reveal her whereabouts to you.
That's okay. I'll just keep looking.
Please, kind friends, help us!
We're lost!
While friendship is outside the range of services we offer,
salvation by way of a personalized spiritual reading will cost you only 100 kwai.
Please, have a seat.

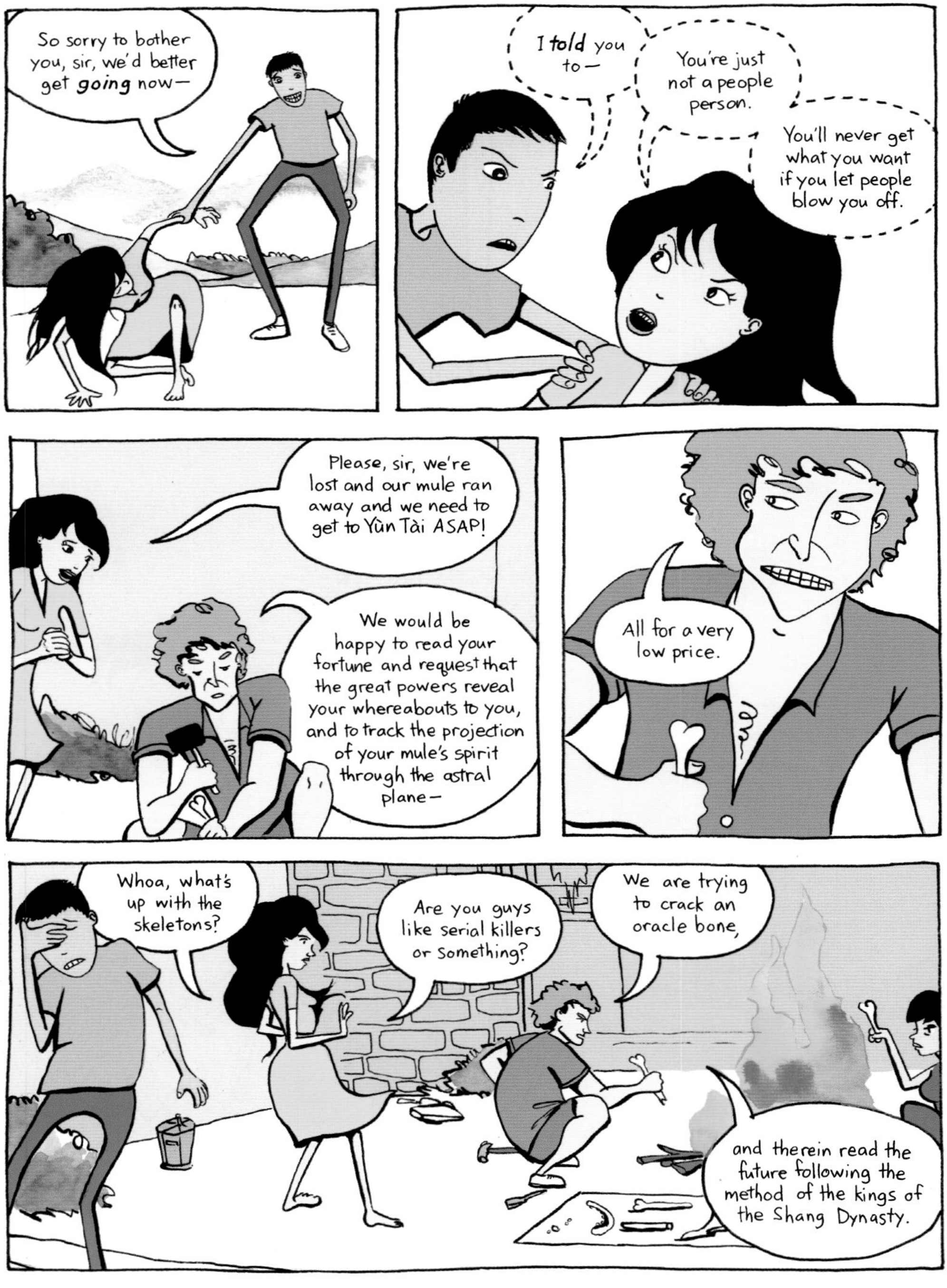

So sorry to bother you, sir, we'd better get *going* now—
I *told* you to—
You're just not a people person.
You'll never get what you want if you let people blow you off.
Please, sir, we're lost and our mule ran away and we need to get to Yùn Tài ASAP!
We would be happy to read your fortune and request that the great powers reveal your whereabouts to you, and to track the projection of your mule's spirit through the astral plane—
All for a very low price.
Whoa, what's up with the skeletons?
Are you guys like serial killers or something?
We are trying to crack an oracle bone,
and therein read the future following the method of the kings of the Shang Dynasty.

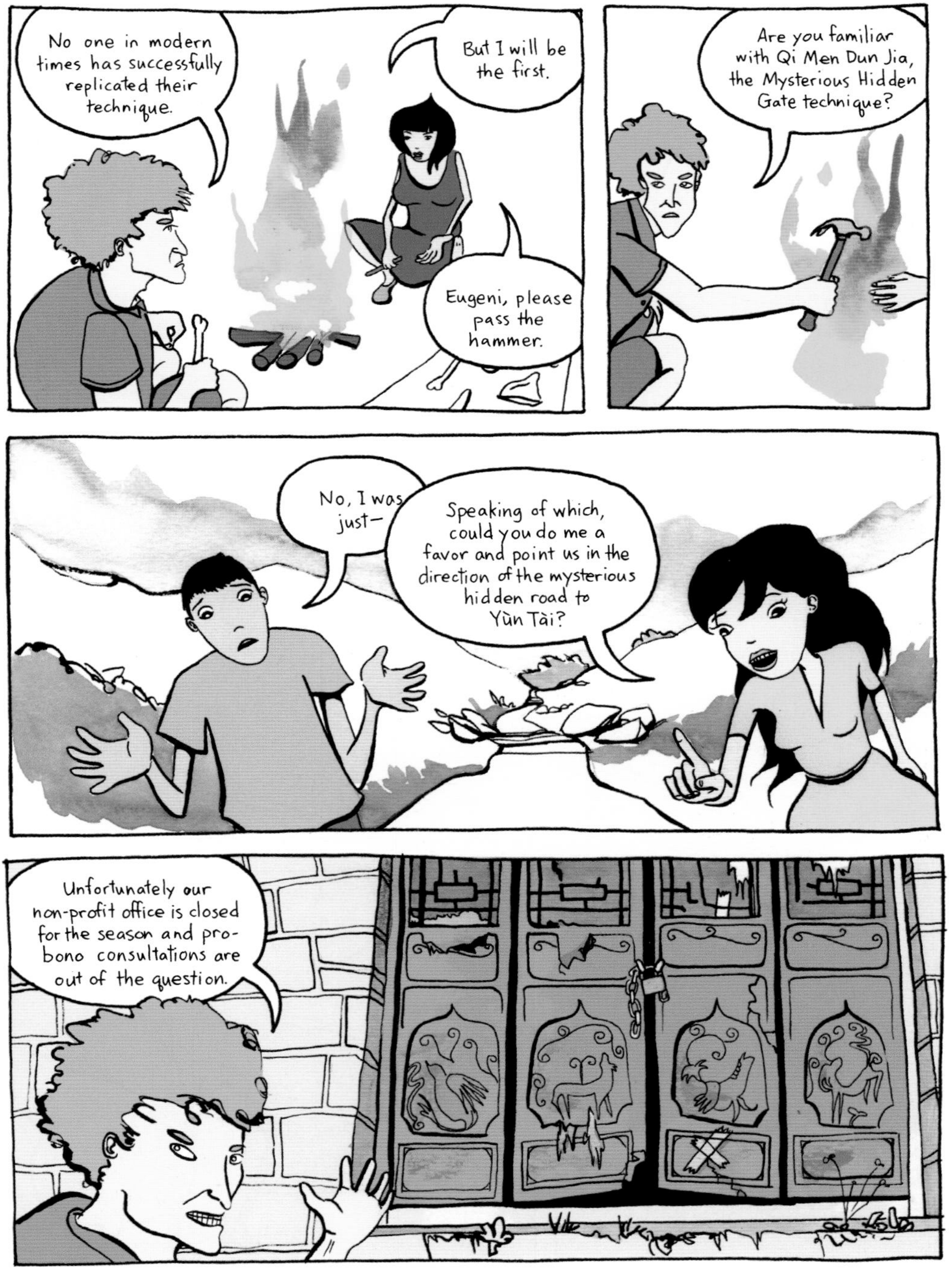
No one in modern times has successfully replicated their technique.
But I will be the first.
Eugeni, please pass the hammer.
Are you familiar with Qi Men Dun Jia, the Mysterious Hidden Gate technique?
No, I was just—
Speaking of which, could you do me a favor and point us in the direction of the mysterious hidden road to Yùn Tái?
Unfortunately our non-profit office is closed for the season and pro-bono consultations are out of the question.

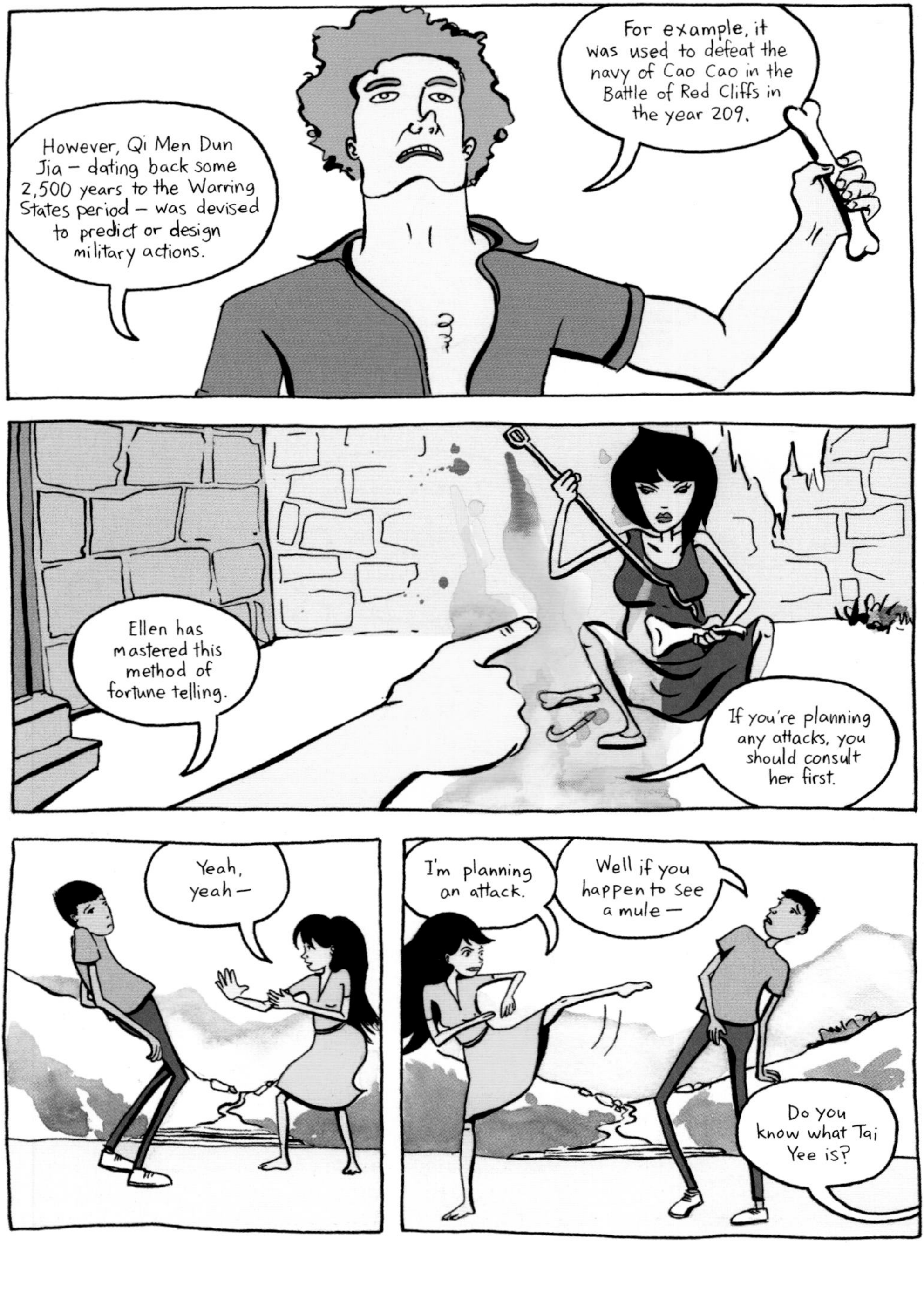
However, Qi Men Dun Jia – dating back some 2,500 years to the Warring States period – was devised to predict or design military actions.
For example, it was used to defeat the navy of Cao Cao in the Battle of Red Cliffs in the year 209.
Ellen has mastered this method of fortune telling.
If you're planning any attacks, you should consult her first.
Yeah, yeah –
I'm planning an attack.
Well if you happen to see a mule –
Do you know what Tai Yee is?

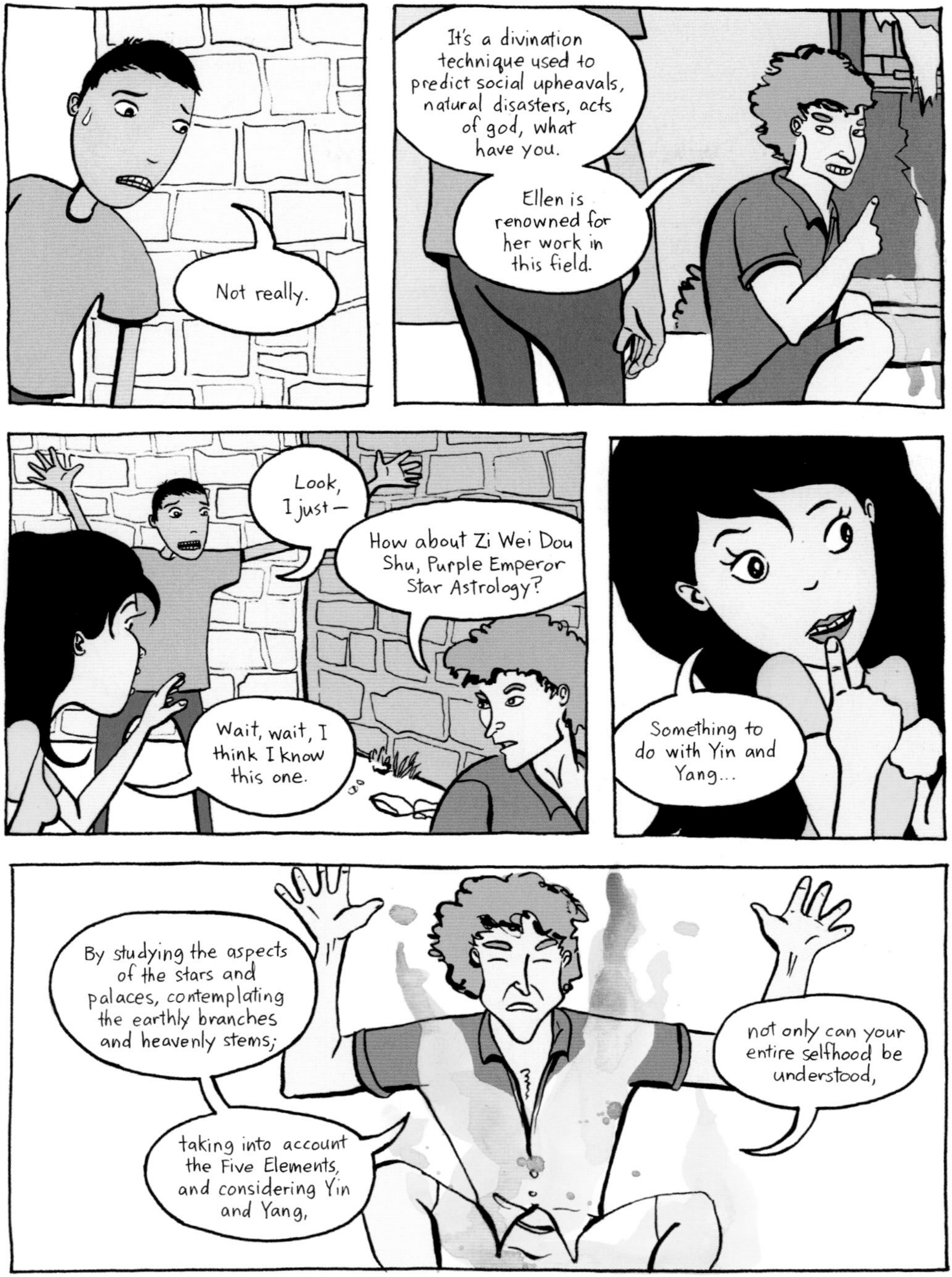
Not really.
It's a divination technique used to predict social upheavals, natural disasters, acts of god, what have you.
Ellen is renowned for her work in this field.
Look, I just—
How about Zi Wei Dou Shu, Purple Emperor Star Astrology?
Wait, wait, I think I know this one.
Something to do with Yin and Yang...
By studying the aspects of the stars and palaces, contemplating the earthly branches and heavenly stems;
taking into account the Five Elements, and considering Yin and Yang,
not only can your entire selfhood be understood,

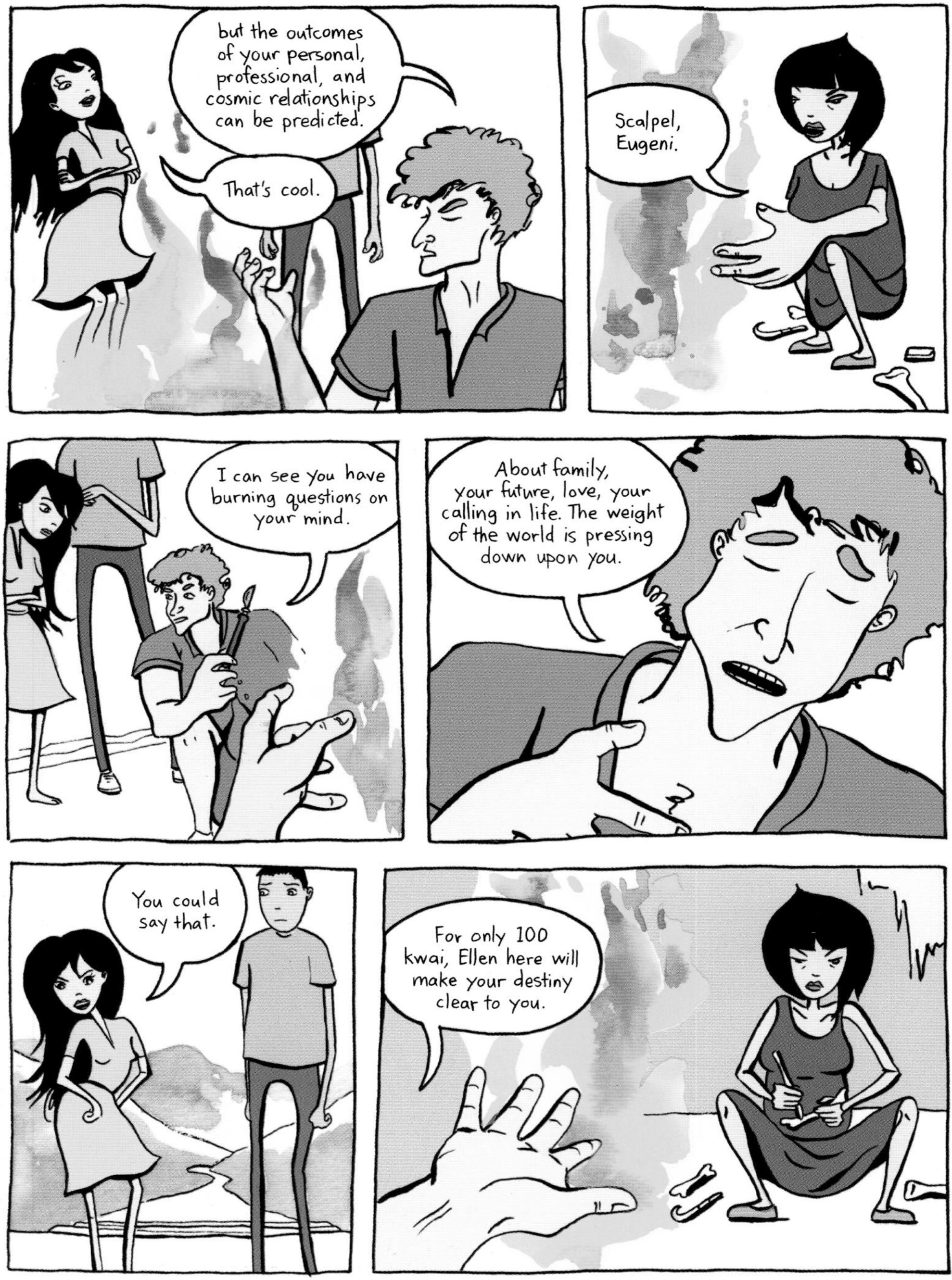
but the outcomes of your personal, professional, and cosmic relationships can be predicted.
That's cool.
Scalpel, Eugeni.
I can see you have burning questions on your mind.
About family, your future, love, your calling in life. The weight of the world is pressing down upon you.
You could say that.
For only 100 kwai, Ellen here will make your destiny clear to you.

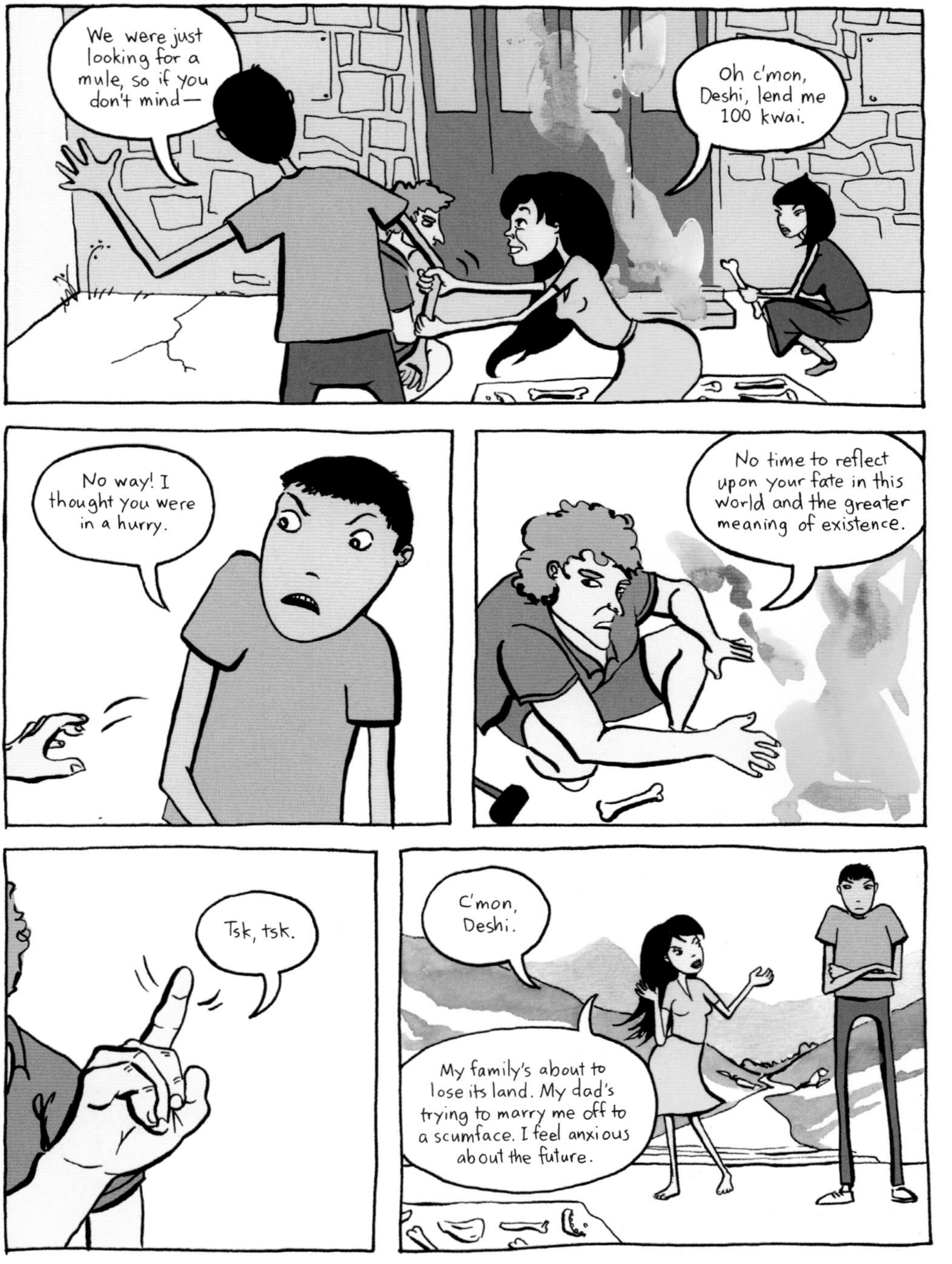
We were just looking for a mule, so if you don't mind—
Oh c'mon, Deshi, lend me 100 kwai.
No way! I thought you were in a hurry.
No time to reflect upon your fate in this world and the greater meaning of existence.
Tsk, tsk.
C'mon, Deshi.
My family's about to lose its land. My dad's trying to marry me off to a scumface. I feel anxious about the future.

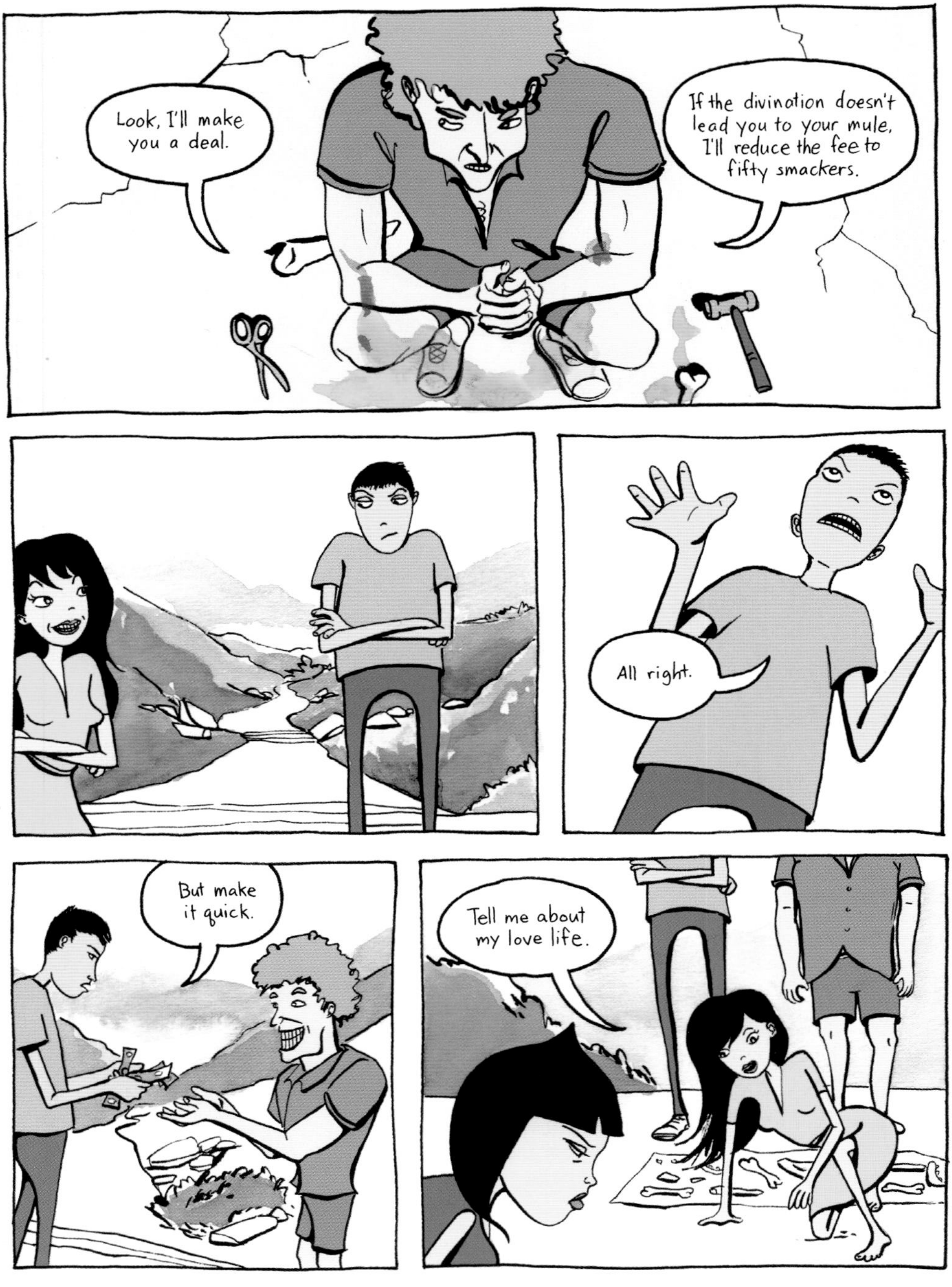
Look, I'll make you a deal.
If the divination doesn't lead you to your mule, I'll reduce the fee to fifty smackers.
All right.
But make it quick.
Tell me about my love life.

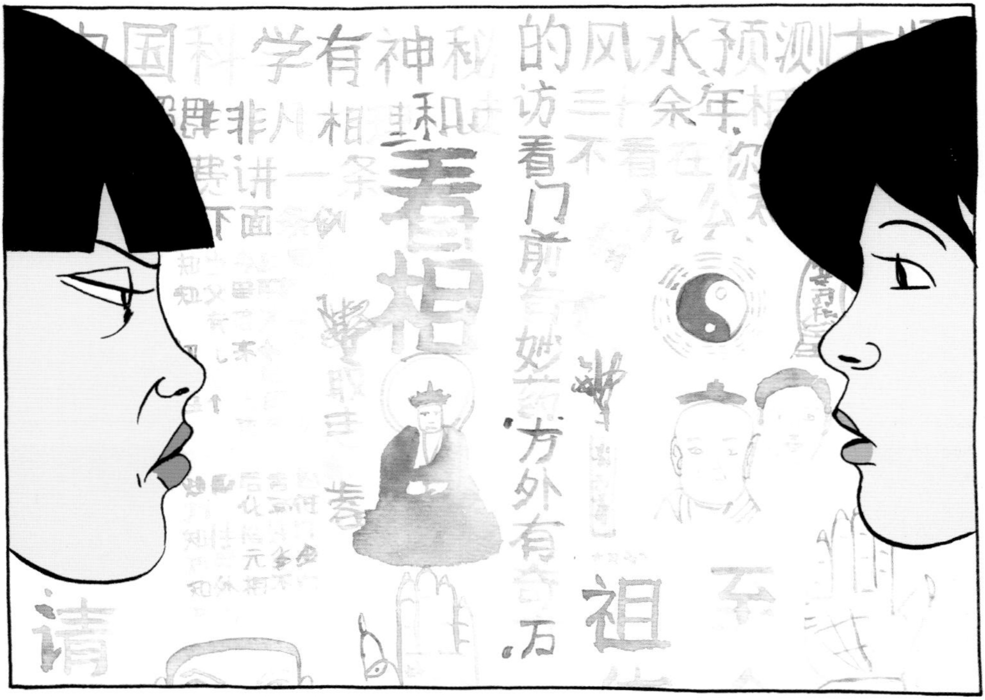
国科学有神秘的风水预测
访看门前
三十余年
看相
方外有
请
祖

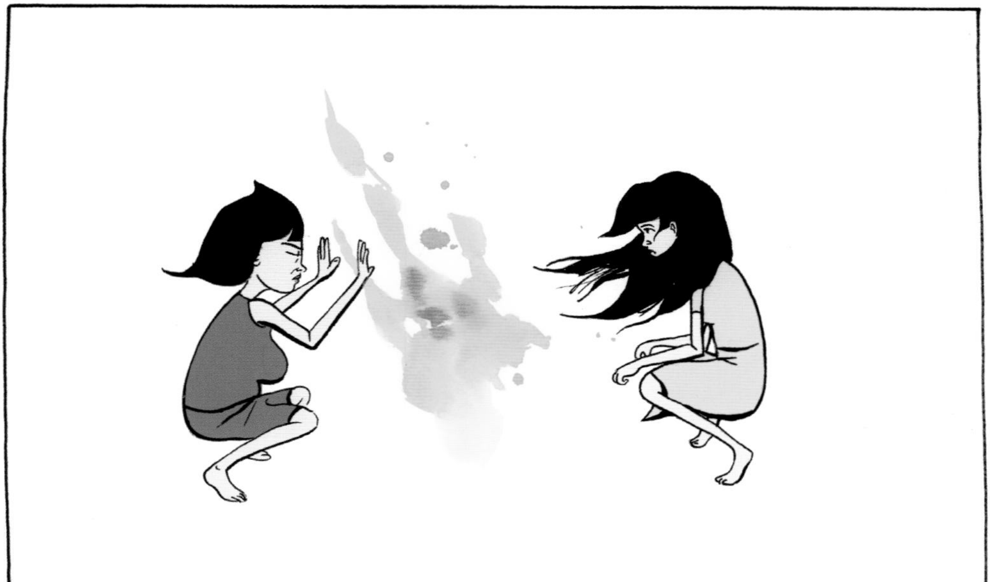

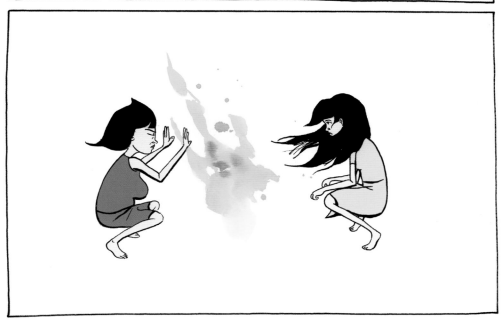

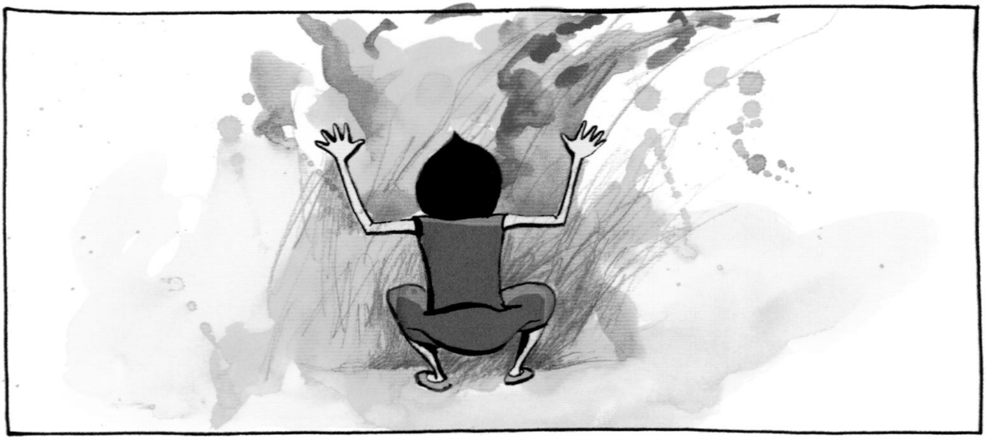

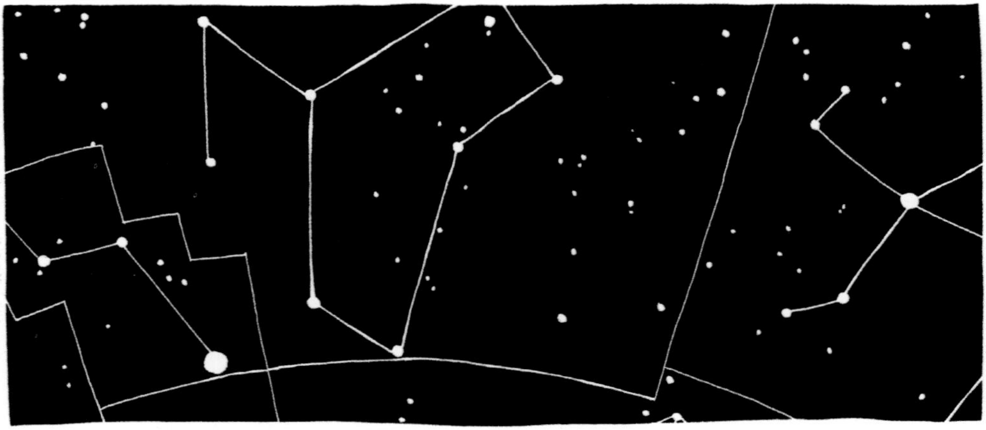

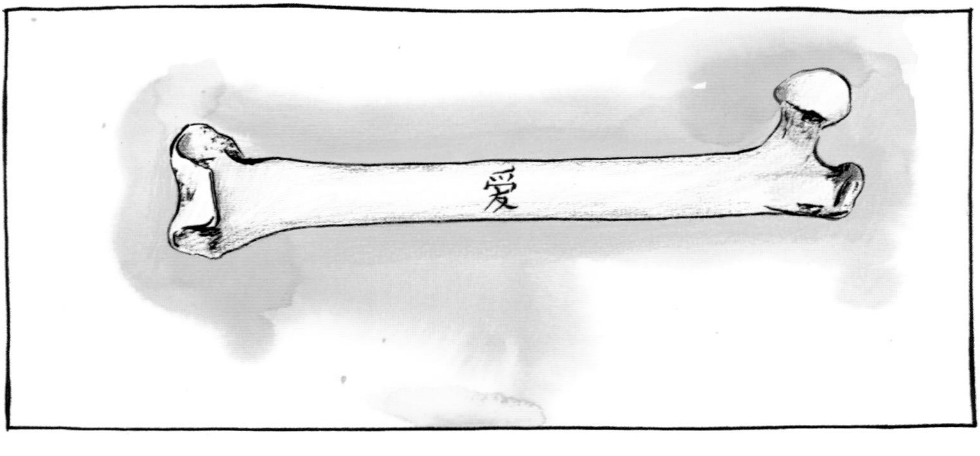
爱

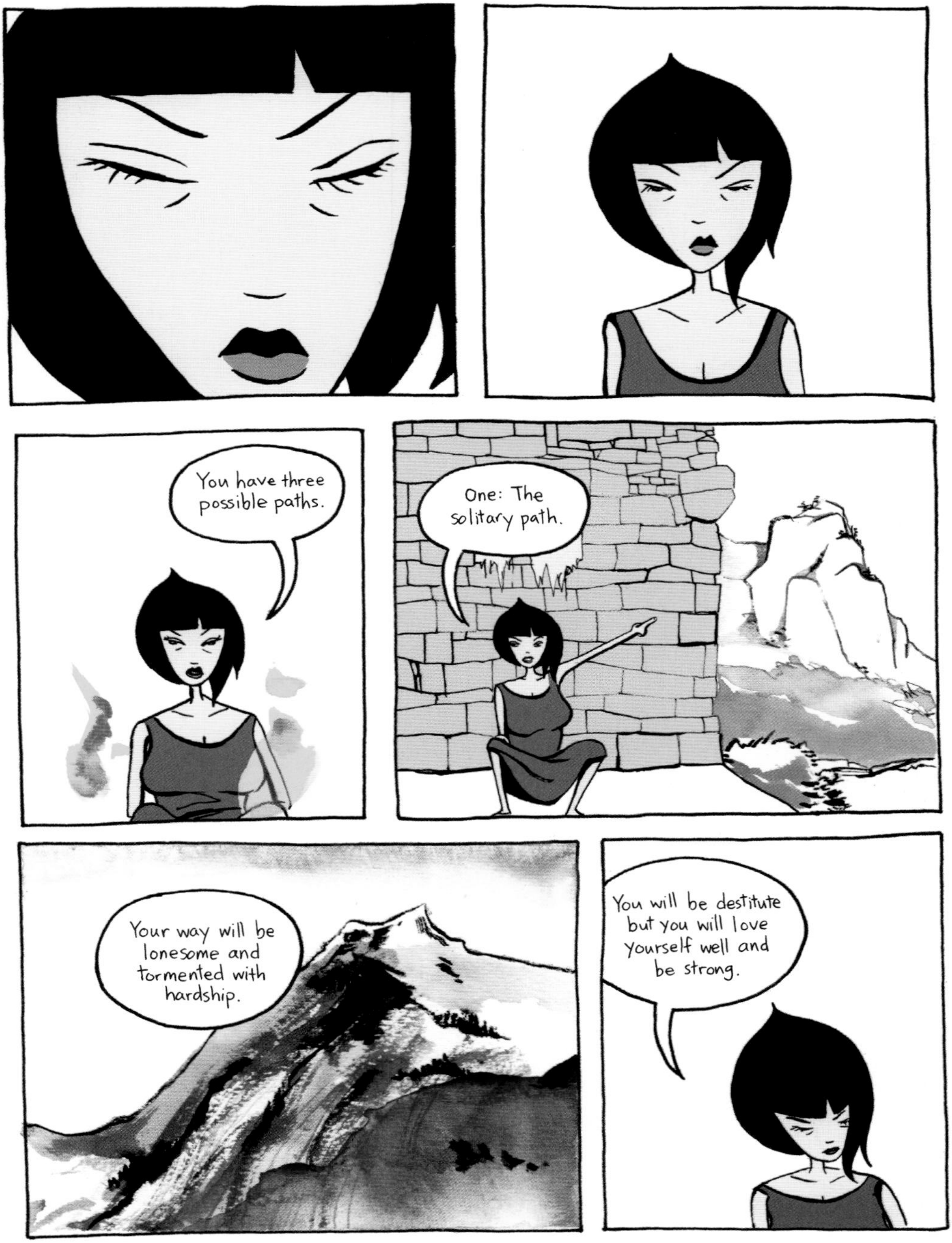
You have three possible paths.
One: The solitary path.
Your way will be lonesome and tormented with hardship.
You will be destitute but you will love yourself well and be strong.

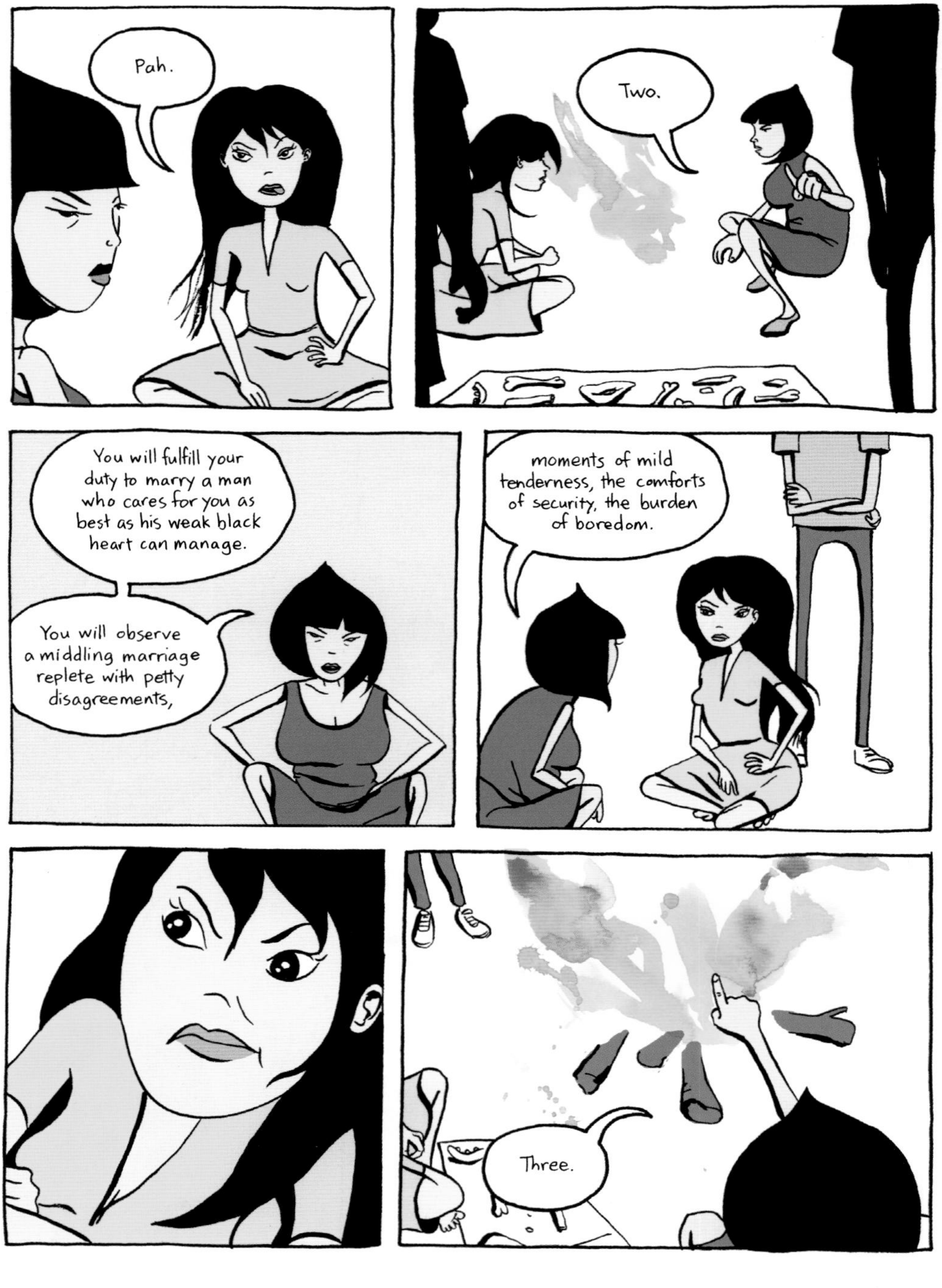
Pah.
Two.
You will fulfill your duty to marry a man who cares for you as best as his weak black heart can manage.
You will observe a middling marriage replete with petty disagreements,
moments of mild tenderness, the comforts of security, the burden of boredom.
Three.

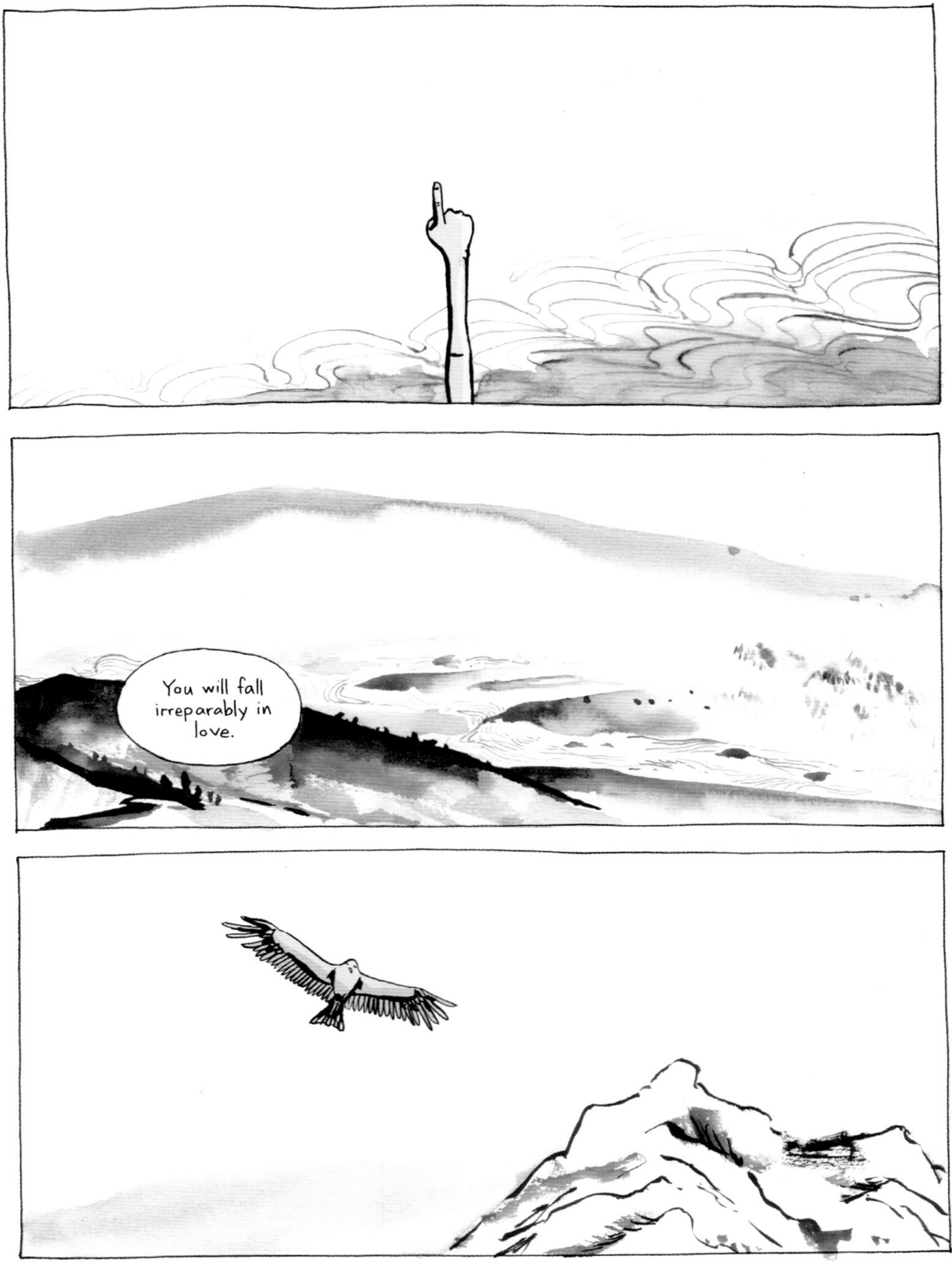
You will fall irreparably in love.

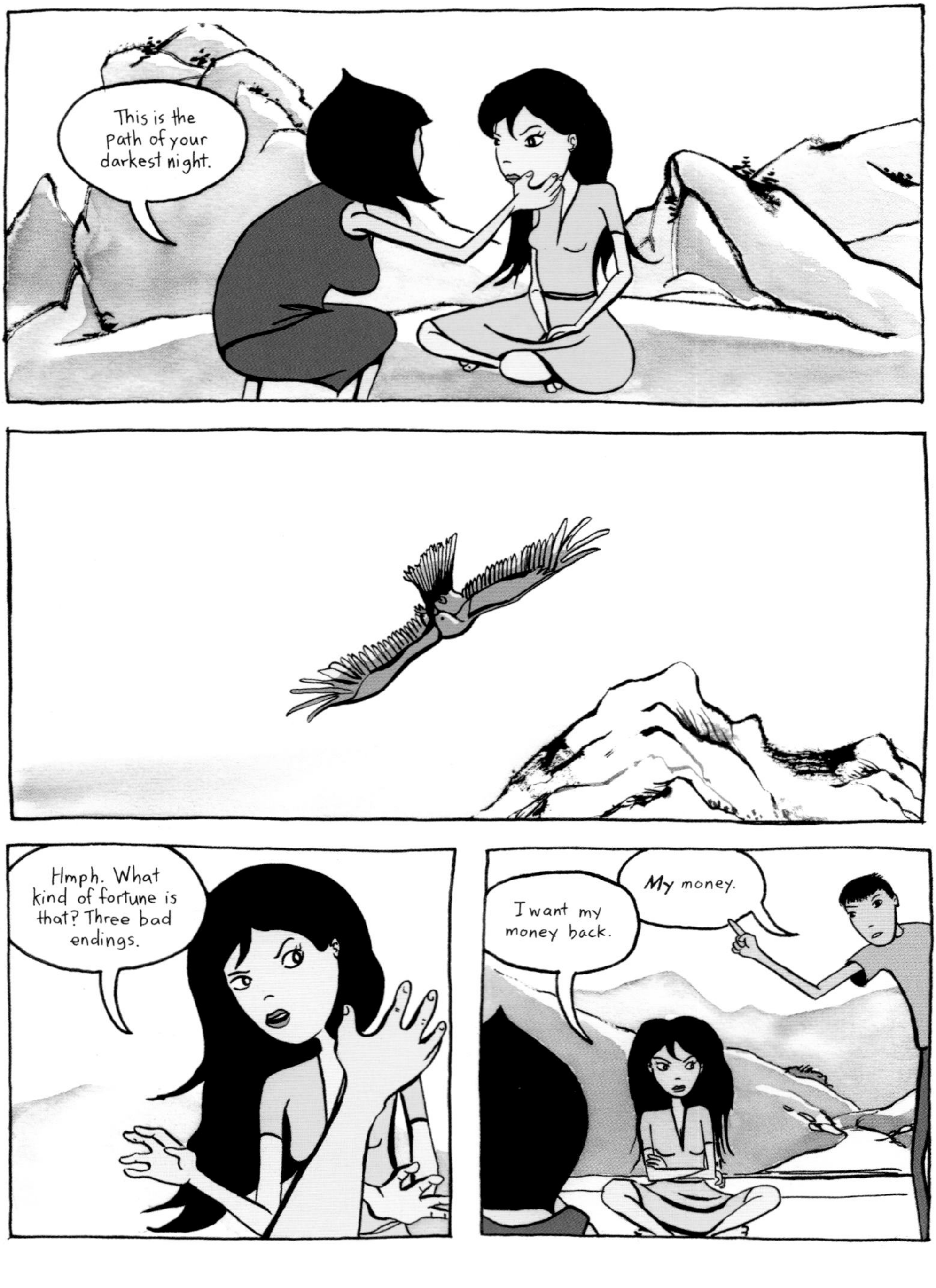
This is the path of your darkest night.
Hmph. What kind of fortune is that? Three bad endings.
I want my money back.
My money.

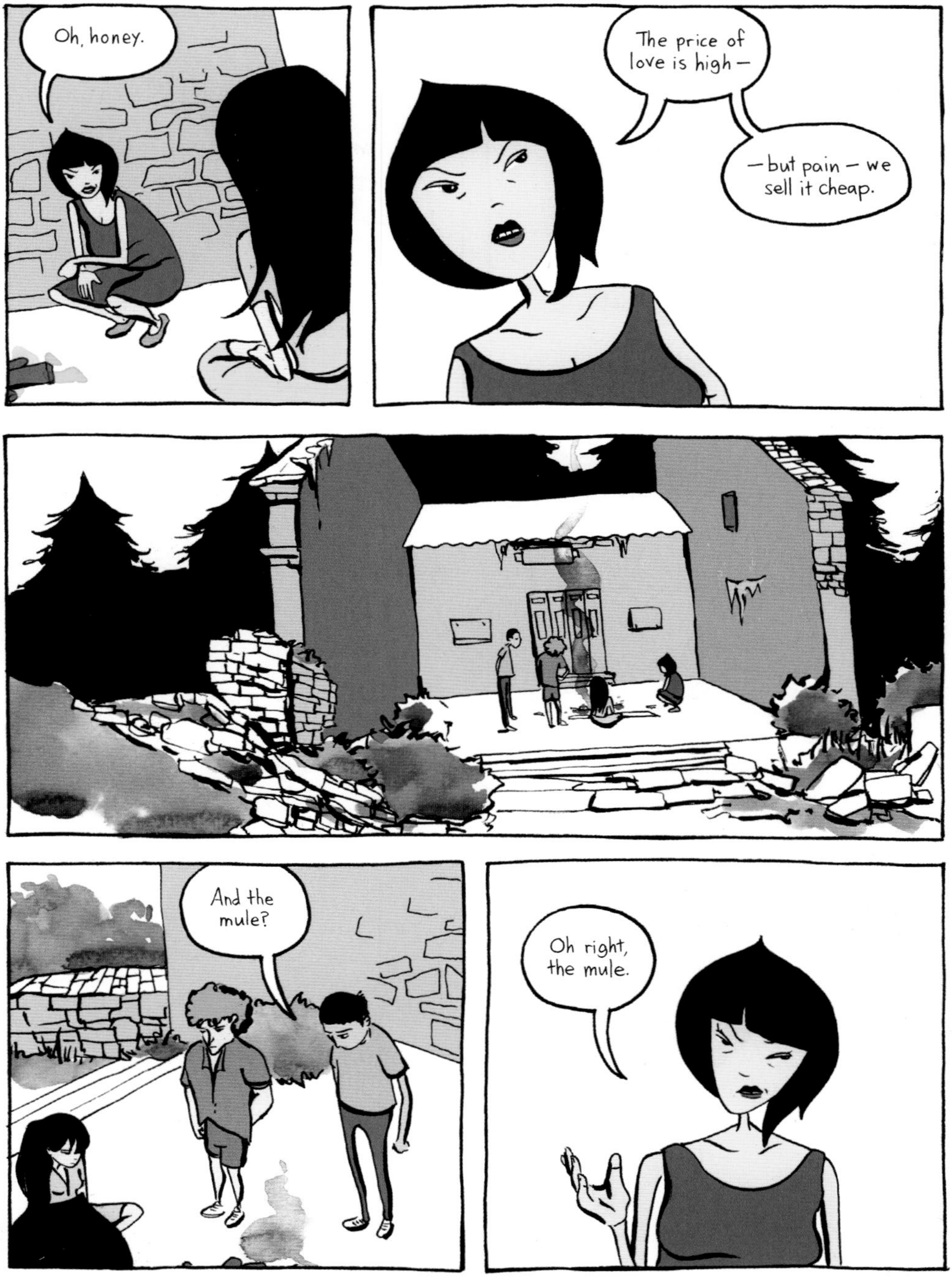

Oh, honey.
The price of love is high —
— but pain — we sell it cheap.
And the mule?
Oh right, the mule.

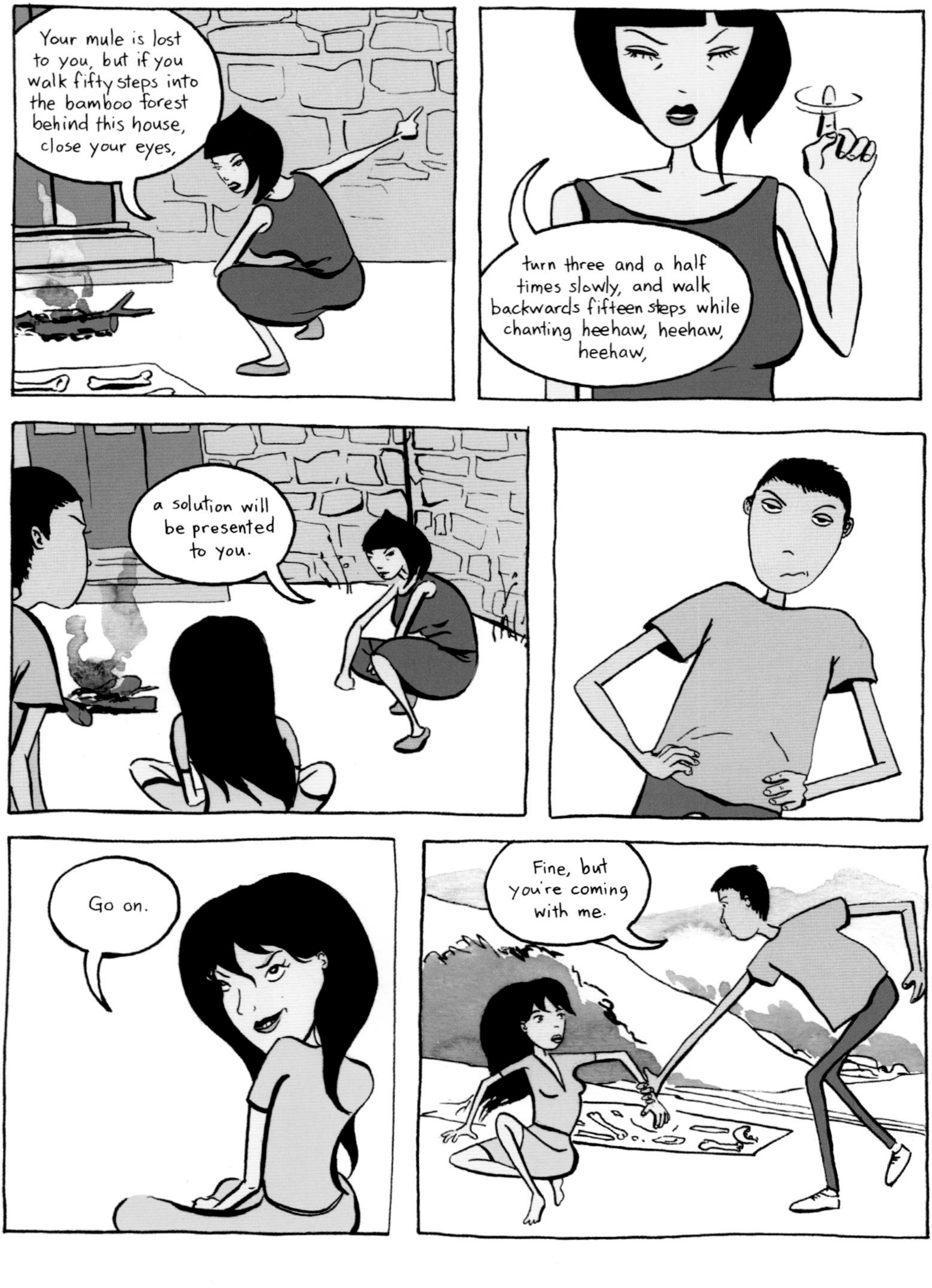
Your mule is lost to you, but if you walk fifty steps into the bamboo forest behind this house, close your eyes,
turn three and a half times slowly, and walk backwards fifteen steps while chanting heehaw, heehaw, heehaw,
a solution will be presented to you.
Go on.
Fine, but you're coming with me.

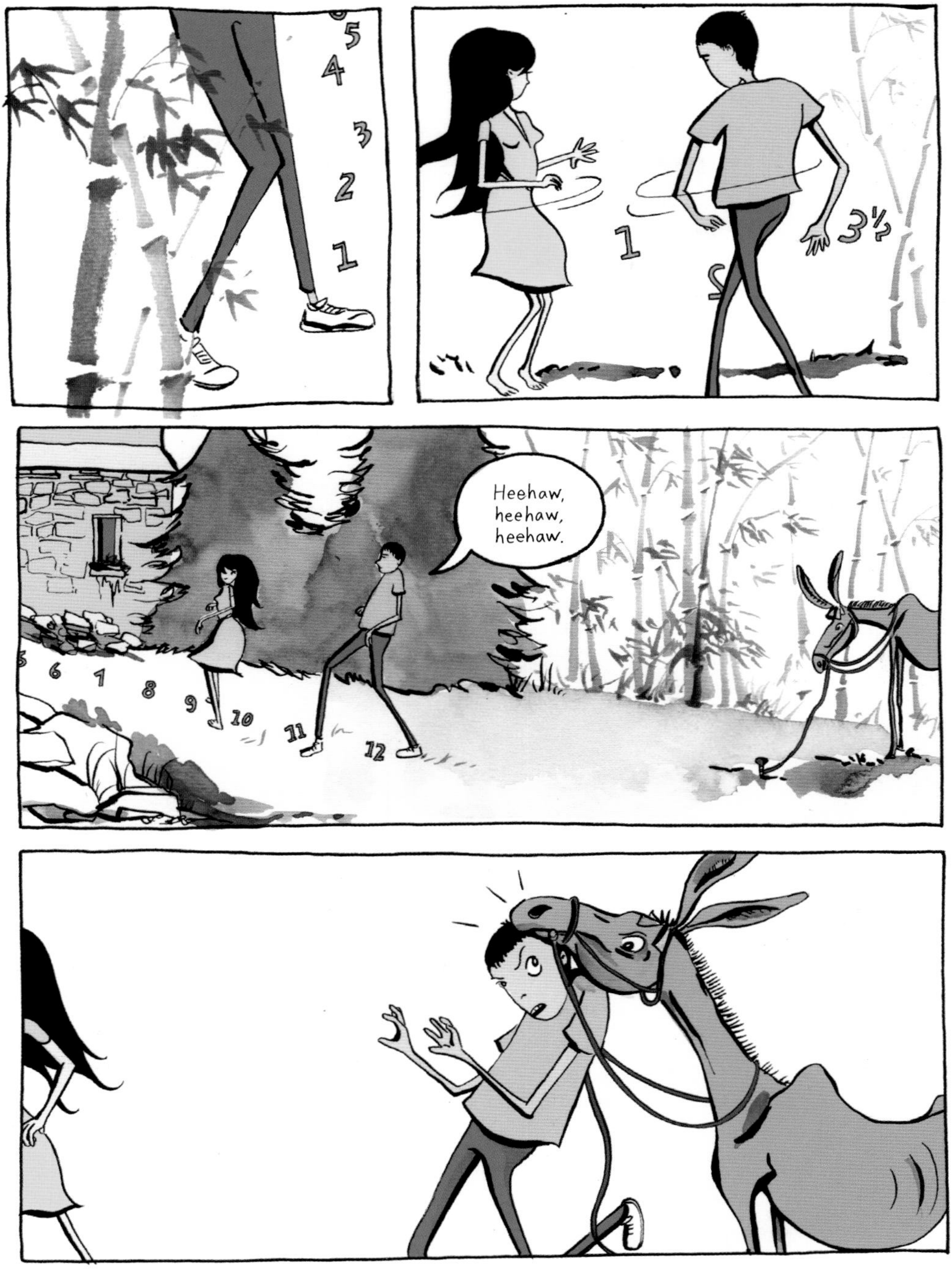
5
4
3
2
1
1
2
3½
Heehaw, heehaw, heehaw.
6
7
8
9
10
11
12

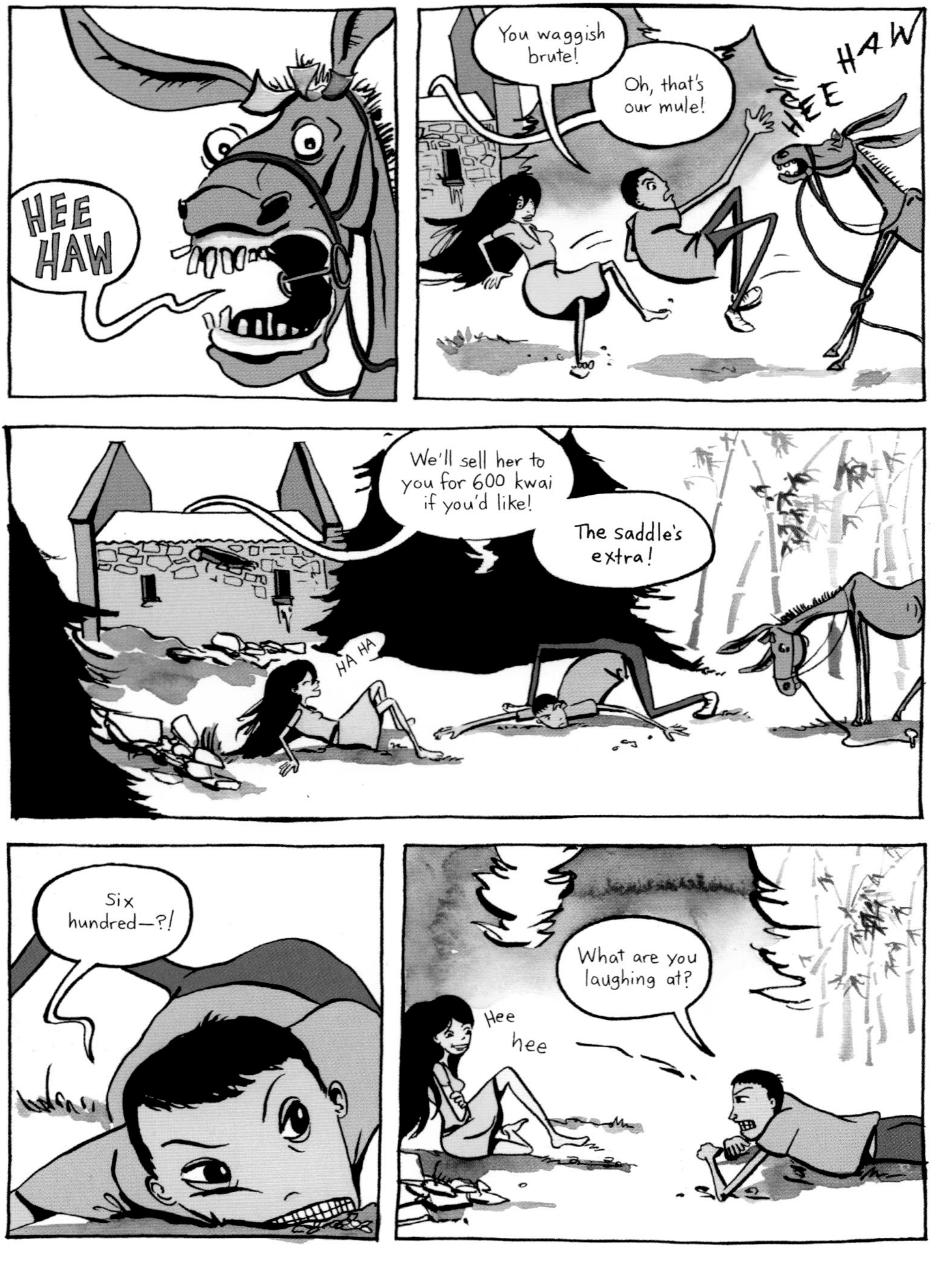
HEE HAW
You waggish brute!
Oh, that's our mule!
HEE HAW
We'll sell her to you for 600 kwai if you'd like!
The saddle's extra!
HA HA
Six hundred—?!
What are you laughing at?
Hee hee

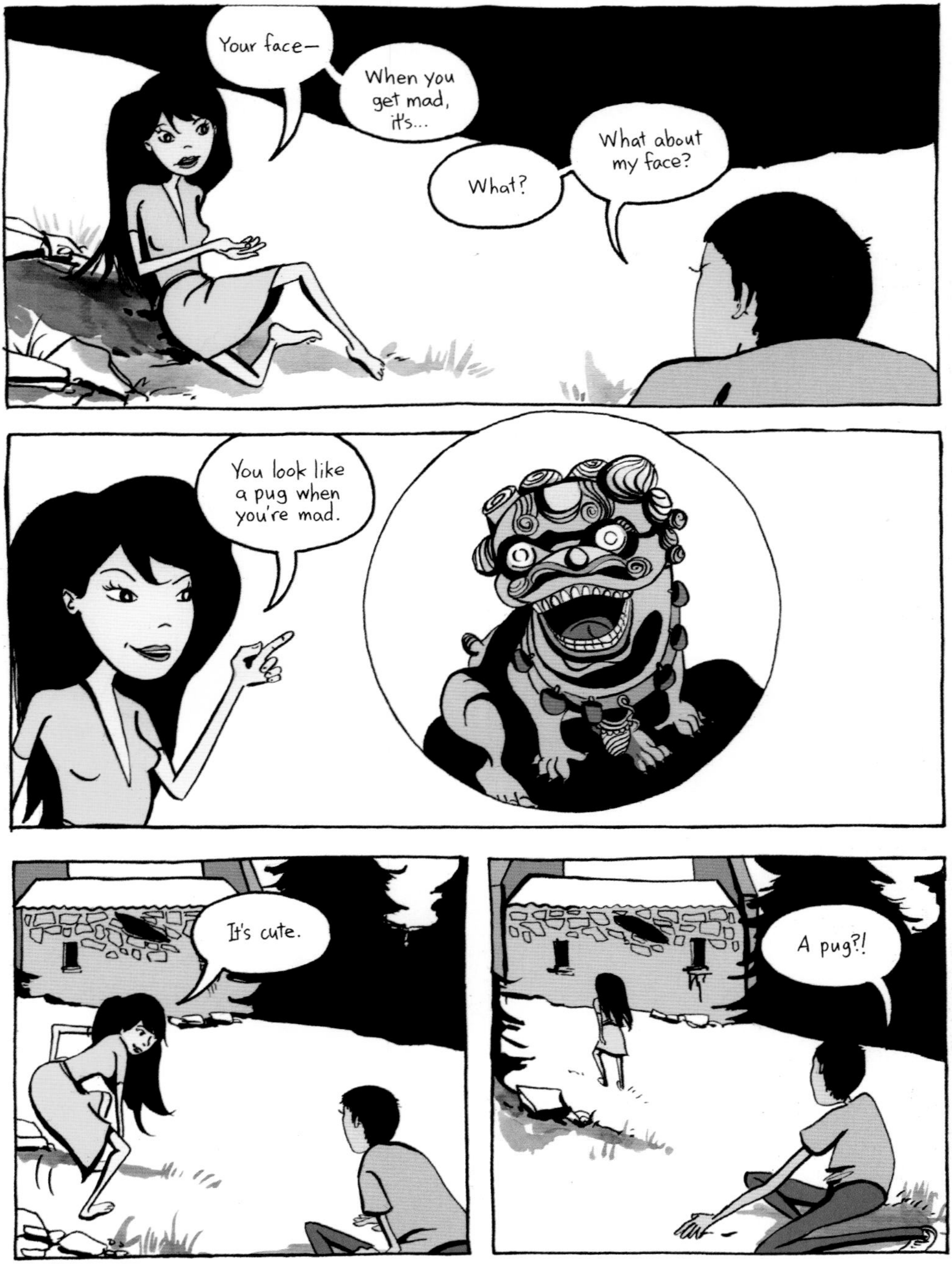
Your face—
When you get mad, it's...
What?
What about my face?
You look like a pug when you're mad.
It's cute.
A pug?!

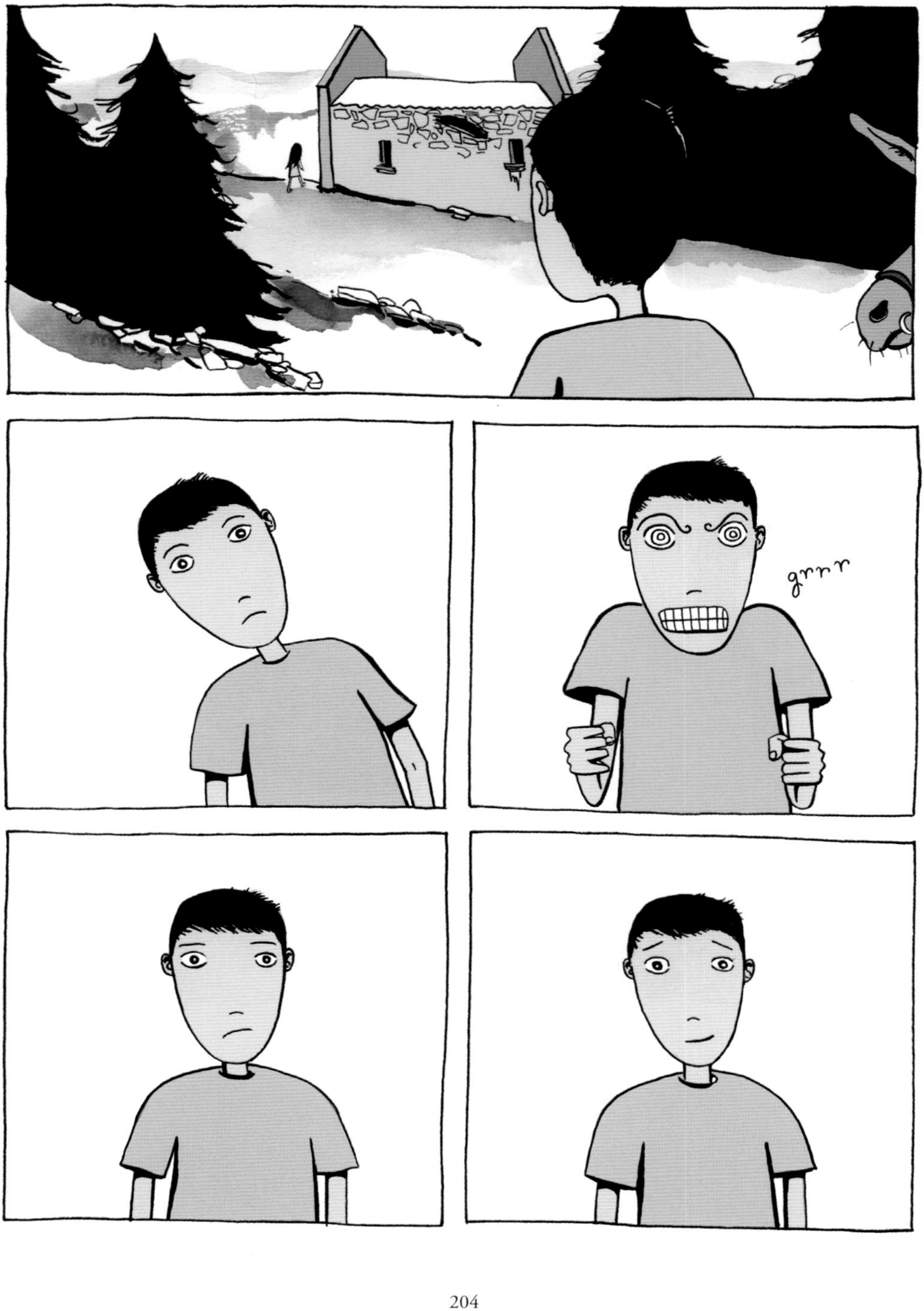
grrr

17. Cockroaches

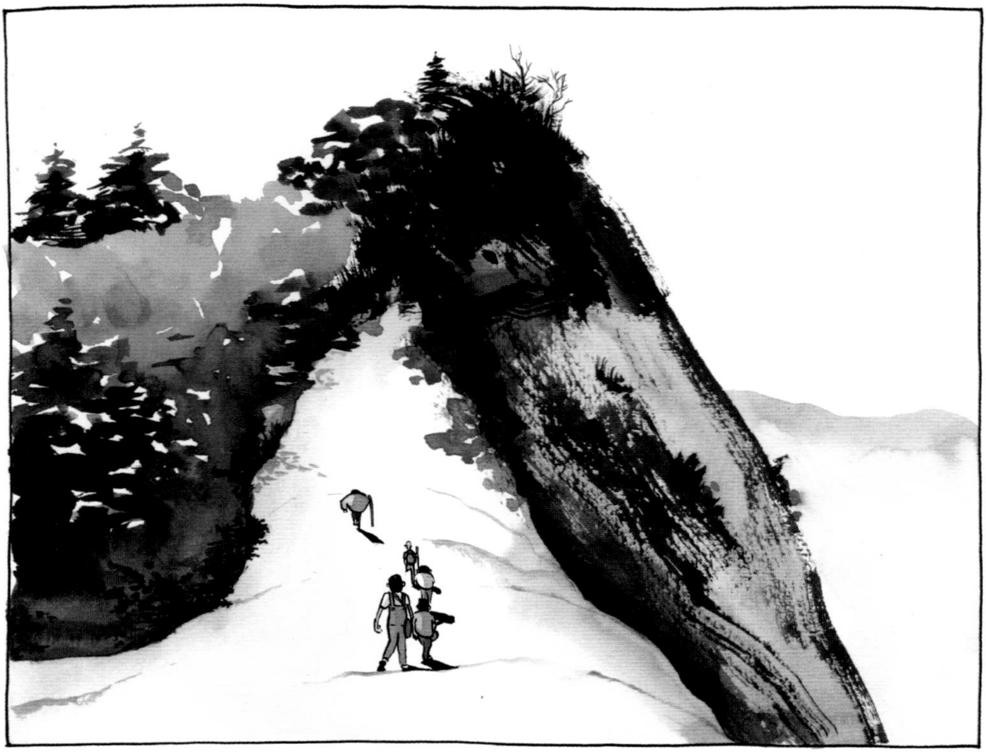

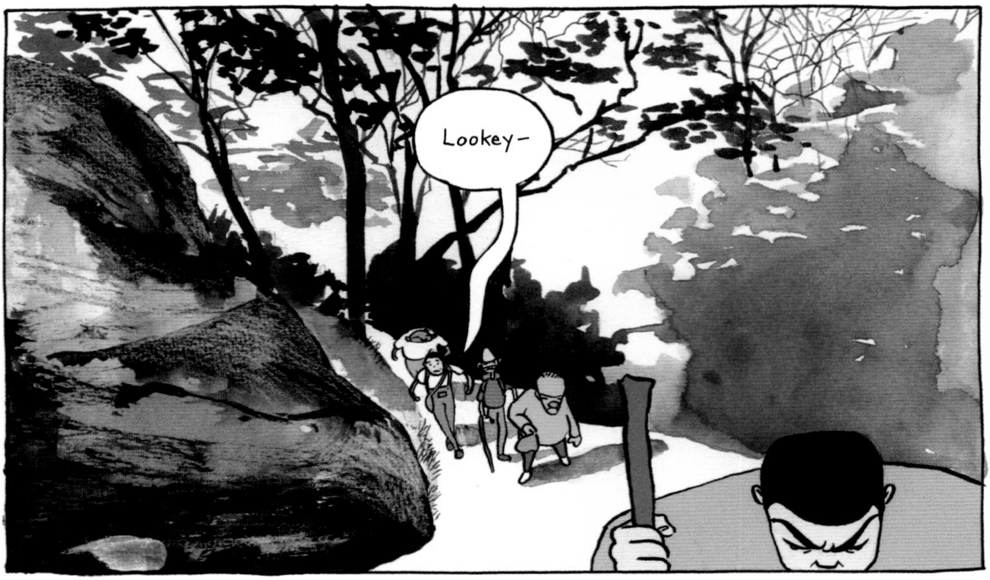
Lookey-

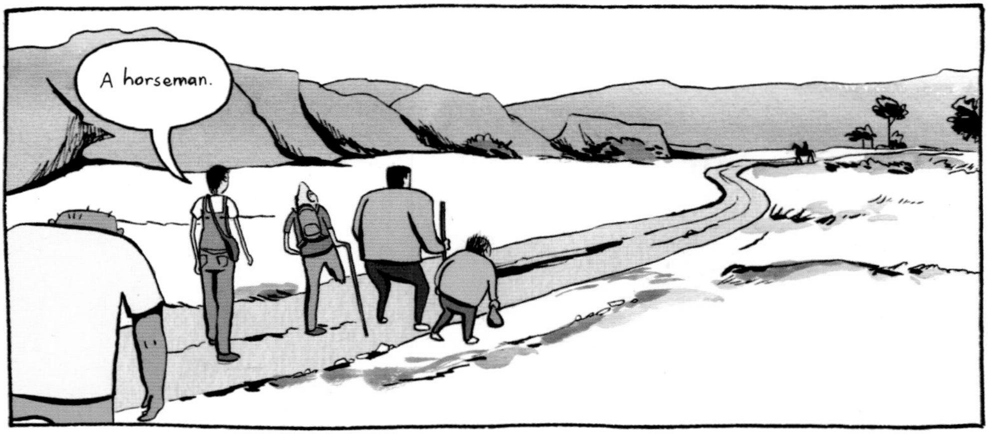
A horseman.

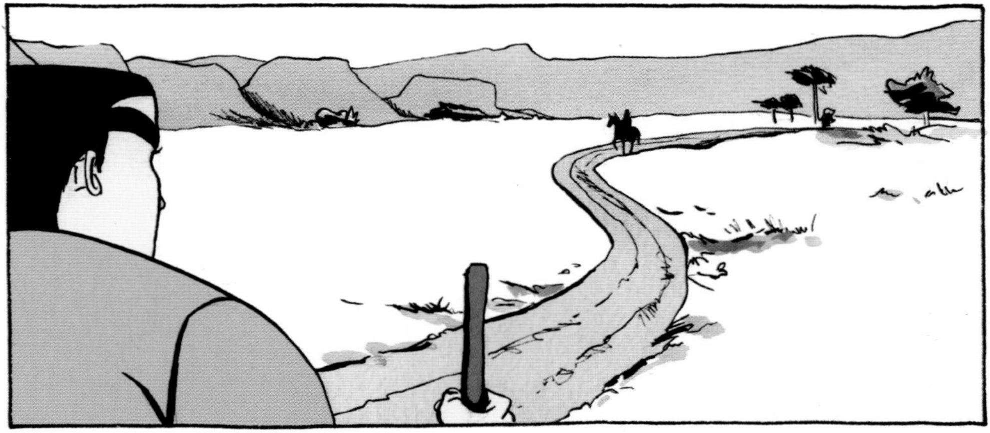

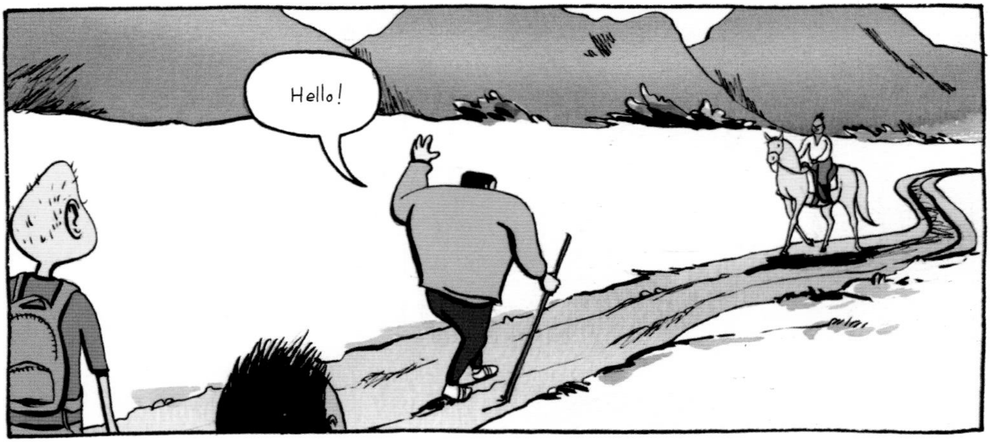
Hello!

I'm looking for my daughter. Have you seen a girl in trouble?

What kind of trouble?

Abducted, swiped by a fool, a son of a bitch with worms in his ears, a cockroach who will never see the pink light of morning.

A cockroach.

Worms, you're saying.

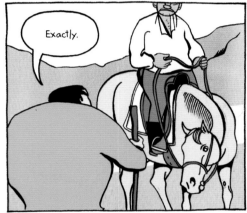

Exactly.

How do you know she was abducted?

Lotta kids run off to the city these days to work in the factories; lotta little bitches run off with their boyfriends—

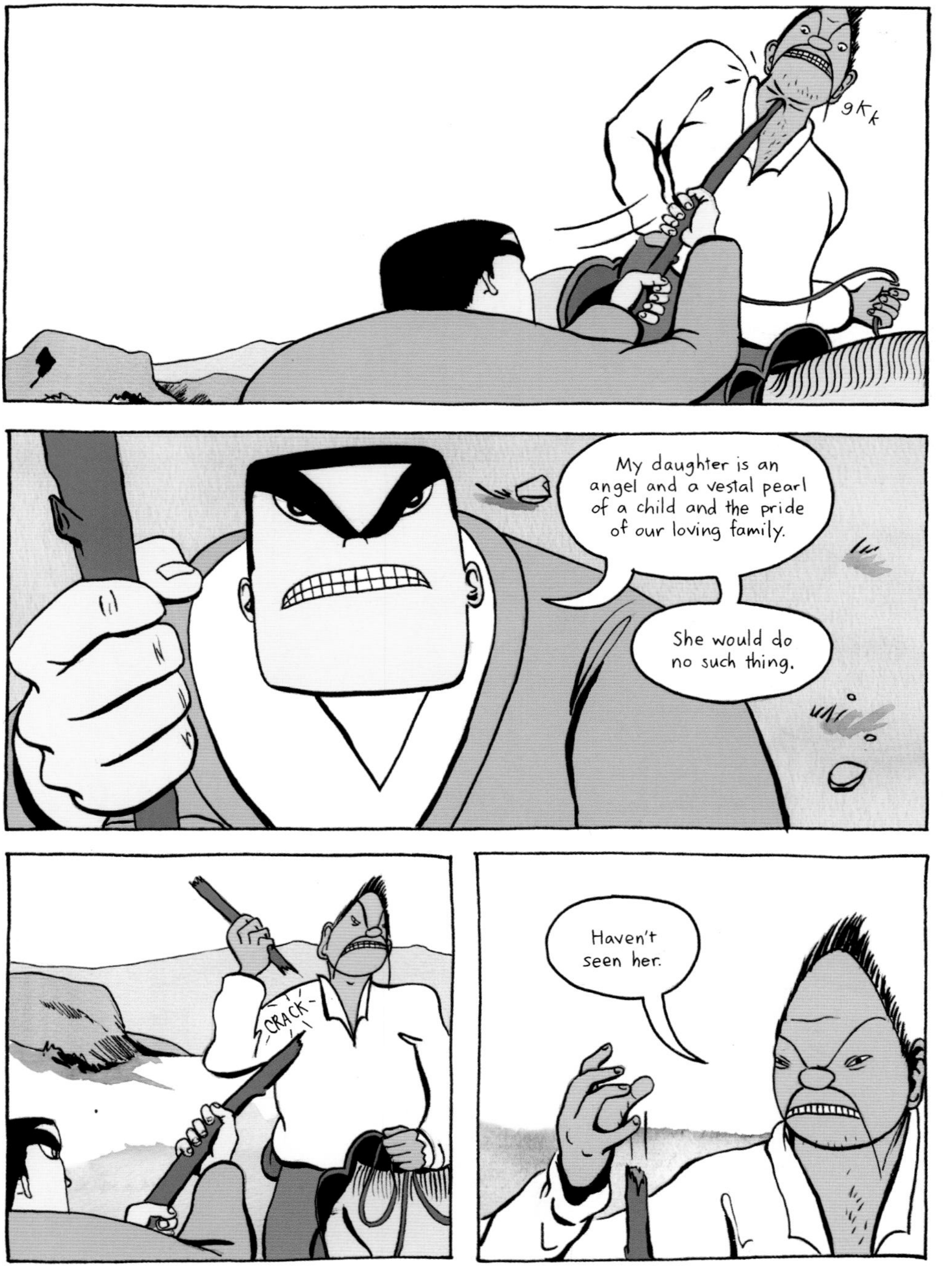
gKk
My daughter is an angel and a vestal pearl of a child and the pride of our loving family.
She would do no such thing.
CRACK
Haven't seen her.

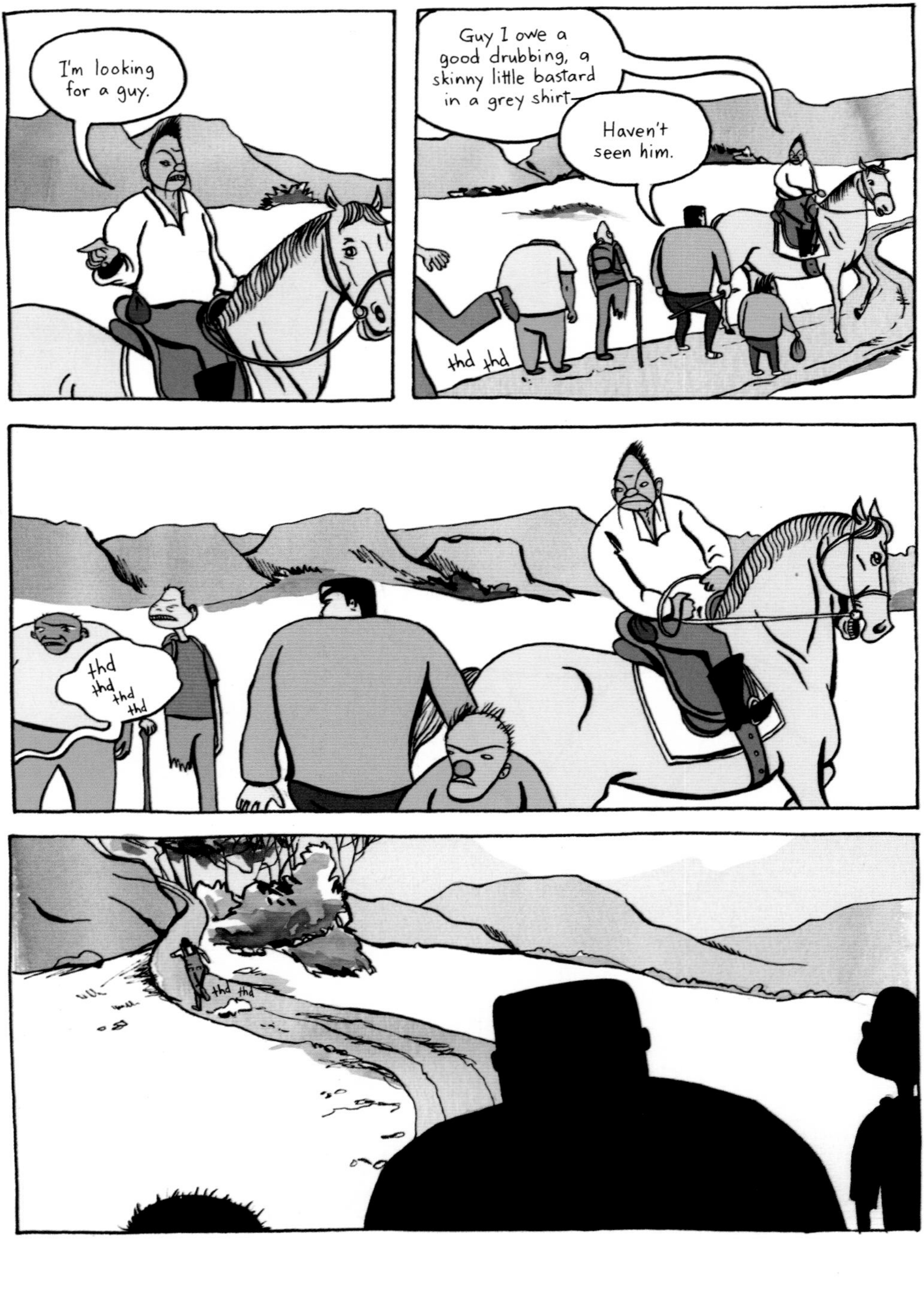
I'm looking for a guy.
Guy I owe a good drubbing, a skinny little bastard in a grey shirt—
Haven't seen him.
thd thd
thd thd thd thd
thd thd

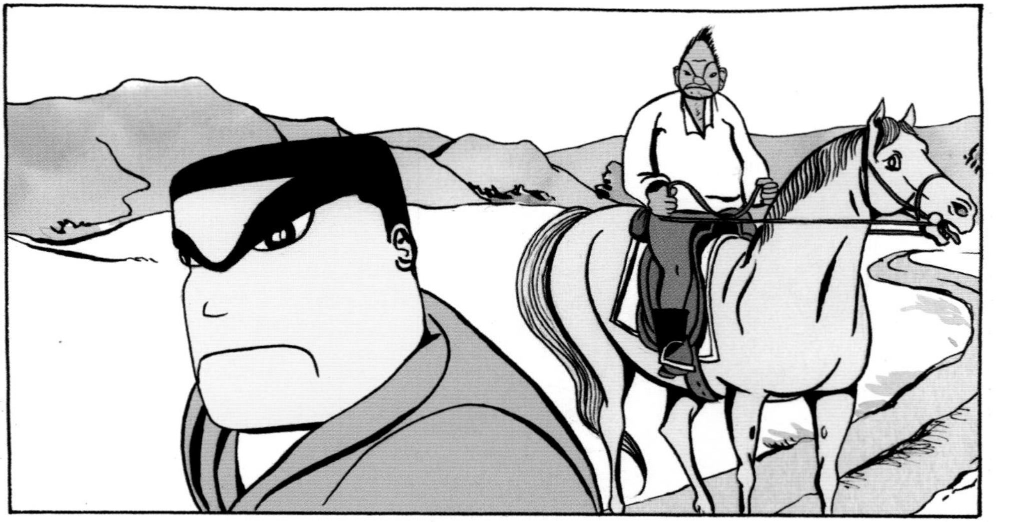

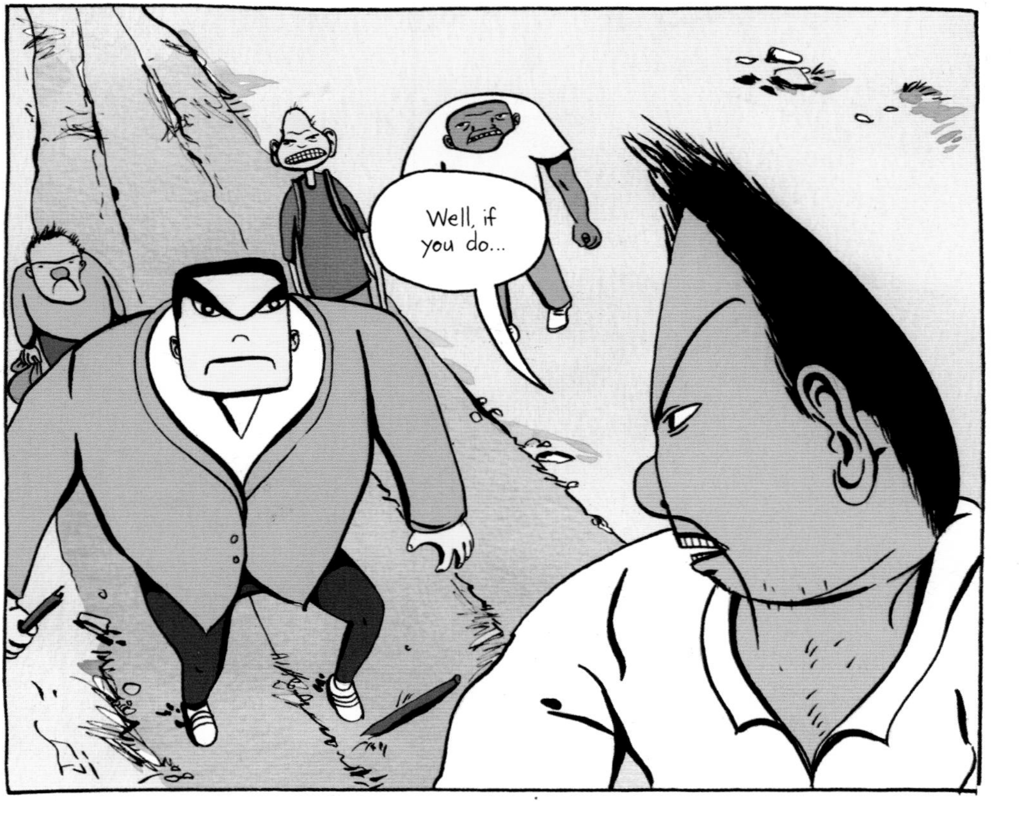
Well, if you do...

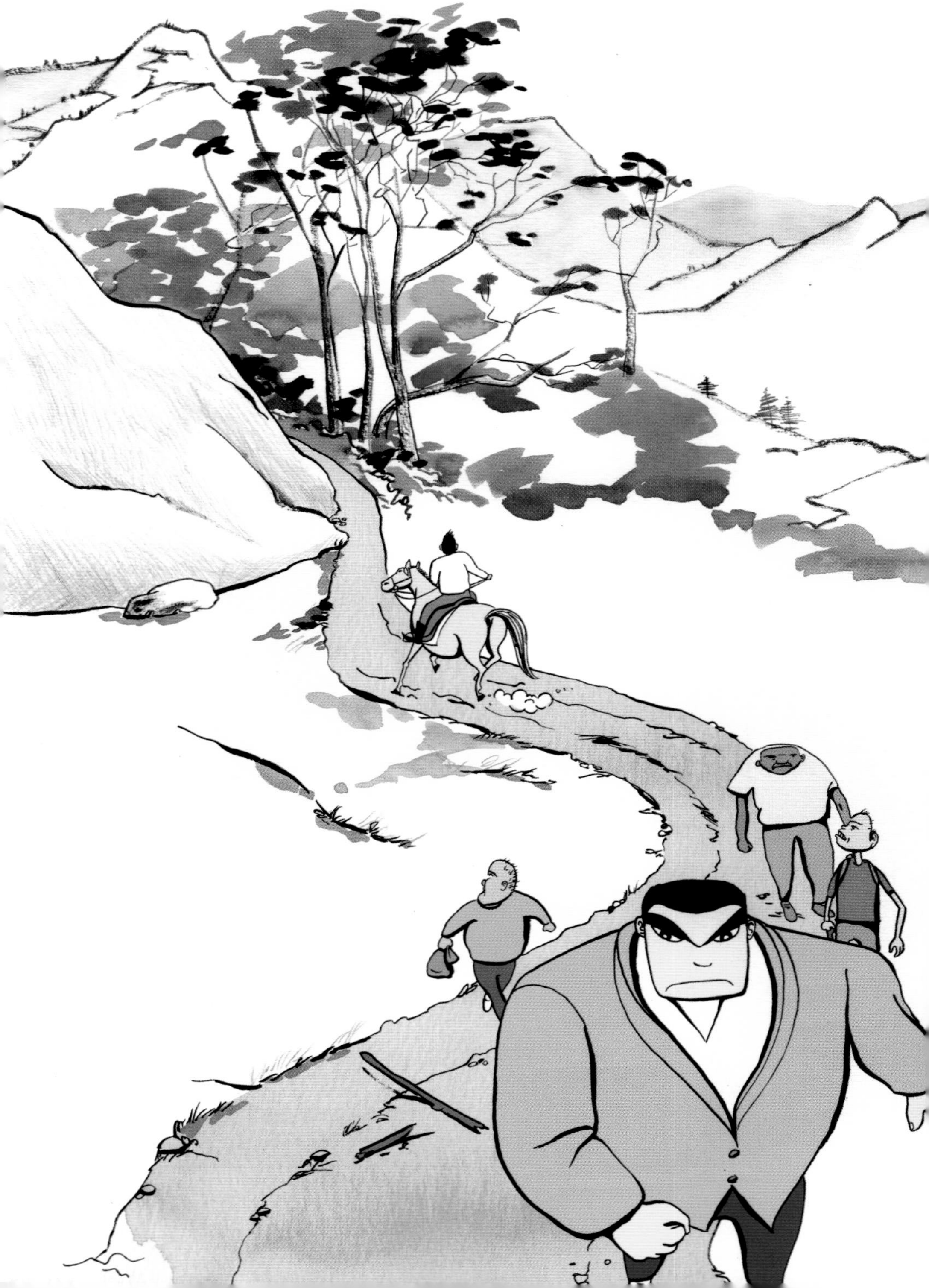

18. Temple

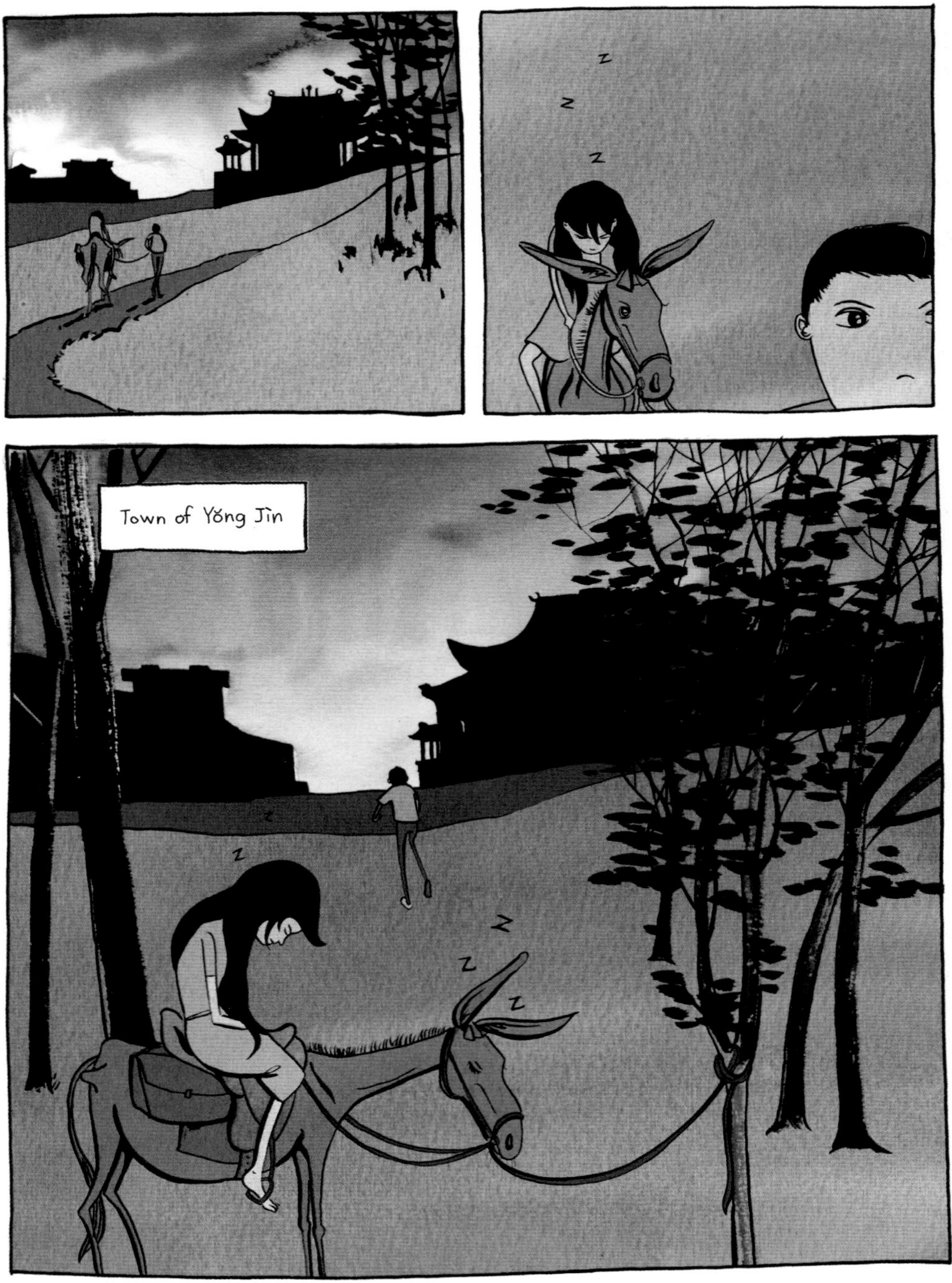
z
z
z
Town of Yǒng Jìn
z
z
z
z
z

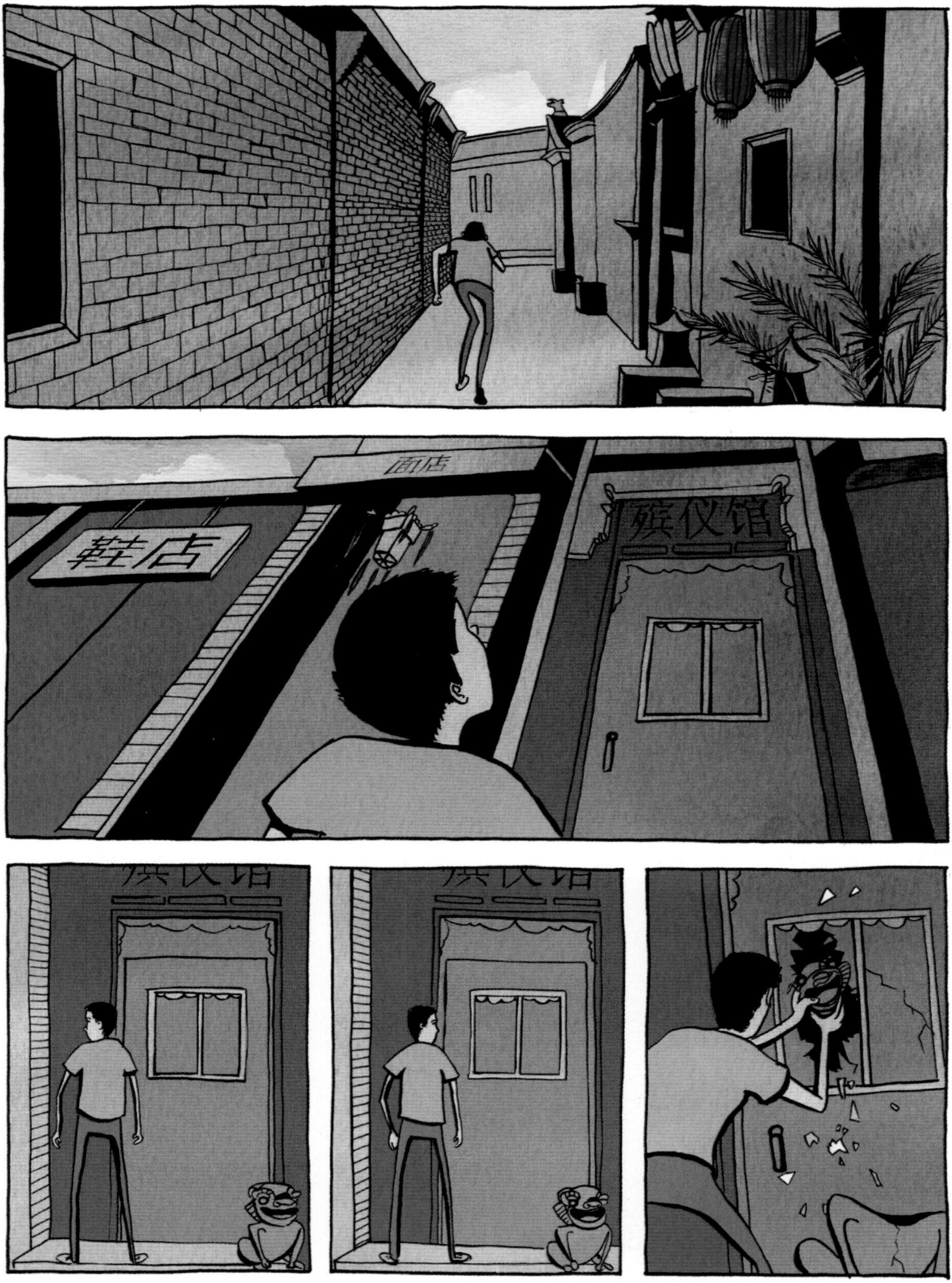
鞋店
面店
殡仪馆

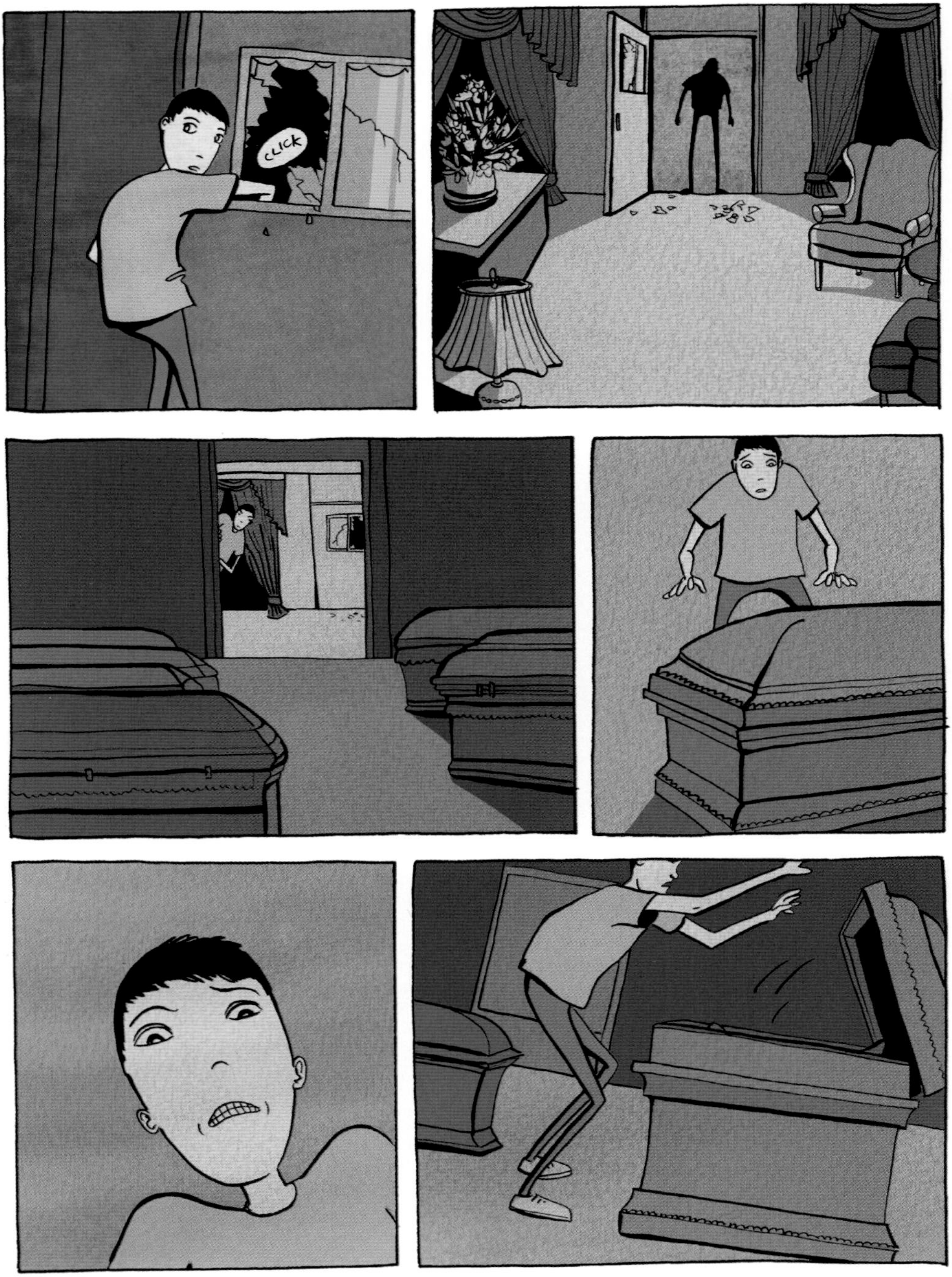
CLICK

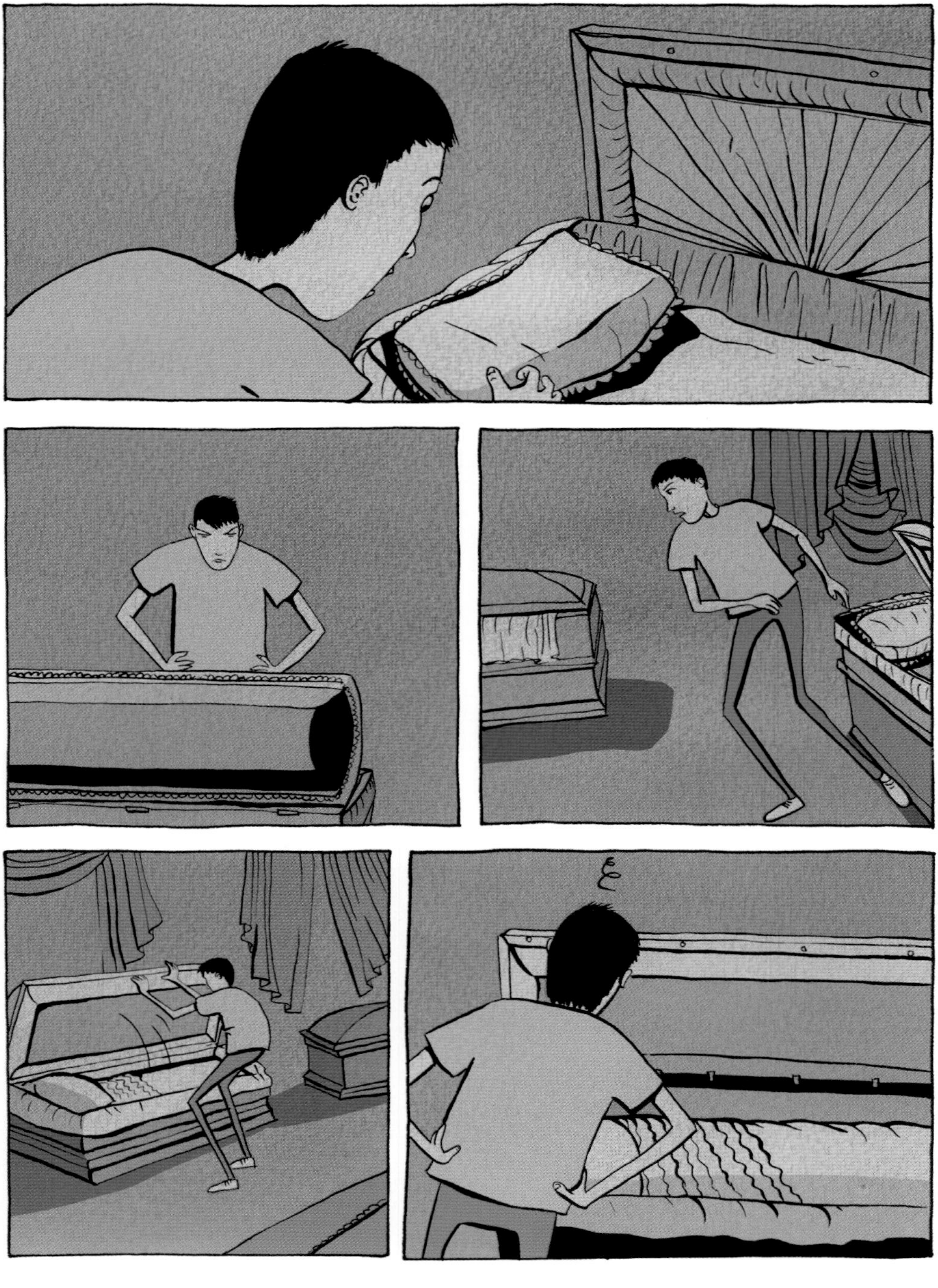

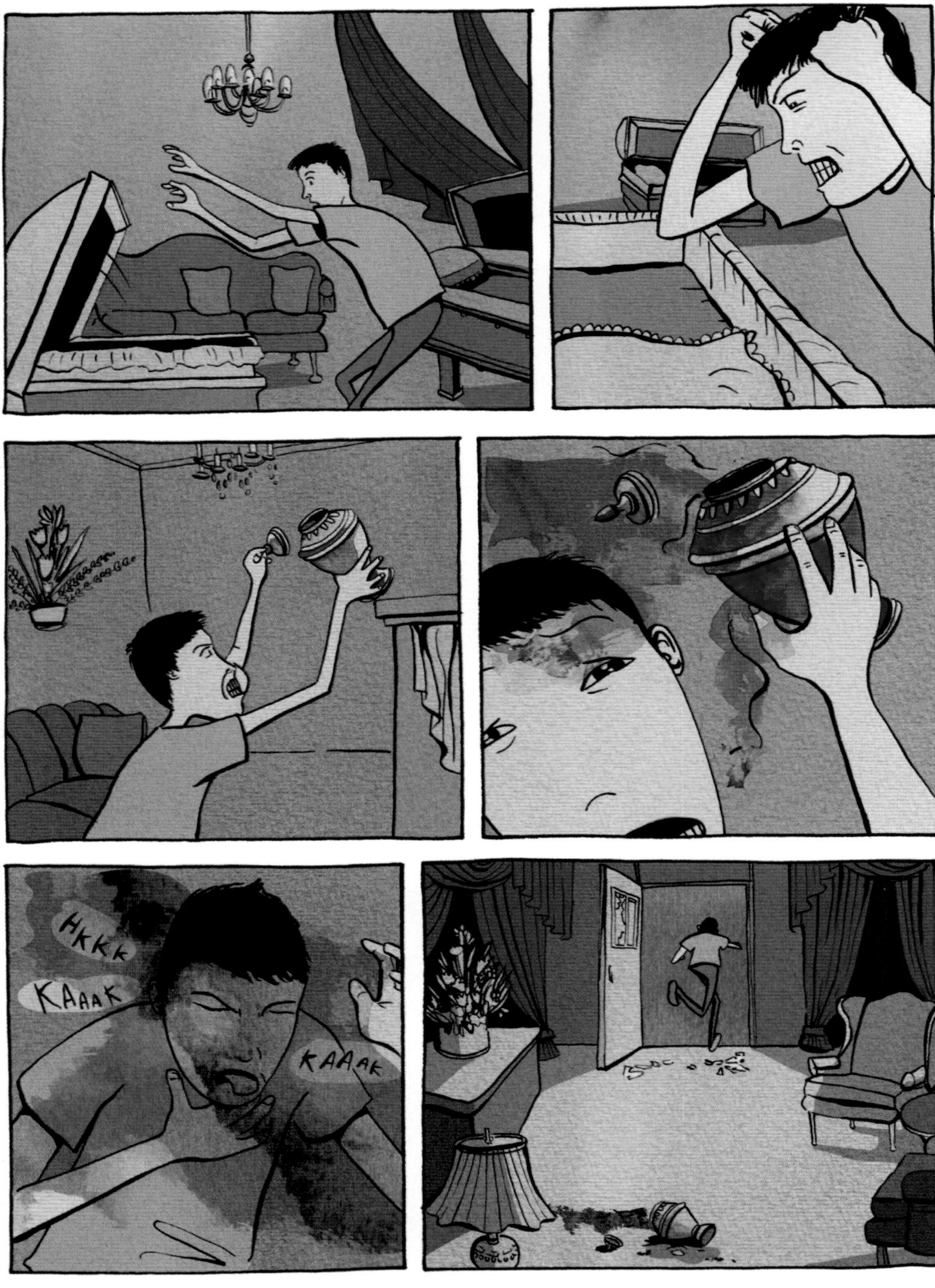
HKKK
KAAAK
KAAAK

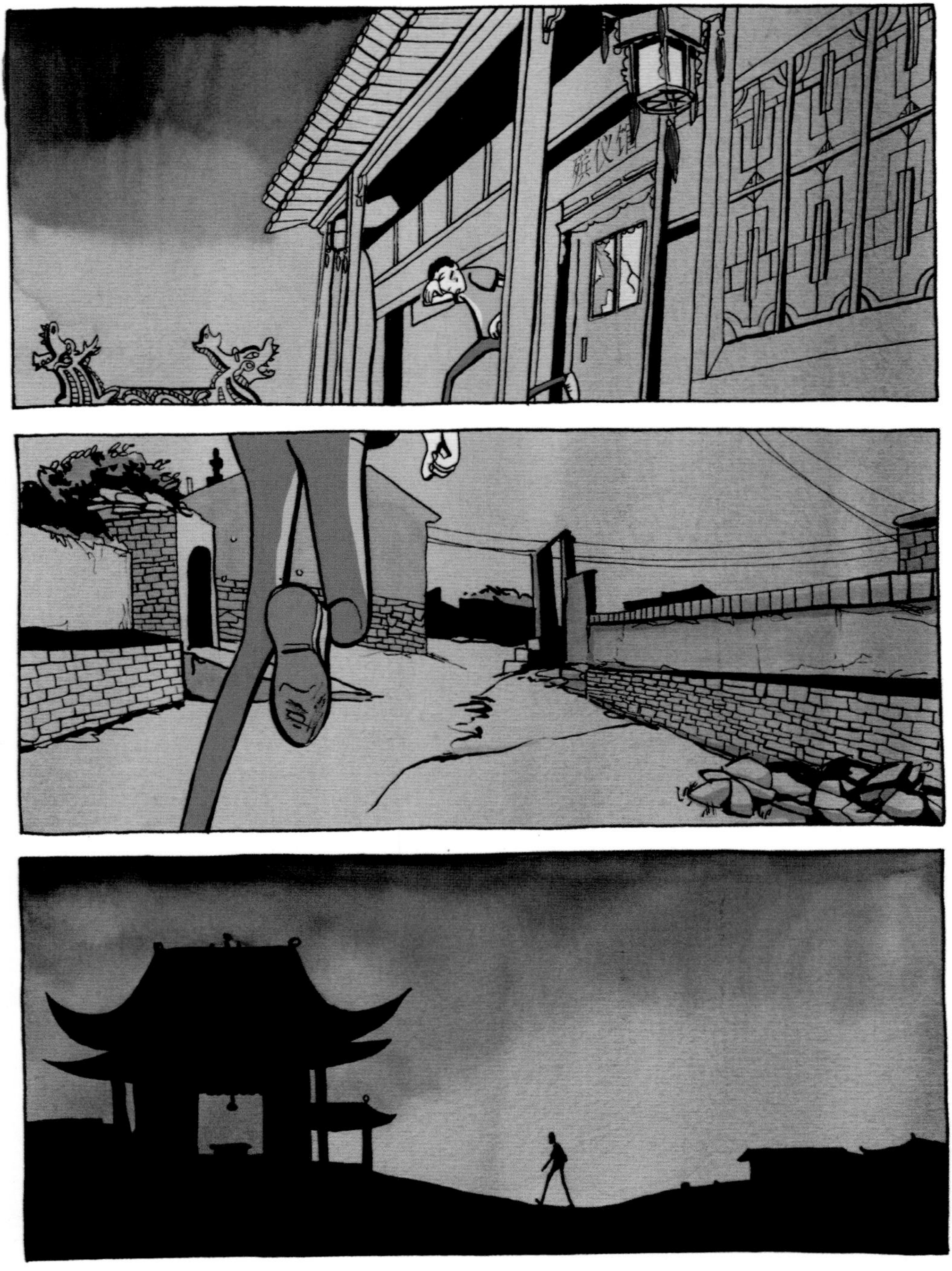
殡仪馆

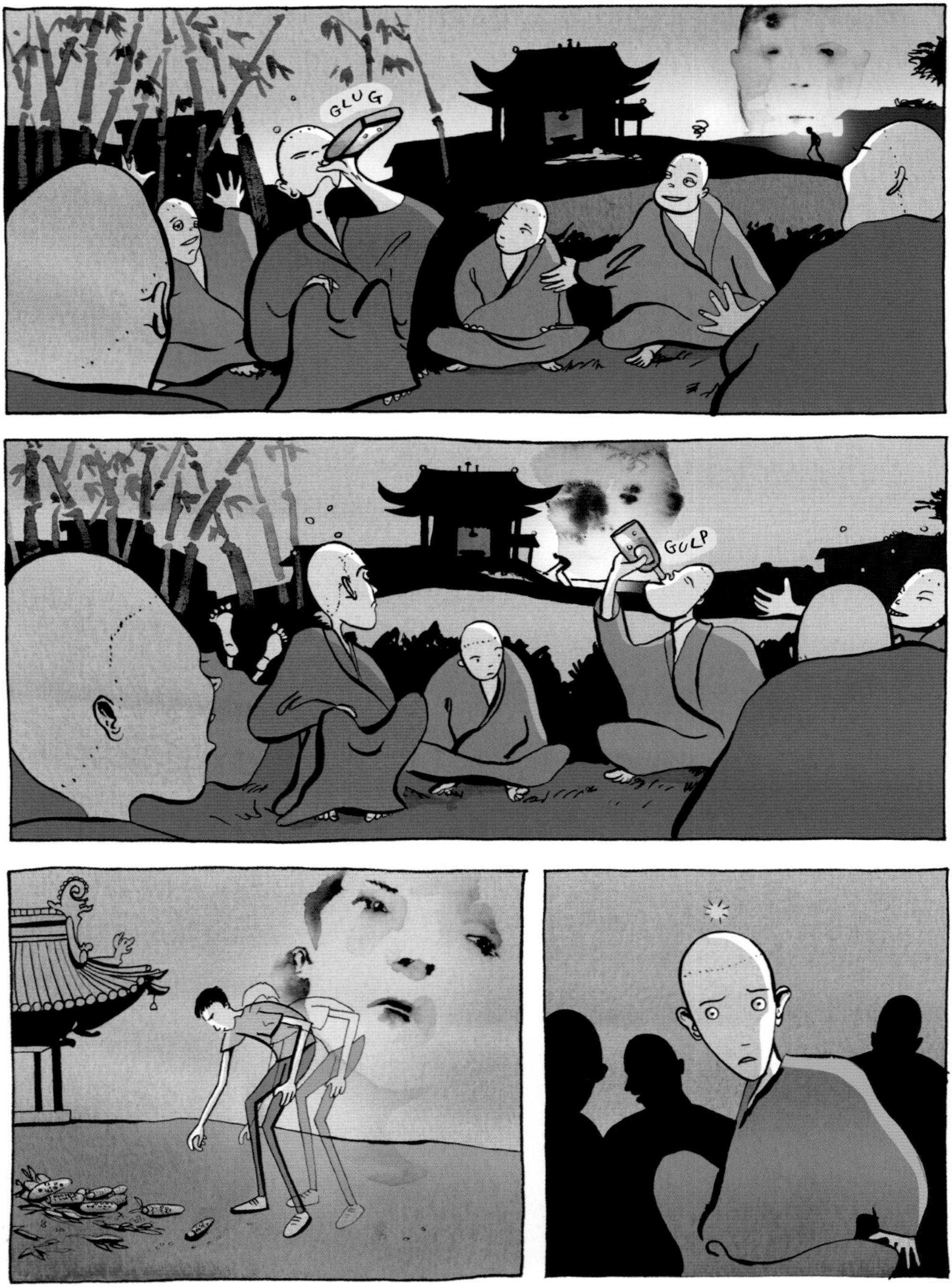
GLUG
GULP

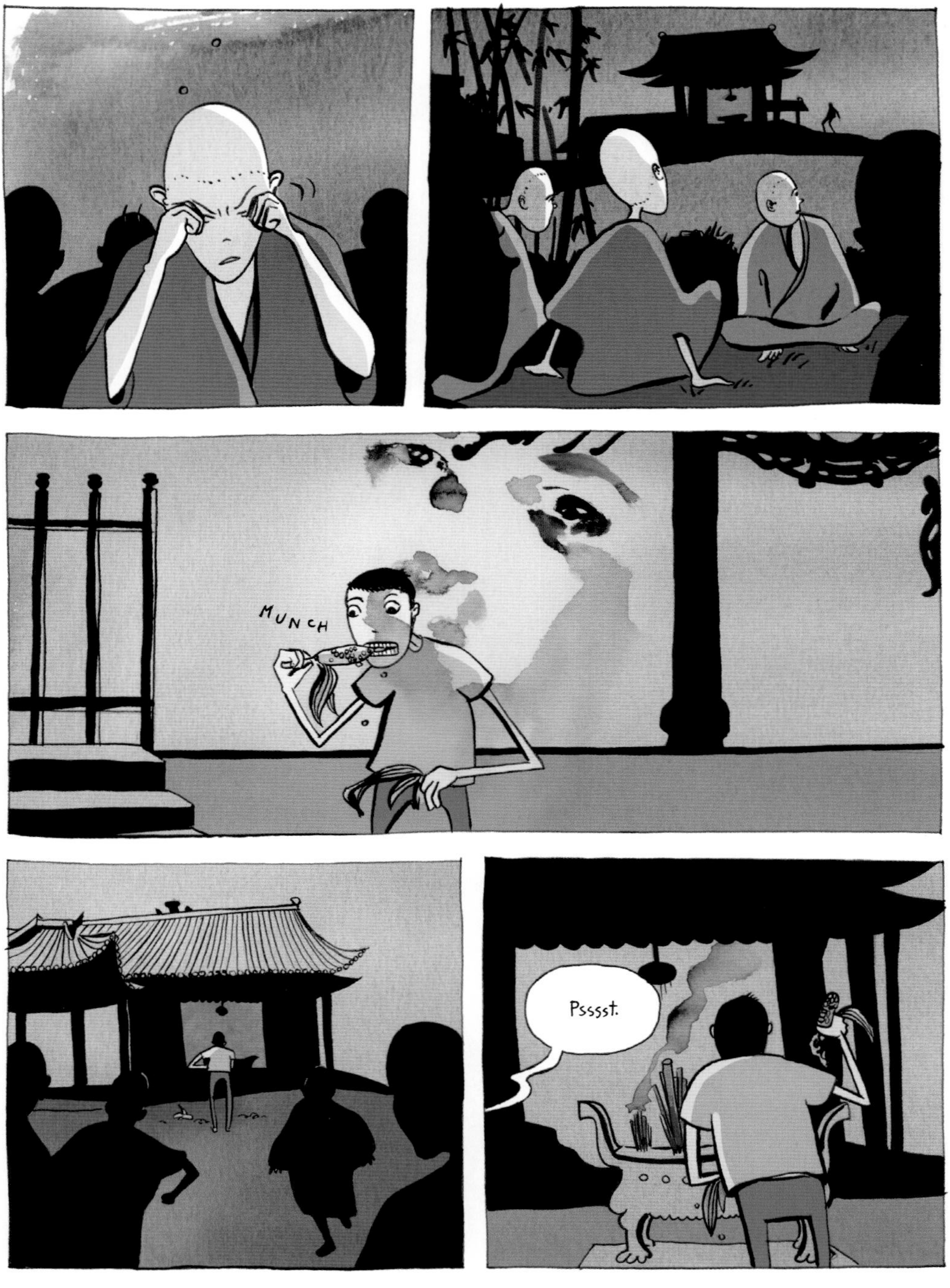
MUNCH
Psssst.

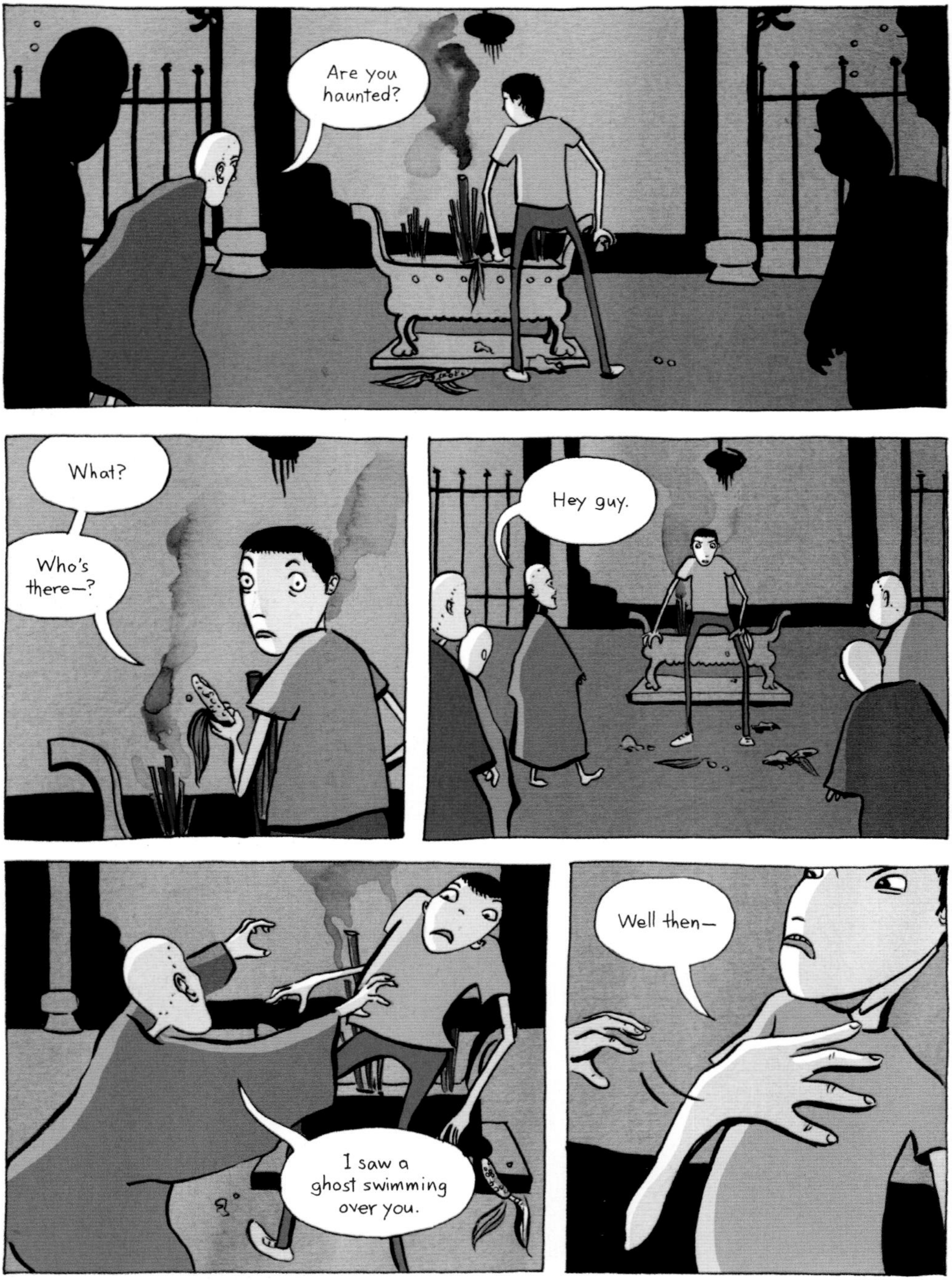
Are you haunted?
What?
Who's there—?
Hey guy.
I saw a ghost swimming over you.
Well then—

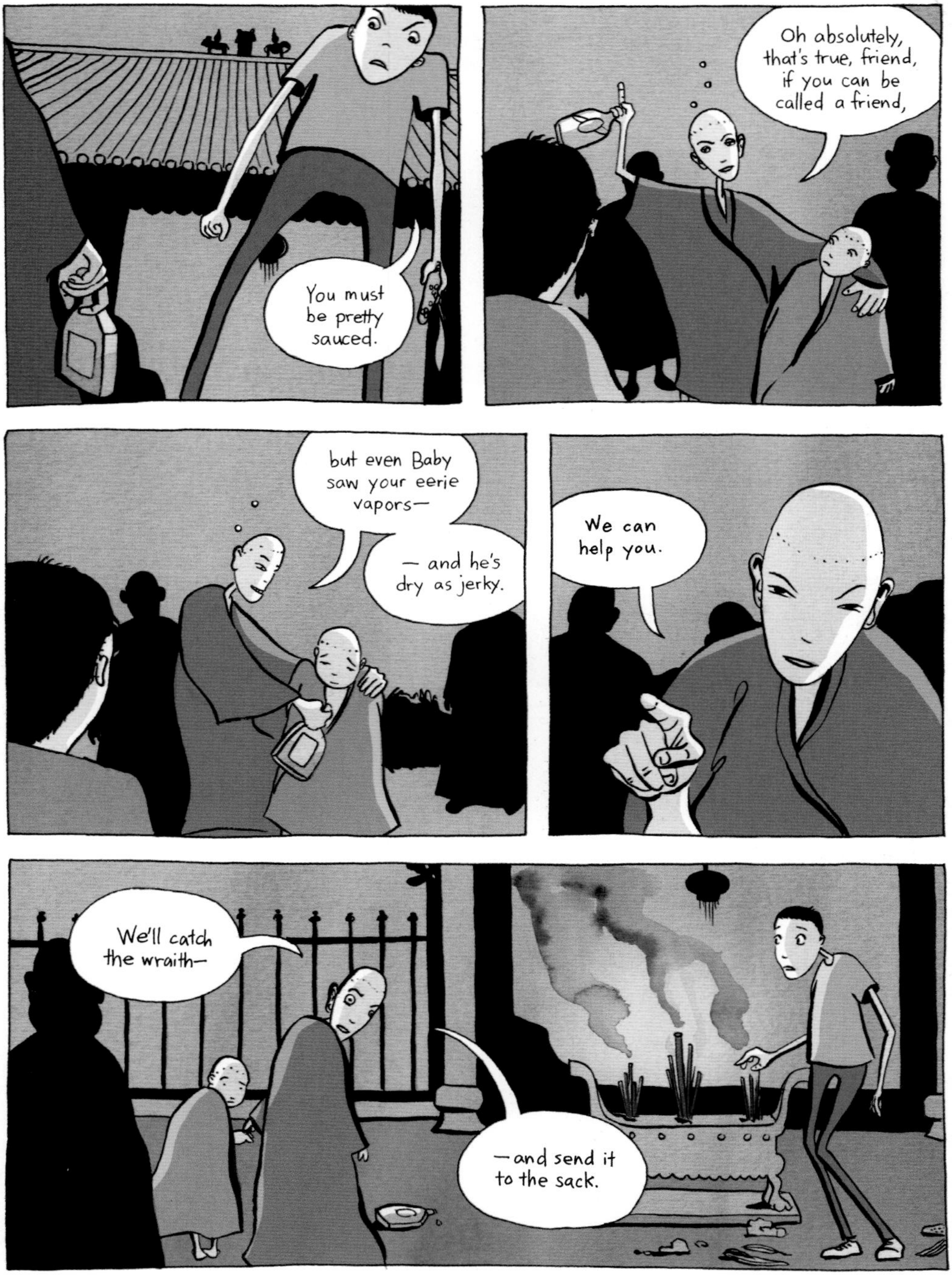

You must be pretty sauced.
Oh absolutely, that's true, friend, if you can be called a friend,
but even Baby saw your eerie vapors—
— and he's dry as jerky.
We can help you.
We'll catch the wraith—
—and send it to the sack.

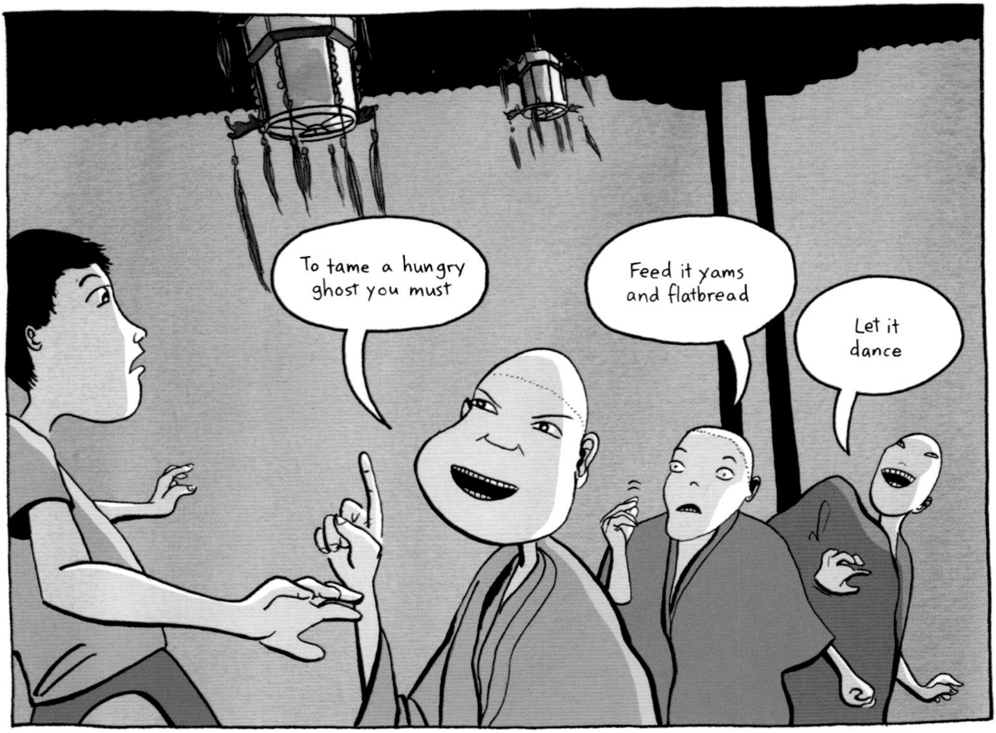
To tame a hungry ghost you must
Feed it yams and flatbread
Let it dance

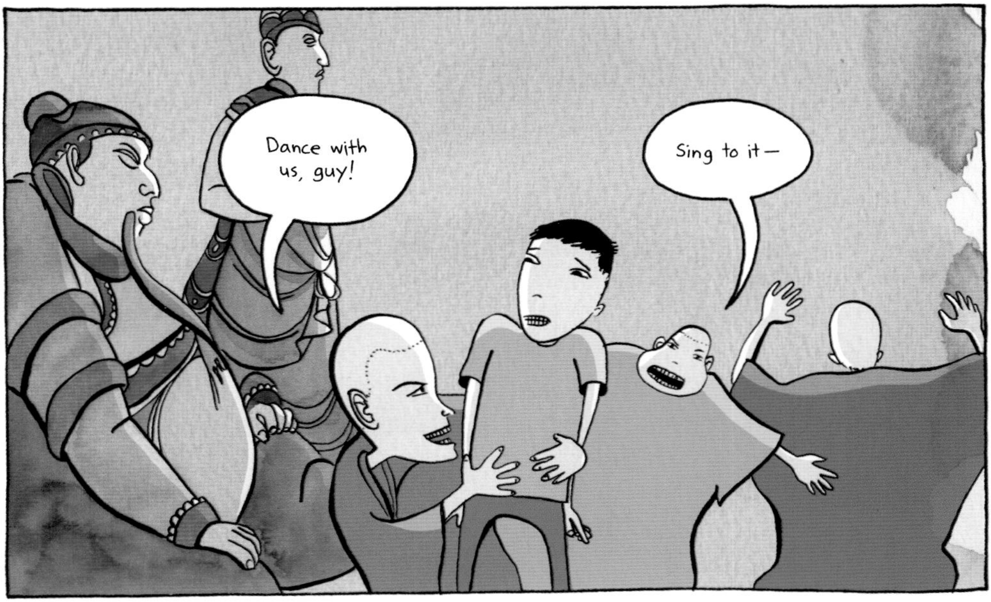
Dance with us, guy!
Sing to it—

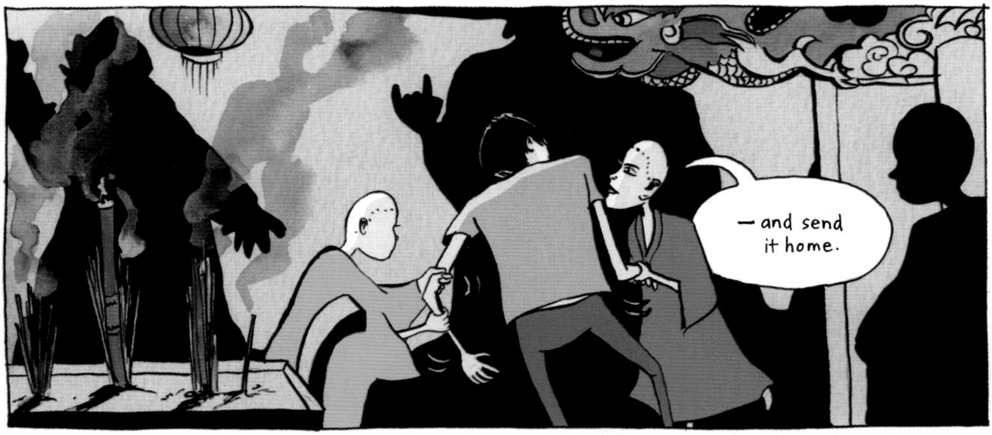
—and send it home.

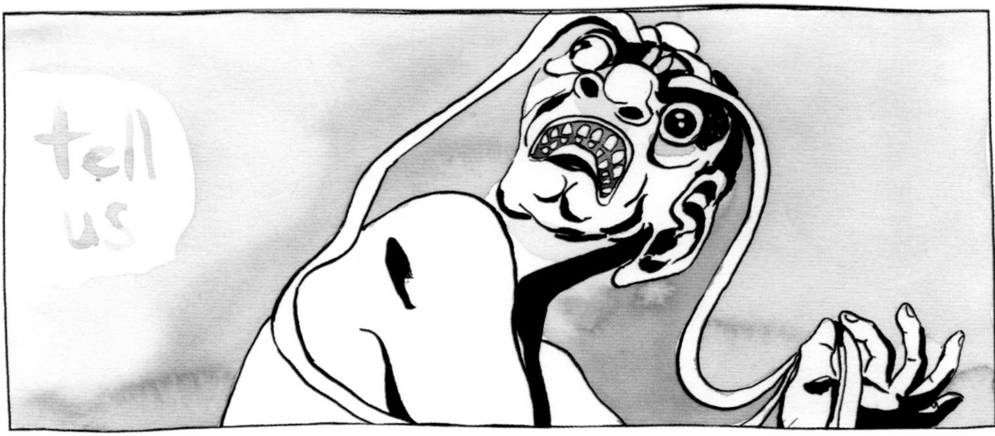
tell us

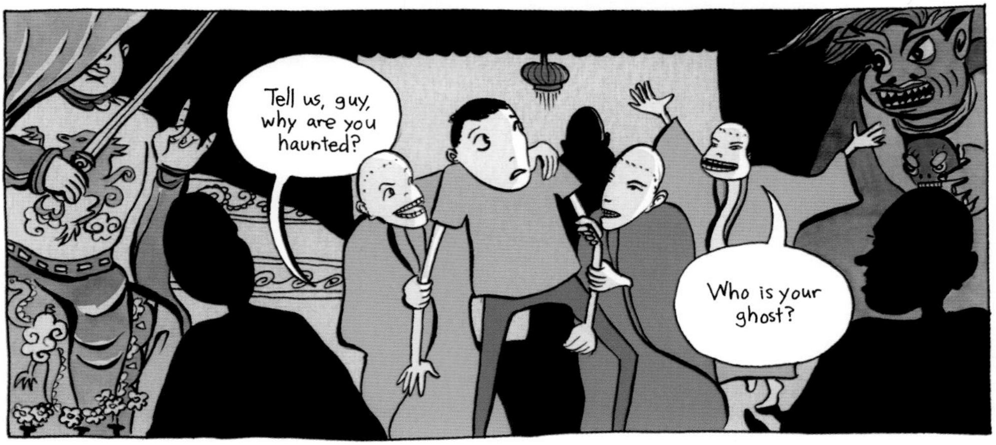
Tell us, guy, why are you haunted?
Who is your ghost?

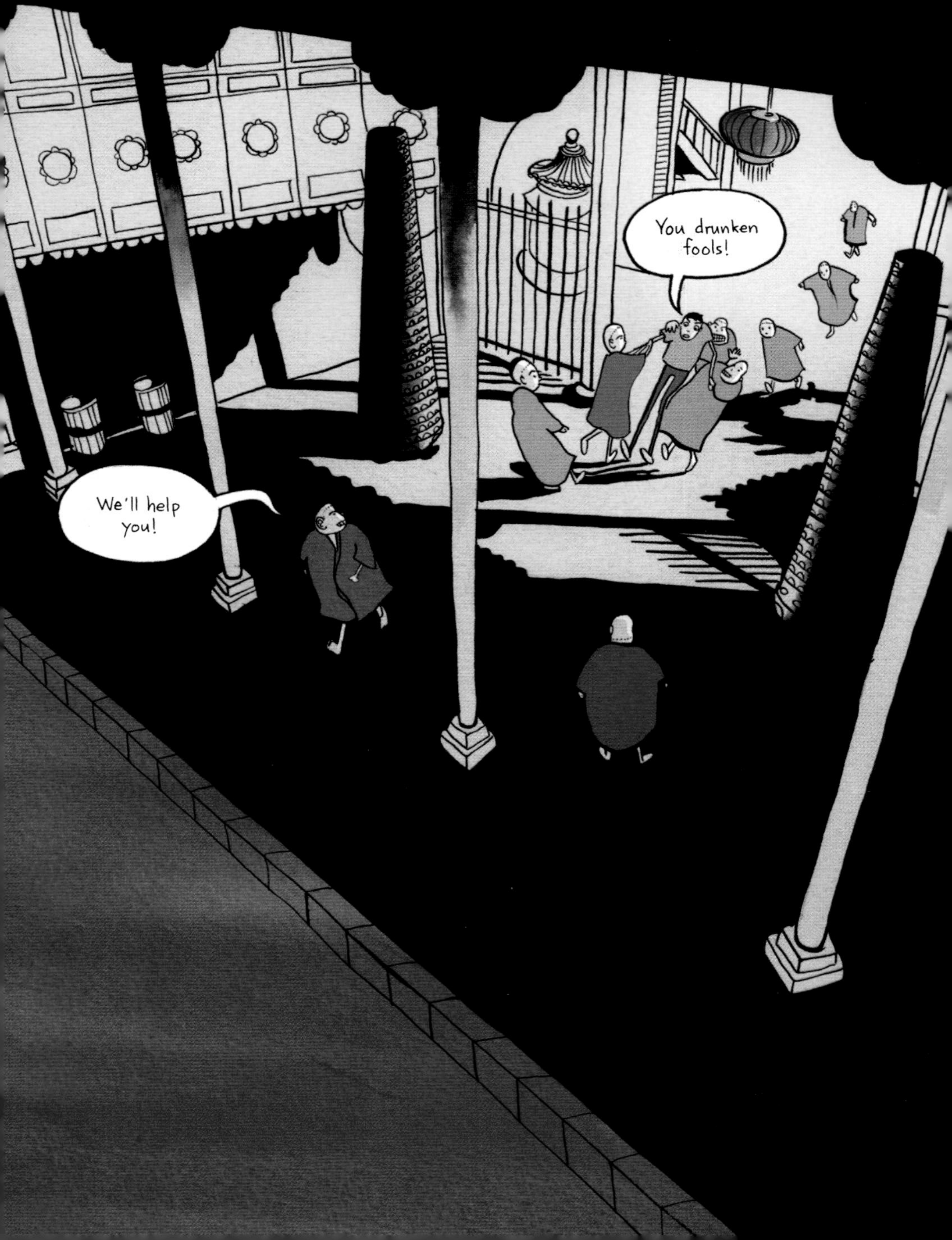
You drunken fools!
We'll help you!

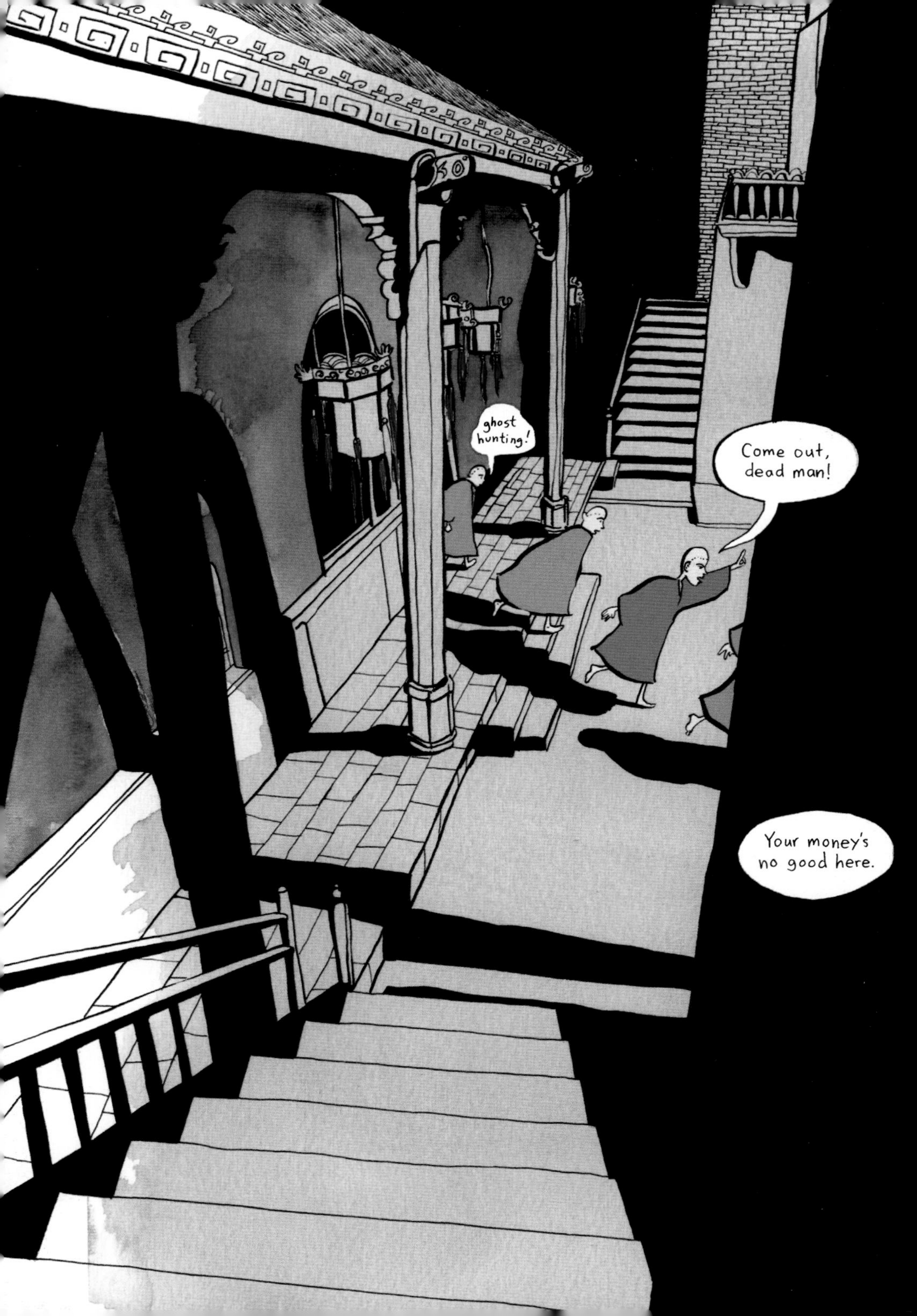
ghost hunting!
Come out, dead man!
Your money's no good here.

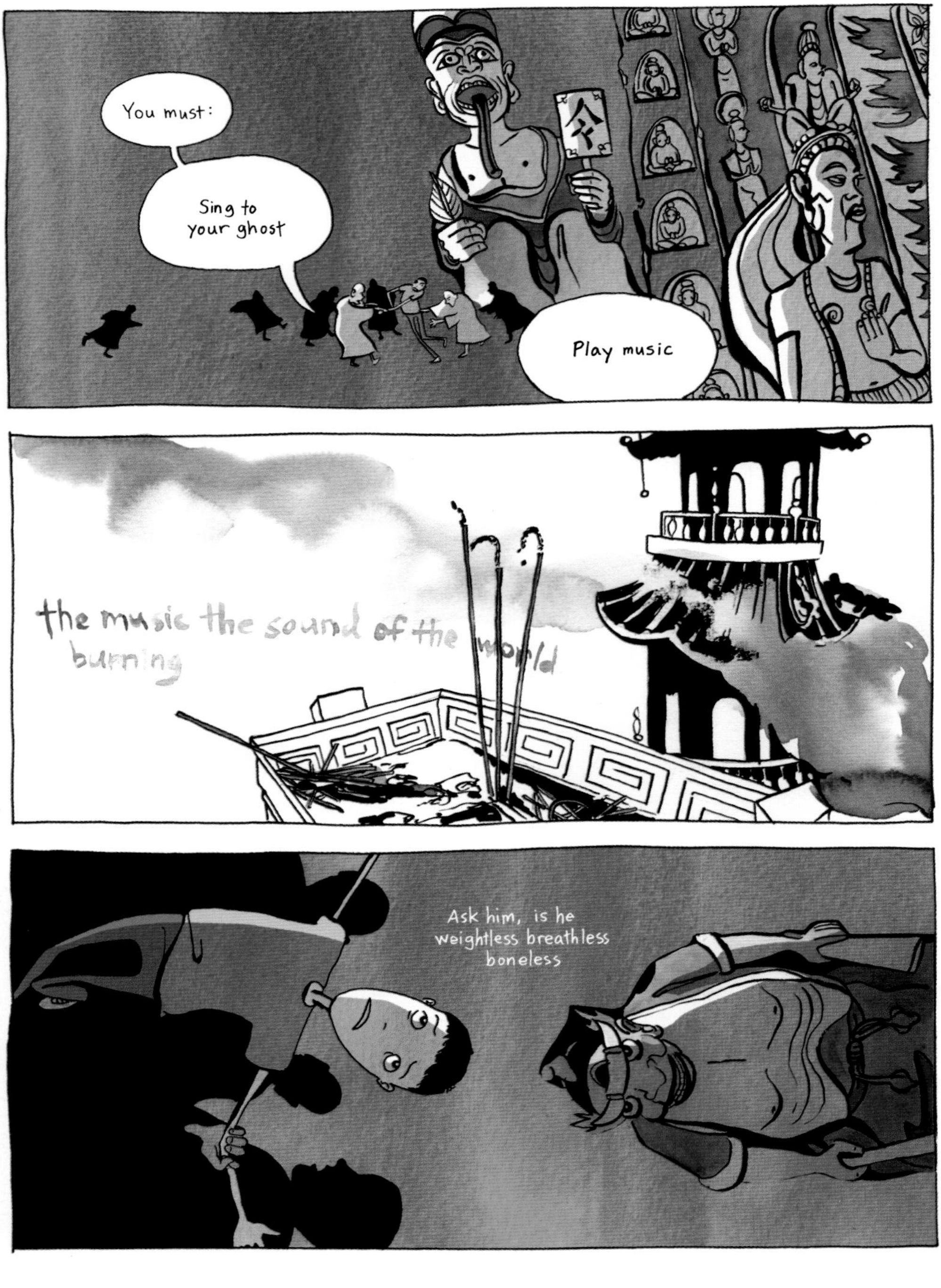
You must:
Sing to your ghost
Play music
the music the sound of the world burning
Ask him, is he weightless breathless boneless

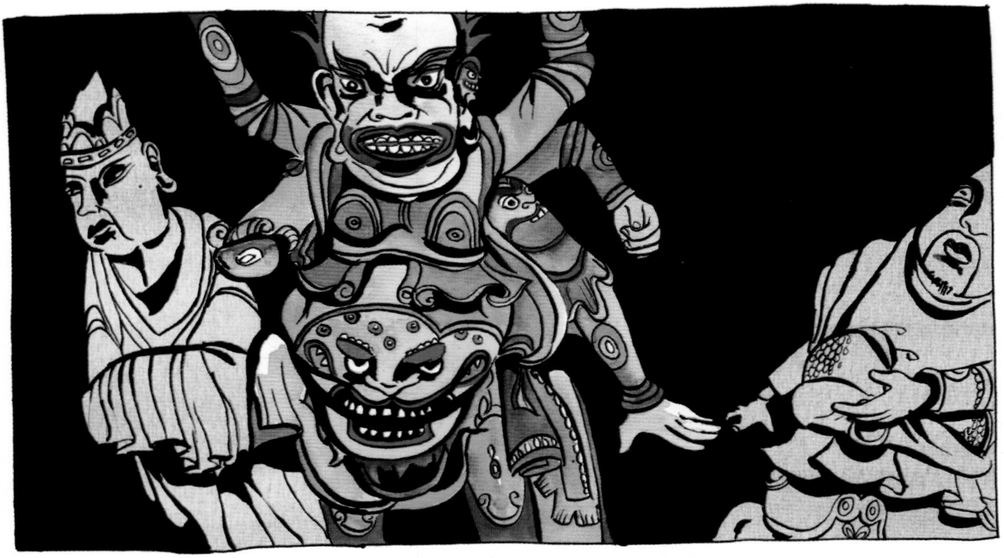

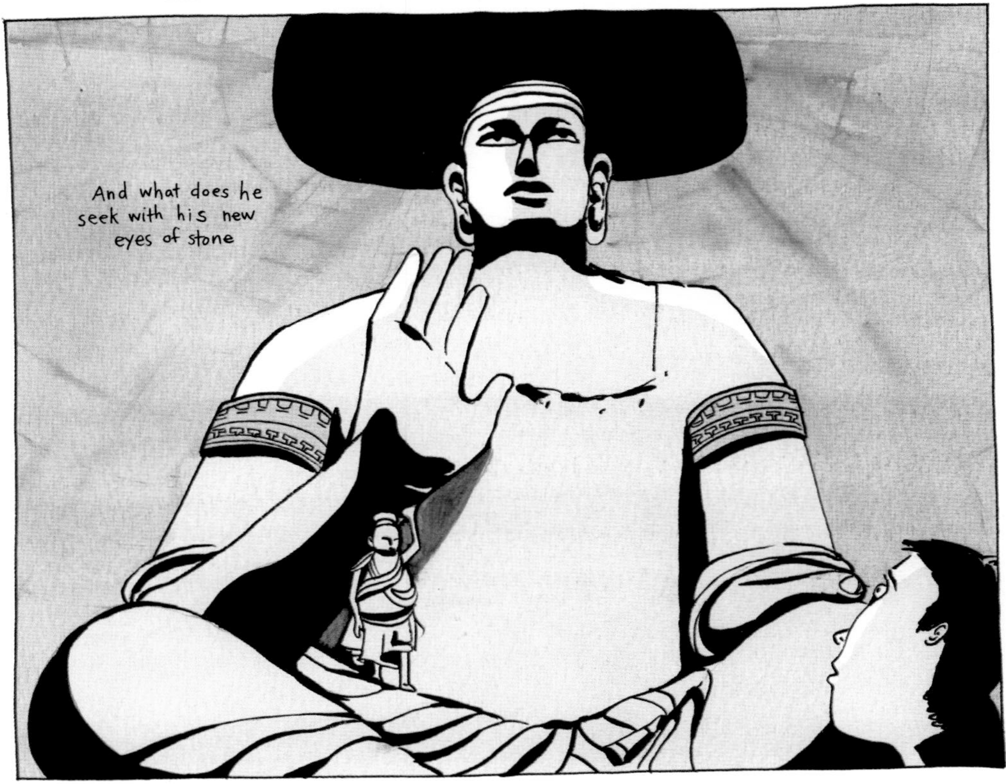
And what does he seek with his new eyes of stone

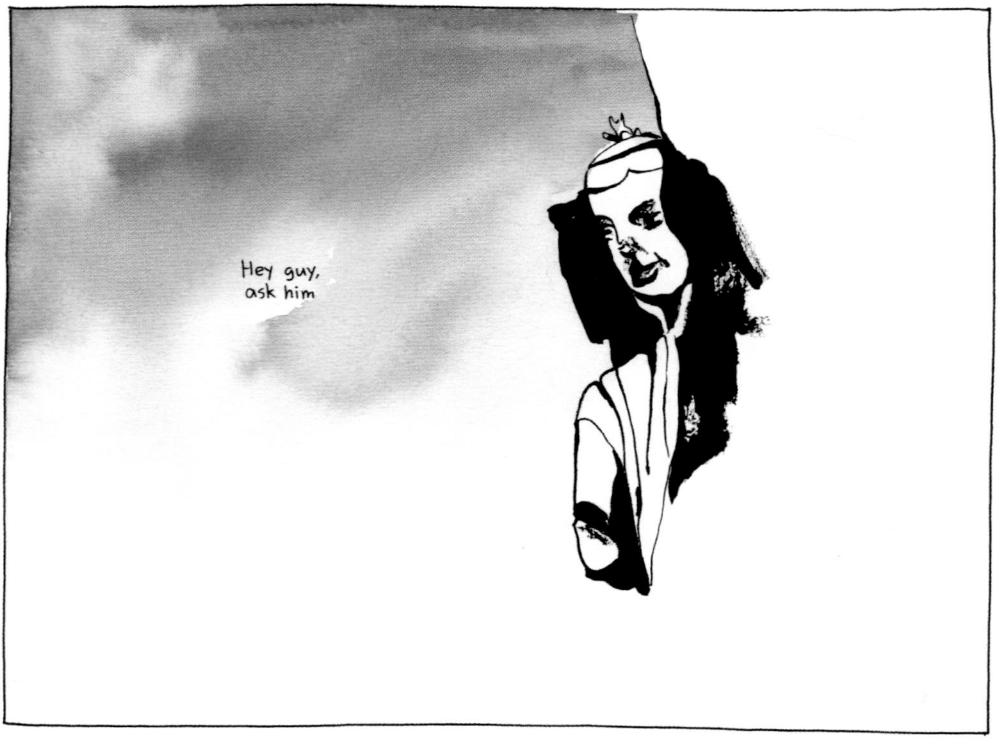
Hey guy,
ask him

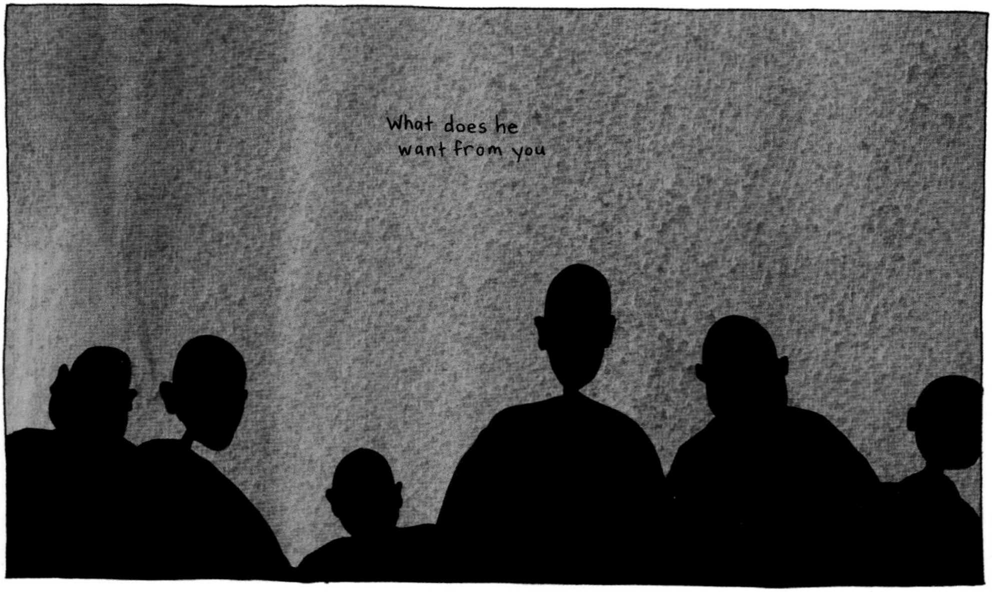
What does he
want from you

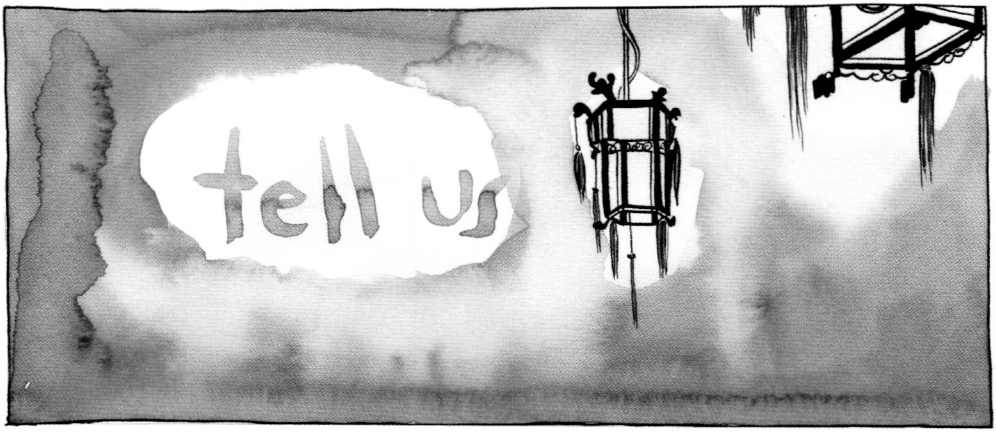
tell us

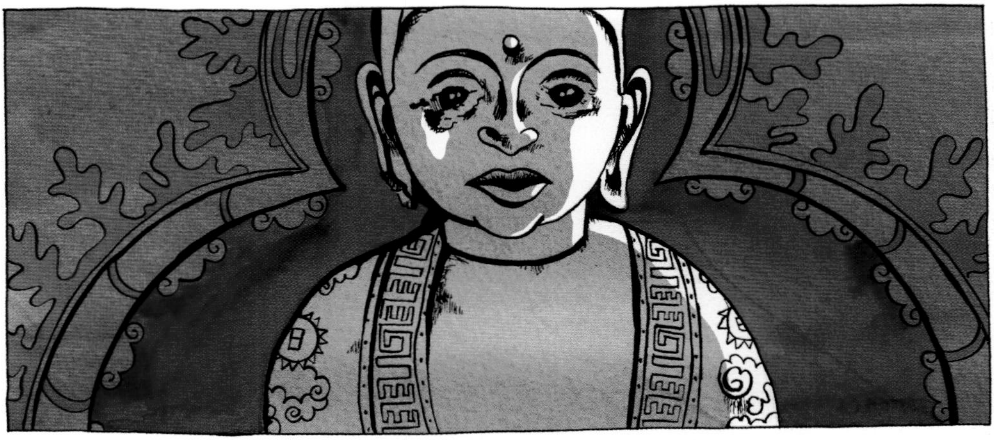

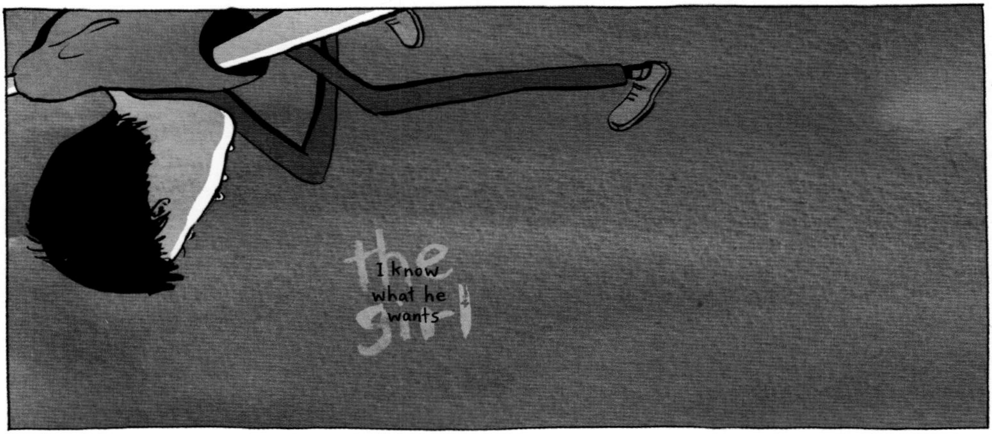
the
I know what he wants
girl

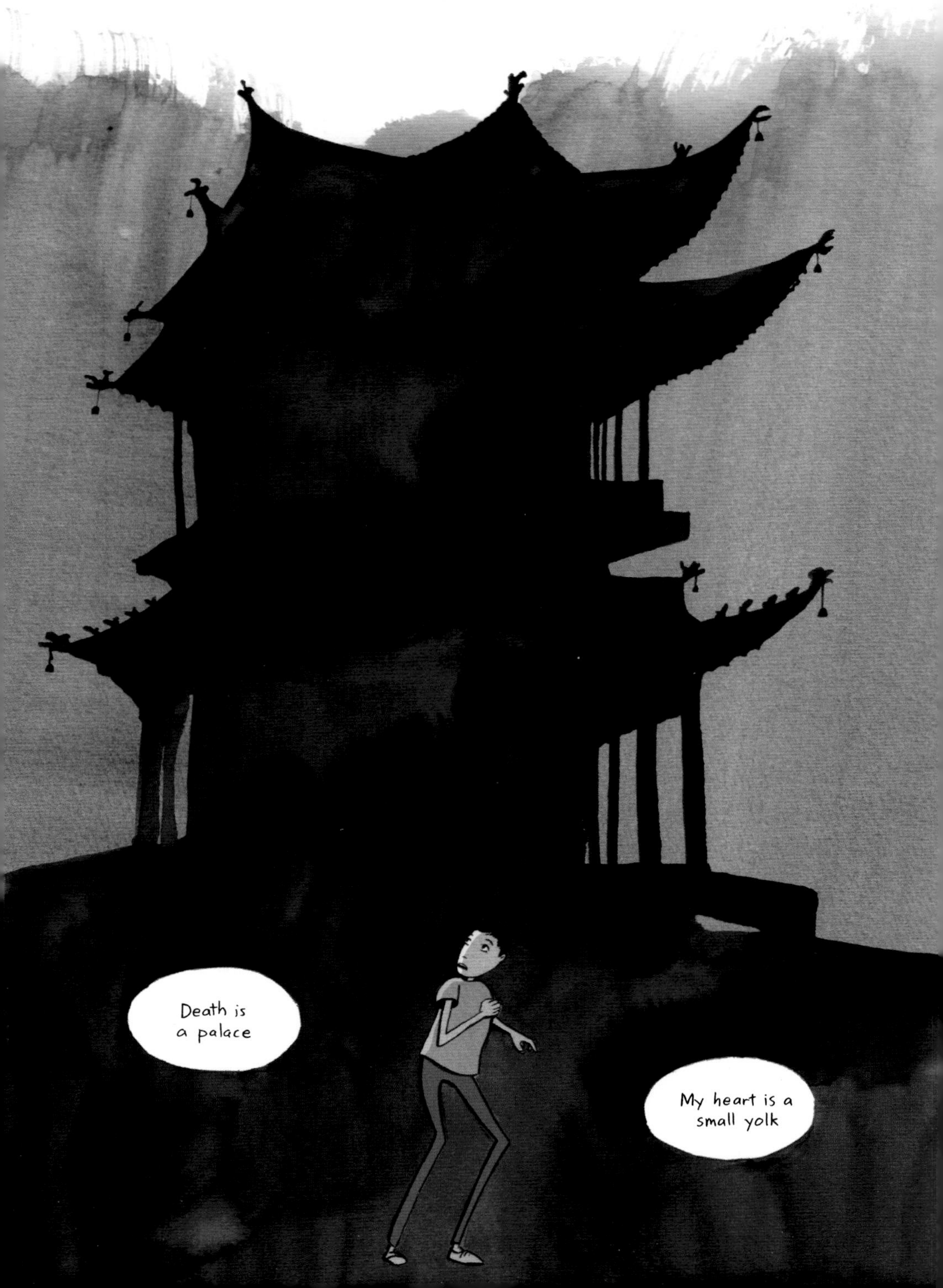
Death is a palace
My heart is a small yolk

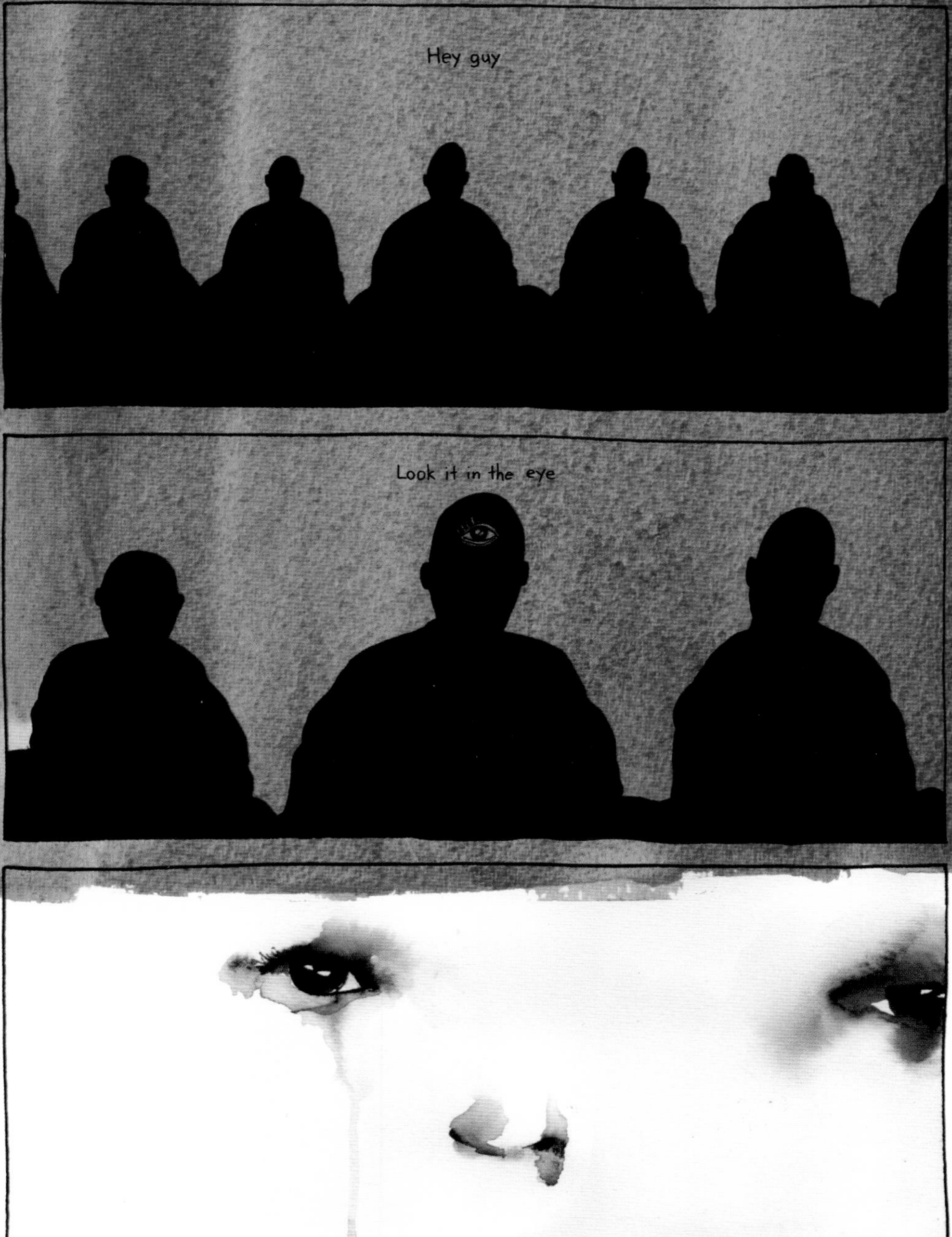
Hey guy
Look it in the eye

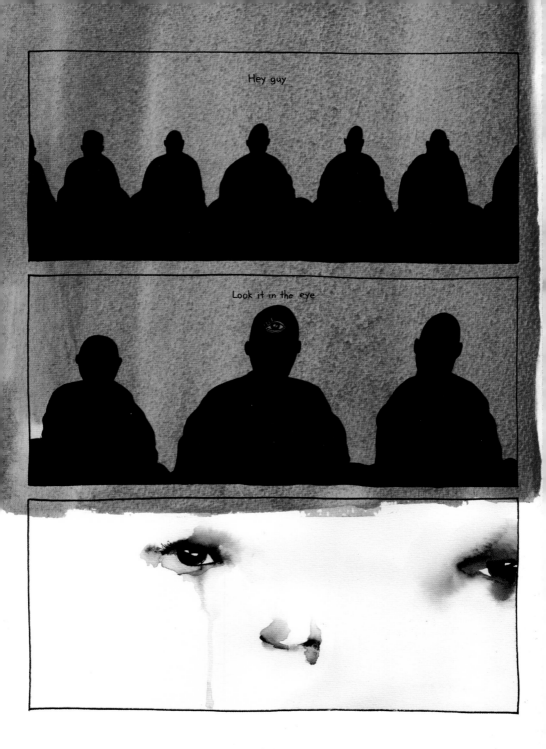

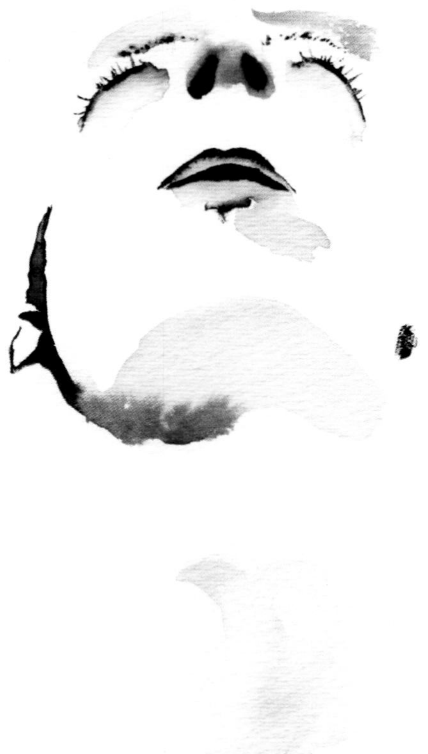

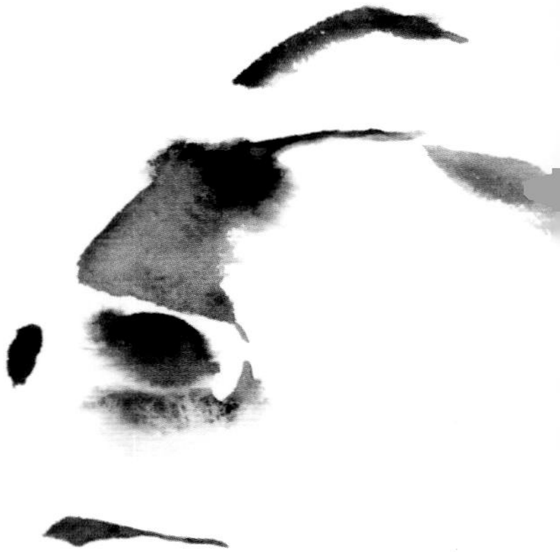

And let it go

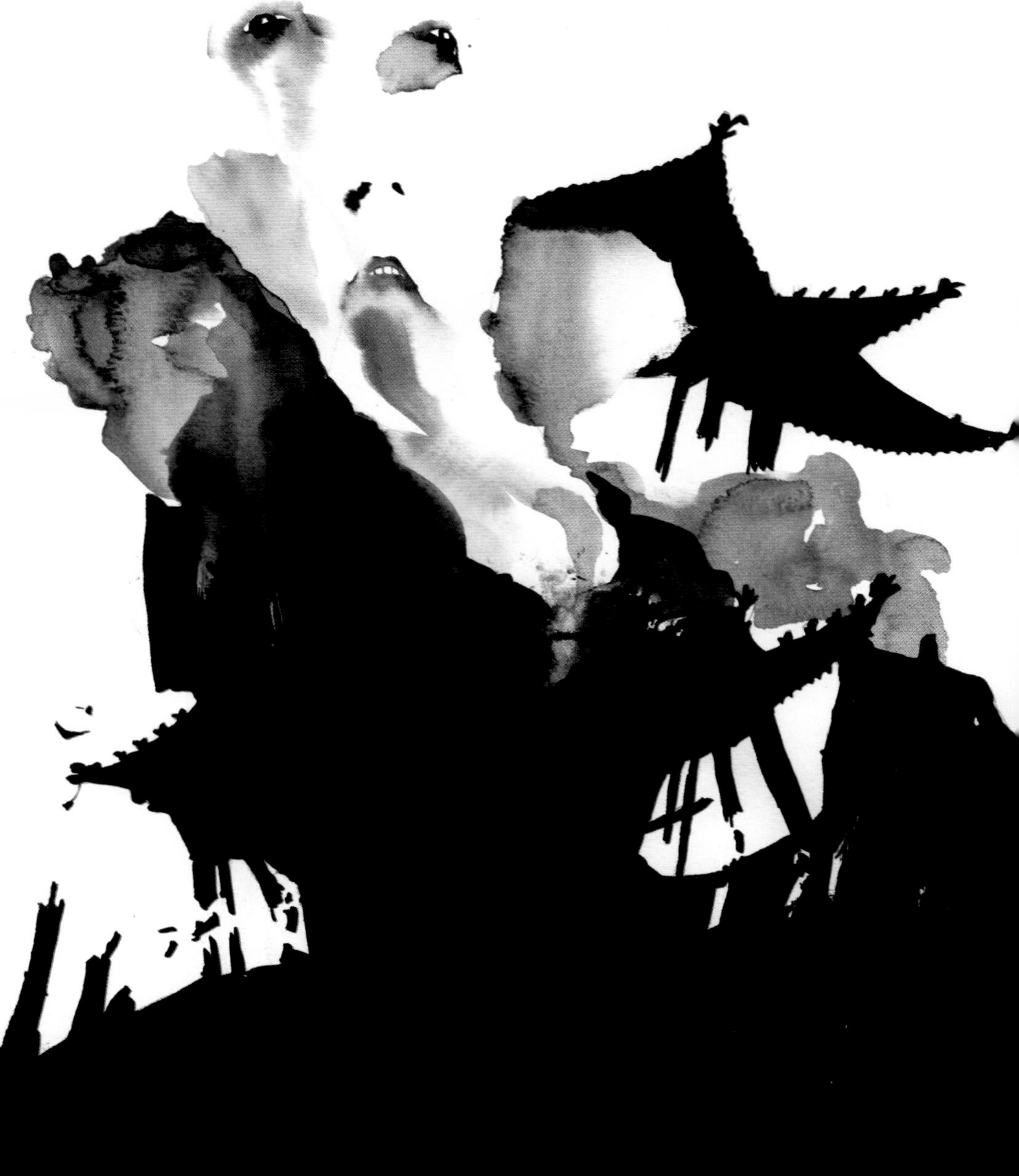

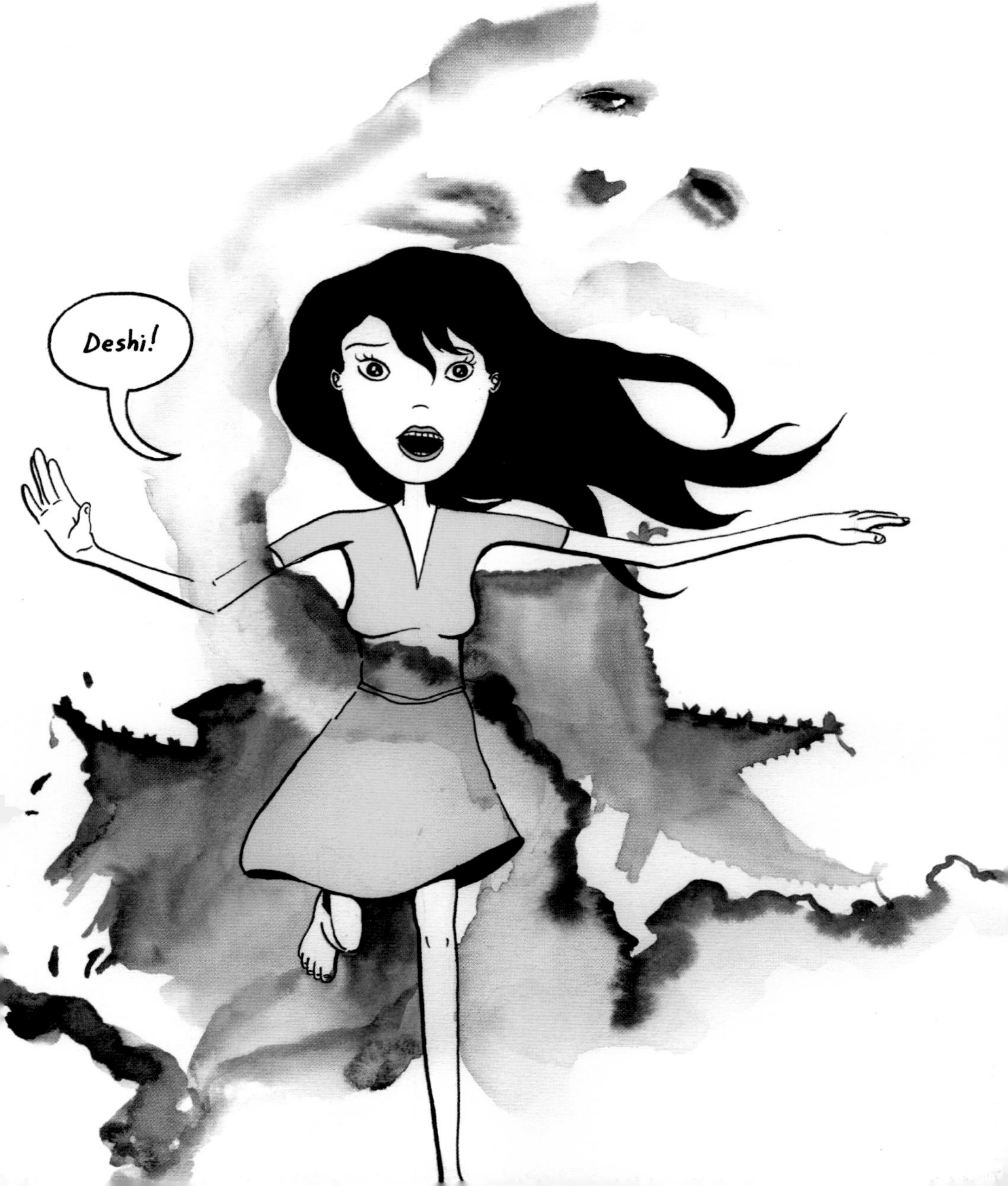
Deshi!

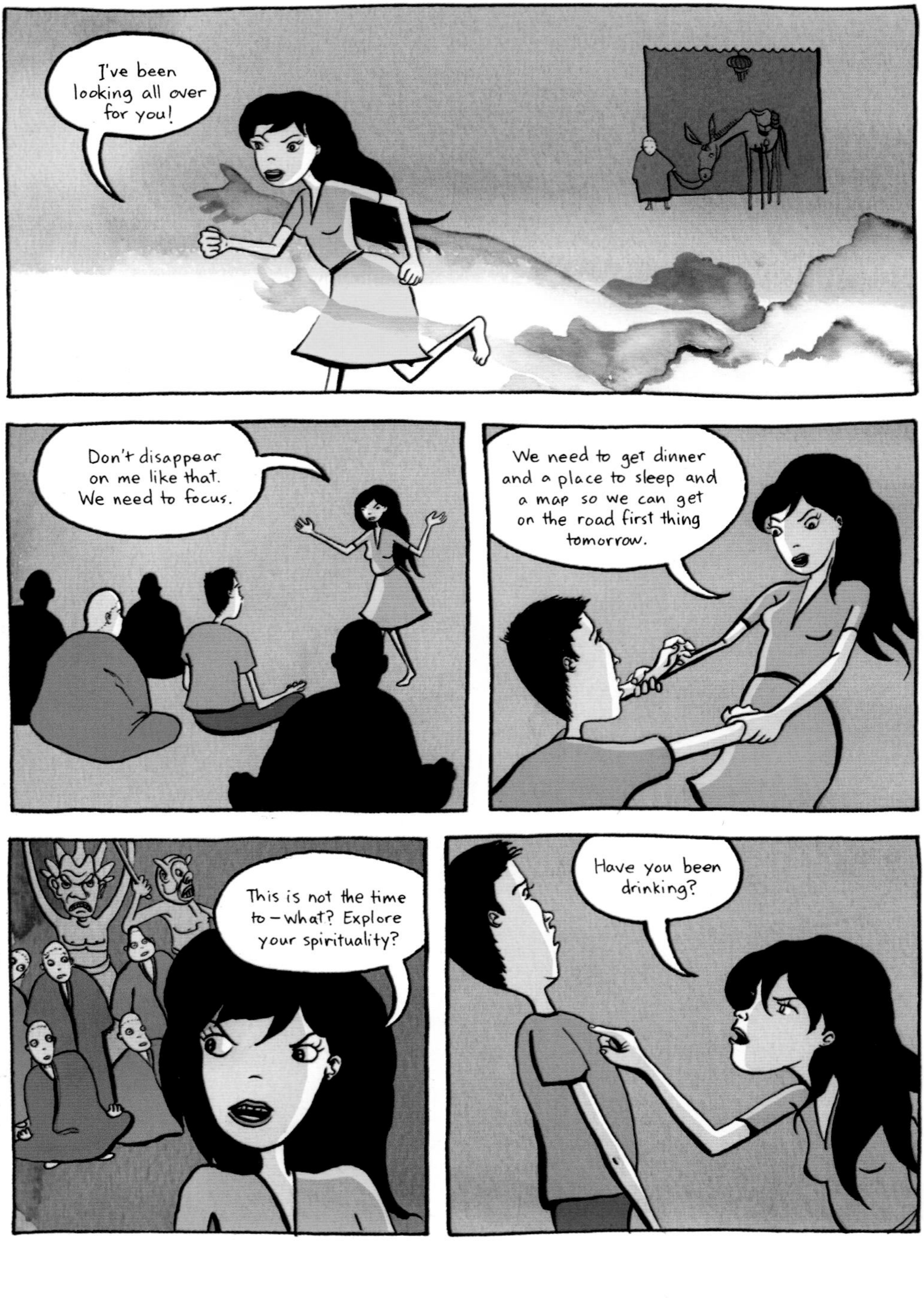
I've been looking all over for you!
Don't disappear on me like that. We need to focus.
We need to get dinner and a place to sleep and a map so we can get on the road first thing tomorrow.
This is not the time to—what? Explore your spirituality?
Have you been drinking?

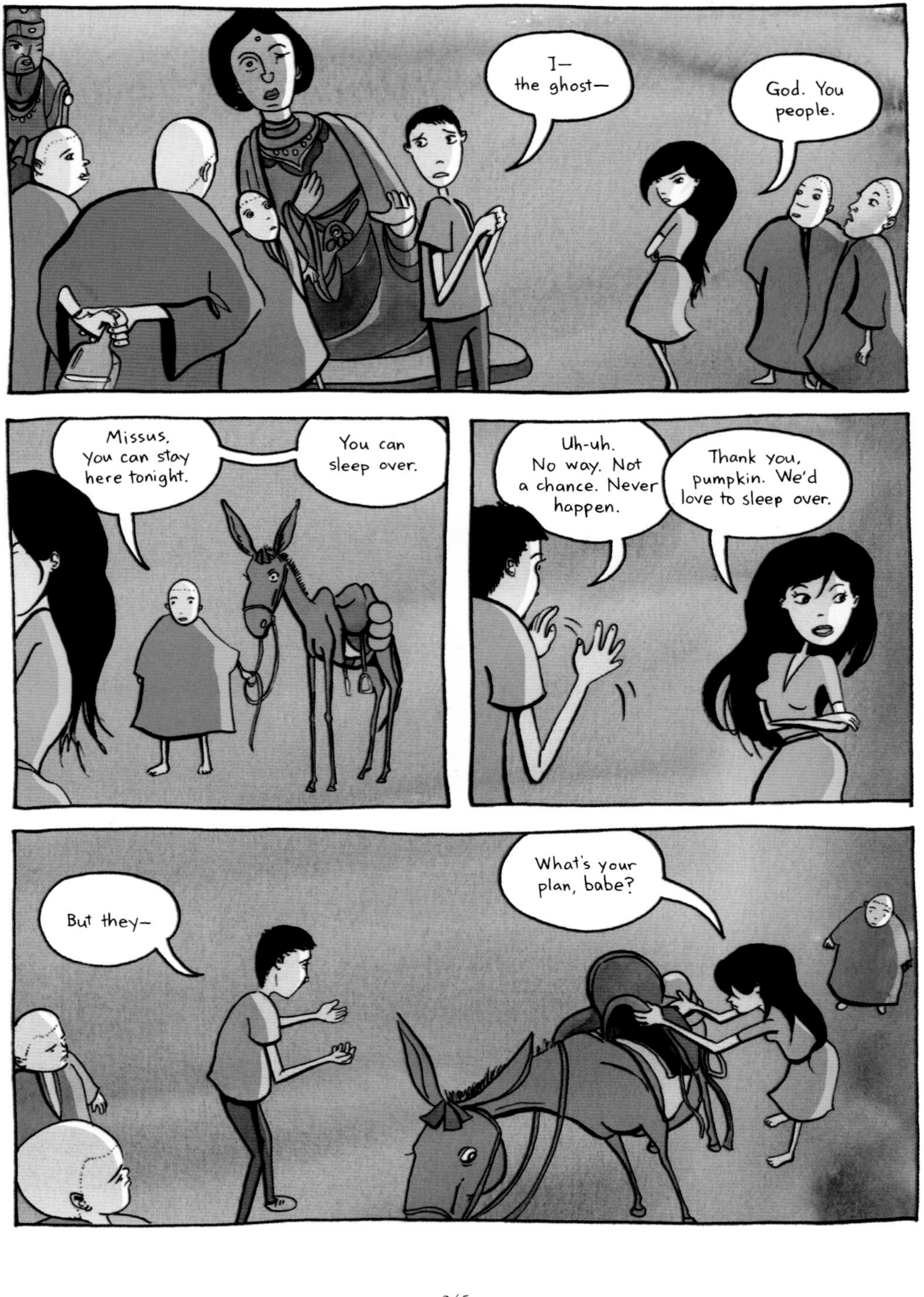
I— the ghost—
God. You people.
Missus, You can stay here tonight.
You can sleep over.
Uh-uh. No way. Not a chance. Never happen.
Thank you, pumpkin. We'd love to sleep over.
But they—
What's your plan, babe?

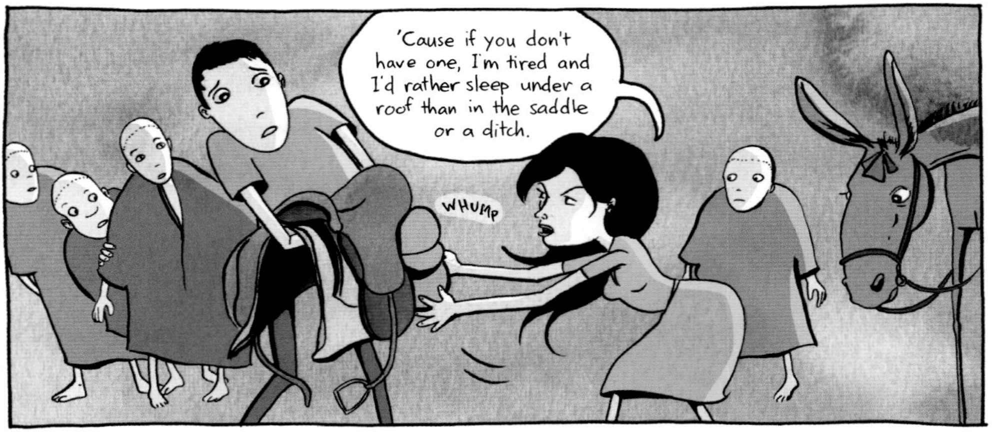
'Cause if you don't have one, I'm tired and I'd rather sleep under a roof than in the saddle or a ditch.
WHUMP

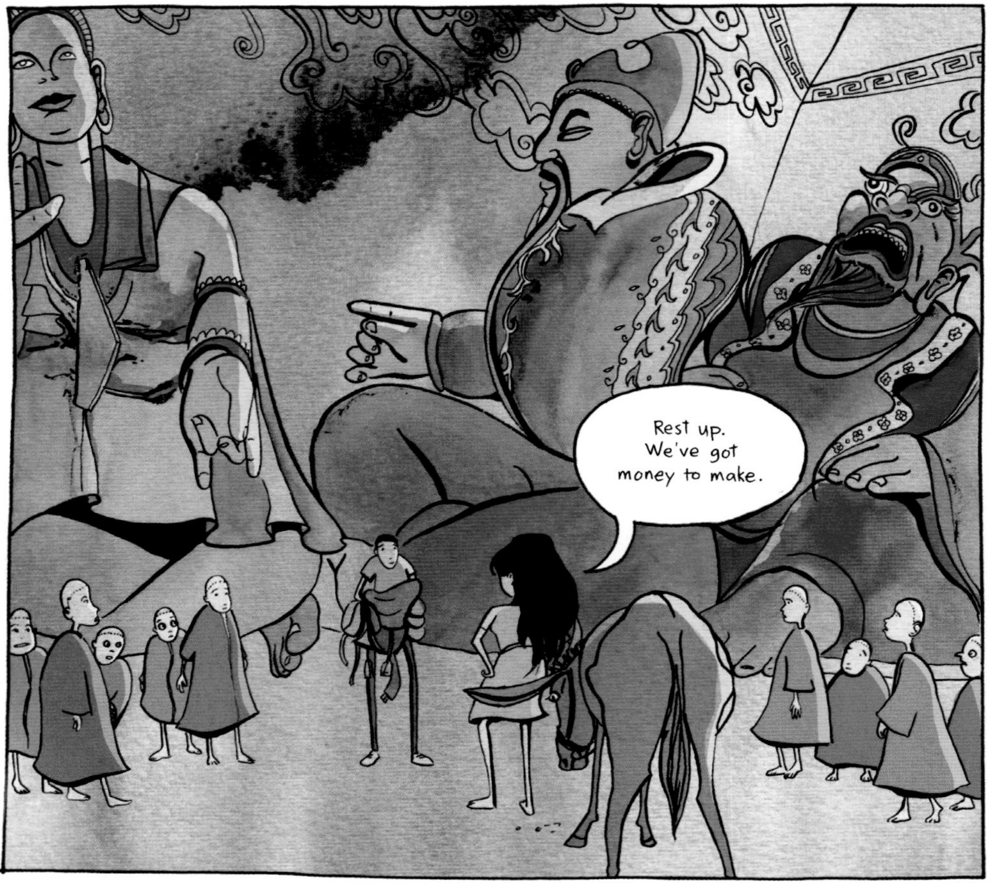
Rest up. We've got money to make.

19. Testimonial of a Washout

FRIDAY

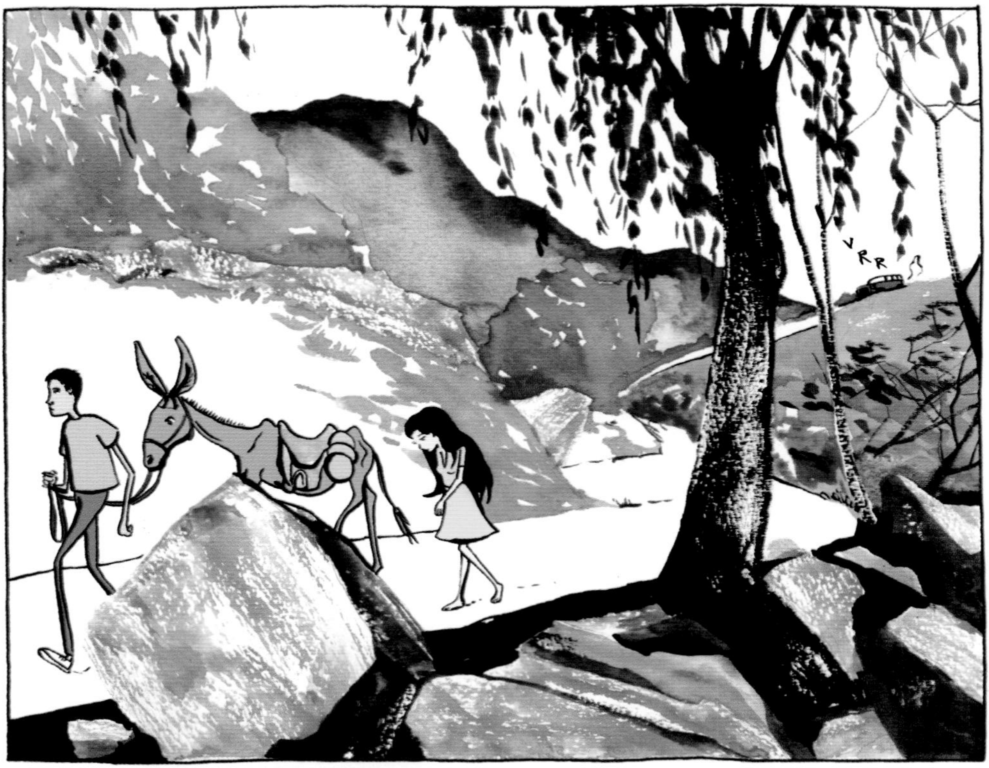
VRR

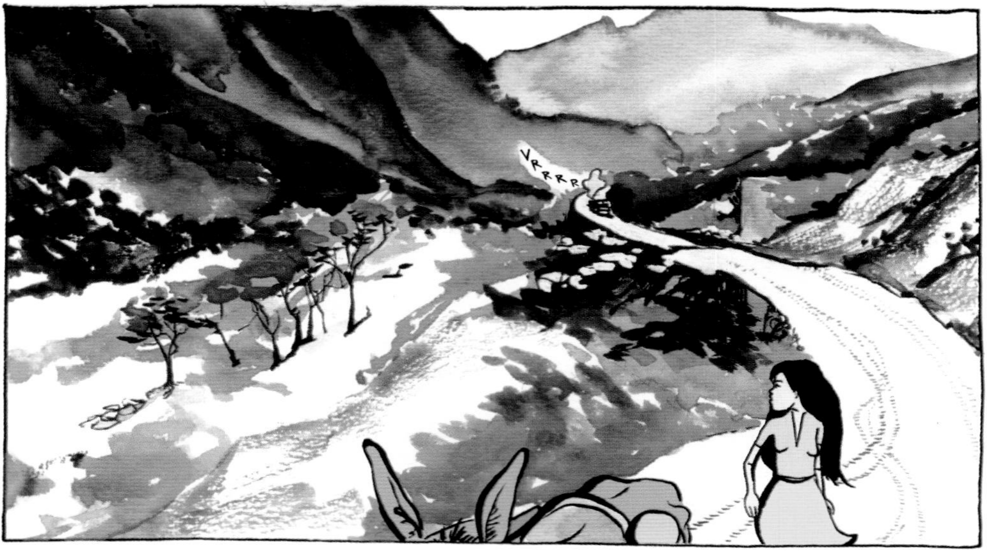
VRRRR

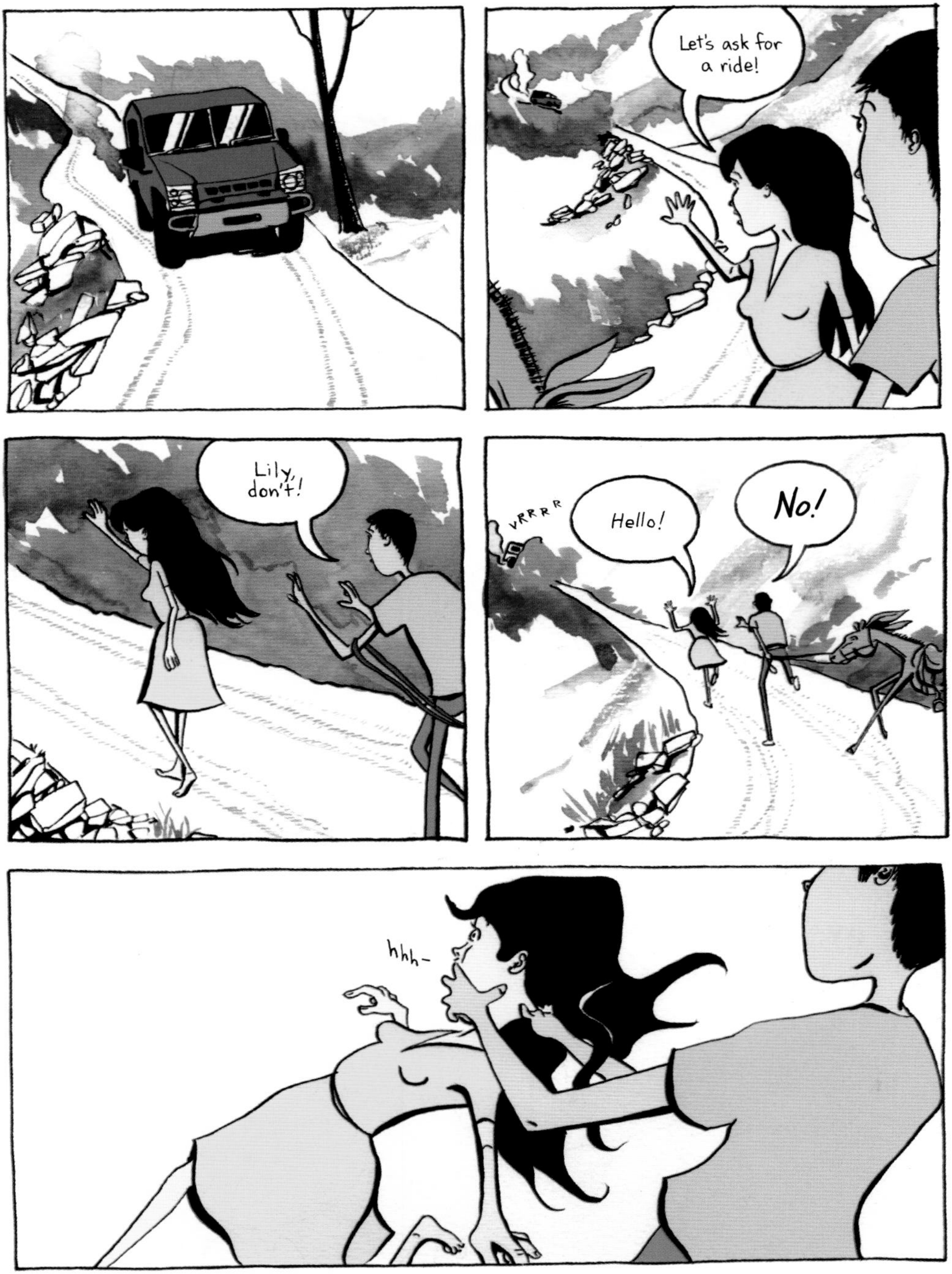

Let's ask for a ride!
Lily, don't!
VRRRR
Hello!
No!
hhh-

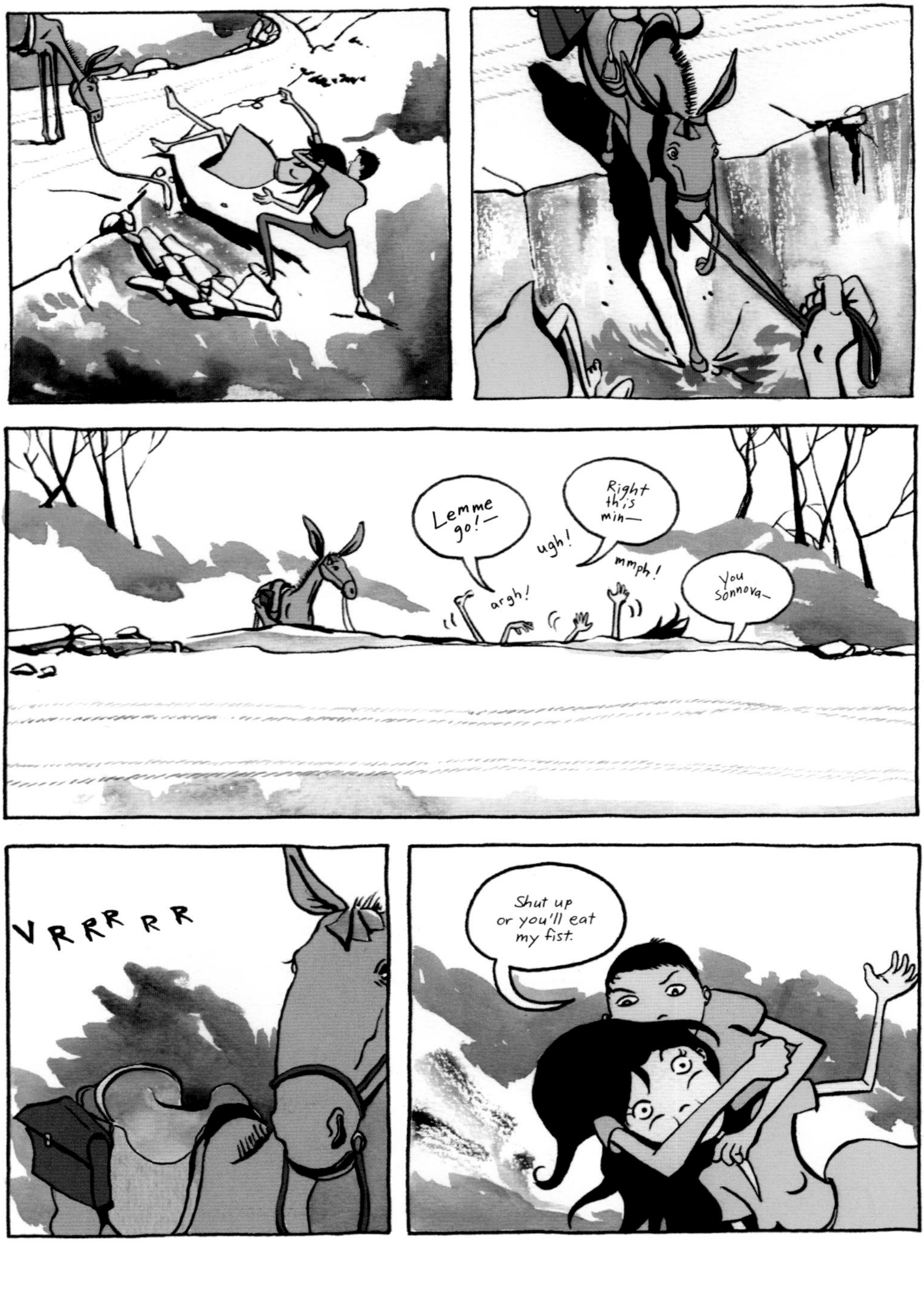
Lemme go!—
ugh!
argh!
Right this min—
mmph!
You sonnova—
VRRRRR
Shut up or you'll eat my fist.

VVRRRRR

251

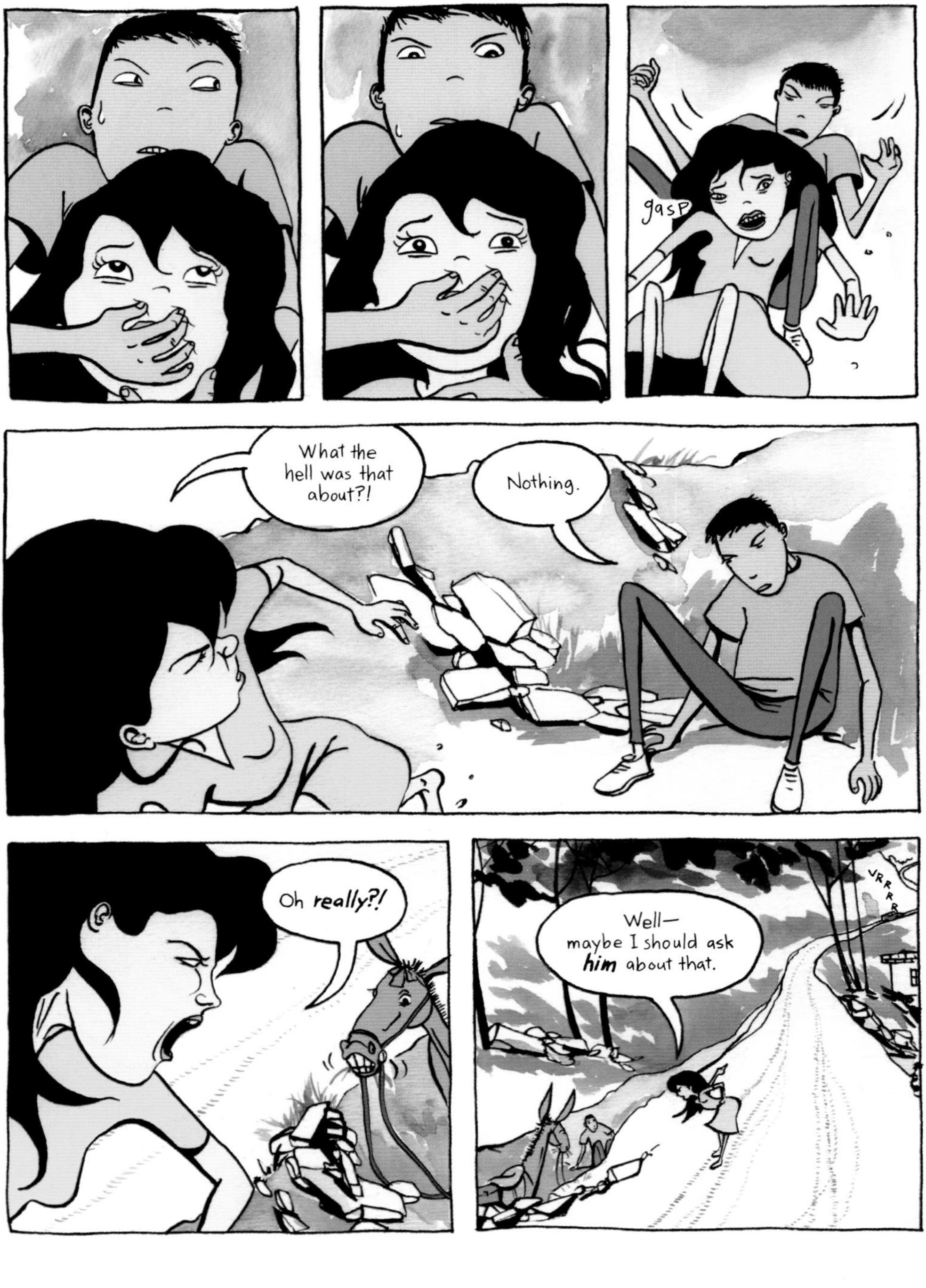
gasp
What the hell was that about?!
Nothing.
Oh really?!
Well— maybe I should ask him about that.
VRRRR

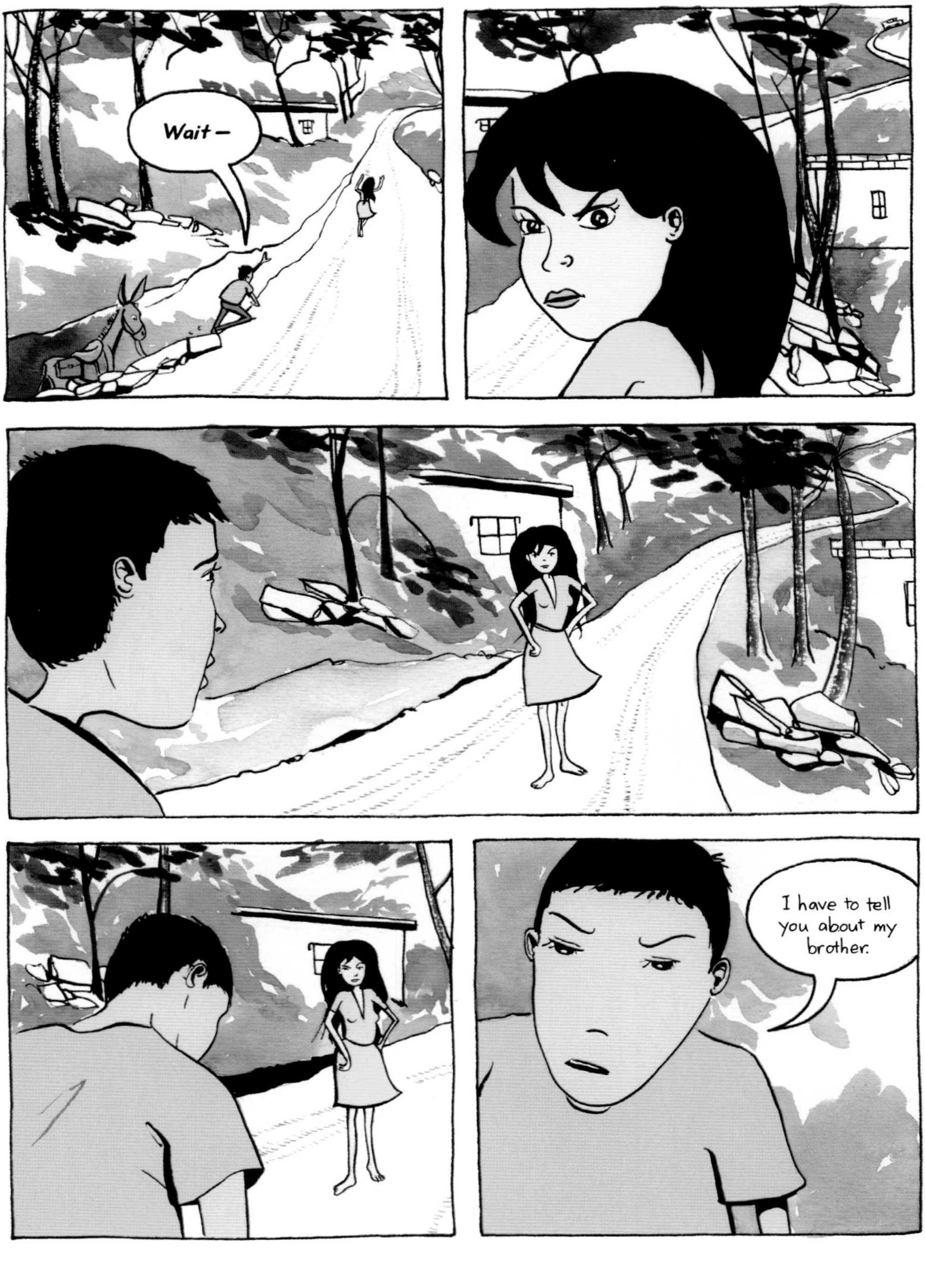
Wait –
I have to tell you about my brother.

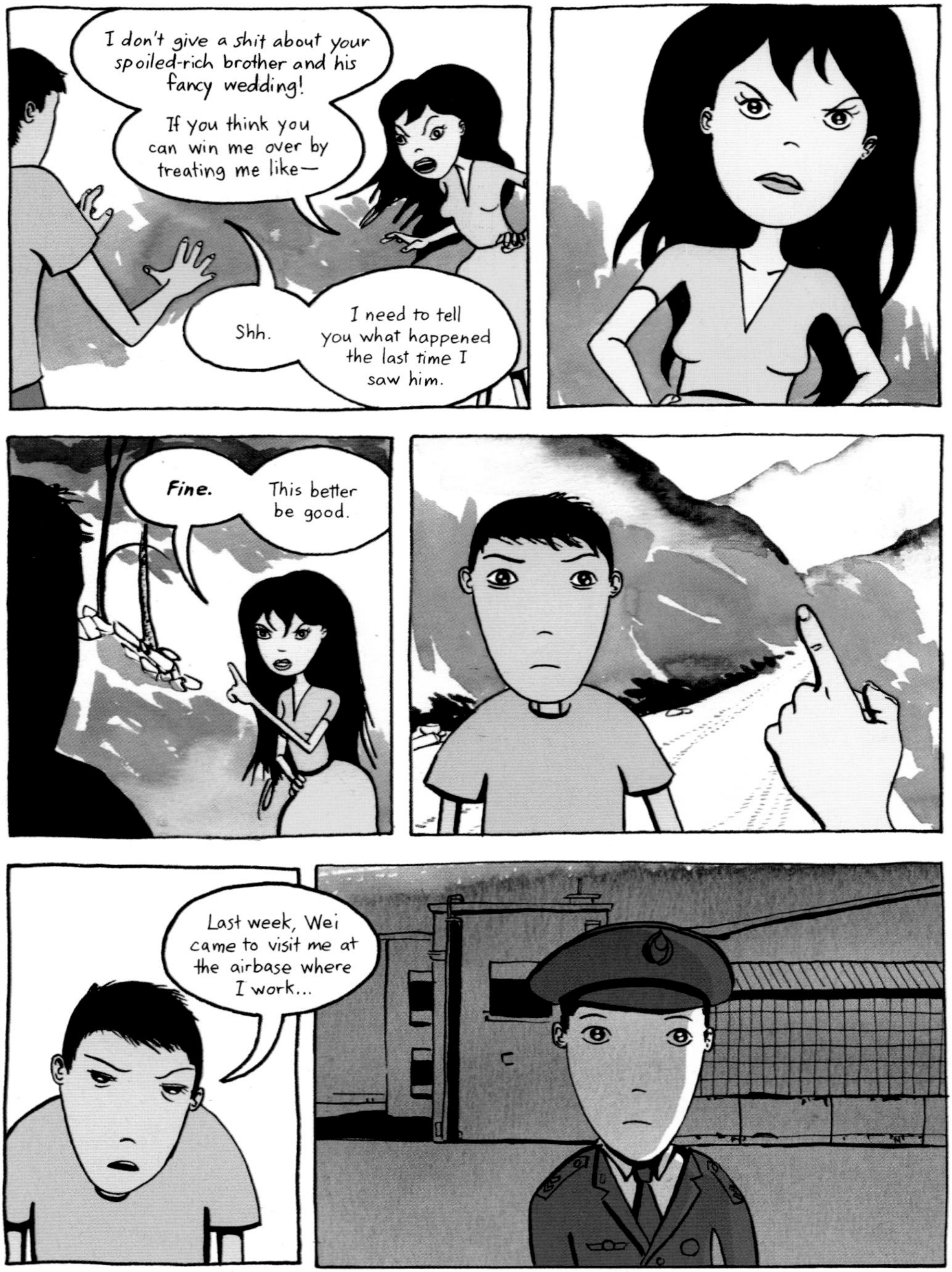
I don't give a shit about your spoiled-rich brother and his fancy wedding!
If you think you can win me over by treating me like—
Shh.
I need to tell you what happened the last time I saw him.
Fine.
This better be good.
Last week, Wei came to visit me at the airbase where I work...

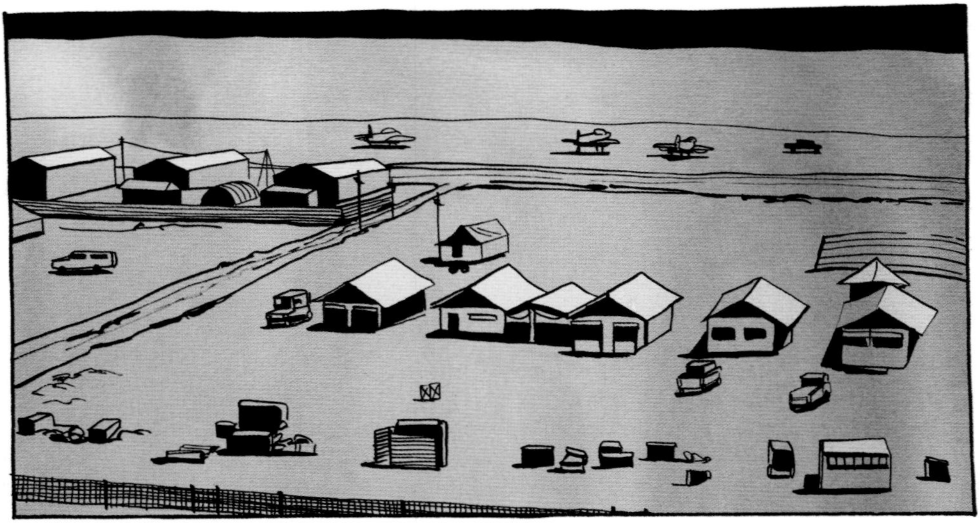

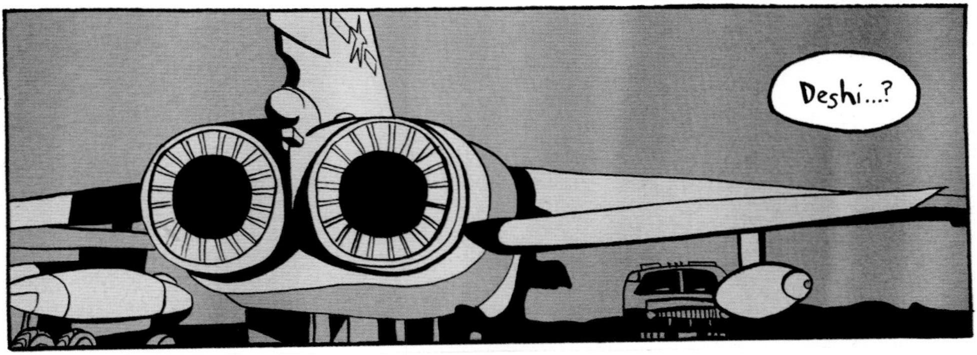
Deshi...?

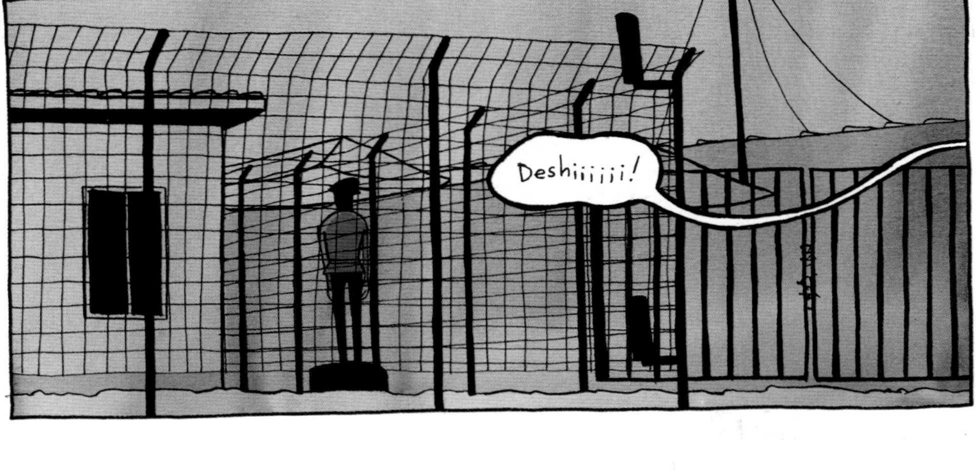
Deshiiiiii!

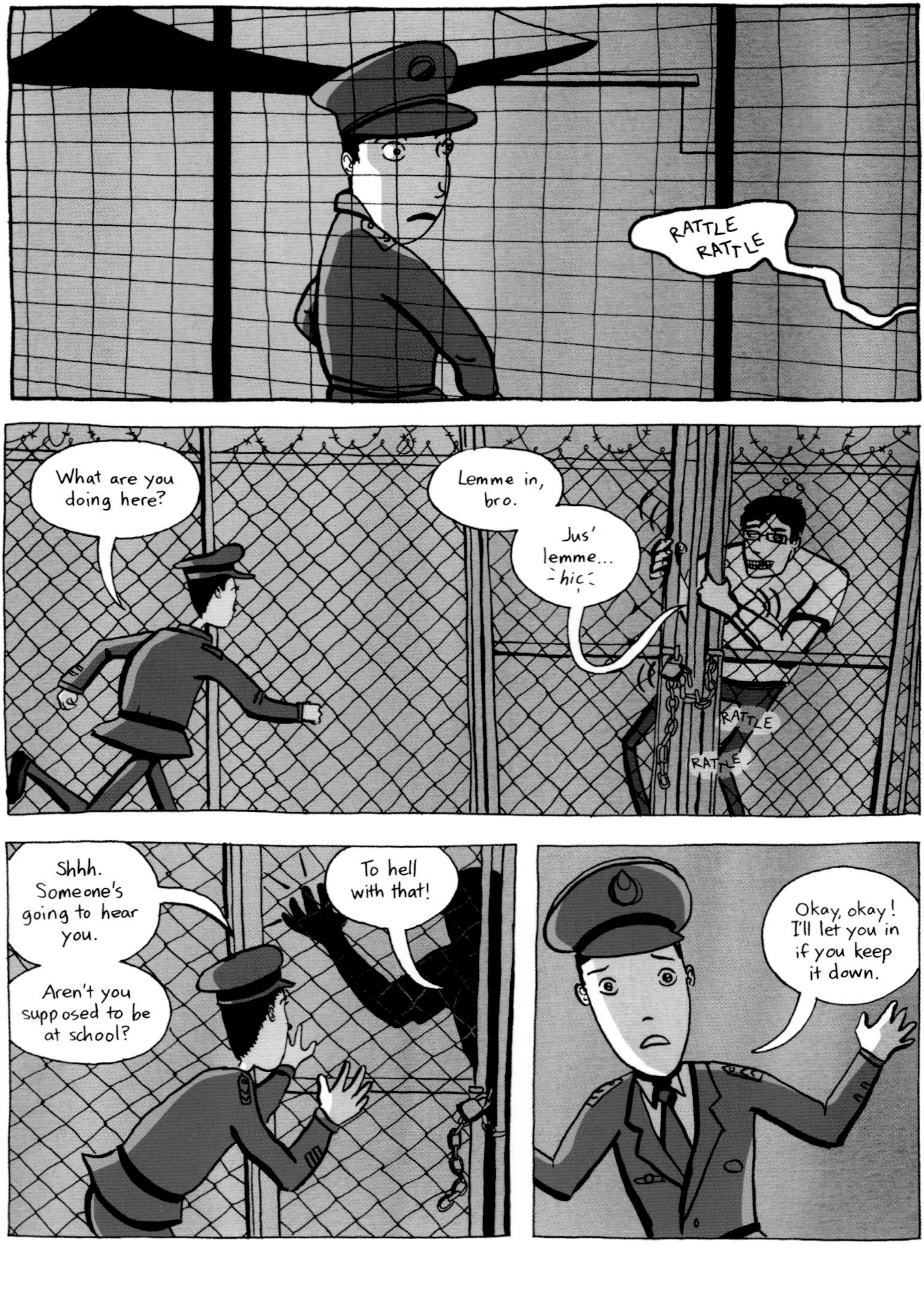
RATTLE RATTLE
What are you doing here?
Lemme in, bro.
Jus' lemme... hic
RATTLE
RATTLE
Shhh. Someone's going to hear you.
Aren't you supposed to be at school?
To hell with that!
Okay, okay! I'll let you in if you keep it down.

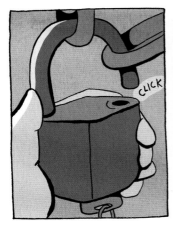

CLICK

hic

He smelled like
sour alcohol and
grinned like a wolf.

My brother,
The Wolf.

Hey, little
man.

I missed
you, kid.

So listen,
Deshi. I need
you to call
Dad.

Why don't
you call Dad
yourself.

Tell him I've
got the bird
flu—no.

Tell him classes have
been canceled due
to a bomb threat—
no, wait.

Tell him I've been
selected for an elite
academic program
in Siberia—no.

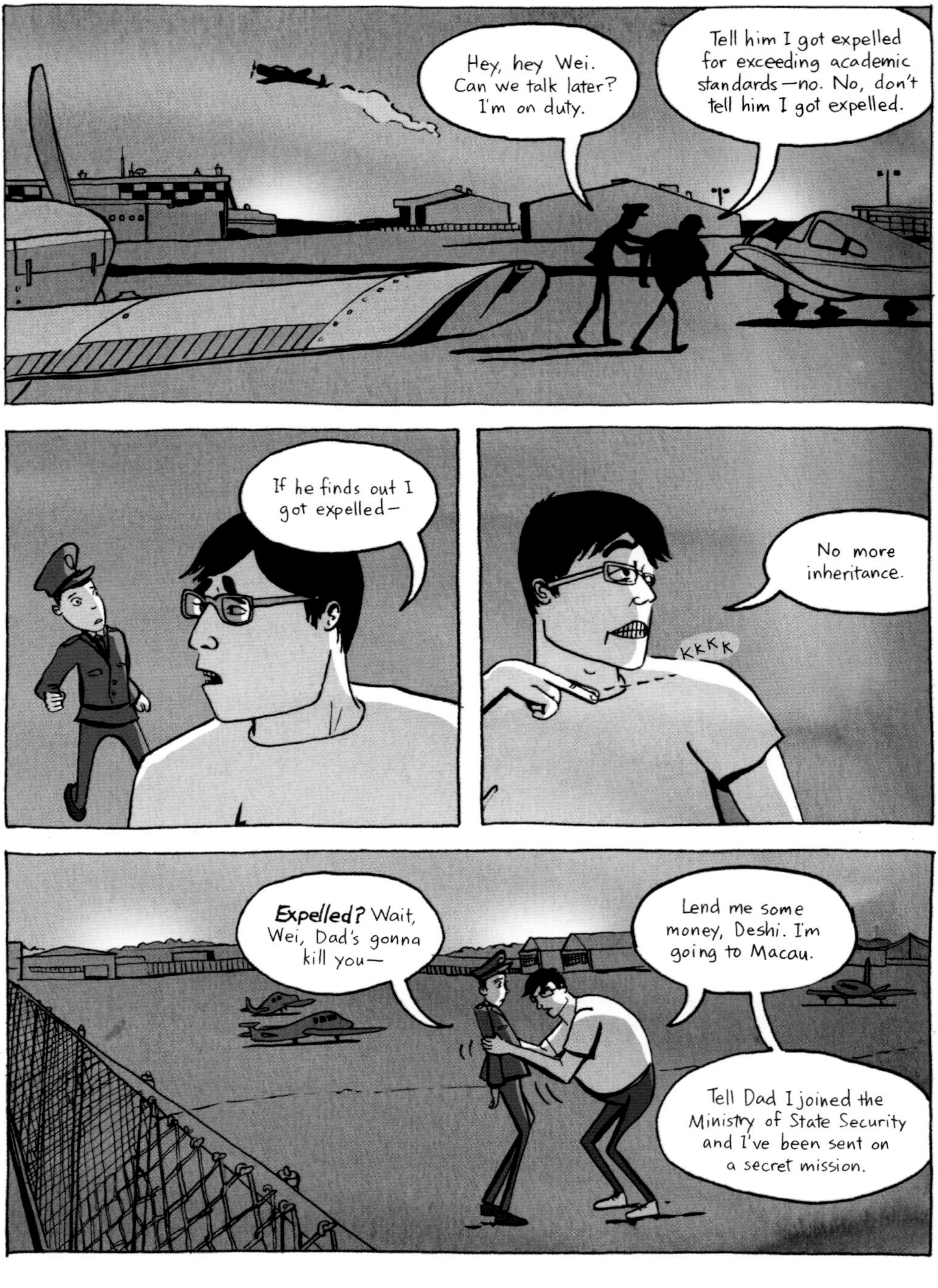
Hey, hey Wei. Can we talk later? I'm on duty.
Tell him I got expelled for exceeding academic standards—no. No, don't tell him I got expelled.
If he finds out I got expelled—
No more inheritance.
KKKK
Expelled? Wait, Wei, Dad's gonna kill you—
Lend me some money, Deshi. I'm going to Macau.
Tell Dad I joined the Ministry of State Security and I've been sent on a secret mission.

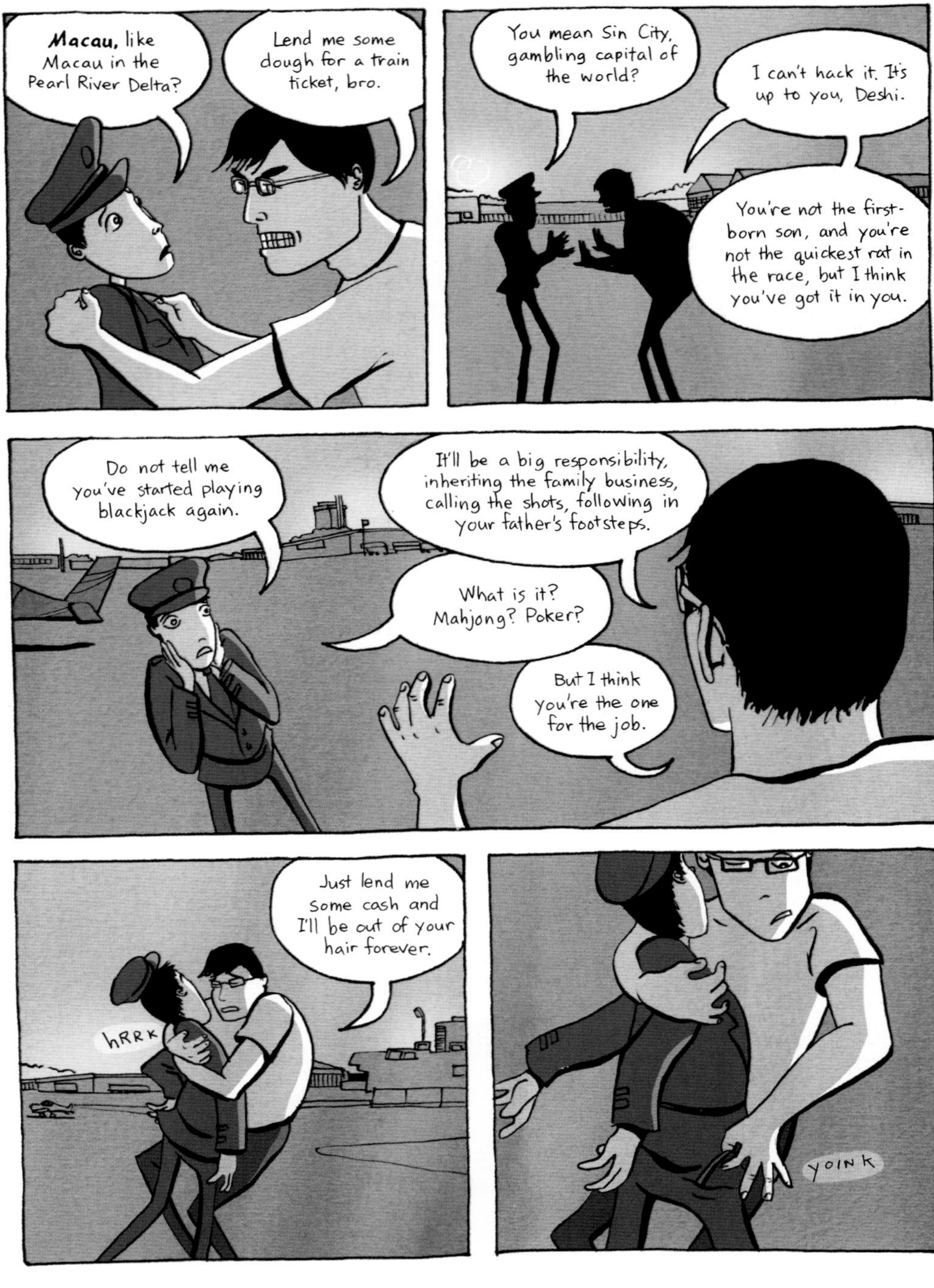
Macau, like Macau in the Pearl River Delta?
Lend me some dough for a train ticket, bro.
You mean Sin City, gambling capital of the world?
I can't hack it. It's up to you, Deshi.
You're not the first-born son, and you're not the quickest rat in the race, but I think you've got it in you.
Do not tell me you've started playing blackjack again.
It'll be a big responsibility, inheriting the family business, calling the shots, following in your father's footsteps.
What is it? Mahjong? Poker?
But I think you're the one for the job.
Just lend me some cash and I'll be out of your hair forever.
hRRK
YOINK

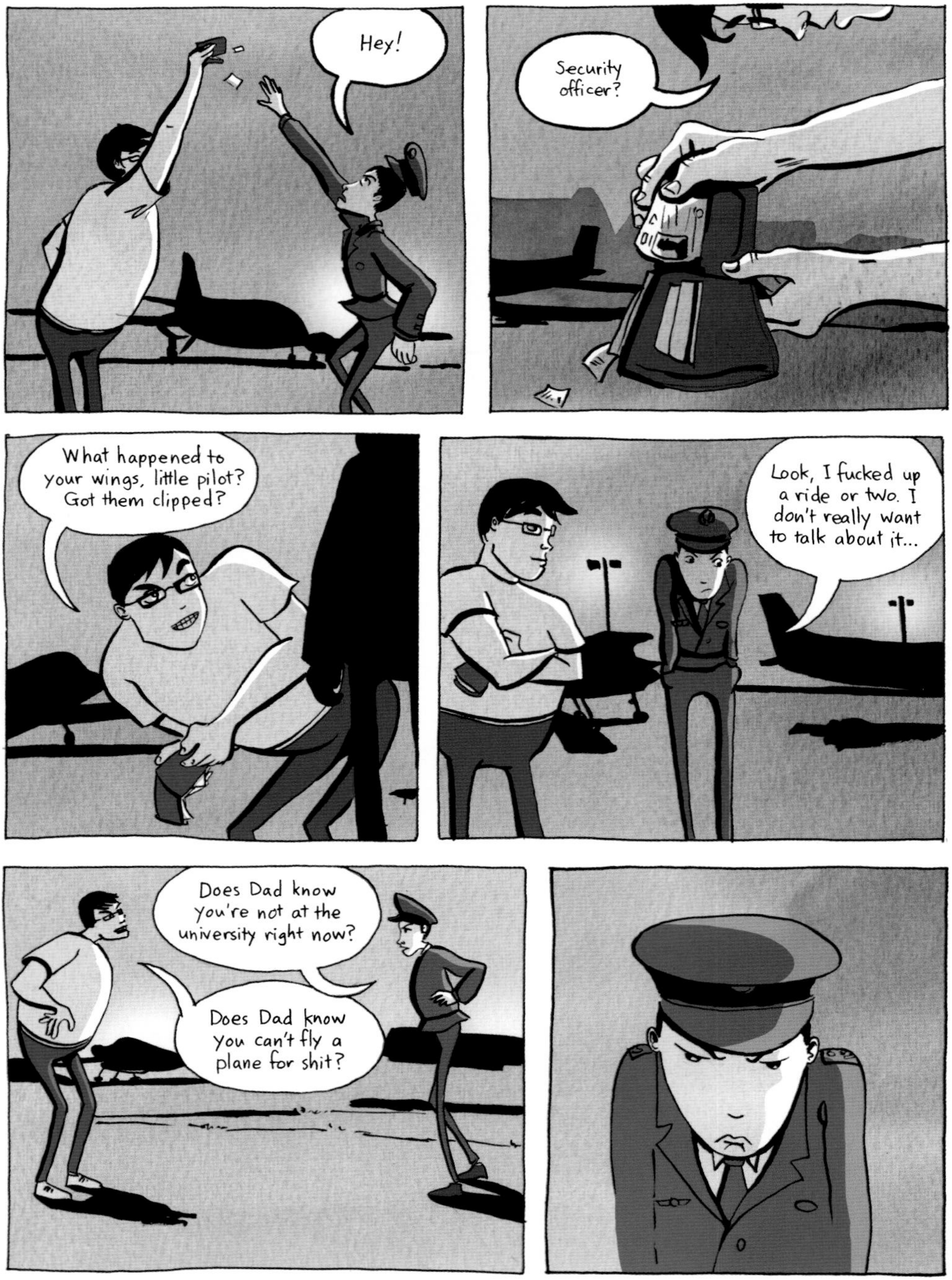
Hey!
Security officer?
What happened to your wings, little pilot? Got them clipped?
Look, I fucked up a ride or two. I don't really want to talk about it...
Does Dad know you're not at the university right now?
Does Dad know you can't fly a plane for shit?

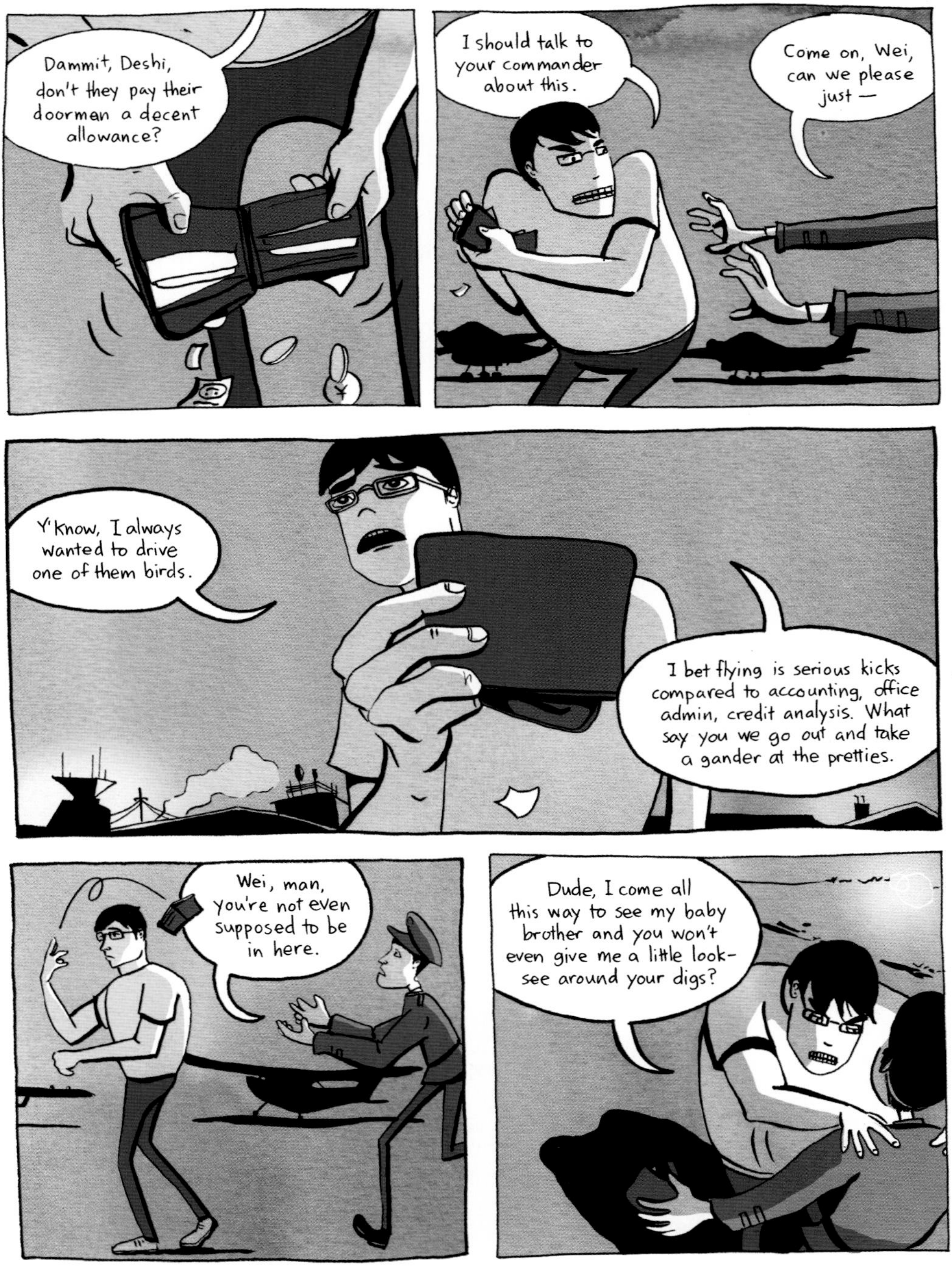
Dammit, Deshi, don't they pay their doormen a decent allowance?
I should talk to your commander about this.
Come on, Wei, can we please just —
Y'know, I always wanted to drive one of them birds.
I bet flying is serious kicks compared to accounting, office admin, credit analysis. What say you we go out and take a gander at the pretties.
Wei, man, you're not even supposed to be in here.
Dude, I come all this way to see my baby brother and you won't even give me a little look-see around your digs?

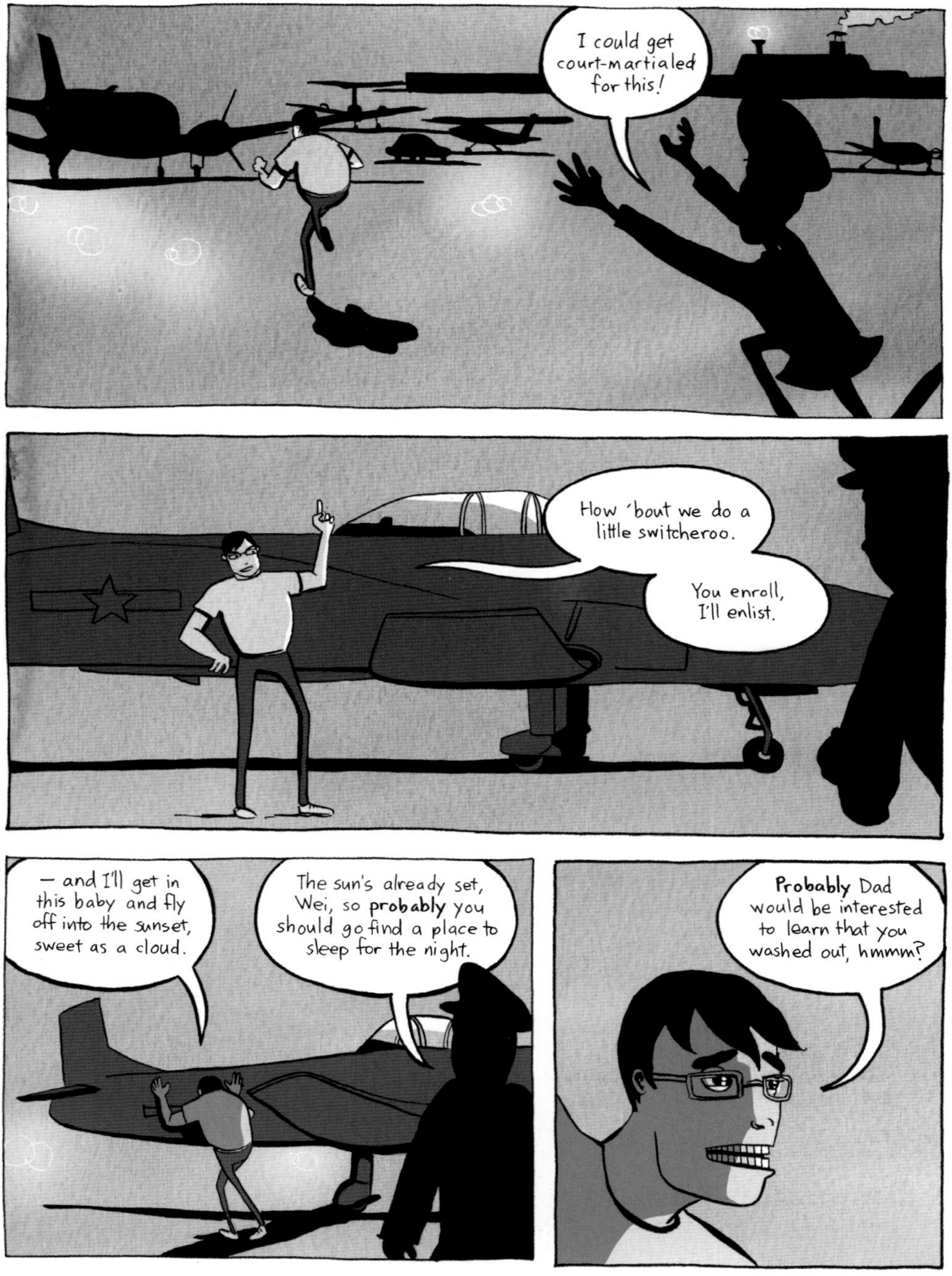
I could get court-martialed for this!
How 'bout we do a little switcheroo.
You enroll, I'll enlist.
— and I'll get in this baby and fly off into the sunset, sweet as a cloud.
The sun's already set, Wei, so **probably** you should go find a place to sleep for the night.
Probably Dad would be interested to learn that you washed out, hmmm?

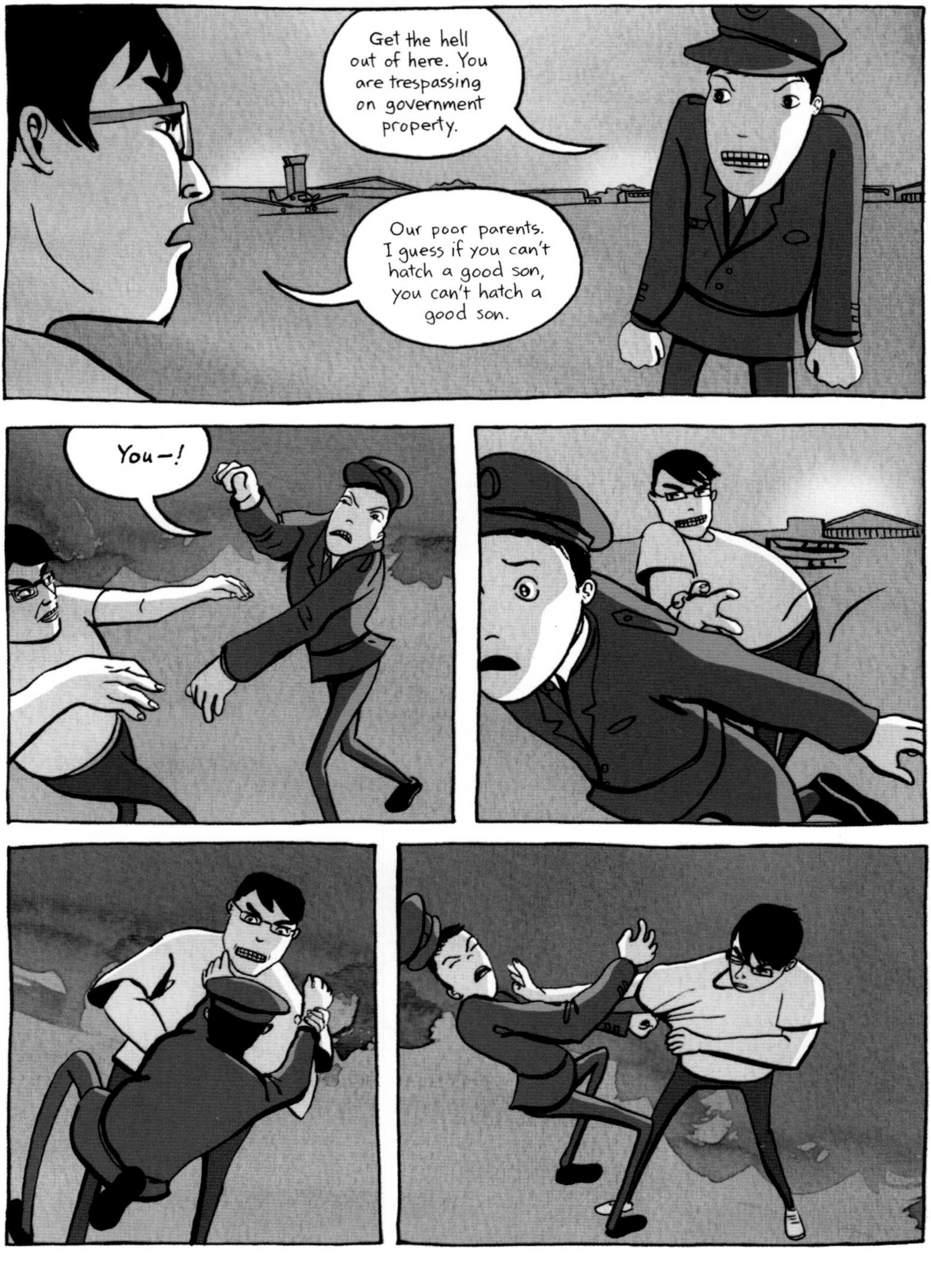
Get the hell out of here. You are trespassing on government property.
Our poor parents. I guess if you can't hatch a good son, you can't hatch a good son.
You—!

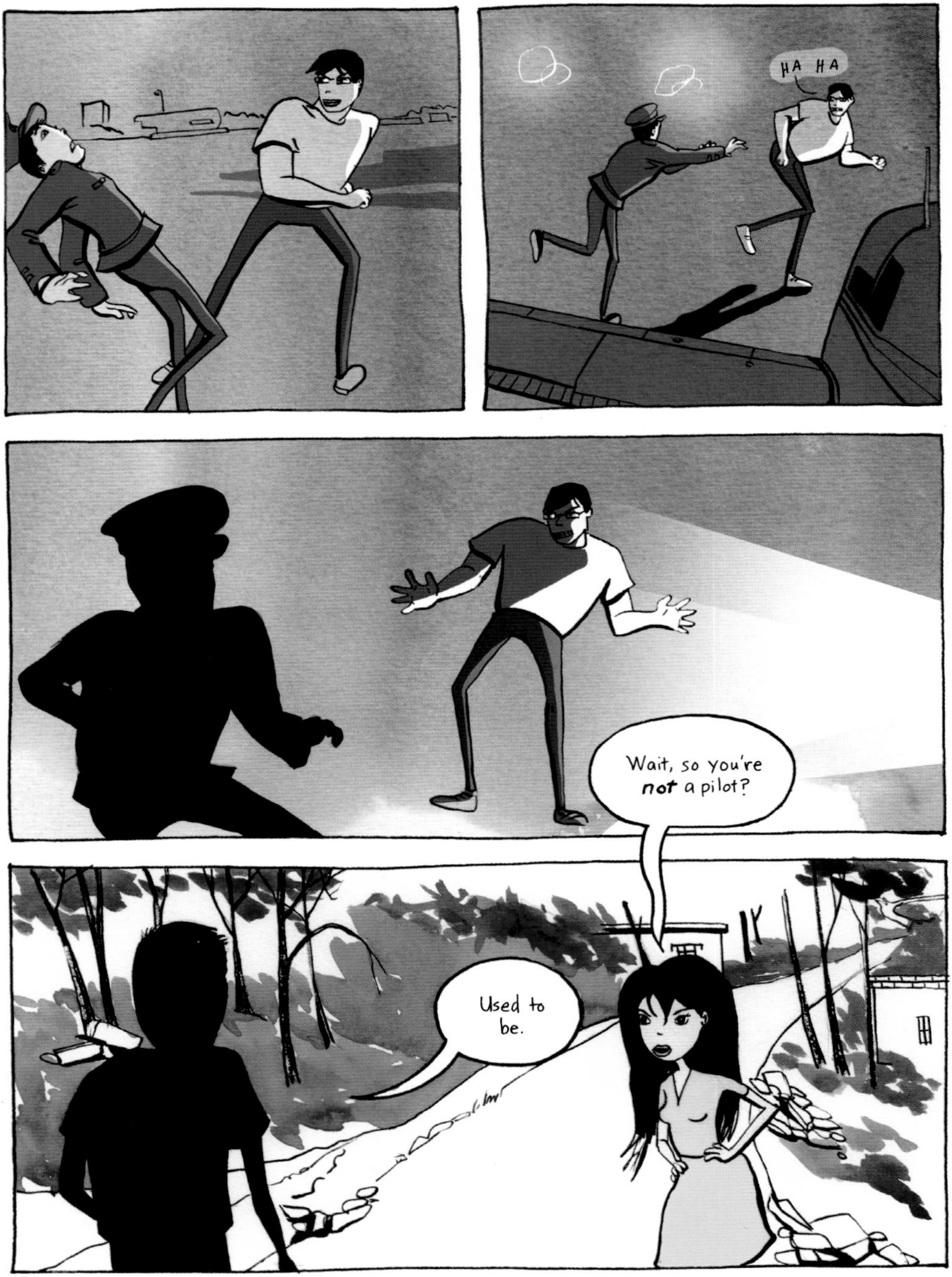
HA HA
Wait, so you're **not** a pilot?
Used to be.

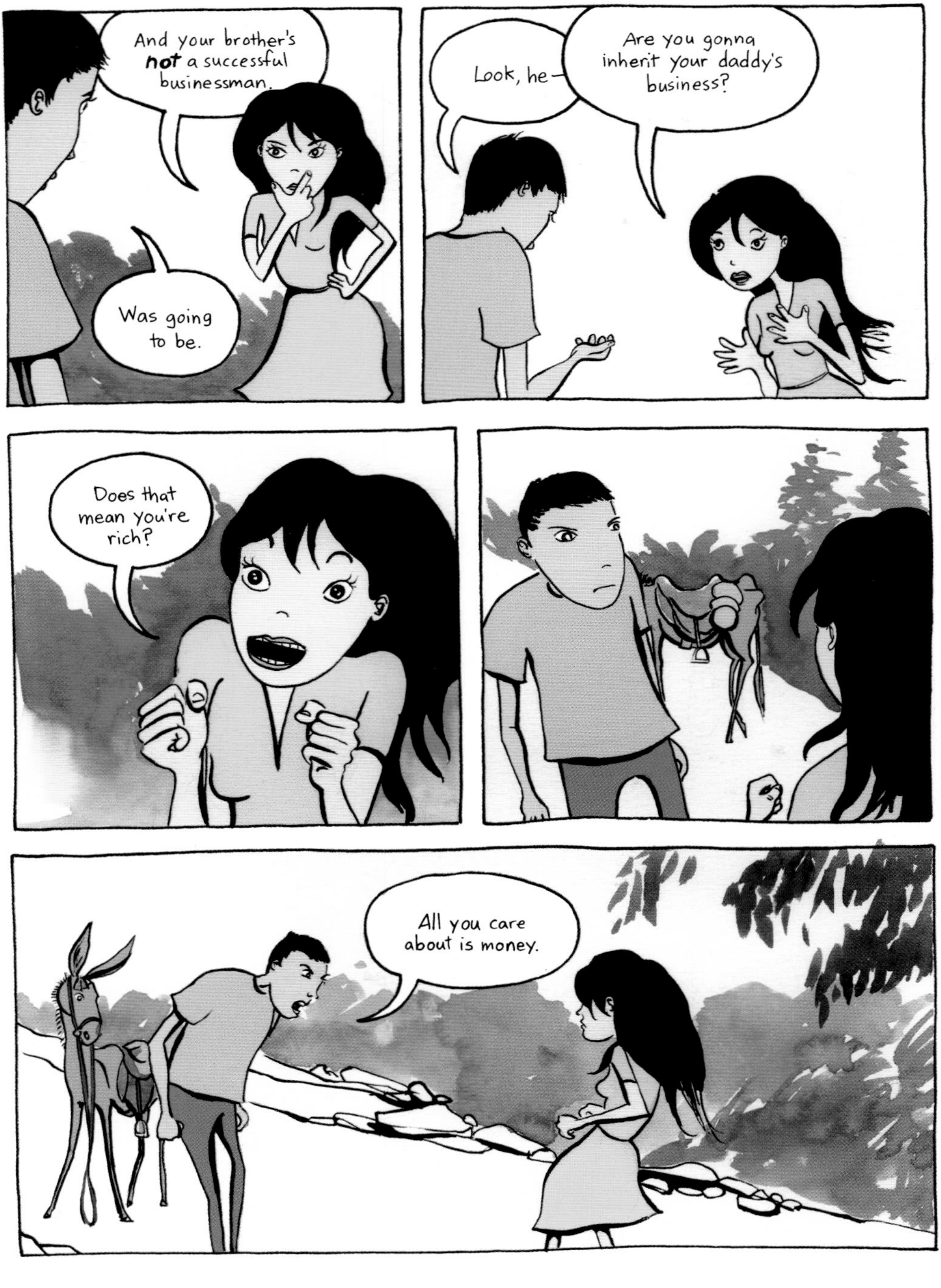
And your brother's **not** a successful businessman.
Was going to be.
Look, he—
Are you gonna inherit your daddy's business?
Does that mean you're rich?
All you care about is money.

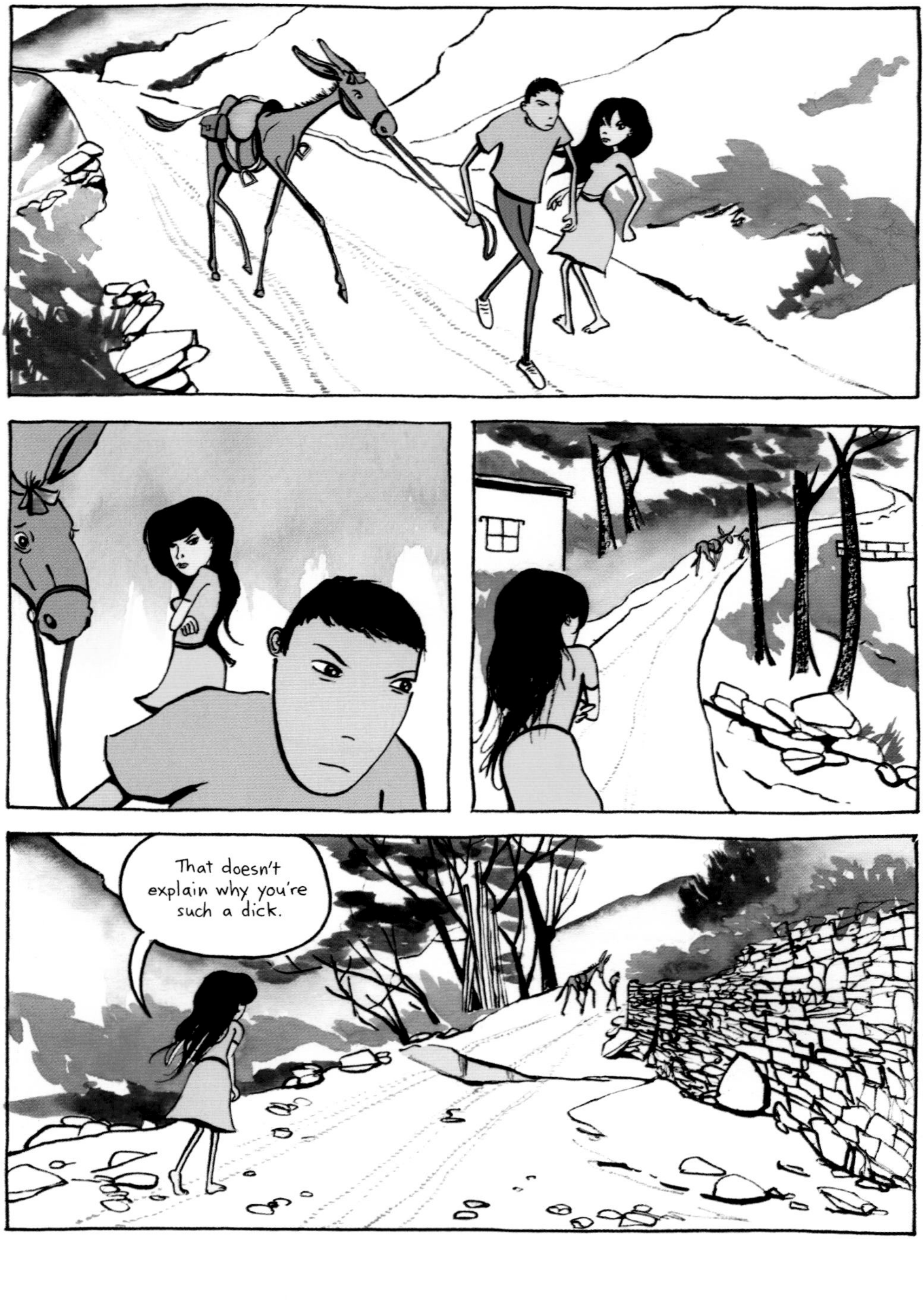
That doesn't explain why you're such a dick.

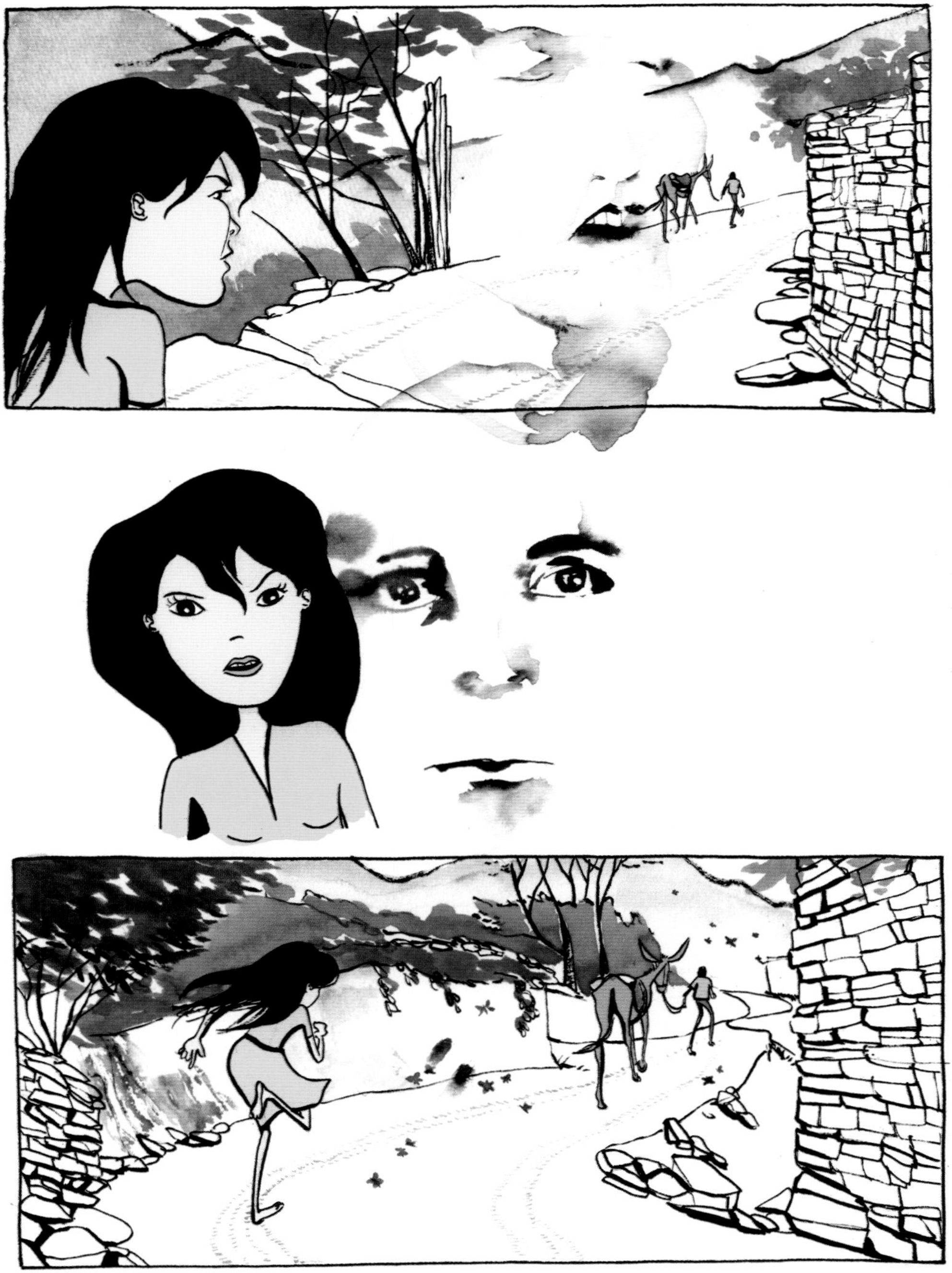

20. The Fortune House

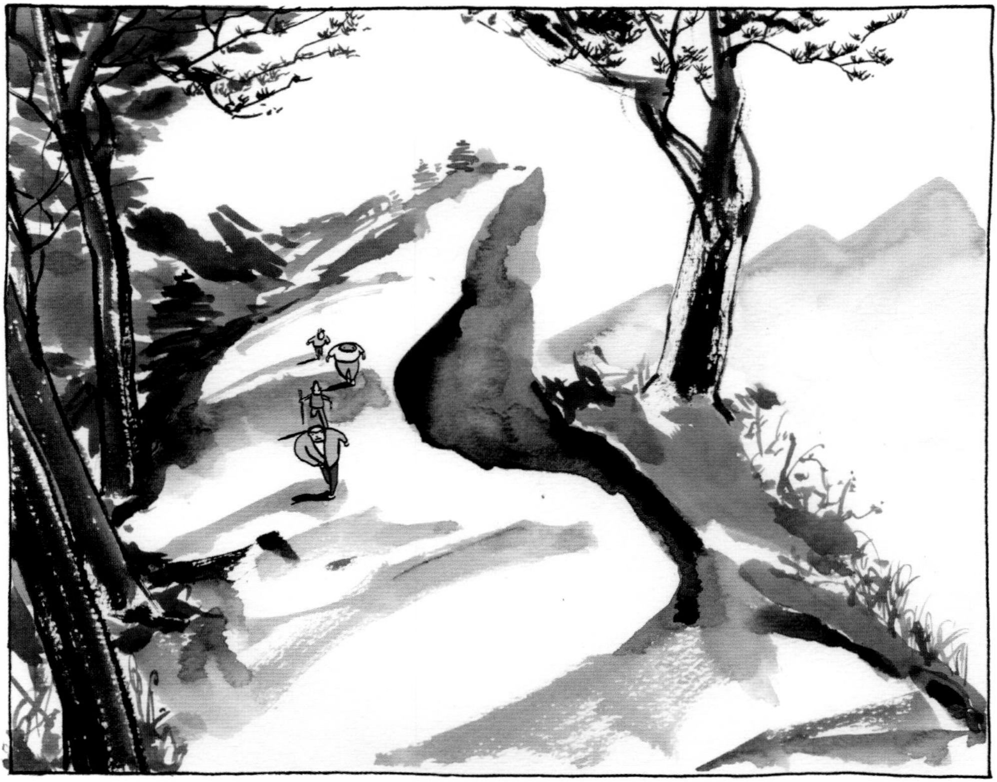

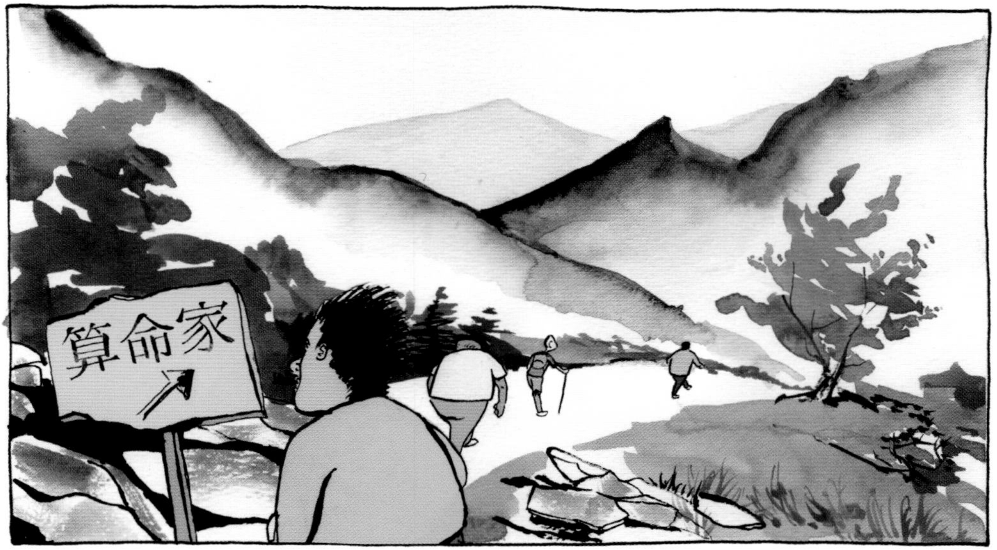
算命家

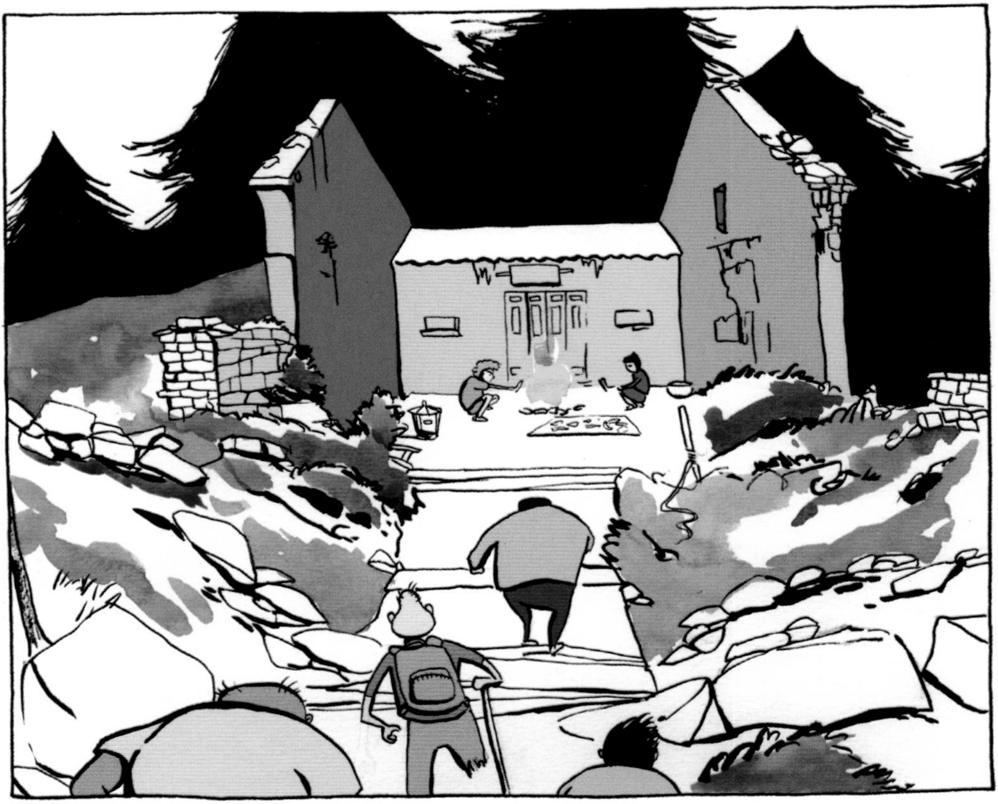

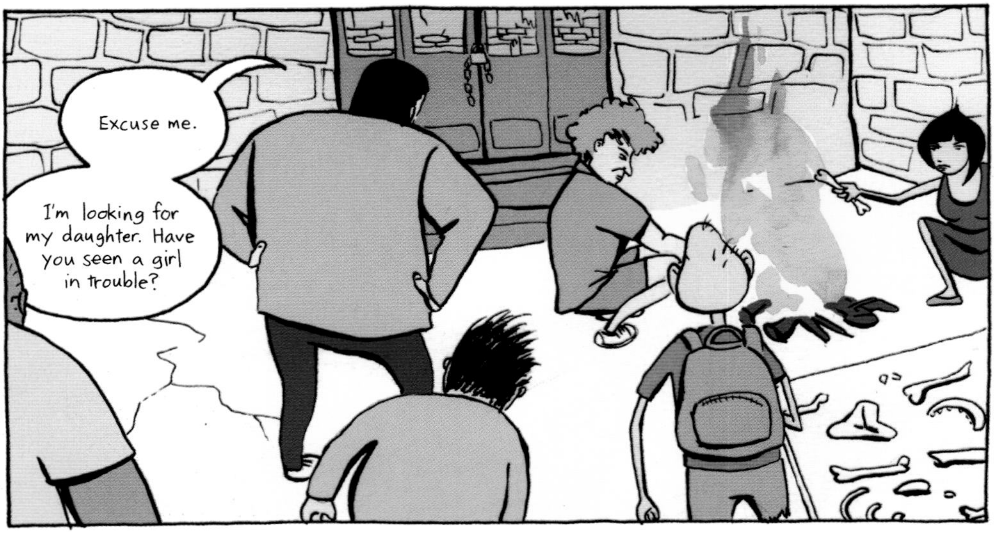
Excuse me.
I'm looking for my daughter. Have you seen a girl in trouble?

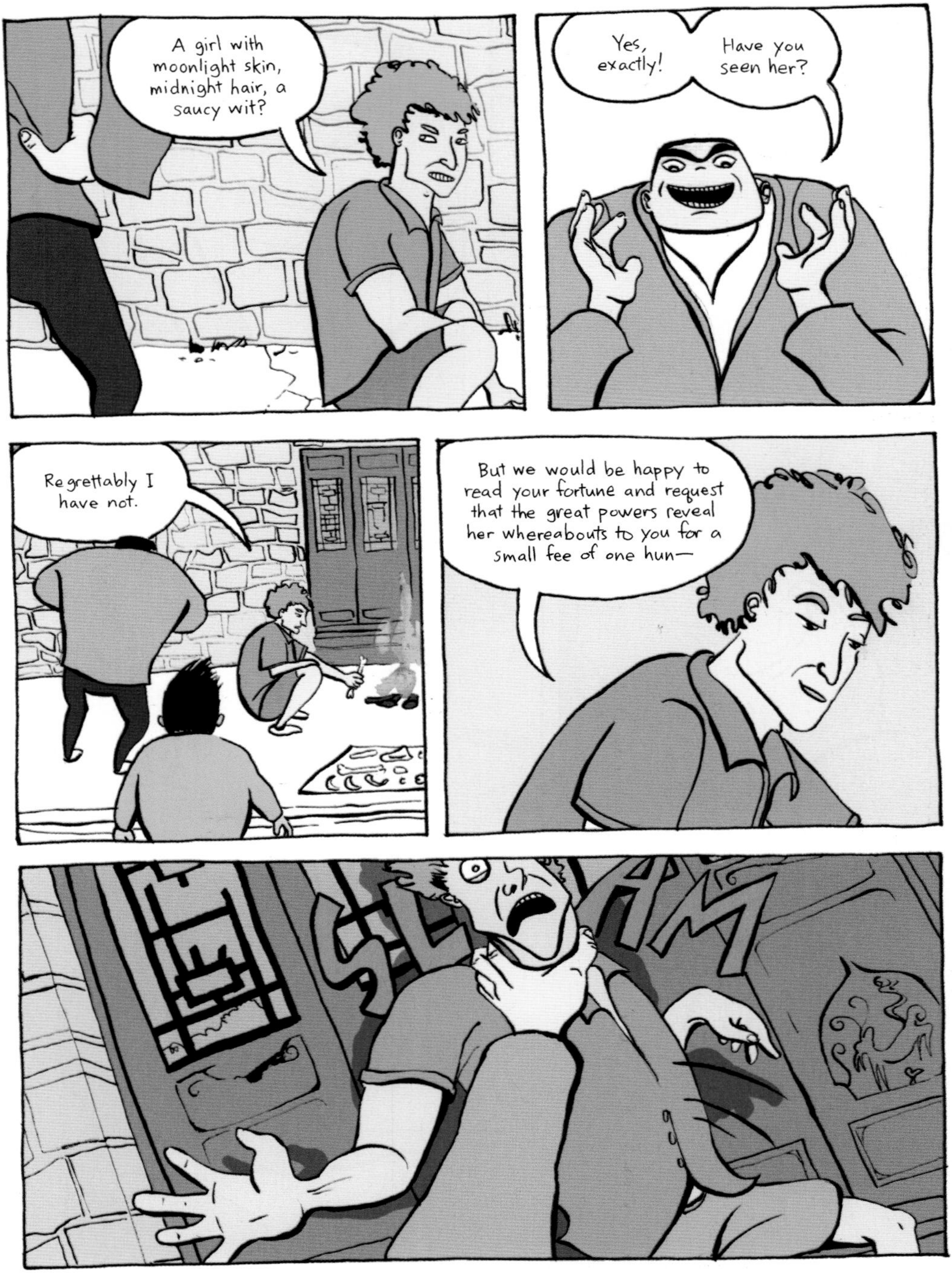
A girl with moonlight skin, midnight hair, a saucy wit?
Yes, exactly!
Have you seen her?
Regrettably I have not.
But we would be happy to read your fortune and request that the great powers reveal her whereabouts to you for a small fee of one hun—
SLAM

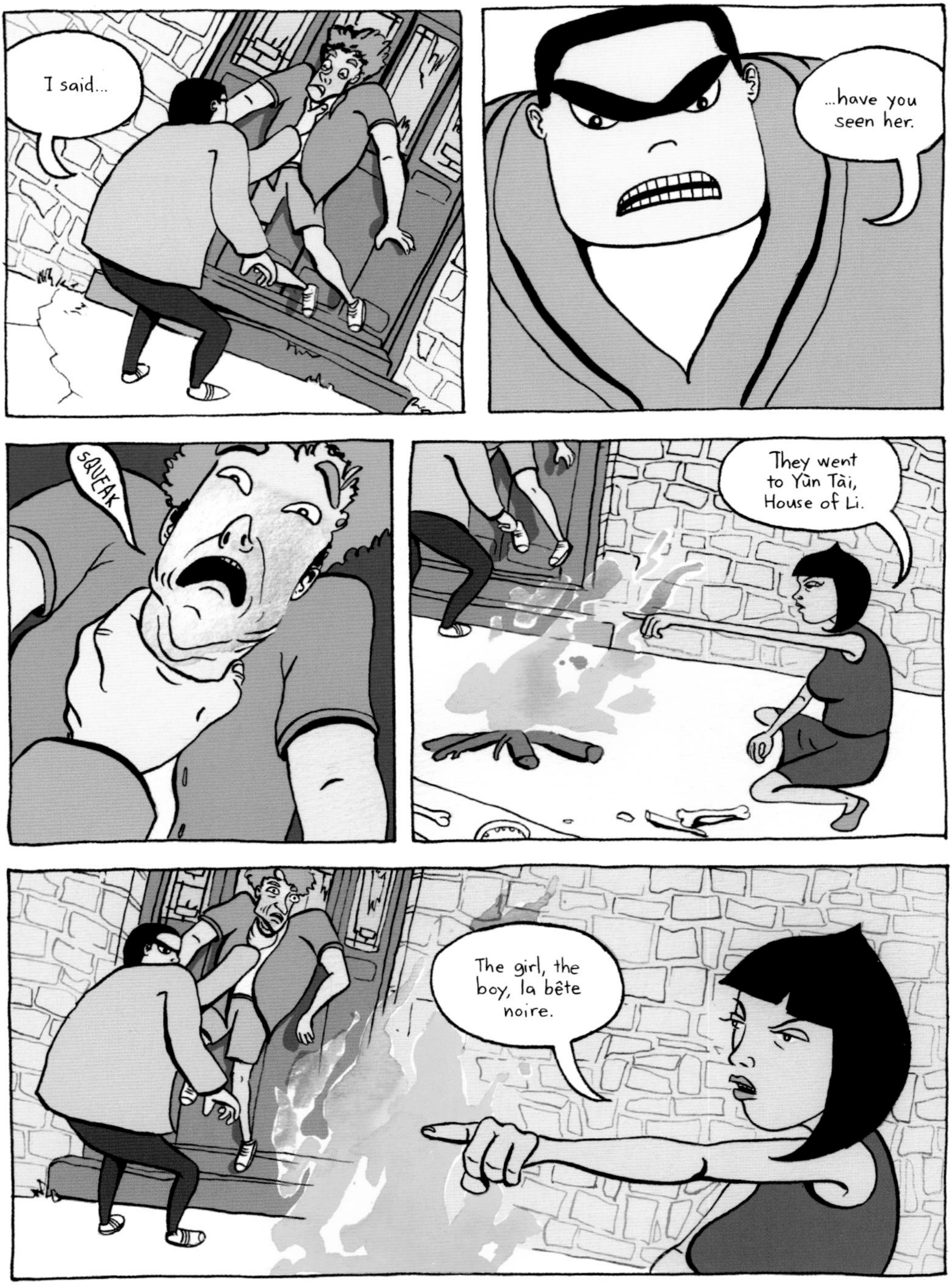
I said...
...have you seen her.
SQUEAK
They went to Yùn Tài, House of Li.
The girl, the boy, la bête noire.

21. The Way Home

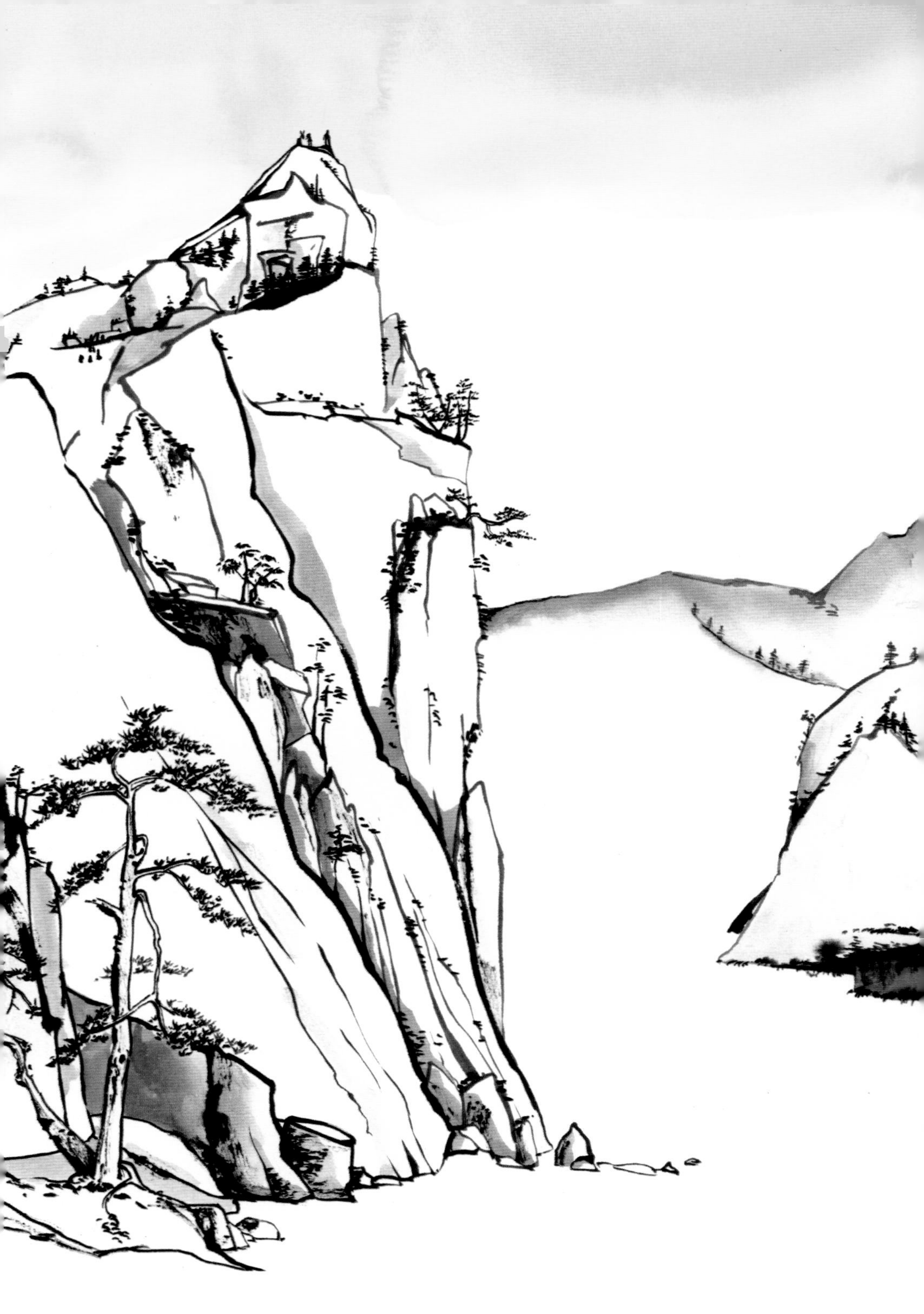

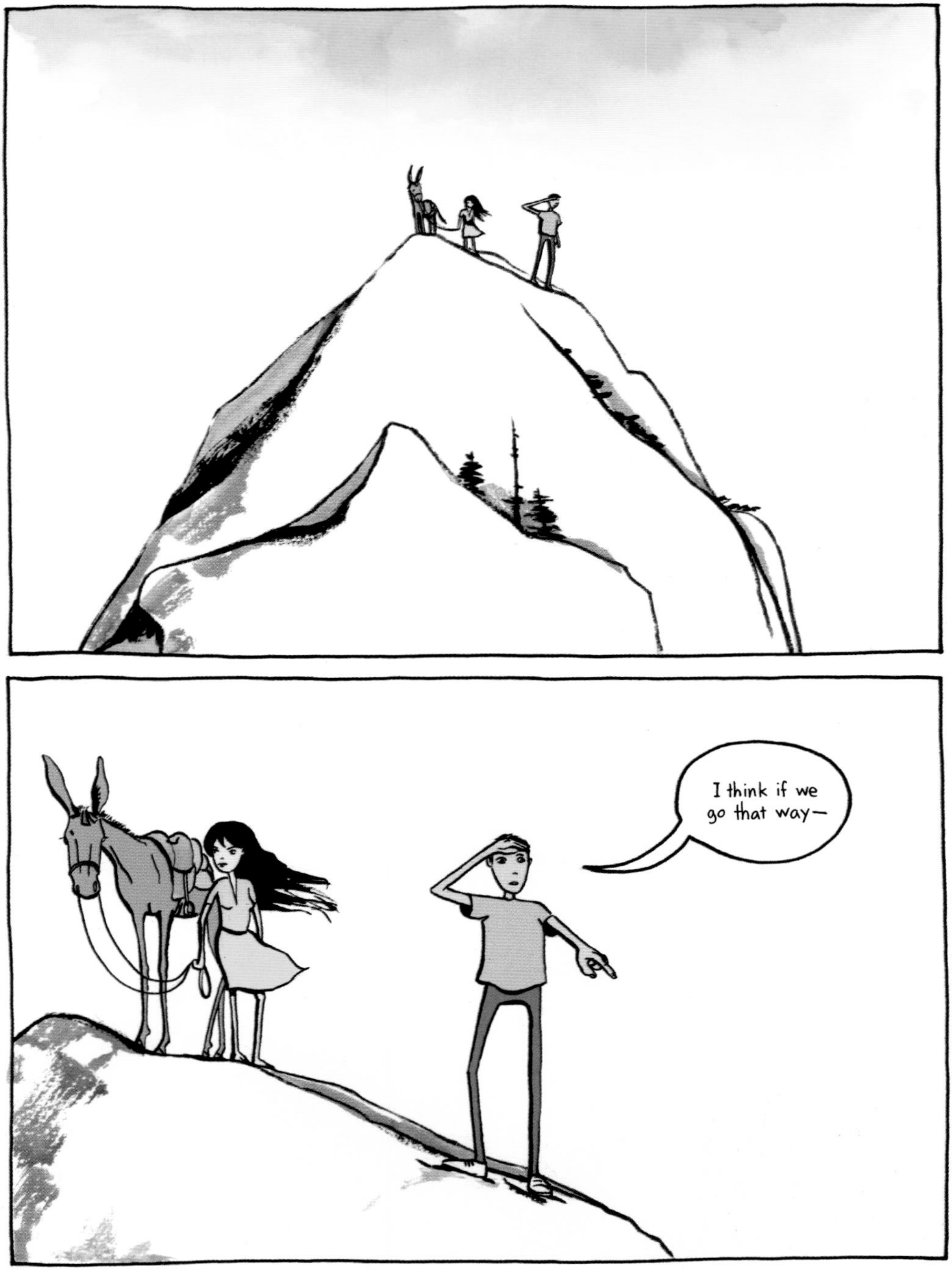
I think if we go that way—

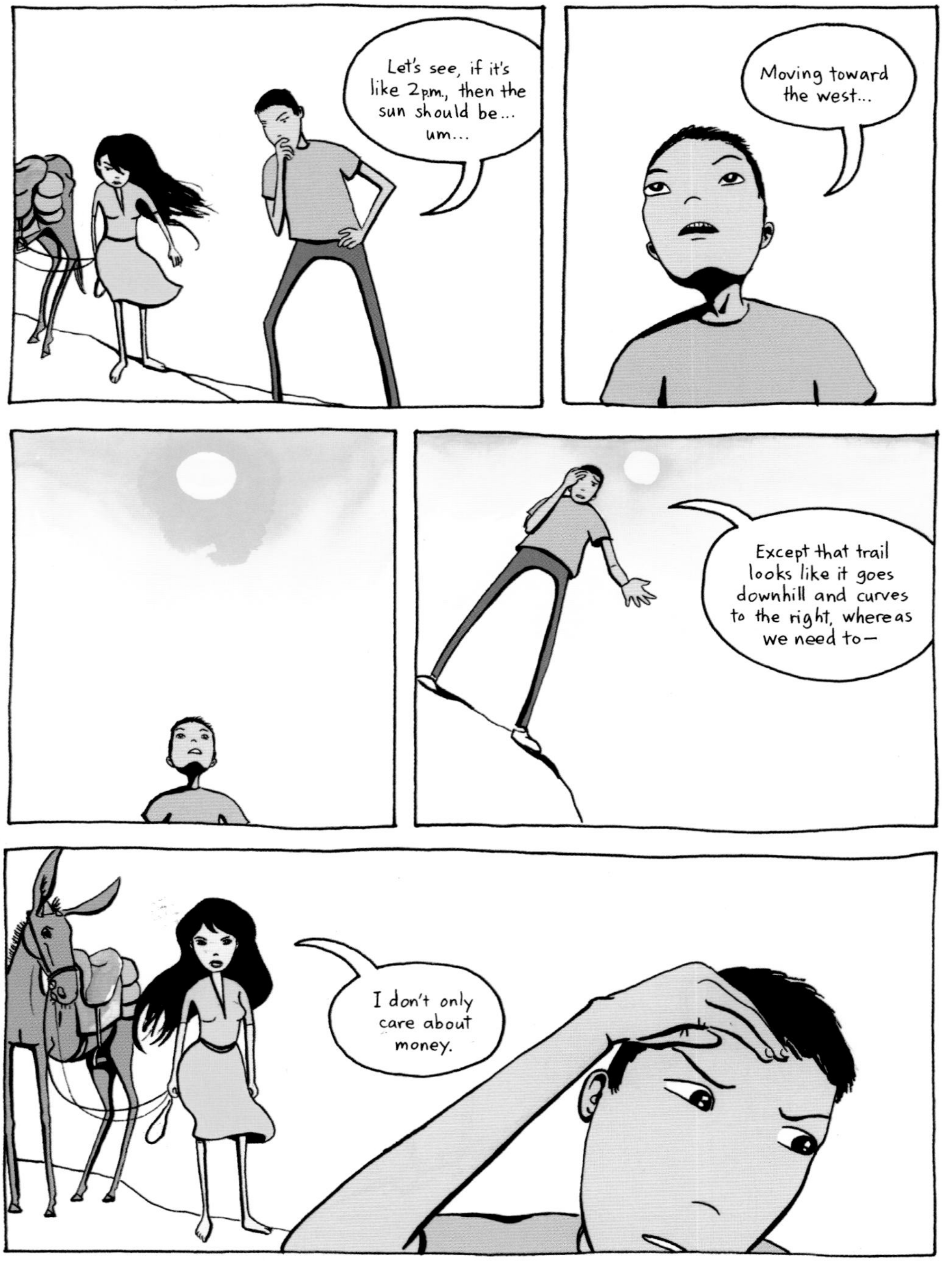
Let's see, if it's like 2p.m., then the sun should be... um...
Moving toward the west...
Except that trail looks like it goes downhill and curves to the right, whereas we need to—
I don't only care about money.

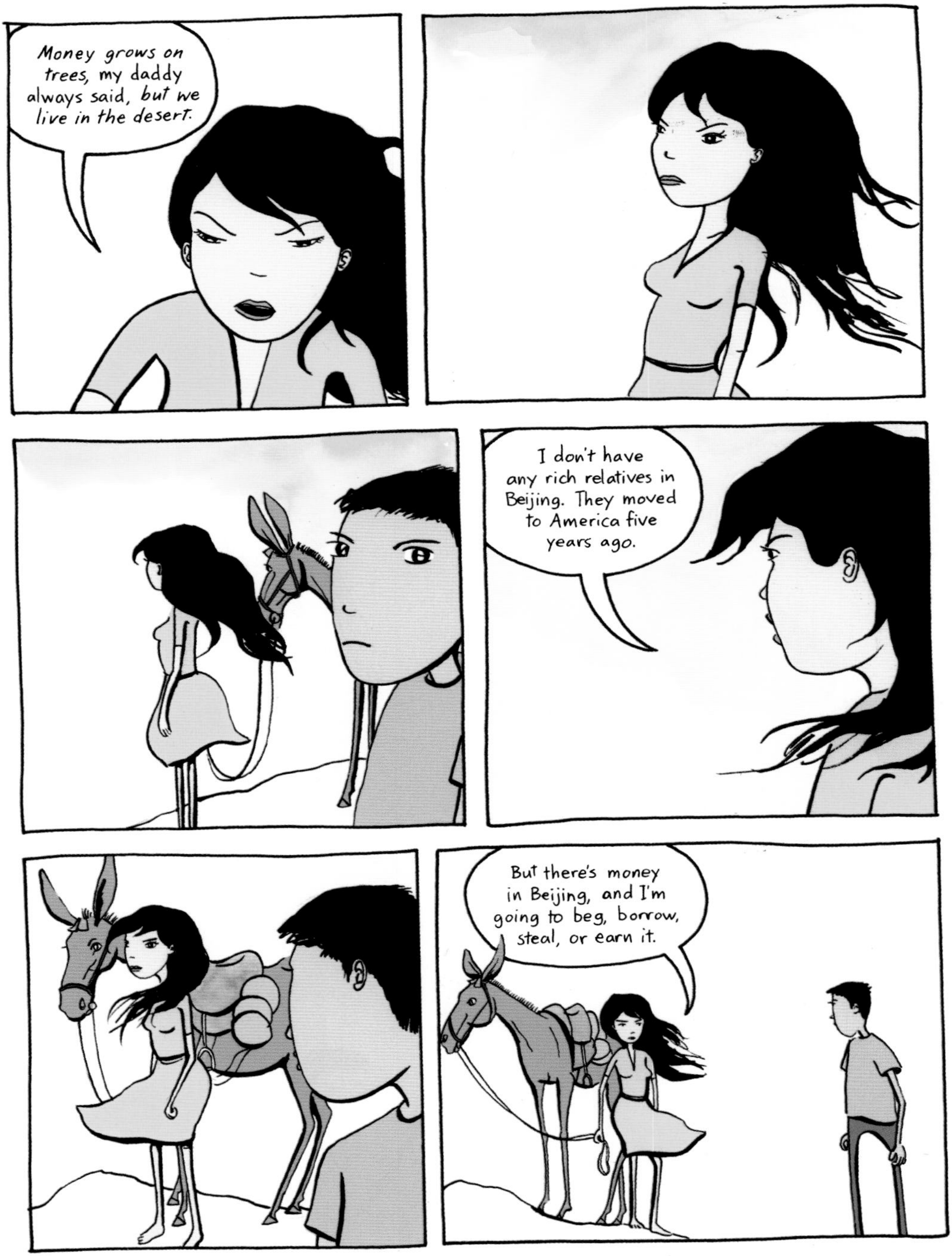
Money grows on trees, my daddy always said, but we live in the desert.
I don't have any rich relatives in Beijing. They moved to America five years ago.
But there's money in Beijing, and I'm going to beg, borrow, steal, or earn it.

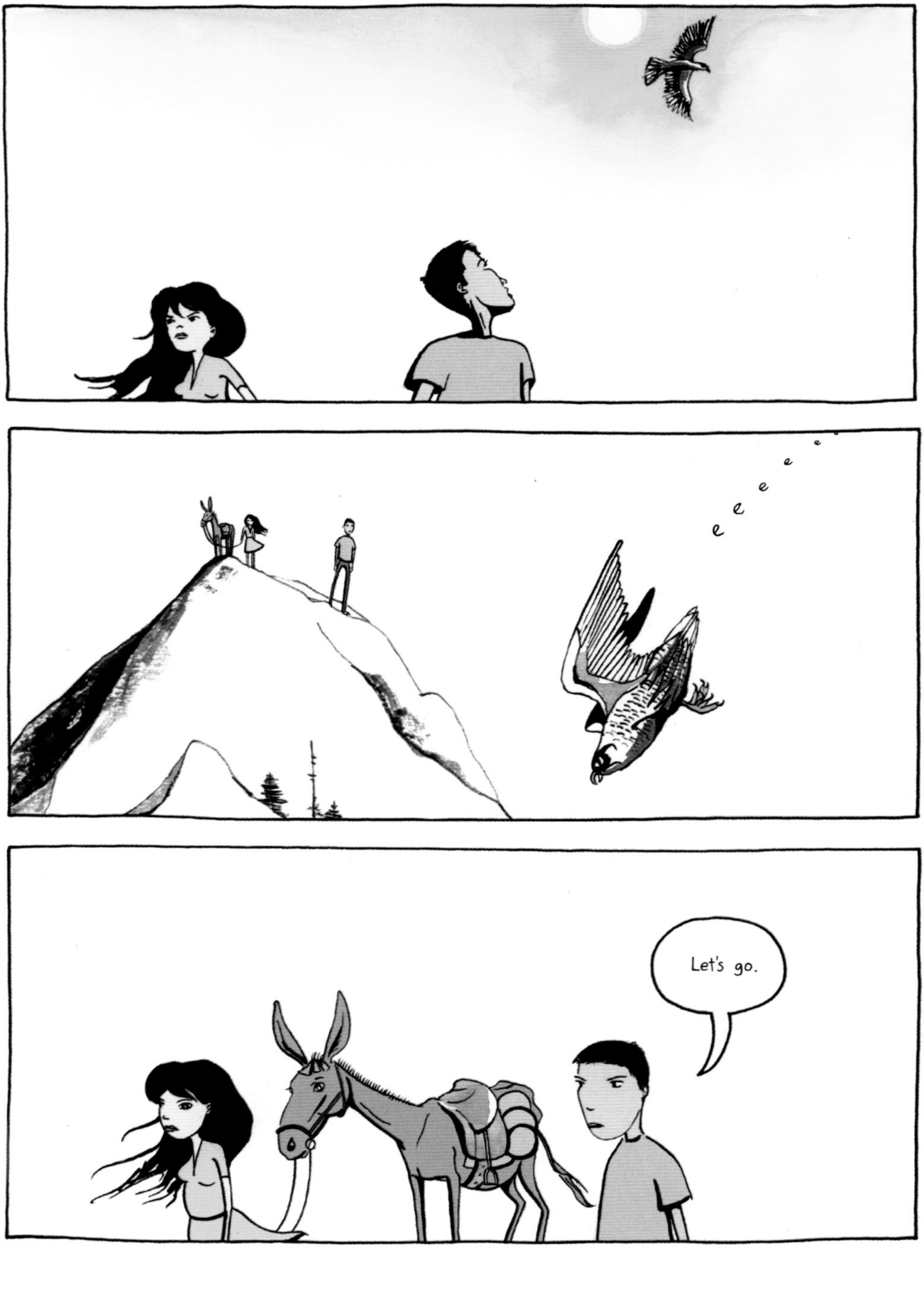
e e e e e e e
Let's go.

22. Dust

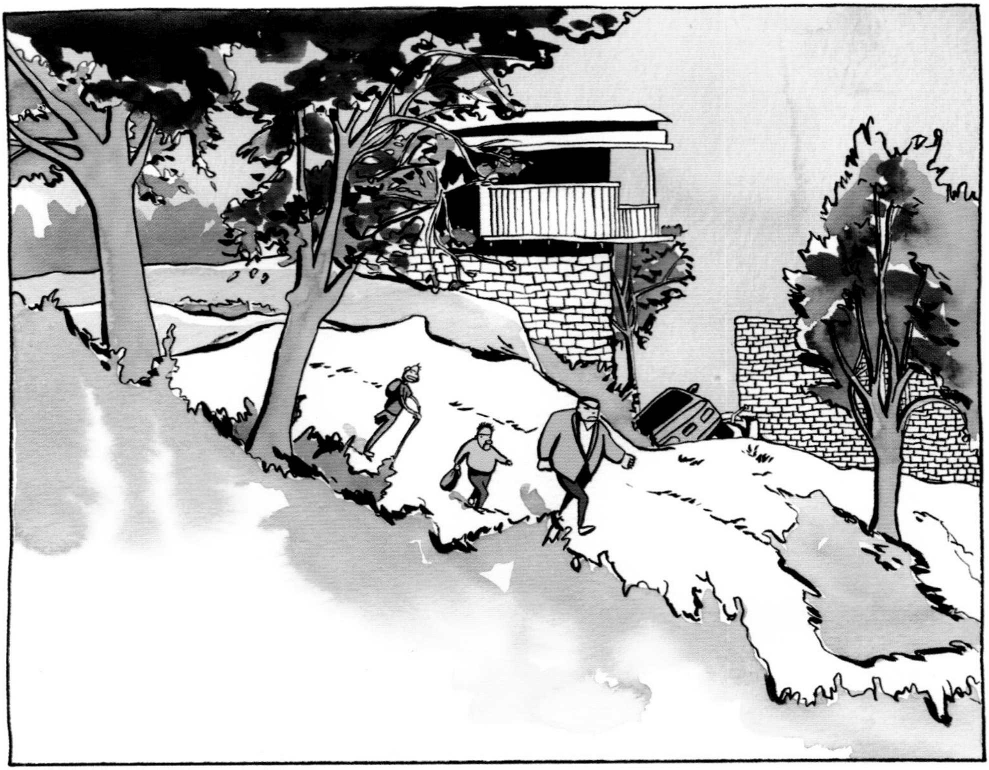

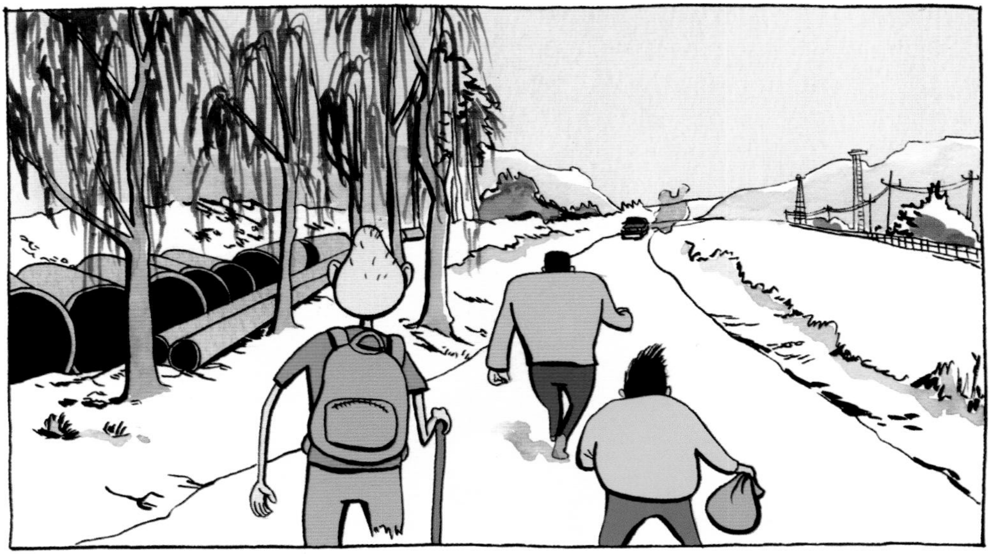

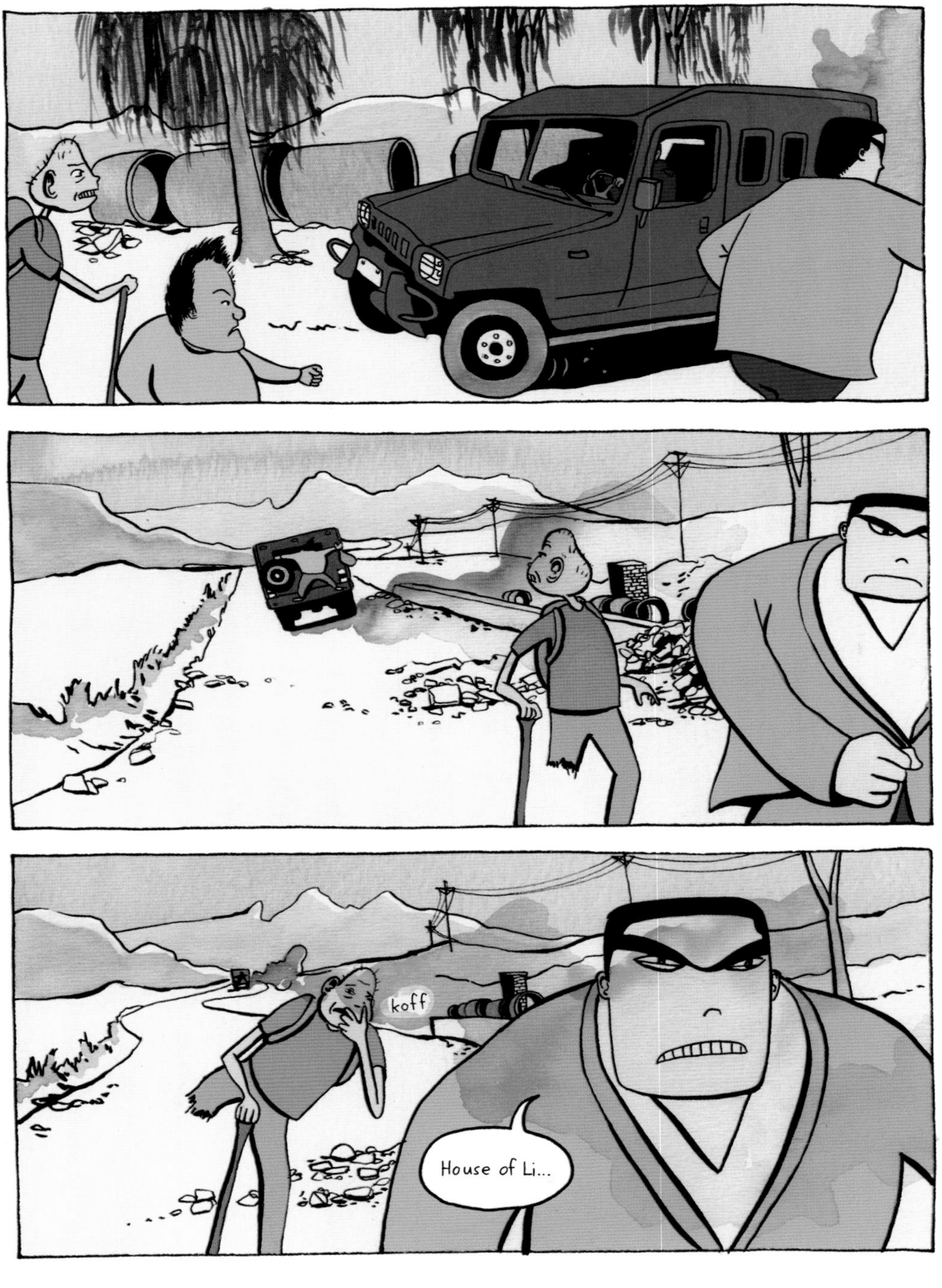
koff
House of Li...

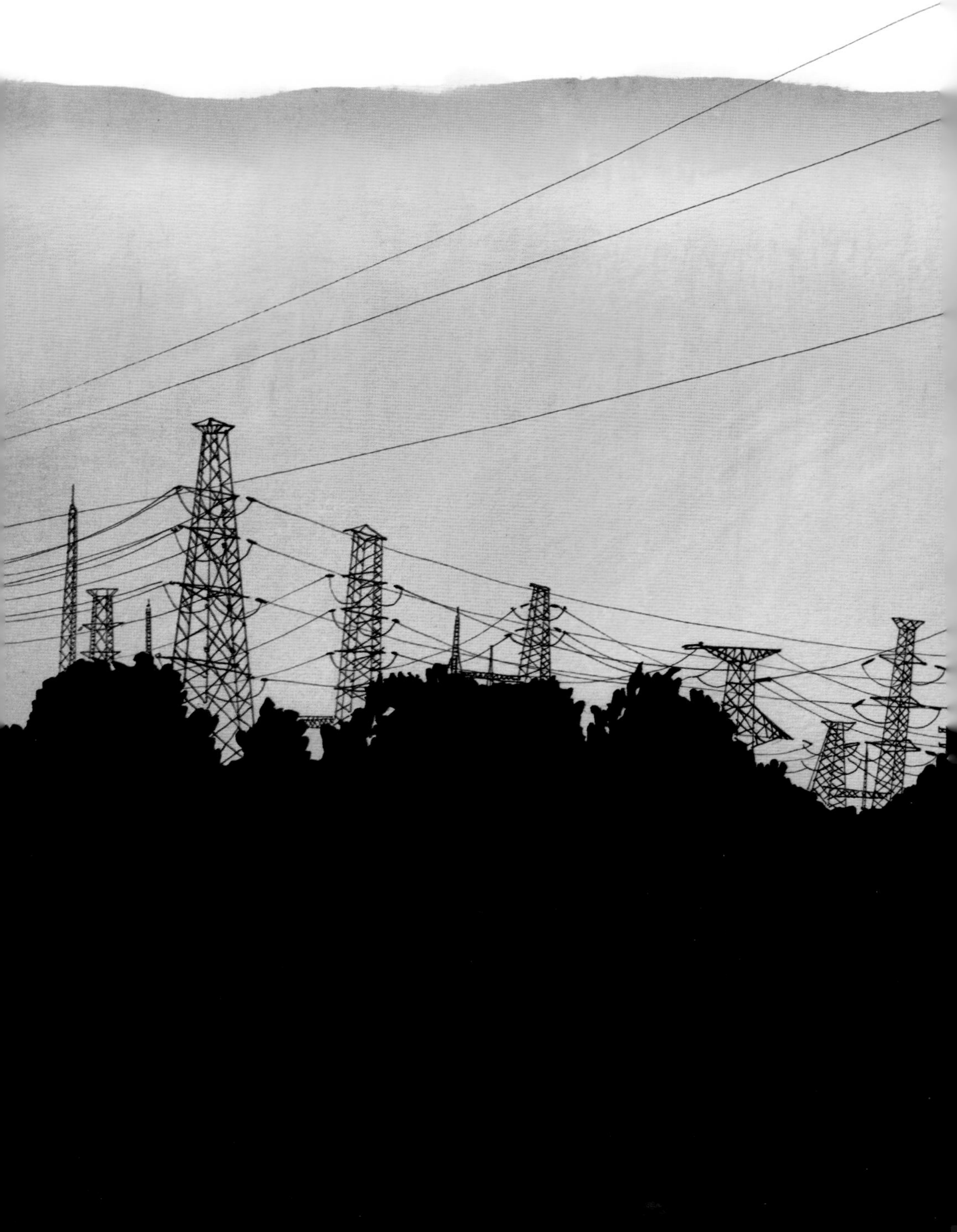

23. Incubus

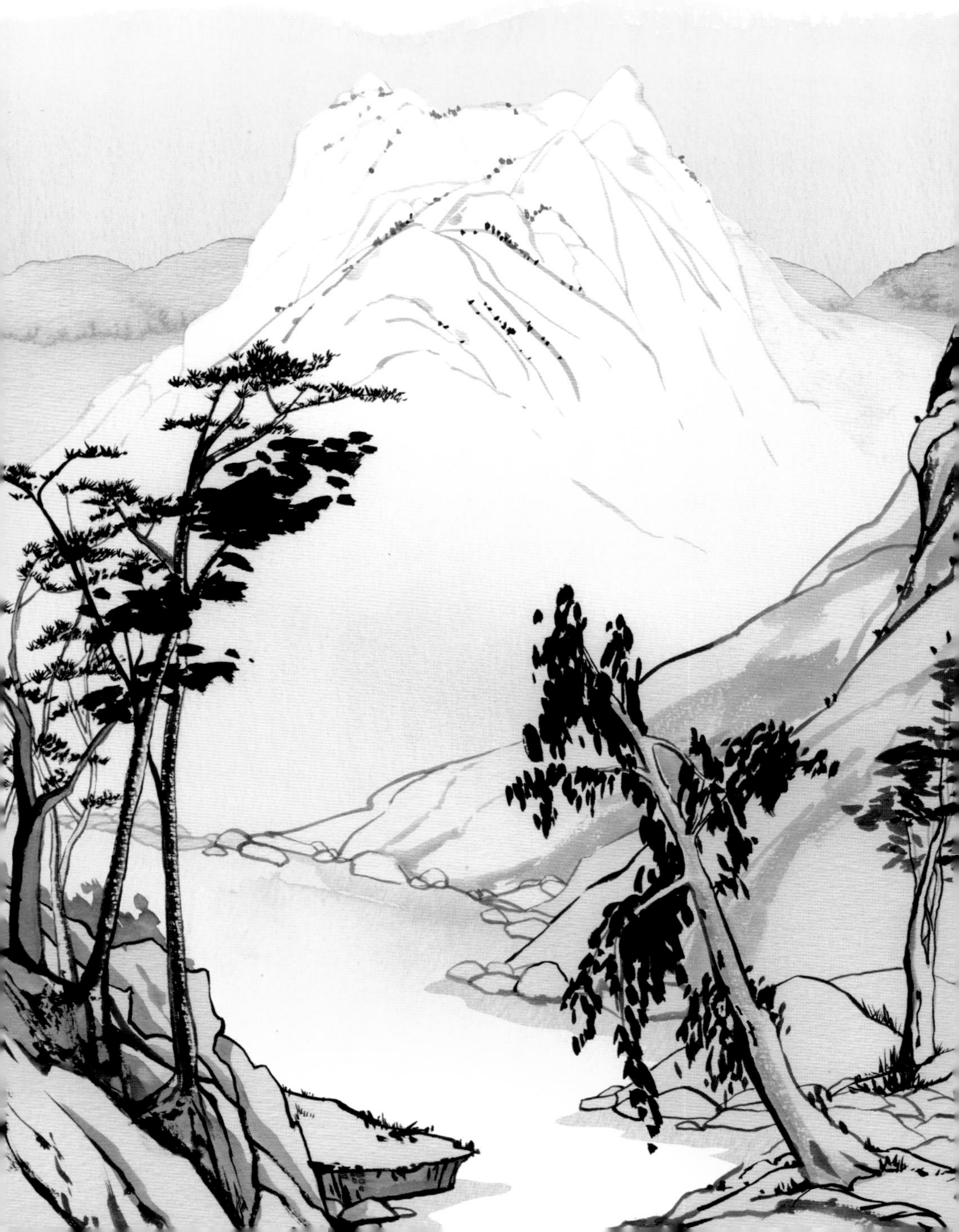

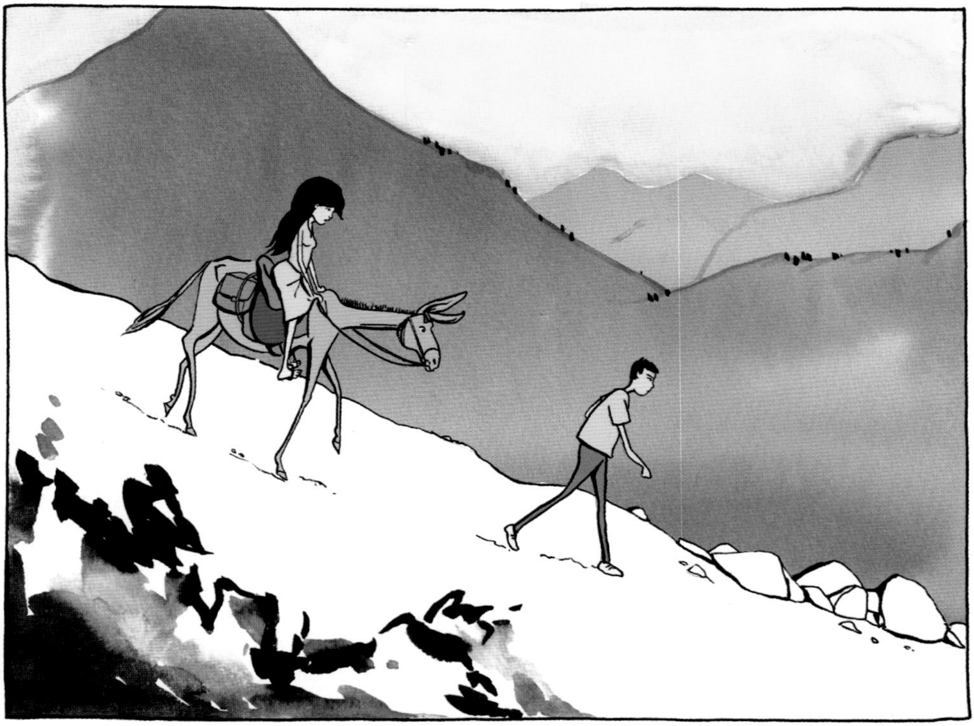

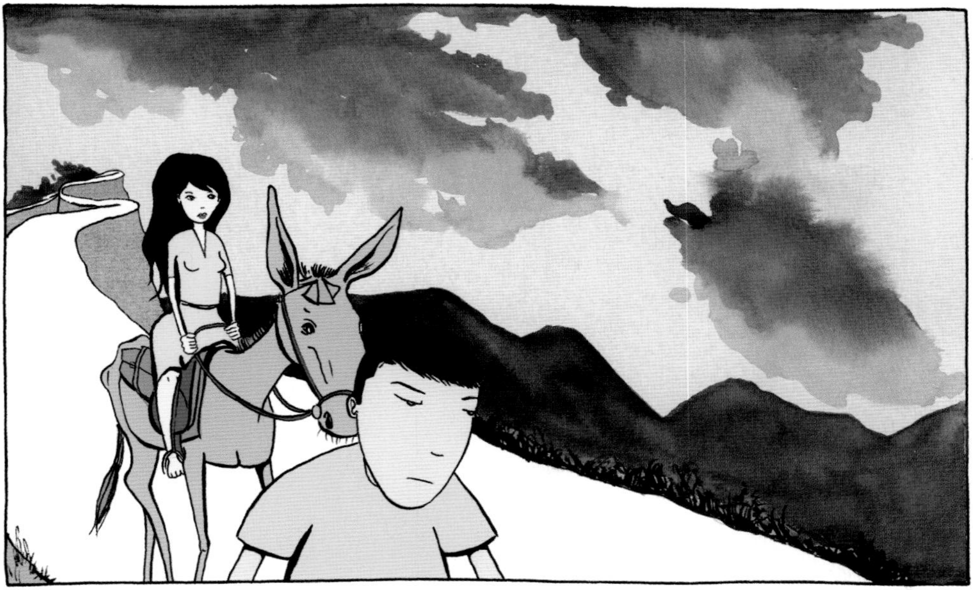

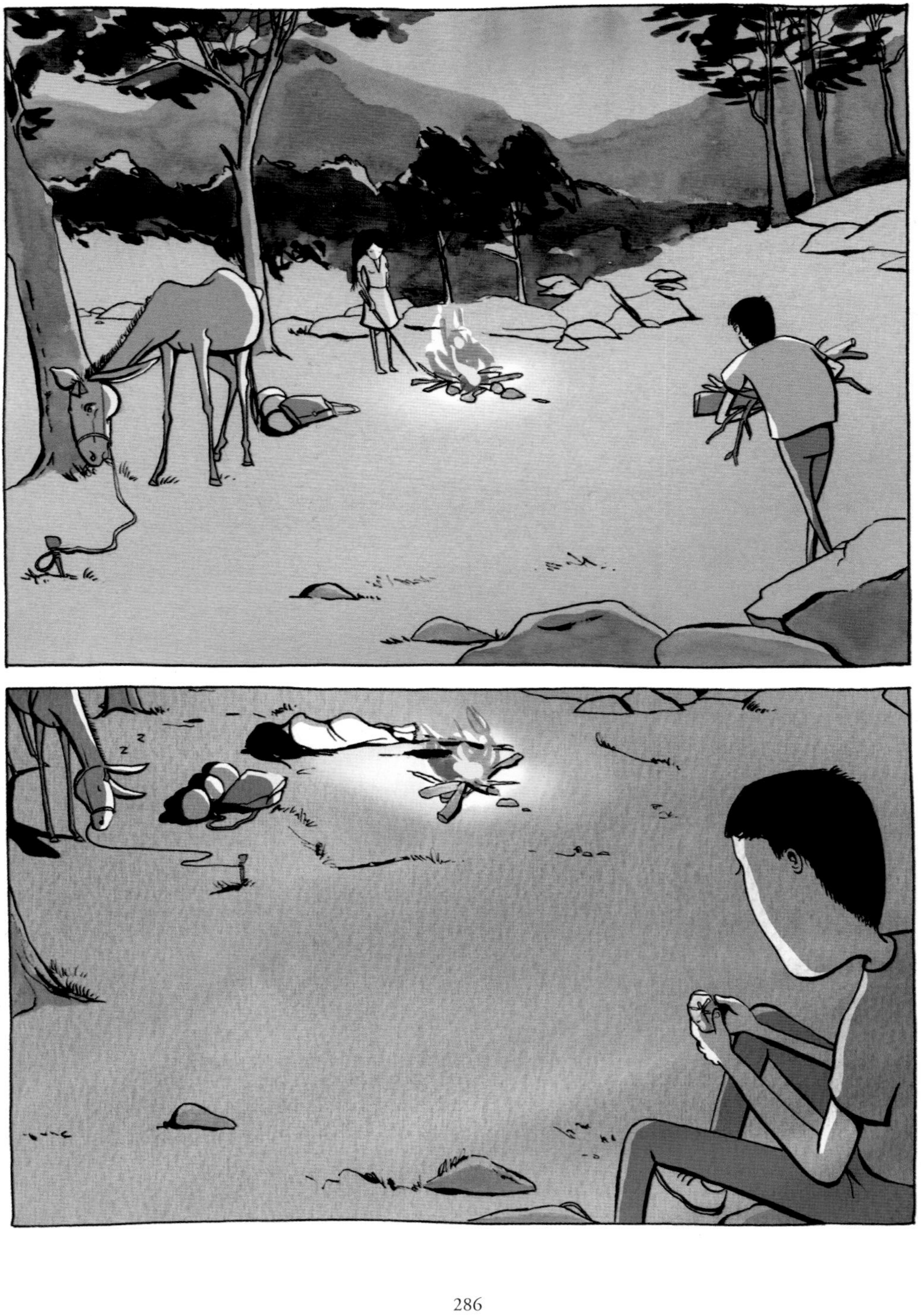

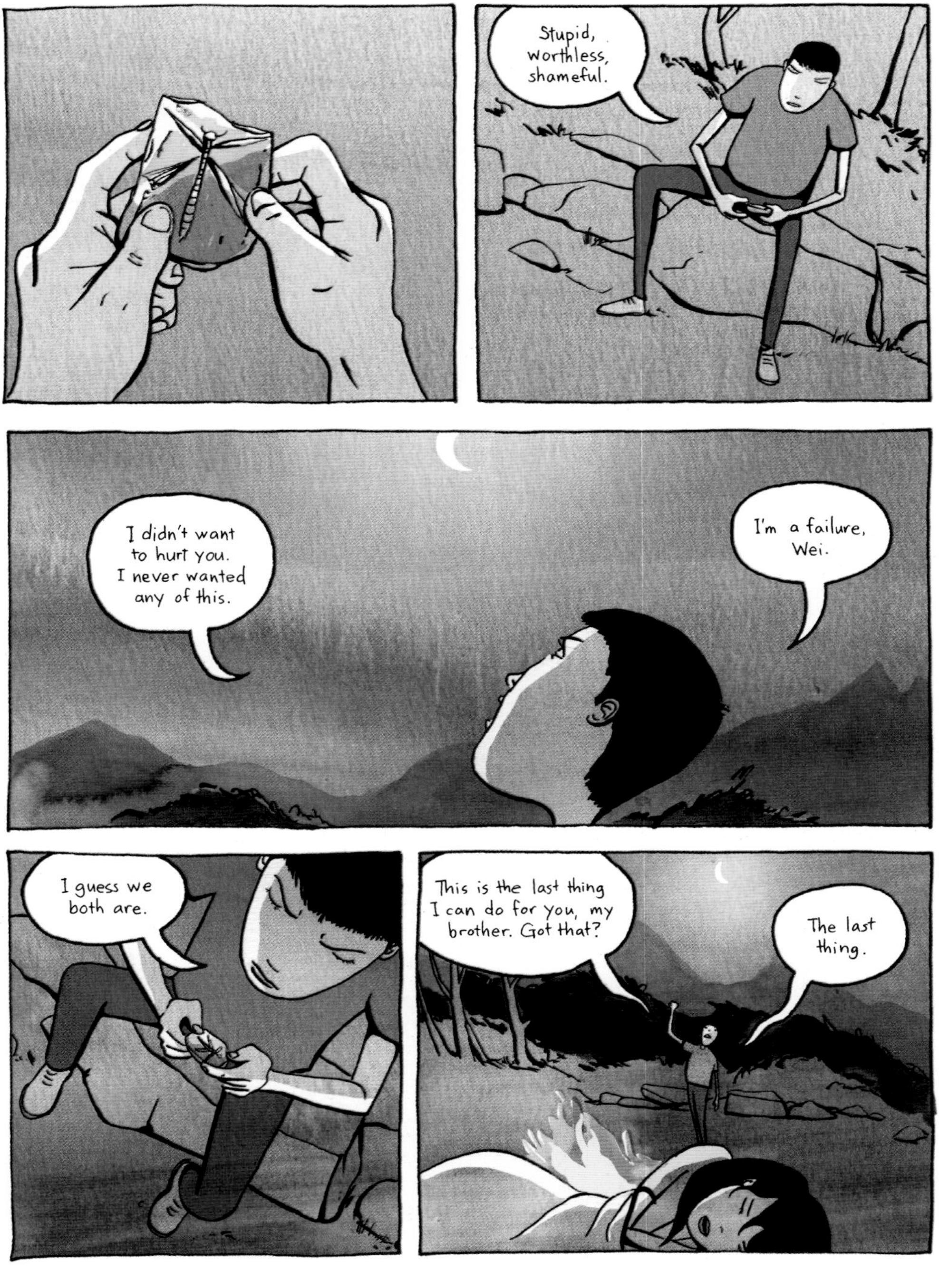
Stupid, worthless, shameful.
I didn't want to hurt you. I never wanted any of this.
I'm a failure, Wei.
I guess we both are.
This is the last thing I can do for you, my brother. Got that?
The last thing.

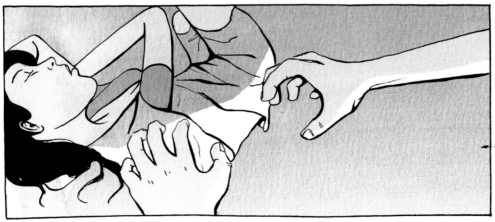

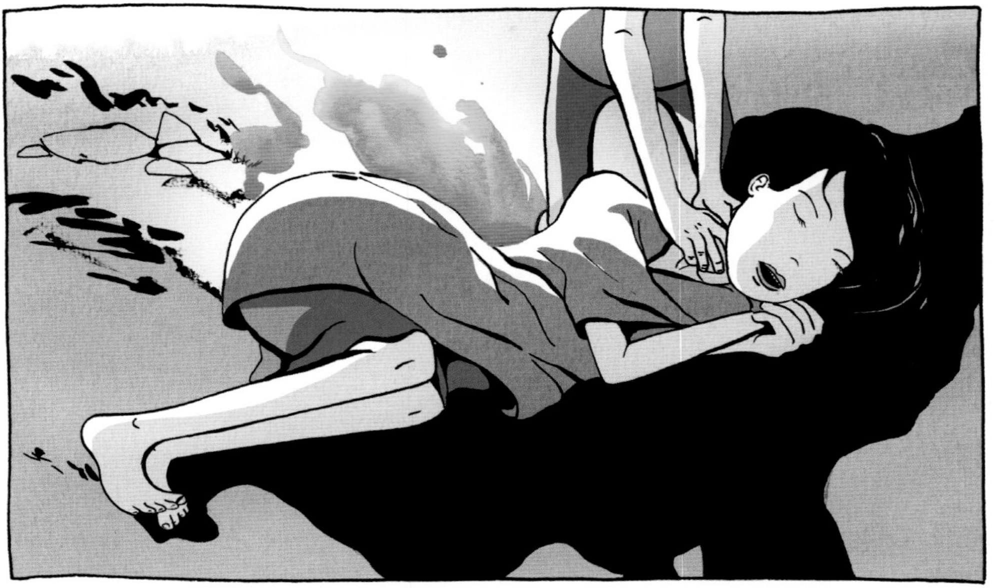

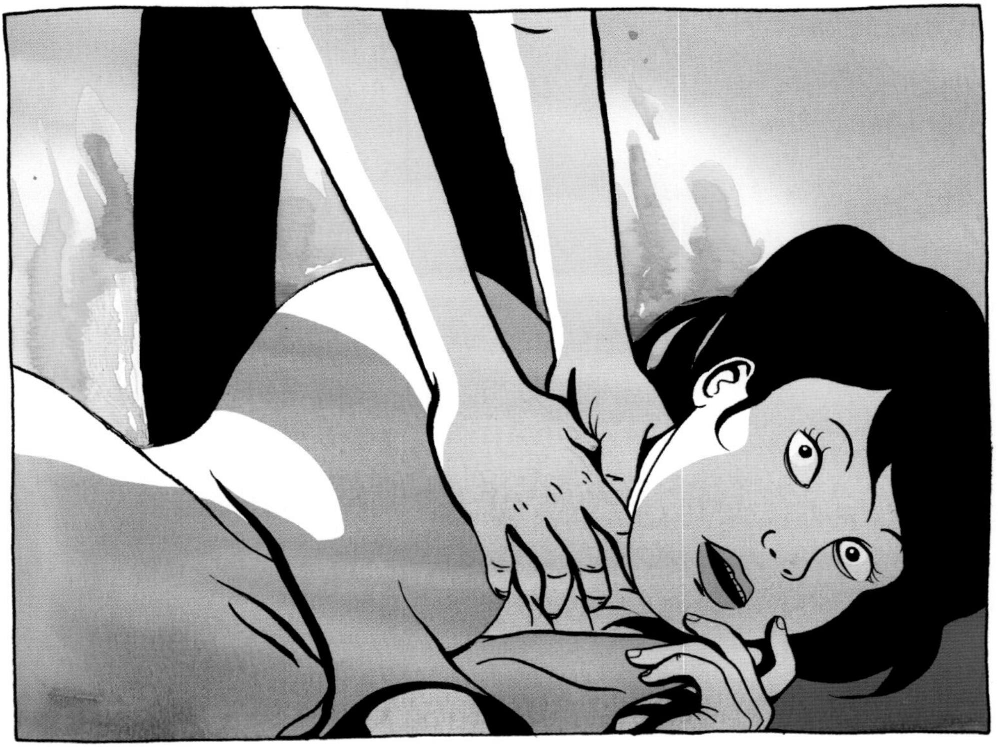

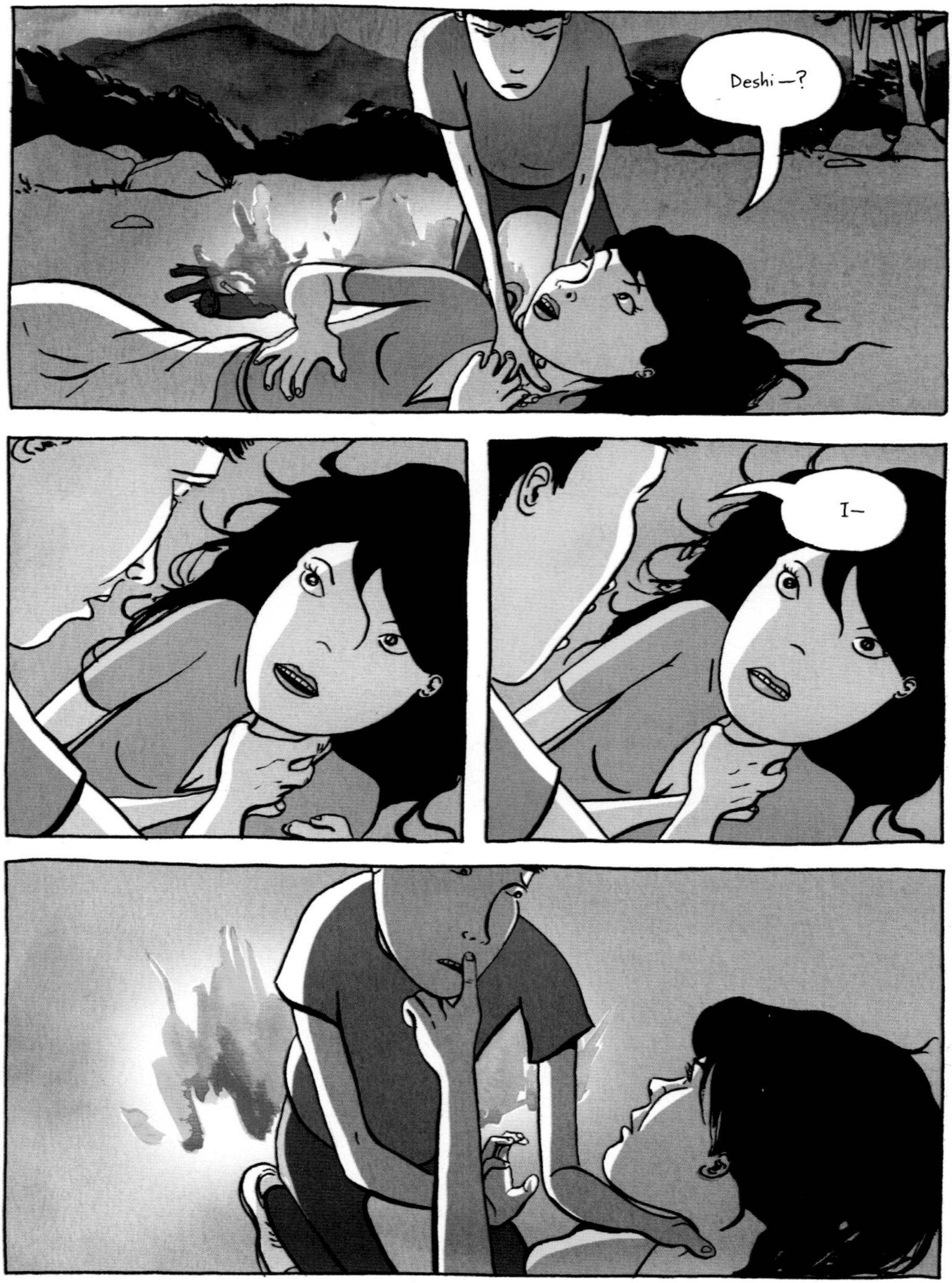
Deshi—?
I—

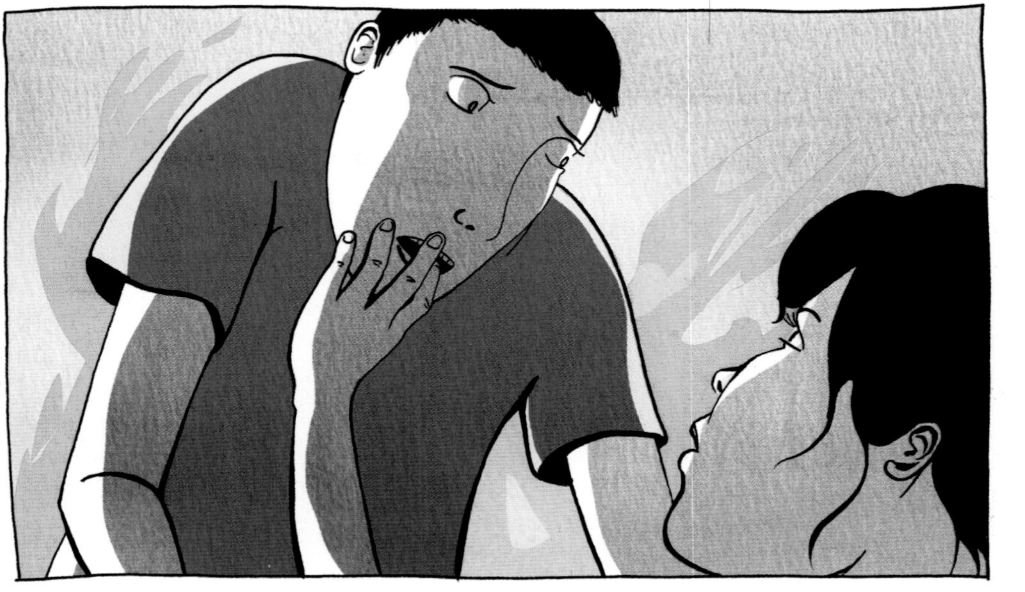

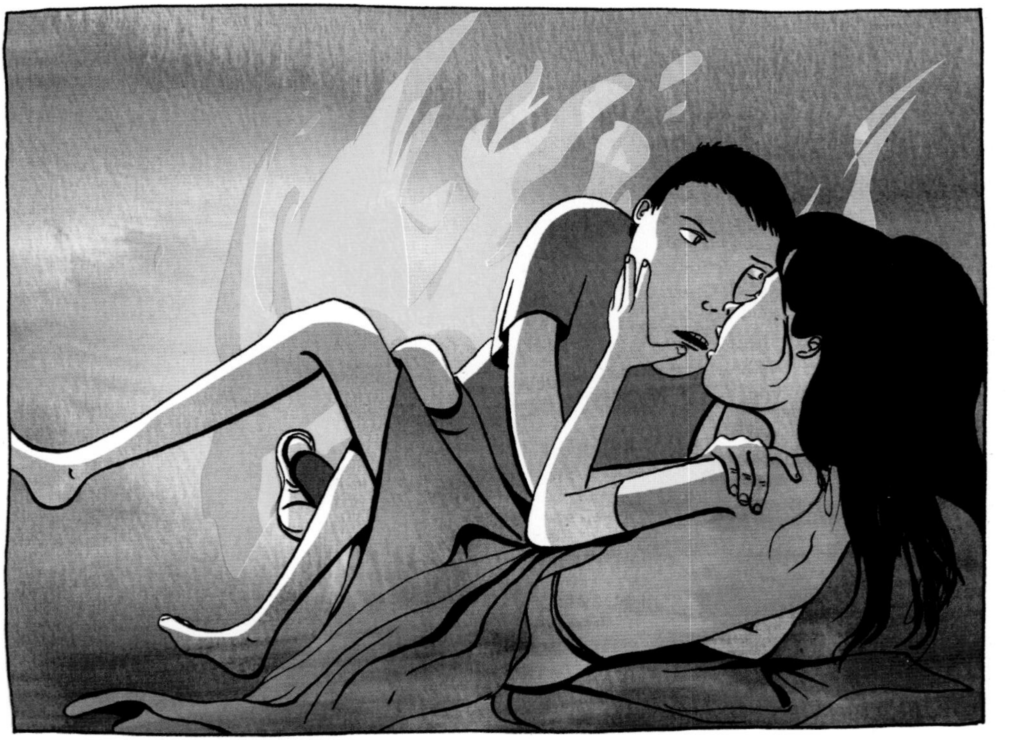

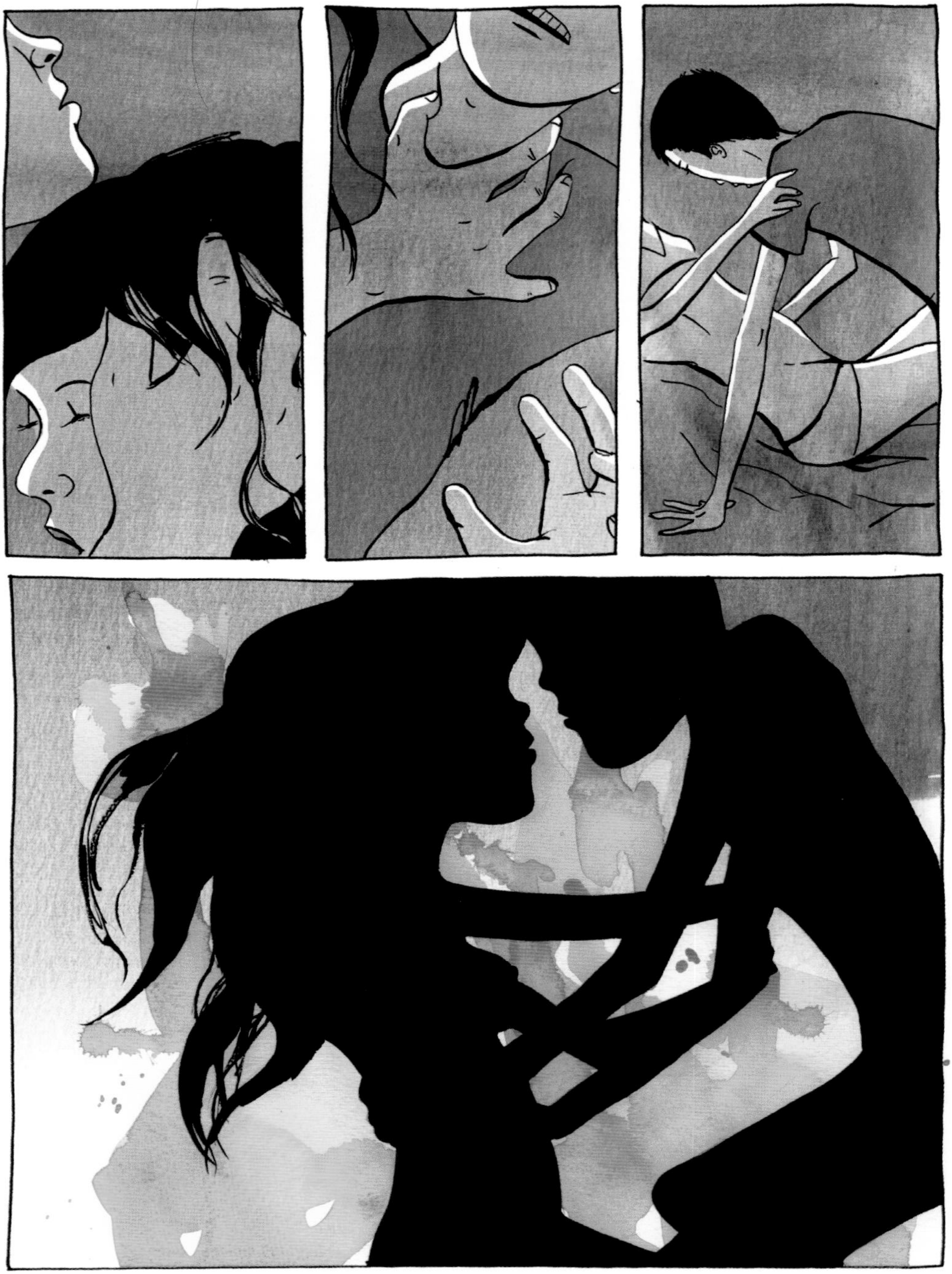

24. The Dream of Cao Chong

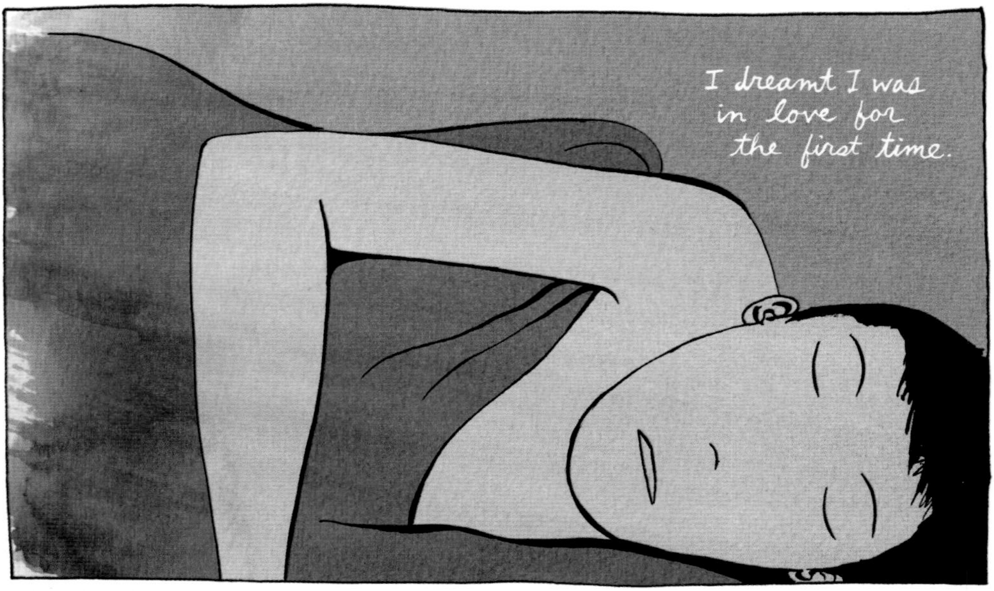
I dreamt I was in love for the first time.

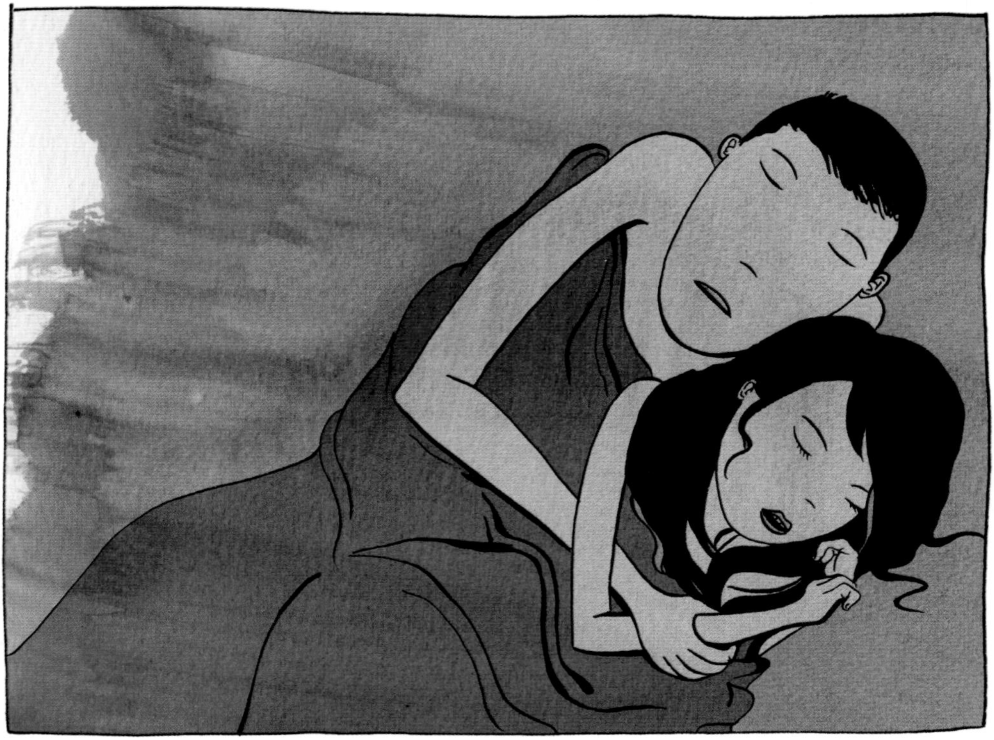

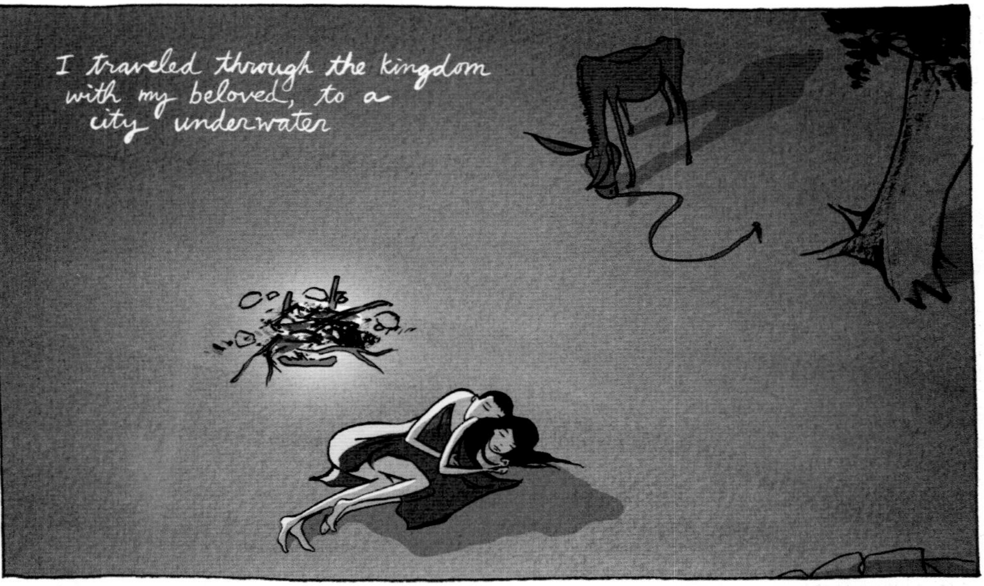
I traveled through the kingdom with my beloved, to a city underwater

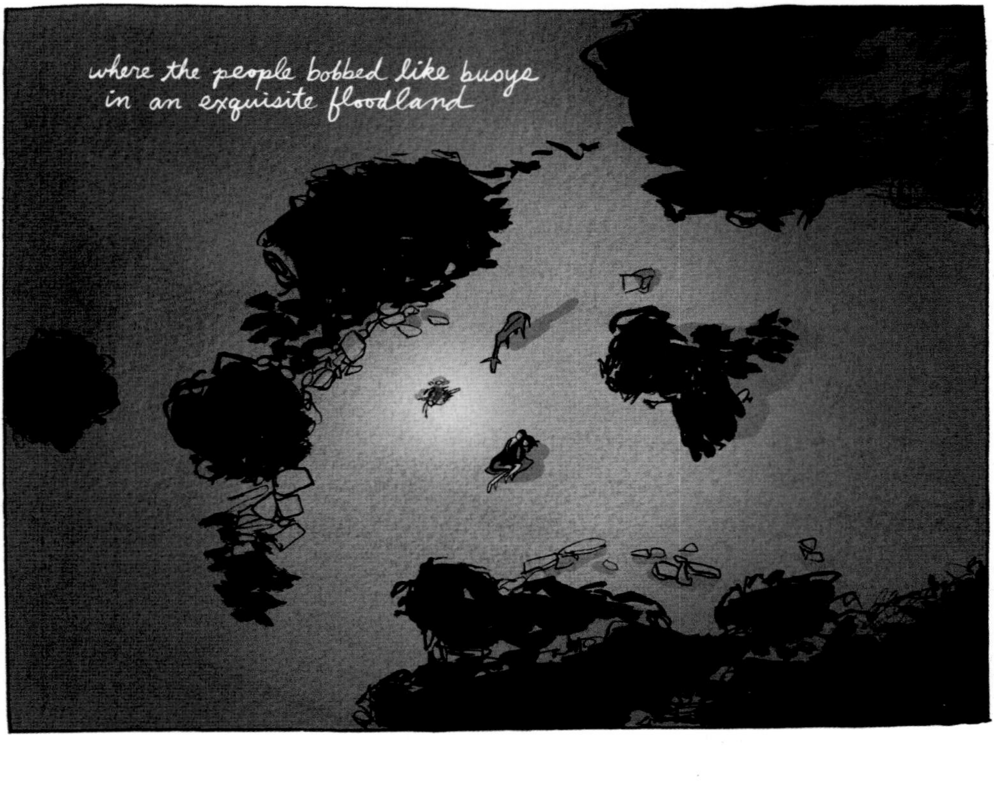
where the people bobbed like buoys in an exquisite floodland

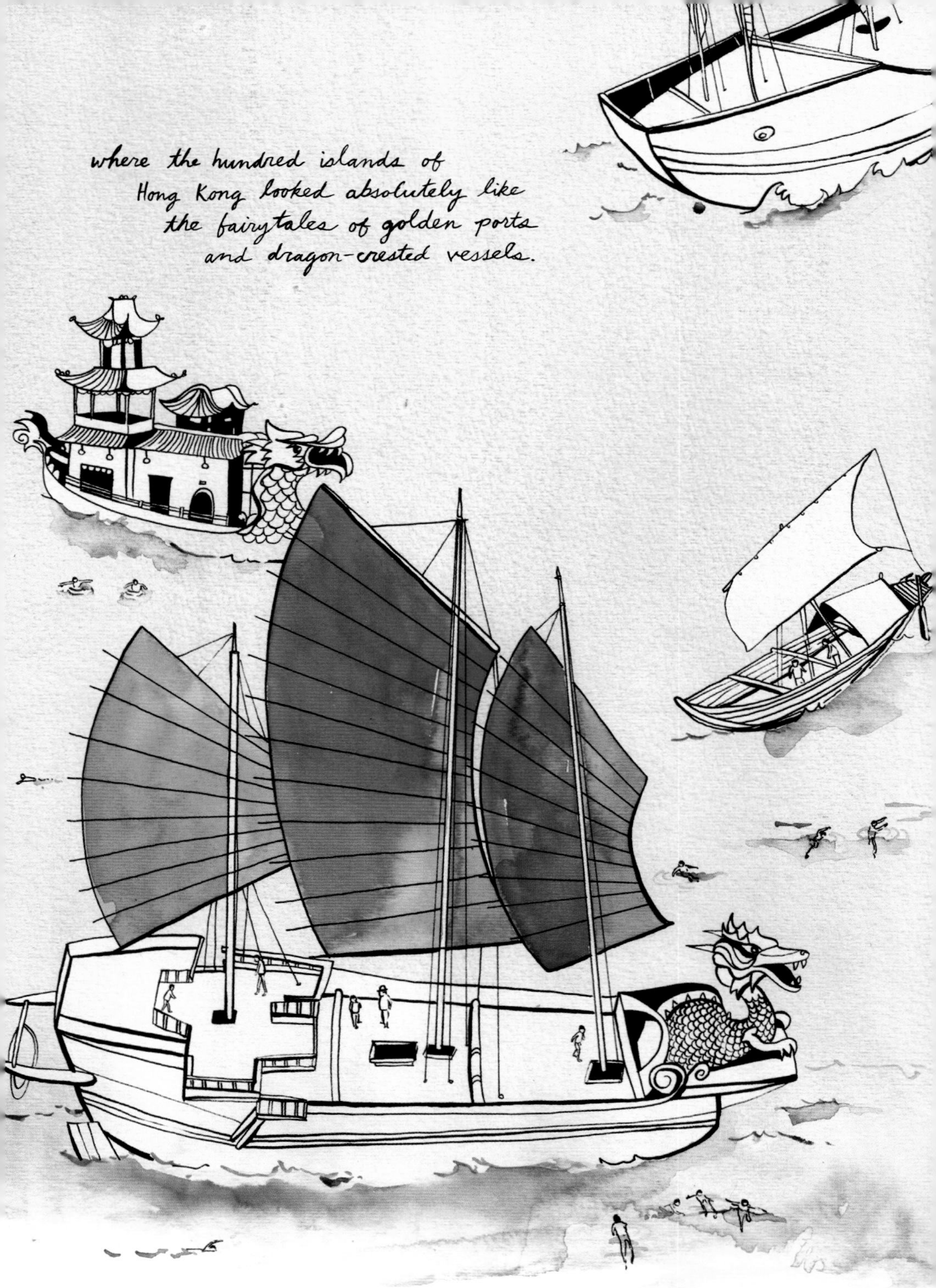
where the hundred islands of
Hong Kong looked absolutely like
the fairytales of golden ports
and dragon-crested vessels.

The summer was ending, the day was waning,
the world was liquid, and soon
she would be gone.

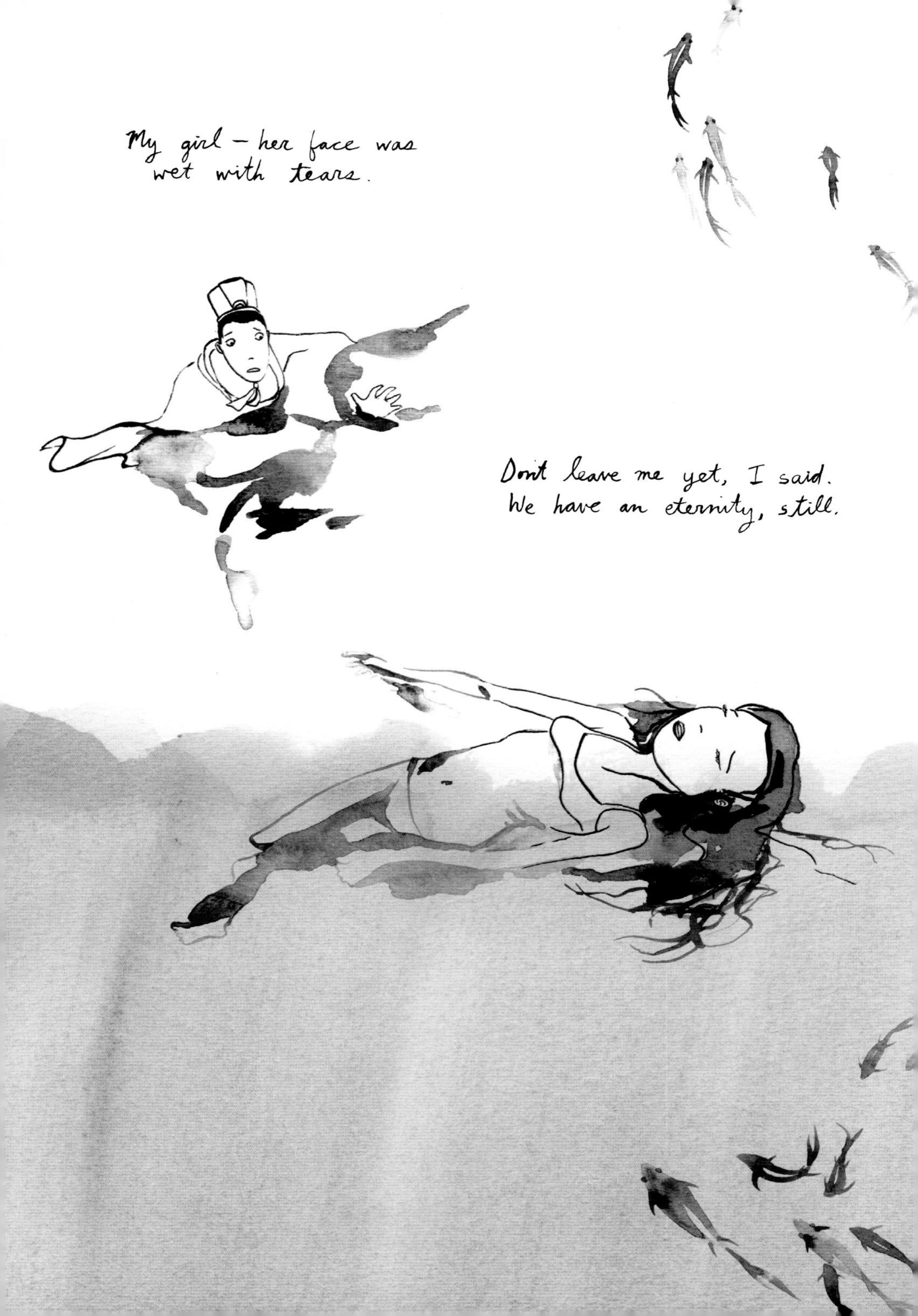
My girl — her face was wet with tears.
Don't leave me yet, I said. We have an eternity, still.

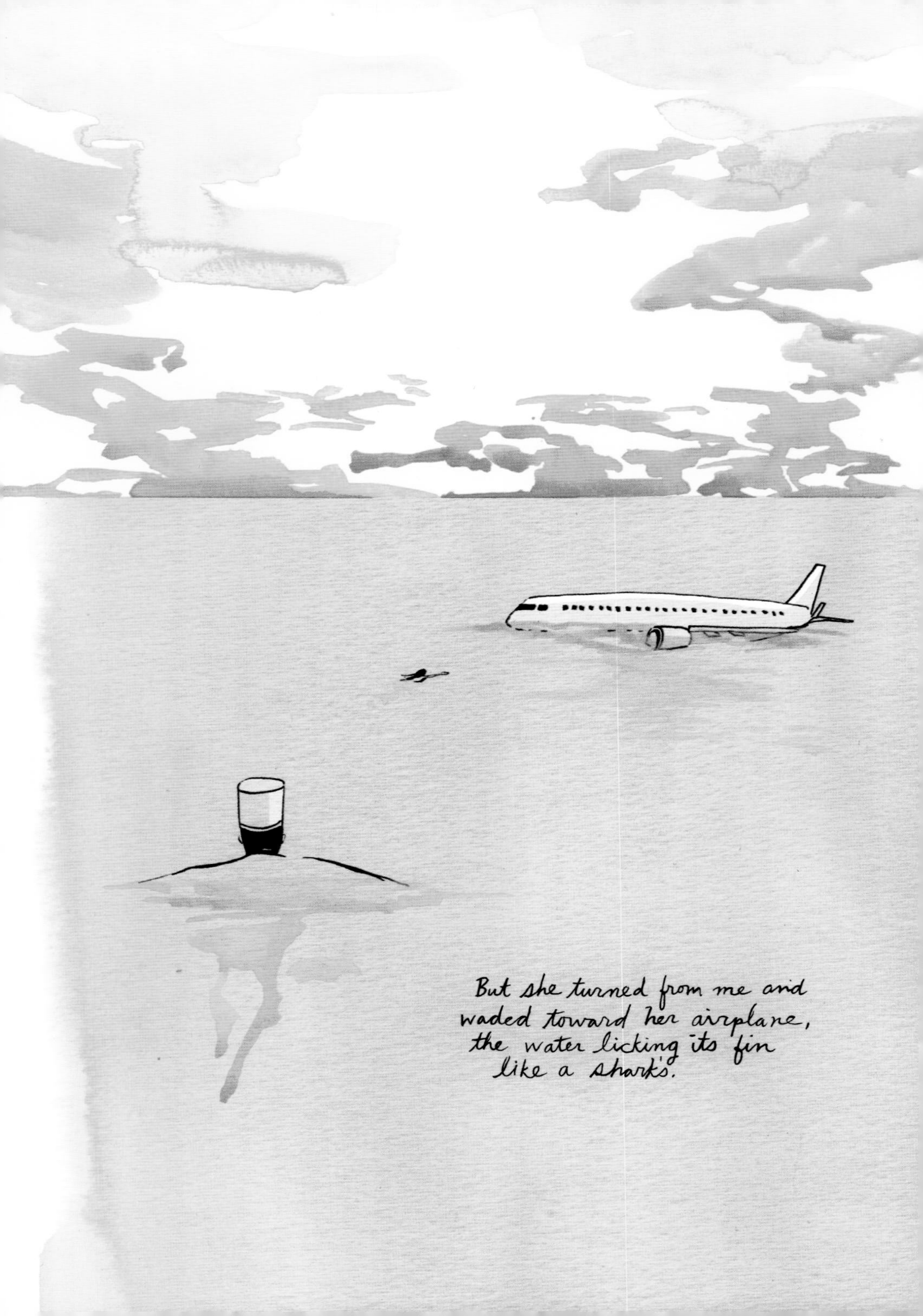
But she turned from me and waded toward her airplane, the water licking its fin like a shark's.

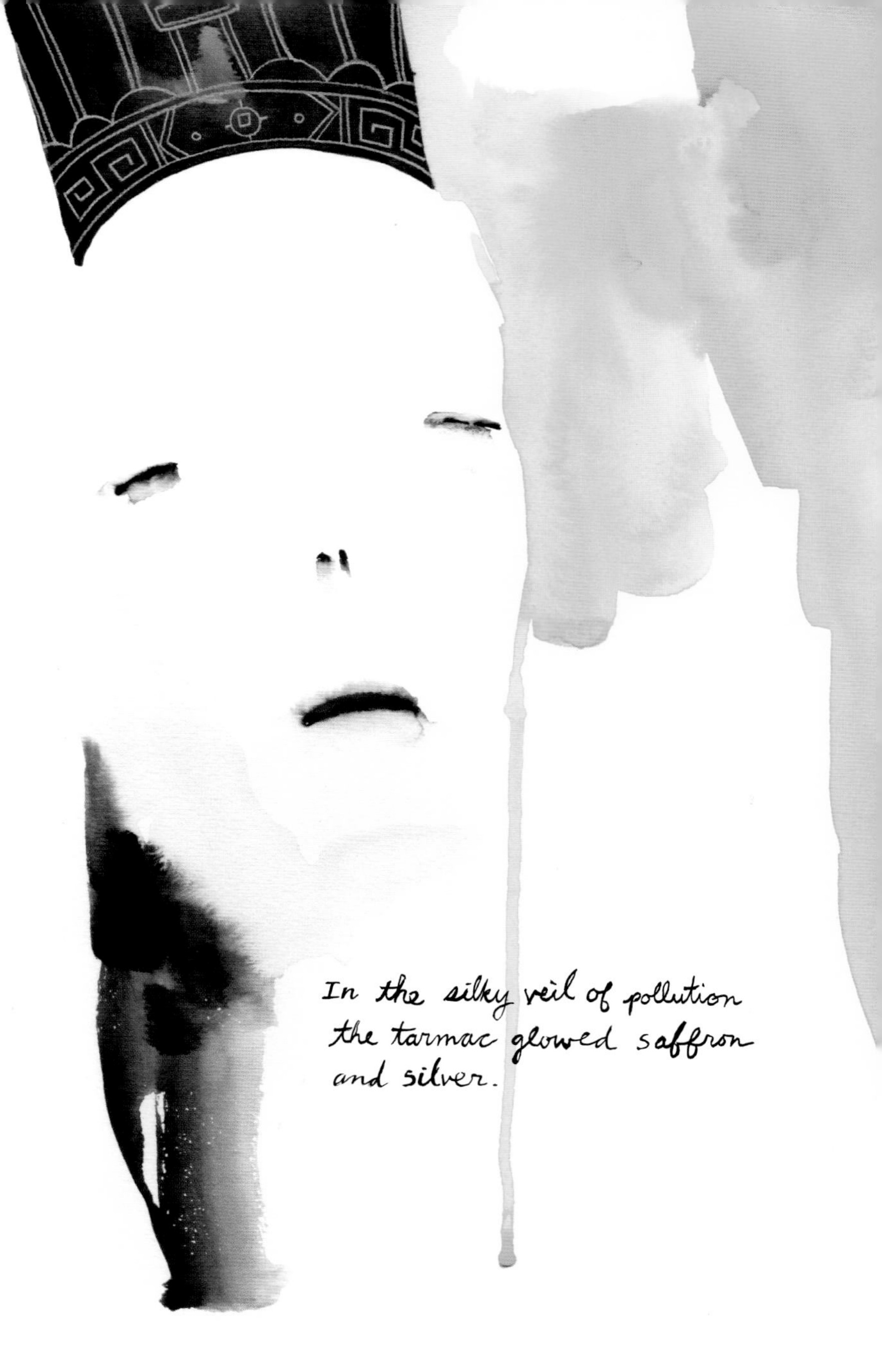
In the silky veil of pollution the tarmac glowed saffron and silver.

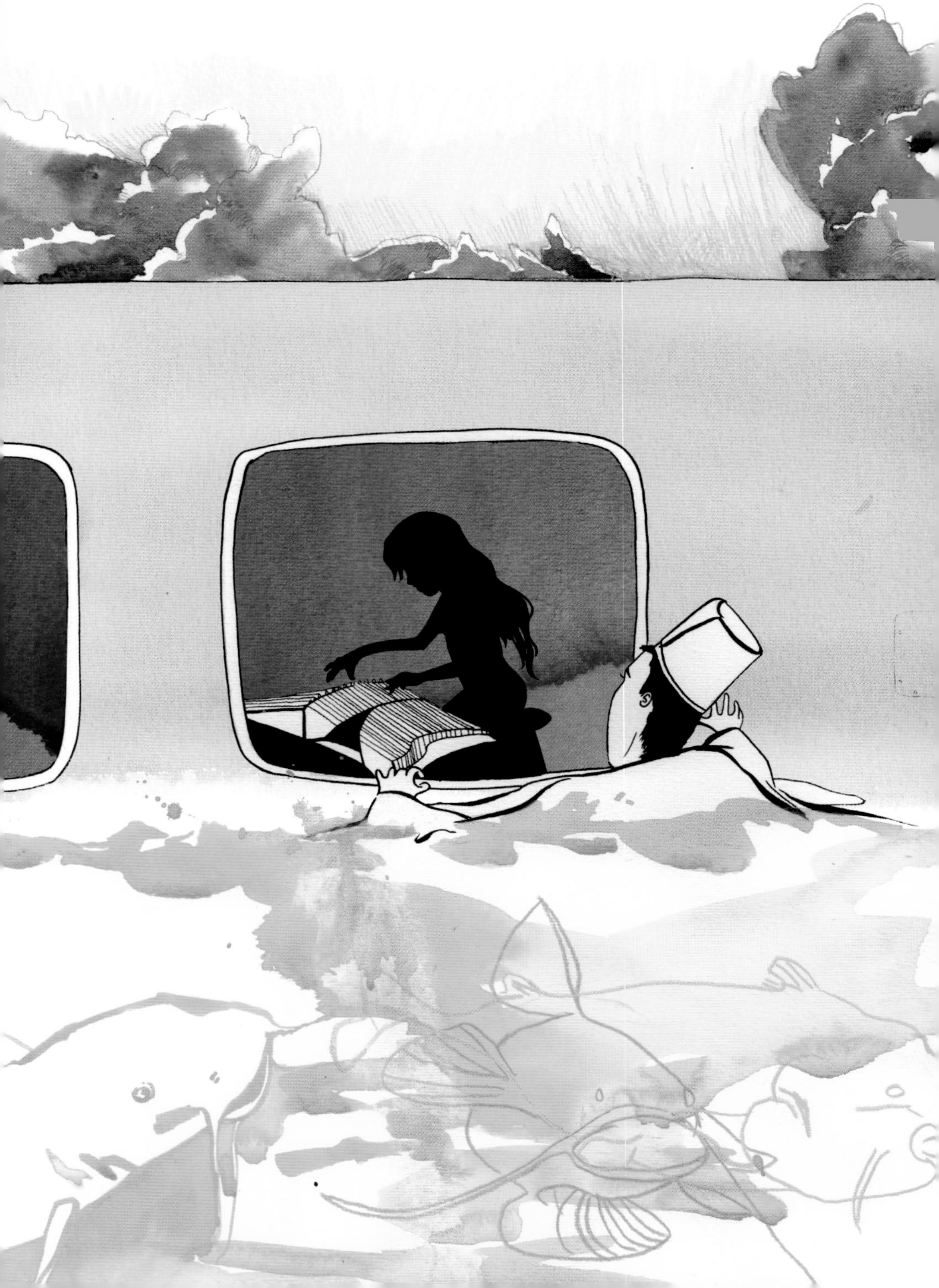

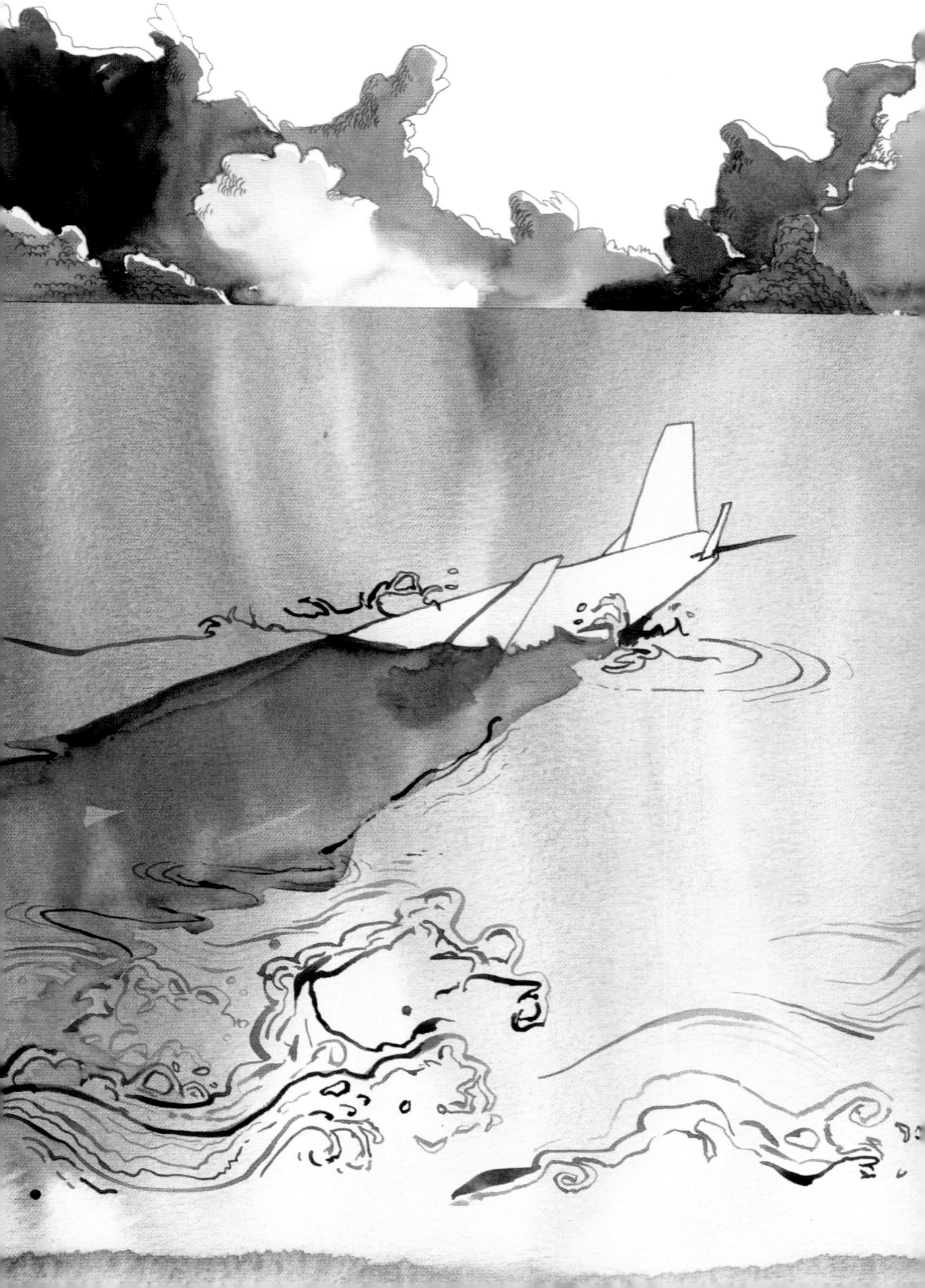

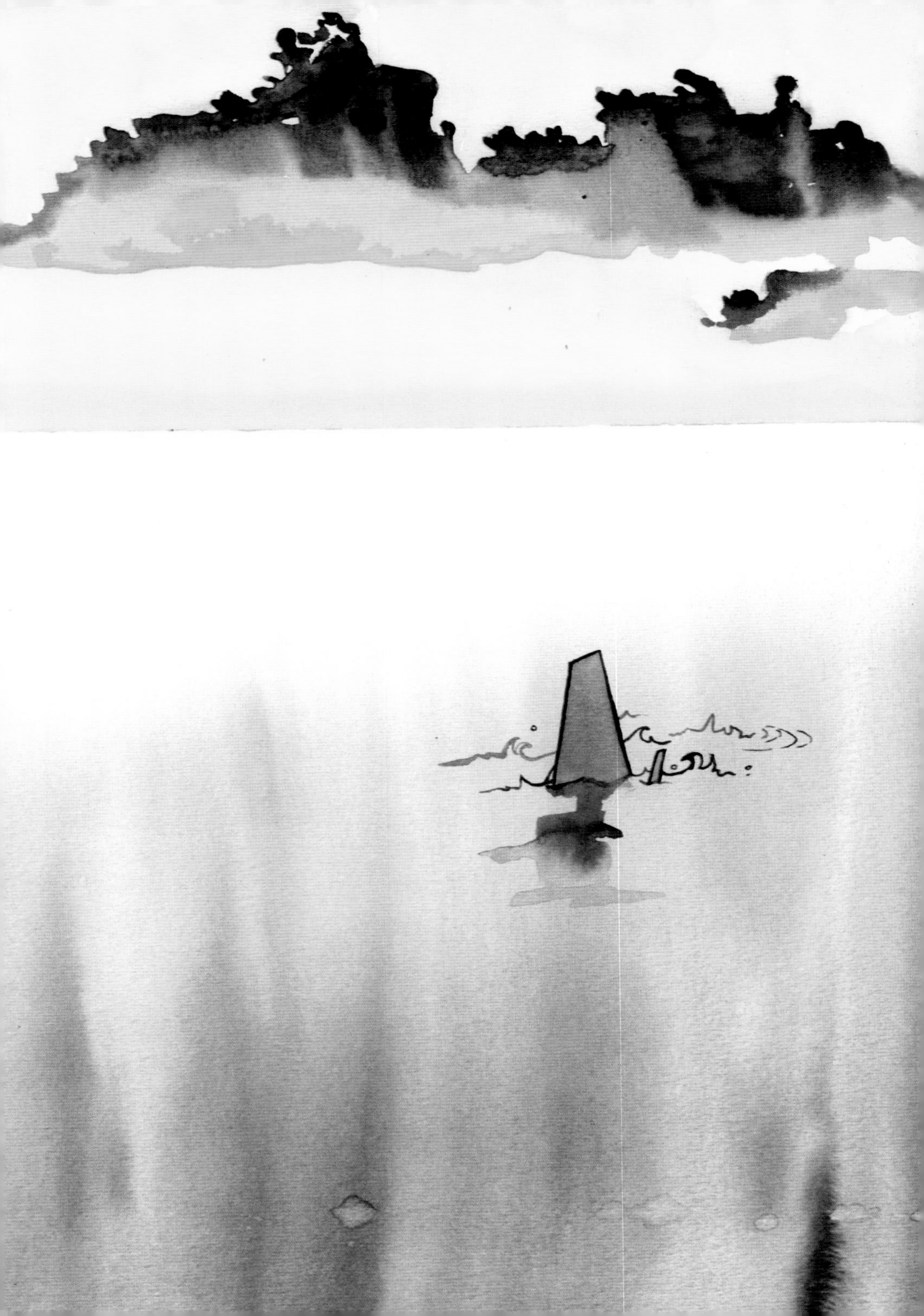

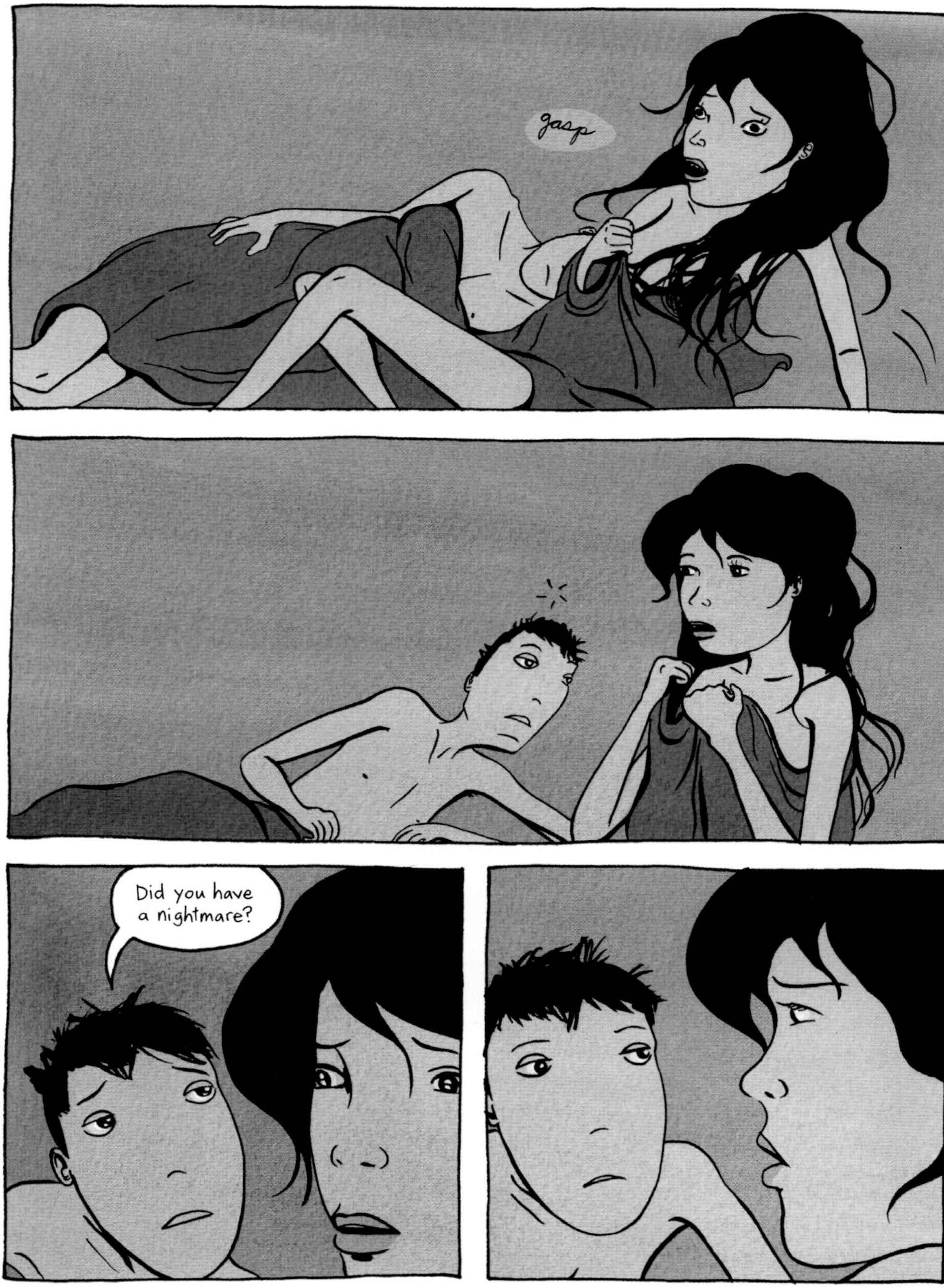
gasp
Did you have a nightmare?

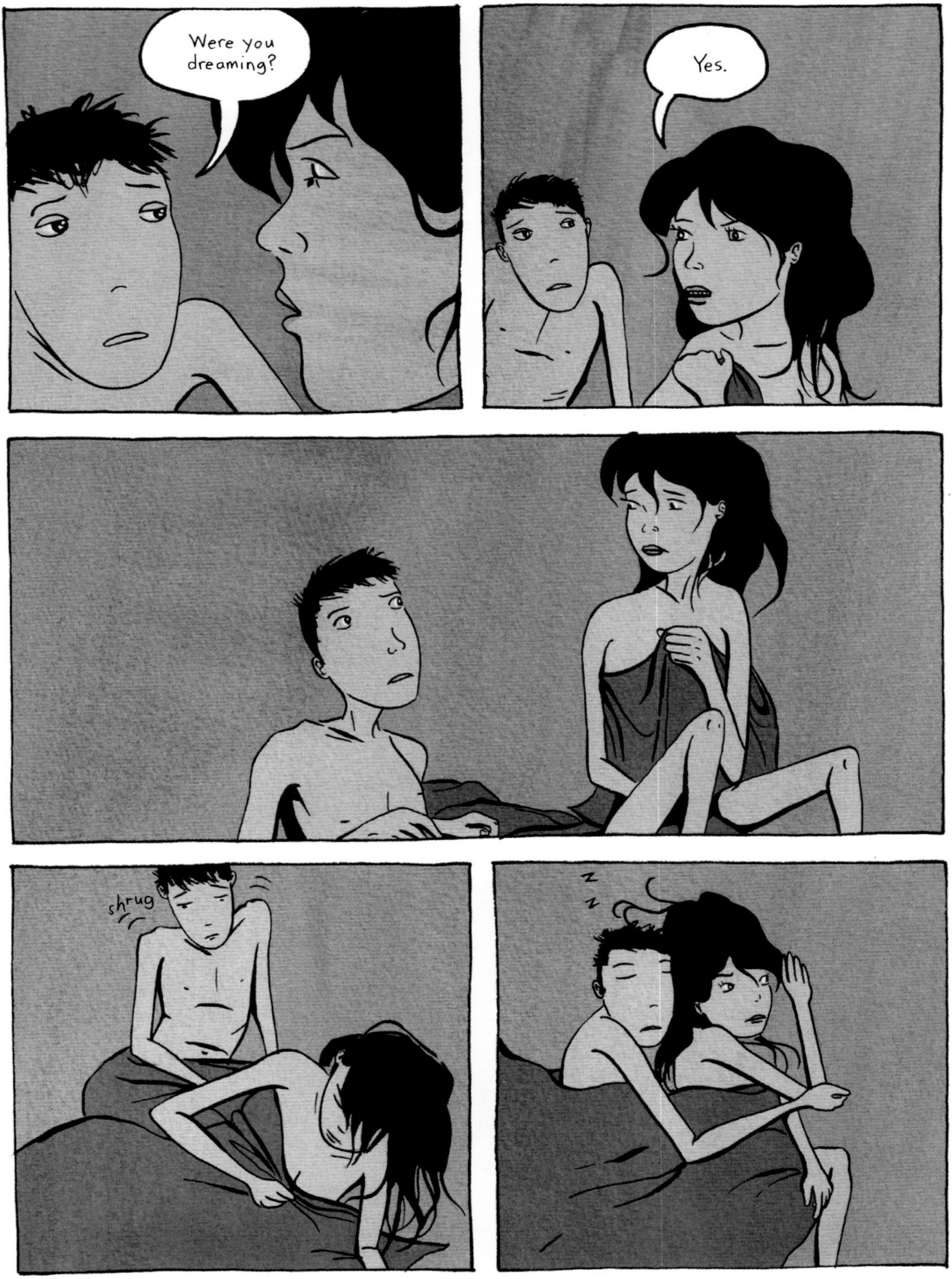
Were you dreaming?
Yes.
shrug
z
z

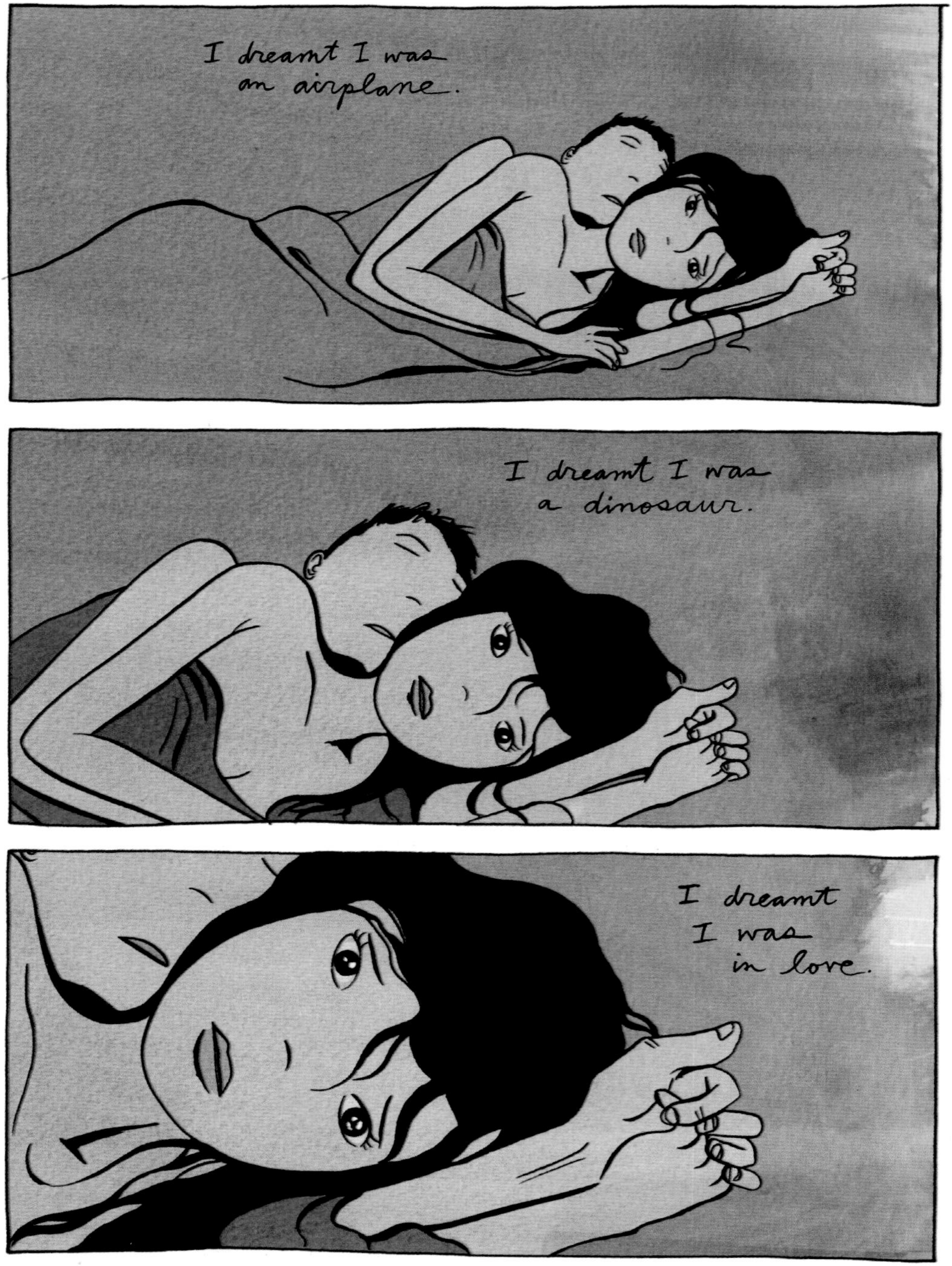
I dreamt I was an airplane.
I dreamt I was a dinosaur.
I dreamt I was in love.

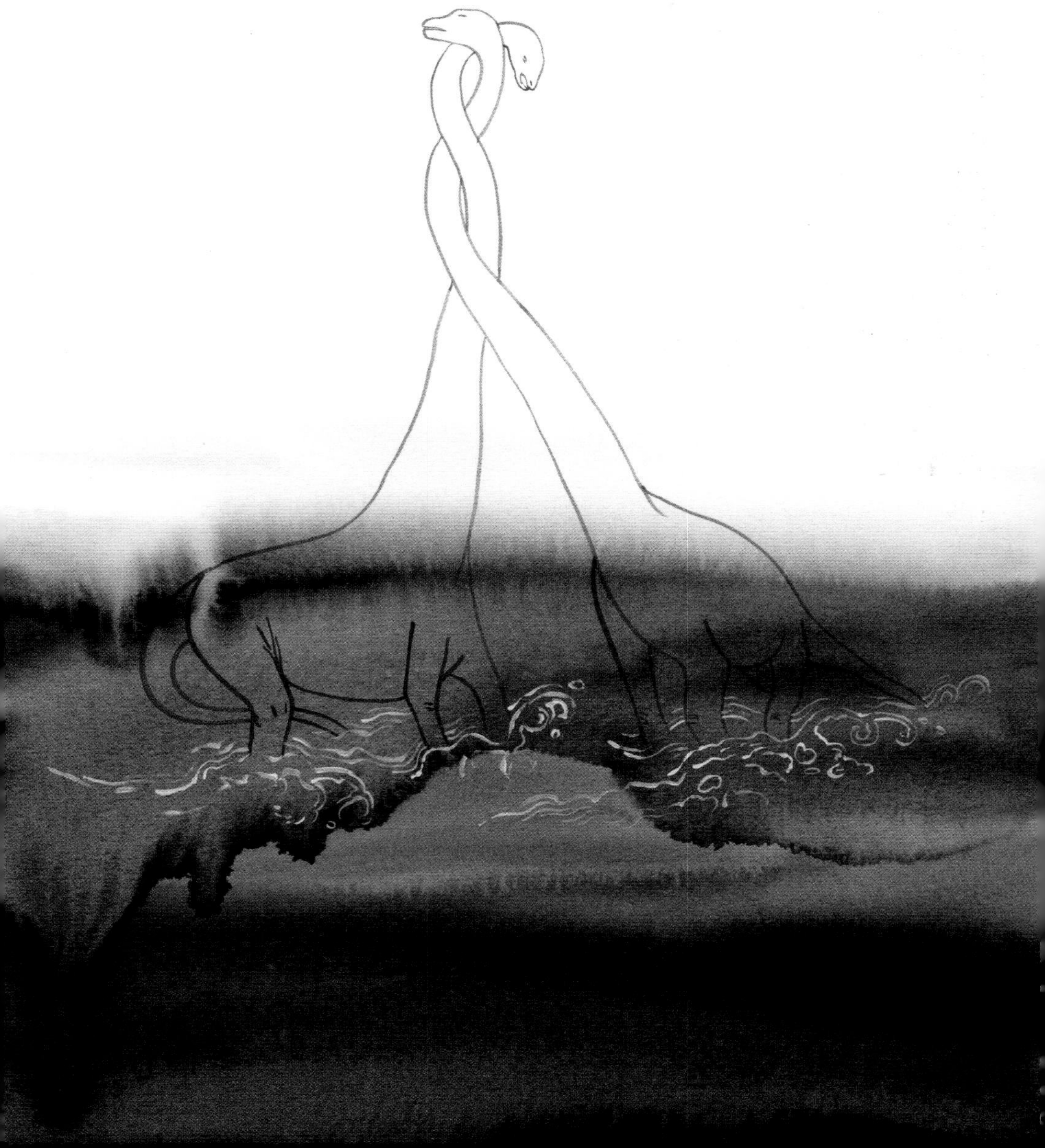

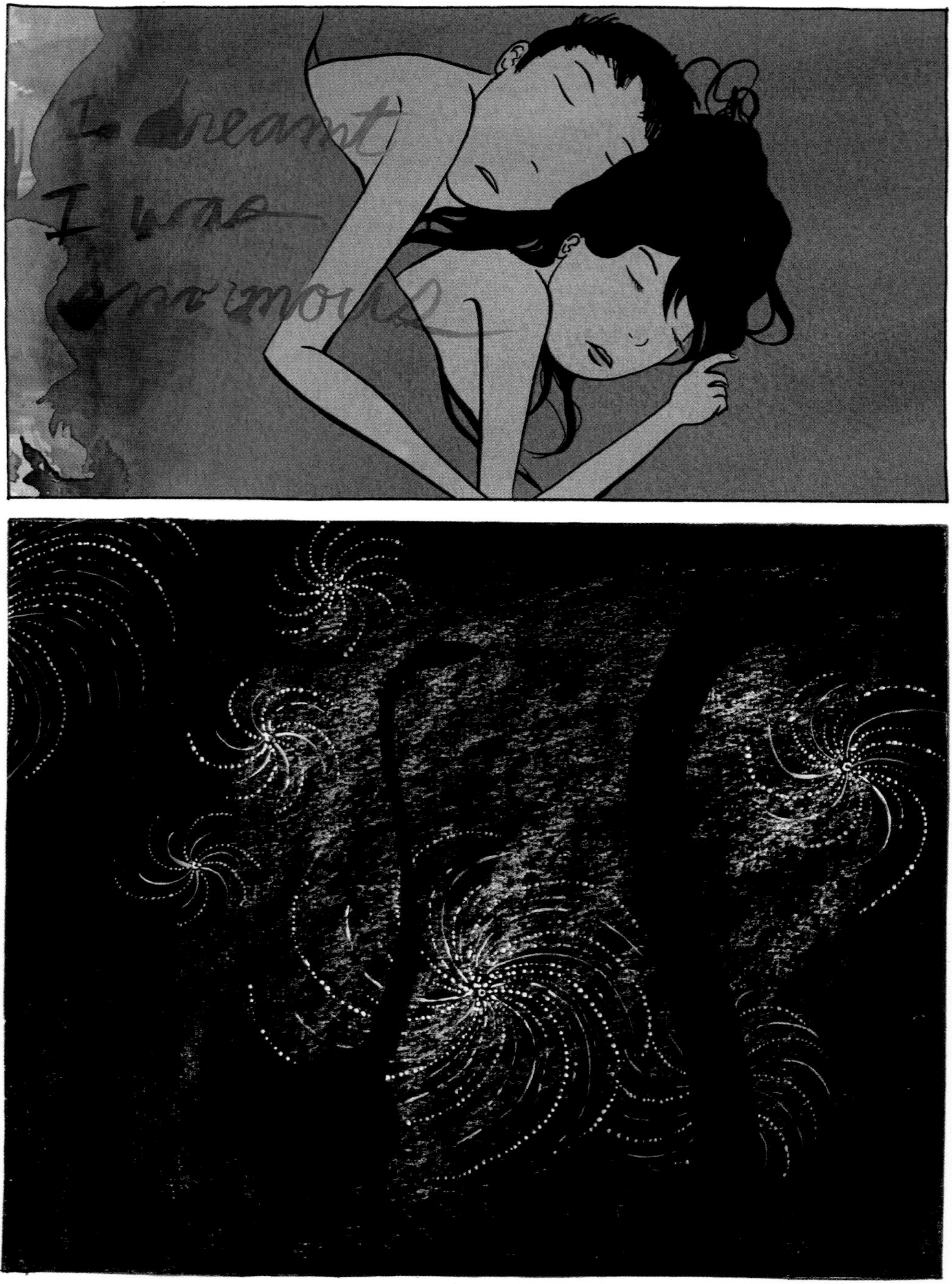
I dreamt I was enormous

25. Ashes

SATURDAY

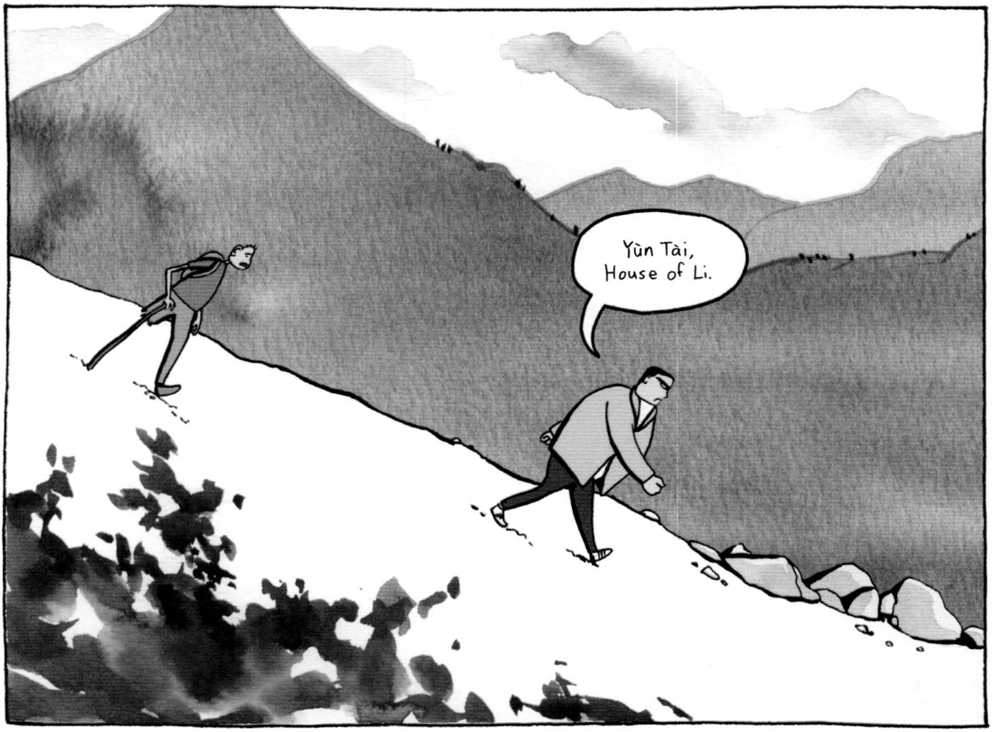
Yùn Tài,
House of Li.

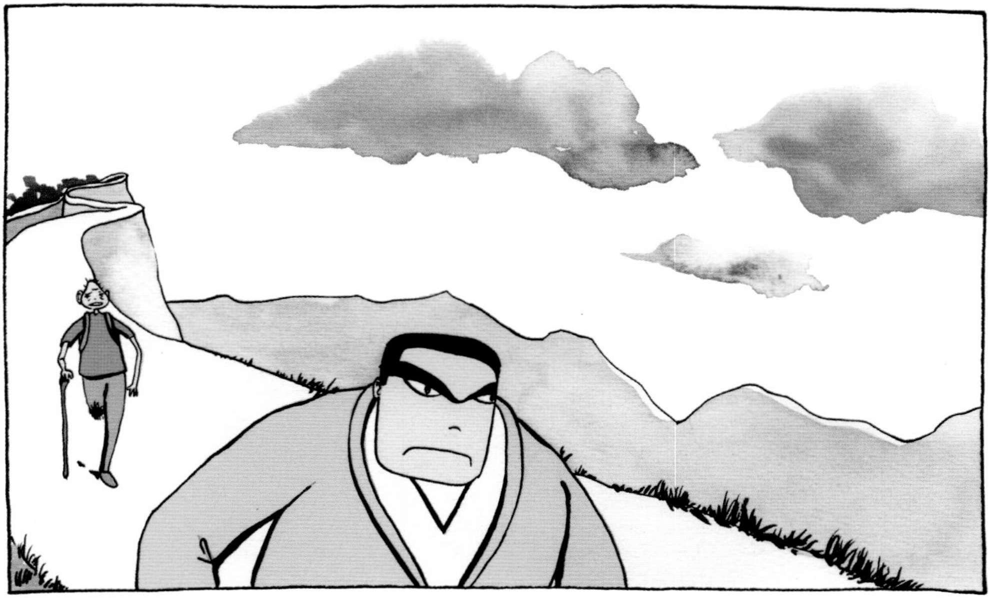

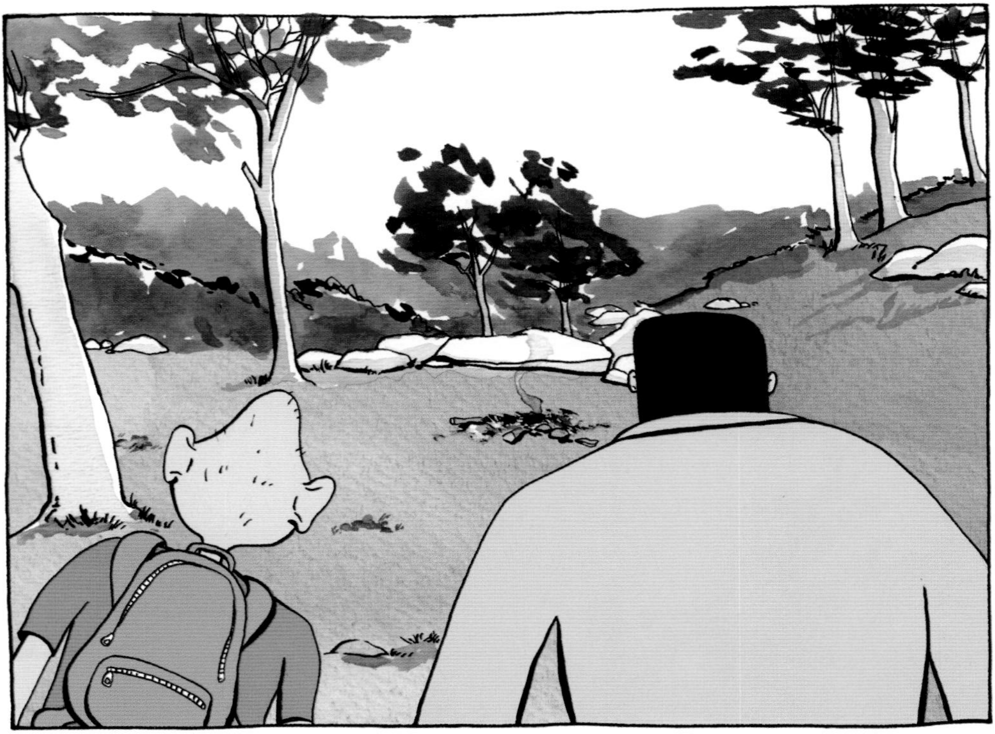

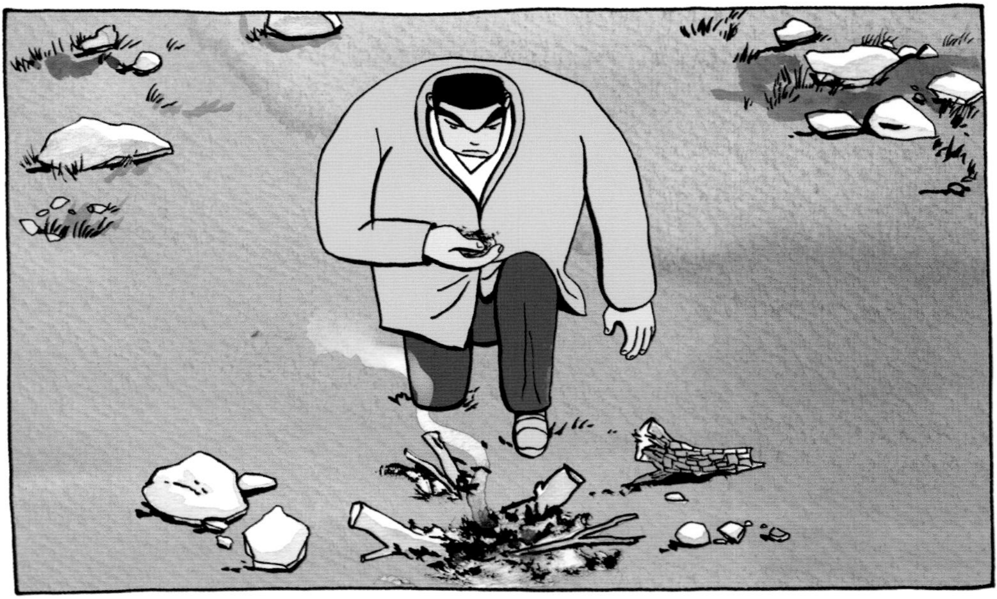

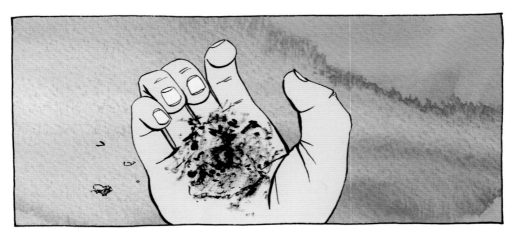

No.

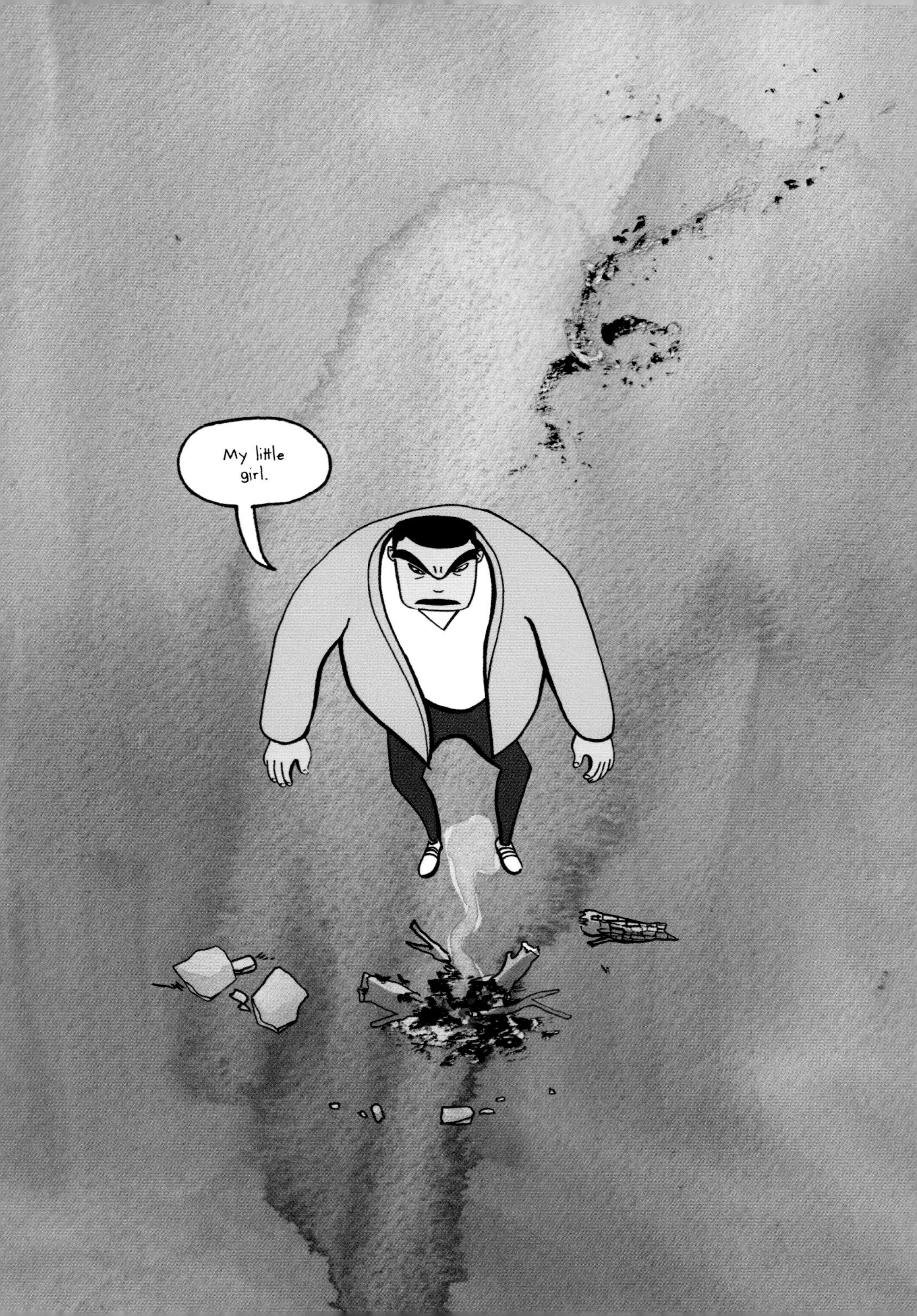
My little girl.

26. Friends

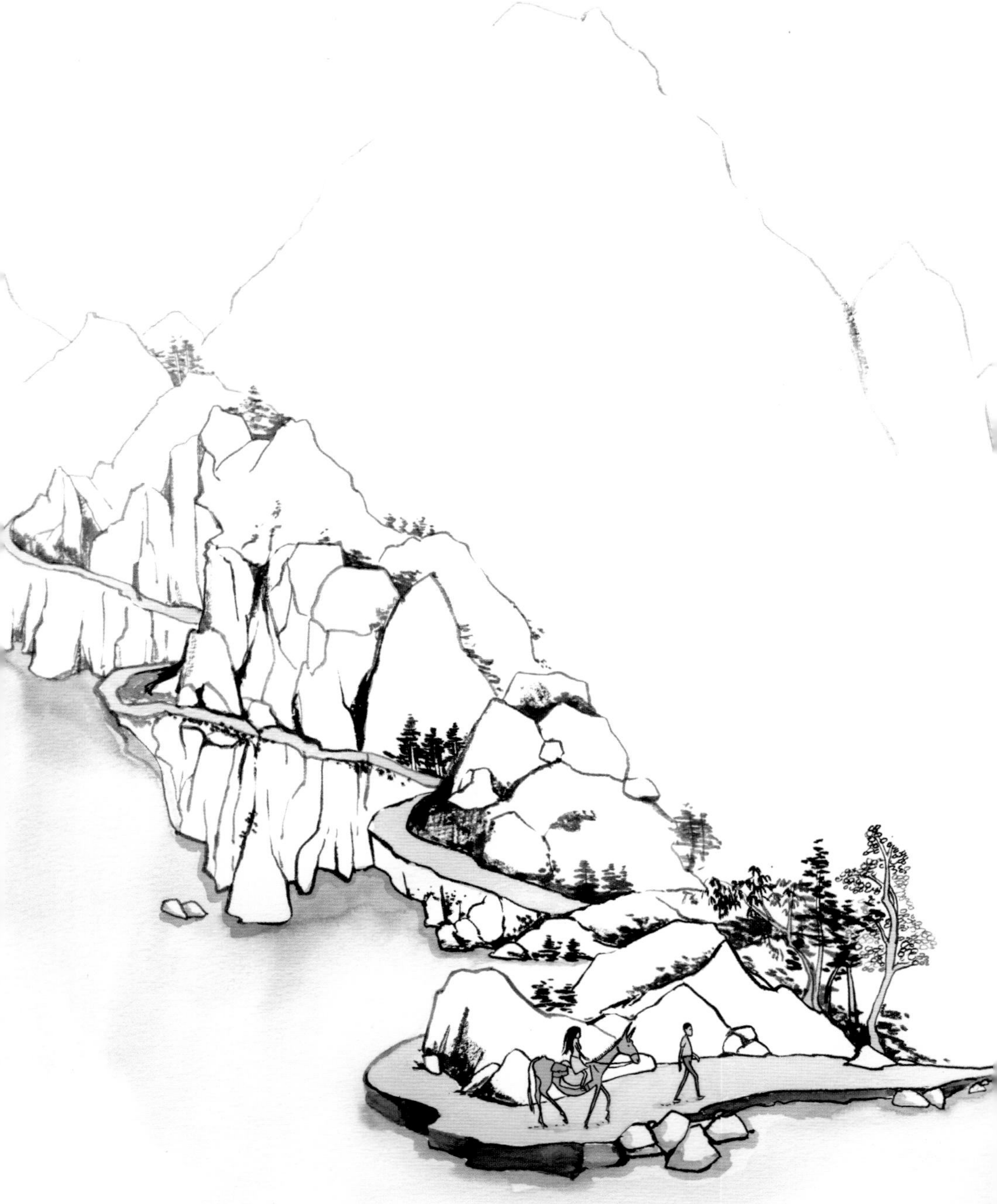

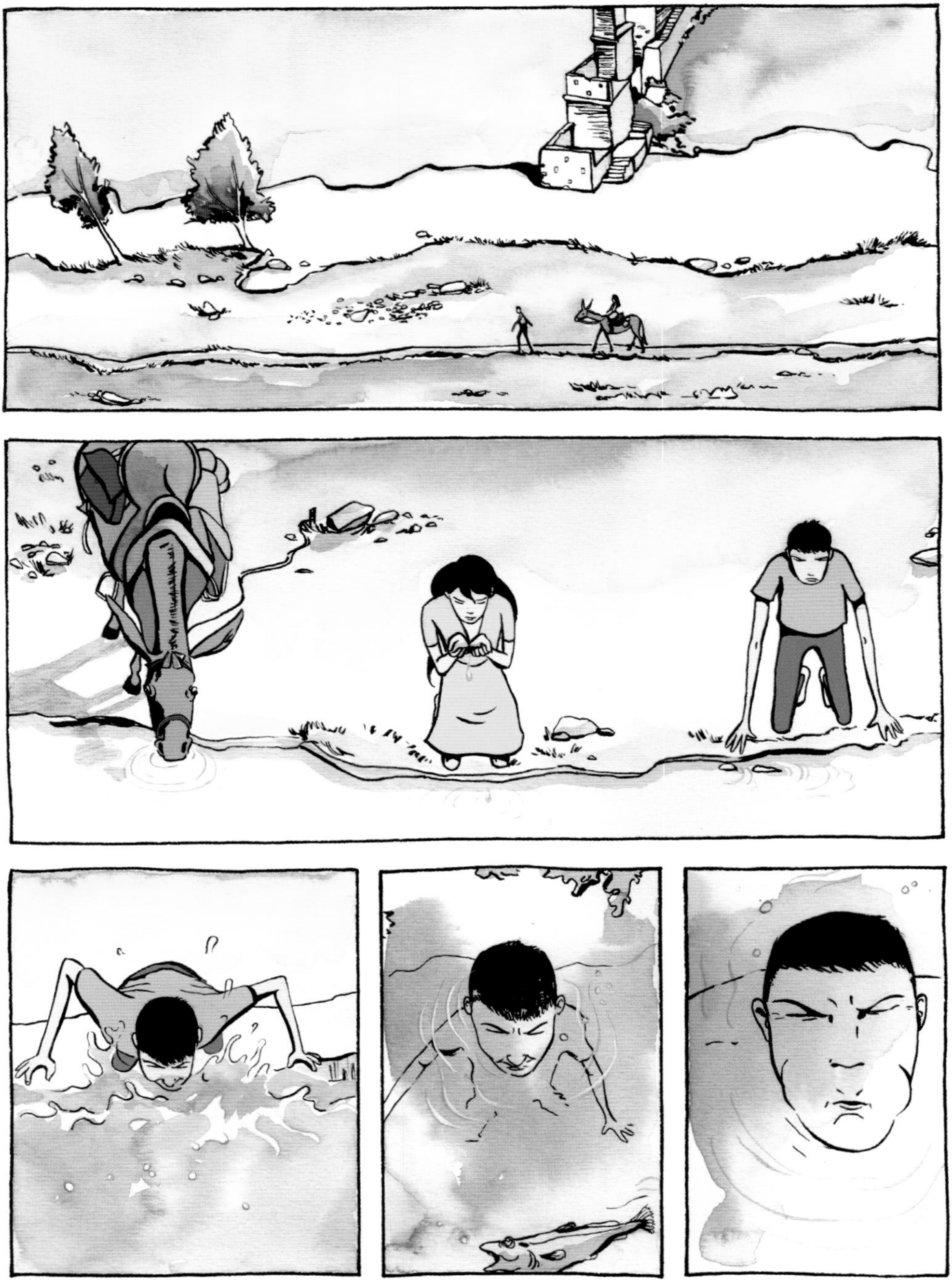

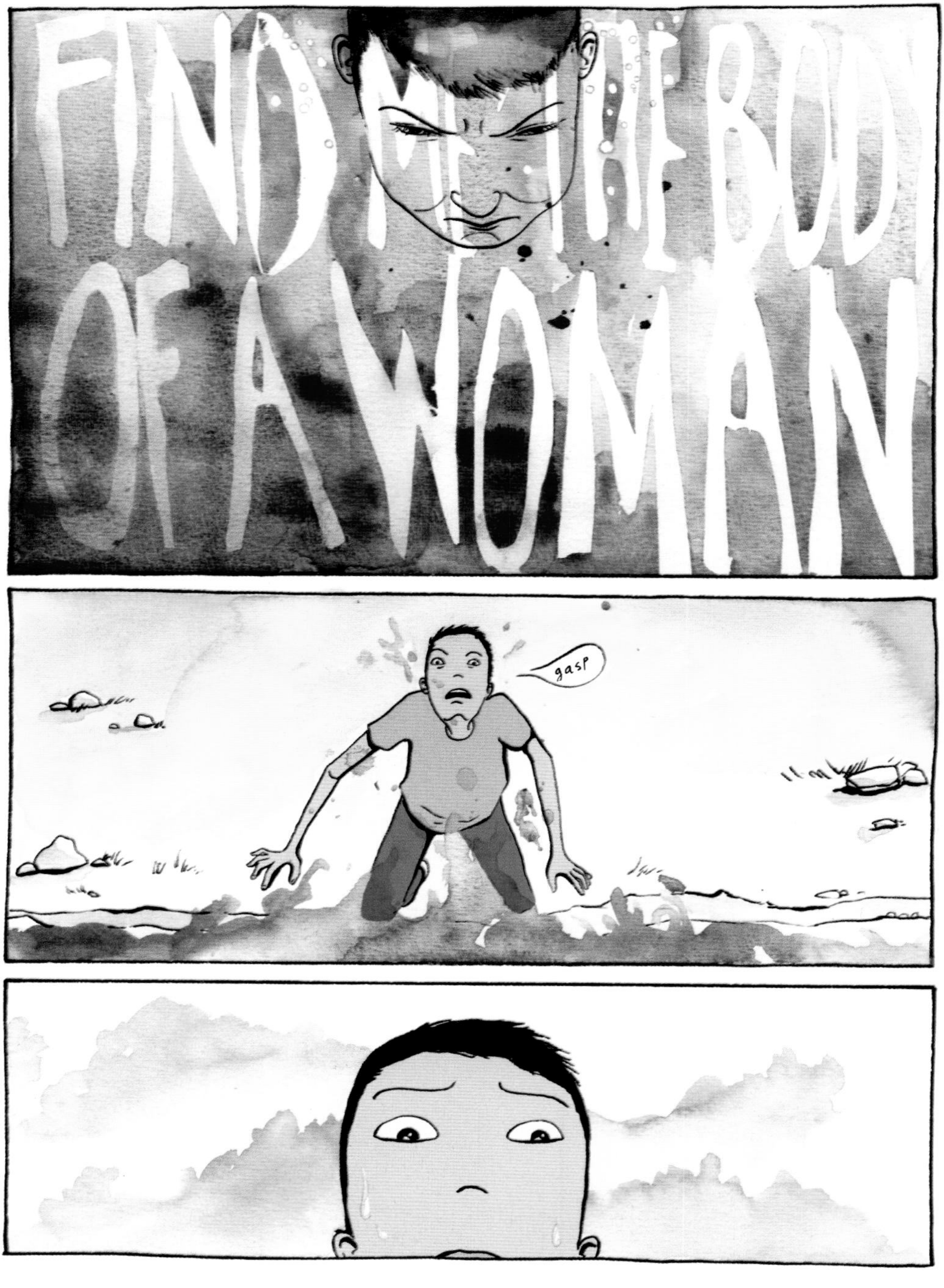
FIND ME THE BODY OF A WOMAN
gasp

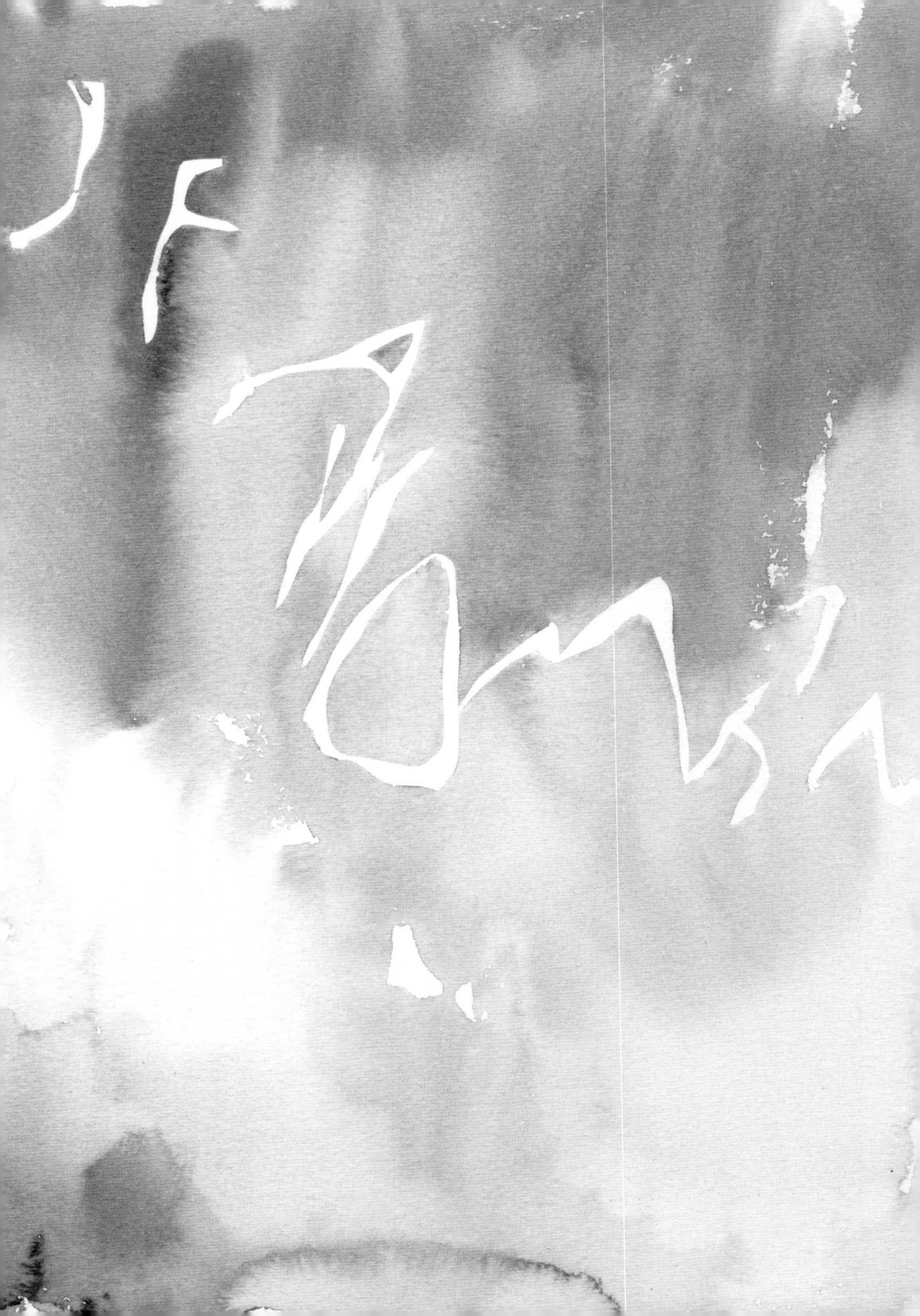

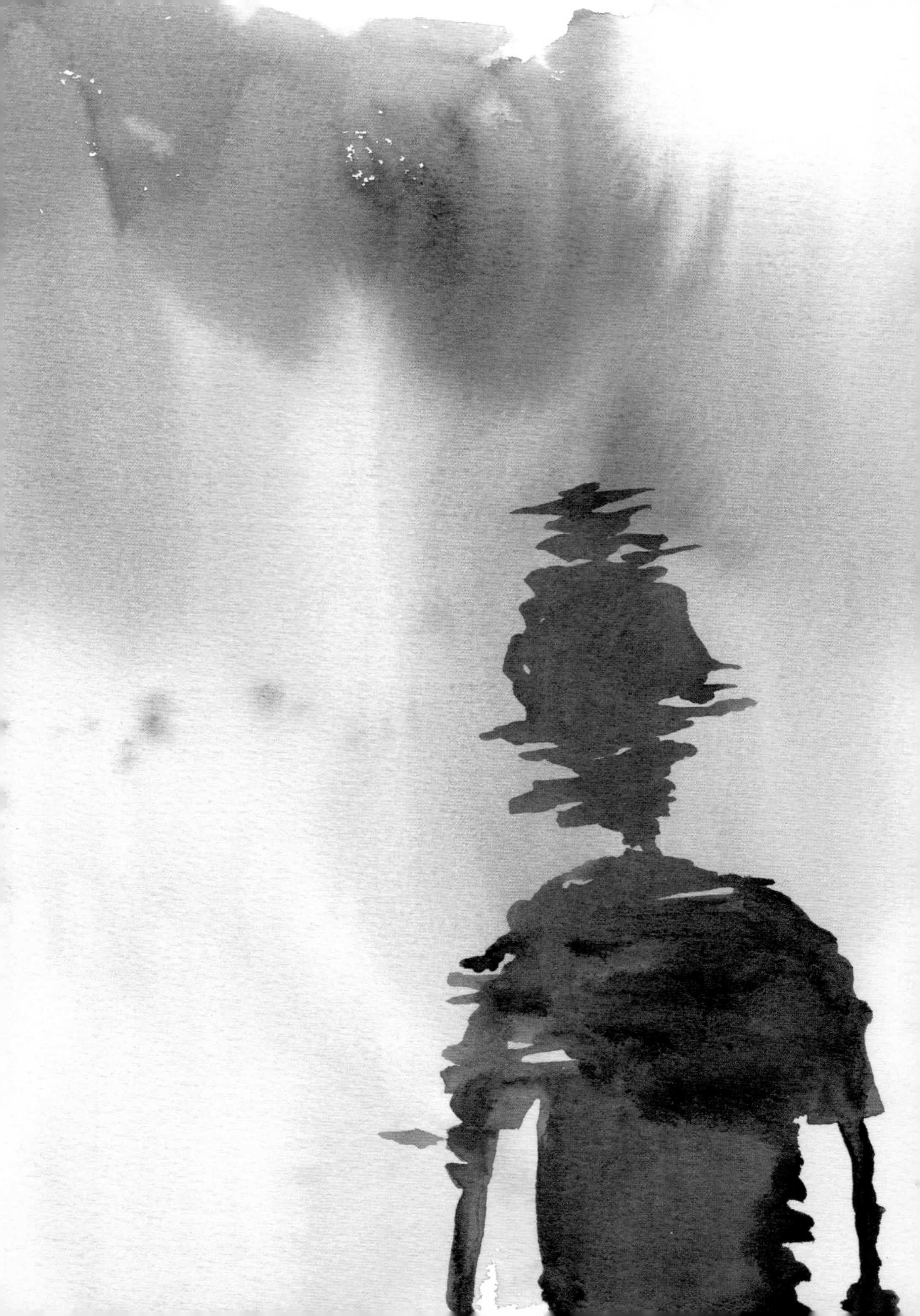

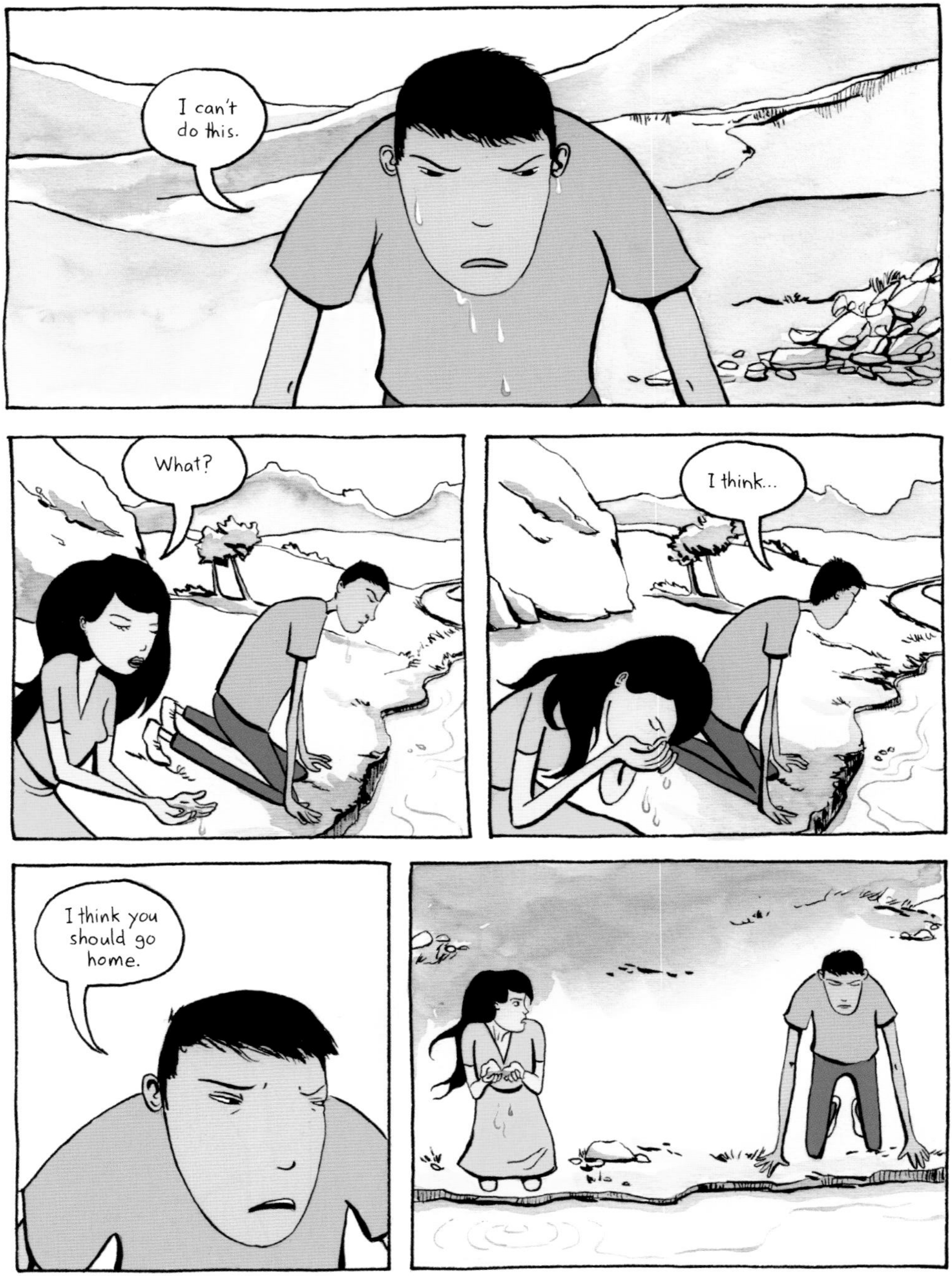
I can't do this.
What?
I think...
I think you should go home.

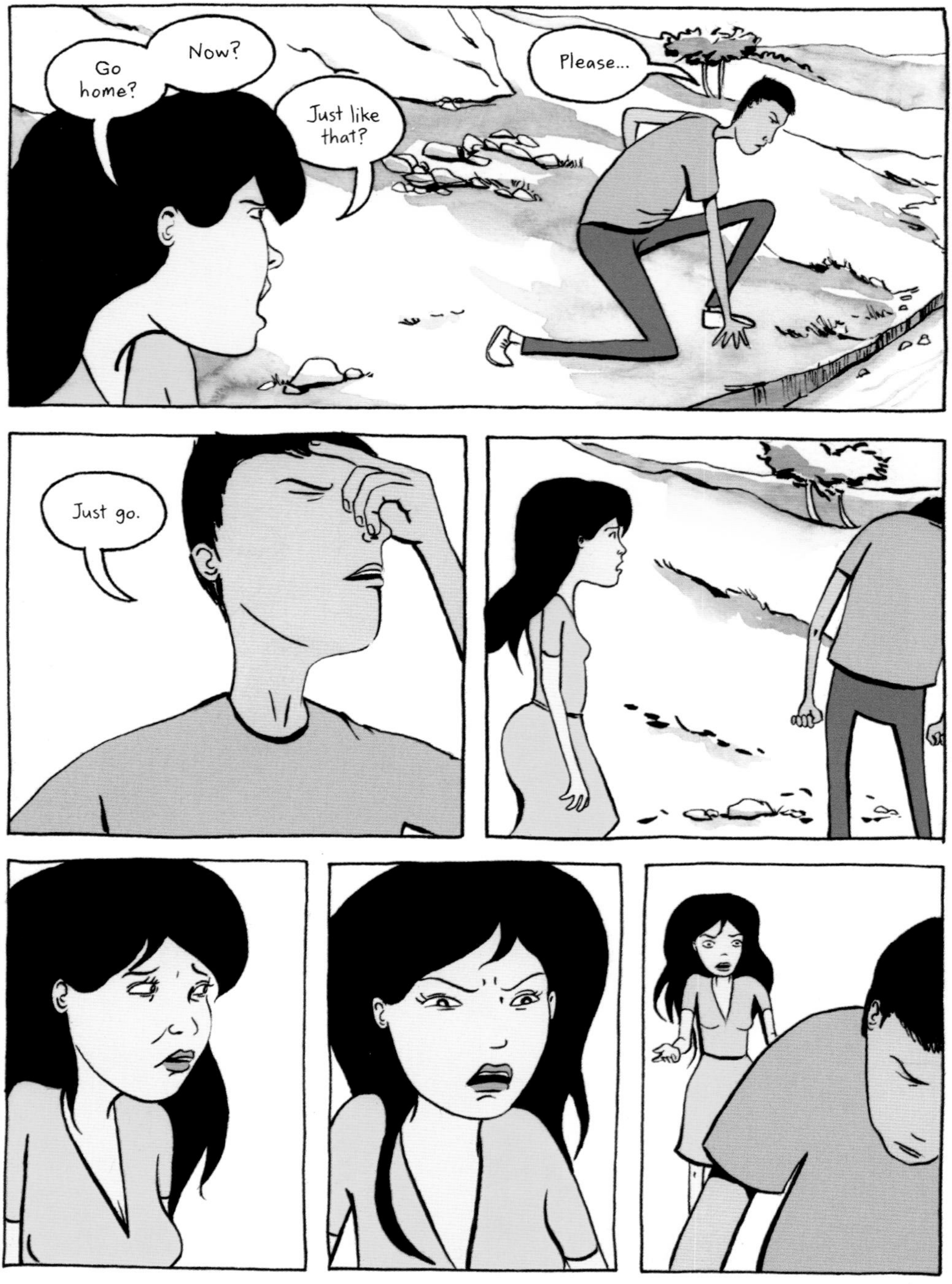
Go home?
Now?
Just like that?
Please...
Just go.

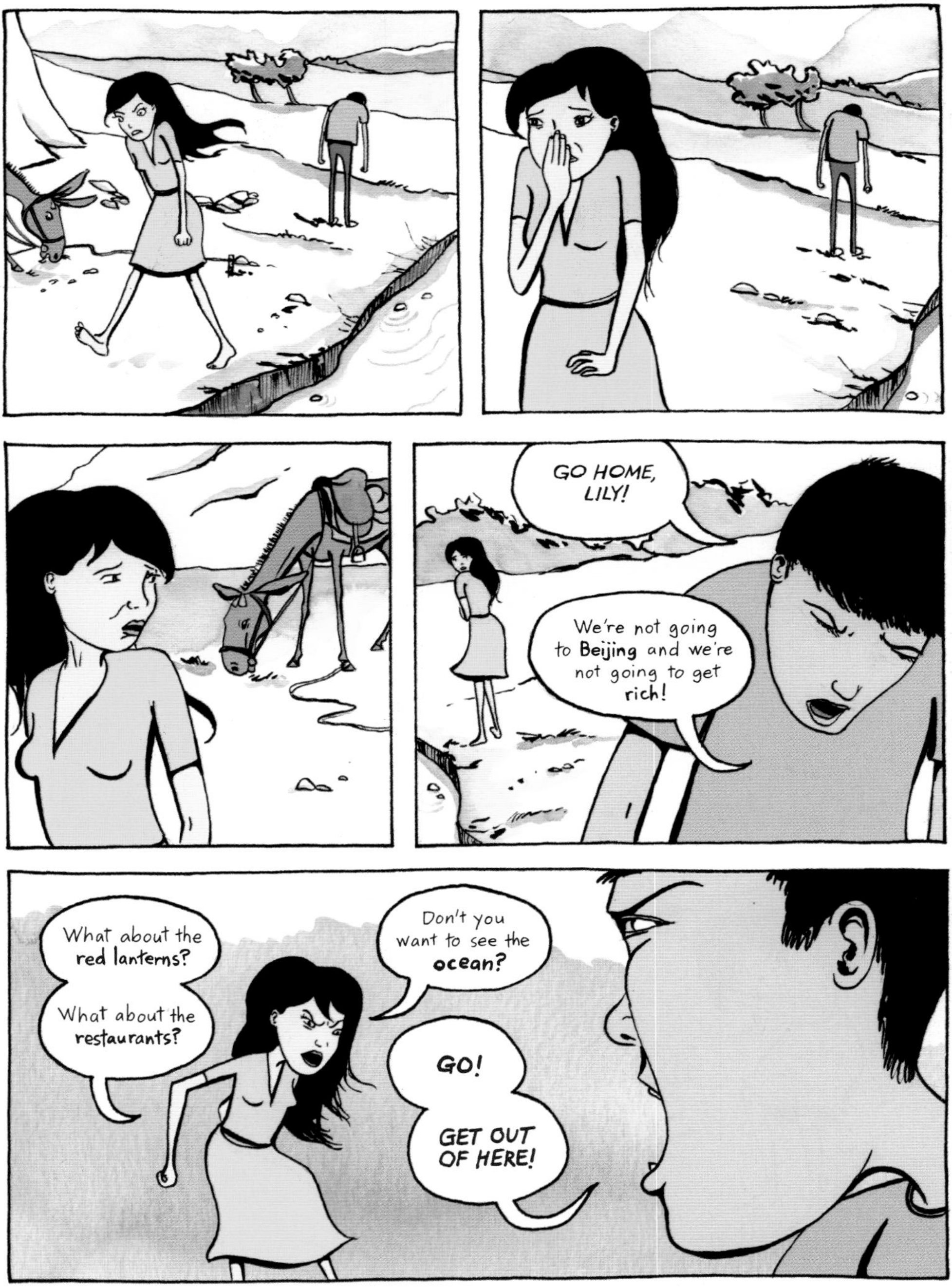
GO HOME, LILY!
We're not going to Beijing and we're not going to get rich!
What about the red lanterns?
What about the restaurants?
Don't you want to see the ocean?
GO!
GET OUT OF HERE!

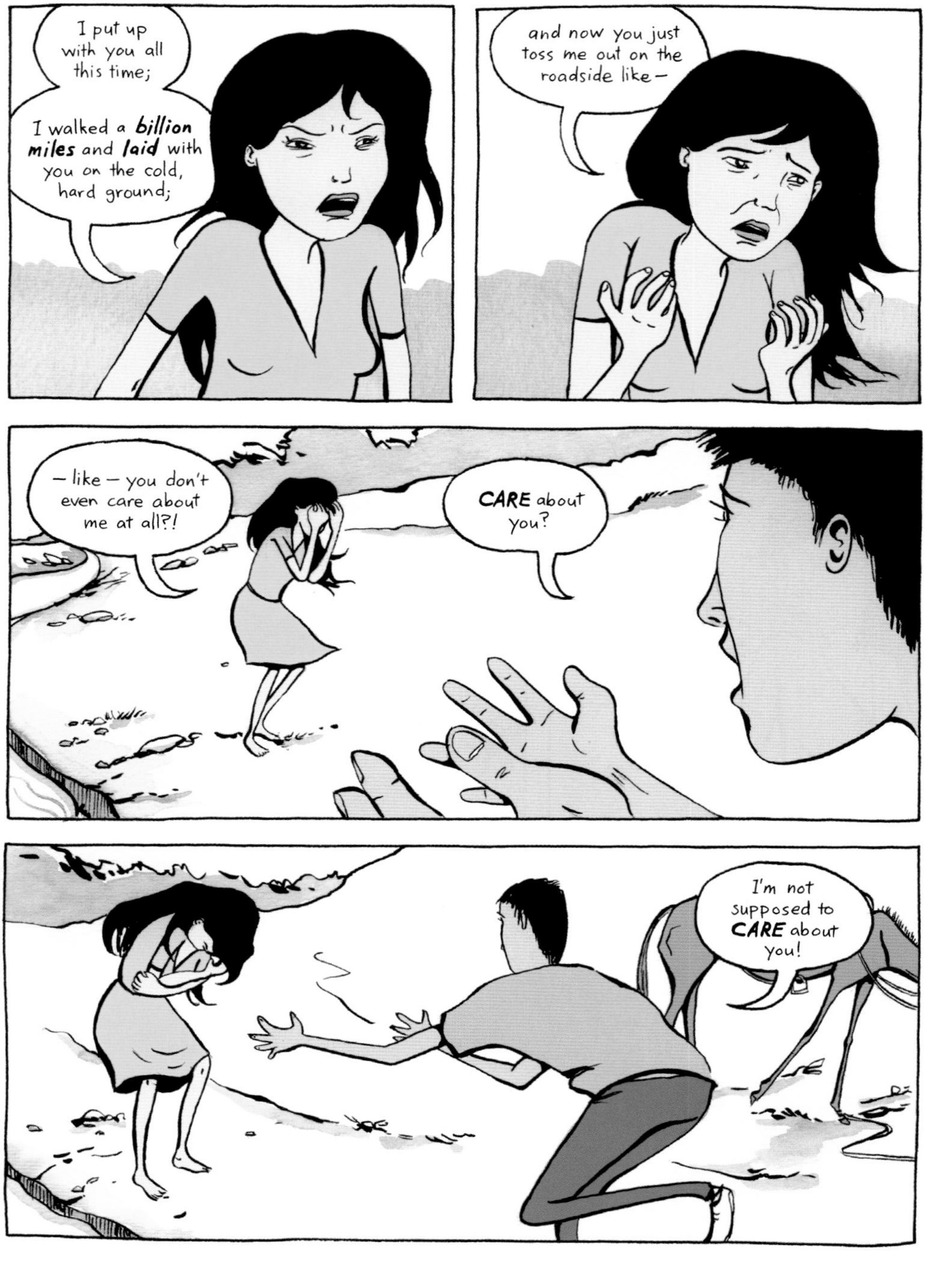
I put up with you all this time;
I walked a **billion miles** and **laid** with you on the cold, hard ground;
and now you just toss me out on the roadside like—
—like—you don't even care about me at all?!
CARE about you?
I'm not supposed to **CARE** about you!

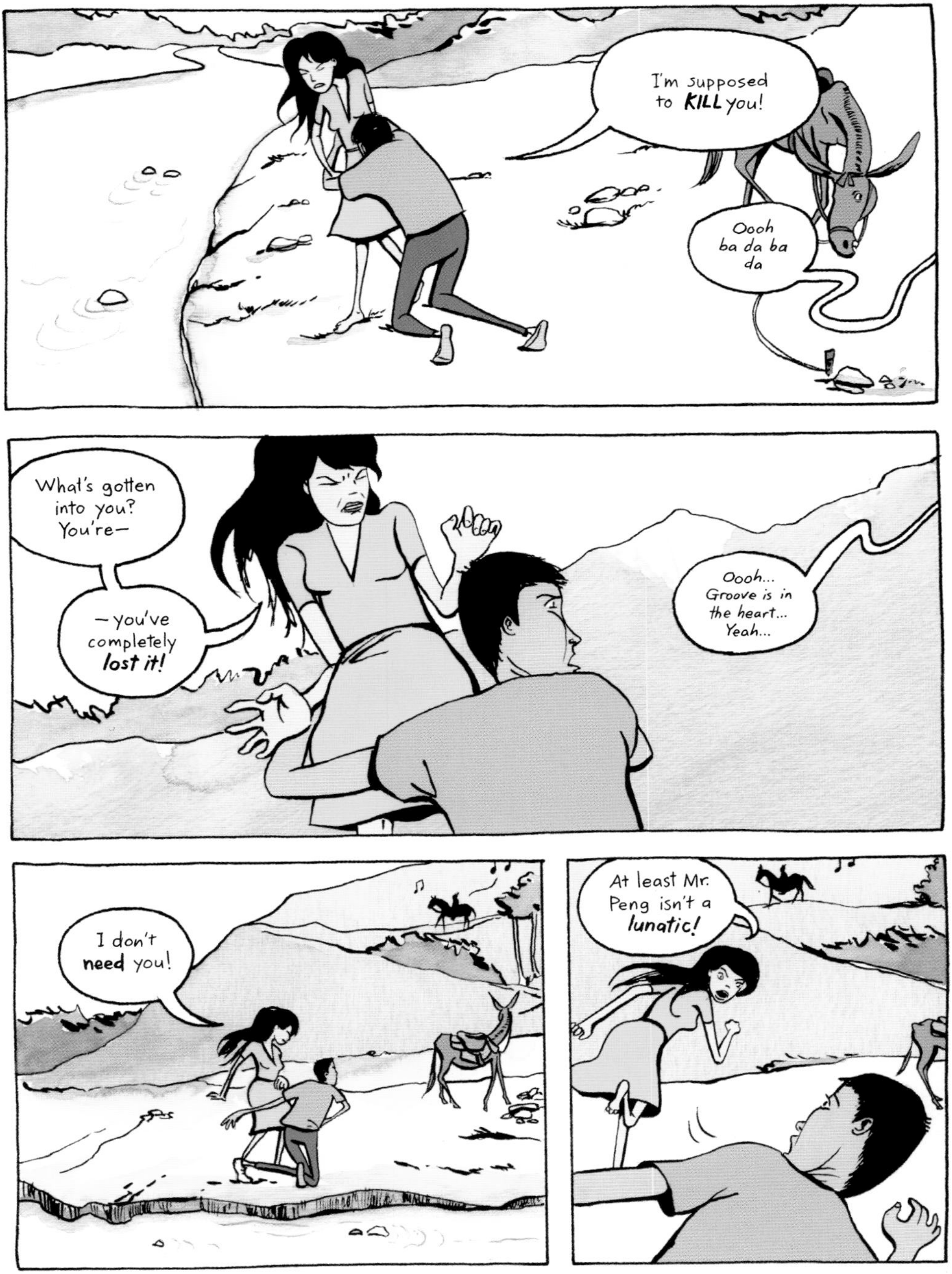
I'm supposed to **KILL** you!
Oooh ba da ba da
What's gotten into you? You're—
—you've completely ***lost it!***
Oooh... Groove is in the heart... Yeah...
I don't **need** you!
At least Mr. Peng isn't a ***lunatic!***

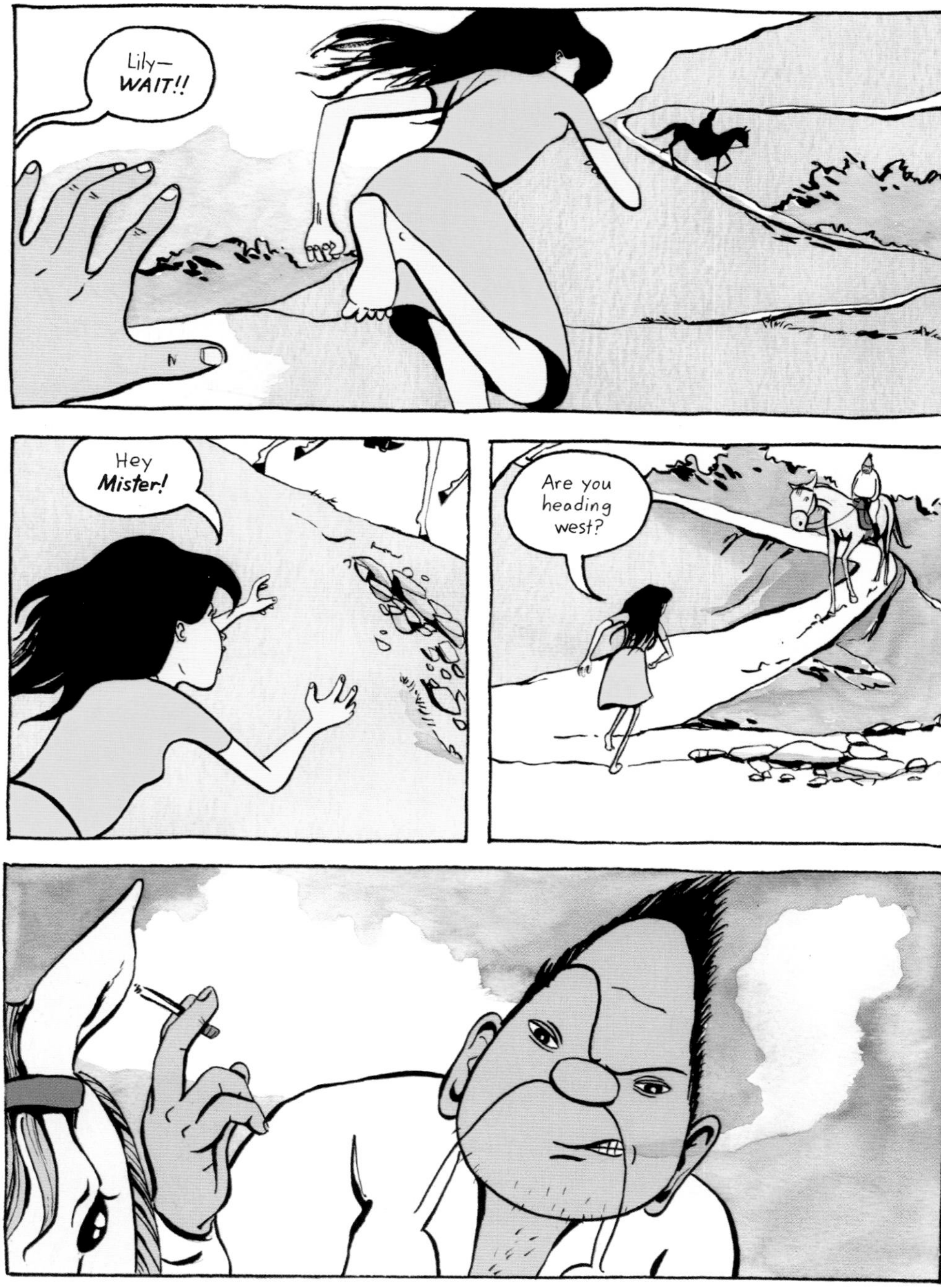

Lily—
WAIT!!
Hey
Mister!
Are you
heading
west?

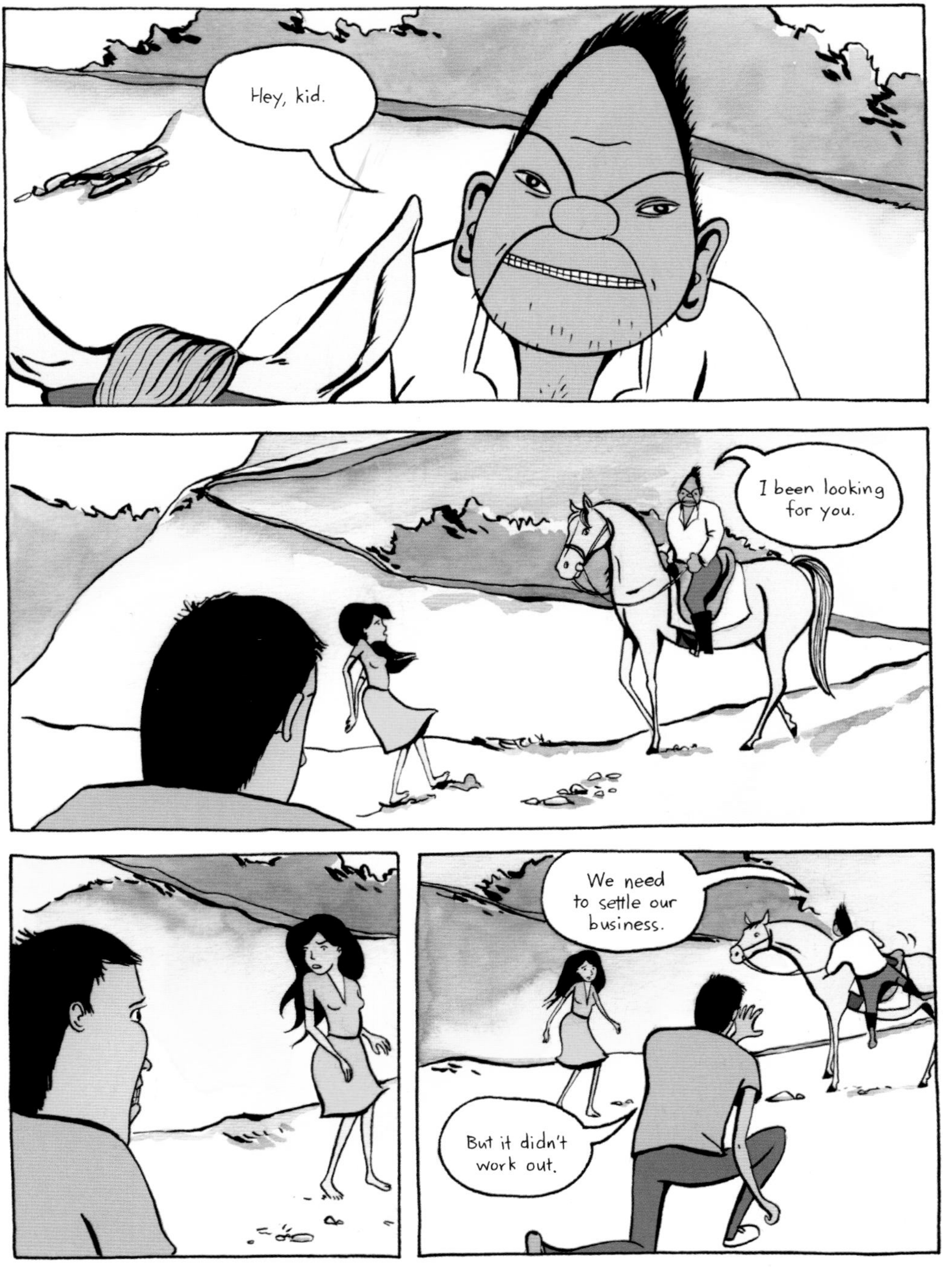
Hey, kid.
I been looking for you.
We need to settle our business.
But it didn't work out.

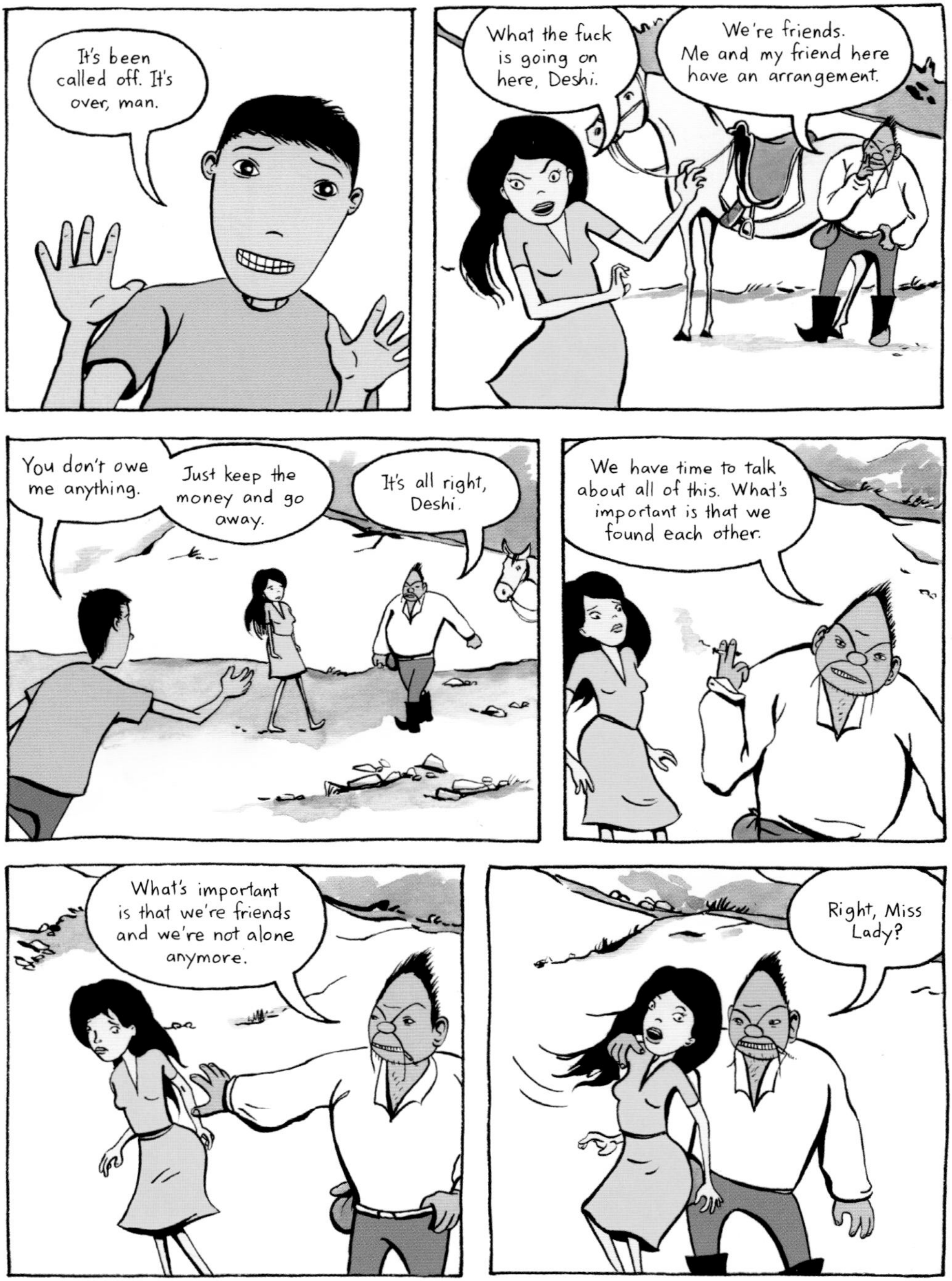
It's been called off. It's over, man.
What the fuck is going on here, Deshi.
We're friends. Me and my friend here have an arrangement.
You don't owe me anything.
Just keep the money and go away.
It's all right, Deshi.
We have time to talk about all of this. What's important is that we found each other.
What's important is that we're friends and we're not alone anymore.
Right, Miss Lady?

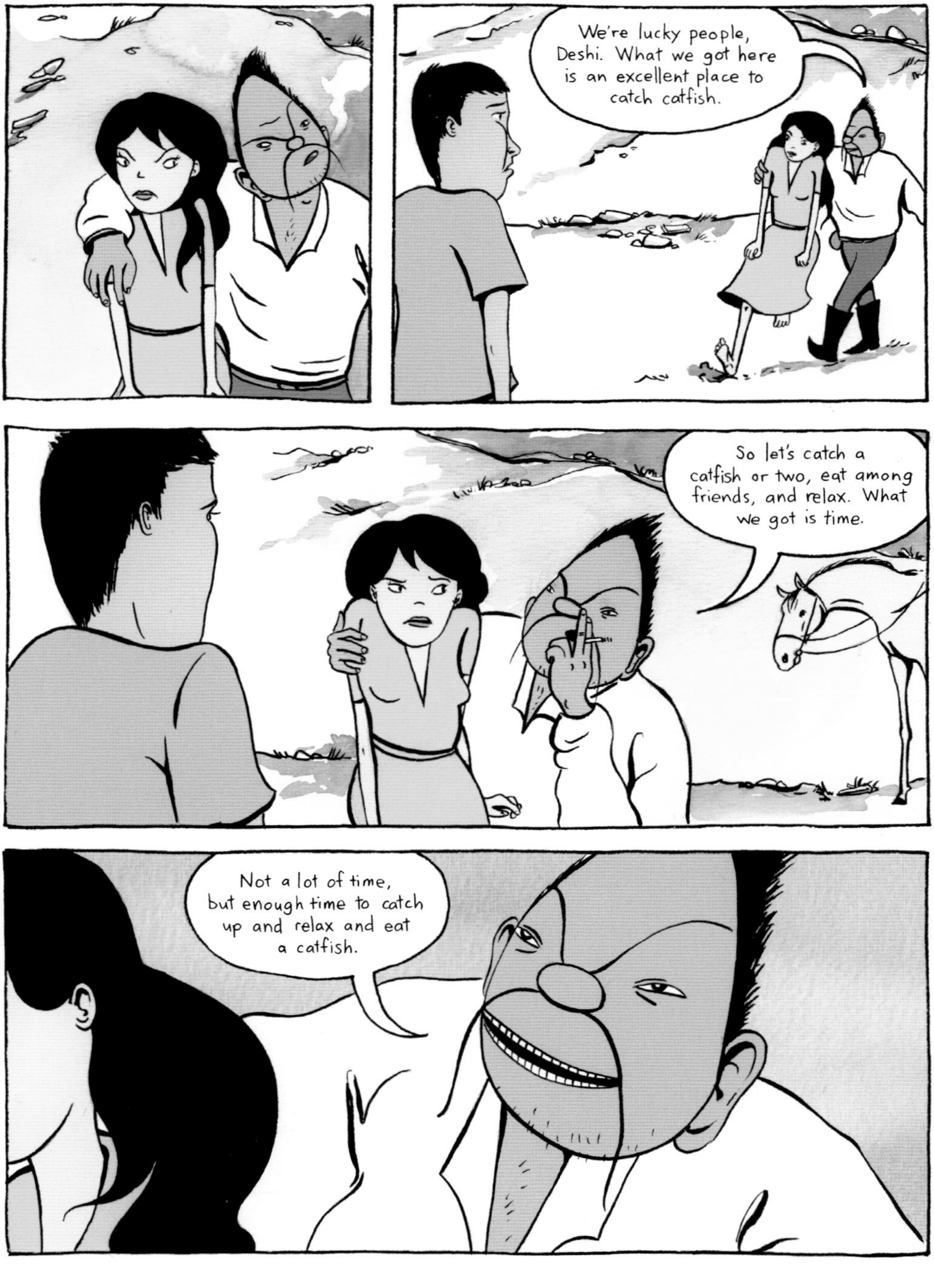
We're lucky people, Deshi. What we got here is an excellent place to catch catfish.
So let's catch a catfish or two, eat among friends, and relax. What we got is time.
Not a lot of time, but enough time to catch up and relax and eat a catfish.

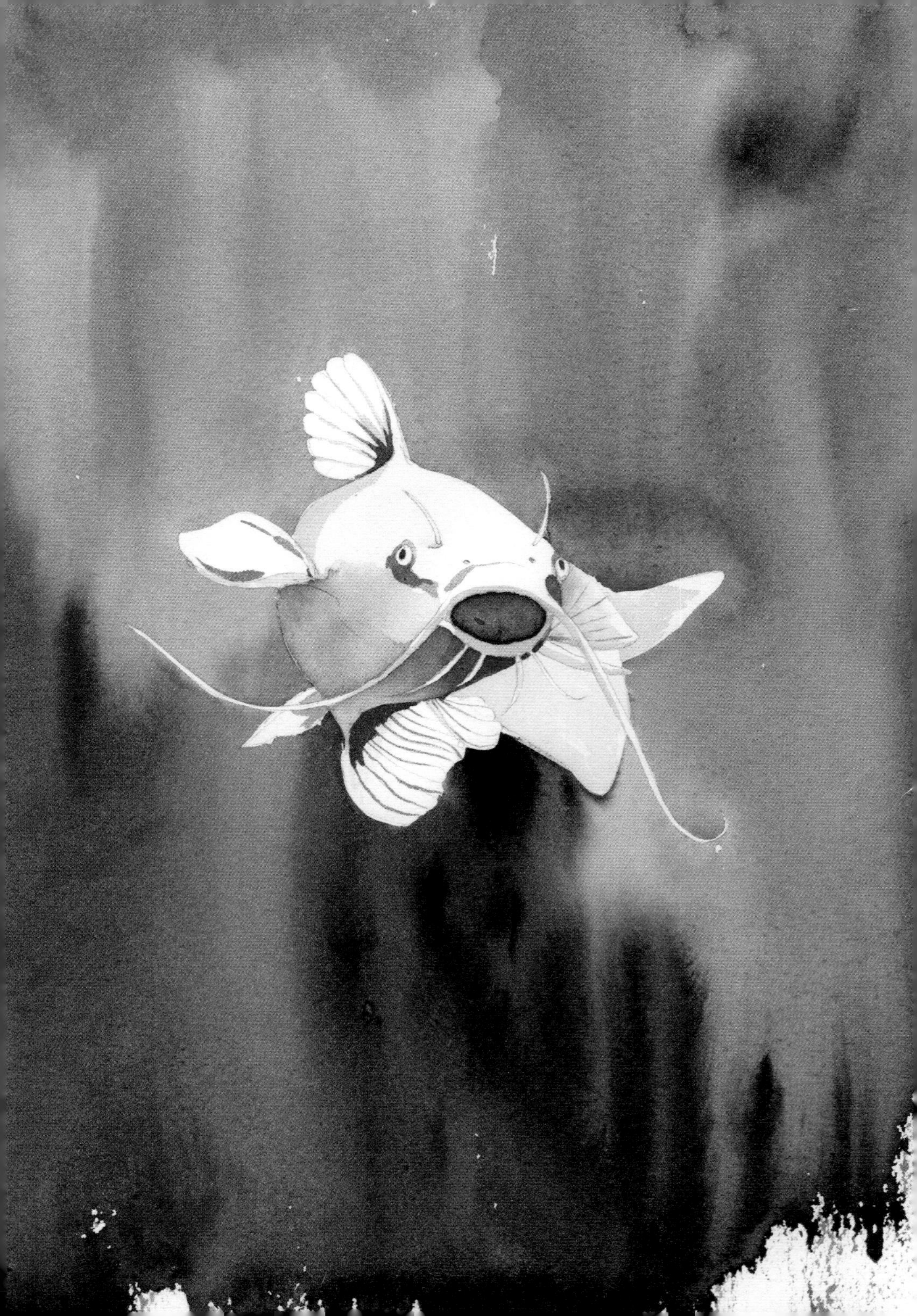

27. Song

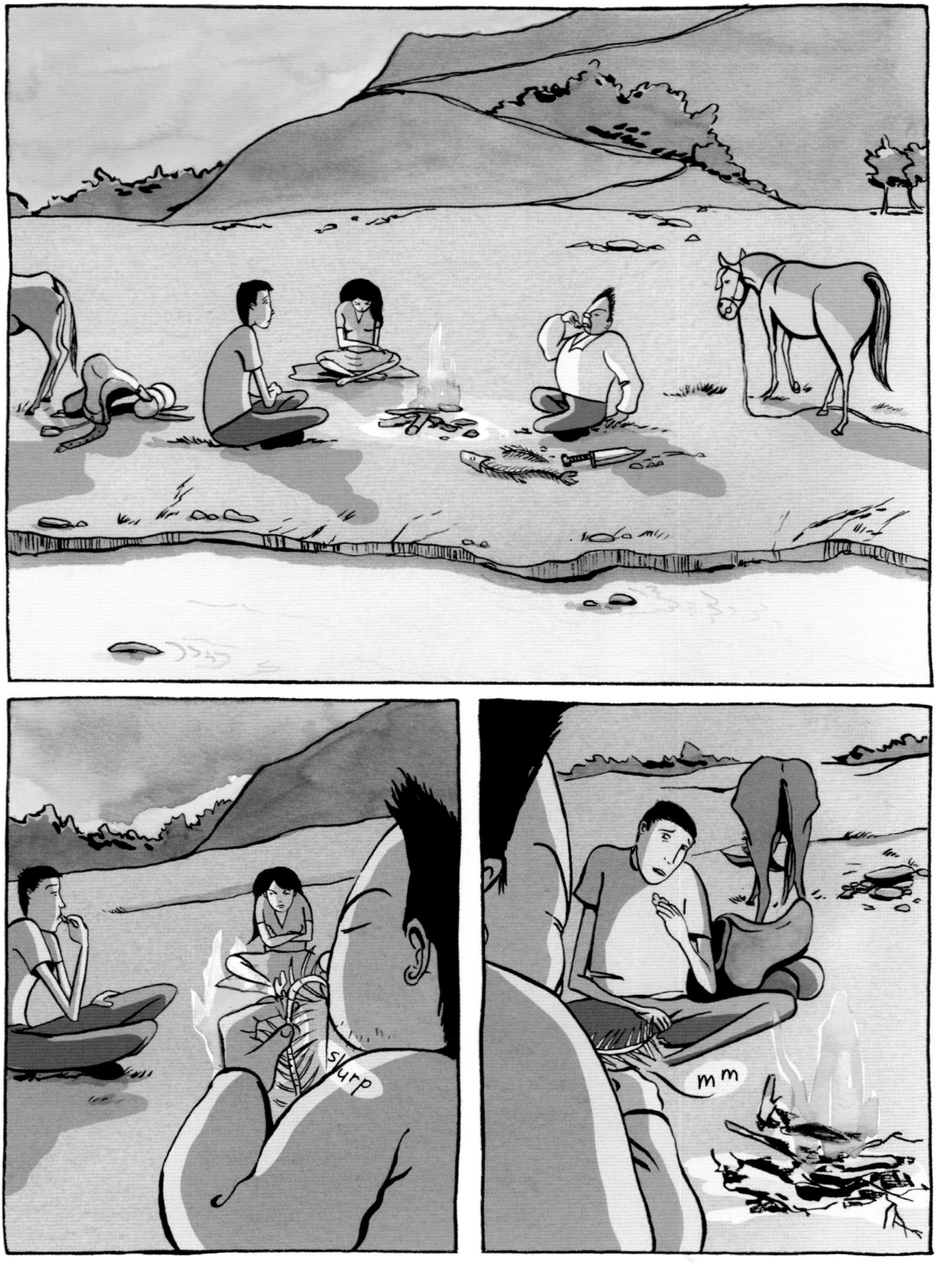
slurp
mm

munch

So, Ladyfriend

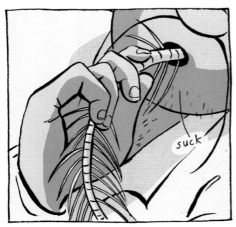

suck

How long have you known my boy Deshi?

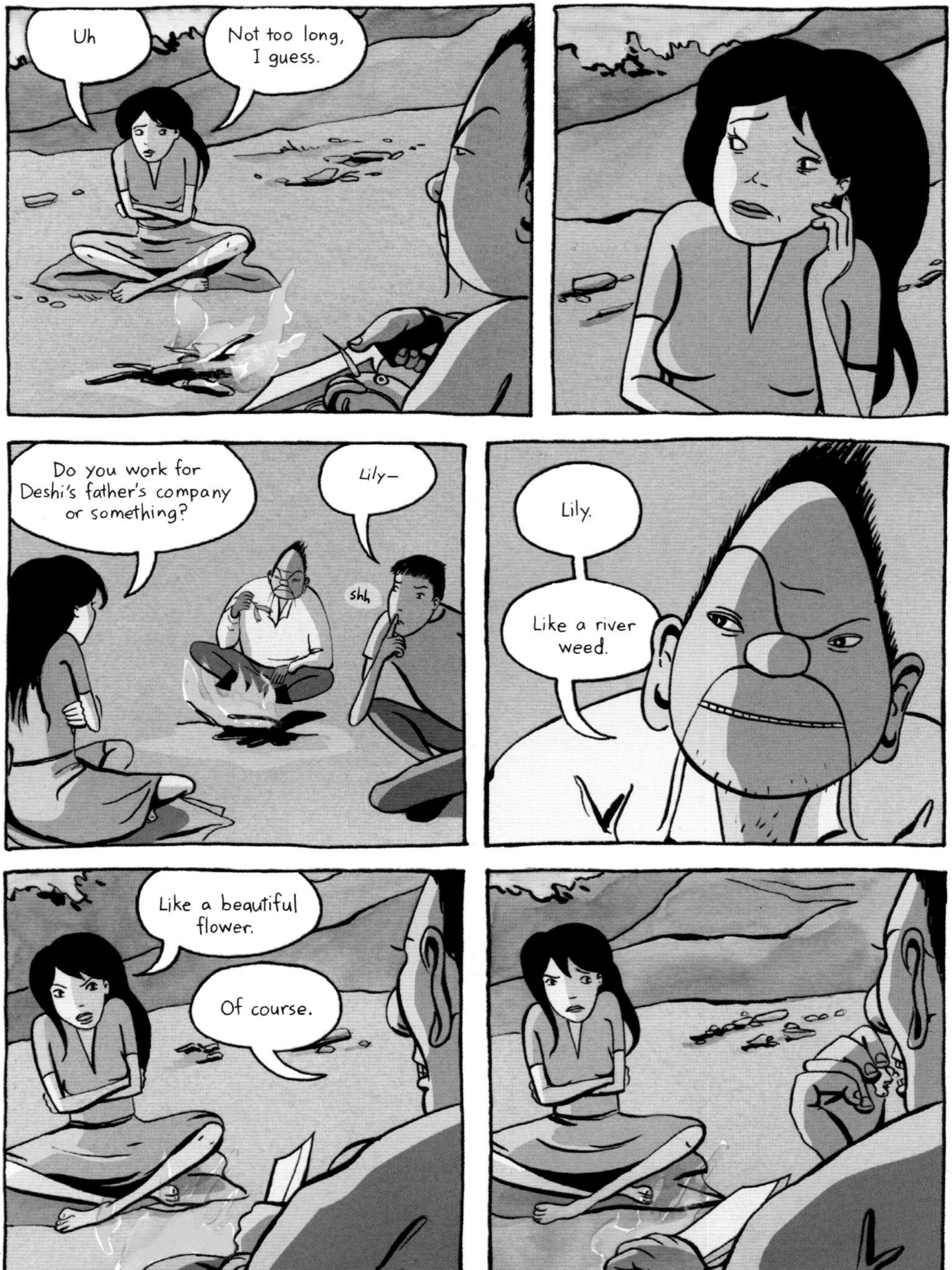
Uh
Not too long, I guess.
Do you work for Deshi's father's company or something?
Lily—
shh
Lily.
Like a river weed.
Like a beautiful flower.
Of course.

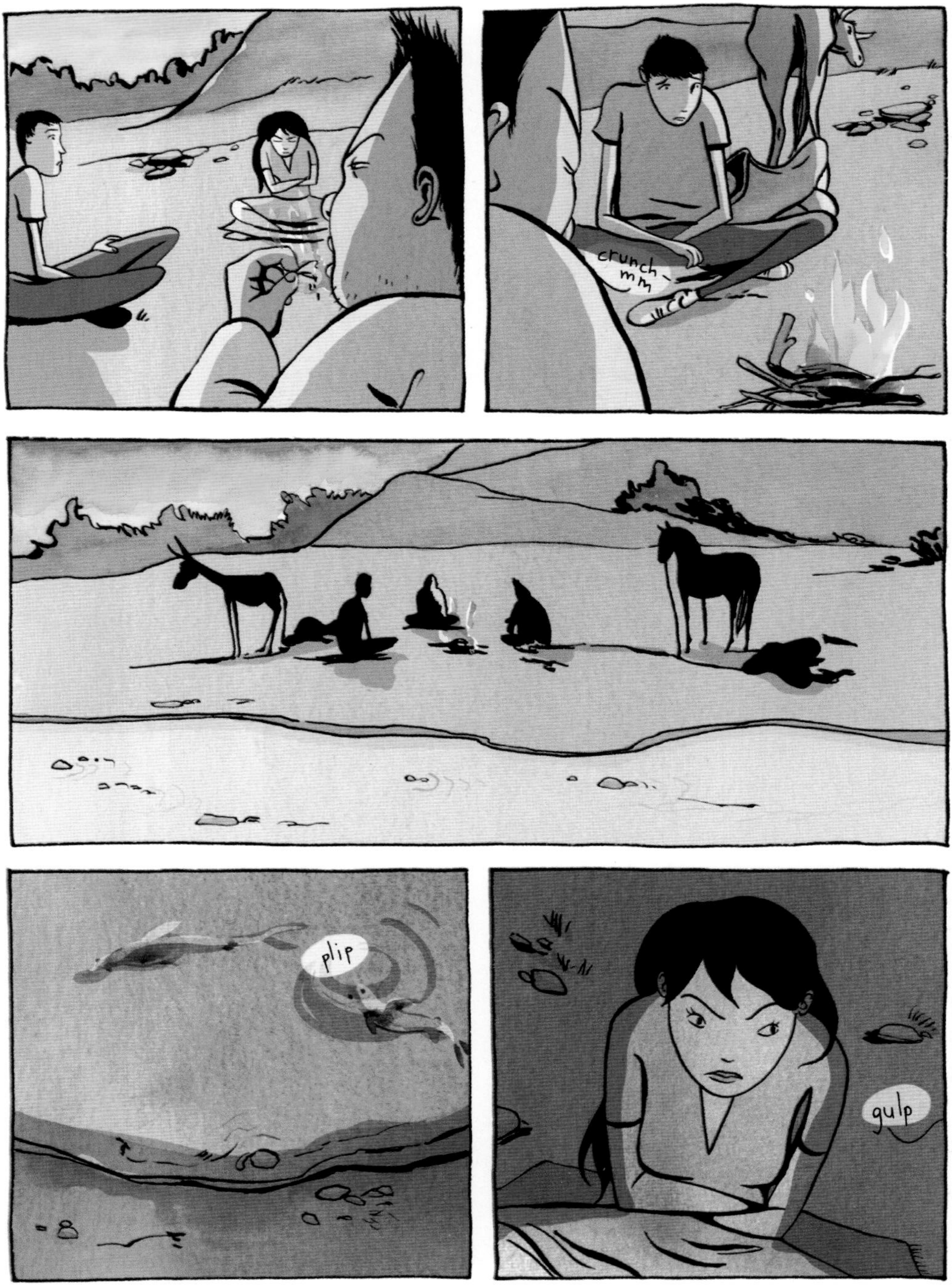
crunch-
mm-
plip
gulp

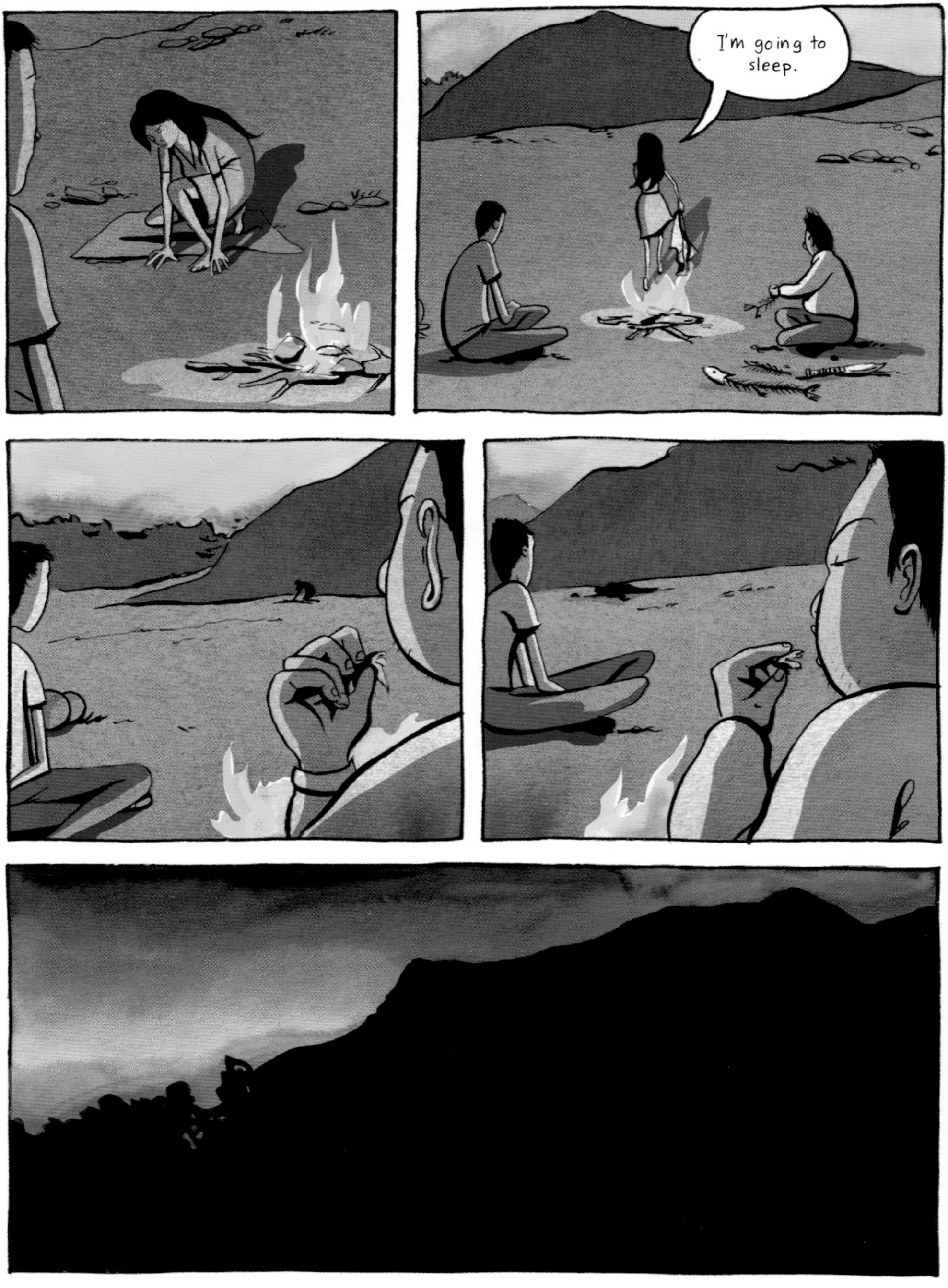
I'm going to sleep.

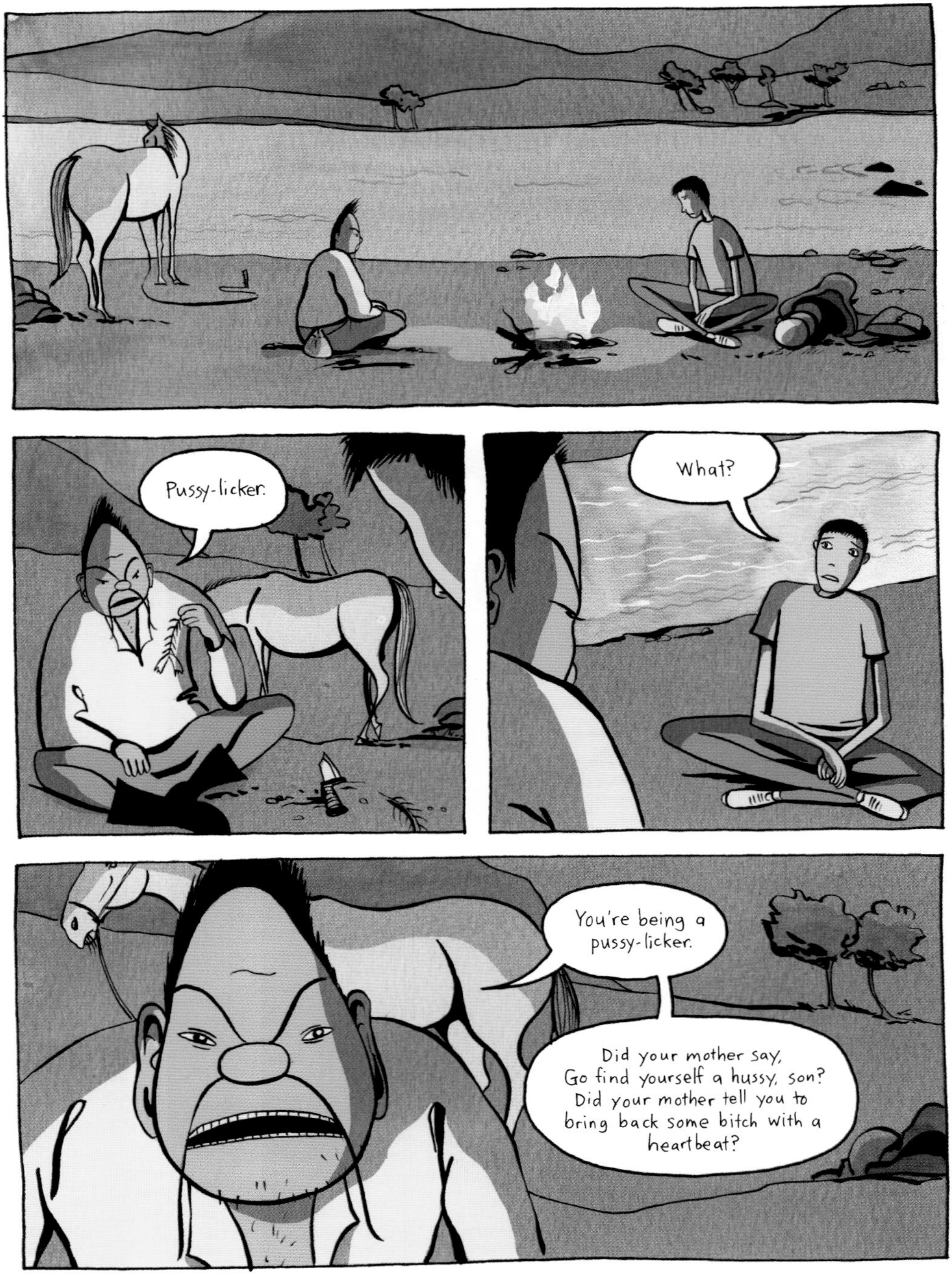
Pussy-licker.
What?
You're being a pussy-licker.
Did your mother say, Go find yourself a hussy, son? Did your mother tell you to bring back some bitch with a heartbeat?

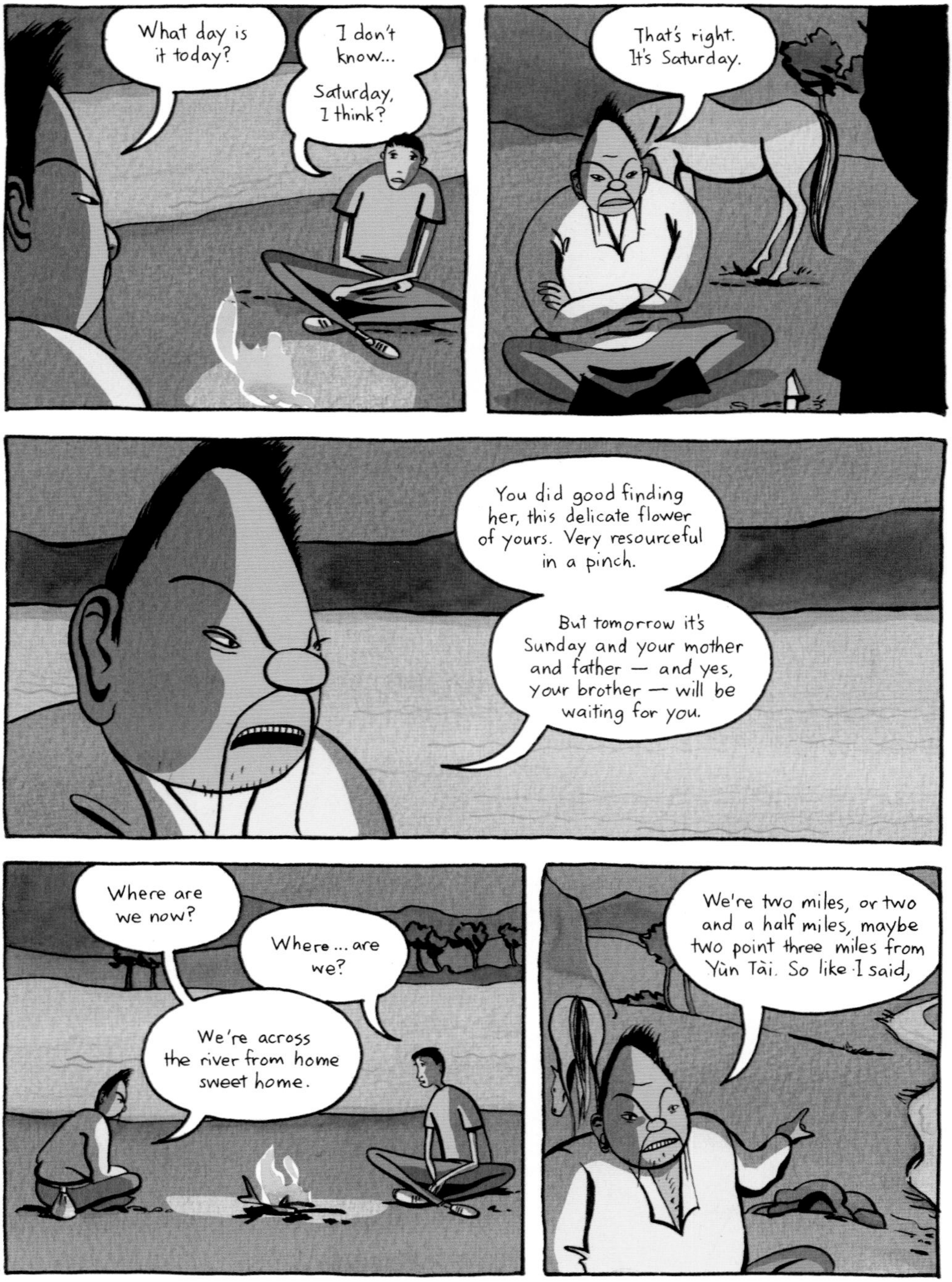

What day is it today?
I don't know...
Saturday, I think?
That's right. It's Saturday.
You did good finding her, this delicate flower of yours. Very resourceful in a pinch.
But tomorrow it's Sunday and your mother and father — and yes, your brother — will be waiting for you.
Where are we now?
Where... are we?
We're across the river from home sweet home.
We're two miles, or two and a half miles, maybe two point three miles from Yùn Tài. So like I said,

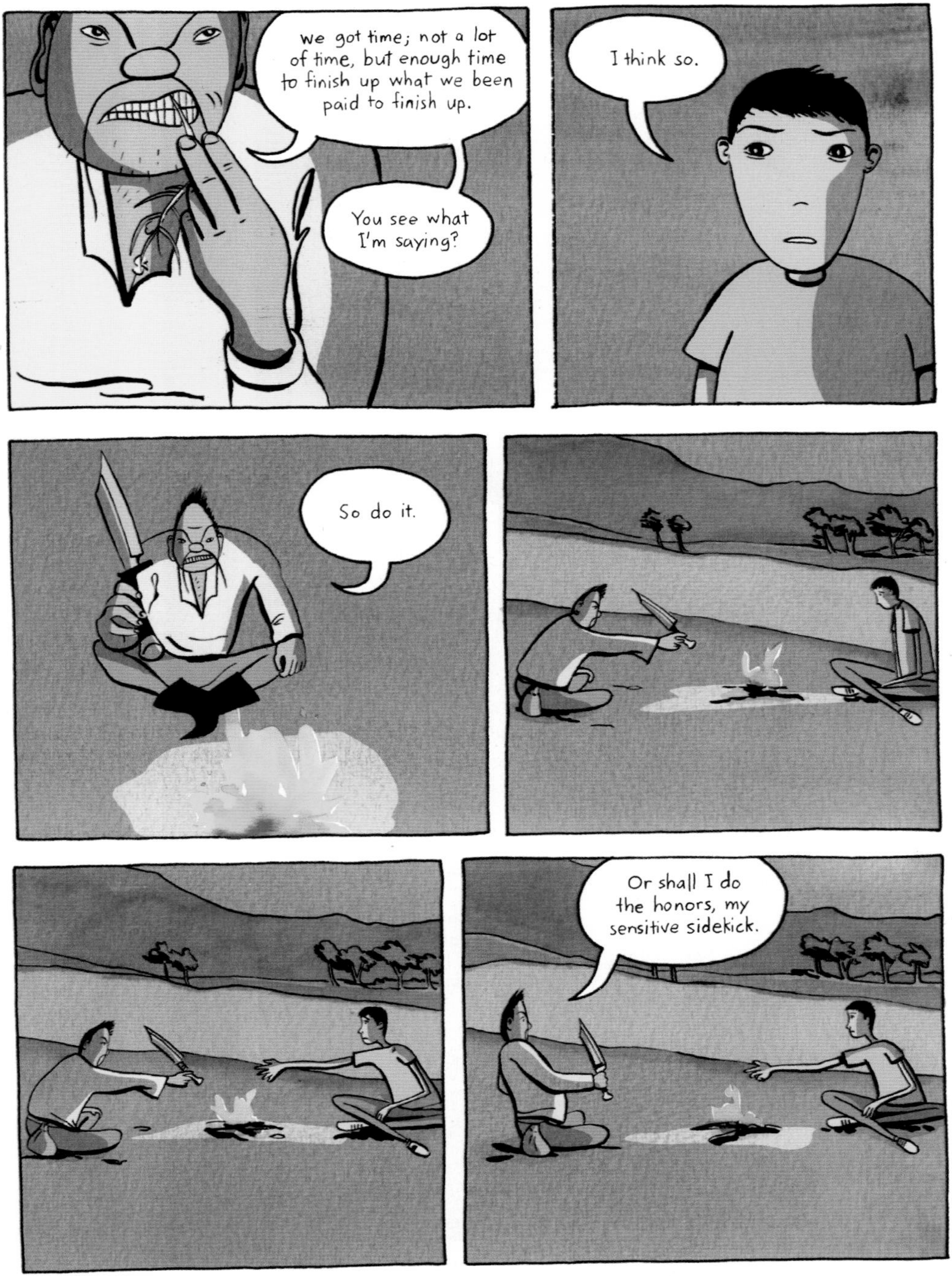
we got time; not a lot of time, but enough time to finish up what we been paid to finish up.
You see what I'm saying?
I think so.
So do it.
Or shall I do the honors, my sensitive sidekick.

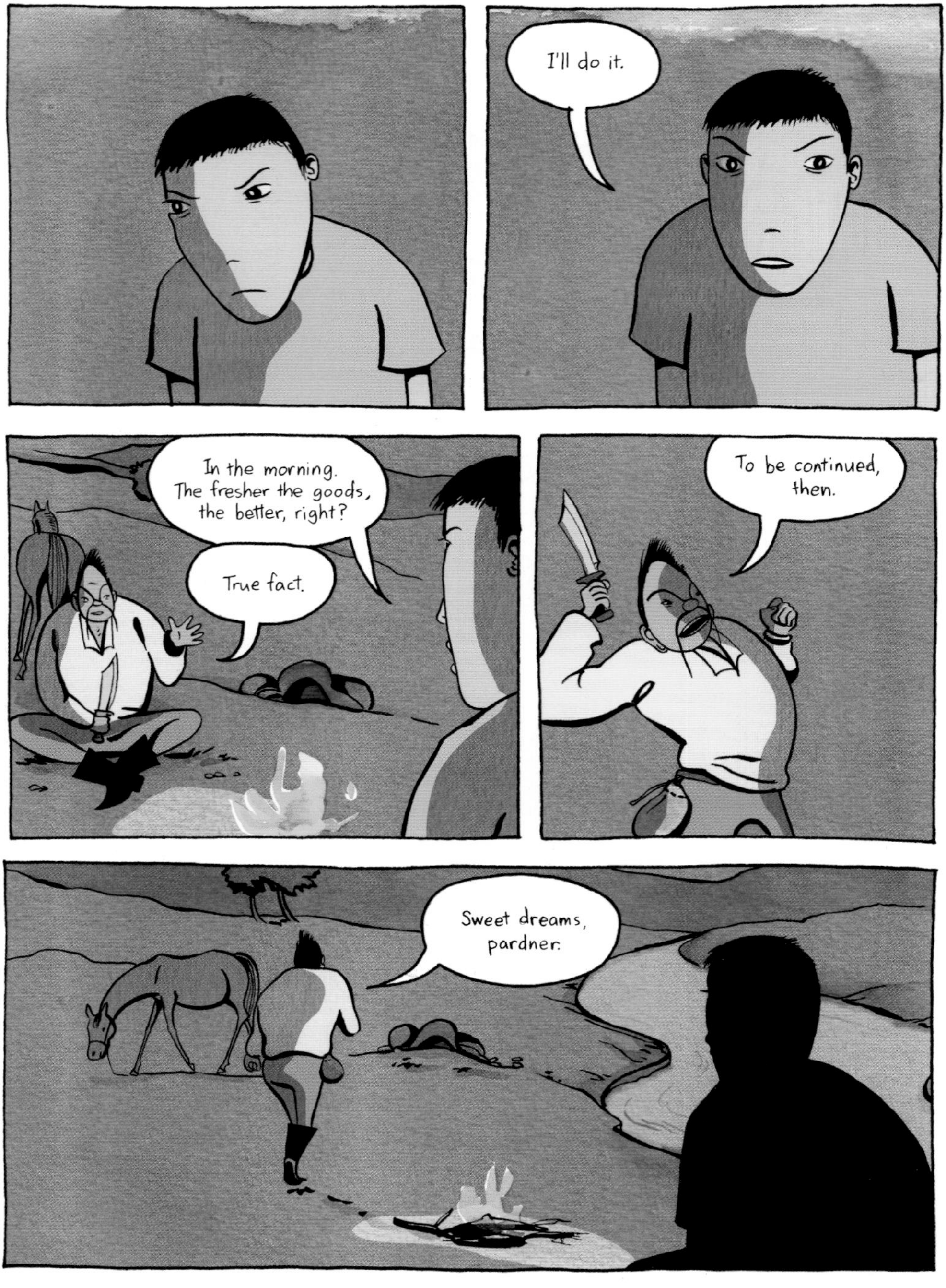
I'll do it.
In the morning. The fresher the goods, the better, right?
True fact.
To be continued, then.
Sweet dreams, pardner.

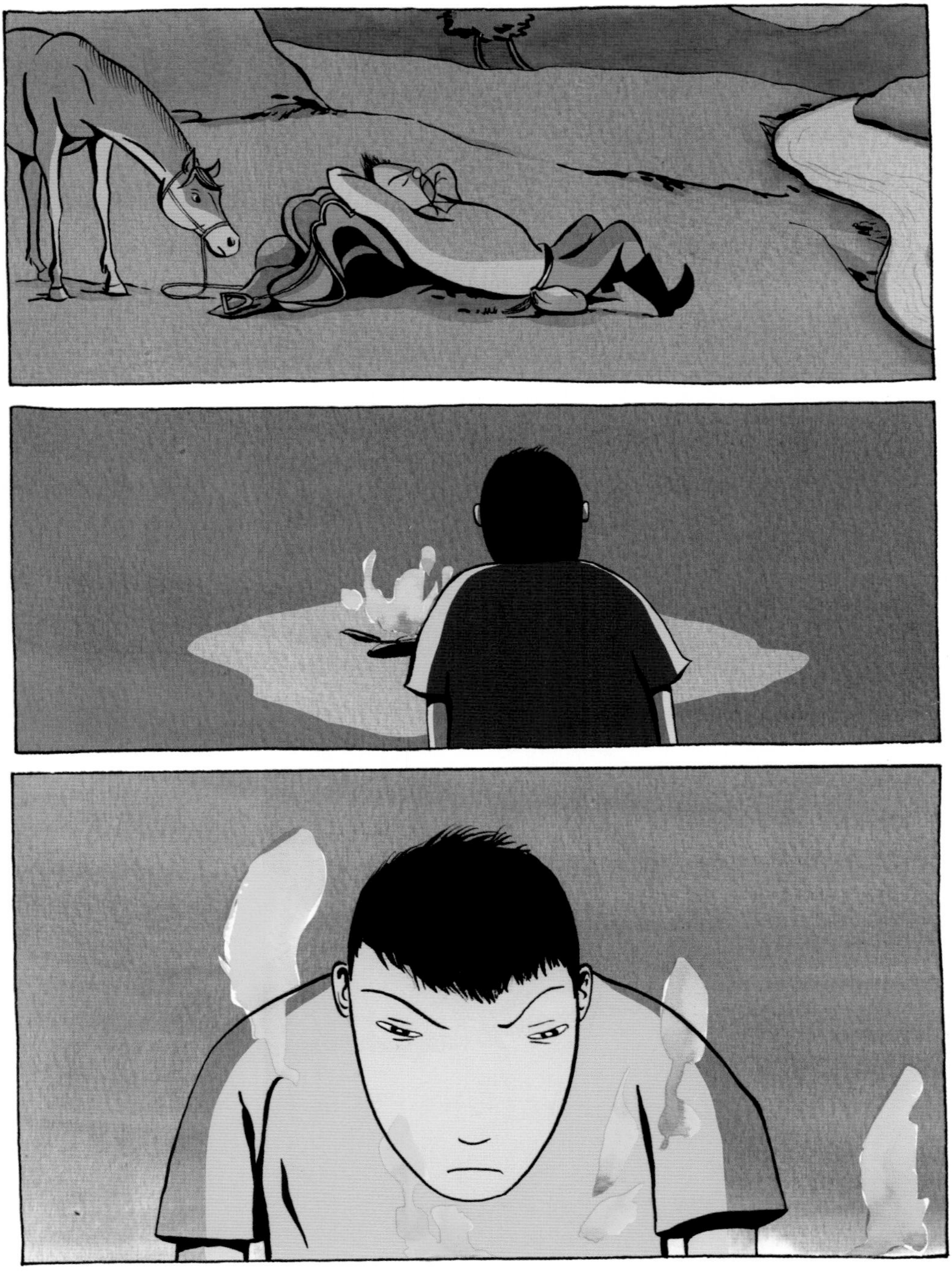

28. Fly By Night

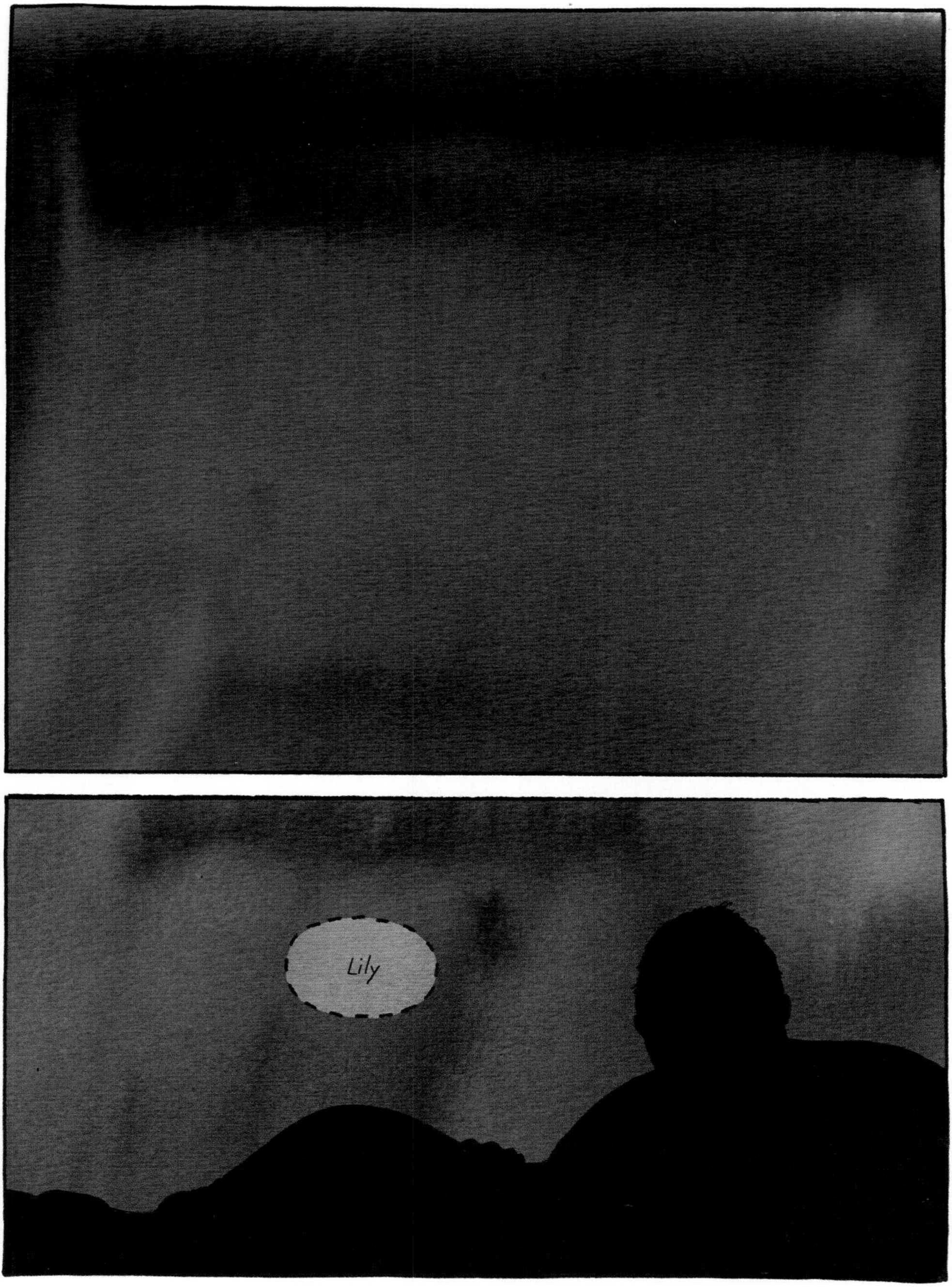
Lily

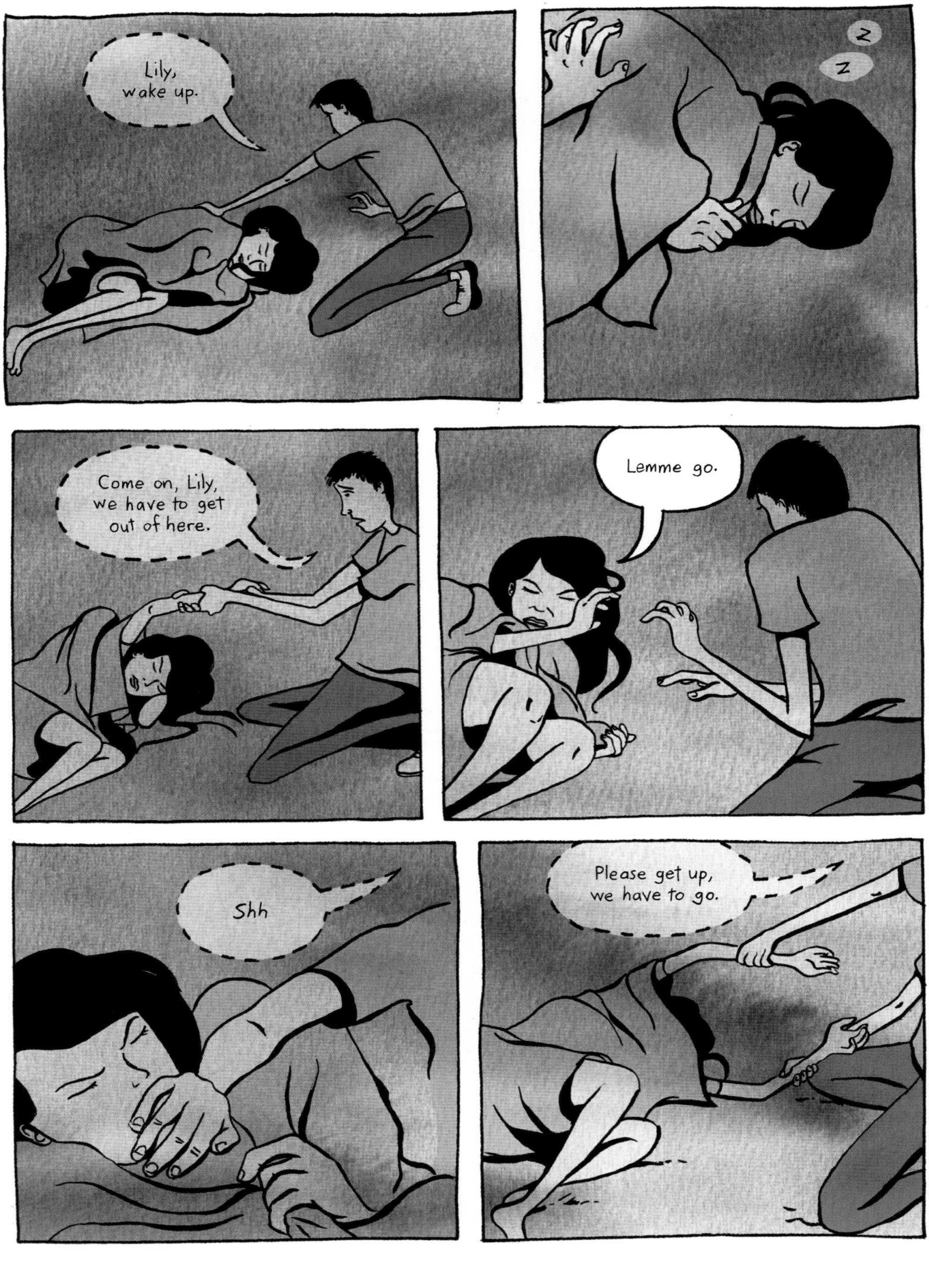

Lily, wake up.
Z
Z
Come on, Lily, we have to get out of here.
Lemme go.
Shh
Please get up, we have to go.

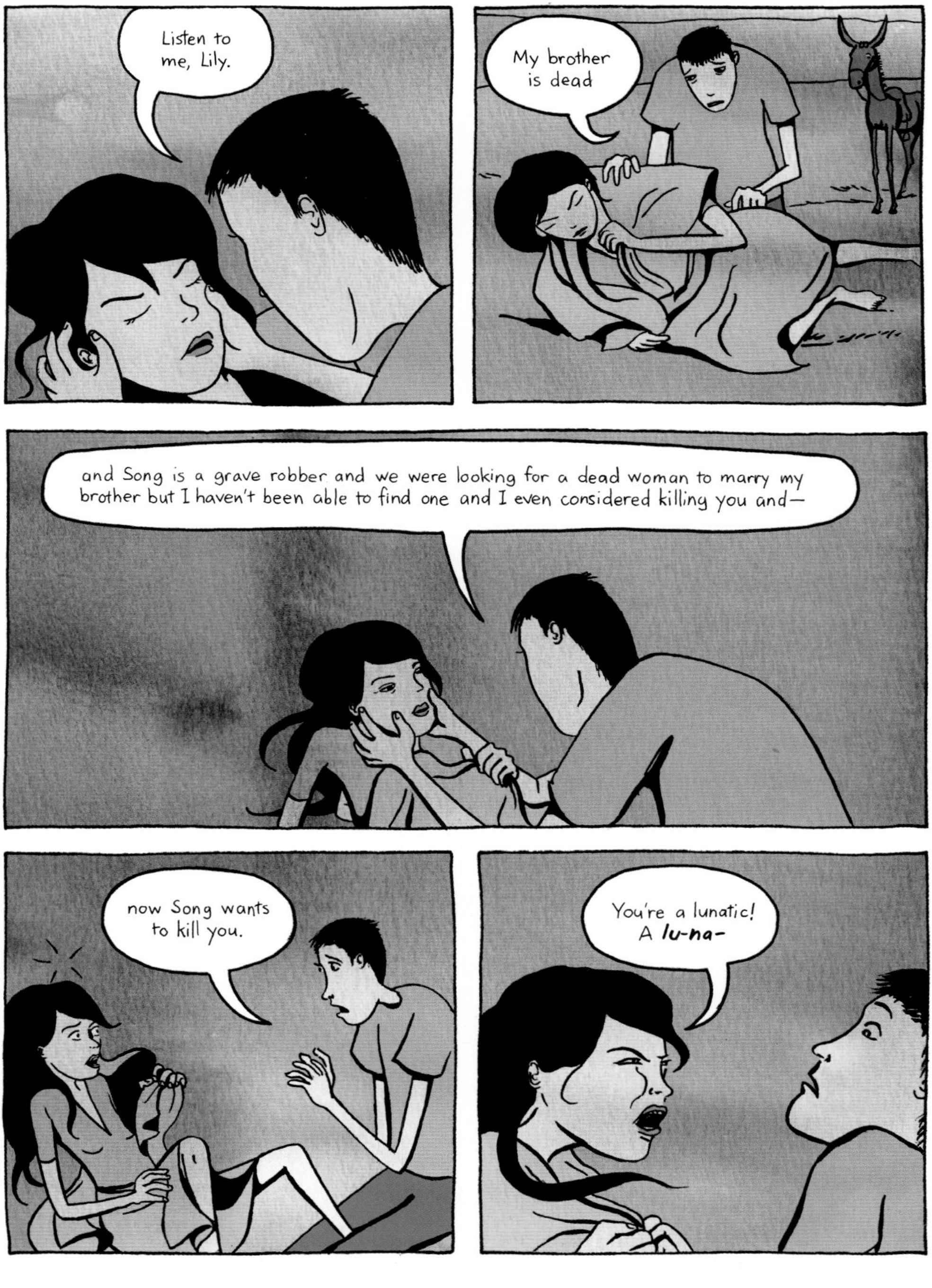
Listen to me, Lily.
My brother is dead
and Song is a grave robber and we were looking for a dead woman to marry my brother but I haven't been able to find one and I even considered killing you and—
now Song wants to kill you.
You're a lunatic! A **lu-na-**

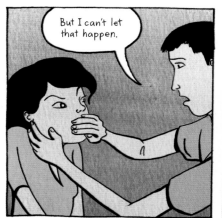

But I can't let that happen.

I want to run away with you to Beijing and be with you and save you from Peng but we need to leave **NOW**.

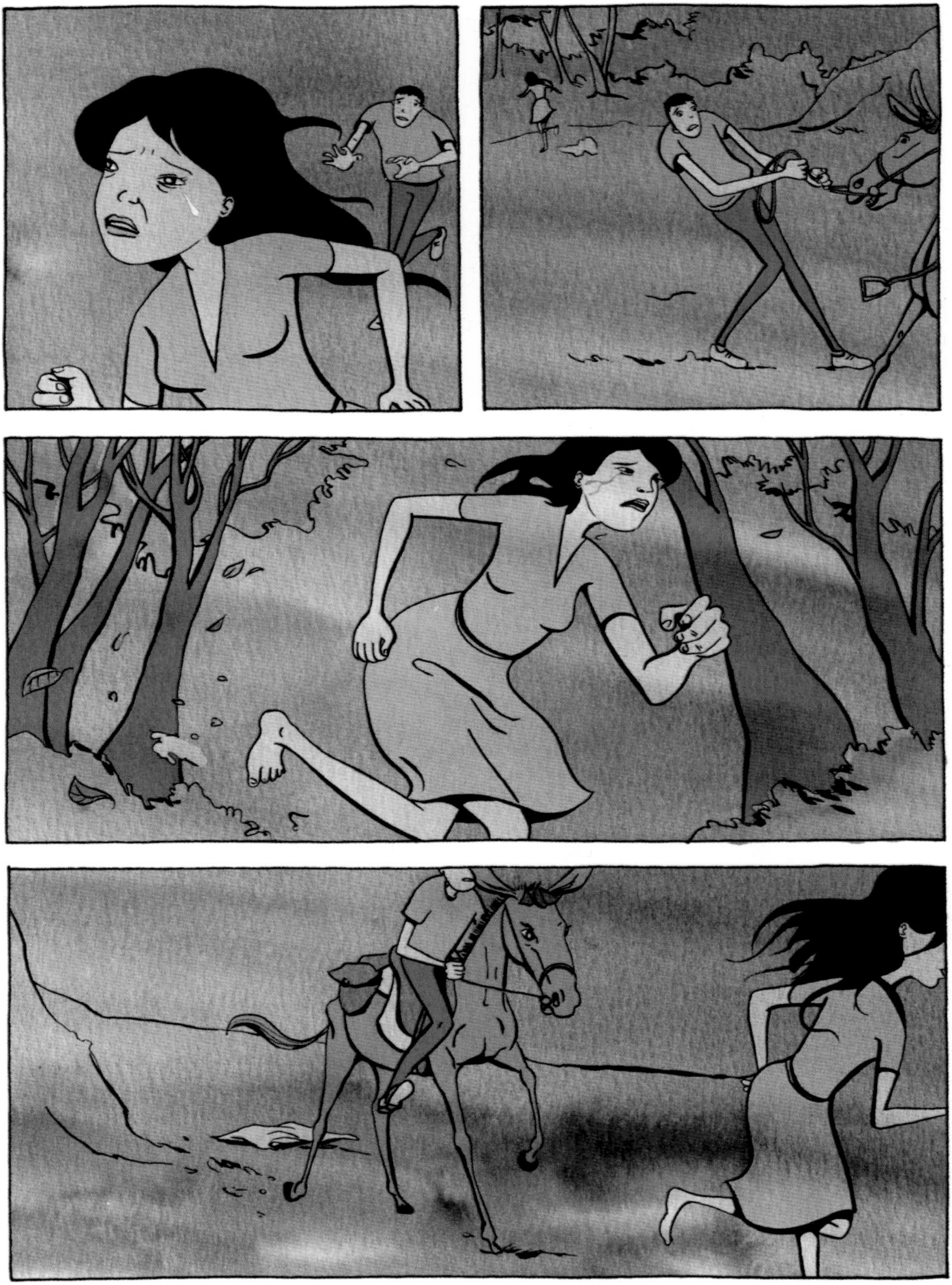

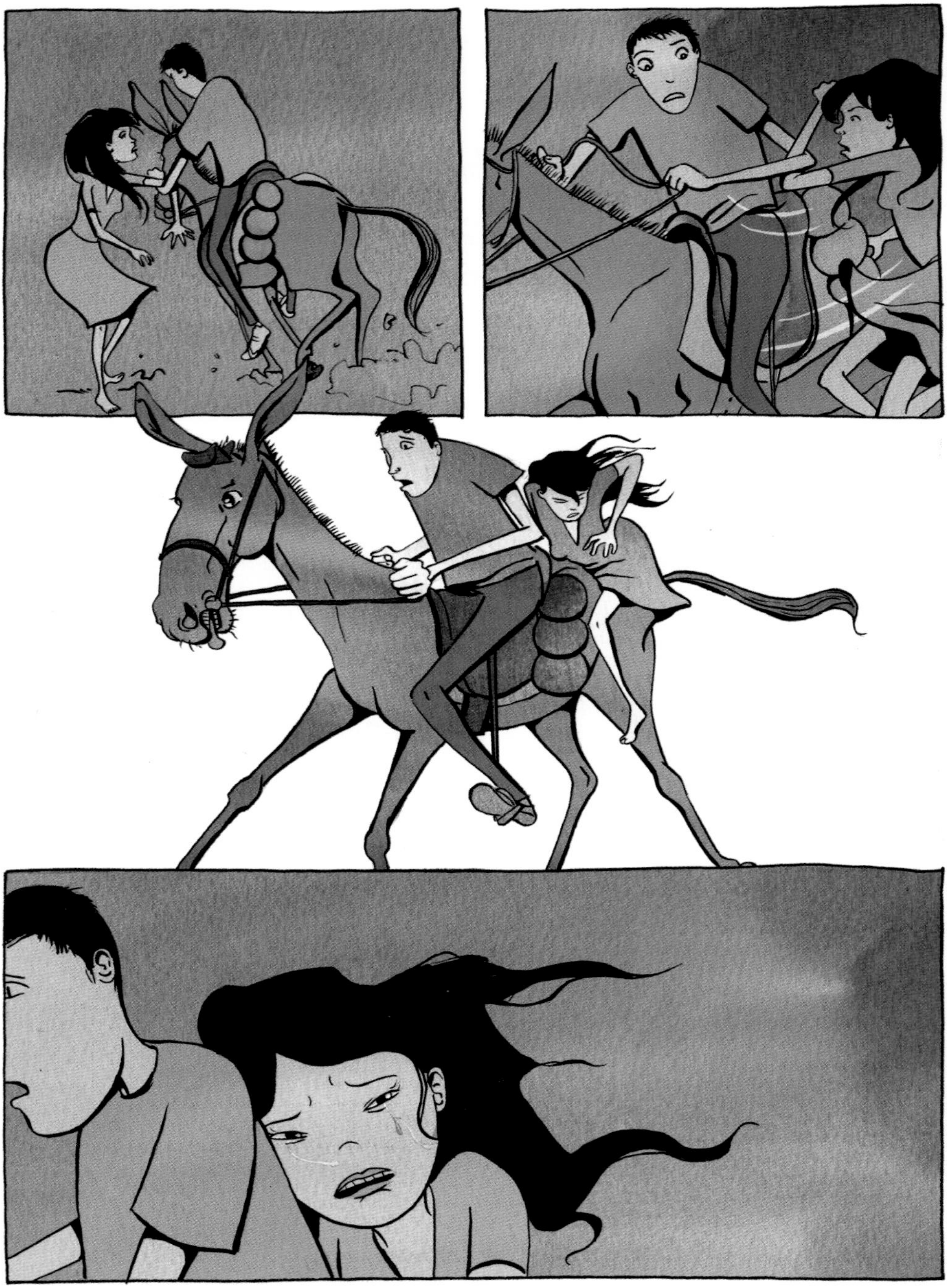

z
z

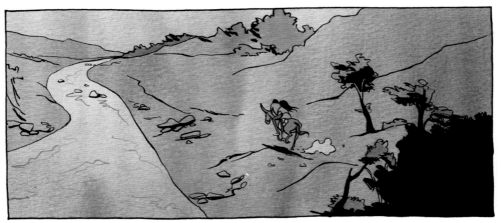

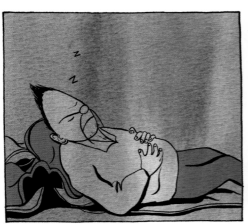

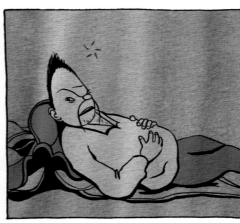

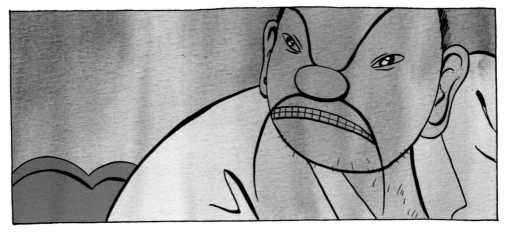

29. Dead Man

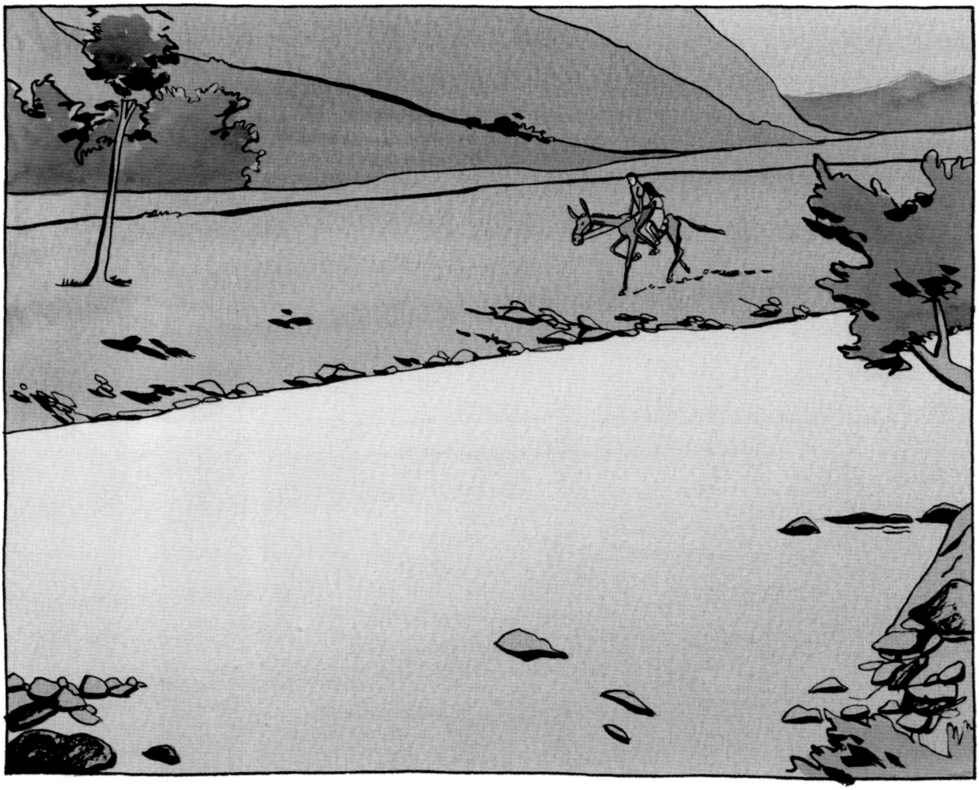

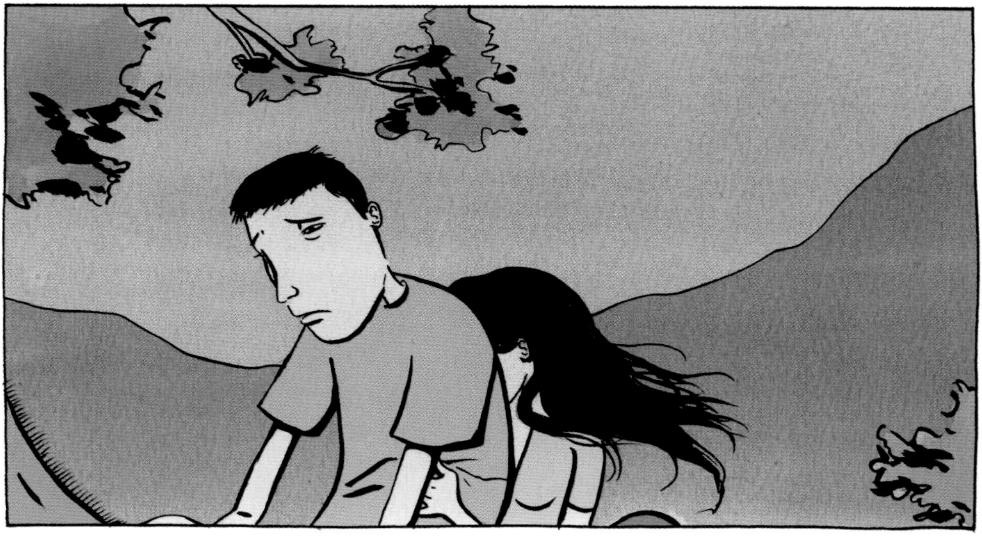

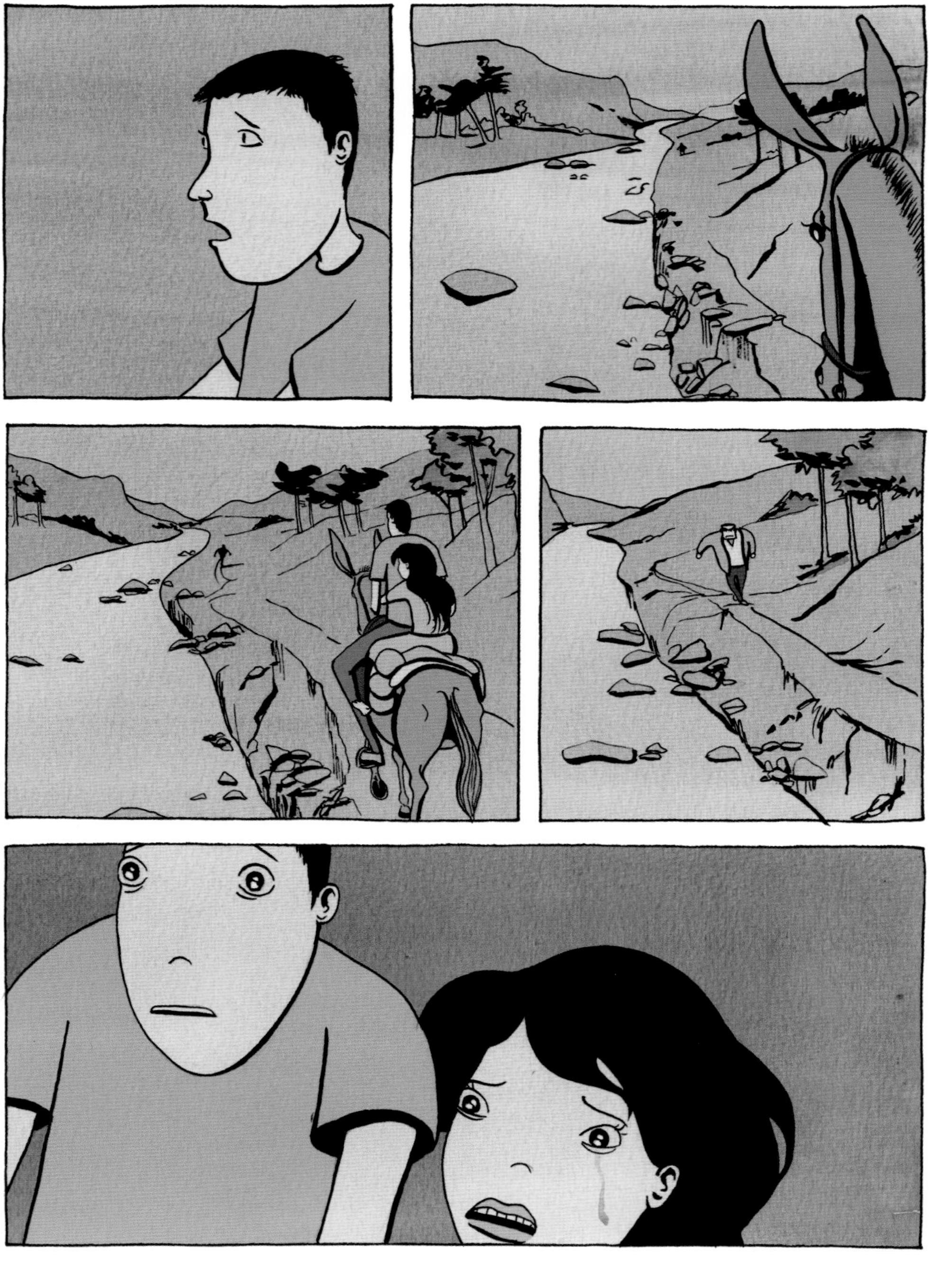

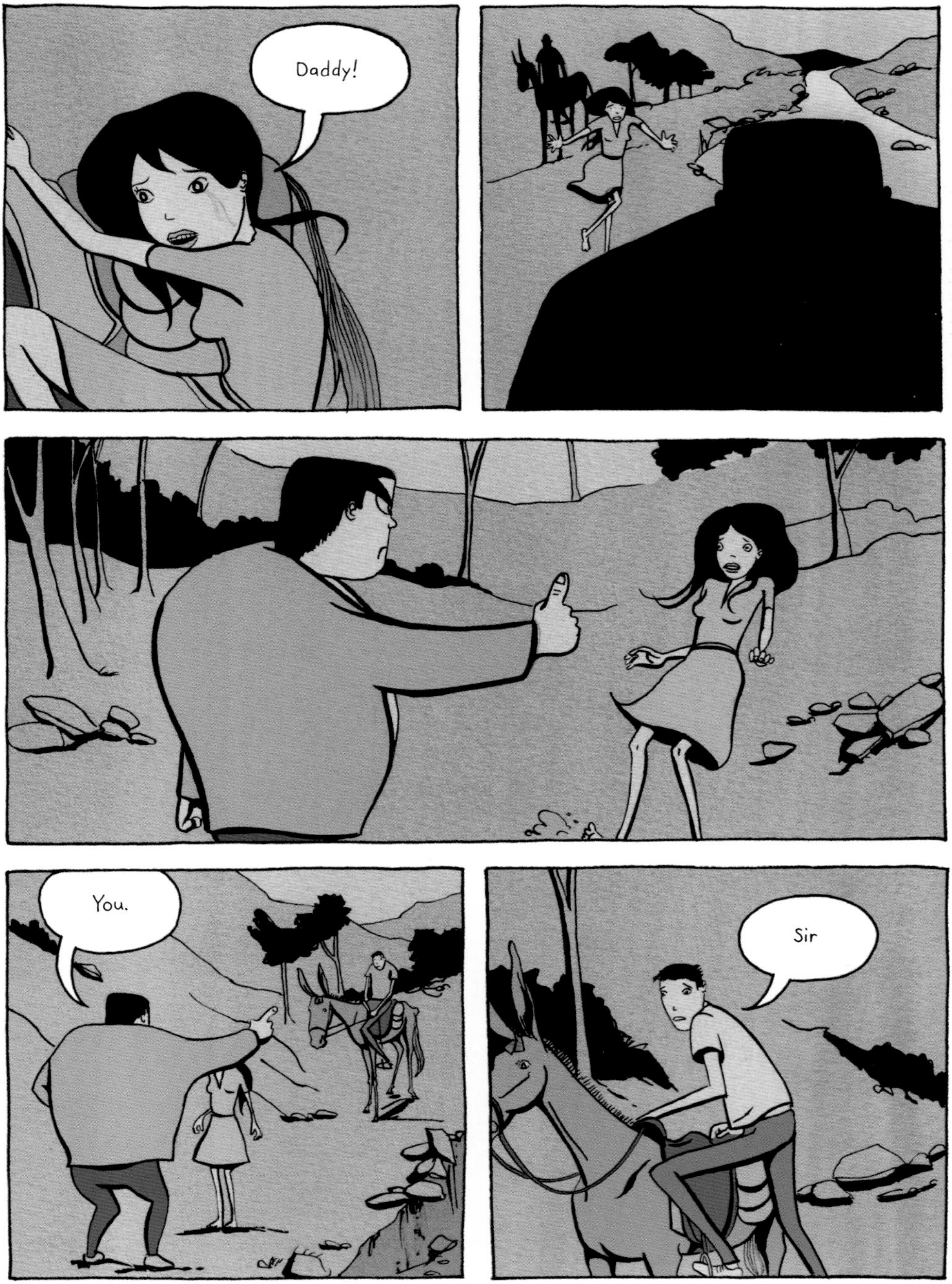
Daddy!
You.
Sir

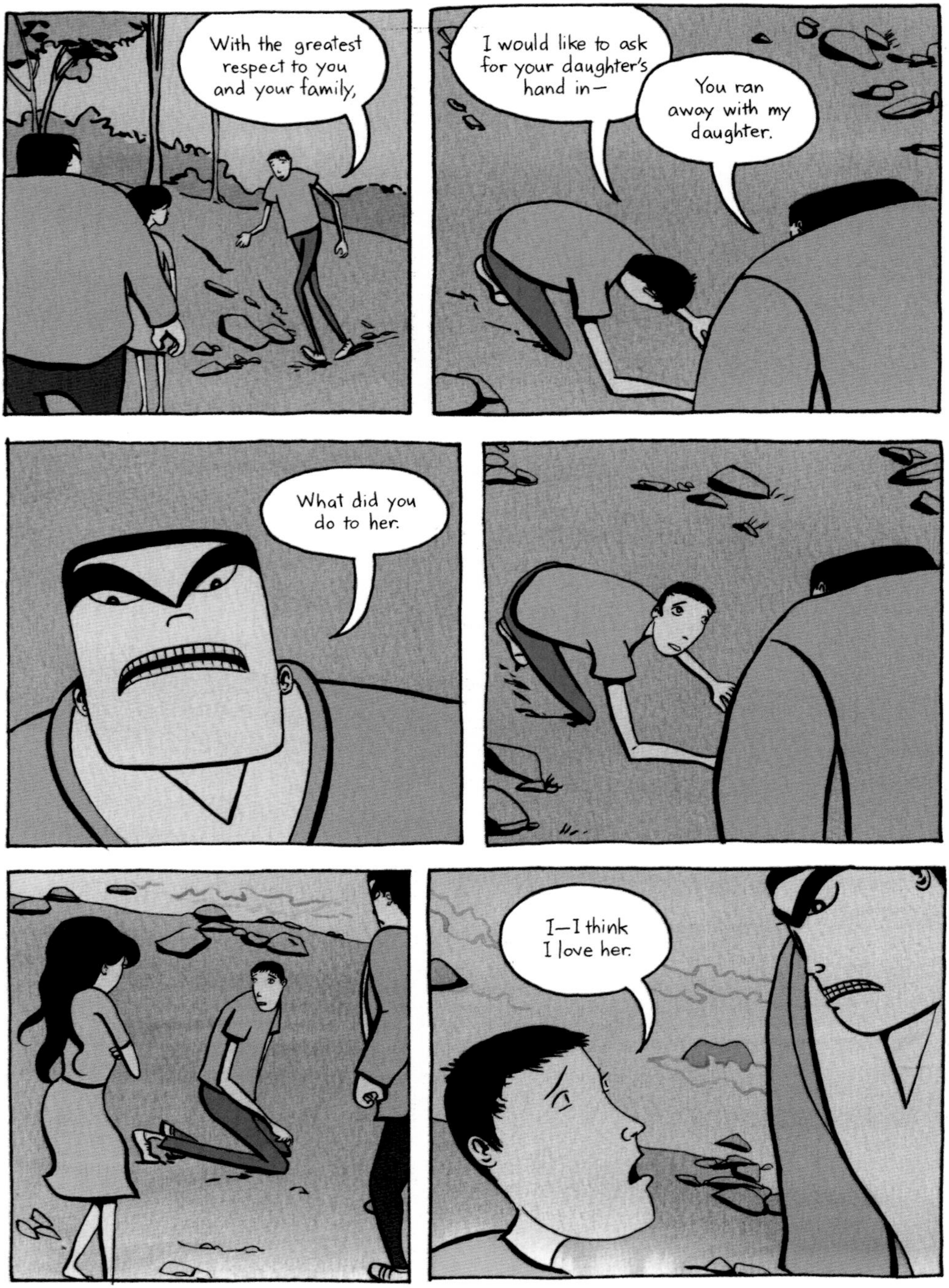

With the greatest respect to you and your family,
I would like to ask for your daughter's hand in—
You ran away with my daughter.
What did you do to her.
I—I think I love her.

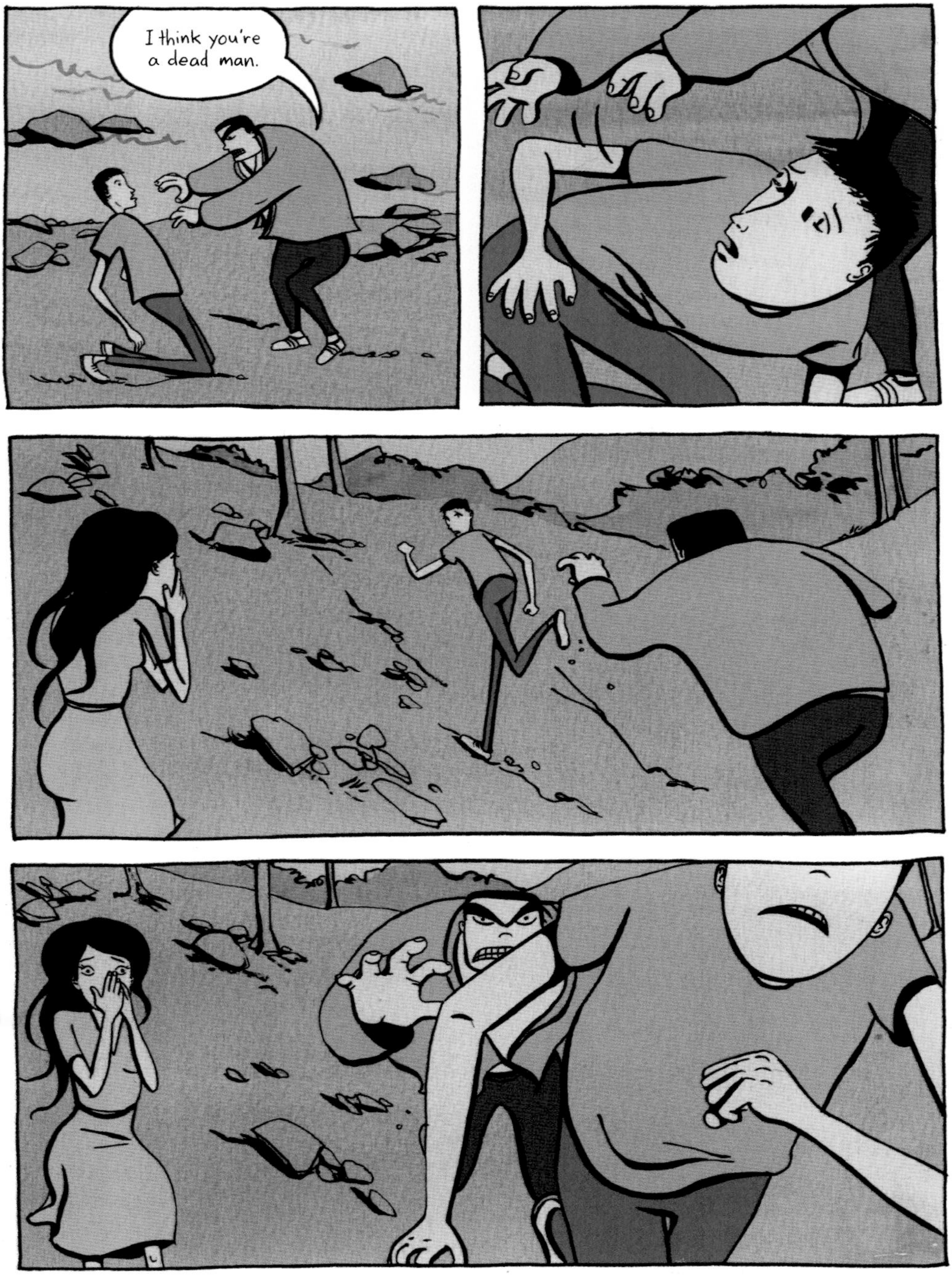
I think you're a dead man.

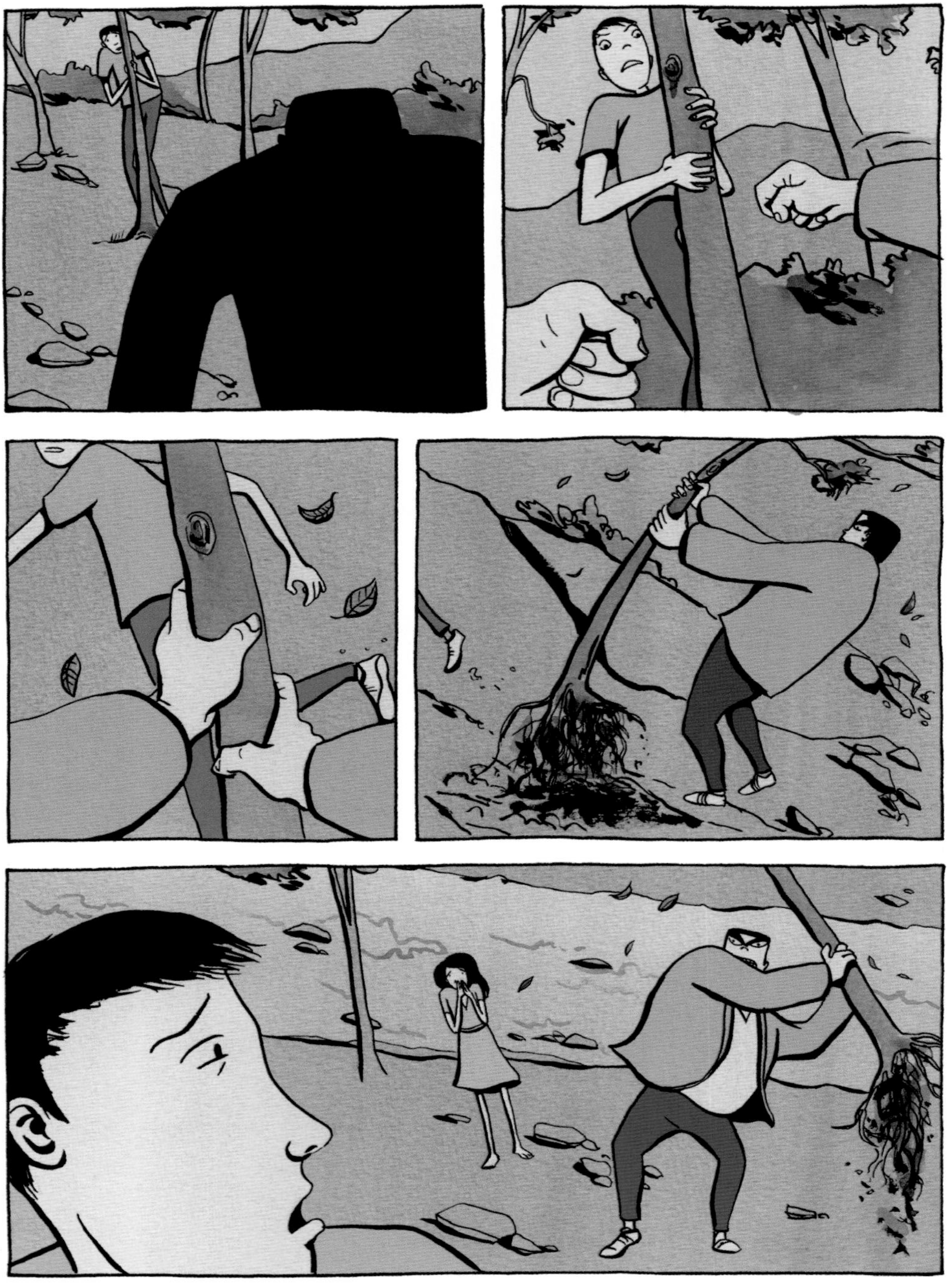

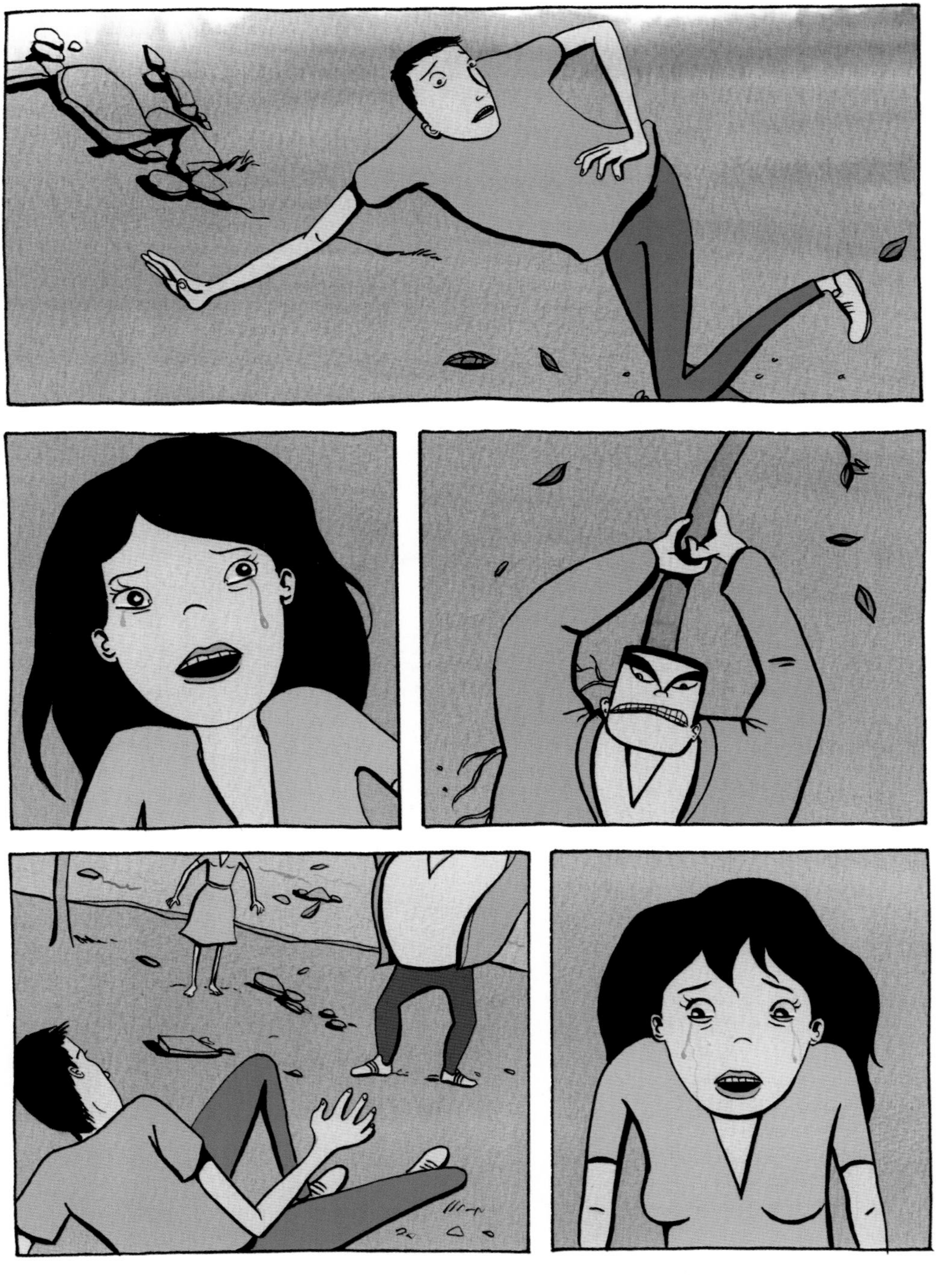

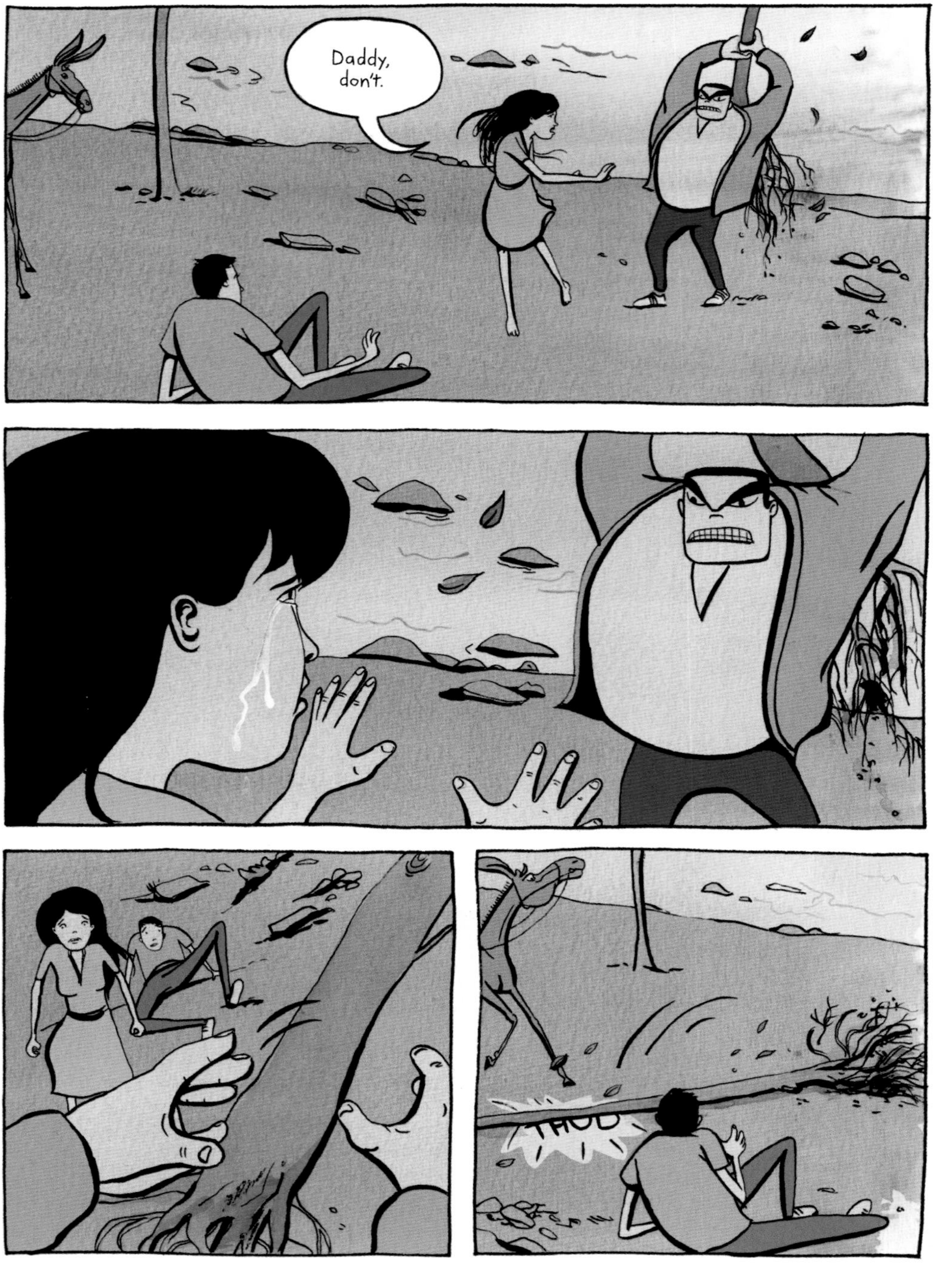
Daddy, don't.
THUD

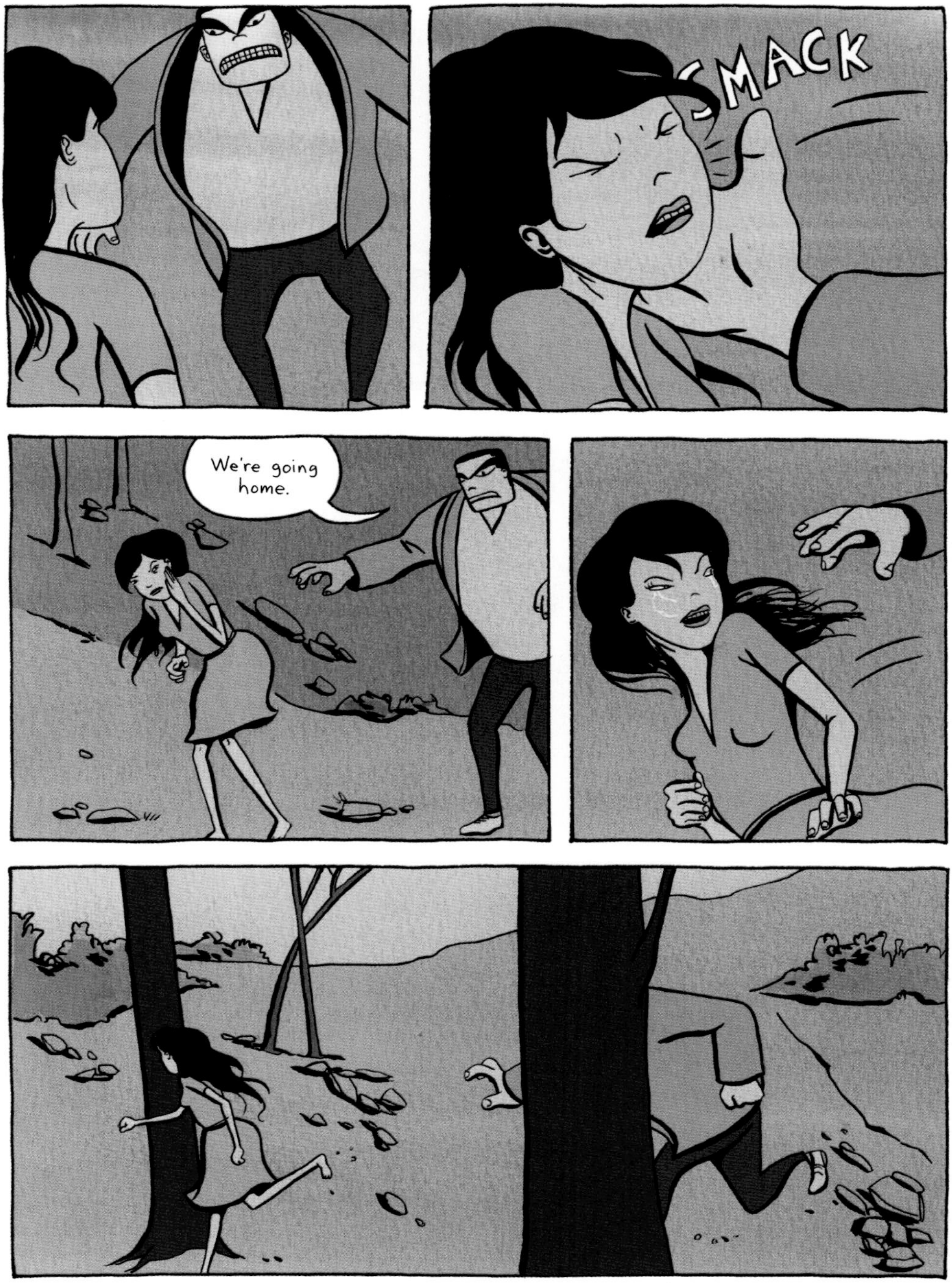
SMACK
We're going home.

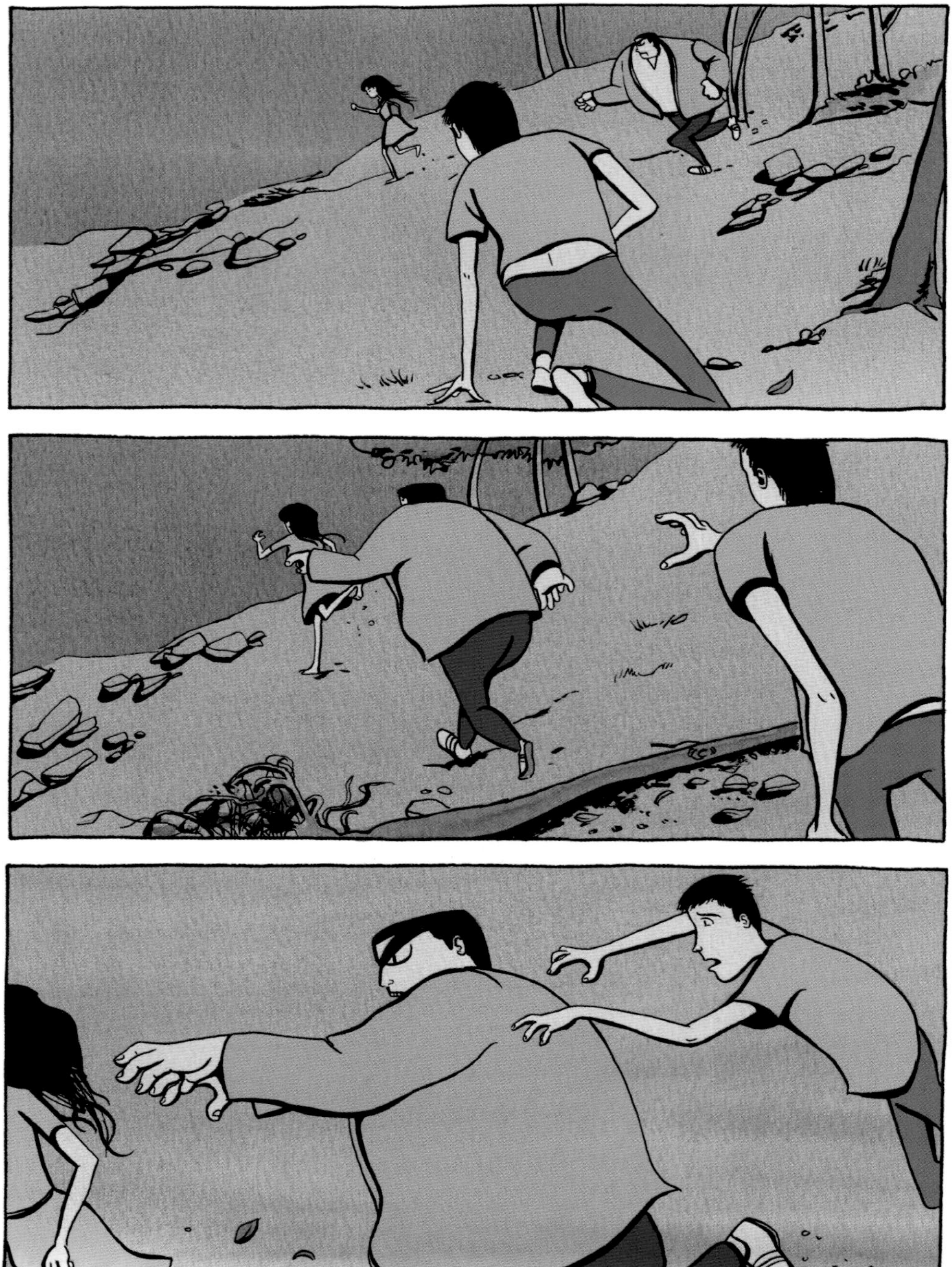

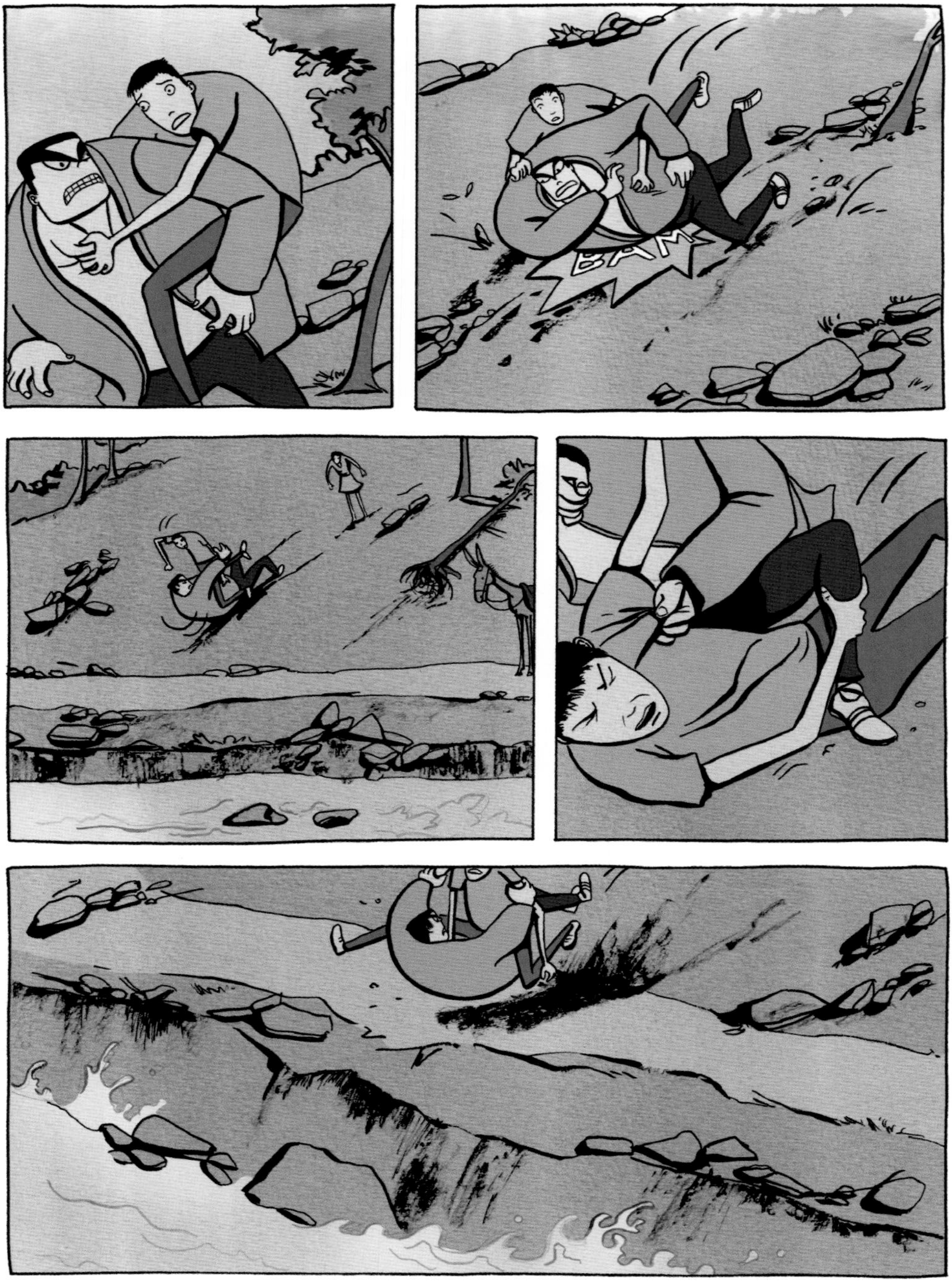
BAM

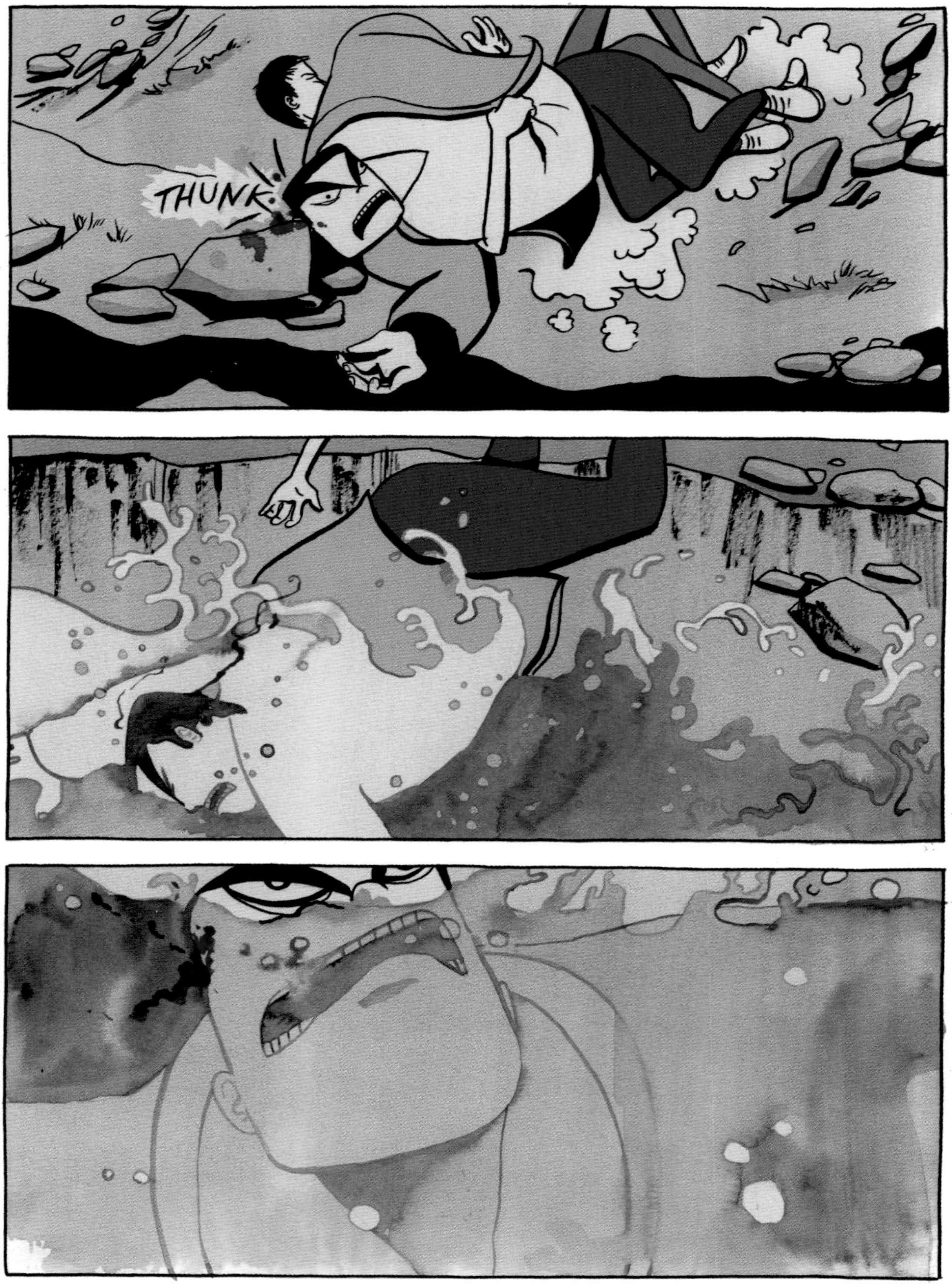
THUNK

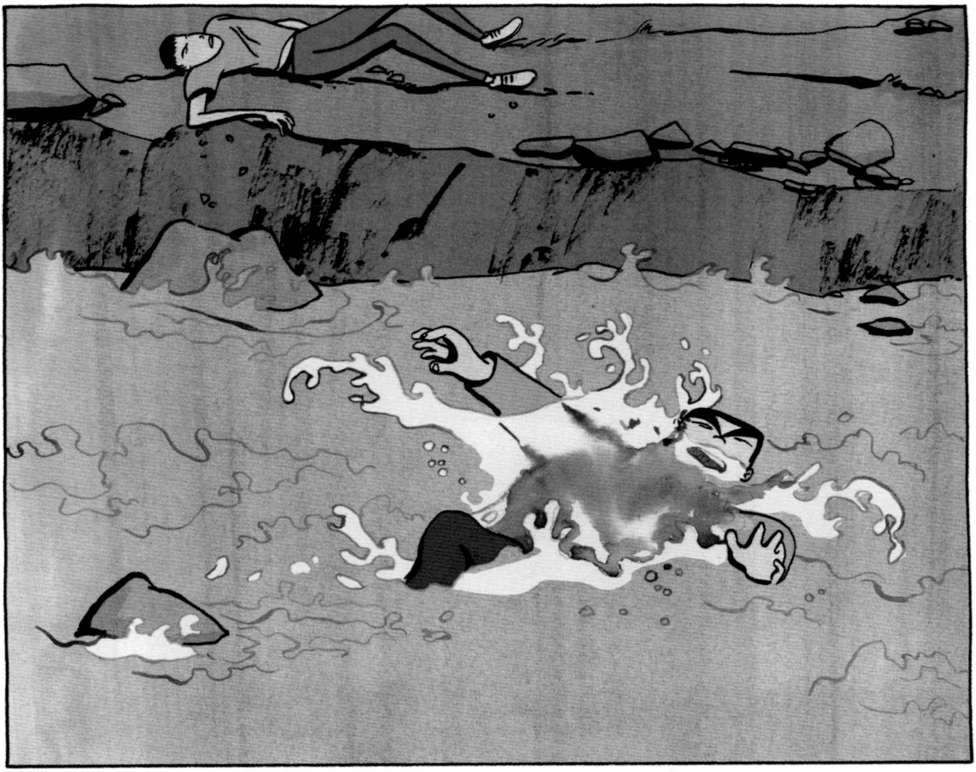

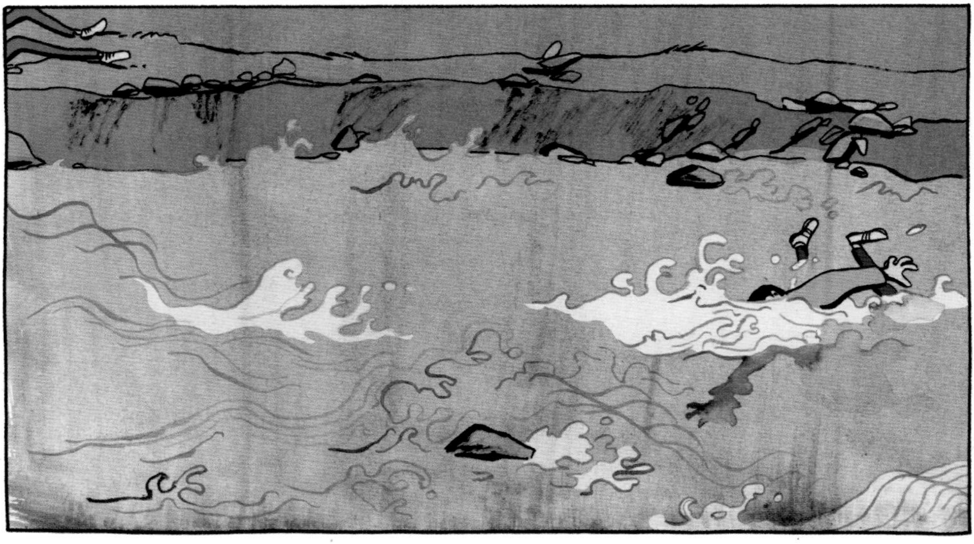

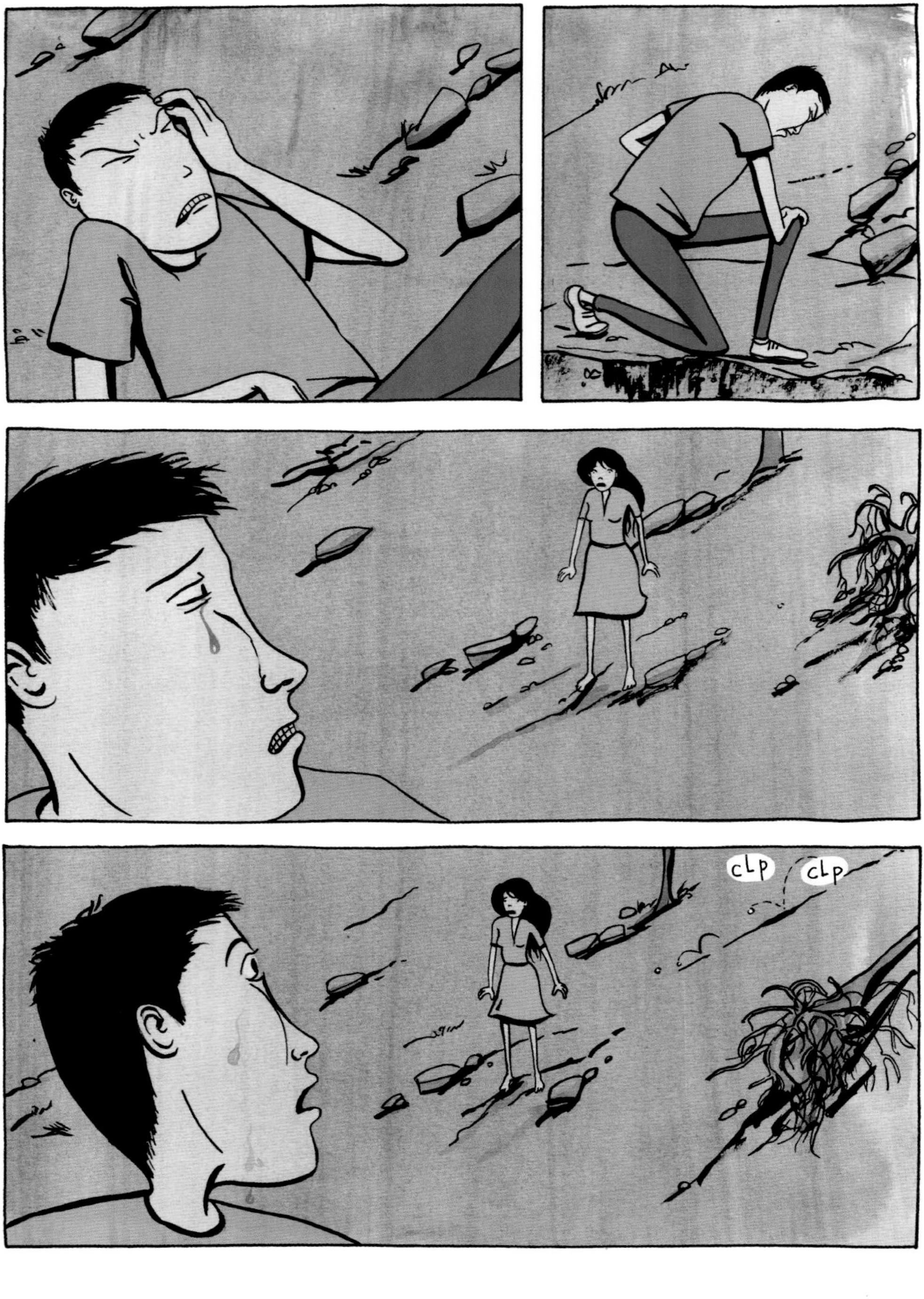
cLp
cLp

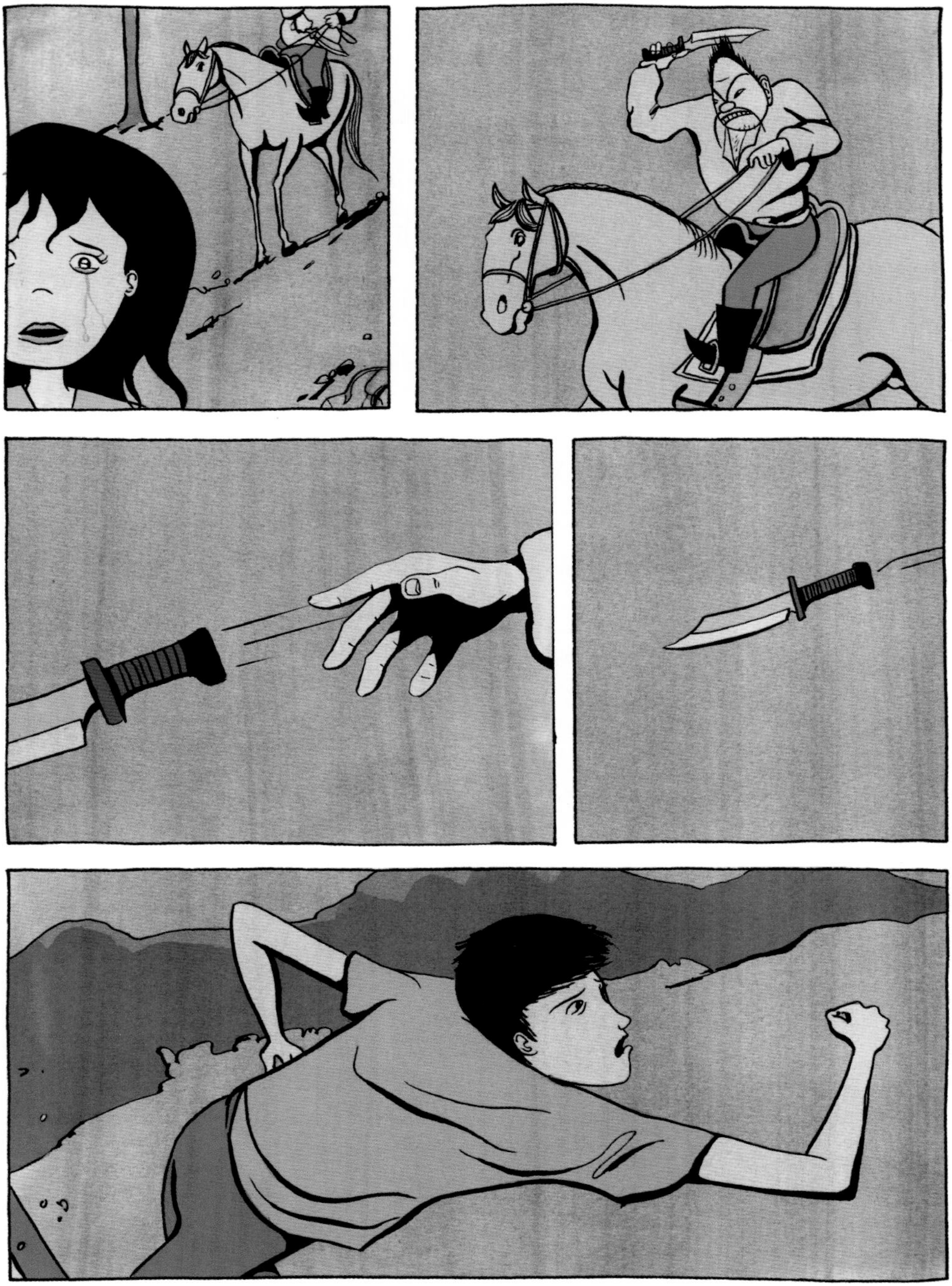

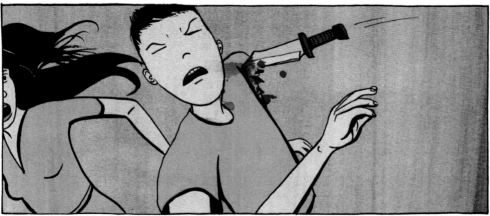

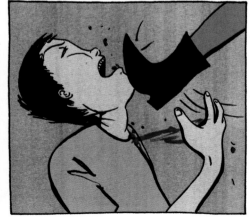

Message from your mother.

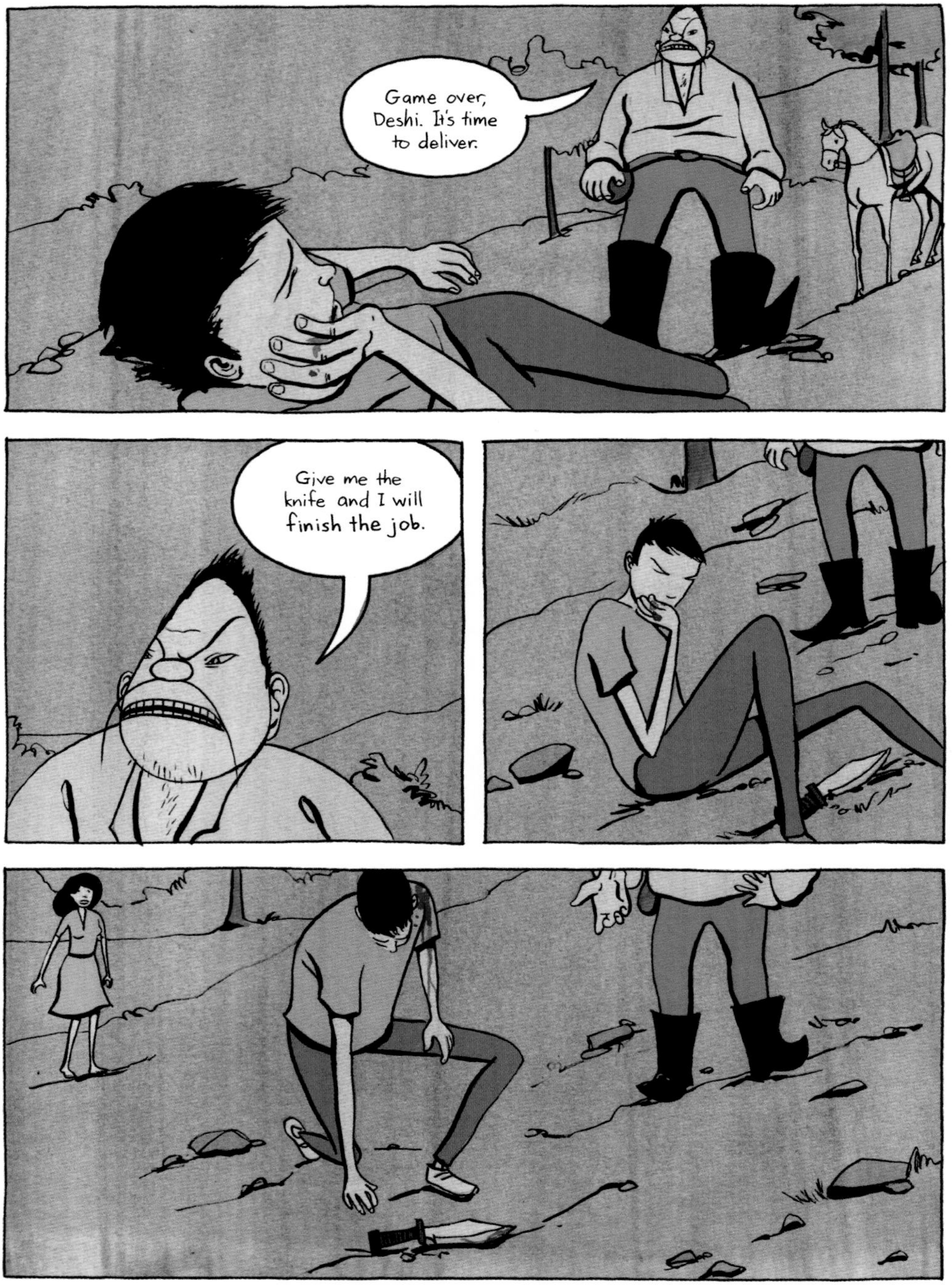
Game over, Deshi. It's time to deliver.
Give me the knife and I will finish the job.

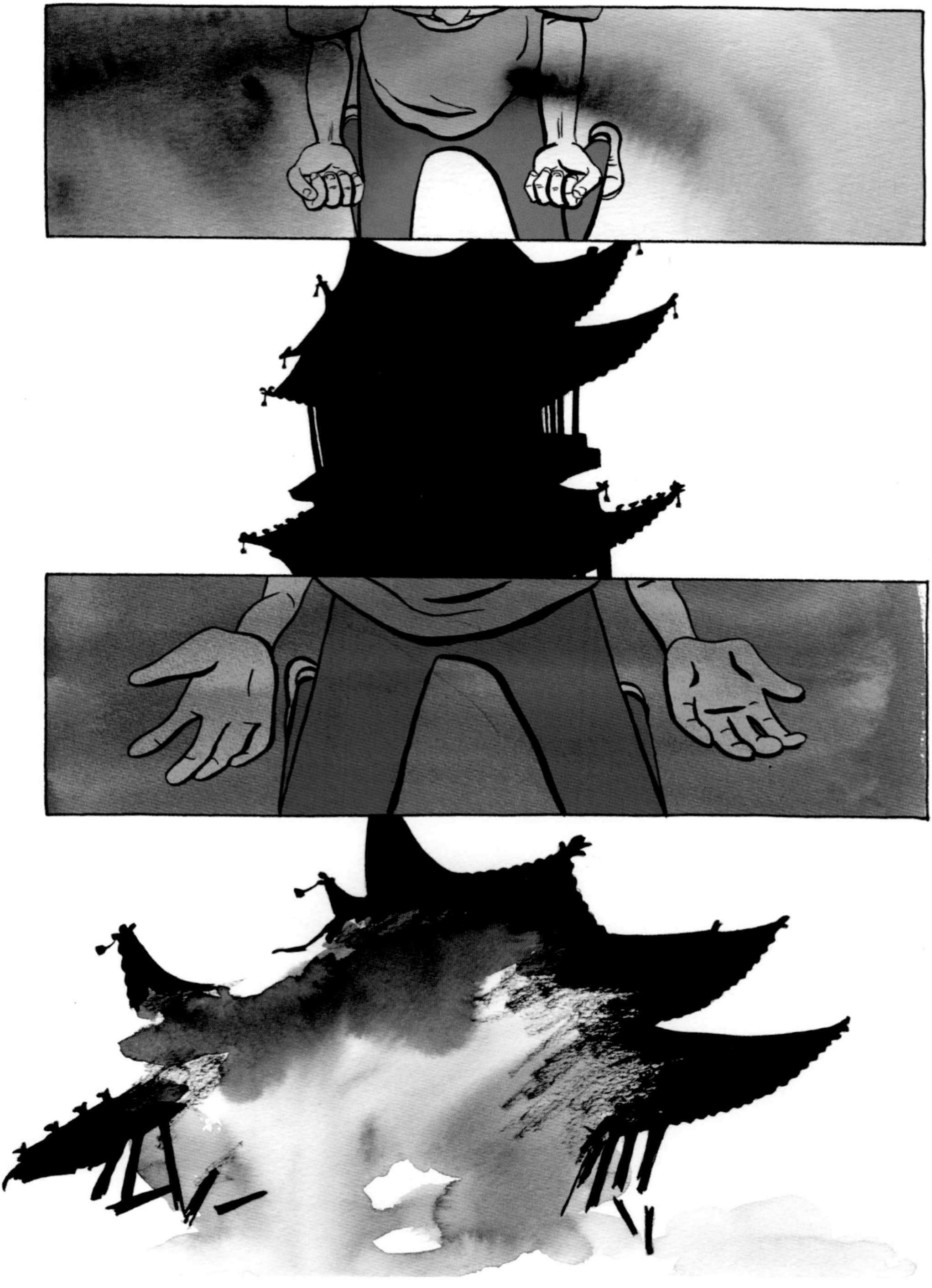

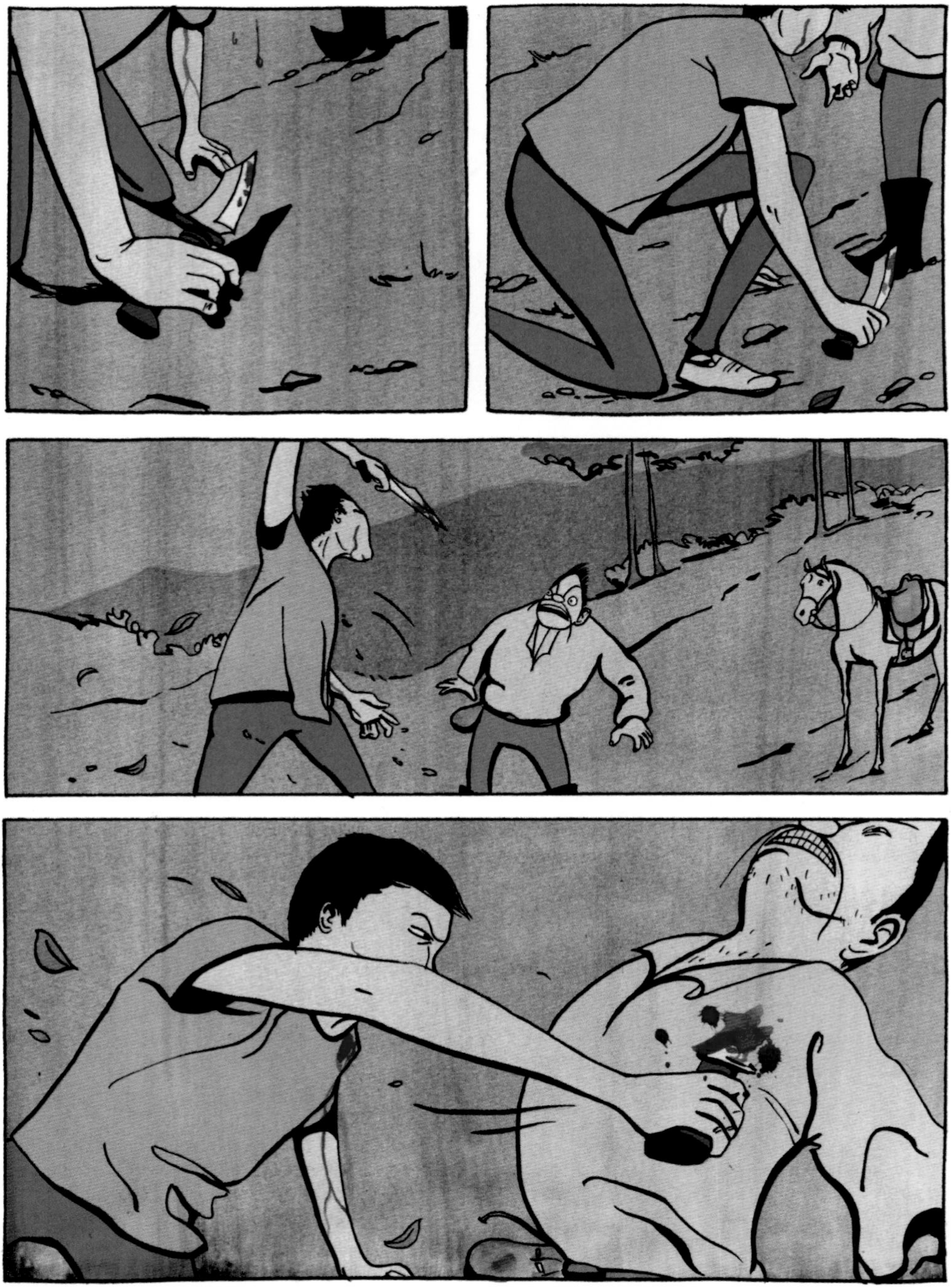

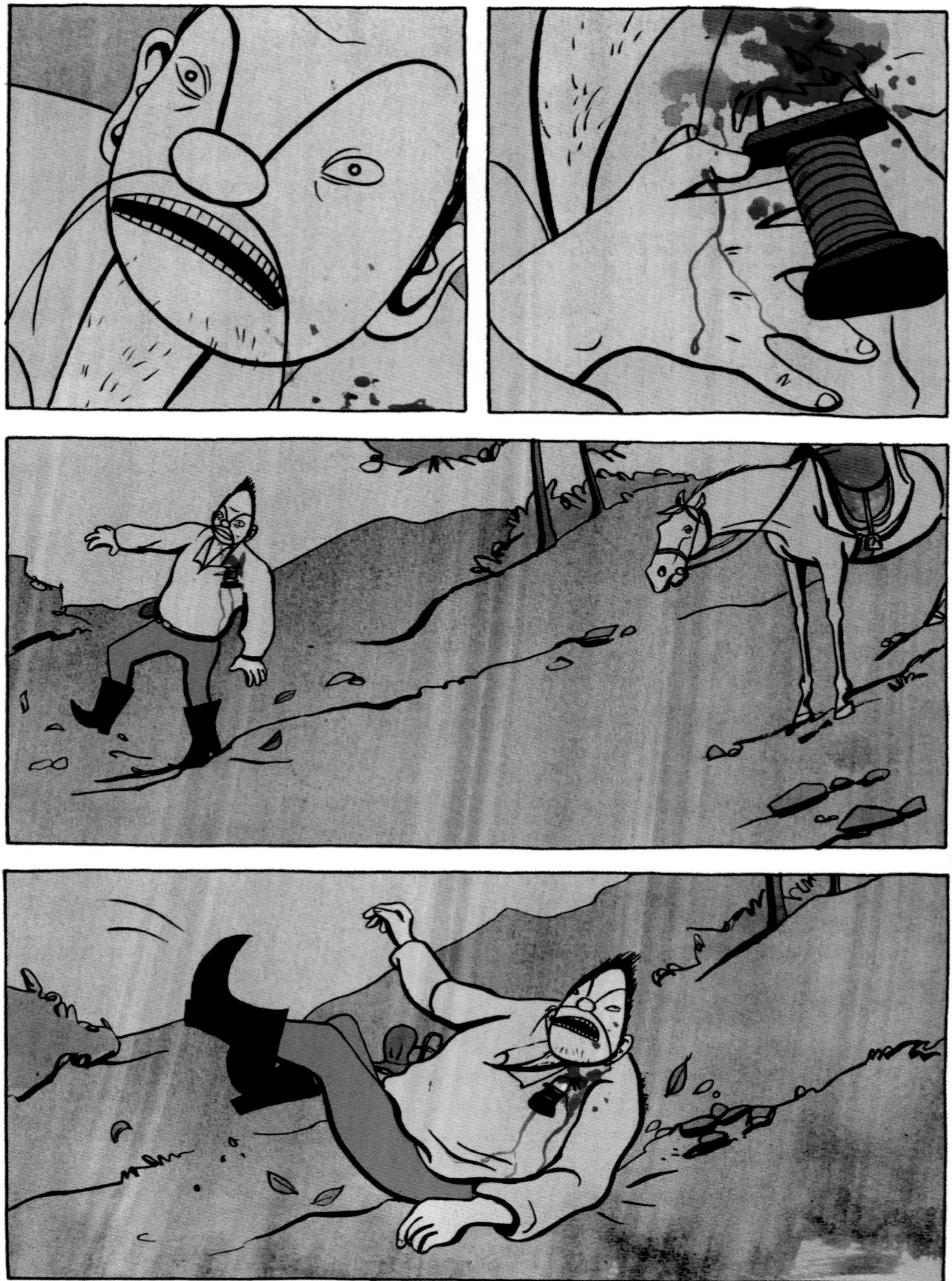

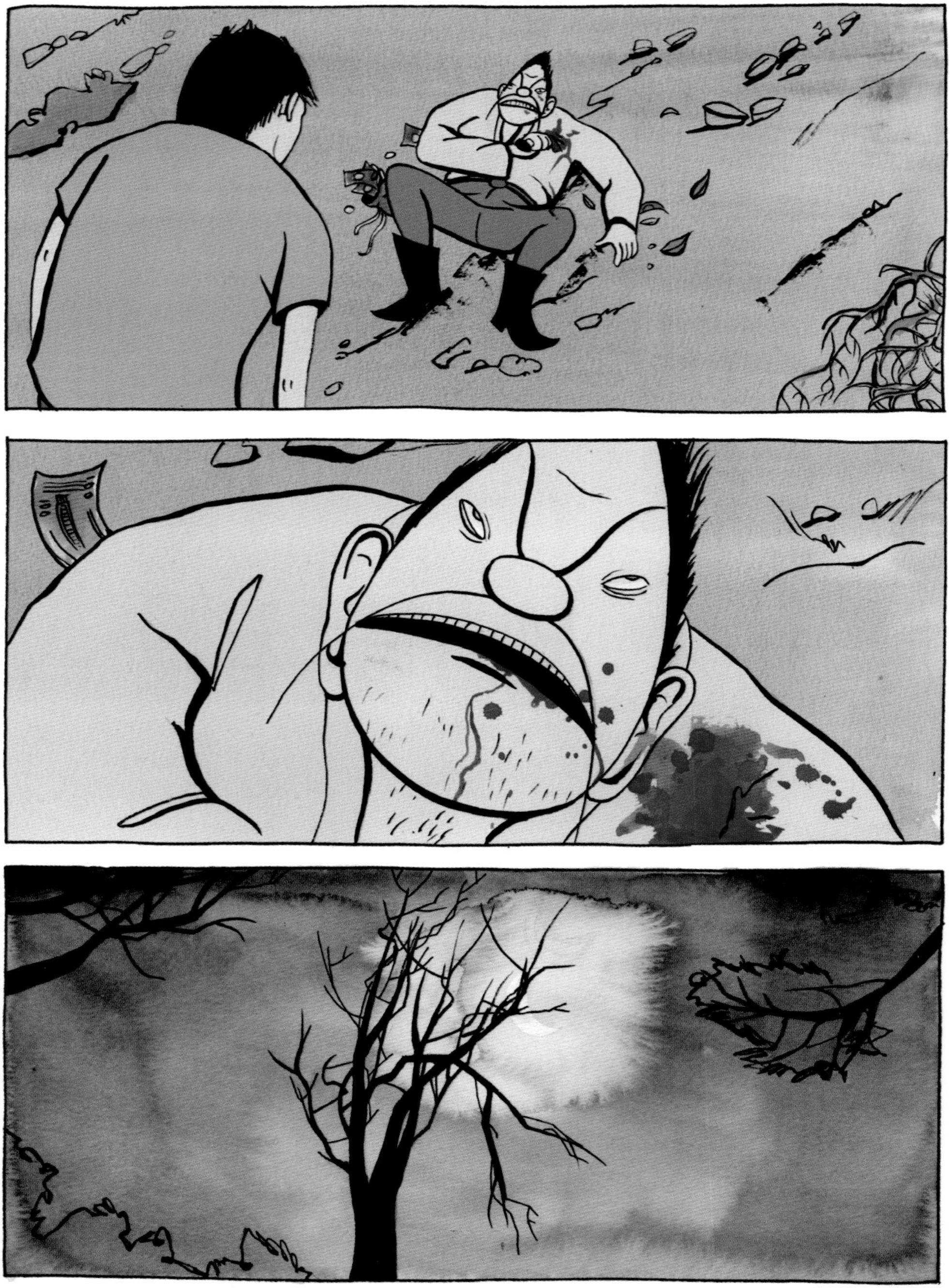

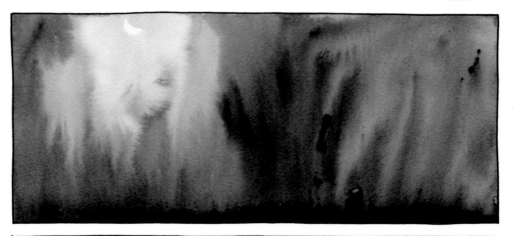

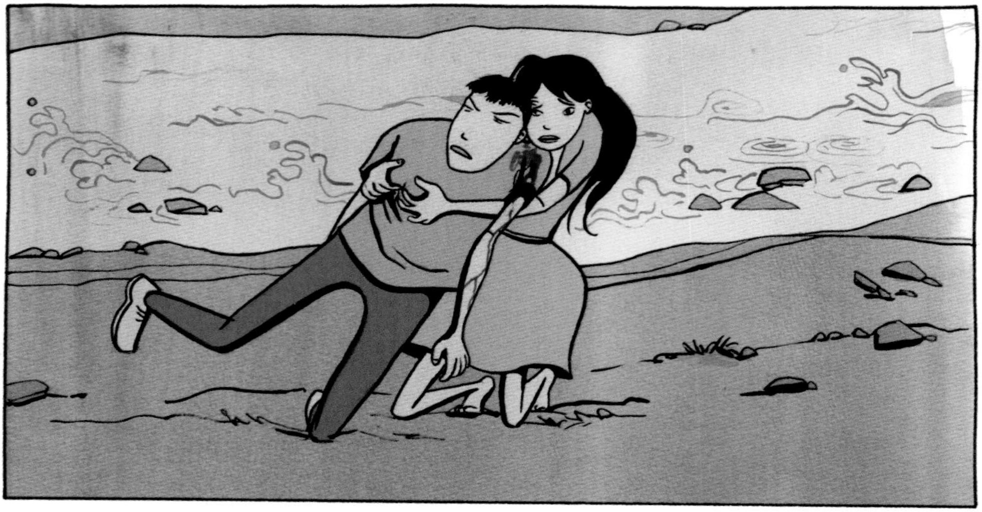

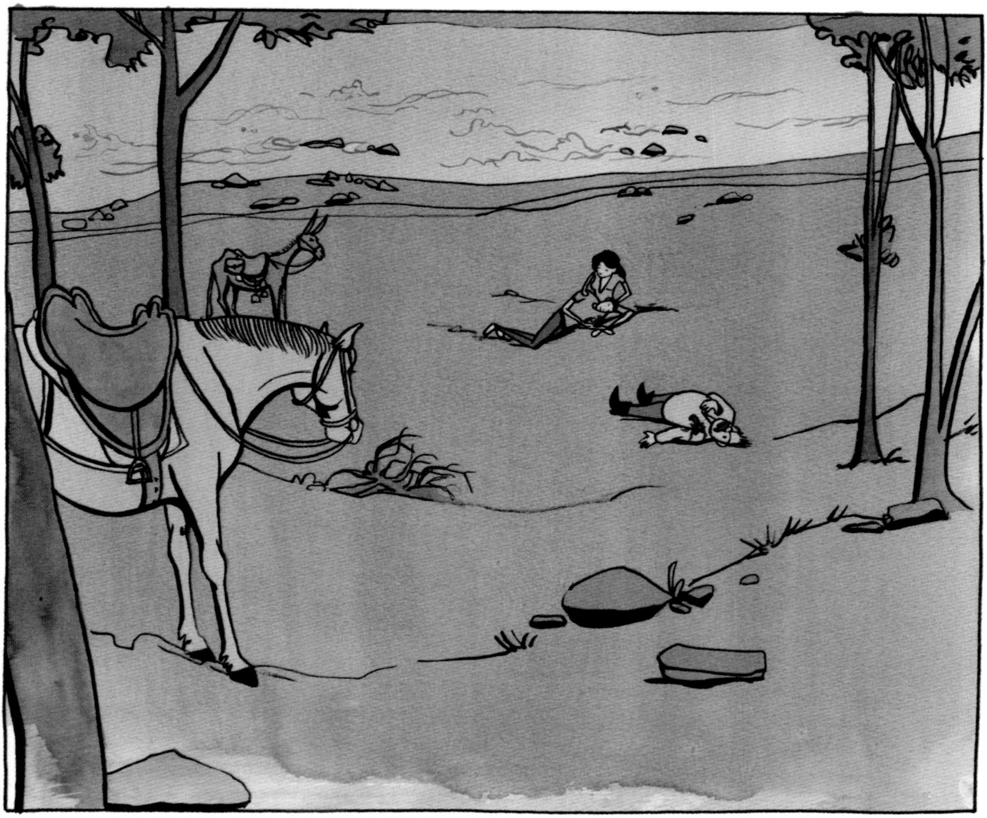

30. Gently Down the Stream

SUNDAY

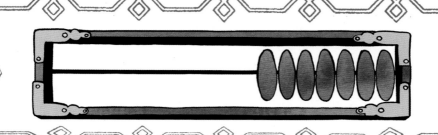

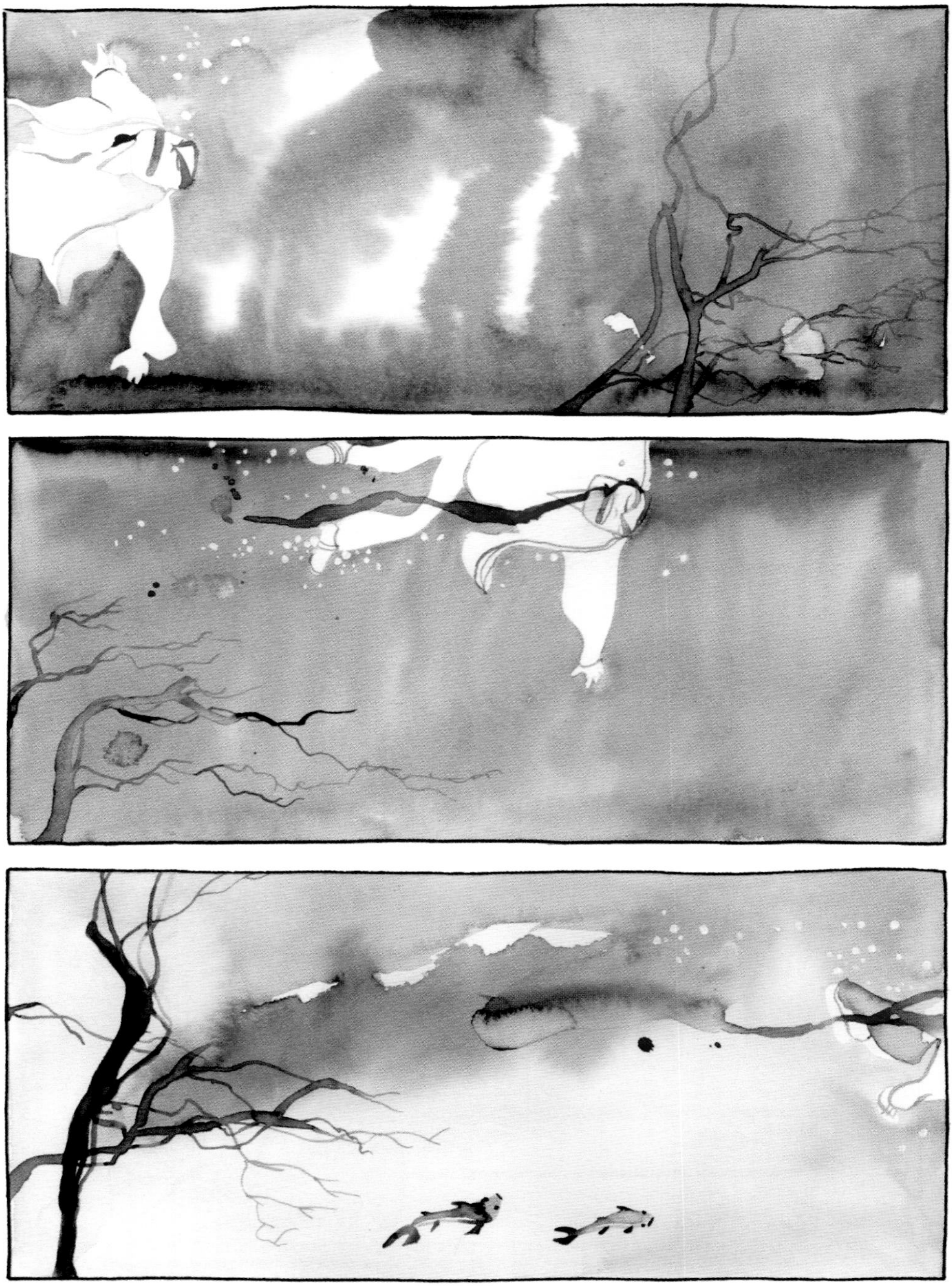

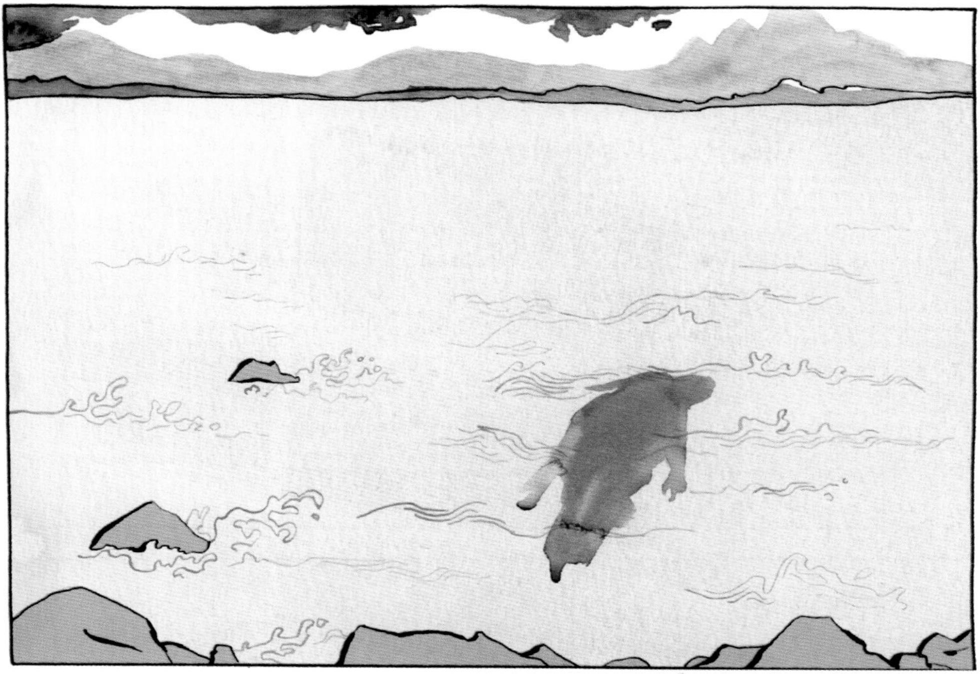

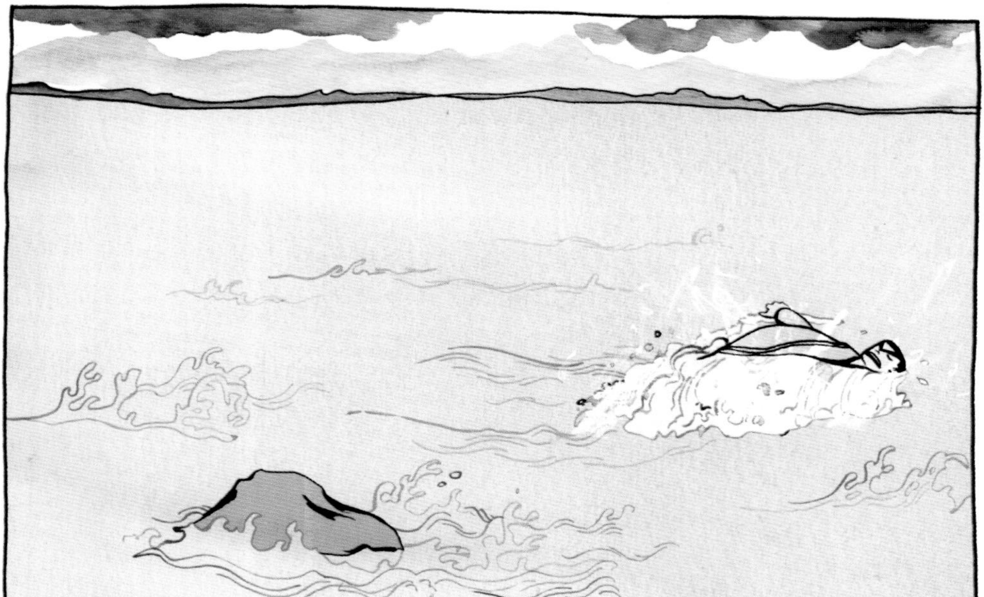

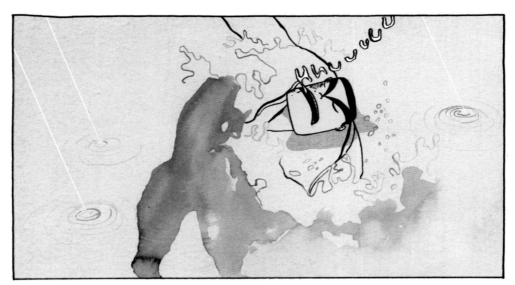

31. The Squall

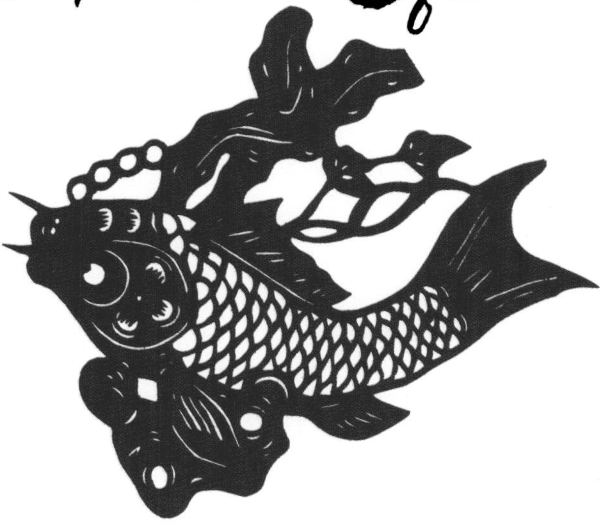

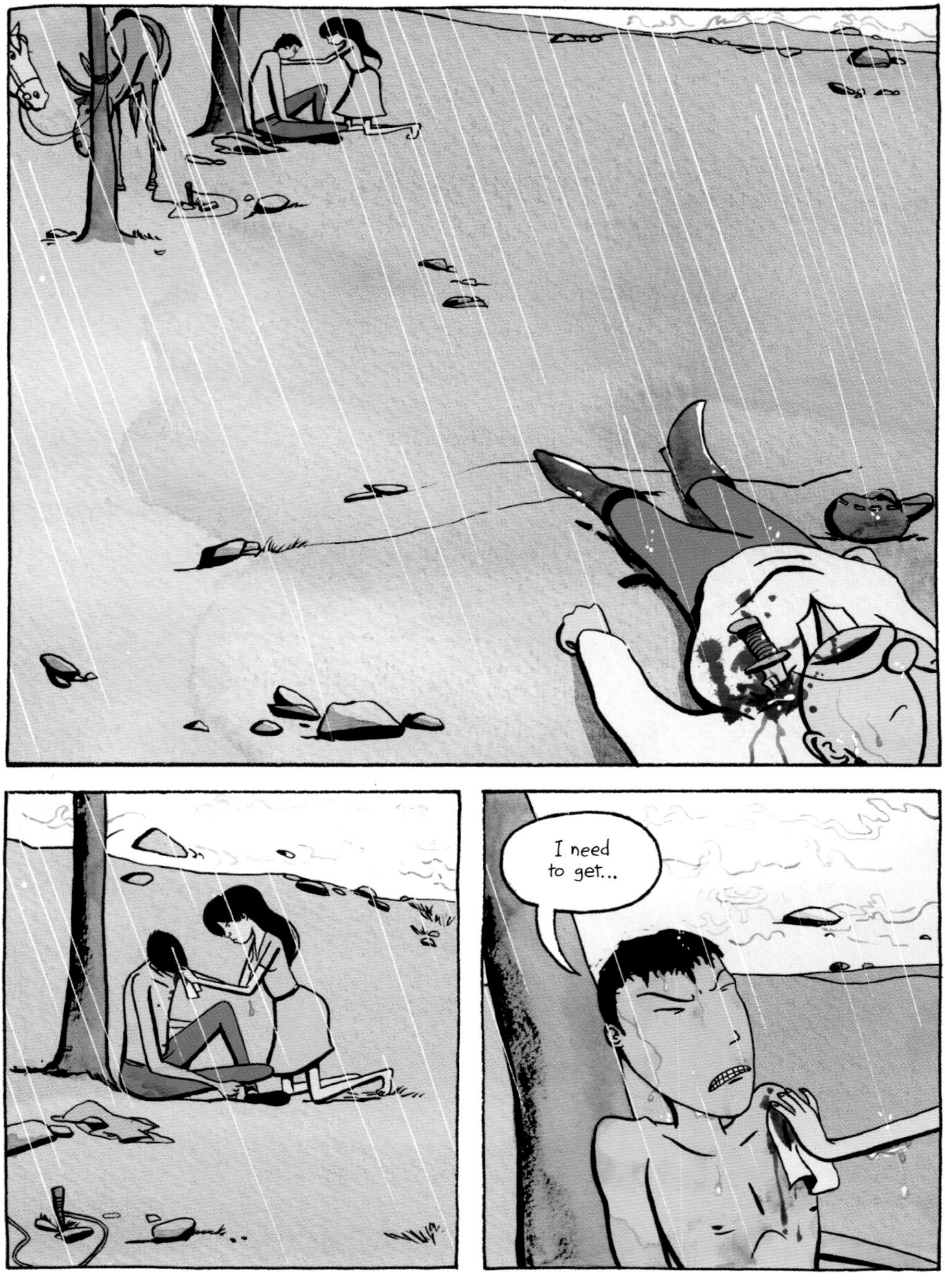
I need to get...

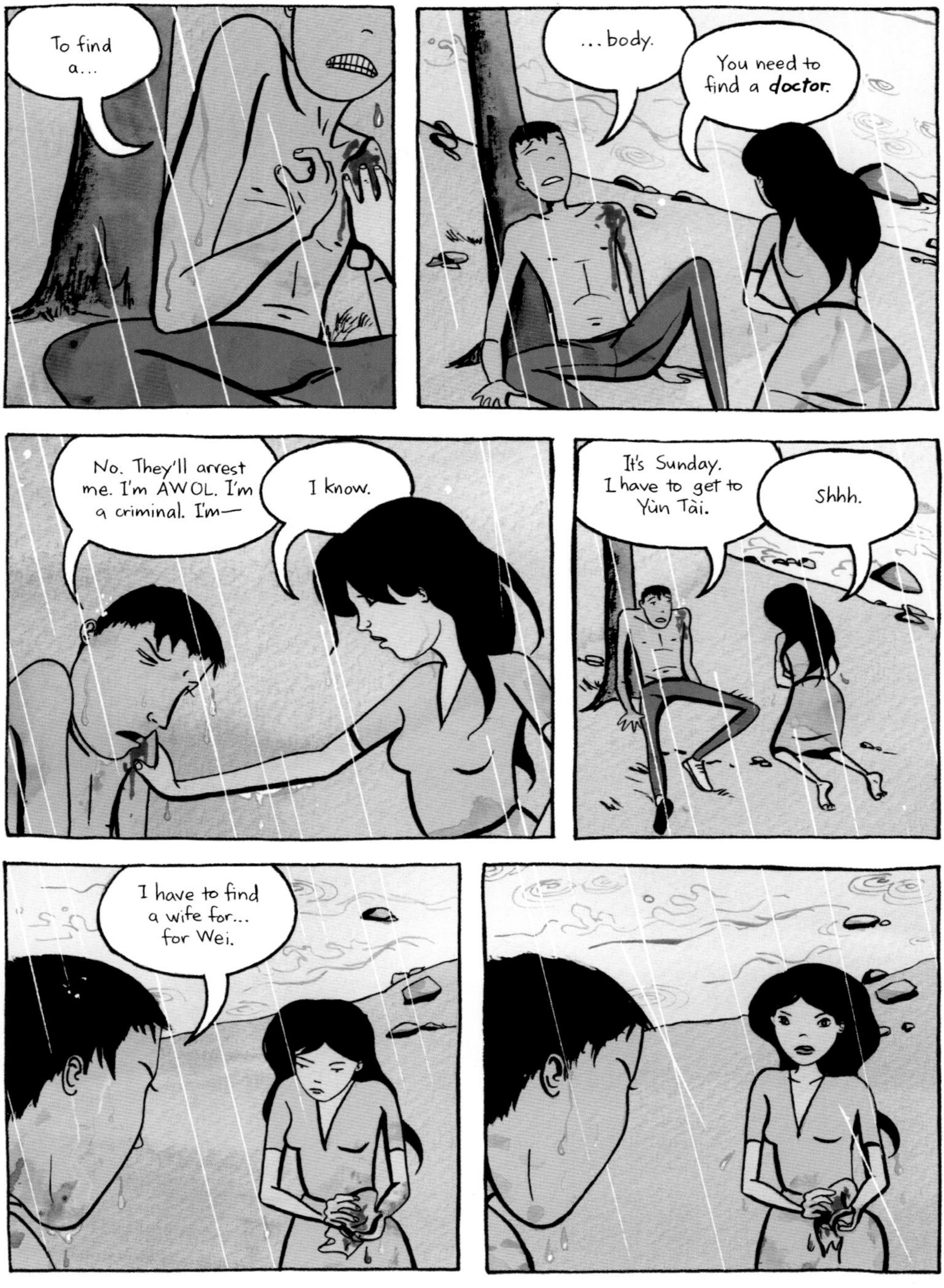

To find a...
...body.
You need to find a **doctor.**
No. They'll arrest me. I'm AWOL. I'm a criminal. I'm—
I know.
It's Sunday. I have to get to Yùn Tài.
Shhh.
I have to find a wife for... for Wei.

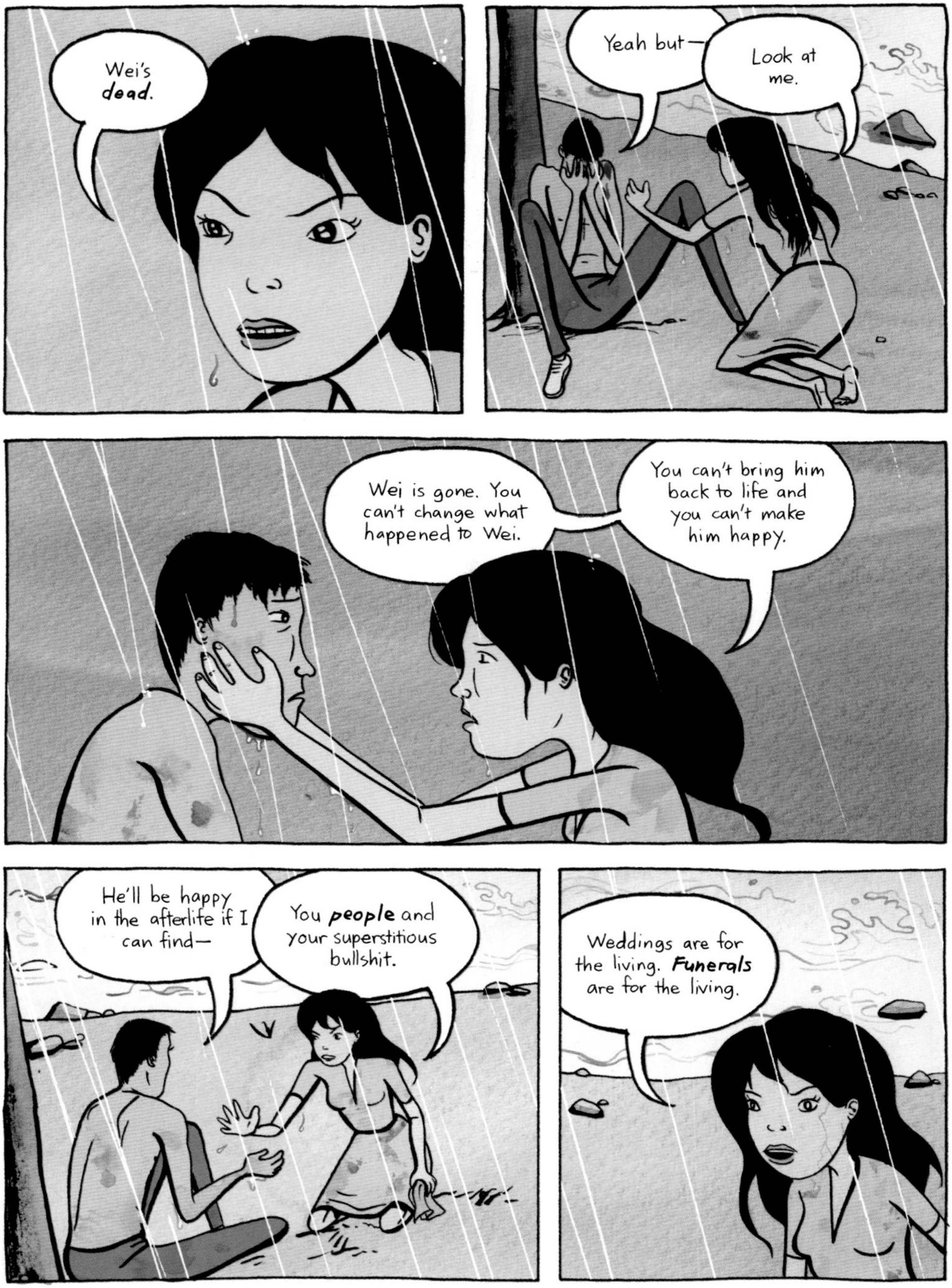
Wei's dead.
Yeah but—
Look at me.
Wei is gone. You can't change what happened to Wei.
You can't bring him back to life and you can't make him happy.
He'll be happy in the afterlife if I can find—
You people and your superstitious bullshit.
Weddings are for the living. Funerals are for the living.

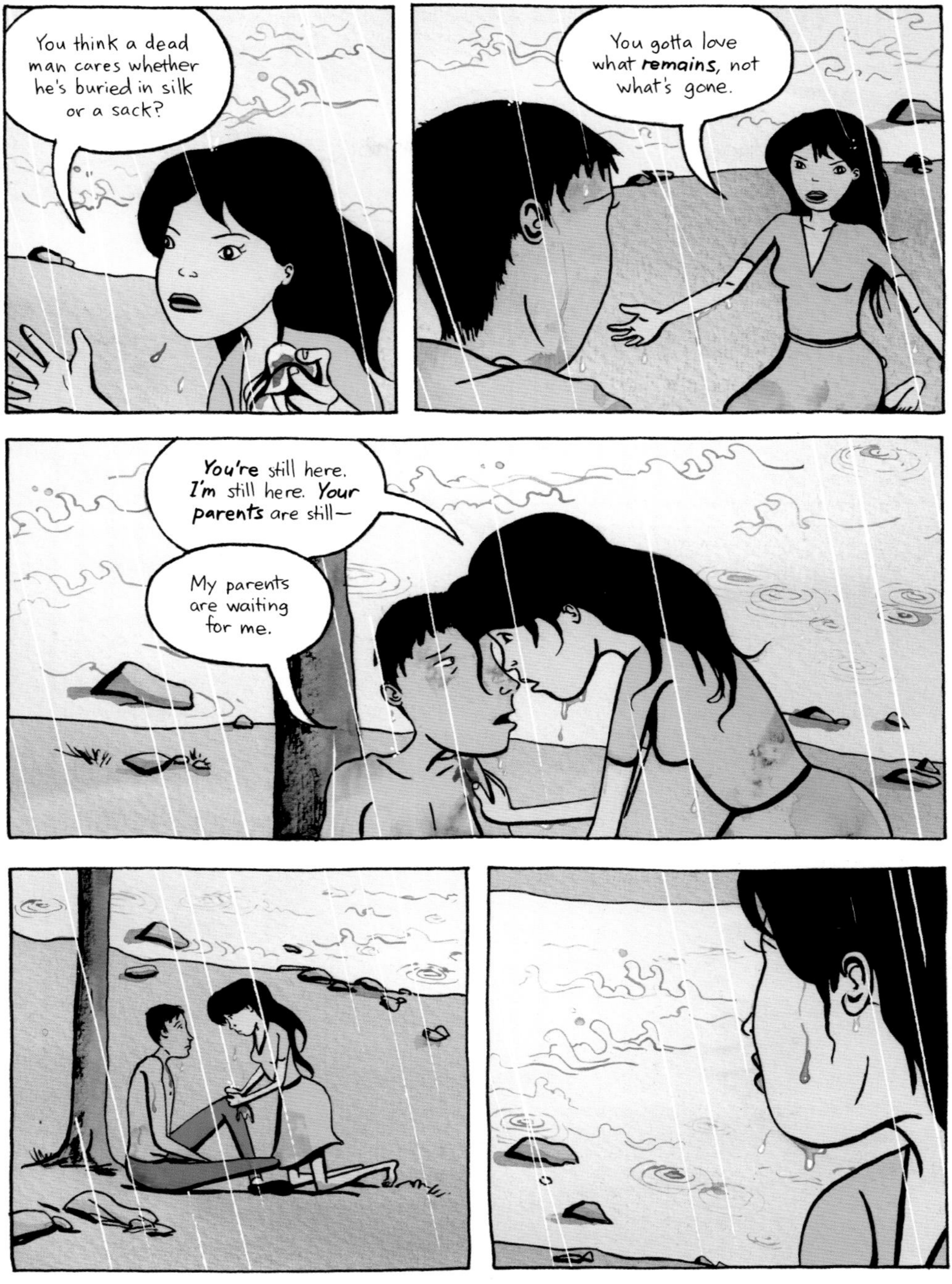
You think a dead man cares whether he's buried in silk or a sack?
You gotta love what **remains**, not what's gone.
You're still here. ***I'm*** still here. ***Your parents*** are still—
My parents are waiting for me.

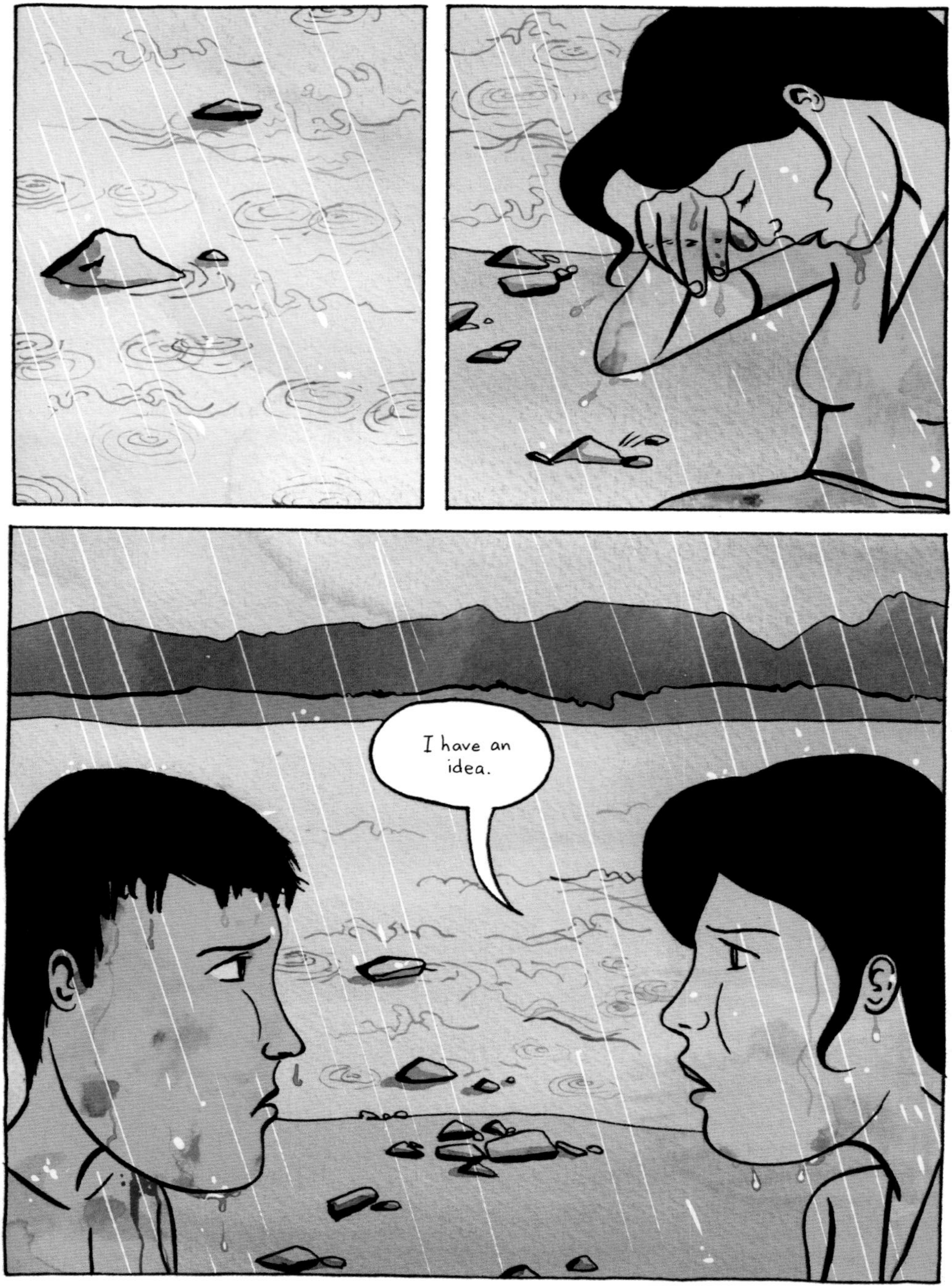
I have an idea.

32. Life is But a Dream

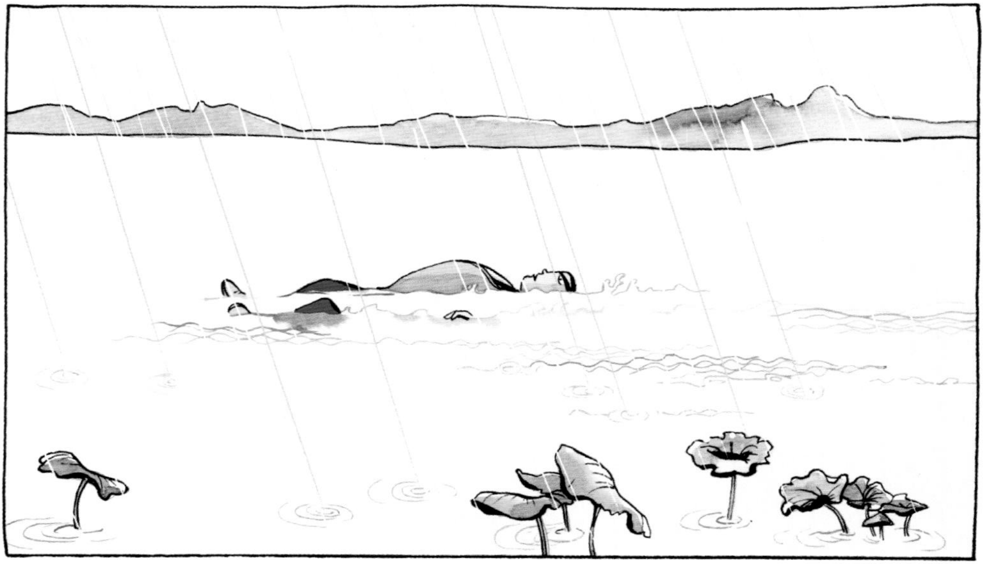

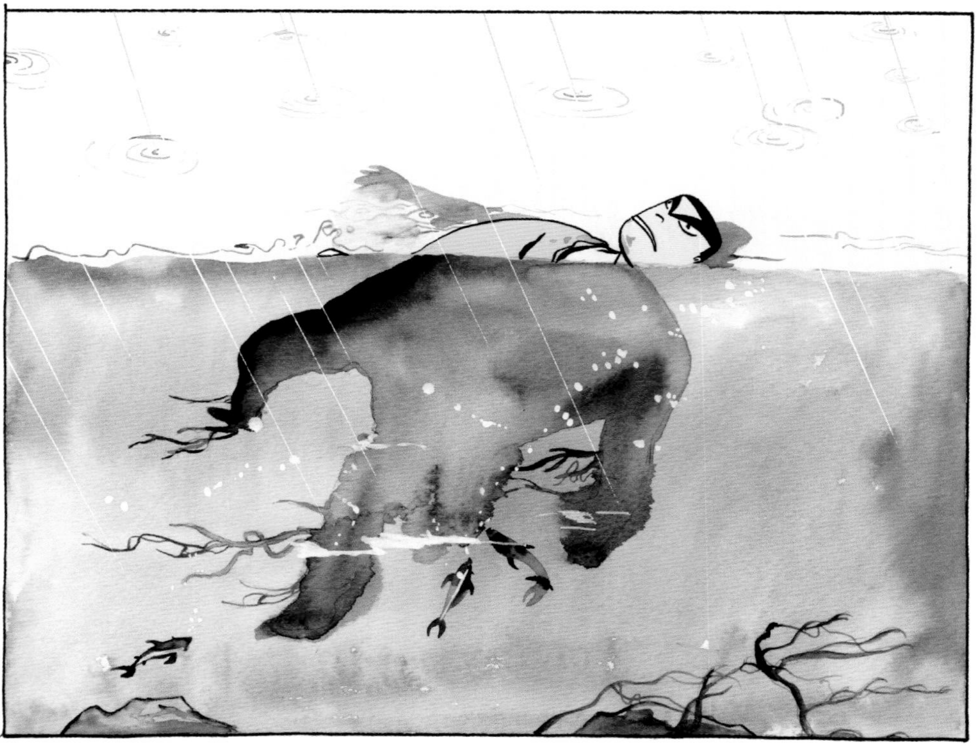

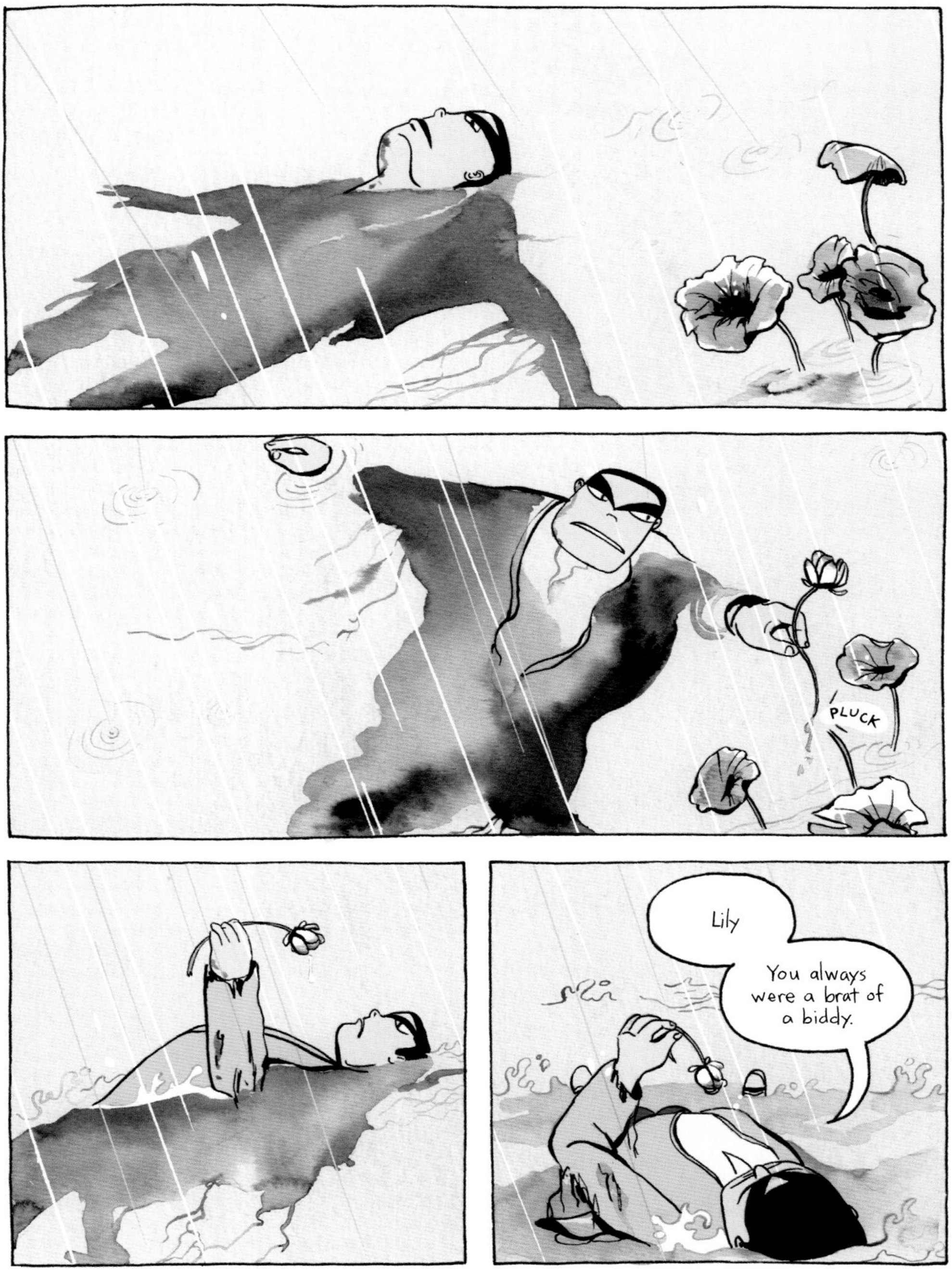
PLUCK
Lily
You always were a brat of a biddy.

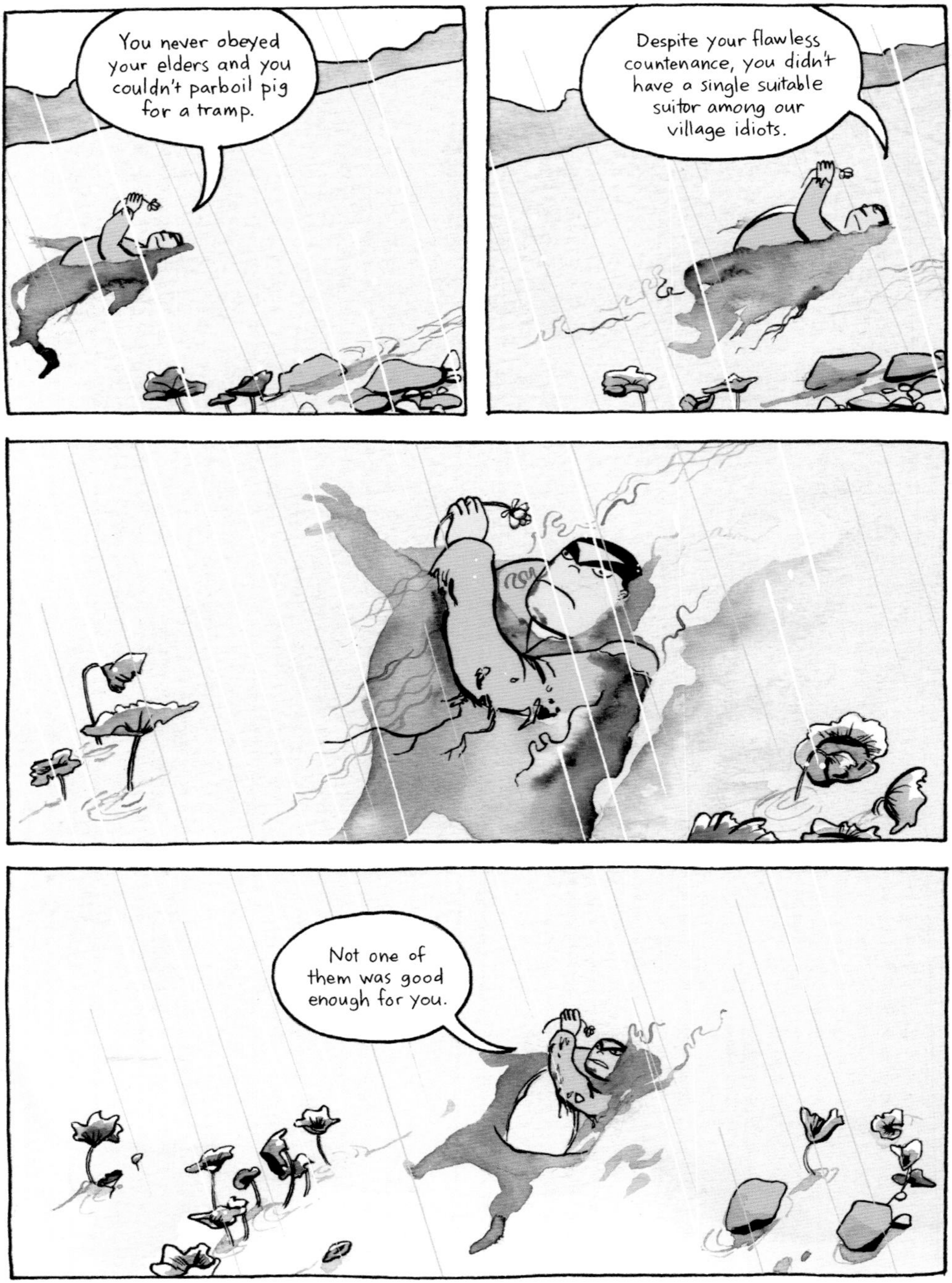
You never obeyed your elders and you couldn't parboil pig for a tramp.
Despite your flawless countenance, you didn't have a single suitable suitor among our village idiots.
Not one of them was good enough for you.

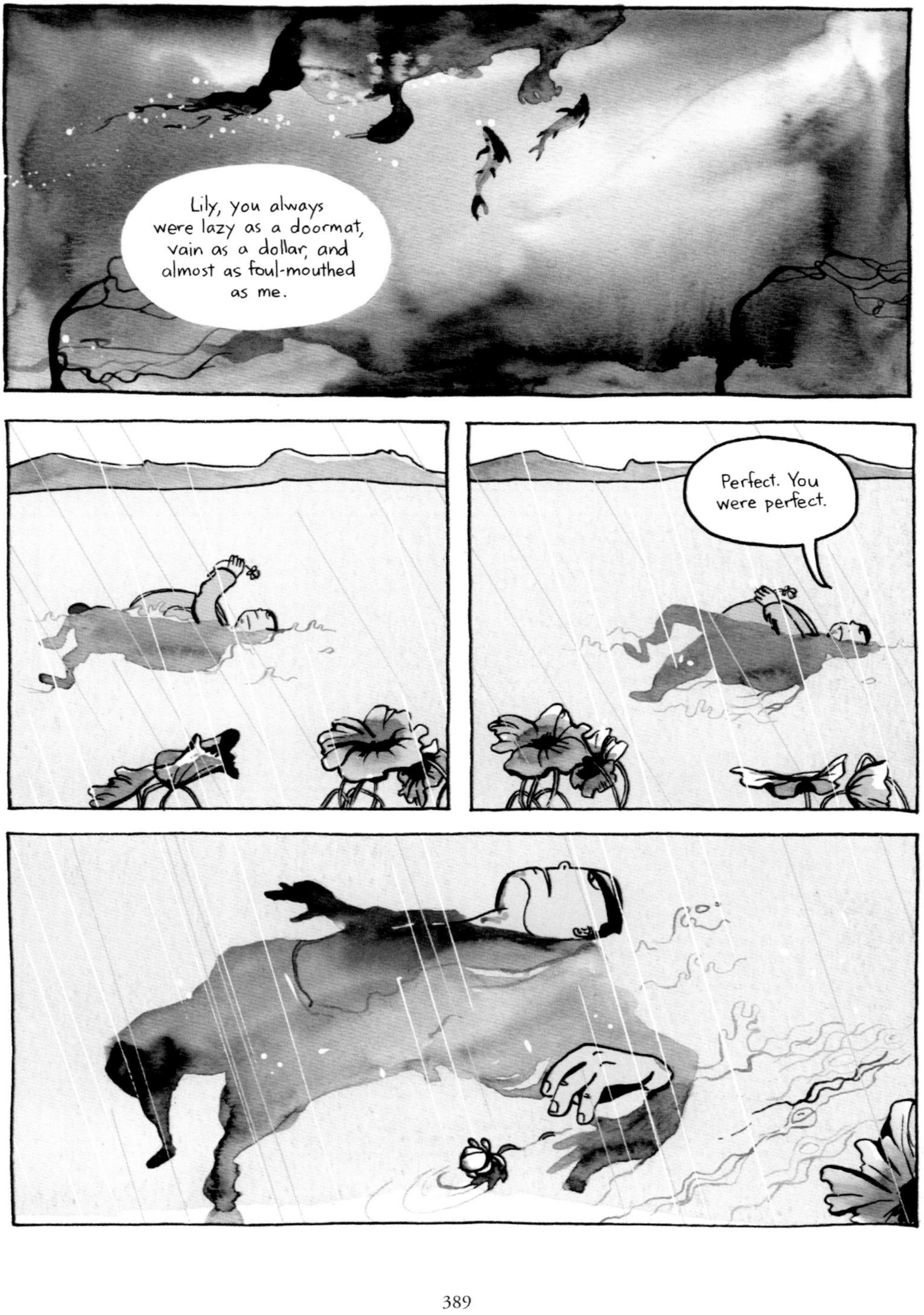
Lily, you always were lazy as a doormat, vain as a dollar, and almost as foul-mouthed as me.
Perfect. You were perfect.

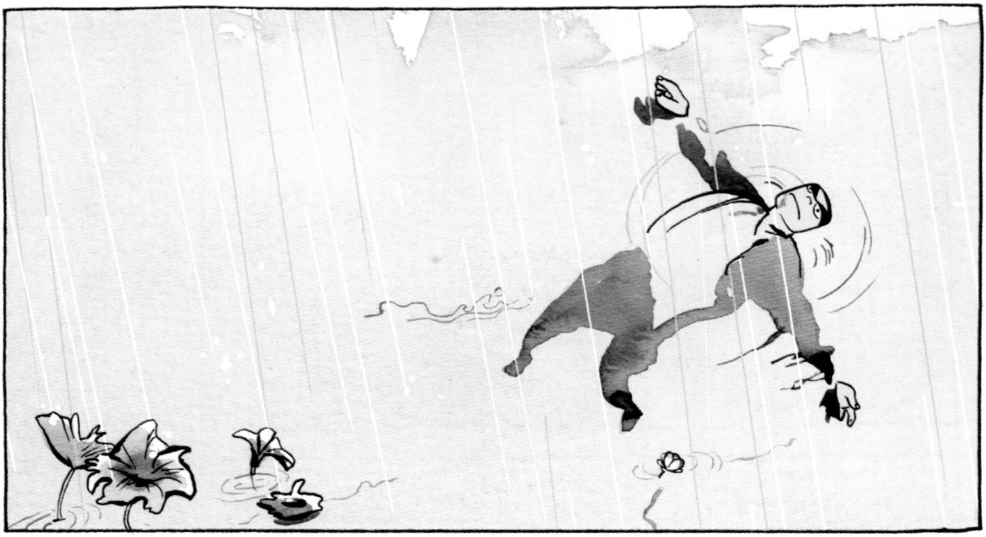

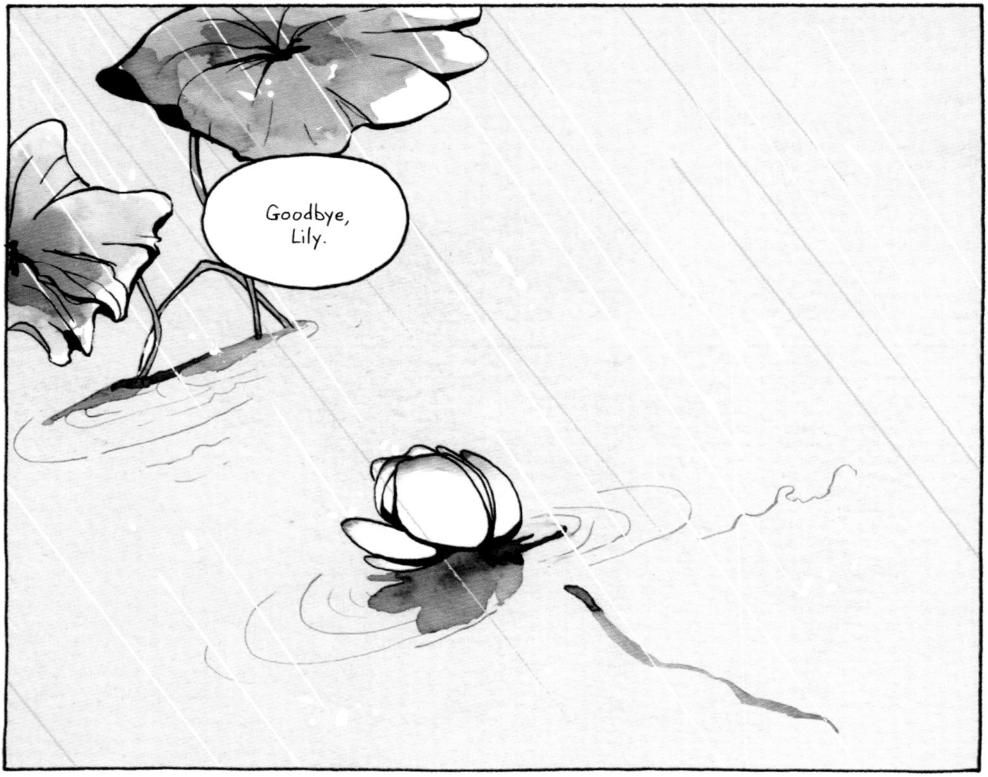
Goodbye, Lily.

33. The Procession

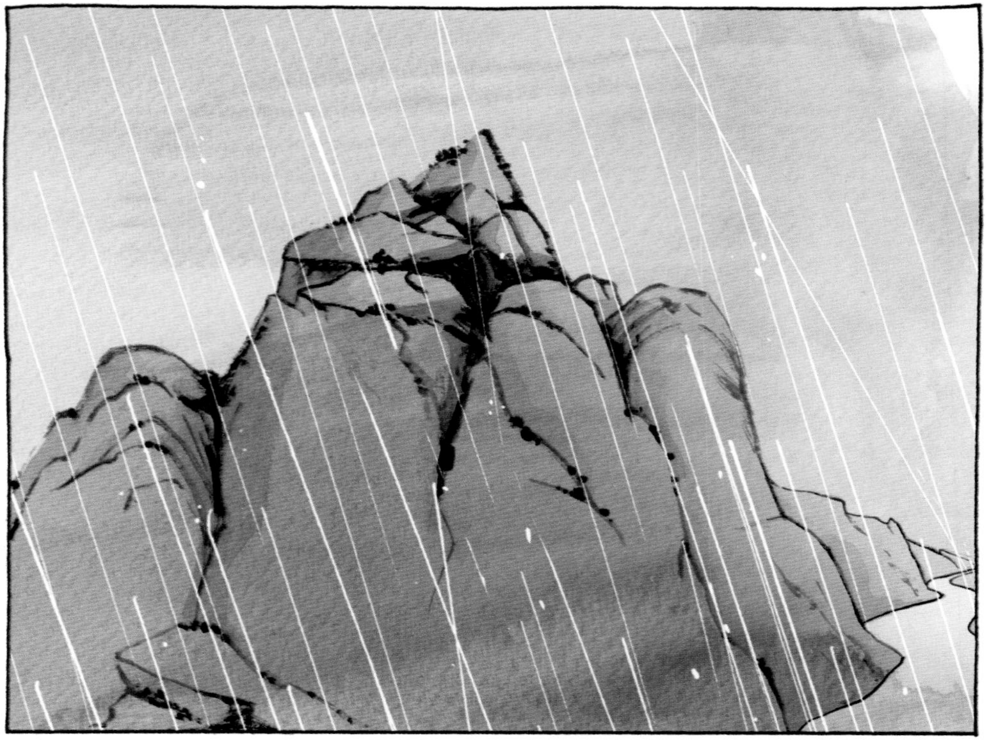

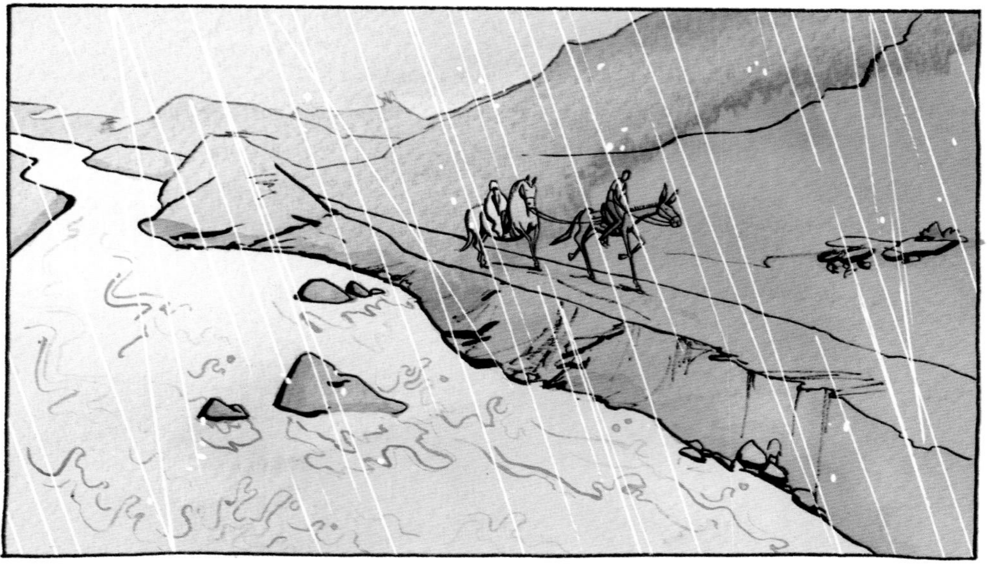

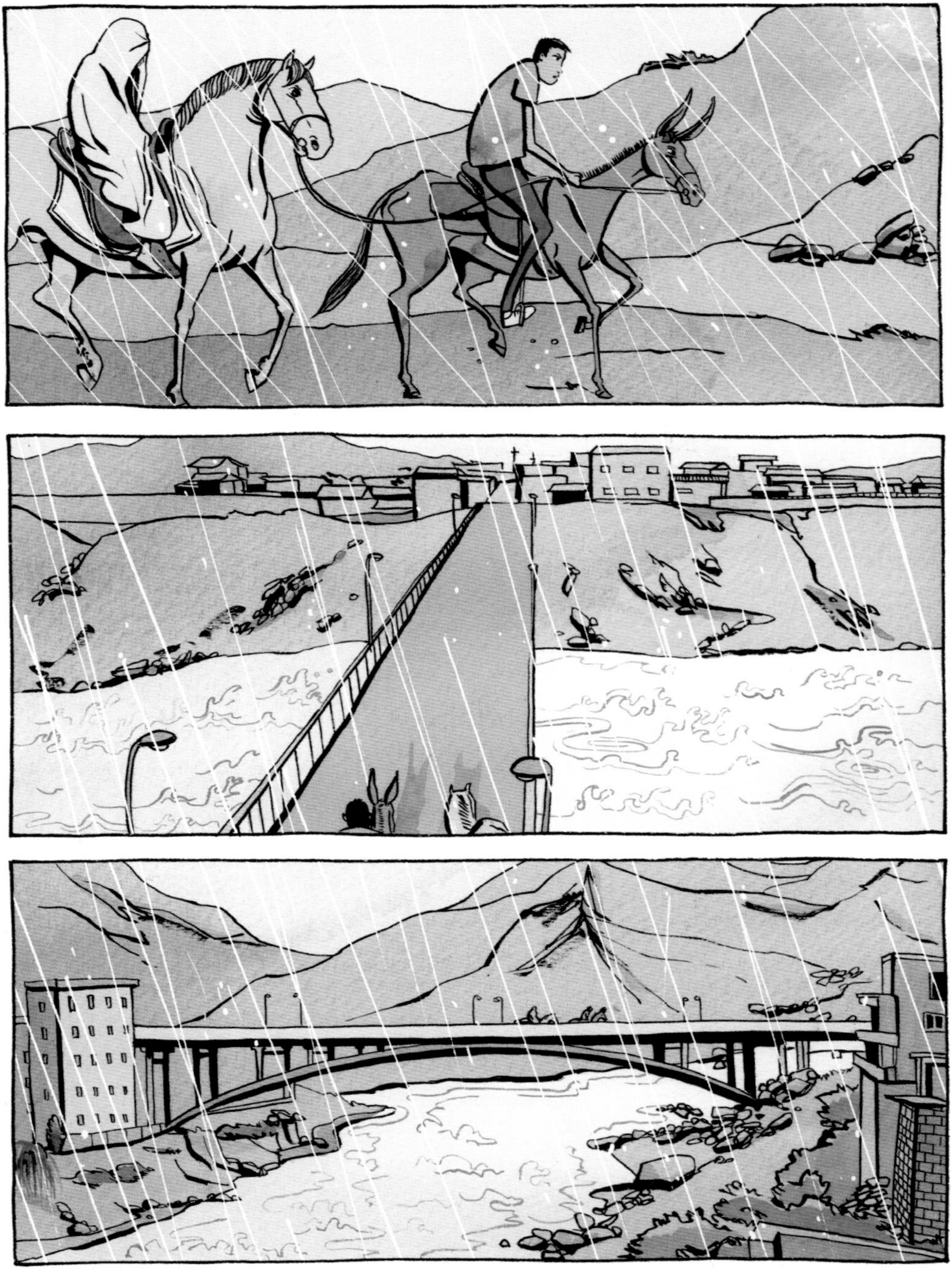

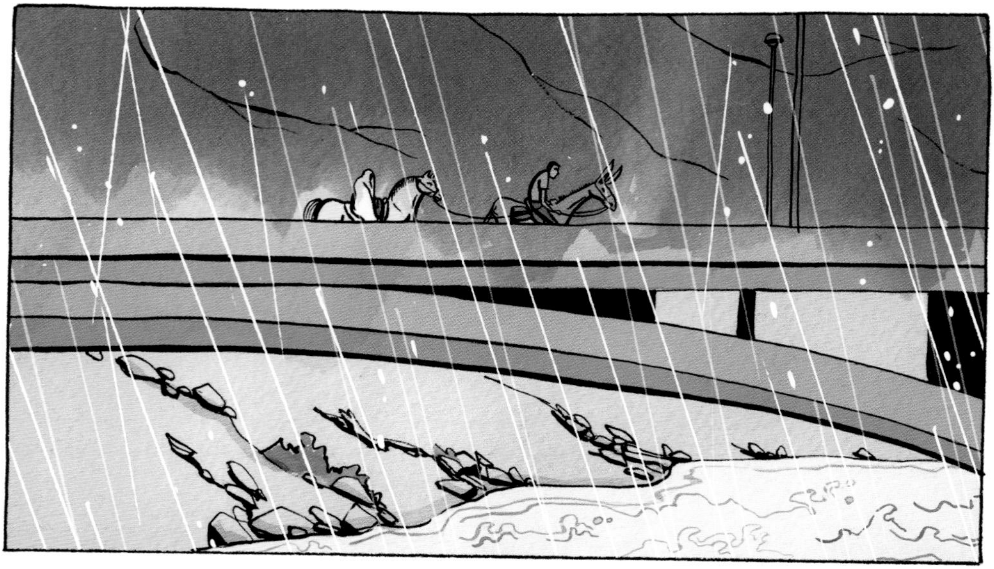

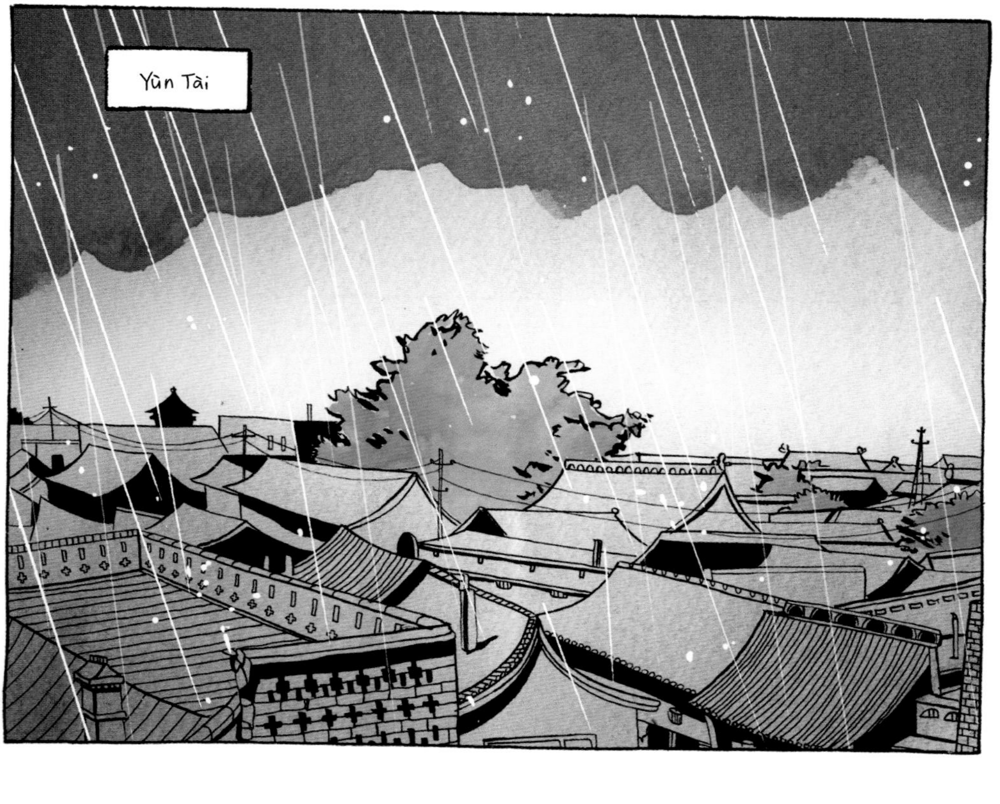
Yùn Tài

34. The Guest

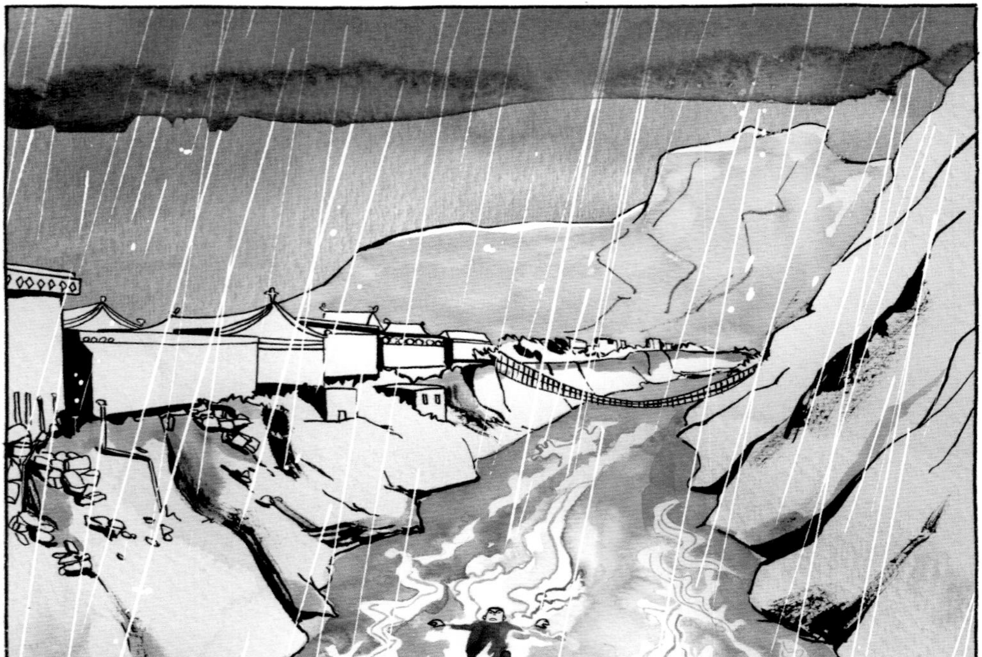

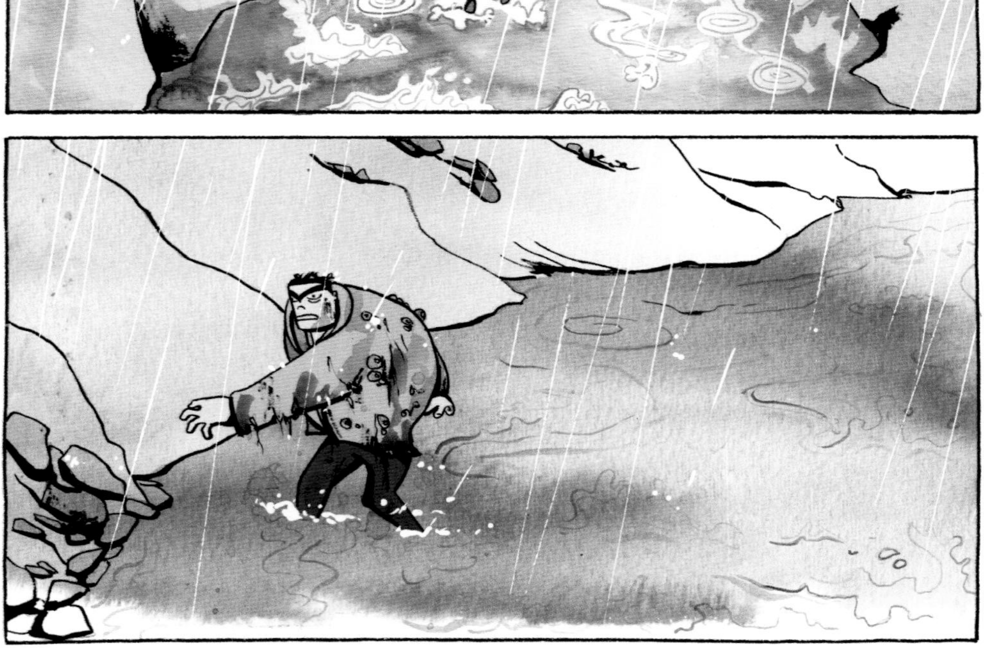

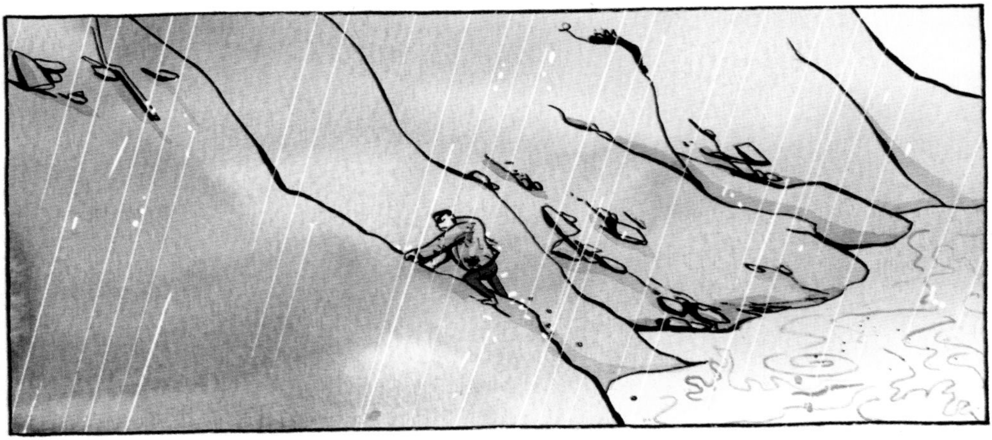

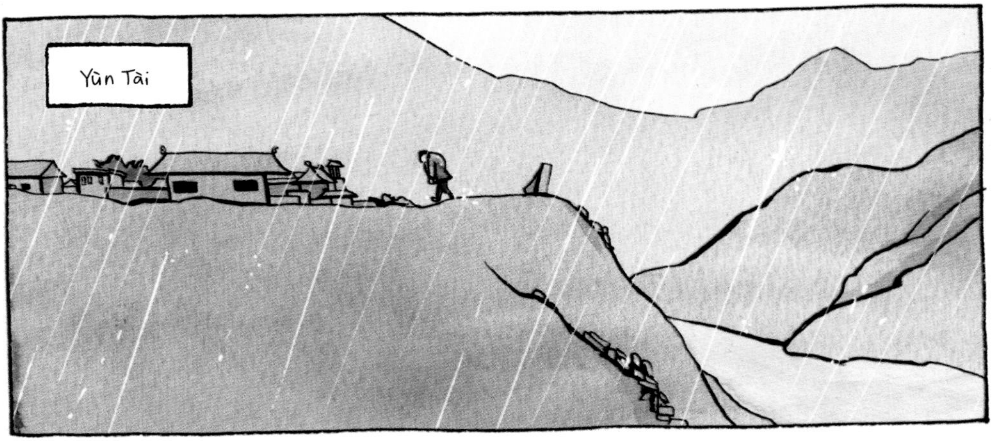
Yǔn Tài

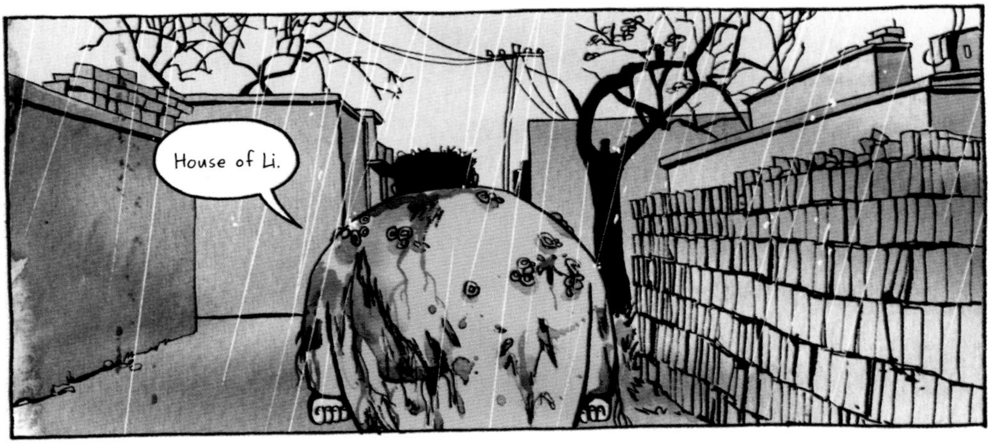
House of Li.

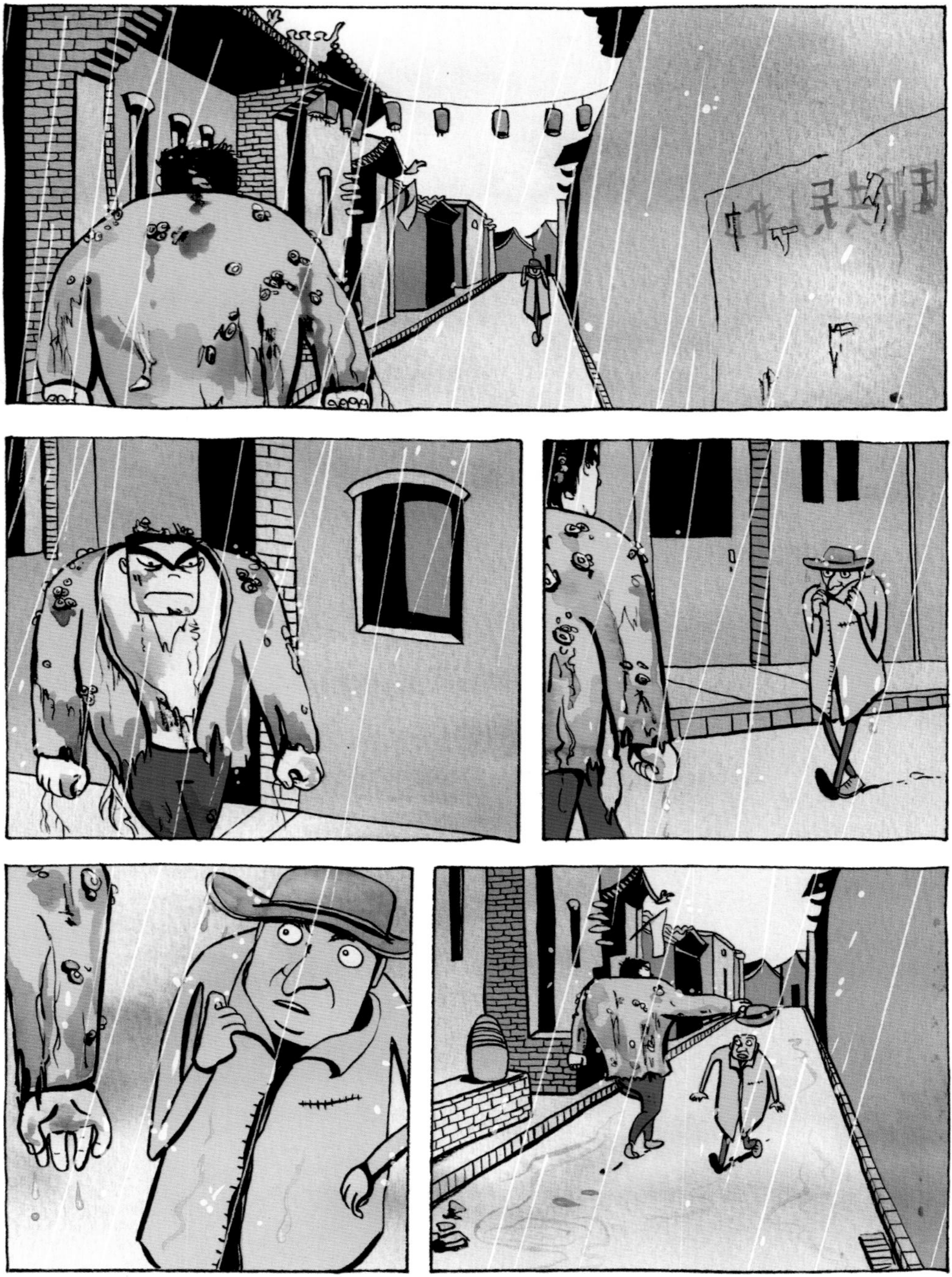

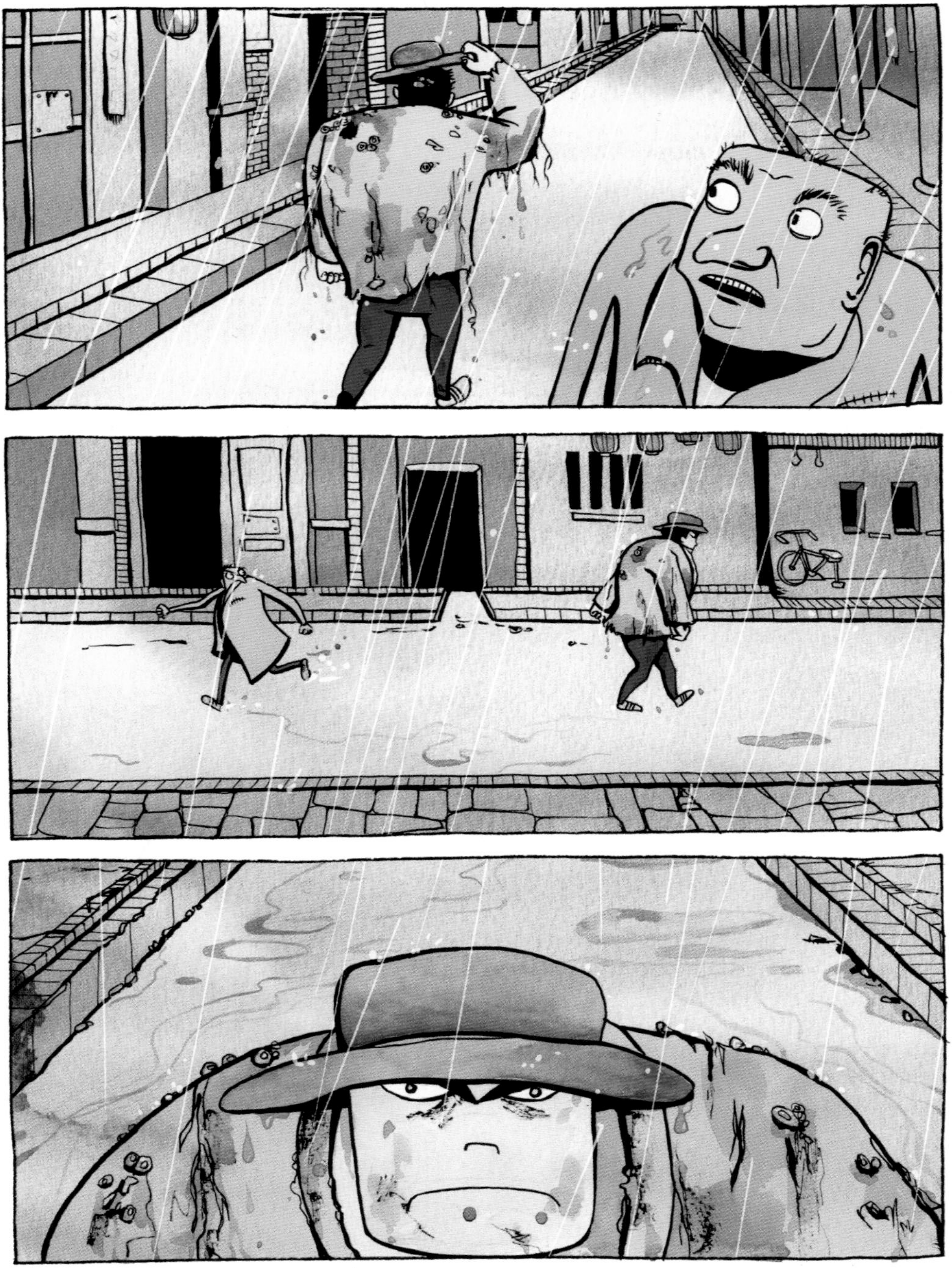

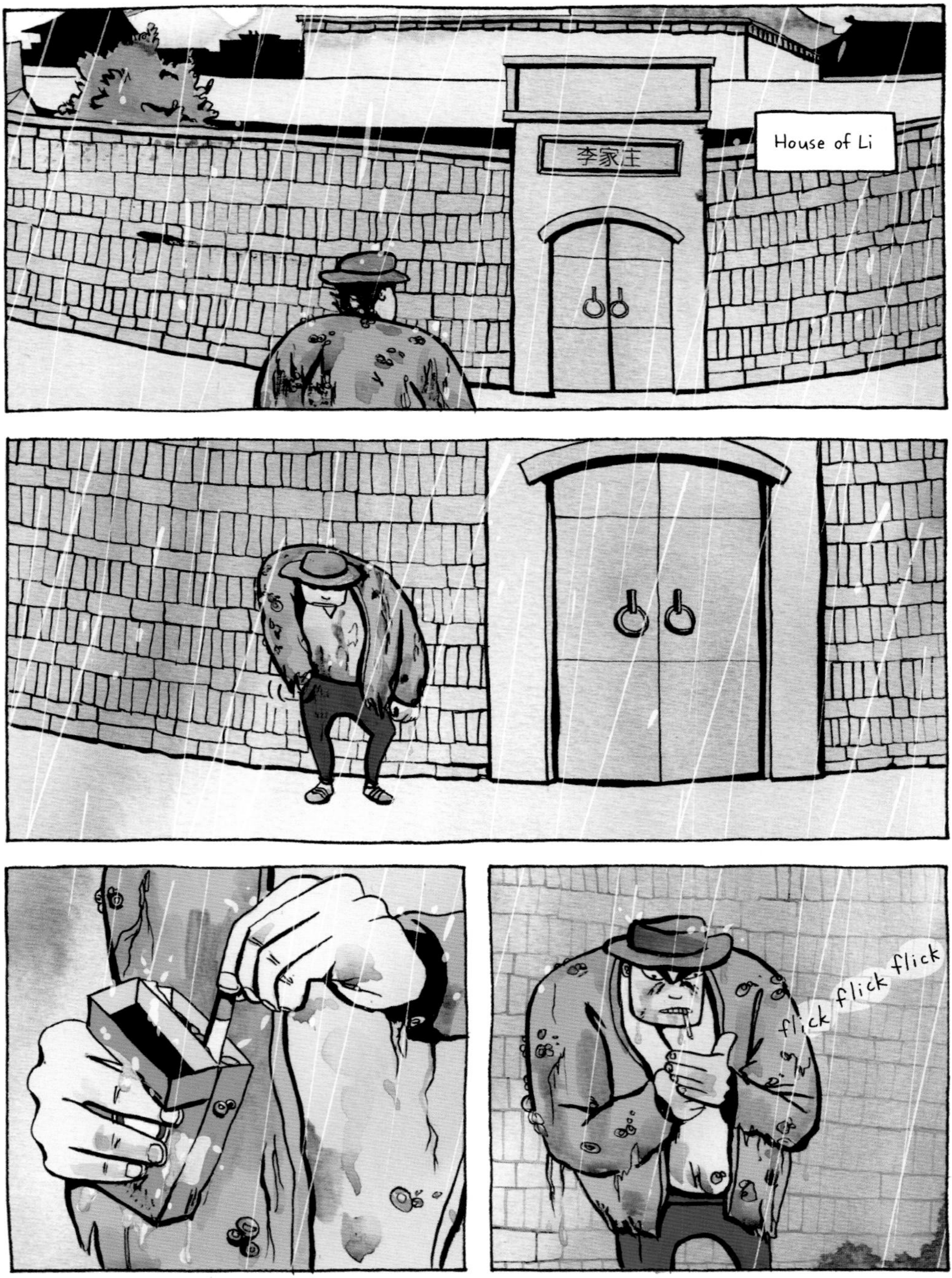
House of Li
李家主
flick flick flick

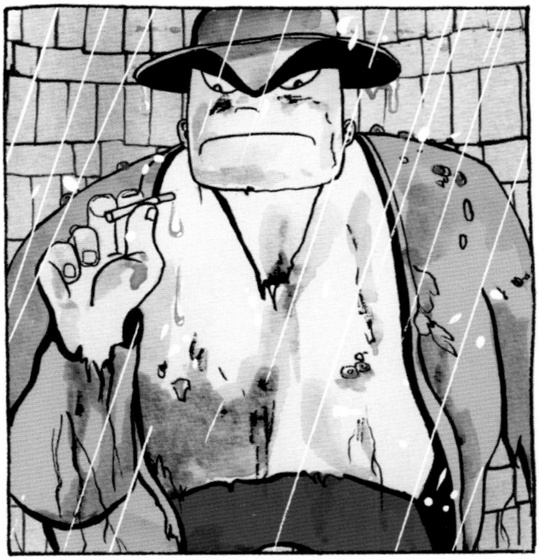

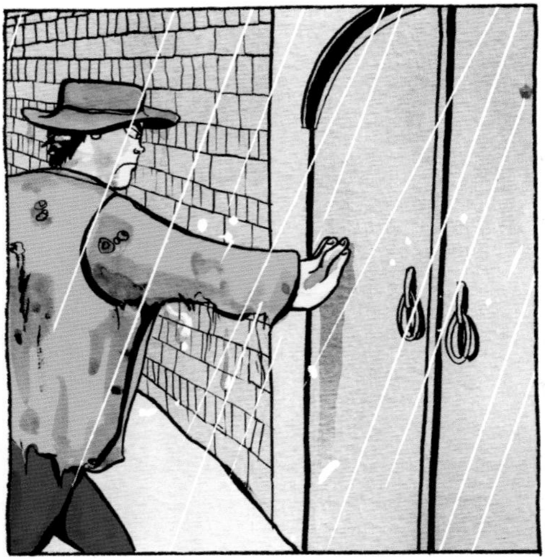

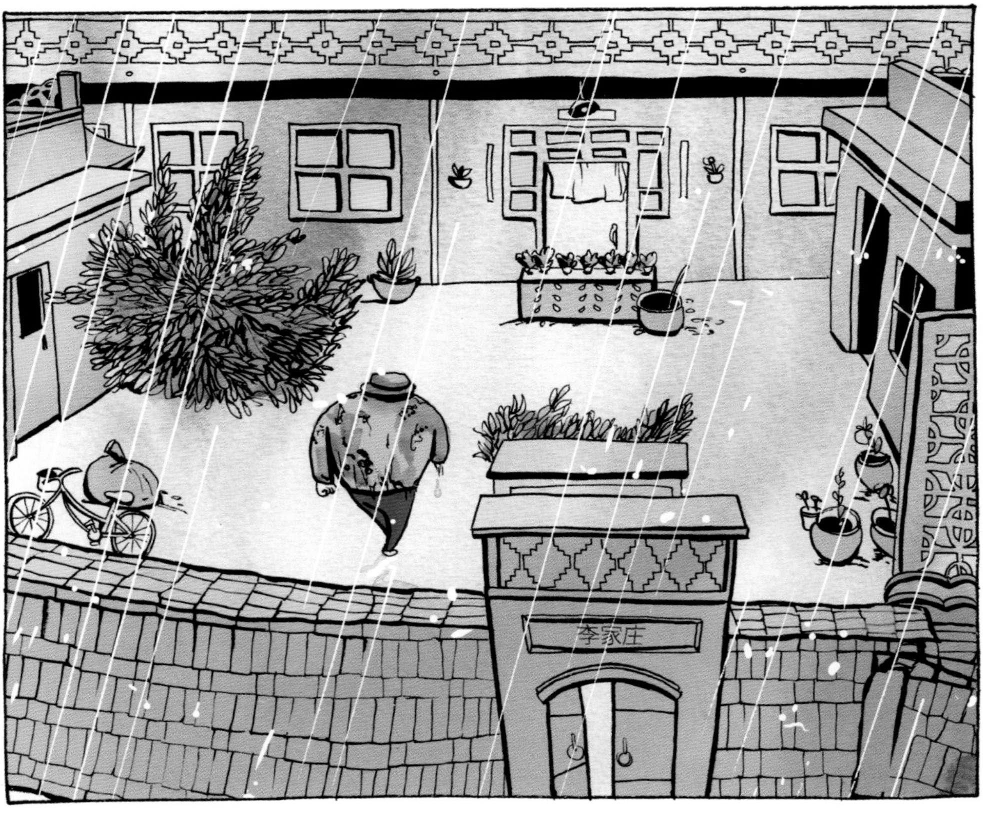
李家庄

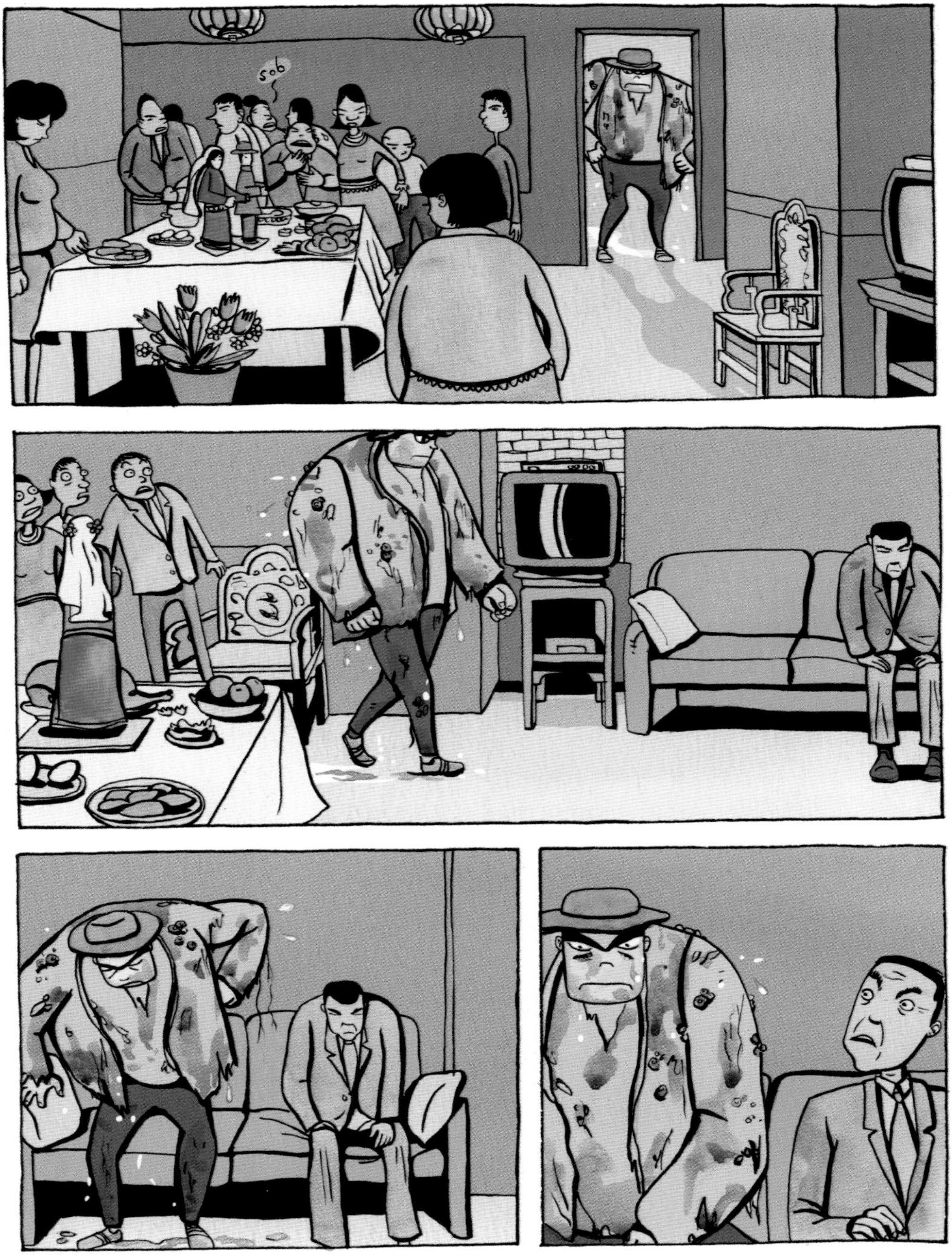
sob

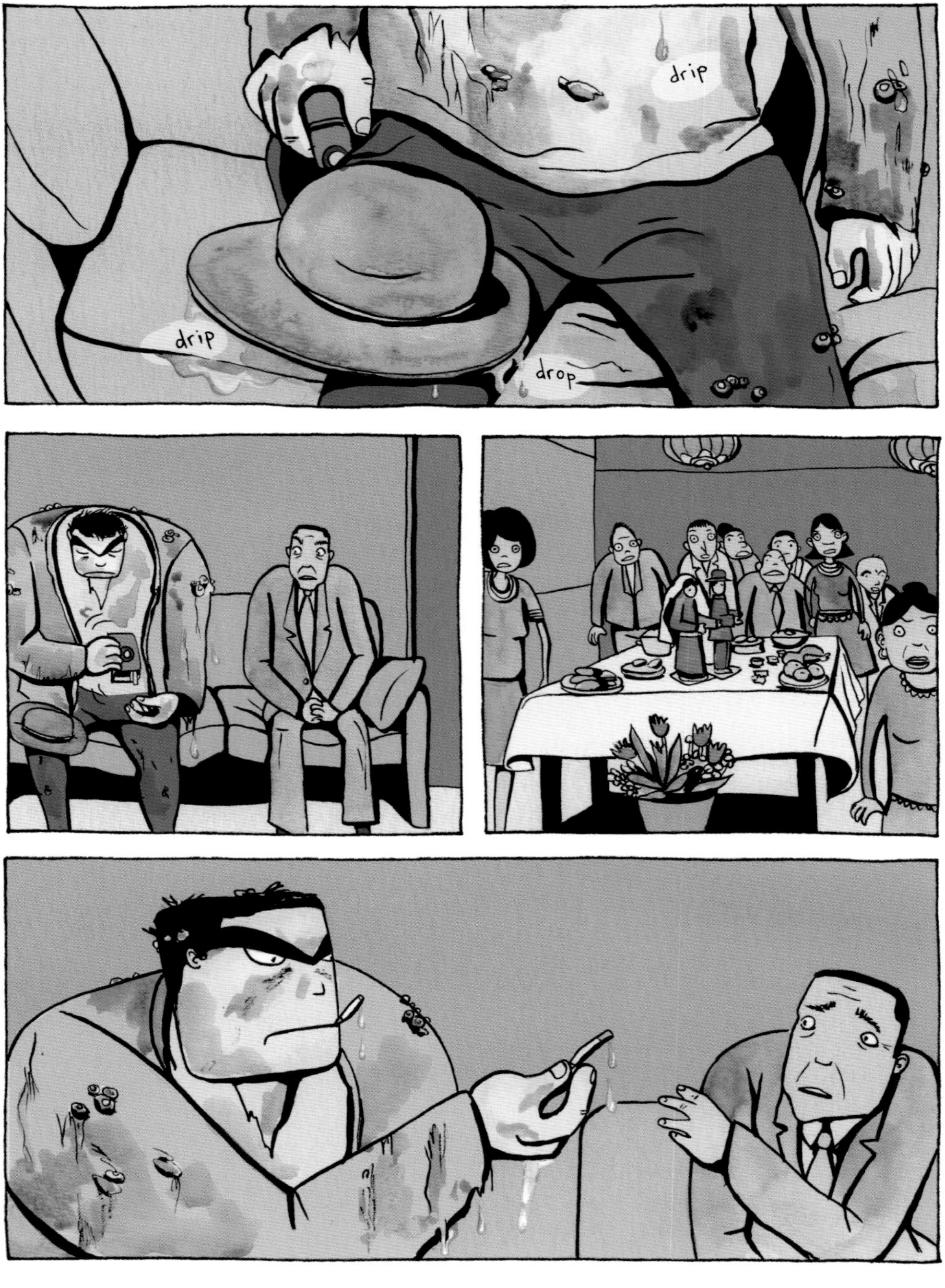
drip
drip
drop

35. The Bride

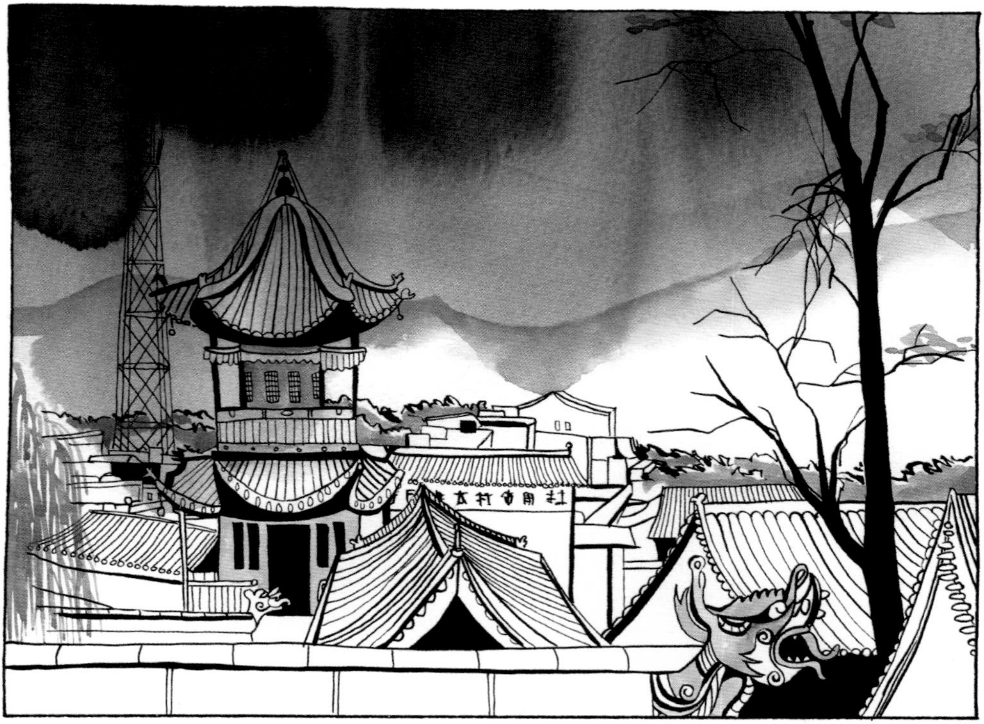

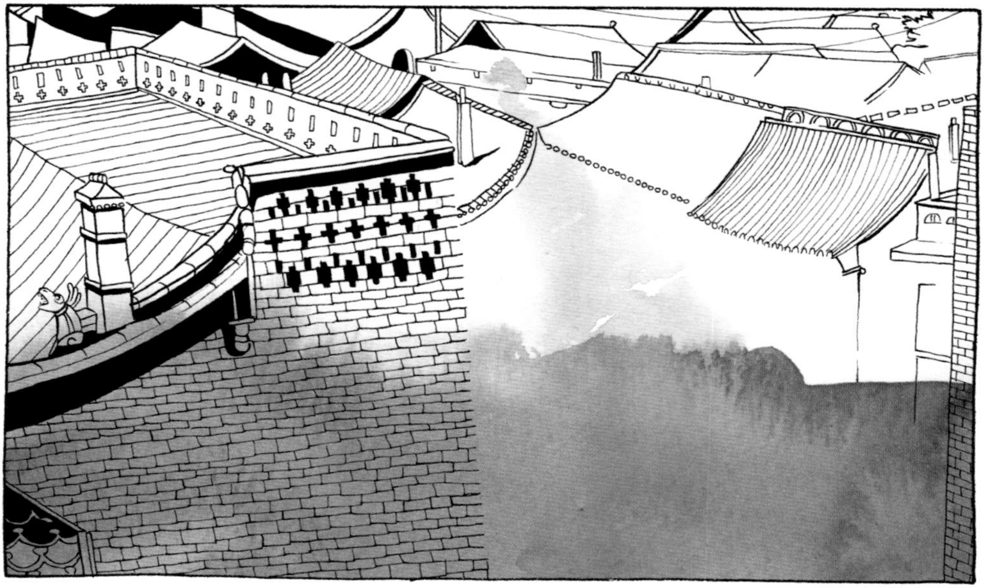

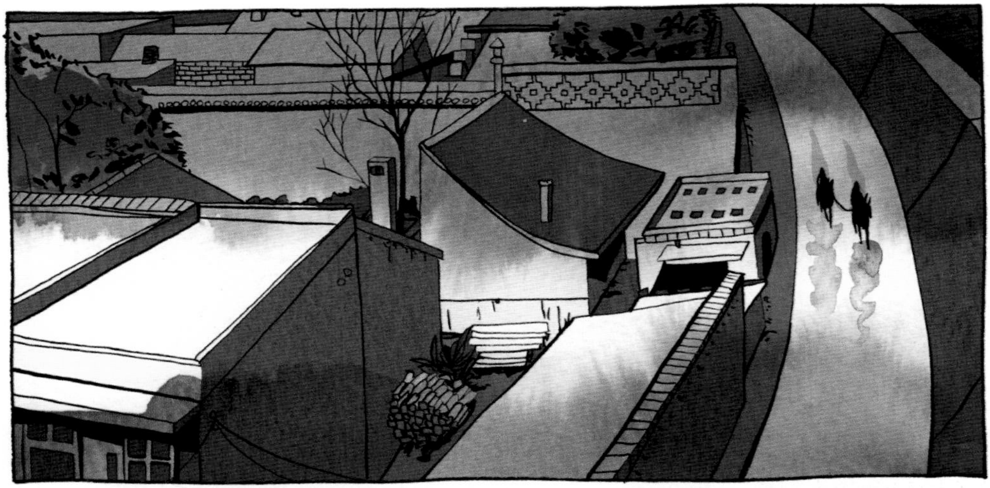

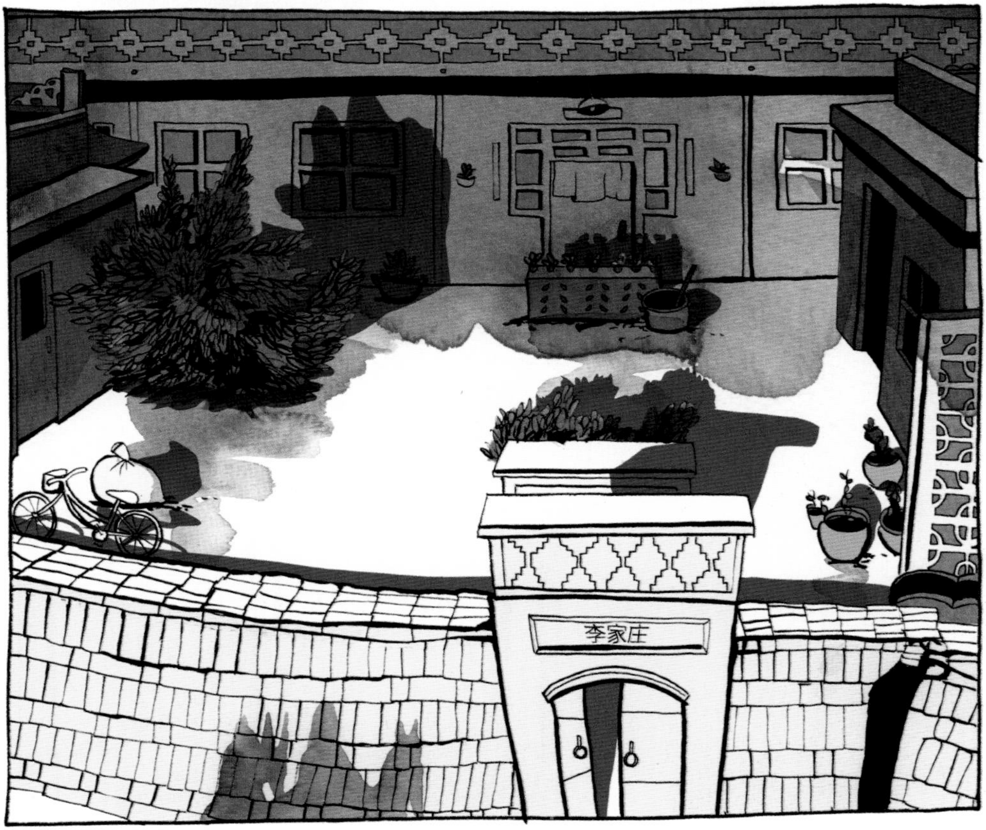
李家庄

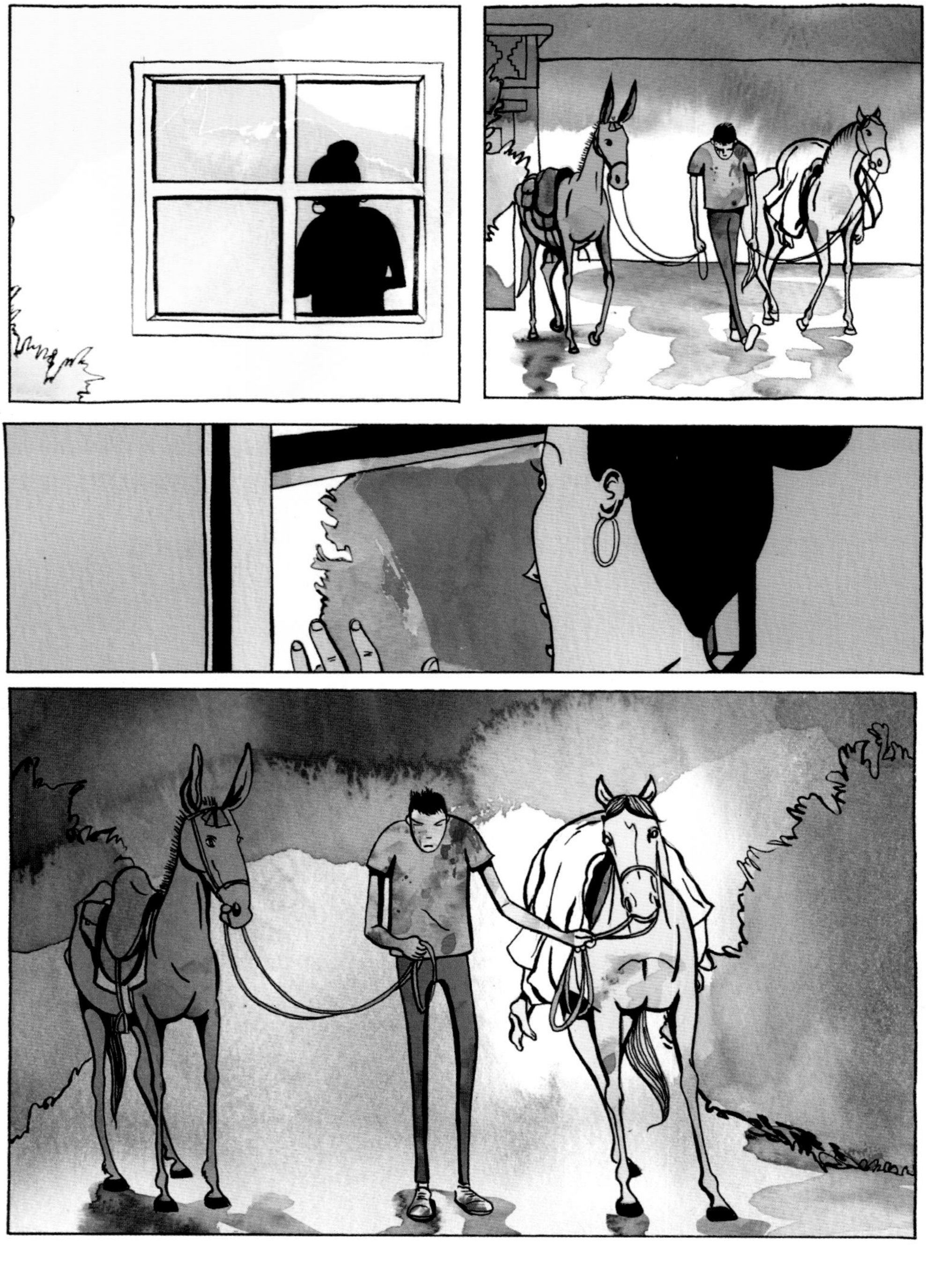

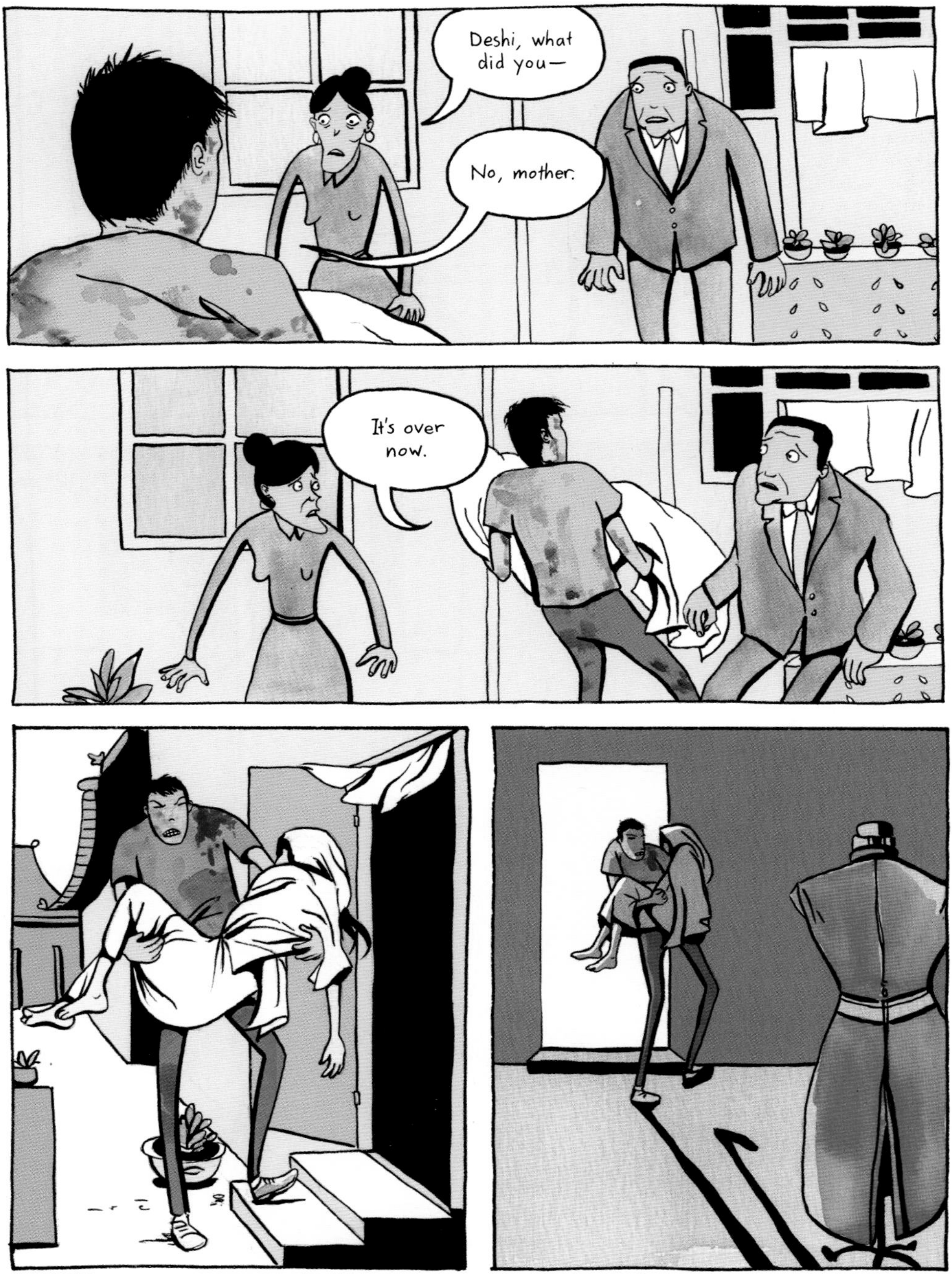
Deshi, what did you—
No, mother.
It's over now.

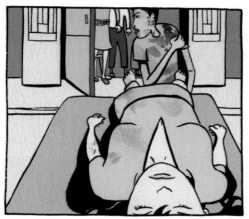

SLAM

ZZIIIP

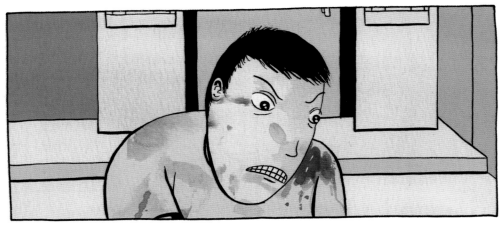

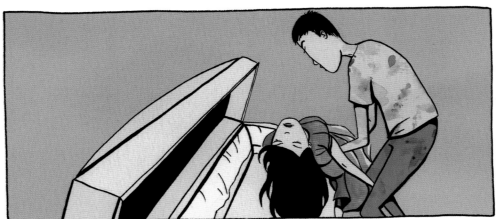

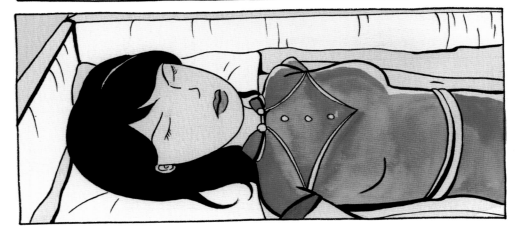

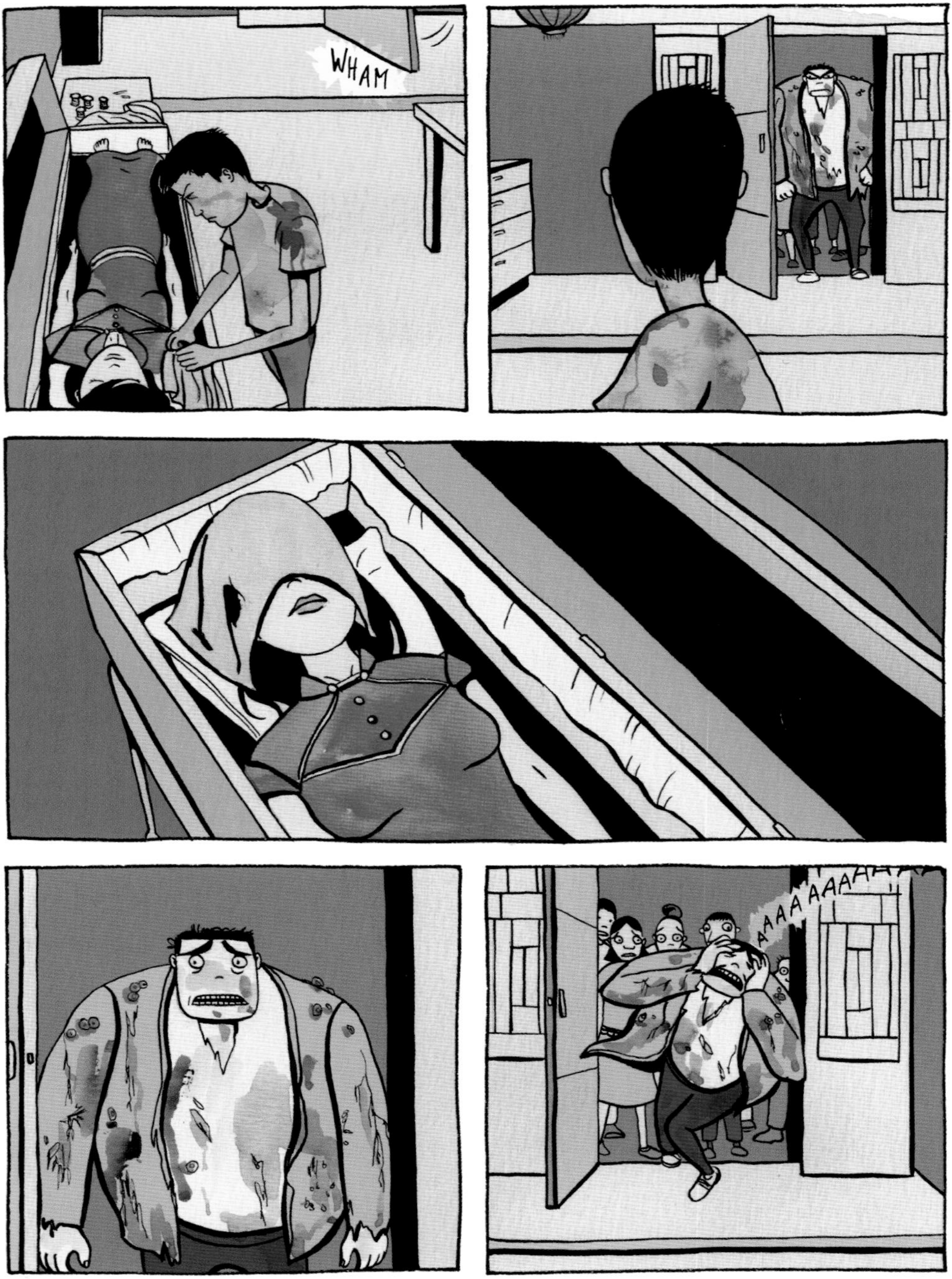
WHAM
AAAAAAAA

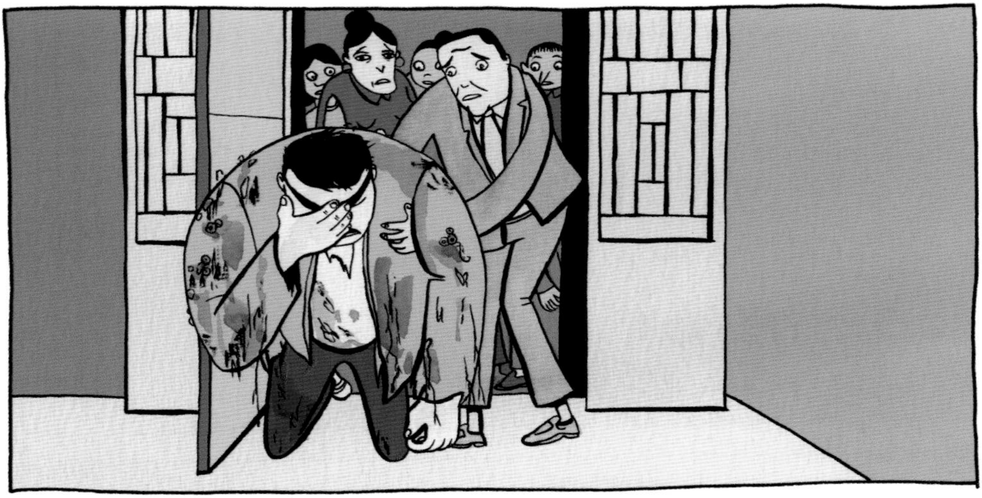

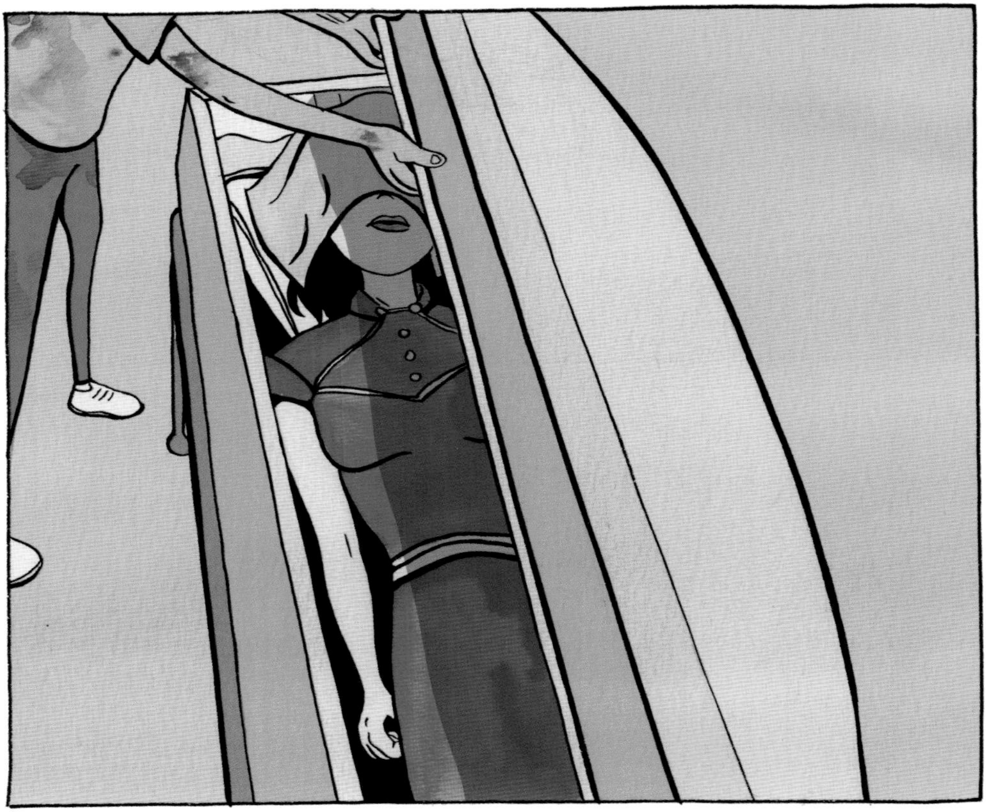

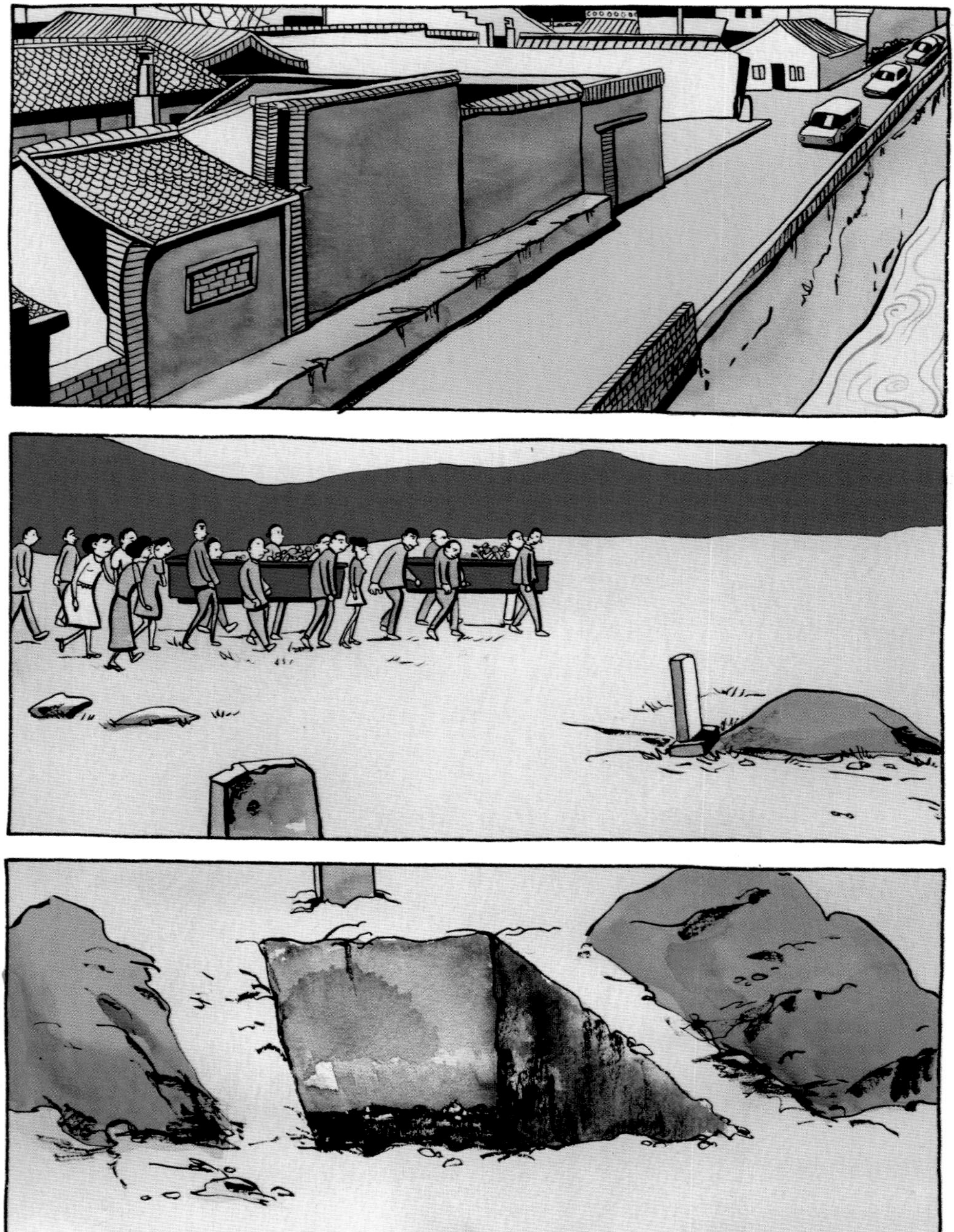

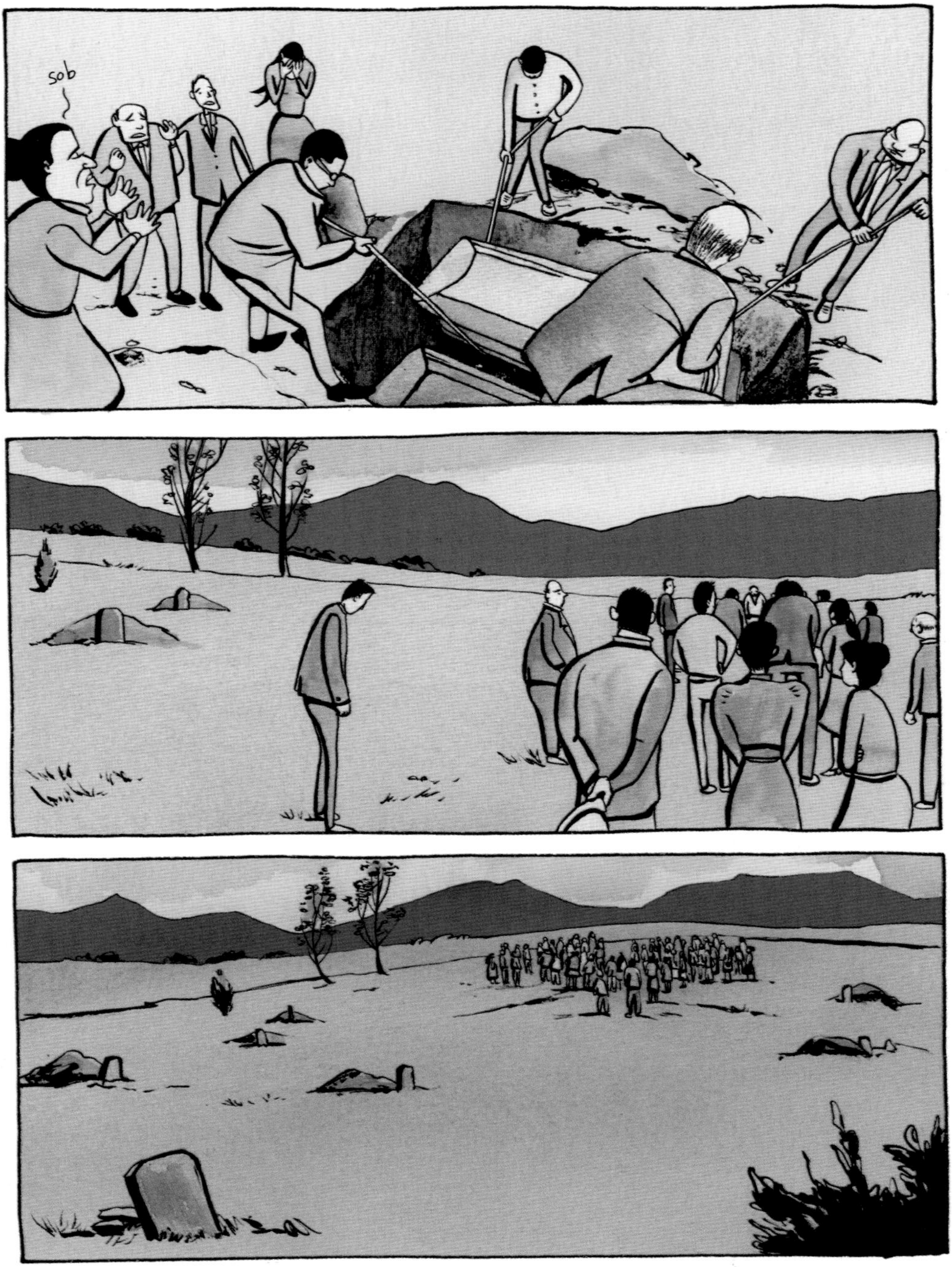
sob

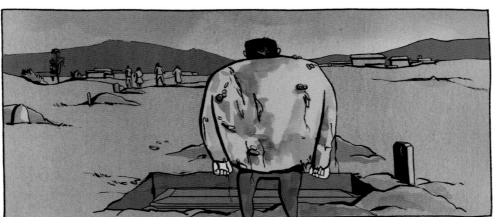

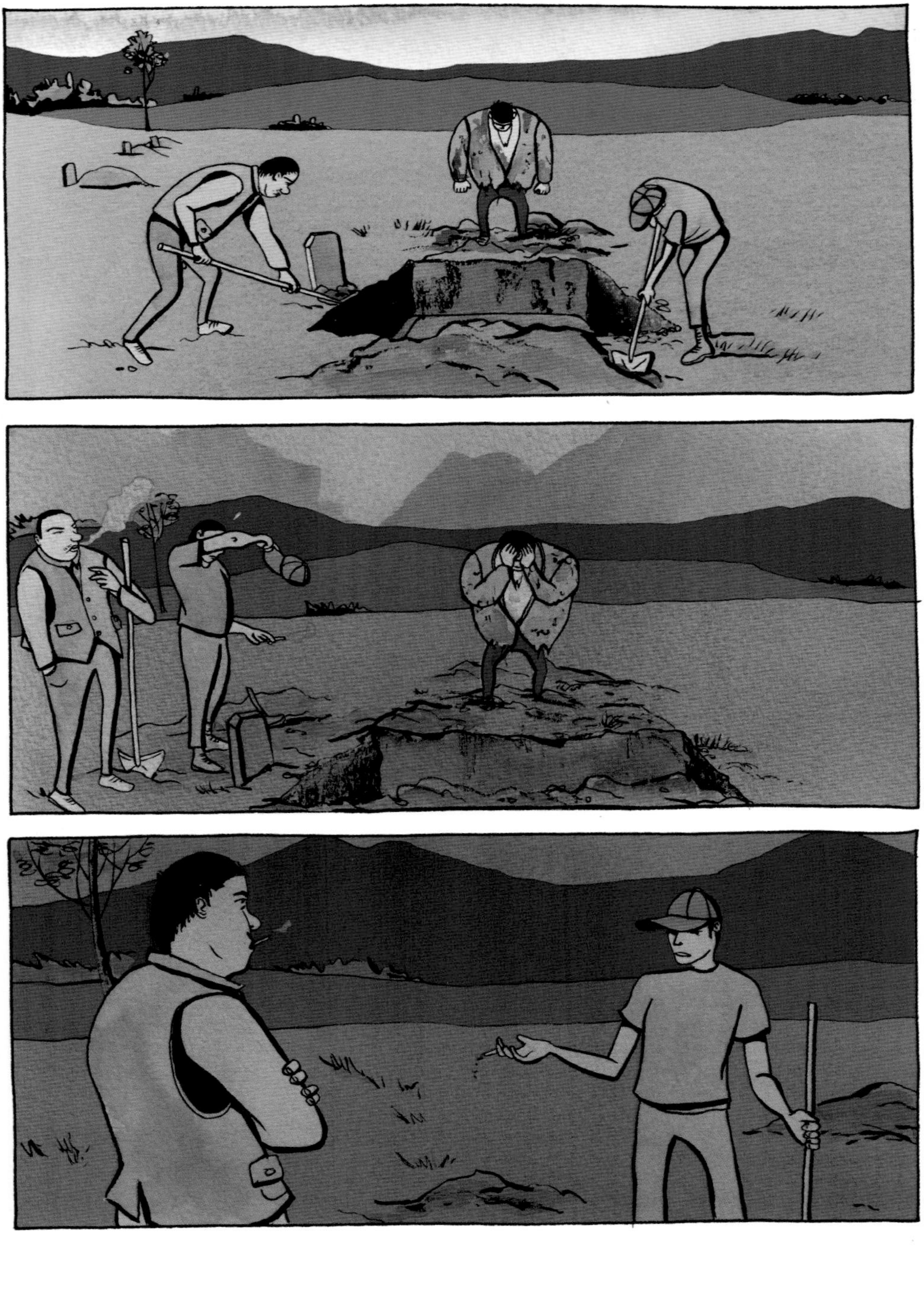

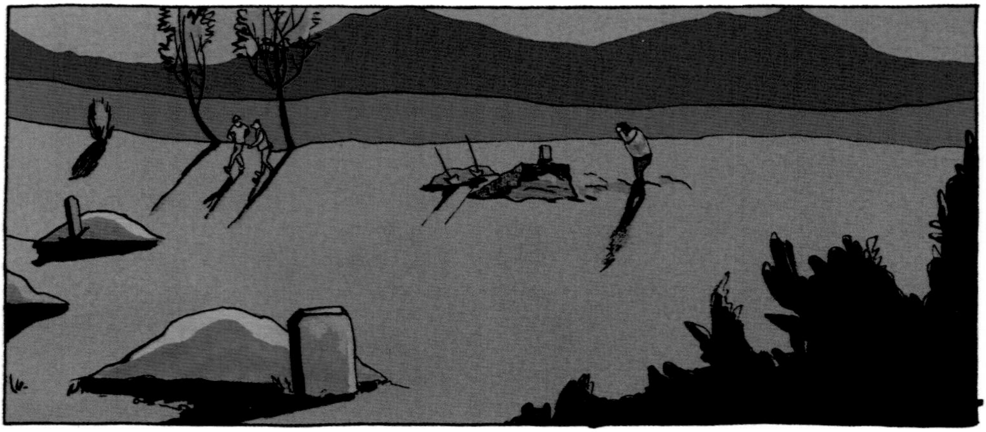
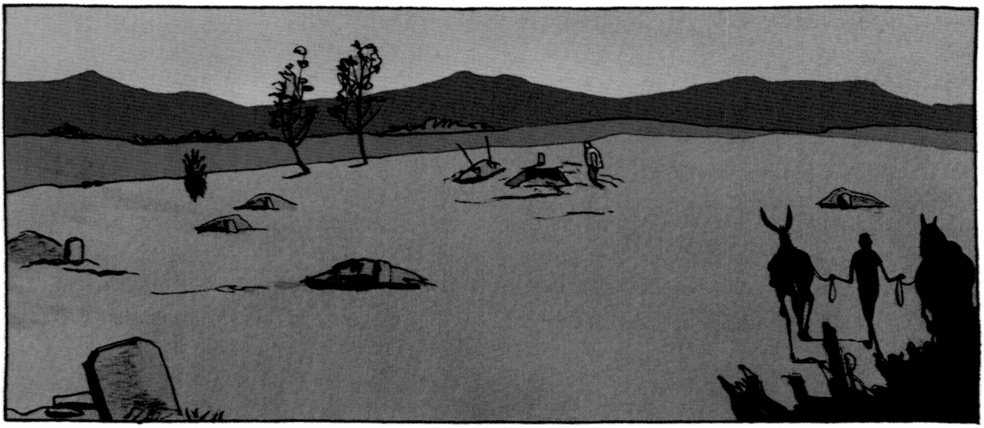
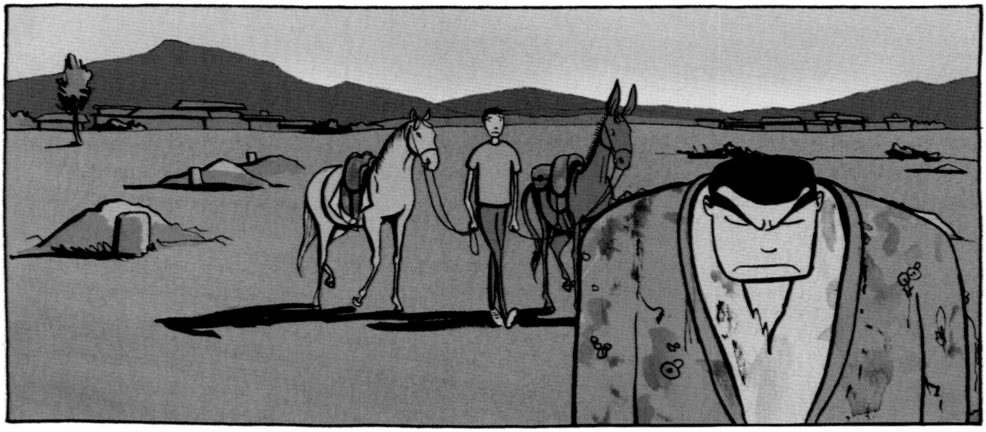

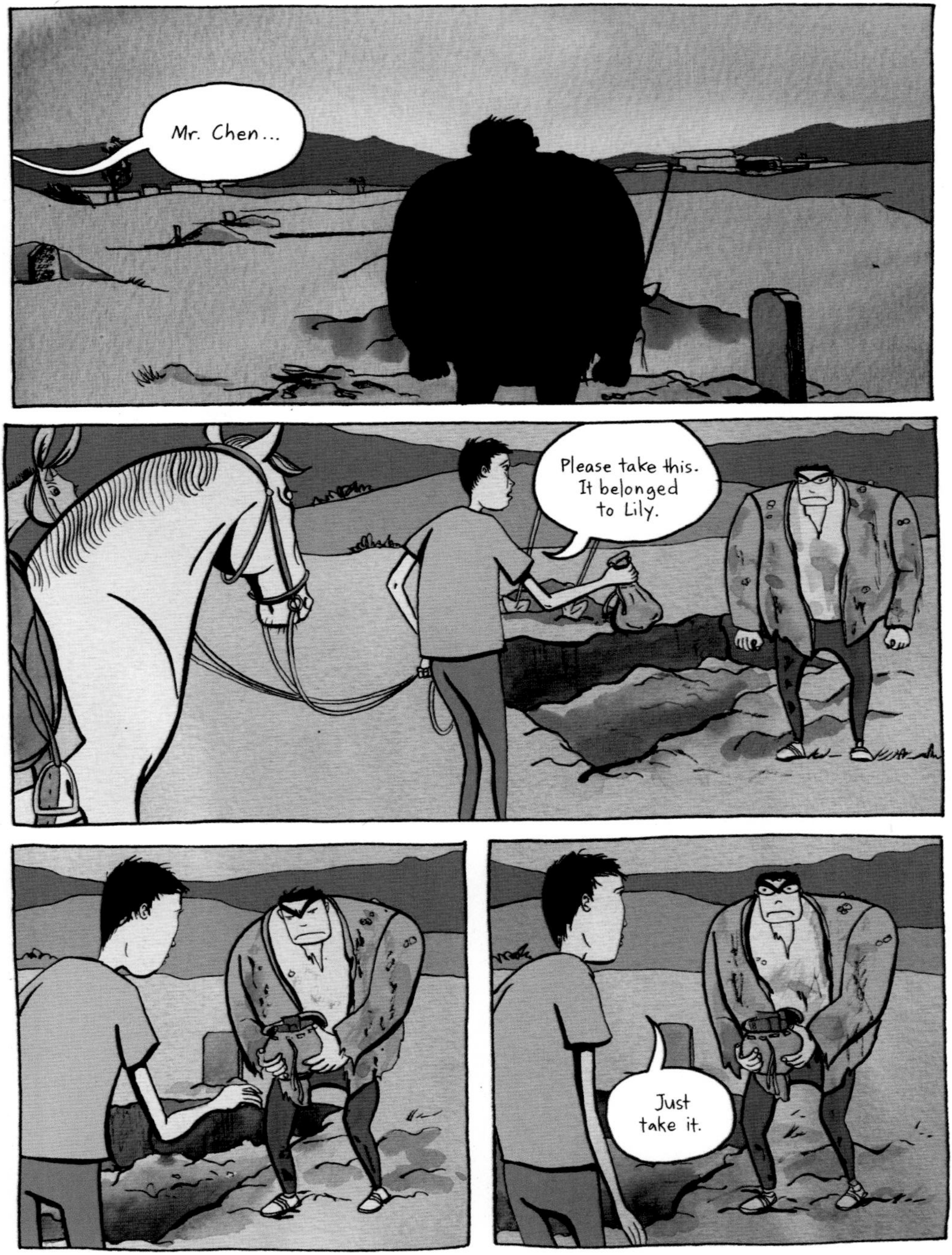
Mr. Chen...
Please take this. It belonged to Lily.
Just take it.

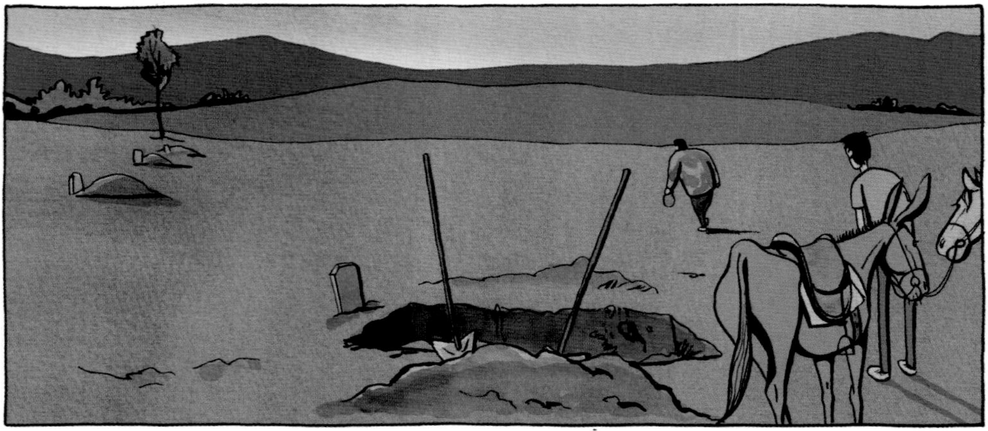

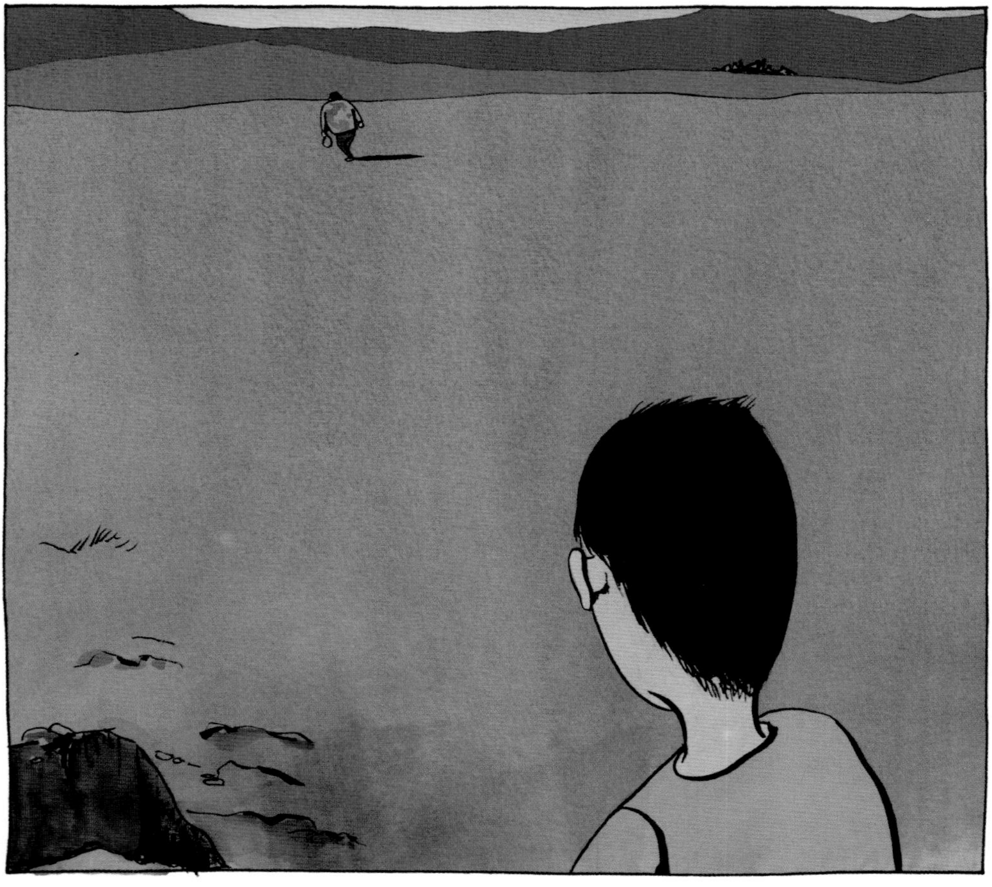

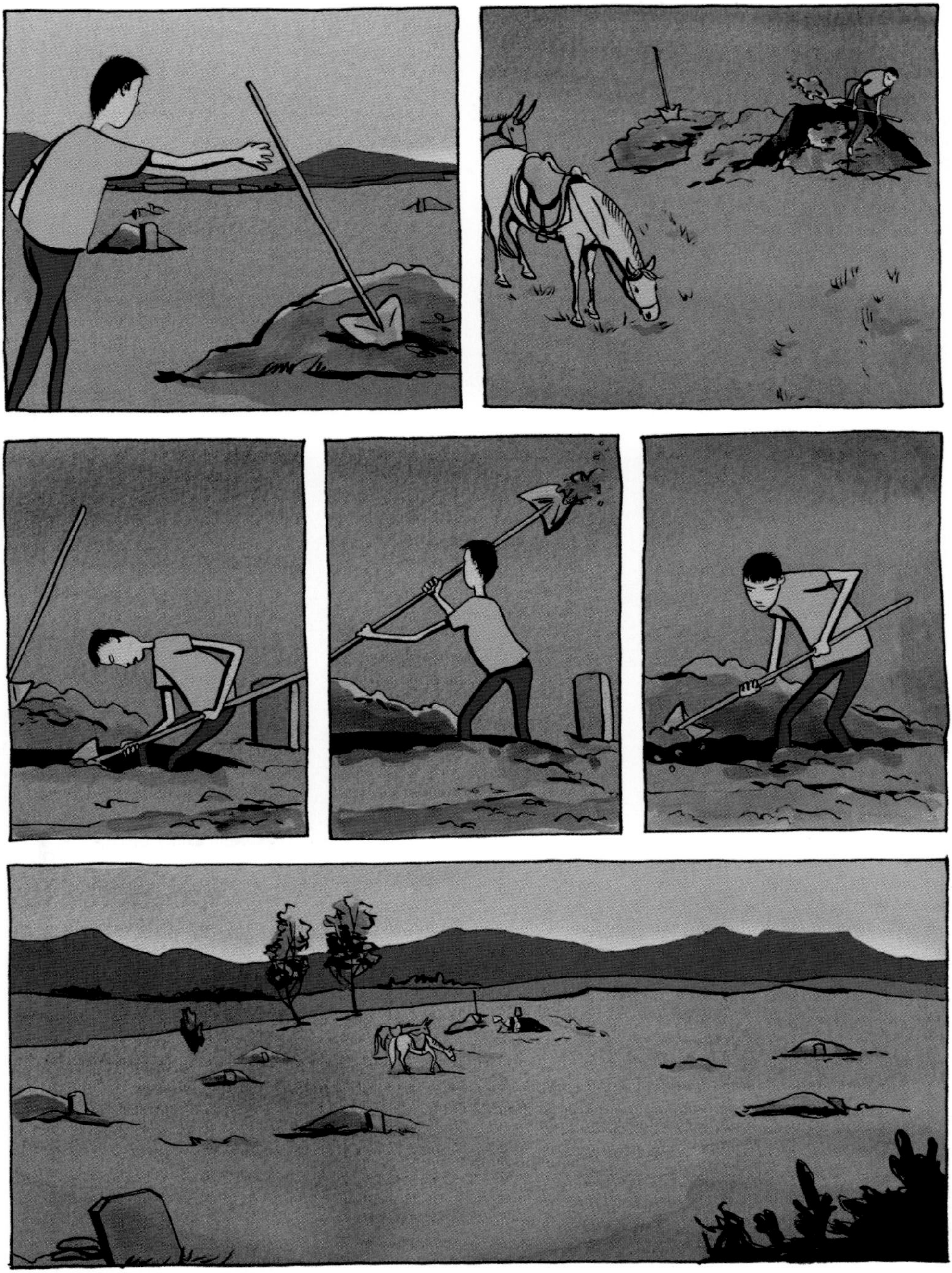

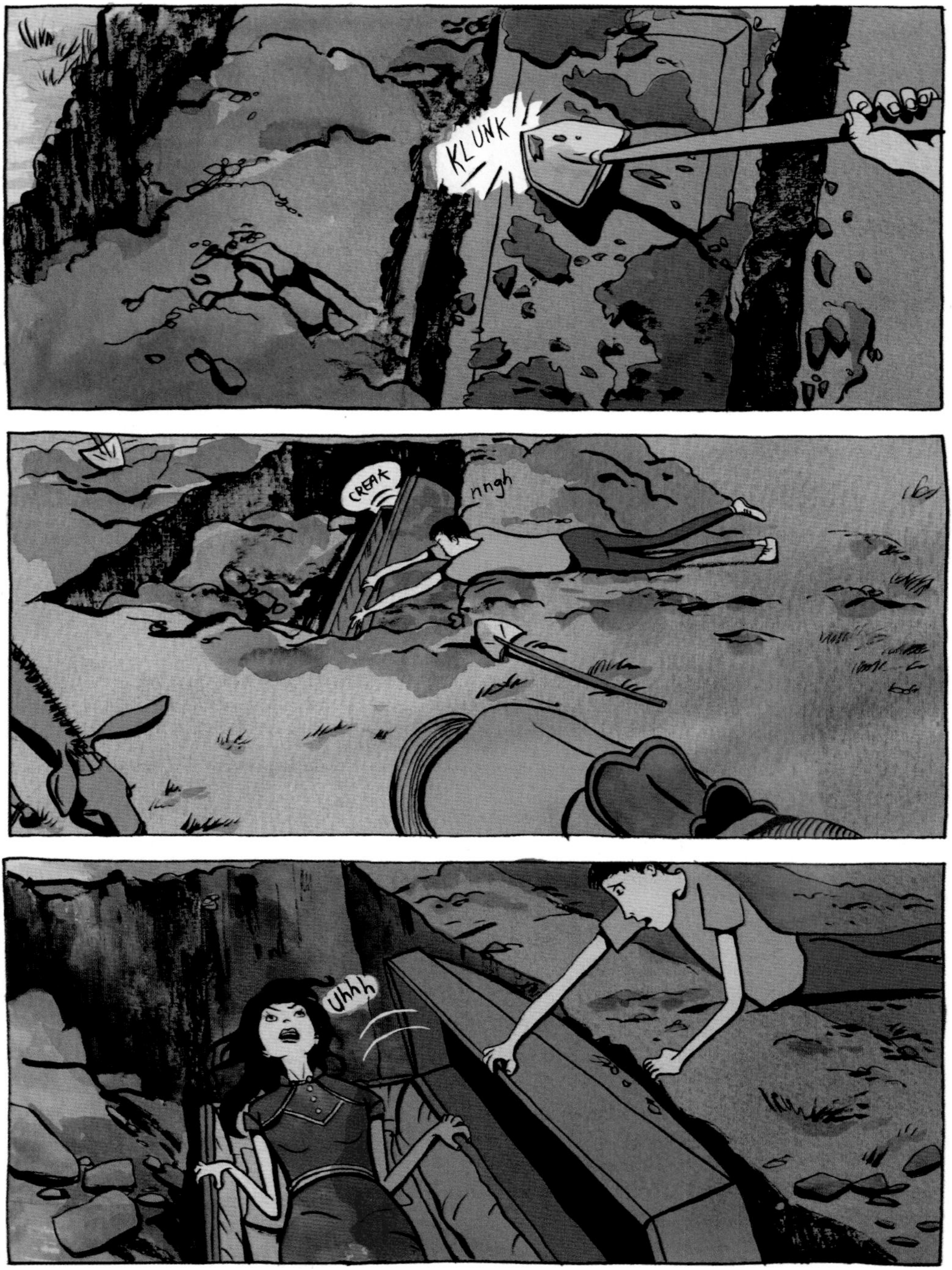
KLUNK
CREAK
nngh
Uhhh

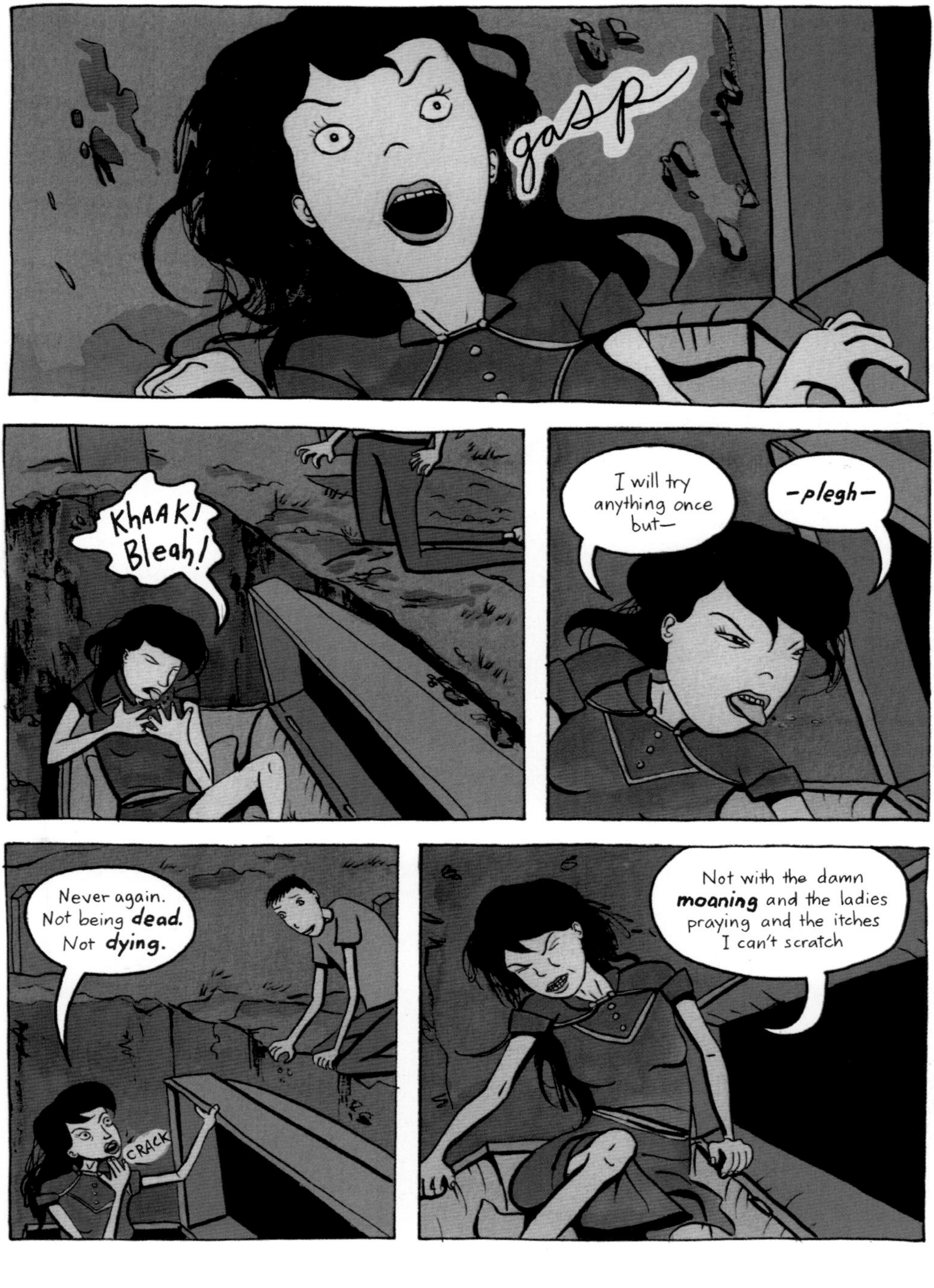
gasp
KHAAK! Bleah!
I will try anything once but—
-plegh-
Never again. Not being dead. Not dying.
CRACK
Not with the damn moaning and the ladies praying and the itches I can't scratch

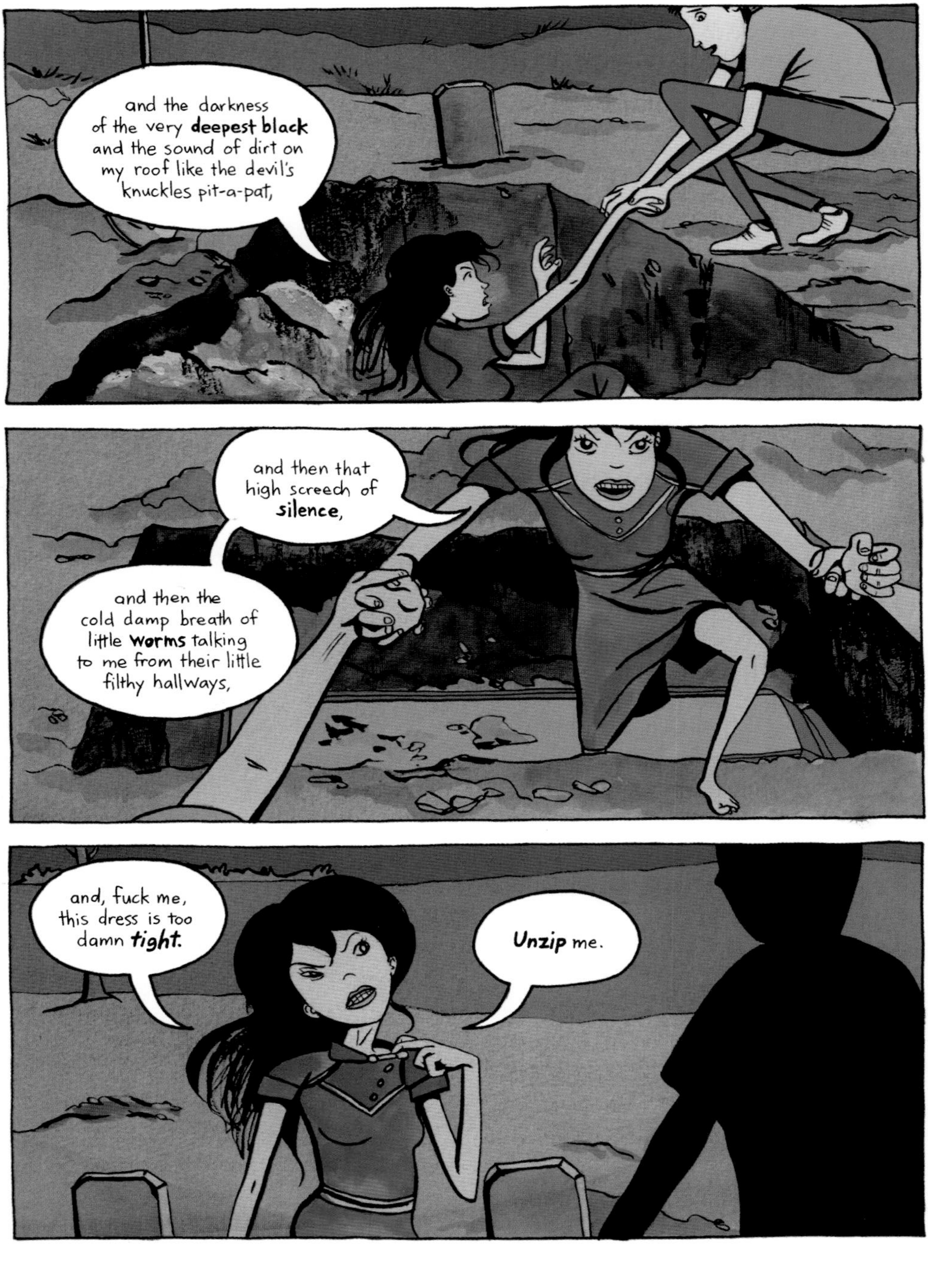
and the darkness of the very **deepest black** and the sound of dirt on my roof like the devil's knuckles pit-a-pat,
and then that high screech of **silence**,
and then the cold damp breath of little **worms** talking to me from their little filthy hallways,
and, fuck me, this dress is too damn ***tight.***
Unzip me.

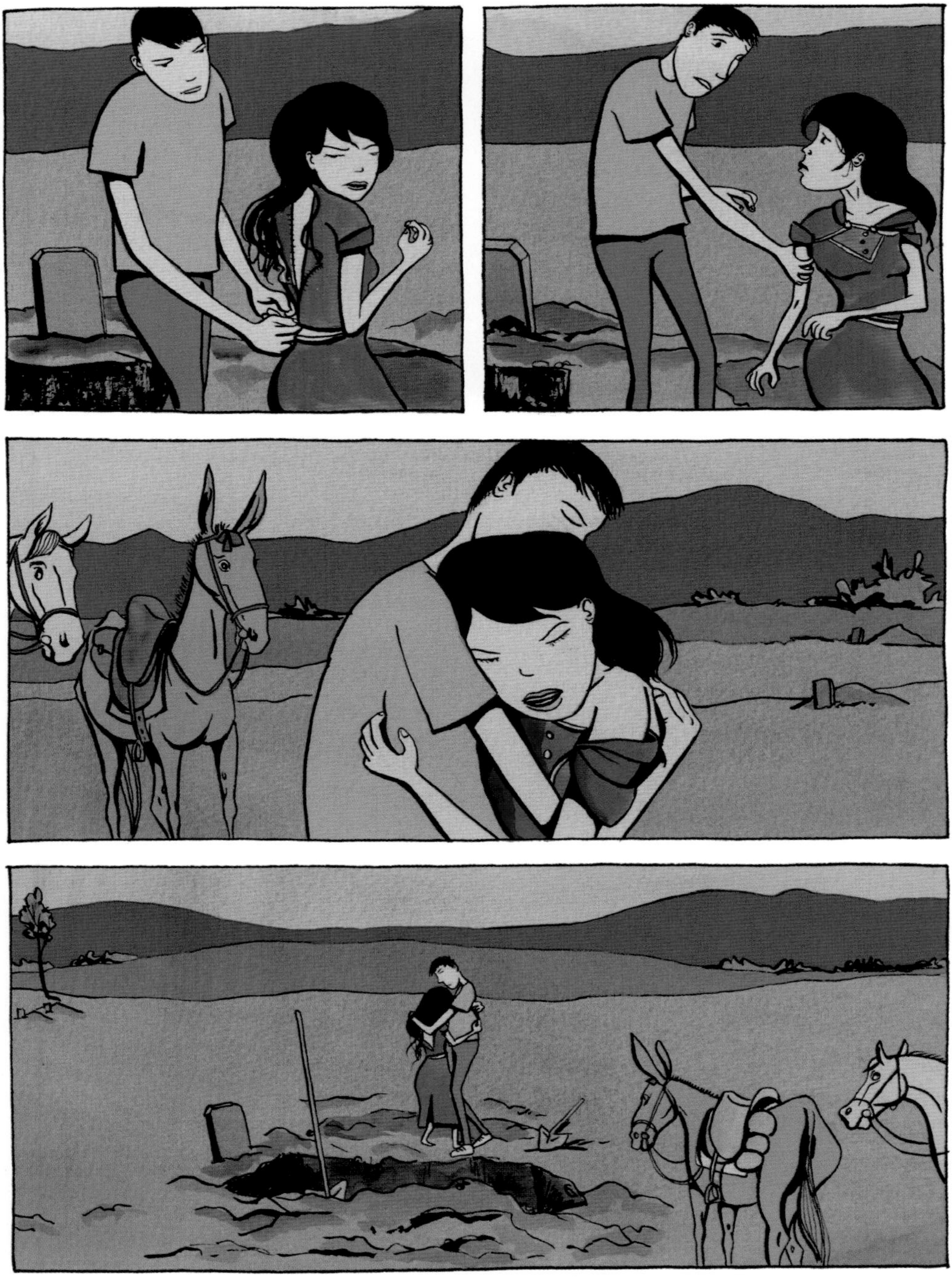

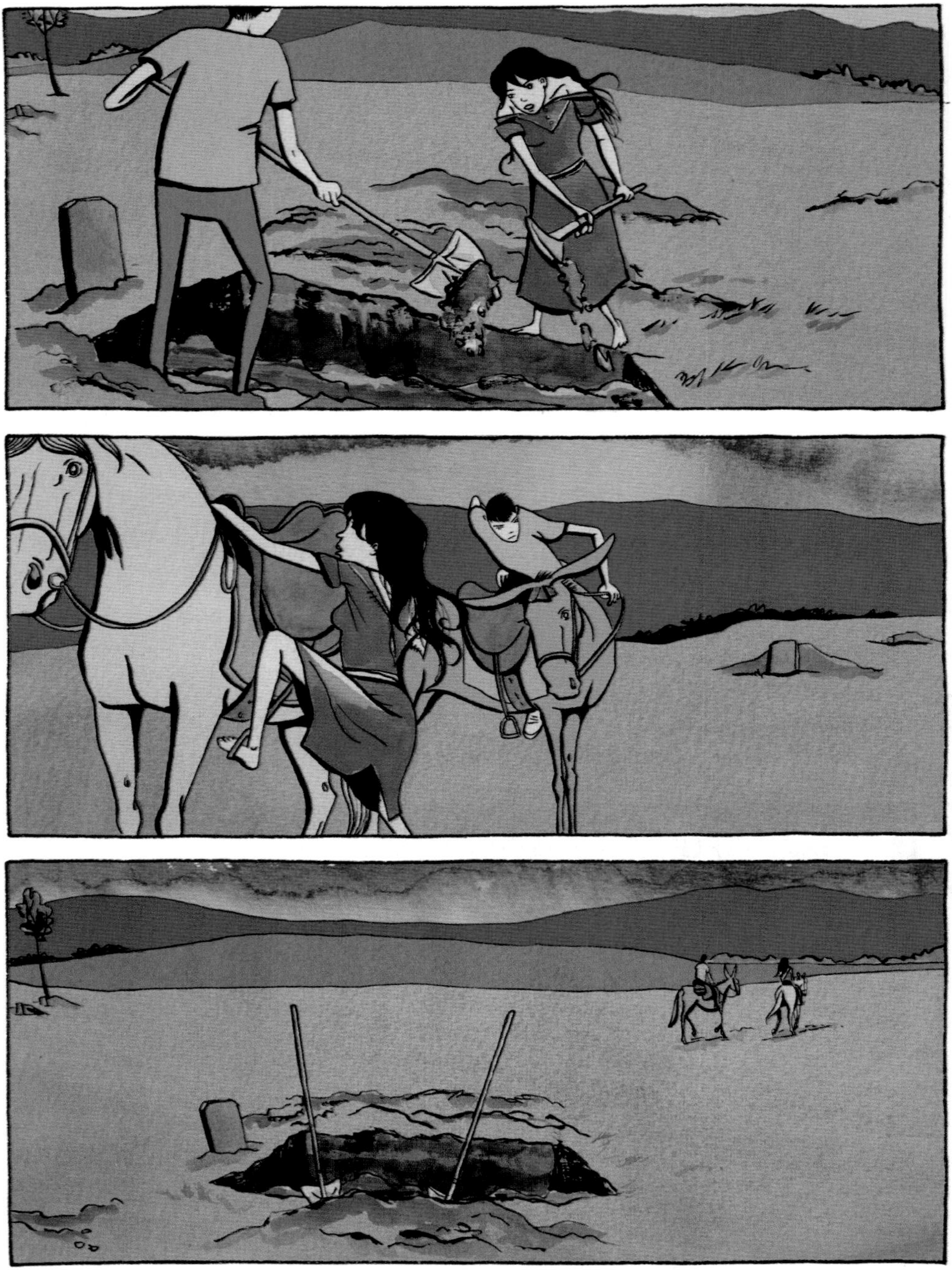

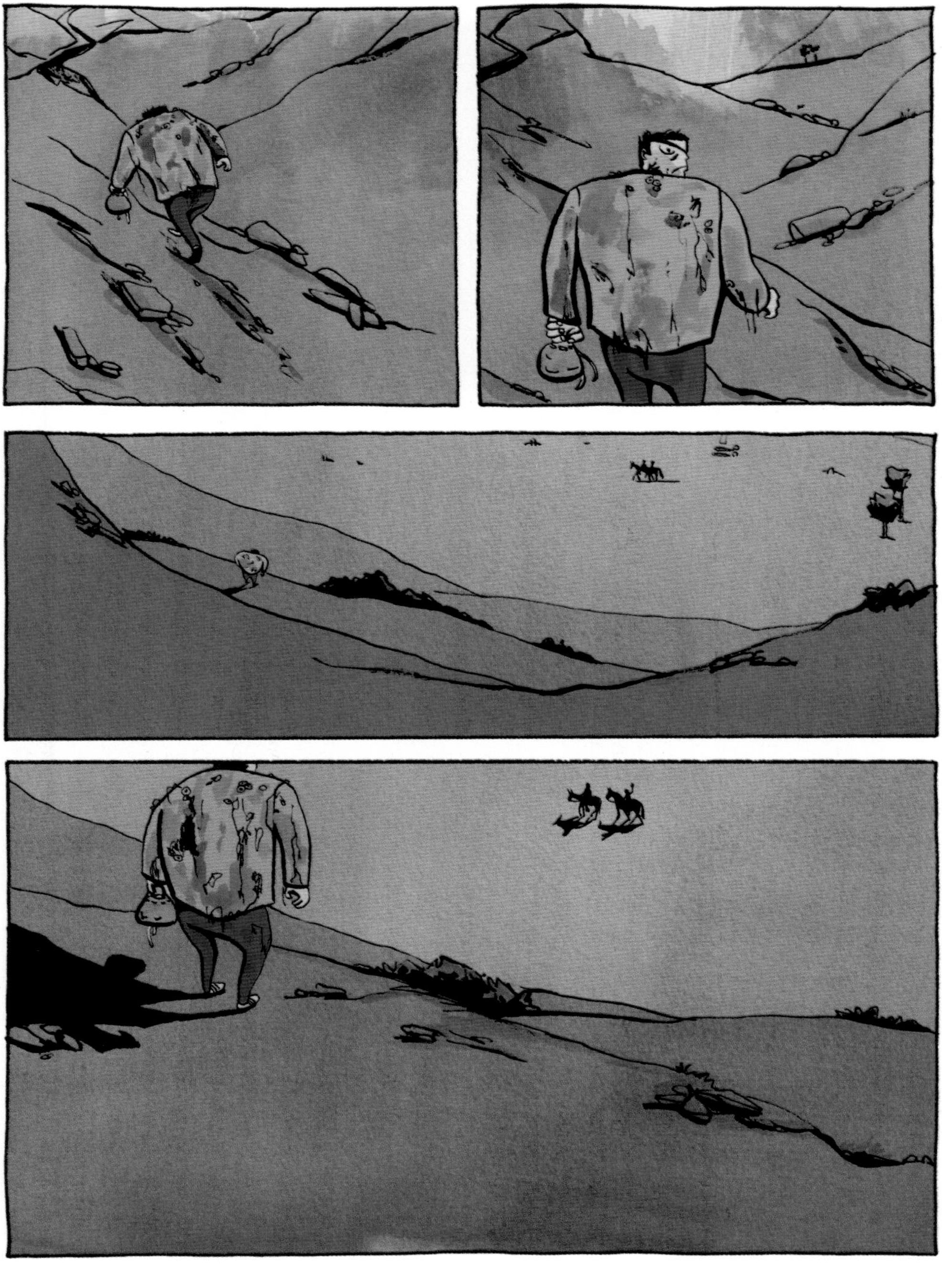

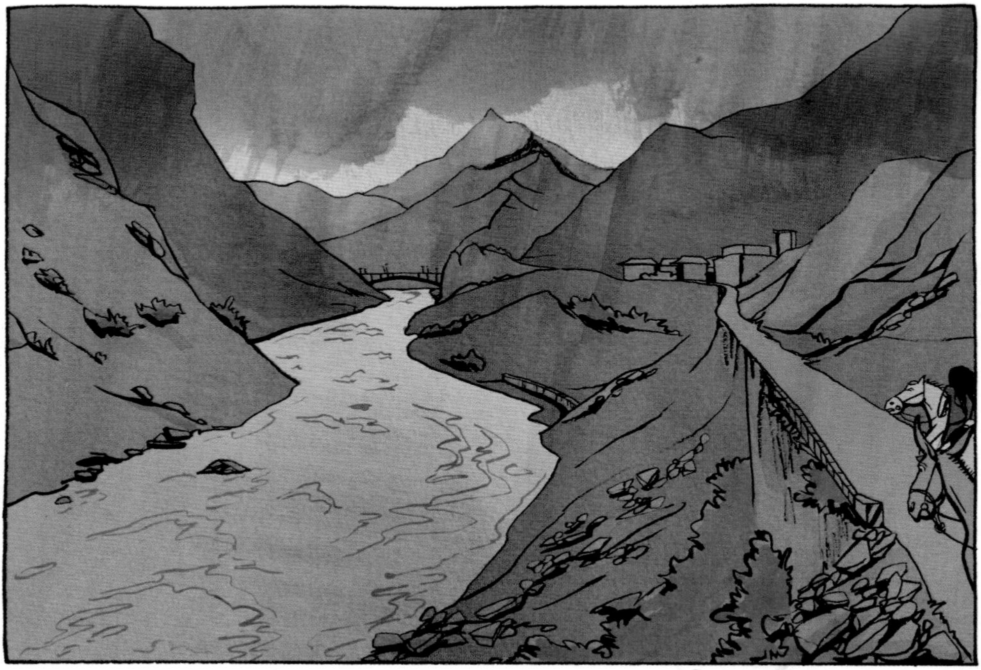

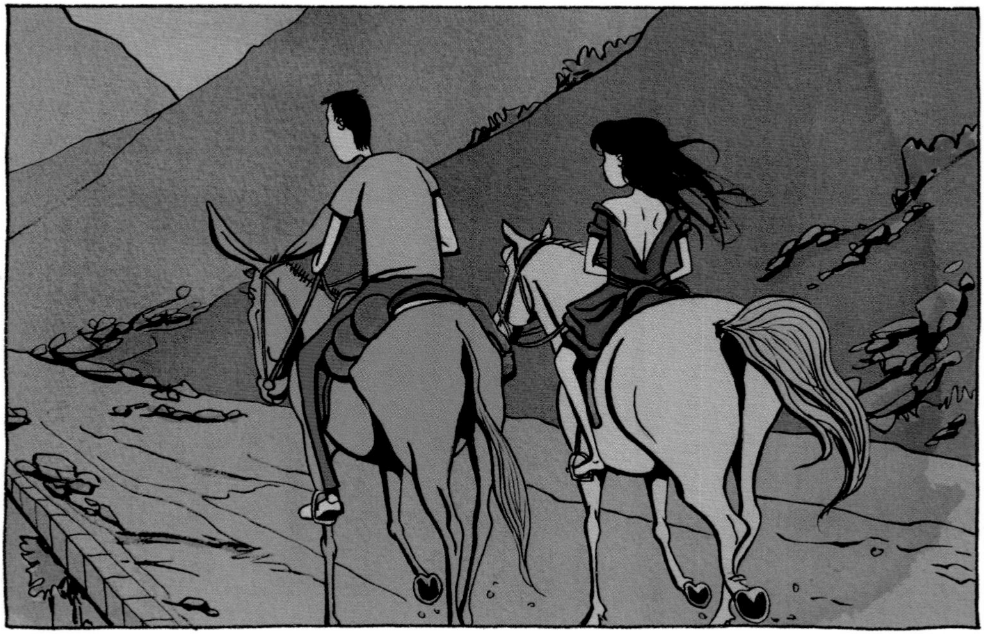

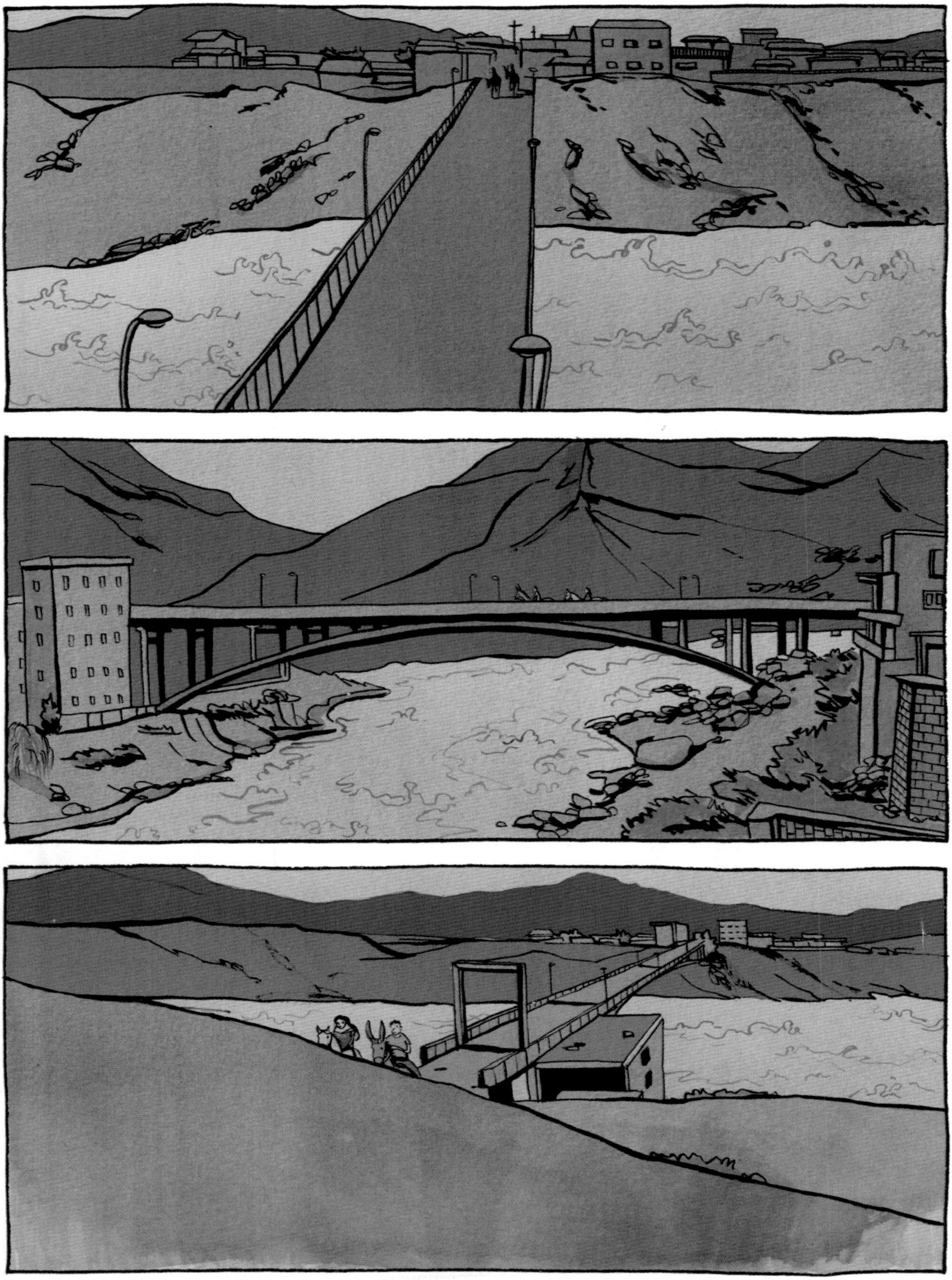

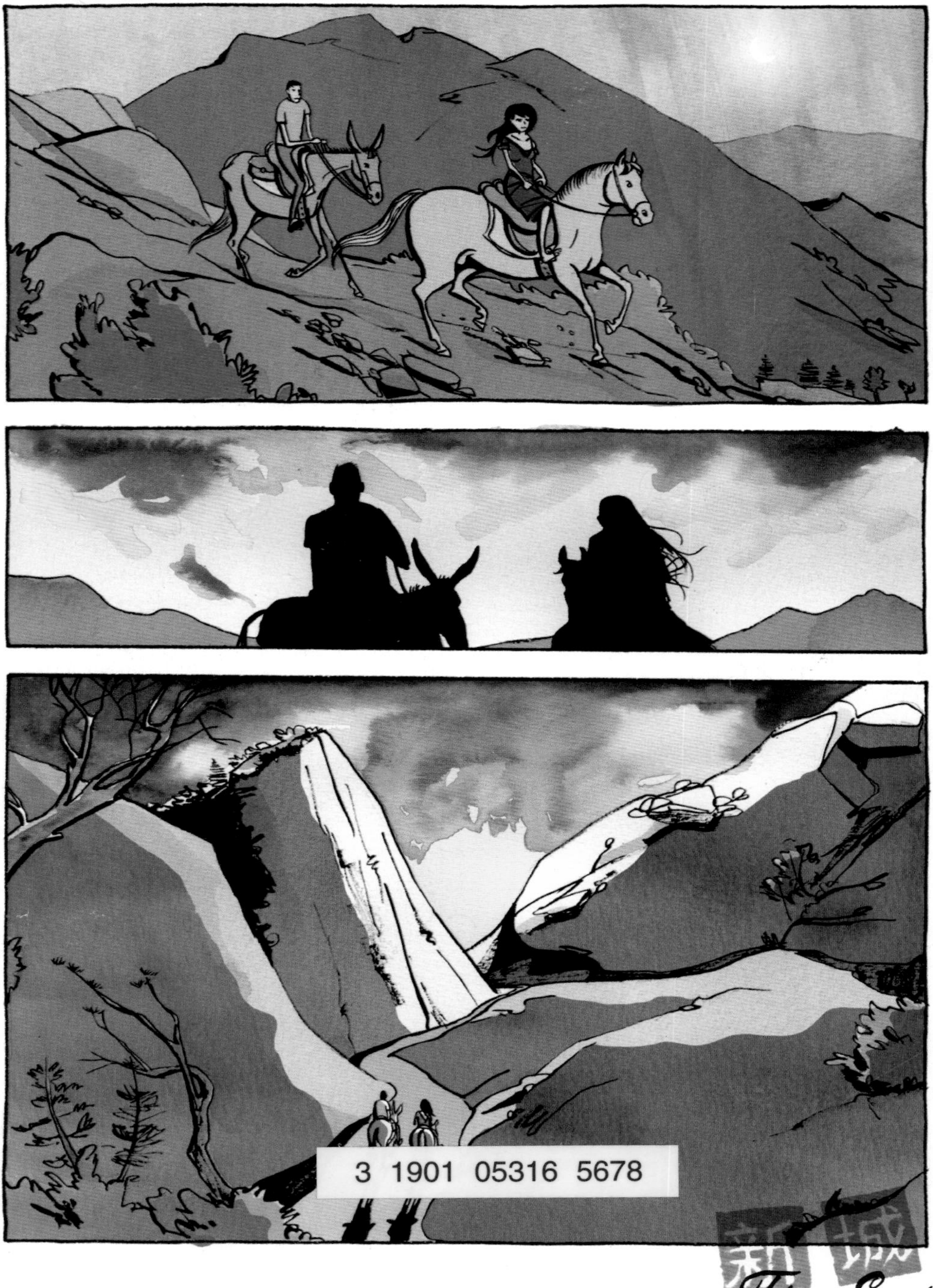
新城

The End